UNIVERSITY OF WOLVERHAMPTON
KNOWLEDGE · INNOVATION · ENTERPRISE

Harrison Learning Centre
City Campus
University of Wolverhampton
St. Peter's Square
Wolverhampton
WV1 1RH
Telephone: 0845 408 1631
Online Renewals: www.wlv.ac.uk/lib/myaccount

THE CRIMINAL JUSTICE ACT 2003

A PRACTITIONER'S GUIDE

Richard Ward
*Professor of Public Law and Head of
the Department of Law,
De Montfort University, Leicester*

Olwen M Davies
Solicitor-Advocate, Crown Prosecution Service

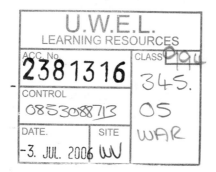

JORDANS
2004

Published by
Jordan Publishing Limited
21 St Thomas Street
Bristol BS1 6JS

British Library Cataloguing-in-Publication Data
A catalogue record for this book is available from the British Library.

ISBN 0 85308 871 3

Typeset by MFK-Mendip, Frome, Somerset
Printed and bound by The Cromwell Press Ltd, Trowbridge, Wiltshire

PREFACE

This book is intended to set out, and explain, the main provisions of the Criminal Justice Act 2003. It is not intended to be an in-depth analysis or critique of the policies which underpin these changes, although, of course, we do explain and evaluate so far as the constraints of the book will allow.

It would be nice to think that this monster piece of legislation was the final chapter in the on-going saga of legislative intervention in the criminal justice process. That, one suspects with some confidence, is unlikely to be the case – although the implementation of the provisions of this Act is likely to take many years. A pause in legislative activity – to enable the range of changes to be digested, understood and made to work – would be welcomed by practitioners, the judiciary, and academics alike.

In its original published form, the Bill comprised 273 clauses and 26 Schedules. Despite the difficulties of ensuring adequate (or, indeed on occasion, any) parliamentary scrutiny, the Act ended its controversial and politically confused passage with 339 sections and 38 Schedules. Authors and publishers do not have the same luxury to endlessly expand coverage. We have, with considerable regret, limited our treatment of certain areas, and took a conscious decision to concentrate emphasis of the book on those matters likely to be of major significance to practitioners and others in the immediate future. It has also not been possible to deal with one or two miscellaneous matters.

We gratefully acknowledge the help and advice that others (both academic and professional) have given us, often with helpful (and caustic!) comments on aspects of the legislation. Professor Michael Hirst read Chapter 5 in draft, but is no way responsible for its contents or opinions. Home Office officials were unfailing helpful in dealing with queries. In addition, particular thanks are due to Tony Hawitt and the team at Jordans who have given us excellent support, and to Helen Hunt who in numerous ways helped in the production of this book. Needless to say, any errors or omissions are ours, and ours alone.

For brevity, we adopt the usual convention of using the term 'him' to refer to 'him' or 'her'.

The law is stated as we understand it to be at 6 February 2004.

Richard Ward
Olwen Davies
Leicester, February 2004

CONTENTS

Chapter 5   **EVIDENCE – BAD CHARACTER**

Chapter 6   **HEARSAY**

Chapter 9 SENTENCING – CUSTODIAL SENTENCES

TABLE OF CASES

TABLE OF STATUTES

TABLE OF STATUTORY INSTRUMENTS

TABLE OF OTHER LEGISLATION

TABLE OF ABBREVIATIONS

the Auld Review   *Review of the Criminal Courts of England and Wales* by Sir Robin Auld
B(A)A 1993   Bail (Amendment) Act 1993
BA 1976   Bail Act 1976
CAA 1968   Criminal Appeal Act 1968
CDA 1998   Crime and Disorder Act 1998
CEA 1898   Criminal Evidence Act 1898
CJA 1967   Criminal Justice Act 1967
CJA 1988   Criminal Justice Act 1988
CJA 1991   Criminal Justice Act 1991
CJCSA 2000   Criminal Justice and Court Services Act 2000
CJPOA 1994   Criminal Justice and Public Order Act 1994
CPIA 1996   Criminal Procedure and Investigations Act 1996
CPS   Crown Prosecution Service
CRE   Commission for Racial Equality
C(S)A 1997   Crime (Sentences) Act 1997
CYPA 1933   Children and Young Persons Act 1933
DPP   Director of Public Prosecutions
DTTO   drug testing and treatment order
ECtHR   European Court of Human Rights
FSS   Forensic Science Service
the Halliday Report   *Making Punishment Work: Report of a Review of the Sentencing Framework of England and Wales* by John Halliday
ICCPR   International Covenant on Civil and Political Rights
LSC   Legal Services Commission
MCA 1980   Magistrates' Courts Act 1980
MHA 1983   Mental Health Act 1983
NOMS   National Offender Management Service
PA 1996   Police Act 1996
PACE Review   *Report of the Joint Home Office/Cabinet Office Review of the Police and Criminal Evidence Act 1984*
PACE   Police and Criminal Evidence Act 1984
PBV   plea before venue
PII   public interest immunity
POA 1985   Prosecution of Offences Act 1985
PRA 2002   Police Reform Act 2002
PSR   pre-sentence report
SA 2000   Powers of Criminal Courts (Sentencing) Act 2000
SCA 1981   Supreme Court Act 1981

SFO   Serious Fraud Office
TA 2000   Terrorism Act 2000
YOT   youth offending team

Chapter 1

INTRODUCTION

1.1 This book deals with the provisions of the 2003 Act which apply to England and Wales.[1] Its purpose is to set out, explain and comment on the provisions of the Act, to explain their rationale, and to set them in context.

References to 'the Act', to 'the new Act', to 'the 2003 Act' or to any section are to the Criminal Justice Act 2003 or to a section of it, unless otherwise indicated. References to other statutory provisions are to those provisions as amended by legislation other than the new Act. For the sake of brevity, the amending legislation has not been referred to unless this is essential to explain the point being made.

References are made occasionally to the date on which this book went to press. That date is 6 February 2004.

1.2 The Parliamentary debates on the Bill were as follows:

HOUSE OF COMMONS
Second reading: HC Deb, vol 395, no 14, 4 December 2002, cols 912–1014
Committee: Standing Committee B, 32 sittings, 17 December 2002–4 March 2003
Proceedings on consideration: HC Deb, vol 405, nos 95, 97, 98, on 13, 19, 20 May 2003, cols 865–983, 697–813, 865–965
Third reading: HC Deb, vol 405, no 98, 20 May 2003, cols 966–983
Consideration of Lords amendments: HC Deb, vol 413, no 160–162, 18–20 November 2003

HOUSE OF LORDS
Second reading: HL Deb, vol 649, no 109, 16 June 2003, cols 558–654
Committee: 11 days, 30 June–18 October 2003, cols 648–744, 876–903, 1025–1036
Report: Four days, 29 October 2003–5 November 2003
Consideration of Commons amendments: 19–20 November 2003

ROYAL ASSENT
20 November 2003

For reasons of brevity, the full titles of Government spokesmen are given only here: David Blunkett MP, Home Secretary; Hilary Benn MP, Parliamentary Under-Secretary of State, Home Office; Lord Bassam, Minister of State, Home Office; Baroness Scotland, Minister of State, Home Office.

---

1   Section 337 prescribes the extent of the Act.

COMMENCEMENT

1.3   Section 336 deals with commencement. It comes into force on such dates as are appointed by the Home Secretary. Different dates may be appointed for different purposes and for different areas (s 336(4)). The provisions referred to at s 336(1) came into effect on 20 November 2003. Those in s 336(2) came into effect on 18 December 2003.

The following commencement orders have been made under s 336(3) of the Act as at the date of going to press.

Criminal Justice Act 2003 (Commencement No 1) Order 2003 (SI 2003/3282)

This Order brought into force on 26 January 2004 certain provisions of Part 12 to permit the passing of a sentence of imprisonment to which intermittent custody relates, and the release on licence of a person serving such a sentence (see **9.21–9.28**). Intermittent custody is being piloted from that date. The Intermittent Custody (Transitory Provisions) Order 2003 (SI 2003/3283) modifies some of the provisions of the Act relating to intermittent custody brought into effect by the Commencement No 1 Order. It does so to limit the power of magistrates in respect of the imposition of terms of imprisonment pending the commencement of the repeal on the restriction of magistrates' powers of imprisonment to a period of six months.

Criminal Justice Act 2003 (Commencement No 2 and Saving Provisions) Order 2004 (SI 2004/81)

The Order brings into effect on various specified dates a number of specified provisions in relation to police powers and sentences. The detailed provisions are noted at various parts of this text. The commencement date for any specific provision is also annotated.

Most parts of the Act do not operate retrospectively. Unless the contrary is indicated, any evidential or procedural provisions created by the Act are applicable after they come into force in respect of conduct occurring before then.

OUTLINE OF THE ACT

1.4   The new Act is the latest in a succession of pieces of major criminal justice legislation over the last few years. Its theme is one of reform and modernisation,[2] trying to ensure that criminal trials are run more efficiently, and with a reduction in the scope for potential abuse of the system. Based on the proposals contained in two White Papers, *The Way Ahead*,[3] published in 2002, and *Justice for All*,[4] published in July 2002, its original 273 clauses (now 339 sections) and 26 (now 38) Schedules

---

2   David Blunkett, MP, HC Second Reading at 912. *Explanatory Notes to Criminal Justice Bill*, published 30 November 2002 (available at www.parliament.uk/bills/).

3   Cm 5074 (available at www.homeoffice.gov.uk).

4   Cm 5563 (available at www.homeoffice.gov.uk).

draw heavily on various reviews and consultation papers. The *Review of the Criminal Courts of England and Wales* by Sir Robin Auld ('the Auld Review')[5] and *Making Punishment Work: Report of a Review of the Sentencing Framework of England and Wales* by John Halliday ('the Halliday Report')[6] underpin and inform many of the key changes, as do various Law Commission Papers, and the *Report of the Joint Home Office/Cabinet Office Review of the Police and Criminal Evidence Act 1984* ('the PACE Review').

1.5 Although the Act covers a wide range of miscellaneous issues, its main provisions can be identified as follows.

– *Amendments to PACE.* Part 1 amends the Police and Criminal Evidence Act 1984 (PACE), to reflect the recommendations of the PACE Review. It does so by extending the law relating to stop and search, by authorising the use of persons other than constables to assist in the conduct of the execution of search warrants, by introducing 'street bail' and by amending provisions relating to length and review of police detention. New procedures are brought in dealing with reviews of, and amendment to the various Codes of Practice. These provisions are dealt with in Chapter 2.

– *Dealing with suspects.* Parts 2, 3 and 4 are concerned with various powers the police have when dealing with suspects. Part 2 gives effect to various recommendations relating to bail. Apart from detailed changes to the Bail Act 1976 to deal with issues relating to offending while on bail, and a presumption against bail in certain circumstances relating to an individual who tests positive for certain Class A drugs, the Act attempts to reform the bail appeals system. The Act, in Part 3, creates a new power to give a conditional caution, whereby the suspect is liable to prosecution if he fails to comply with conditions attached to the caution. Part 4 amends the rules relating to the charging of suspects, by requiring a custody officer to have regard to guidance issued by the Director of Public Prosecutions (DPP) in determining whether the suspect should be released without charge but on bail, released without charge and without bail, or charged. Where a case is referred to the Crown Prosecution Service (CPS) to determine whether proceedings should be instituted, and if so, on what charge, the defendant is to be released on police bail with or without conditions, as appropriate. The commencement of prosecutions is no longer to be by information and summons: instead, a written charge will be issued, accompanied by a 'requisition' indicating details of when and where the accused is to appear in court. All of these changes are discussed in Chapter 3.

– *Disclosure.* Part 5 of the Act amends the disclosure provisions of the Criminal Procedure and Investigations Act 1996 (CPIA 1996). In particular, it replaces the two-stage approach to prosecution disclosure with a single test: a prosecutor will henceforth have to disclose material which might reasonably be considered capable of undermining the case for the prosecution. This new objective test is supplemented by revised rules on review of disclosure. More controversially, a duty is imposed on an accused to supply names, addresses and dates of birth of

---

5   HMSO, 2001. For an overview and critique of its provisions, see the various articles written by Jackson, Malleson and Roberts, and Corker at [2002] Crim LR 249–294.

6   Home Office, 2001. For a critique of the report, see Baker and Clarkson, *Making Punishments Work? An Evaluation of the Halliday Report on Sentencing in England and Wales* [2002] Crim LR 81.

each proposed defence witness. These, and other related changes, are discussed in Chapter 3.

– *Trial.* Parts 6 and 7 of the Act make major changes to the allocation and transfer of offences, designed to ensure that cases are dealt with by the level of court appropriate to their seriousness. Even more fundamental are the changes which introduce trial on indictment by a judge sitting alone. Various provisions reflect this, not all to be brought in for the time being. These are discussed in Chapter 4. A range of provisions empowers a court to hear evidence by way of a live TV link from outside the courthouse (see Chapter 6).

– *Appeals and retrials.* Few provisions of the Act proved more controversial than the power to abolish the double jeopardy rule and, in some circumstances, permit a retrial notwithstanding an earlier acquittal. These provisions, the provisions which allow a right of appeal to the prosecution against a judicial decision to stop a trial, and other miscellaneous appellate changes are discussed in Chapters 7 and 11.

– *Evidence.* A major part of the Act is that dealing with evidence. The Act effectively abolishes the strict application of the hearsay rule. More controversially, it sets out provisions which, in some circumstances, will permit an accused's bad character to be introduced. These provisions are dealt with in Chapters 5 and 6.

– *Sentences.* The insatiable desire of Government and Parliament to introduce major sentencing changes finds its outlet in a major series of provisions largely designed to implement the Halliday Report. These are discussed in Chapters 8, 9 and 10.

1.6 In addition, the Act makes a significant number of miscellaneous changes, not all of which are discussed in the text. Amongst these are:

– changes in respect of jury service (s 321). Section 321 and Sch 33 amend the qualifications for jury service, and the basis for disqualification and discretionary excusal.

– section 328 makes changes to the Police Act 1997 in respect of criminal record certificates.

– section 329 creates immunity from suit in respect of actions for trespass brought by an offender.

Reference should be made as appropriate to the detailed provisions of the Act.

Chapter 2

POLICE POWERS AND PROCEDURES

INTRODUCTION

2.1   In pursuit of the aim of increasing the effectiveness of the detection of crime,[1] and in the context of the bleak statistic that only some 23% of recorded crime is solved,[2] the new Act confers on the police (and other investigators governed by PACE) what *Justice for All* described as 'the tools to bring more criminals to justice'.[3] They include new powers relating to searches, detention, bail, cautioning and charging and investigating afresh cases which ended in a defendant's acquittal. In addition, new provisions are introduced to allow modification and amendment of the PACE Codes.[4]

2.2   The PACE Review was established to identify reforms that would simplify police procedures, reduce administrative burdens on the police, save resources, and speed up the process of justice,[5] without compromising the rights of suspects. Among its recommendations were those in respect of the making and amendment of the Codes, reflected in the provisions of the new Act (see **2.5**). Other recommendations are likewise reflected in legislative action, but many will be implemented by detailed changes to those Codes. The detail of those proposed changes is set out in the Review. Only when the detail of the whole regime is seen will it be possible to assess the efficacy of the changes made by the new Act. Particular consideration was given to seeking to achieve savings of time in relation to custody and detention,[6] which are labour- and paper-intensive. PACE and the Codes require the compilation of often voluminous records for all events while a person is detained (the 'custody record', governed by Code C, para 2.1).

---

1   Cm 5563, Foreword.

2   Home Office Statistical bulletin 7/02: Simmons *et al*, *Crime in England and Wales 2001–02* (2002).

3   Cm 5563, Executive Summary.

4   See **1.4**.

5   See PACE Review, Ch 1, para 8.

6   PACE Review, Executive Summary, para 2.

THE CODES OF PRACTICE

2.3   The PACE Codes provide a fundamental framework for the operation of PACE, binding[7] police officers and others to whom they apply.[8] The new Act (s 11) modifies significantly s 67 of PACE which deals with the making of, or modification of, the Codes. The changes came into effect on 20 January 2004 (see **1.3**).

2.4   The PACE Review[9] considered the relationship between PACE and the Codes to be complex, with a long and complicated modification process leading to considerable delays. There was a need to make the Codes clearer and easier to use. The provisions of s 11 are designed to achieve simpler and quicker processes for modification.[10] It does so by modifying s 67 of PACE by changing the process of consultation.

2.5   The pre-existing modification process was cumbersome and slow, involving publication of a draft, consideration of representations, modification and parliamentary approval. The Government's original proposals were an attempt to shorten the list of consultees, leaving few besides the police with a statutory expectation of being consulted. Following criticism,[11] the Government introduced what is now a statutory obligation on the Home Secretary to consult with the police, the General Council of the Bar, the Law Society and the Institute of Legal Executives, and 'any other persons as he sees fit' (s 67(4) of PACE). The Government is mindful of the desirability of groups such as those concerned with mental health problems or children's welfare having some input.[12]

2.6   Under the pre-existing s 67, new or revised Codes were required to be laid before both Houses of Parliament, and subject to the affirmative resolution procedure. The Bill sought to dispense totally with the need for such a resolution, although a dual approach was mooted for new Codes or major modification to a Code, intending to maintain effective parliamentary scrutiny.[13] The proposals would nonetheless have left discretion in the hands of the Home Secretary, albeit subject to an undertaking to consult with the Home Affairs Committee.[14] On-going concern led to what is now the requirement, in s 67(7), for the use of the affirmative resolution procedure for new

---

7   For exclusion of evidence obtained where there has been a 'significant and substantial' breach of the Codes, see *Walsh* (1990) 91 Cr App R 161, CA; *Absolom* (1989) 88 Cr App R 332, CA; *Delaney* (1989) 88 Cr App R 38, CA.

8   Including persons who are charged with the duty of investigating offences or charging offenders (PACE, s 67(9)). See, eg, *Okafor* 99 Cr App R 97, CA (Customs & Excise officers); *RSPCA v Eager* [1995] Crim LR 59, DC (RSPCA investigators); *Serious Fraud Office, ex parte Saunders* [1988] Crim LR 837, DC (SFO). A head teacher investigating an incident at school is not bound by the Codes: *DPP v G* (1997) *The Times*, 24 November, DC. Those designated under the Police Reform Act 2002, s 38, s 39 or s 41 are subject to the Codes.

9   Chapter 2, para 2.2.

10 HC Consideration of Amendments, 19 May 2003, cols 702–708; HL Committee, 7 July 2003, cols 36–46.

11 See Second Report of Joint Committee on Human Rights 2002/2003.

12 HL Committee, 7 July 2003.

13 Baroness Scotland, HL Committee, 7 July 2003, col 38.

14 Baroness Scotland, *ibid*.

Codes, and a modified affirmative resolution procedure in respect of revisions to Codes (s 67(7A)).

NEW STOP AND SEARCH POWER IN RESPECT OF CRIMINAL DAMAGE

2.7 Section 1 amends s 1 of PACE. It does so by adding to s 1 the power to stop and search for prohibited items connected to offences of criminal damage. This change is in response to growing complaints from the public about vandalism and graffiti.[15] Debate saw MPs give vivid descriptions of the depressing nature of constituents' surroundings in graffiti-ridden estates dominated by yobbish behaviour. These new powers are part-and-parcel of a strategy to act to curb the activities of those who diminish the quality of life for others in this fashion, further illustrated by the Anti-Social Behaviour Act 2003 and by the anti-social behaviour provisions of the Crime and Disorder Act 1998, as amended by s 322 of the new Act. The new s 1 came into force on 20 January 2004 (see **1.3**).

Under the amended s 1, if a police officer reasonably suspects a person in a public place to be in possession of an article made or adapted for the purpose of an offence under s 1 of the Criminal Damage Act 1971,[16] or intended by the person carrying it for that purpose, the officer may stop that person and search for that article.

The breadth of this provision is obvious. Many everyday articles (such as spray paints) potentially fall within the scope of the stop and search power. But a whole host of everyday articles can be used to cause criminal damage – combs, keys, pens, cans, bottles, even books. Despite the desirability of curtailing undesirable anti-social behaviour, the dangers inherent in an ever-widening stop and search power (which depends solely for its legality on the state of mind of the officer) are obvious. The officer will need to justify the reasonableness of the suspicion he holds, if challenged in criminal or civil proceedings, but the history of the use and misuse of stop and search powers suggests that it is, in reality, very difficult to counter an assertion of suspicion.[17] The Home Office intends to issue guidance as to how the power is used to minimise some of the dangers, although PACE Code A applies.[18]

Home Office Circular 60/2003 states that all stop and search powers must be used fairly, objectively and without bias against ethnic or other groups within the community. The powers involving criminal damage may bring officers into greater contact with juveniles. Officers are expected to be fully aware of, and ready to take account of, the special needs of juveniles and other vulnerable groups.

---

15 HC Committee, 17 December 2002, cols 11–30.

16 Under s 1(1): 'A person who without reasonable excuse destroys or damages any property belonging to another intending to destroy or damage any such property or being reckless as to whether any such property would be destroyed or damaged shall be guilty of an offence.'

17 See Miller, Bland and Quinton, *The Impact of Stops and Searches on Crime and the Community* (Home Office, 2000) (www.homeoffice.gov.uk/rds).

18 Lord Bassam, HL Committee, 30 June 2003, col 605.

ENTRY AND SEARCH

2.8   Government policy is to seek to make better use of police time so that detection and successful prosecution of crime overall will increase.[19] One way of achieving this is by permitting the greater use of civilians in the execution of search warrants, a trend facilitated by the Police Reform Act 2002 (PRA 2002). Section 2 of the new Act develops this further. It inserts a new s 16(2A) and (2B) into PACE. These confer the same powers on civilians assisting police officers under s 16 of PACE as the constables they accompany have in respect of the execution of the warrant and seizure of items to which the warrant relates. The civilian must be in the company of the constable and act under his supervision (PACE, s 16(2B)). By this is meant that the officer must be on the premises.[20] The change takes effect from 20 January 2004 (see **1.3**).

One consequence may be to lessen the number of officers needed to effect a search unless other operational issues arise, such as anticipated resistance from an occupier. It will facilitate the bringing to bear of technical expertise, of particular value in the context of specialised searches, such as of IT, media or financial records,[21] or counterfeiting of products (such as, for example, CD recordings). Of course, if resistance is encountered, and violence occurs, those accompanying the constables in the execution of the warrant will not be in the same legal position as the constables: their powers of arrest are those of a private citizen, while any assault on them will not constitute an offence of assault on a constable in the execution of duty under s 89 of the Police Act 1996 (PA 1996), because they are not constables. If they are authorised persons within the meaning of s 38 of PRA 2002, an assault on, or wilful obstruction of, them while acting within the execution of their duty will be an offence under s 46 of PRA 2002. The problem is largely unimportant because the constable who is present to oversee the search can make an arrest.

2.9   Civilians are also empowered under s 21 and s 22 of PACE (access and copying and retention) to act as auxiliaries to constables (CJA 2003, Sch 1, paras 3 and 4). The deployment of civilians in this fashion under other statutes will also be permitted (Sch 1, paras 11–19).[22] There will be a need for vigilance to ensure that civilians are being used only where statute permits and that they remain controlled by constables. A failure to keep within the limits of these powers will obviously lead to the legality of a search being questioned.

---

19   PACE Review, Ch 2, para 17.

20   Lord Bassam, HL Committee, 30 June 2003, col 609.

21   PACE Review, Ch 2, para 20.

22   The relevant statutes are Criminal Justice Act 1987, s 2; Criminal Justice and Police Act 2001, s 56; PRA 2002, Sch 4.

EXTENSION OF POWERS OF ARREST UNDER SECTION 24 OF PACE

2.10   Section 3 amends Sch 1A to PACE, which sets out specific offences which are to be regarded as arrestable offences,[23] and for which arrest without warrant is permitted under s 24(1)(c) of PACE. It does so by adding three new offences to the list. It came into effect on 29 January 2004 (see **1.3**).

Offences under s 36 of the Criminal Justice Act 1925 (making an untrue statement for procuring a passport)

2.11   Under pre-existing law, those involved in 'identity frauds' are summonsed to attend court. Terrorists and organised criminals, for whom obtaining false documents is sometimes a first step to the commission of numerous other offences, and those engaged in illegal immigration, are unlikely to respond.[24] Because of the use to which passports are put by organised crime,[25] a power of arrest is conferred, which also triggers the power conferred by s 18 or s 32 of PACE, to search for evidence.

Offences under s 5(2) of the Misuse of Drugs Act 1971 (possession of a Class C drug) in respect of cannabis or cannabis resin

2.12   Although possession of cannabis was an arrestable offence, the downgrading of cannabis from a Class B to a Class C drug[26] reduced the maximum sentence to two years' imprisonment and therefore removed the arrestable offence status, although (despite popular misconception) possession remains unlawful. The change made by s 3 maintains possession of cannabis as an arrestable offence. During the year 2000, some 70,306 people were dealt with by police for possessing cannabis.[27] It is estimated that some 12% of all 16- to 59-year-olds in the United Kingdom had taken an illicit drug, and 3% had used a Class A drug in the period 2001–2002. Some 11% of 16- to 59-year-olds used cannabis in the same period (some three million people), with a youngest mean age of 15½ years. Seizure of cannabis accounted for 71% of all drug seizures in 2000–2001.[28] The potential scope of the change is therefore obvious. The reclassification to Class C is intended to free up police manpower, with arrest being exceptional.[29] In the majority of cases the matter will be dealt with by an informal warning on the street and confiscation of the drug, or the granting of street bail, or by a conditional caution (see **3.14**). A power of arrest is retained, for certain

---

23   An offence is also arrestable if it is an offence for which the sentence is fixed by law, or if it is an offence for which a person aged 21 years or over (not previously convicted) may be sentenced to imprisonment for a term of five years (or might be so sentenced were it not for the restriction contained in the Magistrates' Courts Act 1980 (MCA 1980), s 33).

24   Baroness Scotland, HL Committee, 30 June 2003, cols 613–614.

25   *Ibid*, col 614.

26   See Misuse of Drugs Act 1971 (Modification) (No 2) Order 2003 (SI 2003/3201), which came into effect on 29 January 2004.

27   Home Office Findings, no 202.

28   See British Crime Survey 2001/2002 (to be found at www.homeoffice.gov.uk/).

29   Baroness Scotland, HL Committee, 30 June 2003, col 615. Guidance has been issued by the Association of Chief Police Officers to that effect. See Home Office Circular 05/2004.

situations identified in Home Office Circular 05/2004: examples include where public order is at risk, repeated flouting of the law and where children are put at risk (by, for example, the possession of cannabis near a school). A fourth, more surreal, example is where a person deliberately blows smoke into the face of a police officer.[30]

Offences under s 174 of the Road Traffic Act 1988 (false statements and withholding material information)

2.13 Issues relating to identity fraud are equally applicable to driving documents as to passports (see **2.11**). Difficulties arise for police officers where the true identity of a potential offender cannot be determined.[31] Hitherto there has not necessarily been a power of arrest available. If the police henceforth reasonably suspect they have been given false details which are germane to their enquiries, they can arrest.

STREET BAIL

2.14 Not everyone who is arrested needs to be taken to a police station to be questioned. The arrest and detention of a suspect frequently involves several hours of waiting around and form-filling by officers. Where a suspect's identity and address are clearly established and the offence is minor, there is often no need to interview, particularly in strict liability offences, motoring or minor public order matters. The processing of such suspects brings no advantage and seemingly every disadvantage to the officers involved, with the formality and procedural requirements that follow.[32]

Section 4 of the new Act introduces a power that permits the police to bail a suspect before reaching the police station, and does so by amending s 30 of PACE (which currently sets out the general requirement to take an arrested person to the police station). It also adds new ss 30A–30D to PACE. Consequential amendments are made to other provisions in the light of the new street bail provisions: Sch 1 to the new Act amends s 34 (limitation on police detention), s 35 (definition of 'designated police station'), s 36 (custody officers at police stations), s 41 (calculation of time periods under s 30A) and s 47 (bail after arrest) of PACE. These changes came into effect on 20 January 2004 (see **1.3**).

2.15 The new, and amended, provisions in s 30 and ss 30A–30D of PACE permit one of three possibilities once an arrest is made.

– arrest and removal of the suspect to a police station as soon as practicable after the arrest (s 30(1), (1A));
– arrest but subsequent release before arrival at the station because there are no longer any grounds to continue detention (s 30(7), (7A)); *and now*
– release of the suspect on bail before reaching the police station (s 30A).

The suspect who is granted street bail is under an obligation to attend the nominated police station at the time and on the date specified, just as would be the case if he had been bailed under any of the provisions of the pre-existing s 30. The details of the

---

30 Examples given by Baroness Scotland, HL Committee, 30 June 2003, cols 614–615.

31 See *Barnes v DPP* [1997] 2 Cr App R 505, DC; *Karia v DPP* 166 JP 753, DC.

32 PACE Review, Ch 2, paras 27–31.

police station to attend can be modified by subsequent notification (PACE, s 30A(3), (5), s 30B(3), (4)).

Street bail must be unconditional, and it will not be appropriate if it is necessary or desirable to impose conditions (eg not to visit a particular place). A suspect who is street bailed must be given notice in writing of the offence for which he was arrested and the grounds on which he was arrested, on the spot before release (PACE, s 30B(2)).

The powers contained in the Bail Act 1976 (BA 1976) do not apply to a suspect who has been granted street bail, the operation of that Act being excluded (PACE, s 30C(3)).

2.16   The amended s 30(1) of PACE maintains the general duty to take the arrested person to a police station as soon as practicable, but, in future, an officer may instead decide to grant street bail. In either case, the officer may, as now, delay taking the suspect to the police station if his presence at a place other than a police station is necessary in order to carry out such investigations as it is reasonable to carry out immediately (PACE, s 30(10), (10A)). A period of time may therefore elapse before the officer decides to grant street bail, but s 30(2) requires release within six hours unless the suspect is going to be taken to a designated police station and detained in the usual way under Part IV of PACE. Any prolonged detention (within the six-hour limit) may well be justifiable, for example to attend a search of premises, and it can scarcely be in the interests of the police to delay release longer than is necessary.[33] One safeguard against abuse is the requirement that the reasons for any delay must be recorded as soon as the suspect is released on bail or arrives at the police station (PACE, s 30(11)).

2.17   The notice granting street bail must specify the police station which the suspect is required to attend, and the time of such attendance (PACE, s 30B(3), (4)). That police station does not have to be proximate to the place of residence of the suspect, and will be the choice of the arresting officer. Lack of funds for travel, the convenience of or practicability for the suspect or other interested parties, and lack of consultation about any changes are all issues, and the sort of factors that may contribute towards non-surrender, but arguably are no different from the pre-existing position where a suspect is bailed at the police station.

It may be that it is not practicable to specify immediately the identity of the police station, or the date and time of attendance. That information need not necessarily be provided at that stage but, if it is not, those details must be included in a supplementary notice (PACE, s 30(4), (5)). There is no time-limit either as to the date of attendance, or even when a supplementary notice may be issued. Suggestions from the Law Society that a maximum four-week period should exist were resisted by the Government, which was keen to maintain maximum flexibility.[34] Home Office Circular 61/2003[35] suggests that the period of street bail should not be greater than six weeks, and, in most cases much sooner, two weeks being the norm.

---

33   Lord Bassam, HL Committee, 30 June 2003, col 631.

34   Lord Bassam, *ibid*, col 637.

35   Circular 61/2003, Bail Elsewhere Than At a Police Station, December 2003.

The details specified on grant of street bail, or in a supplementary notice, may change for a whole variety of reasons. The new provisions permit the issuing of more than one supplementary notice (PACE, s 30B(7)). This, together with the lack of any finality, is surely unsatisfactory and a matter of some concern.

2.18 The use of the word 'must' in the various notice provisions[36] confirms that these notice requirements are mandatory. How effective such notices will be at producing a suspect's attendance at the police station is a different matter. A bail notice may be lost. Supplementary notices may not be received – suspects are sometimes itinerant, changing addresses with frequency, so if an amended notice is issued, it may not reach them. A suspect who does not speak English, or who is illiterate, may have difficulties comprehending the contents of the notice, and non-comprehension could arise for a whole host of other reasons, such as alcohol or substance abuse, learning difficulties or dyslexia.[37] The importance of the process may simply escape the inadequate, laid-back or feckless. There will be no duty solicitor to spell out the consequences of not surrendering bail to a suspect in the street and the very lack of formality may leave a suspect unaware of the fact he is actually on bail. For these reasons, how the police use these powers will be crucial.

2.19 Home Office Circular 61/2003 identified four key considerations as to how 'front-line officers' should use their discretion at the point of arrest. These are: the nature of the offence; the ability to progress the investigation at the police station; the level of confidence in the suspect answering bail; and the level of awareness and understanding of the procedure by the suspect. These matters address, at any rate in part, some of the concerns and issues highlighted above.

Officers must ensure that the power is used fairly, objectively and without any bias against ethnic or other groups within the community, and the use by officers of street bail powers should be monitored, so to ensure that decisions to use or decline to use street bail are not on the basis of stereotypical images or generalisations.

The Circular states that among the matters that the officer should take into account are the following:

– the type of offence. It is unlikely that street bail will be granted in respect of a serious arrestable offence;
– the impact of the offence on the victim or offender;
– whether delay in dealing with the offender would lead to the loss of vital evidence;
– whether the arrested person it fit to be released back onto the streets;
– whether the arrested person understands what is happening, a factor which applies particularly to juveniles or vulnerable suspects who may need the help of an appropriate adult;
– the likelihood of commission of a further offence;
– whether the arrested person has provided a correct name and address;
– the level of risk to the safety and welfare of a juvenile or vulnerable person.

---

36 See PACE, ss 30(11), 30B(1), (2), (3), (5), (7).

37 For the problems faced by those with learning difficulties or dyslexia see *Magistrates' Courts Criminal Practice 2003* (Jordans), Procedural Guide Section P, p 351.

This list is, of course, not definitive.

2.20 Concerns were raised during the passage of the Act regarding the position of children. The PACE Codes require the parents or guardians of an arrested child to be notified immediately of any arrest. That safeguard will not exist in the new street bail provisions. An amendment, which would have permitted the granting of bail to a child only in the presence of an appropriate adult, was not accepted.[38] Guidance is contained in Home Office Circular 61/2003. The Minister stated:[39]

> '. . . the very nature of street bail means that an appropriate adult will probably not normally in any event be available on the spot to participate in the process . . . we intend [in the Guidance] to emphasise that an officer considering such action in relation to a juvenile must be satisfied that the juvenile fully understands the implications of street bail and the obligations that flow from it . . . we are likely to specify that street bail should be given only to a juvenile who is able to provide a satisfactory name and address of a parent, guardian or some other person responsible for his welfare . . . In those circumstances the police will be able to post a copy of the street bail notice to the parent or guardian, with an indication that it would be helpful if that person could attend the police station with the juvenile when he answers to his bail . . . '

So, the parent or guardian will eventually be told (assuming the details given by the juvenile are in fact correct). That does not alter the fact that at a crucial time there is no safeguard for the welfare of the child through the appropriate adult provisions. The Guidance addresses these issues, and it is likely to be the case that street bail is more likely to be granted to the 17- to 18-year-old group.[40] Whether it is satisfactory to have safeguards only in the form of Guidance, and the potential for young children to be granted bail without the accepted safeguards, is an altogether different question. Clearly, an officer will only use the street bail power where, because of the nature of the alleged offence and suspect, it is considered appropriate to do so. One situation where it will not be appropriate is where an officer is not satisfied as to the suspect's true identity. In that situation, an officer will need to arrest.[41] Once at the police station, a suspect's fingerprints can be taken without consent, and without charge, to verify his identity.[42] In any event, it may not be appropriate to grant street bail to a child. Of course, nothing prevents the child (or indeed any other suspect) being granted bail in the normal way at the police station, even if street bail has been refused. A designated officer should make telephone contact as soon as practicable with the parent or guardian of a person under 17, to inform that person of the arrest, of the alleged offence, that bail has been granted, that the suspect has a copy of the bail notice and that a further copy of the notice will be forwarded to them setting out the reporting requirements.

2.21 The new s 30D of PACE deals with the consequences of failure to answer to street bail. In such cases an officer has a power of arrest, and the suspect must be taken to a police station as soon as practicable (although that need not be the police station

---

38 Proposed by Baroness Walmsley, HL Committee, 30 June 2003, col 640.

39 Lord Bassam, HL Committee, 30 June 2003, cols 643–644.

40 Lord Bassam, *ibid*, col 647.

41 Either for the offence itself (assuming it is an arrestable offence within PACE, s 24) or under the general arrest conditions in PACE, s 25.

42 See **2.36**.

specified in the street bail notification). This power is a power to arrest for an offence (s 30D(4)), and that arrest will, in turn, be governed by the terms of s 30. It would, potentially, be open to an officer to grant further street bail, but that is probably unlikely.

A failure to answer street bail may well significantly prejudice the suspect: he may be regarded in the future as a bad risk for bail, because of his initial failure to surrender to bail. Although the amendments in the new Act relating to bail[43] do not directly relate to this position (because street bail is not governed by the BA 1976) such a failure can only increase the risk of objections to bail, and might have the unfortunate effect of increasing the numbers of individuals on remand in custody.[44]

2.22 There is no time-limit for the period of street bail. During that period, the circumstances may change or new information may come to light. It is open to the police to write to the suspect removing the requirement to attend. The effect of that is that the suspect is no longer on bail and therefore no longer subject to the criminal justice process.

POLICE DETENTION

Reviews of detention

2.23 Section 6 amends s 40A of PACE, modifying the arrangements for telephone reviews of detention. It came into effect on 20 January 2004.

Section 40 of PACE requires that periodic reviews of the detention of a suspect should be carried out, by a review officer. In the case of a person who has been arrested and charged, that review officer is the custody officer. In the case of a person arrested but not charged, the review officer must be an officer of at least the rank of inspector, who has not been involved in the investigation of the case. These periodic reviews must occur no later than six hours after the initial detention and then at intervals of no greater than nine hours (PACE, s 40(3)).

Section 40A of PACE confers a power to conduct that review by telephone, where it is not reasonably practicable to have the review officer (of at least the rank of inspector) present in person in the police station to carry out that review. Section 40A came into force on 1 April 2003, but even before it had been brought into force, the police considered that s 40A could cause logistic and resource problems, particularly at night.[45] The reasons why such difficulties do not fall within the concept of 'not reasonably practicable' are far from clear, even allowing for the qualities of

---

43 See **3.25–3.41**.

44 See Harriet Harman MP, Solicitor-General, HC Committee, 18 May 2003, col 721: 'The intention is that fewer people will be on remand, because the message will be clearly sent that people cannot take a risk by not turning up to court because it will be one strike and they are out, so to speak. There will be no misunderstanding in the minds of defendants, because it will be clear if they have been granted bail by the court to return ... they will have to return ... Otherwise, when they are brought before the court, they will be remanded in custody. The aim will be that people will be clear about the need to turn up at court.'

45 PACE Review, *op cit*, Ch 2, para 38.

operational efficiency and effectiveness underpinning the change.[46] The police complain that the logistics of inspectors' reviews in person were not fully addressed in the enacting of s 40A. Although the police may welcome the new provisions, others (including the Youth Justice Board) remain concerned about the loss of face-to-face reviews, and the loss of potential safeguards, especially for juveniles. Indeed, during the passage of the original s 40A, the then Minister of State observed that review by telephone was not entirely satisfactory, and should be reserved for circumstances where there is no reasonable scope for alternatives.[47]

2.24   The amended s 40A provides that a telephone review of the detention under s 40(1)(b) (ie of a person who has been arrested but not charged) must be carried out by means of a telephone discussion with one or more persons at the police station where the arrested person is held. The new s 40A(1) does not specify who that person should be, but the review officer will, as now, be an officer of at least the rank of inspector. The other preconditions in s 40A remain as enacted in 2001.

Two points should be noted. The first is that the requirement in the pre-existing s 40A relating to the impracticability of holding a review in person has gone. Although it is not intended that telephone reviews become the norm,[48] there are no *legal* safeguards to prevent this. Guidance is contained in Home Office Circular 60/2003. The choice of whether to conduct a review in person or by telephone is that of the review officer, who must take into account the needs of the person in custody. The benefits of carrying out a review in person should always be considered, based on individual circumstances, with specific additional consideration if the person is a juvenile (and of the age of that juvenile), mentally vulnerable, has been subject to medical attention for other than routine minor ailments, or there are 'presentational or community issues around the person's detention'. Secondly, despite the fact it is not expected that a telephone review will occur if there is a facility for video conferencing,[49] the original version of the Bill (which would have given legal effect to this) was removed by Government amendment. Reliance on Guidance to provide safeguards for suspects is not entirely satisfactory.

2.25   One important issue is the question of access to legal advice. Section 40 of PACE requires the review officer to give the arrested person, or any solicitor representing him who is available at the time of the review, an opportunity to make representations (PACE, s 40(12)). That remains the case. There is, however, no right to be *present*. The person providing legal advice will be advised of the review and will be able to make representations.

Extending periods of detention without charge

2.26   Under s 42(1) of PACE, if the preconditions are satisfied an officer of the rank of superintendent or above may authorise an extended period of detention of a person under arrest for a *serious arrestable offence*, for up to a total of 36 hours. This has

---

46   Lord Bassam, HL Committee, 30 June 2003, col 655.

47   Charles Clarke MP, Criminal Justice and Police Bill, HC Committee, 20 March 2001, col 560.

48   Lord Bassam, HL Committee, 30 June 2003, cols 651–652.

49   See Circular 60/2003, *Changes Affecting PACE*, para 3.8.

attracted considerable criticism.[50] Statistical evidence suggests that the use of this power, which amounts to a considerable inroad into the liberty of the citizen, is infrequent. In 2001, there were 1.25 million people detained by police, yet only 697 of those were detained for over 24 hours.[51] Of those 697, some 192 of them were in Gwent and only three other forces detained 50 people or more in excess of 36 hours. Some forces had not invoked the power and others had done so less than ten times.[52] There was no obvious explanation for the huge use of it in Gwent. The disparity might indicate wrong or inappropriate use.[53]

2.27   Section 7 of the new Act replaces s 42(1), and came into effect on 20 January 2004 (see **1.3**). The effect of a new s 42(1)(b) is that this power to extend detention applies not simply to serious arrestable offences[54] but to all *arrestable offences*.[55] Nothing in s 7 affects other provisions: the power to apply to a magistrates' court for a warrant of further detention continues to apply only to a person under arrest for a serious arrestable offence.

The scope of the power to extend the period of detention is thus significantly widened, a change opposed by the Home Affairs Committee.[56] It amounts to a lowering of the threshold, and brings within its scope not only extremely serious offences but also others which do not always have that level of seriousness: theft, robbery, burglary, handling stolen goods, riot, threats to kill, actual bodily harm, indecent assault, blackmail, conspiracy to defraud, counterfeiting and criminal damage are all examples. The change will also bring into this category many other relatively minor offences which clearly do not call for extended detention powers: for example, possession of cannabis or cannabis resin, or procuring a driving licence by deception.[57] One approach considered but rejected by the Government was to increase the list of specified offences within Sch 5 to PACE: it concluded that to specify all these offences would open up a whole set of additional powers, some of which were unlikely to be appropriate.[58] It considered that a need for more general extended detention powers existed, pointing to examples of investigations being hampered by delays caused by access to legal advice, appropriate adult availability, and the need for medical treatment or interpreters.

Arguably, if the seriousness criteria in s 116 of PACE cannot be satisfied, there can be no justification for what is a significant intrusion into liberty. The fact that these criteria are sometimes applied in a doubtful way[59] points to the operational and administrative frustrations created by the current law. By definition, if the powers are

---

50   See Second Report of Joint Committee on Human Rights, HL Paper 402, paras 16–23.

51   Baroness Scotland, HL Committee, 30 June 2003, col 93.

52   Second Report of Joint Committee on Human Rights, *op cit*.

53   Simon Hughes MP, HC Committee, 19 December 2002, col 93.

54   Defined by PACE, s 116.

55   Defined by PACE, s 24.

56   Second Report of Joint Committee on Human Rights, *op cit*, para 20.

57   See definition of arrestable offence, PACE, s 24. See **2.10–2.12**.

58   Eg the capacity to detain up to 96 hours under s 43 of PACE by way of warrant of further detention, and the power to delay access to legal advice under s 58 of PACE.

59   Baroness Scotland, HL Committee, 30 June 2003, cols 667–668.

extended we should expect to find a corresponding increase in their use, for otherwise the exercise is pointless. Extended detentions in individual cases may give rise to potential challenges under the Human Rights Act 1998: extended detention may, for non-serious offences be disproportionate[60] and give rise to a breach of Art 5.[61]

2.28 Under the amended s 42, the authorising officer may simply authorise detention for 36 hours, although that does not require detention for the whole of that period, even if authorised. The existing criteria must be satisfied. In particular, the right to consult a solicitor and the obligation to conduct the inquiry diligently and expeditiously remain. Legal advisors will need to be pro-active in ensuring that inquiries are conducted expeditiously, and the powers of extended detention not used for simple administrative convenience. Although the Government points to examples of investigations being hampered by delays caused by access to legal advice, the appropriate adult availability, need for medical treatment or interpreters and so forth, the current use of the extended detention power does not suggest a problem of sufficient size to justify interfering with the carefully constructed balance between ensuring effective investigation and the rights of a suspect that is at the heart of the current PACE regime.

Where extended detention is sought, two issues arise. One is the potential for challenge under Art 5; the other is whether any confession made during a period of extended detention is admissible. Although it is unlikely that in normal circumstances the admissibility of a confession would be affected, even by the disproportionate use of extended detention powers, in the case of a child or vulnerable suspect, issues of reliability or, in an extreme case, oppression cannot be discounted.

2.29 The extended detention powers are also a matter of concern to the Commission for Racial Equality (CRE).[62] It considered that this provision might have a disproportionate effect on black and Asian citizens. Its assessment showed that, while white people had a higher tendency to be arrested for burglary and criminal damage, black people were more likely to be arrested for robbery, which, because of its serious nature, might lend itself to longer detention compared with those arrested for relatively minor criminal damage or non-dwelling house burglary. Black and Asian people tended to be arrested more than other groups for forgery, drugs and fraud, again offences which often require more investigation, and thus were particularly susceptible to prolonged detention. Arrest figures show that different ethnic groups face greater arrest rates in some age groups as well as for different offences, and the CRE felt s 7 could exacerbate those trends. The Home Office believes that the power to monitor arrest statistics for notifiable offences under s 95 of the Criminal Justice Act 1991 (CJA 1991) will provide safeguards for minority groups against disproportionate use of the extended power.

---

60 Second Report of Joint Committee on Human Rights, *op cit*, paras 20–21.

61 Article 5(3) and (4) – the right to be brought *promptly* before a judge following arrest and detention and the right to challenge detention after charge speedily.

62 *Initial Partial Race Equality Impact Assessment*, 7 August 2003.

Extended detention of terrorist suspects

2.30   Section 306 amends Sch 8 to the Terrorism Act 2000 (TA 2000). It does so by permitting a court to authorise detention of a terrorist[63] suspect under a warrant for further detention for a period of up to 14 days, without charge or release. It came into force on 20 January 2004 (see **1.3**). Home Office Circular 02/2004 gives guidance as to its use.

2.31   The need for a potentially longer period of detention is rooted in the ever increasing sophistication of modern terrorists.[64] An investigation can be delayed while dangerous substances are made safe and analysed, forensic tests are carried out, health and safety regulations are observed, computers are examined and interpreters are sought for suspects who lack sufficient English to be questioned by police. Given the fact that terrorism is international, counter-terrorism measures taken in a co-ordinated way between police forces, agencies and governments often require liaison between national police forces which may be time consuming. Nonetheless, there are clear human rights issues which arise from extended detention without charge, which must be balanced against the interest of the State in preventing acts of terrorism.

2.32   The current provisions, which permit extended detention of up to seven days, are used sparingly. Only 16 out of the 212 suspects arrested under this provision in the first quarter of 2003 were detained for six days,[65] so the number of cases affected by the new extended power may be few. Further, the detailed nature of the changes preserves the important role of the court, introduced in the TA 2000 as a response to the judgment of the European Court of Human Rights in *Brogan v UK*.[66] Under the amended Sch 8, para 36 to the TA 2000, following the initial detention of up to 48 hours, the first application for extension of detention can (but need not) extend the detention for up to seven days. If further time is needed, a further application can be made for a period not exceeding another seven days. That application can be made prior to the seventh day, if applicable. On each occasion when an application is made[67] the court will have to be satisfied that the conditions for extension of detention are fulfilled. It would be considered 'perfectly routine' if the courts granted further extensions in periods of only 24 or 48 hours.[68]

---

63   The term 'terrorist' is defined at s 1 as including a use or threat of action defined by s 1(2), and the use or threat is designed to influence the Government or intimidate the public or a section of the public (s 1(1)(b)), and the use or threat is made for the purpose of advancing a political, religious or ideological cause (s 1(1)(c)). Action falls within s 1 if it: (a) involves serious violence against a person; (b) involves serious damage to property; (c) endangers a person's life, other than that of the person committing the action; (d) creates a risk to the health or safety of the public or a section of the public; or (e) is designed seriously to interfere with or seriously to disrupt an electronic system. The use or threat of action involving the use of firearms or explosives is terrorism irrespective of whether or not s 1(1)(b) is satisfied.

64   Beverley Hughes MP, HC Consideration of Amendments, HC Deb, vol 405, no 98, cols 942–943.

65   Beverley Hughes MP, *ibid*, col 941.

66   (1989) 11 EHRR 117, ECtHR. The 7-day system under the old Prevention of Terrorism (Temporary Provisions) Act 1984 breached Art 5(3) because of the lack of judicial involvement.

67   There may be more than one such application, provided the total time-limits are observed.

68   Beverley Hughes, *op cit*, col 945.

This potentially raises human rights concerns.[69] The judicial scrutiny introduced by the TA 2000 does provide some answer to the potential Art 5 challenge.[70] The United Kingdom, following the September 11 terrorist atrocities, temporarily derogated from its obligations under Art 5(3).[71] The Joint Committee considered[72] that the extended detention of up to 14 days, despite the requirement for judicial involvement, may well be unfair to a suspect because his ability to challenge the lawfulness of further detention would be considerably hindered by being refused access to the evidence or intelligence in the hands of the investigators. Because of the nature of the subject matter, the evidence on which further detention was sought would be likely to attract a claim of public interest immunity. Patently, it is difficult to argue a case in the absence of knowledge of the facts,[73] although in special circumstances representation by 'special counsel' might be appropriate as a last resort.[74]

Detention may also be disproportionate to the legitimate aim pursued by the investigator.

The Home Secretary, in a letter to the Joint Committee,[75] pointed to the complex nature of these types of investigation. There comes a point when a period of pre-charge detention *might* be out of all proportion to the needs of investigators. Given the reluctance of courts to second-guess the judgments of the executive on matters of national security,[76] this would be a rare and extraordinary case. The fact remains that this extended power amounts to a significant erosion of the right to liberty and security under Art 5. Extending police powers, where the statistics establish no pressing need for such an extension, creates the risk that people suspected of these grave offences will face routine lengthy pre-charge detention for no good reason. The fact that their personal views or the events leading to their arrest may cause outrage is no justification of itself for a lessening of their rights. Parliamentary concerns about this change were not focused on denying the authorities the extended power if a genuine need exists: the question is whether a case has been made out to demonstrate that need.

---

69 See Eleventh Report of Joint Committee on Human Rights, HL Paper 118.

70 The relevant part of Art 5 provides that a suspect should be brought promptly before a judge or other officer authorised by law to exercise judicial power and shall be entitled to trial within a reasonable time or release pending trial. Release may be conditioned by guarantees to appear for trial.

71 Under Art 15 ECHR. A derogation may be challenged: see, eg, *Brannigan v United Kingdom* (1993) 17 EHRR 539, ECtHR.

72 Eleventh Report of the Joint Committee on Human Rights, paras 97–105.

73 See *R v Secretary of State for Home Department, ex parte Cheblak* [1991] 2 All ER 720, CA. For the difficulties for the defence of making legal submissions where the Crown will not disclose evidence or intelligence following a PII ruling, see *Edwards and Lewis v UK* (2003) *The Times*, 29 July, ECtHR.

74 See *H; C* (2004) *The Times*, 4 February, HL.

75 *Op cit*, paras 103–104.

76 *R v Secretary of State for Home Department, ex parte Cheblak* (above).

Property of detained persons

2.33 Section 8 amends s 54 of PACE by deleting the requirement that a custody officer must 'record or cause to be recorded' the property of a detained person. This change, which came into effect on 20 January 2004, is intended to reduce unproductive police time, and to reduce the obligations placed on police officers by PACE and the Codes of Practice.[77] Much police time can be spent retrieving belongings from a detained person, and logging them individually. This task falls to the custody officer, who must reach a decision about which items a detainee may be allowed to keep with him in his cell, and which need to be withheld from him.[78] The withheld items are then sealed in a property bag. The seal can be broken to remove items but, although there is no PACE requirement to log this event, custody officers, to protect themselves and other staff from allegations of theft or damage, normally like to record the fact of opening the bag and re-sealing it, often double-checking the contents before re-sealing, and often doing all of this in front of the suspect for transparency's sake.

2.34 The amended s 54 obliges the custody officer to 'ascertain' items rather than individually recording each item of property. The problems with these changes were noted in the Eleventh Report of the Joint Committee on Human Rights,[79] which highlighted the risk of complaint if loss or damage is occasioned to a prisoner's belongings. It considered that items of value were more likely to be recorded, leaving open the question as to what is individually recorded – the term 'ascertain' gives the custody officer wide discretion. Value is not necessarily an indicator of importance: a bus ticket in the possession of a detained person who wishes to establish an alibi may be crucial, yet not thought to merit inclusion in any list of property.

The Committee was also concerned that there would be little effective redress for a person who suffered some loss or damage to his possessions, because of the difficulty of establishing what was, or was not, in the presence of the police. It may, for example, be difficult to establish that the item was lost, or that it had not been left with the suspect. There would be no evidential basis on which to found a complaint. From another perspective, the lack of detailed recording may leave officers prone to unfounded complaints, made by those who may have a motive to make unfounded allegations.

The approach to be taken by custody officers is suggested by Home Office Circular 02/2004. Custody staff should consider whether the circumstances of the case suggest any particular need to record property at all, or in detail, because, for example, it might amount to evidence or proceeds of crime. The nature of the property is relevant: drugs, money and property of significant value should always be specifically recorded, but items of low value need not, or might be recorded in general terms (eg 'contents of handbag'). The detained person should be asked whether there are items he would specifically wish to be recorded. The record of property may, or may not, be part of the custody record, but cross-reference should always be made to that record, and,

---

77 PACE Review, *op cit*, paras 34–35.

78 PACE, Code C, para 4; PACE, s 54(1).

79 *Op cit*, paras 22–26.

wherever the record of property is made, the detainee should be allowed to check and sign as correct.

TAKING FINGERPRINTS AND NON-INTIMATE SAMPLES WITHOUT CONSENT

2.35 Sections 9 and 10 significantly extend the power to take fingerprints and non-intimate samples. The powers to retain fingerprints and non-intimate samples remain unchanged, but, in the light of case-law relating to retention,[80] the effect of the changes is to greatly increase the amount of data potentially available for storage on the Police National Computer or the DNA database.[81]

Fingerprints

2.36 Section 9 amends s 61 of PACE. The amended s 61 permits the taking of fingerprints without consent where a suspect is detained for a recordable offence.[82]

Under the pre-existing s 61, fingerprints could only be taken without consent under the authority of a police officer of at least the rank of superintendent, and where the detained person had been charged with a recordable offence, or informed that he would be reported for it. Even if that criterion were satisfied, fingerprints could be taken only if the detained person had not had his fingerprints taken during the course of the investigation of the offence in respect of which he had been charged or reported. The authorising officer had to have reasonable grounds for suspecting that person's involvement in a crime, and for believing that those fingerprints would confirm or eliminate the suspect's involvement with the offence or confirm his identity (if there was reasonable doubt as to who the suspect actually was). Fingerprints could not be taken solely to prove a person's identity.

The change is primarily intended to enable the police to identify those who might seek to evade justice by the giving of a false identity.[83] The police can link to the Police National Computer, which may reveal relevant information not only about identification but, perhaps, whether the individual is a danger to themselves, requires medication or an appropriate adult. It also enables speculative searches to be made against the Police National Computer, even where identity is known.

2.37 The effect of the change is that fingerprints may be taken routinely from those detained in consequence of an arrest for a recordable offence, or charged with a recordable offence, provided that he has not had fingerprints taken in the course of the investigation by the police. Unlike under the pre-existing s 61, no senior officer authorisation is required. Many will regard the power to take, and retain, fingerprints of those who are detained, but not proceeded against, with some concern. Certainly, in previous legislation care had been taken to strike a balance between the collection and retention of data in respect of those charged and those not. This change tilts the

---

80 See **2.38**.

81 See **2.40**.

82 Defined by the National Police Records (Recordable Offences) Regulations 2000 (SI 1139/2000).

83 Mr Bob Ainsworth MP, HC Consideration of Amendments, HC Deb, 19 May 2003, col 699.

balance in favour of the police. An individual wrongly arrested for, say, a public order offence, but wrongly identified (and later released without charge) can be finger-printed (if the police so wish). This amounts to a significant extension of the law. Fingerprints may be retained under s 64 of PACE (see **2.39**).

Non-intimate samples

2.38   Section 10 makes similar changes to s 63 of PACE in respect of non-intimate samples.[84] As with fingerprints,[85] the amended s 63 permits a non-intimate sample to be taken without consent where a suspect is detained following arrest for a recordable offence,[86] and no such sample has yet been taken, or any which have were not good enough for the purpose for which they were taken. There is no requirement that the suspect be charged or cautioned. Arrest for a recordable offence is all that is required. The rationale for this change is similar to that in respect of fingerprints.

The wider issues

2.39   Modern technology clearly aids both crime detection and crime prevention.[87] The power to take and retain samples and fingerprints, and to engage in speculative searches, was extended in 1994 to reflect the recommendation of the Royal Commission on Criminal Justice for the creation of a DNA database.[88] The size of the criminally active population could be as high as three million, and one half of those are on the national database.[89] It is intended that the latter figure should reach 2.6 million by April 2004.[90]

Anyone charged, cautioned or convicted of an offence already has his sample added to the database because of s 63 of PACE. Fingerprints or sample data of those charged can be added under the pre-existing provisions. Furthermore, the provisions relating to destruction of data mean that much data can be retained.[91] In *Chief Constable of South Yorkshire (Marper) v Chief Constable of South Yorkshire*,[92] the applicants argued unsuccessfully that the retention of their fingerprints etc breached their right to respect for their private lives under Art 8 ECHR. The Divisional Court held that the taking and retention of prints and other samples was not incompatible with Art 8, there

---

84 A 'non-intimate sample is defined by PACE, s 65, as: (a) a sample of hair other than pubic hair; (b) a sample taken from a nail or from under a nail; (c) a swab taken from any part of a person's body including the mouth but not any other body orifice; (d) saliva; (e) a footprint or similar impression of any part of a person's body other than a part of his hand.

85 See **2.36**.

86 Now PACE, s 63(2B).

87 See Earl Ferrers, Minister of State, Home Office, Criminal Justice and Public Order Act 1994, HL Deb, vol 554, col 383.

88 Cm 2263 (1993), Ch 2.

89 White Paper *Criminal Justice – the Way Ahead*, Cm 5074, Feb 2001, para 1.28.

90 Cm 5563 (2002), para 3.16.

91 PACE, s 64 allows retention of fingerprints or samples (and information derived therefrom) unless they fall within s 64(3). Fingerprints or samples taken from a person in connection with the investigation of an offence, where the person is not suspected of having committed the offence, must be destroyed.

92 (2002) *The Times*, 4 April. An appeal to the House of Lords is pending.

being the legitimate and proportionate aim of preventing (or detecting) crime permitted by Art 8(2).

2.40 The effect of the changes is therefore to increase still further the potential for the taking, and retention, of data from individuals who have not been convicted of a crime. The Government argued[93] that the database will help to eliminate suspects and identify perpetrators, thus making the perceived interference with people's privacy justifiable. The provisions hold 'social value',[94] with statistics showing that once a speculative search was made, there was a 40% chance of a match. Thus, the more samples are kept, the more detection occurs. The effect of the changes will be to catch the additional 1.2 million people each year who are arrested for recordable offences.[95]

That the potential for solving crime increases the more data is held is undeniable, as is the value to the police and other law enforcement agencies. There is, however, a balance to be struck, which was inherent in the original provisions of PACE. The Joint Committee on Human Rights in its Eleventh Report had real concerns about this extension of police power. The taking of non-intimate samples can be far more invasive than may first be assumed.[96] It can involve uncomfortable, embarrassing, and potentially degrading interference with intimate parts of a person's body, including the taking of samples from inside a person's mouth and the taking of impressions or casts from any part of a person's body. The use of this power is therefore likely to interfere significantly with a person's bodily integrity and dignity.[97]

2.41 The Joint Committee was also concerned about the storage of highly personal data and who would control it or take responsibility for its maintenance. This raises issues that go beyond the scope of the new changes, and which arise in any event. The information stored is sensitive, and could be of interest to a variety of persons (perhaps insurers, employers, drug companies and others). Issues of confidentiality arise with the increasing use of the private sector for activities such as checking the criminal records of prospective teachers, with the provisions in s 328 of, and Sch 35 to, the new Act to privatise the Criminal Records Bureau and possible developments with the Forensic Science Service (FSS). The Joint Committee was satisfied that current arrangements were satisfactory, and provided appropriate protections under the Human Rights Act 1998 for the individual,[98] but the position if changes were to be made is more uncertain, although the balance of authority suggests that a privatised service handling individual data would fall to be regarded as a 'public body' and thus retain the protections of the 1998 Act.[99]

---

93   HL Committee, 30 June 2003, cols 713–714.

94   Hilary Benn MP, in a letter to the Joint Committee on Human Rights.

95   Lord Hunt, HL Committee, 30 June 2003, col 713. The databases will not necessarily increase by 1.2m new individuals each year: some samples taken here will belong to individuals already on the database.

96   The Lord Bishop of Chester, HC Committee, 30 June 2003, col 716.

97   Joint Committee, *op cit*, para 42.

98   See *ibid*, paras 44–54.

99   For the application of the HRA 1998 to private bodies, see *Poplar Housing & Regeneration Community Association Ltd v Donoghue* [2001] EWCA 595, CA; *Heather v Leonard Cheshire Foundation* [2002] All ER 936; and *Aston Cantlow & Wilmcote with Billeslley Parochial Church Council v Wallbank* [2003] 3 All ER (D) 1213, HL.

The Committee was, however, concerned by the informal manner in which responsibility is allocated in the case of the national DNA database. A Memorandum of Understanding between the FSS, the Association of Chief Police Officers and the National DNA Database Board sets out who is expected to do what, but this is not legally binding.[100] It was concerned that in the event of a complaint or litigation by an aggrieved person there would be considerable difficulty in establishing who was accountable for what under the terms of the Memorandum. In practice, this means that the lack of clarity as to responsibilities or functions would make it difficult to identify the party to be pursued in respect of any grievance, raising the spectre of litigation between parties to the Memorandum. The potential loss of control over information takes on an added dimension now that cross-jurisdiction investigation of crime is more prevalent, so that there is greater co-operation, for example, by way of sharing potential forensic evidence allowing other States to access to a UK resident's samples. The Committee (para 54) was very concerned at the giving away by the State of its citizens' personal information to other countries, as well as the general lack of accountability in respect of retention and storage.

DRUG-RELATED MATTERS

Summary and background

2.42 Drug misuse has long been recognised as one of the major causes of offending. Around 80% of male remand prisoners and around 75% of female remand prisoners admit to prior drug use, and 54% of males and 51% of females confess to drug dependency.[101] The White Paper estimated that those who test positive for crack cocaine or heroin on arrest are responsible for 50% of all acquisitive crime (ie crime to raise funds to support the drug abuse). Such a habit is estimated to cost £15,000 a year for an individual to fund.[102] On its back often comes levels of other acquisitive or violent crimes.[103] A Home Office survey[104] of the results of drug testing of arrested persons was revealing. Some 47% of those in the survey arrested for shoplifting tested positive for opiates, some 30% for cocaine; 23% and 31% of arrestees for theft of a motor vehicle tested positive for opiates and amphetamines respectively; and 11% of arrestees for burglary tested positive for opiates. Of arrestees for burglary, taking a motor vehicle without consent, theft of a motor vehicle, or shoplifting, some 80% tested positive for at least one drug (although this also includes alcohol).

In recent years, various initiatives have been taken to address the drug-taking issue. The provisions relating to drug treatment and testing orders, introduced in 1998,[105]

---

100 Eleventh Report of Joint Committee of Human Rights, *op cit*, paras 54–55.

101 *Justice for All*, Cm 5563, para 131.

102 *Ibid*, para 137.

103 See the Proceeds of Crime Act 2002 which facilitates seizure of 'dirty money' pending investigation of a crime, and the provision to confiscate monies equivalent to the value of any benefit derived from drug trafficking, in the Drug Trafficking Offenders Act 1987.

104 Home Office Research Study 183, *Drugs and Crime: The results of research on drug testing and interviewing arrestees* (Home Office, 2002).

105 See ss 52–57 of Powers of Criminal Courts (Sentencing) Act 2000 ('SA 2000'), now repealed: see **8.23**.

were part of that. The White Paper *The Way Ahead*[106] suggests that drug problems are best tackled by identifying the users as early as possible, which is on arrest. There have been pilot drug-testing procedures for Class A drugs at police stations in Stafford, Nottingham and Hackney, under Criminal Justice and Court Services Act 2000 (CJCSA 2000) which permits testing of arrestees over 18 who are arrested for a 'trigger' offence, including acquisitive offences, and also possession or supply of certain drugs. Some 47% of those tested during the pilot in Stafford, 63% of people tested in Hackney and 58% tested in Nottingham tested positive for Class A drugs.[107] However, an evaluation of the pilot studies has overall proved inconclusive as to the relationship between mandatory testing and any reduction in crime.[108] It is in that context that the new Act provides a range of additional measures.

Possession of cannabis or cannabis resin

2.43   As noted at **2.13**, possession of a Class C drug becomes an arrestable offence.

Extension of drug-testing to juveniles in custody

2.44   The CJCSA 2000 created a new s 63B of PACE. Section 63B(1) allows the police to administer a test for the presence of Class A drugs where (a) the suspect has been charged with one of the trigger offences,[109] or (b) an officer of the rank of inspector or above has reasonable grounds for suspecting that the charged person has misused Class A drugs and that misuse has caused or contributed to the offence. The suspect had to be aged 18 or over. Section 5 reduces that age minimum to 14.[110]

2.45   The introduction of the power to drug-test *suspects* was a significant extension of police powers. As recently as 1997 the Government said that it had no intention to extend compulsory testing to those who had not been convicted of any offence.[111] Some might regard as curious the second part of s 63B (dealing with the reasonable suspicion that misuse of Class A drugs may have caused or contributed to the offence), given that at this stage the 'offence' itself may not have been proved or admitted. Any misgivings about the s 63B power, enforced on pain of criminal sanction,[112] are heightened in the context of its use against juveniles.

2.46   The test amounts to the taking of a sample of urine, or a non-intimate sample (PACE, s 63B(1)). The suspect must be asked to give a sample, having been given the

---

106 Cm 5074, paras 2.46–2.54.

107 David Kidney MP, HC Committee, 7 January 2003, col 150.

108 Home Office Findings No 180, Research, Development and Statistics Directorate (Home Office, 2003).

109 'Trigger offence' is defined by Sch 6 to the CJCSA 2000.

110 This may be varied by the Home Secretary by statutory instrument (PACE, s 63B(6A)).

111 See Consultation Paper *Breaking the Vicious Circle* (Home Office, 1997).

112 See **2.49**.

warning or information required by s 63B(5).[113] The section is silent as to when this may occur, and it appears to be open for the police to make such a request at any time while the suspect is in police detention, irrespective of whether he has been charged.

In the case of a suspect under the age of 17, the request for a sample, the warning identified above or the taking of the sample itself may only occur in the presence of an appropriate adult (s 63B(5A)).[114] Should a parent, guardian, or social worker be unavailable (for whatever reason) the appropriate adult for this purpose will be 'any responsible person over 18 so long as they are neither a police officer or employed by the police' (s 63B(10)). Since the wording of this mirrors that of PACE, Code C, para 1.7, the restriction on the solicitor acting as appropriate adult (contained in Note 1F) presumably applies equally.

2.47   Section 63B(7) provides that where a test is made, the information obtained from the sample may be disclosed for any of the following purposes:

(a)   to inform any decision about the grant of bail;

(b)   where a suspect is in police custody or remanded into custody by the court, to help make a decision about his supervision in custody;

(c)   to provide information to a court to reach a decision about sentencing and any decision about his supervision and release;

(d)   to ensure that appropriate advice and treatment can be given to a suspect or defendant.

This empowers the police to tell others in the criminal justice system about the drug usage in order to assist in the rehabilitation of a defendant or to ensure that anyone else dealing with him knows of the drug usage to protect his welfare, or to assist in arriving at the right sentence, or the right requirement in a community order. It thus prevents the use of the information for forensic or investigative purposes. That protection may not be quite what it seems: the police will have, or have access to, that information, which might prompt a demand for a non-intimate sample if the preconditions in s 63 are satisfied, and the defendant is marked, for the future, as a Class A drug user. Despite reassurances given during the passage of the Act as to the purpose of the extension, the fact that juveniles can be labelled in this way is a cause for some concern.

2.48   The retention and destruction of the sample fall within the provisions of PACE, s 64.[115] Section 64(1A) provides that, except when s 64(3) applies, samples may be retained after they have fulfilled the purposes for which they are taken, but must not be used by any person except for purposes related to the prevention or detection of crime, the investigation of an offence or the conduct of a prosecution. Thus the data will

---

113 Section 63B(5) requires an officer to warn the suspect (a) that, if when so requested, he fails without good cause to do so he may be liable to prosecution, and (b) in a case falling within s 63B(1)(b), of the authorisation of the officer and of the grounds for it. That authorisation may initially be verbal, but must be recorded as soon as practicable (PACE, s 63C). Modifications to s 38 of PACE (duties of custody officer after charge) are made by s 12, the effect of which is that the custody officer is under no obligation to release the detained person if he is being detained further to enable the use of this power.

114 As defined by s 63B(10), inserted by 2003 Act, s 15.

115 See **2.39**.

remain, and may inform decisions about the individual in future investigations or dealings with the detained person, subject to the limits on the use of the information in s 63B(7).

2.49 Failure to comply, without good cause, with the request for a sample will be a criminal offence punishable on summary conviction by imprisonment for a term not exceeding 3 months or a fine not exceeding Level 4 on the Standard Scale (currently £2000). The usual provisions relating to custodial sentences and fines on juveniles will apply.

2.50 The House of Lords expressed considerable concern at this extension of s 63B to juveniles. The very need for the change was doubted, given known levels of Class A drug usage by juveniles. One survey[116] showed that among 15-year-olds, cannabis (Class C) was the most frequently used drug, and the use of Class A drugs was very rare, although those figures could be atypical because regular Class A users might be unlikely to be at school to participate in such a survey. Home Office research[117] reveals that, when just under 300 young offenders were interviewed, the results indicated that most had used cannabis, a quarter had used cocaine and LSD, but only 18% had used crack cocaine and 11% heroin. The levels of usage of Class A drugs by juveniles are far from clear.

There are also concerns as to the nature and exercise of the powers.[118] The offence for which the suspect is arrested need not have a connection, direct or indirect, with the taking of drugs. There is no requirement that the offence be directly a drug or drug-related offence, merely that it be a 'trigger' offence.[119] The test will be carried out at the police station, which is not a place where young people charged with offences are customarily received with warmth. The test may be carried out in the presence of a total stranger if a friend or relative is unwilling or unavailable to attend. The information will then be passed on to those with a legitimate interest, who may be ready to conclude the suspect is an habitual drug-user. Indeed, the more this is denied, the more some may conclude that the defendant has a problem which he declines to acknowledge. There will, at this stage, be no evidence to distinguish the habitual user from the dabbler, or even the one-off experimenter who tries a drug through peer pressure. There are also concerns to ensure that the information from test results is handled sensitively. These results should be used only to inform a course of treatment, rather than influencing criminal proceedings where they have no bearing on the crime and do not relate to problematic behaviours.

2.51 There is also the issue of consent. Medical practitioners called by the police to take samples will not take them where a suspect declines to give permission as this is unethical and may constitute a civil battery, because even s 63B does not permit the compulsory taking of a sample. Indeed, such consent may not always be genuine, informed consent. Most medical practitioners require a parent or guardian's consent, which may not be forthcoming. Where no doctor or nurse is needed, consent must still

---

116 A school lifestyle survey undertaken jointly by the Department of Health and Youth Justice Board, cited by Lord Hodgson, HL Committee, 7 July 2003, cols 55–60.

117 Home Office Research Studies 192 and 261.

118 See Lord Adebowale, Chief Executive of Turning Point, HL Committee, cols 51–53.

119 Defined by CJCSA 2000, Sch 6.

be given, but there will be individuals who might decline for fear of embarrassment or pain, out of awkwardness or through fear of parental reaction to any discovery that drugs have been used. These may, depending on the evidential base established and the attitude of the court, fall within the description of 'good cause'.

2.52   There are also HRA 1998 issues, as to whether the Art 8 rights of the juvenile are infringed. Limitations to the right to respect for private life must fall within one of the purposes identified in Art 8(2), be proportionate and address a pressing social need. A s 63B search is for 'the prevention of crime' and, possibly, the 'protection of health or morals', given that the purpose of the s 63A sample procedure is to enable any drug-related issue of the juvenile to be addressed. Nonetheless, the younger the individual, the greater the justification for the intrusion on the right which must be shown. Given the low levels of Class A drug misuse to be found among this age group, it by no means follows that such justification can be established. Any blanket use of this power would be open to challenge. The police must be able to demonstrate that it was appropriate to take a sample from *this* suspect. So, too, with the transmission of the information obtained from the test, although if that has proved Class A drug positive, the terms of Art 8(2) will often be satisfied, provided that the wider transmission is appropriate to the prevention of crime or ensuring the welfare of the suspect. Care will need to be taken to ensure that information is not used for inappropriate purposes: it would be inappropriate to use it for the purposes of the trial, other than sentencing, but that, in any event, is not within the scope of the section. It is not intended that the record of the test be used as a 'tool to beat the offender [sic] in any adverse way'.[120] The Minister stressed that information from the test could not be used as additional evidence for the offence which was charged, for investigative purposes nor would the court be entitled to view drug use as an aggravating feature of the offence charged. This last point sits somewhat uneasily with the terms of s 63B(7), which allows the court to have regard to such information when sentencing. It may not aggravate the offence itself, but nonetheless is relevant information that will be relevant in determining what sentence is to be passed and what requirements, if any, that sentence should contain. Nor does it sit easily with the 'joined up' approach to criminal justice that the new Act, and the Courts Act 2003, promote.

---

120 Baroness Scotland, HL Committee, 7 July 2003, col 78.

Chapter 3

PRE-TRIAL PROCESS

INSTITUTING CRIMINAL PROCEEDINGS

3.1 Under pre-existing provisions, proceedings are commenced by summons, charge and information. The White Paper *Justice for All* described some of these methods and procedures as 'cumbersome'.[1] It proposed that all cases should begin life as a charge, whether the defendant had been arrested or not. Part IV of the new Act simplifies the system by providing for the issuing of a charge and a 'requisition'. It gives the prosecution much greater involvement in the choice of charge at the outset. It also attempts to divert suitable people from the court system entirely, by the use of conditional cautions.

3.2 These changes reflect the current failure always to get the charge right in the first place. Only some 23% of crime reported is solved. Of those cases where an offender has been charged, 13% of cases have to be discontinued by the CPS, either because there is not enough evidence to convict or because it is not in the public interest to proceed against the offender.[2] Some 45% of police files submitted to the CPS are not properly compiled, with the result that some of those charged are not convicted because of the lack of evidence. Some 40% of cases which do get as far as a trial then collapse due to inadequate preparation, costing £80 million to the taxpayer and resulting in acquittal, sometimes without the evidence being heard.

Research also shows that failure to get the charge right early makes the plea before venue (PBV) process less useful than it could be.[3] Pilot projects placing prosecutors and police officers or civilian employees under the same roof ('co-location') saved 14% of what would otherwise have been spent, and in one area, the number of cases disposed of at the first hearing increased by 20%.[4]

The changes are intended to create a system where the choice of charge is made by the CPS, in the expectation that more guilty pleas will occur at an earlier stage in proceedings and that proceedings can be commenced in a more efficient manner.

---

1   At p 52.

2   *Justice for All*, Cm 5563, Ch 3 'Getting the Process Right from the Start', p 52.

3   See Herbert 'Mode of Trial and Magistrates' Sentencing Powers: Will increased powers inevitably lead to a reduction in the committal rate?' [2003] Crim LR 314.

4   See *Justice for All, op cit*, p 51.

The new section 37 of PACE

3.3   Section 28 of, and Sch 2 to, the new Act amend s 37 of PACE. They came into force on 29 January 2004 (see **1.3**). Section 37 provides three possibilities as to how a detained suspect will be dealt with:

–   release without charge but on bail (s 37(1)(a));
–   release without charge and on bail but not for that purpose (s 37(1)(b));
–   release without charge and without bail (s 37(1)(c));
–   charge (s 37(1)(d)).

Where the suspect is released without charge, the police will be under a duty to inform him that he is being released so that the file can go to the CPS to make a decision as to whether to charge, or to caution conditionally, with which offence or on what terms.

Bail pending decision

3.4   If the CPS are to decide on charge, or as to whether a new conditional caution is appropriate,[5] the police will normally need to bail the suspect in order to send a file about the offence to the local CPS, because, except in straightforward cases, the maximum limits of detention under PACE (now increased to 36 hours except in terrorist cases),[6] will not generally be long enough for the prosecutor's view to be ascertained. This leaves an offender on bail, because there is no power to remand a person in custody until he has been charged. Once a suspect is charged, s 38 of PACE permits the custody officer to detain him until the next court hearing, or to place conditions on bail to prevent absconding, commission of offences or interference with witnesses, for his own protection or where there are doubts about his real identity. But no such conditions could be attached to pre-charge bail: a suspect could re-offend, or attempt to dissuade a witness from persisting with his complaint, or destroy evidence or, especially in the case of a Class A drug addict, carry on criminal activity to fund his addiction, without being in breach of any bail conditions. In future the police will be able to attach conditions to bail granted pre-charge (see **3.9**). Although this involves restrictions on the liberty of an individual before charge, if this procedure were not adopted, an early charge might otherwise result, thus triggering normal bail arrangements including the power to impose conditions.

The decision-making process

3.5   Section 37(7A) makes the custody officer the sole arbiter as to which of the permitted courses of action should be taken. In order to assist in deciding that question, Guidance will be issued and published[7] by the DPP pursuant to a new s 37A (Sch 2, para 3). Police officers must have regard to that guidance, which may be revised from time to time (s 37A(1)–(3)). Suspects will need clear advice about the likely attitude of the custody officer to their release. Guidance may vary from region to region, or cover certain types of cases or circumstances. Recently, 'fast-track' squads of Crown Prosecutors have worked with police and courts in certain

---

5   See **3.14** and **3.22**.

6   See **2.30**.

7   See s 37A(5).

high-crime inner city areas to deal speedily with street robbery.[8] Specific guidance may be drawn up for particular localities to tackle locally prevalent crimes, for example drugs in police areas covering airports or seaports, gun crime in inner-city areas or public order offences during major football tournaments. With the addition of this possibility of regional or offence-related Guidance to that of potentially differing PACE Codes, the task of legal representatives at the police station in some areas is likely to become increasingly complicated.

The DPP's powers

3.6   An entirely new s 37B (inserted by Sch 2, para 3) sets out the duties of the police in liaising with the CPS, and the reciprocal obligations of the CPS. Once a person has been bailed under s 37(7)(a), an officer involved in the investigation must, as soon as practicable, notify the DPP of any information that the DPP requires. The information required will, again, be specified in Guidance issued by the DPP.[9]

The DPP (in reality, a suitably authorised Crown Prosecutor) must then decide whether there is sufficient evidence of the commission of an offence by the suspect to lead to a charge,[10] using the present 'sufficiency of evidence' and 'public interest' tests. In considering the public interest, the DPP must consider whether it is possible to dispose of the matter by way of a conditional caution (s 37B(5))[11] or in the case of juveniles, a reprimand or final warning.[12]

The prosecutor's decision must be communicated in writing to the officer. If no prosecution is to follow, or the suspect is to be offered a caution, then the custody officer must notify the suspect in writing. The prosecutor's decision (to proceed, to caution or to take no further action) will be binding upon the police. However, if a caution is offered and it is not possible in fact to administer it, then the suspect must be charged instead.

Any caution will be administered on the 'bail back' date (that is, when the suspect returns to the police station on the day he is required to answer his police bail). A caution can also be administered to a person already in police detention. Charging, if it is to happen, can occur on the bail back date or by service of a written charge and requisition[13] upon the defendant at any time (CJA 2003, s 29).

3.7   Section 37B thus hands the decision about charge to the CPS in many, although not all, cases. Minor and road traffic offences will be capable of being dealt with by the police alone where the suspect admits guilt to the police. It also by implication removes the police discretion as to whether to caution, as this is not an option retained by s 37(7)(a)–(c), although presumably officers can, and are likely to, make recommendations when communicating with the DPP under s 37B(1). The police will still be able to charge without referral to the CPS (s 37(7)(c)), but the choice of charge

---

8   *The 'Premium Service'*, Ch 3, para 3.19; *Justice for All, op cit.*

9   Section 37A(2)–(6).

10   Section 37B(2)–(3).

11   See **3.14**.

12   Under Crime and Disorder Act 1998 (CDA 1998), s 65.

13   See **3.22**.

will be limited by the DPP's guidance, which will have to be followed. Further, the CPS will no longer need to serve proposed notices of discontinuance upon the police offering them an opportunity to comment before a decision is taken.

These developments are unlikely to be welcomed by all police officers, who now lose control over the choice of charge or choice as to whether to charge or caution. They will be seen by some as taking away a degree of autonomy from the investigatory agency. However, the research for the Auld Review,[14] and that cited by the White Paper *Justice to All*,[15] highlighted the fact that the laying of the wrong charge, or overcharging, were real obstacles to securing guilty pleas, and something that had to be tackled if the objectives set by the Government for reform of the criminal justice system were in fact to be achieved.

Release under s 37(7)(a) – breach of bail following release

3.8 A suspect may be released on conditional bail and breach those conditions, or he may be in breach of a new s 37C by failing to attend on the bail back date. Providing that the preconditions in s 37C apply, he may now face arrest for one, or both, of these failings.

Section 37C will apply where the person has been released on bail under s 37(7)(a) (ie while the CPS are deciding whether to charge him and with what offence). A person who had been charged could have bail conditions imposed under s 38 of PACE (police station to court bail), so s 37C only applies to the new situation of being bailed pending a DPP decision).

Section 46A of PACE (which confers a power to arrest for failure to answer police bail) is amended to allow arrest for breach of the bail conditions: the DPP must not, at the time of the arrest, have given notice of that decision. The police must then either release the suspect without charge, either on bail or without bail (presumably while the decision is still awaited from the DPP) or, alternatively, may charge the suspect with the original offence for which he was arrested and bailed (PACE, 37(2)).

3.9 The potential that a failure to surrender can precipitate being charged might, perhaps, be seen as an incentive to answer to the bail. In addition, a suspect who is charged under s 37C(2)(a) risks being refused bail under s 38 of PACE (post-charge bail) because he has demonstrated that there are reasonable grounds for believing that he would fail to attend court if he were bailed once again.

The police cannot simply charge as a punitive measure: the custody officer must be satisfied that there is sufficient evidence to charge the suspect with the offence for which the arrest was initially made. He must also be satisfied that the suspect did not have reasonable cause for the failure to attend at the police station at the time appointed for him to do so (PACE, s 37C(3)).

Breach of any condition imposed under the new s 37D now becomes arrestable (PACE, s 46A(1A), added by Sch 2, para 5). Again, the suspect may be charged if: (a) there is, in the opinion of the custody officer, sufficient evidence to charge for the

---

14   *Op cit*, Ch 10, paras 35–38.

15   *Op cit*, Ch 3.

offence for which that person was arrested, or (b) any bail condition was broken and the suspect had no reasonable cause to do so (PACE, s 37C(4)). What amounts to 'reasonable cause' under the BA 1976 is a matter of fact for any tribunal asked to deal with breach proceedings to assess, aided by representations from the defence and, perhaps, the prosecution. A custody officer operating under the new s 37 will find himself in an analogous position save that in the police station the police act as prosecutor, and a defence solicitor can make representations to dissuade the police from taking any action adverse to the suspect.[16]

Section 37D(5) requires the custody officer to 'take reasonable steps' to consult the DPP before charge following arrest for one or other breach. What is reasonable will depend upon the individual facts of the case, but it would seem this exercise would only be worthwhile if a Crown Prosecutor were either present at the police station, or, alternatively, willing to advise over the phone, possibly without having seen the police file. Prosecutors may be reluctant to advise by telephone without seeing some evidence. Contacting a prosecutor outside working hours or during unsociable hours may not be easy either, although the CPS is introducing a prosecution version of the Duty Solicitor scheme, whereby advice may be obtained from a prosecutor 24 hours a day.[17]

3.10 If the DPP has not yet taken a decision, or there is insufficient evidence to charge, the suspect will have to be bailed again (s 37A(6)) and the conditions previously laid down will continue to apply. The words of the subsection say: 'shall ... be subject to the same conditions ... which applied immediately before his arrest' and thus appear to remove any discretion to vary conditions, which could be very burdensome for a defendant. The conditions might, for example, deal with residence out of town, non-contact with a spouse or partner who genuinely wants to reconcile, or with a curfew which affects employment prospects. It is of crucial importance that legal representatives negotiate manageable bail conditions from the outset, as the client may have to live with them for some weeks pending the decision of the DPP. Indeed, the new provisions do not contain any limits as to the period of time during which pre-charge bail can extend. One proposed amendment to the Act would have permitted s 37 bail to last no more than 28 or 30 days,[18] thus ensuring matters were concluded swiftly, and avoiding the costs of appeals against conditions of bail imposed by custody officers. In response, the Government[19] stated that this should be left to guidelines drawn up by the DPP and Association of Chief Police Officers, but reassured critics that public funding would be available to fund a challenge to the magistrates' court over conditions attached to pre-charge bail.

Guidelines are welcome, but there is no apparent opportunity for professional bodies or groups, or groups with interest in the welfare of mentally ill offenders or young people, to be consulted about the guidelines. They will not be debated by Parliament, and will not have the force of law. Not all of those arrested will be charged and, of those charged, not all will be guilty. Innocent people may be placed under onerous or

---

16 BA 1976, s 6(4).

17 'CPS Direct' or the Pre-charging Advice Scheme has been introduced across the country as part of co-location during 2003.

18 HL Committee, 14 July 2003, col 683.

19 Lord Goldsmith, HL Committee, *ibid*, col 864.

impracticable conditions while a decision from the DPP is awaited. The lack of a legal deadline is a matter for concern. Given inevitable pressures on CPS time, these cases, where there is no deadline in law by when a decision must be reached, may attract lower priority than cases where the suspect has been charged and thus is subject to deadlines imposed by the court for progress, or those where the suspect may be subject to the custody time-limit provisions under s 22 of the Prosecution of Offences Act 1985 (POA 1985). These defendants will necessitate a higher priority in consequence than someone not yet charged.

3.11 Section 47 of PACE is amended, with a new s 47(1)(b)–(e). No application under s 5B of the BA 1976 by the prosecutor can be made to the magistrates to vary bail imposed under s 37(7)(a) (bail on charge) or s 37C(2)(b) (breach of bail following charge). Section 47(1)(c) prevents a defence application in the same circumstances as above. Section 47(1)(d) disallows an application under s 43B (applications where bail was granted under Part IV of PACE or under s 3(8) of the BA 1976 (committals to the Crown Court for trial or sentence)). However, s 47(1)(e) grants a right for an application 'by or on behalf of the person' to vary conditions. This appears to be only a defence application, but s 47(1) makes it plain that if bail is varied it does not lapse following that variation. This complex route is designed to make it plain that pre-existing provisions cannot be used to deal with conditional bail. A specific right to match the new s 37 regime is introduced.

3.12 Limited redress exists for a suspect whose bail extends over, say, many weeks and whose liberty is curtailed by conditional bail. Article 5 of the ECHR may not assist, as conditional bail has not been held to be a restriction of liberty, unlike detention.[20] In *McDonald v Procurator Fiscal, Elgin*[21] the court left the door open to the argument that a condition which compelled a person to remain where the court had put him may become a deprivation of liberty. Further, this interference with liberty by the custody officer has no independent judicial input, of a type envisaged by Art 5(3) and (4). Arguably, prolonged bail conditions become an interference with one's rights to respect for one's private life under Art 8. Those conditions could become disproportionate to the infringement, founding an Art 5 or Art 8 challenge, and delay also raises issues under Art 6. Conditional bail may encompass conditions such as not to enter a certain locality or contact a named person, not to drive, or not to leave the country. Such conditions could prevent a person going to work or socialising, earning a living, working abroad or taking a holiday. There is thus the scope for arguments based on infringement of Art 8 rights (right to respect for private and family life). The key question will then be whether the restriction of the Art 8(1) right is necessary for, and proportionate to, the prevention of crime under Art 8(2), and depend upon the nature of the condition, and of the crime for which the arrest was made and bail granted, and the length, nature and effect of the restriction, and whether the alternative to conditional bail would be charge and remand in custody.

Section 37D – supplementary provisions

3.13 The police have the power to arrest for breach of bail while awaiting a decision under s 37(7)(a) or s 37C(2)(b). They may vary the date, time and place when bail is to

---

20 See *R v HM Advocate* (2000) *The Times*, 14 April, HC Just.

21 (2003) *The Times*, 17 April, HC Just.

be answered, but that variation must be in writing under s 37D(2) and either served by post or in person when the person attends to answer the original bail back date.

A postponing of bail has no effect upon any conditions which will continue to apply (s 37D(4)). There is now a power to keep a suspect in custody following arrest to enable the formalities under s 37B and s 37C to be attended to (PACE s 46A, added by s 37D(4)) and, in the case of drunks or others who are unfit to be dealt with, to keep them detained until sober or otherwise fit enough to be dealt with under s 37D(5). Presumably this will be part of the maximum 36 hours' detention time, otherwise a suspect's liberty could be deprived beyond the usual PACE limits.

CONDITIONAL CAUTIONS

3.14 Part III of the new Act introduces conditional cautions. A conditional caution is a caution which is given in respect of an offence committed by the offender, and which has conditions attached to it with which the offender must comply. Failure to comply with those conditions renders the offender liable to be prosecuted for the offence in respect of which the caution was given.

3.15 Not everyone who commits a crime needs to be dealt with by a court. In minor cases, mentally ill offenders are often diverted to seek treatment or other help. Juveniles may receive a graduated scheme of reprimands and final warnings under s 65 of the CDA 1998. These are a record of the fact that the individual has offended and admitted the offence, but no penalty is imposed. They become part of the record of the character of the individual. Adults may receive a caution in a similar fashion: they must admit their guilt and there must be sufficient evidence to justify a conviction.[22]

There has been until now no sanction for an adult who accepts a caution and then commits another offence, save that he may lose the prospect of receiving another caution. There is no requirement for reparation, although it may be intimated by the police that they might be prepared to deal with the crime by way of caution should the individual pay compensation for damage done, for example in a case of vandalism. However, officers are specifically discouraged from becoming involved in negotiations between offenders and victims about reparation.[23] With juveniles, as each step on the graduated scale is exhausted, they come closer to having to appear before a youth court and having to face sentence.

3.16 The Auld Review[24] observed that some 266,000 cautions were issued in 1999, amounting to some 25% of 'solved' offences. This is a significant number of extra-court disposals. However, it noted that the system paid no heed to the feelings of victims; it lacked rigour and posed a temptation to hard-pressed police forces to use cautions to effect a better clear-up rate of crimes. It therefore proposed 'Caution-plus' – a new scheme where cautions would be administered on certain conditions which, if unfulfilled by an offender, would permit him to be prosecuted instead. This was the basis for the subsequent recommendations in the White Paper *Justice for All* and the provisions for conditional cautions contained in Part 3 of the Act.

---

22 National Standards of Cautioning, Home Office Circular 18/1994.

23 See Circular 59/1990, para 14.

24 *Op cit*, Ch 10, paras 41–47.

The order

3.17 Section 22 defines a conditional caution as one 'given in respect of an offence and which has conditions attached with which the offender must comply'. Conditions can only be imposed to the extent that they either 'ensure or facilitate the rehabilitation of the offender' or to make sure he effects some reparation (s 22(3)). A conditional caution may be administered by a constable, an investigating officer[25] or someone authorised by the DPP (s 22(4)). This adds two new possible categories of persons entitled to administer the caution, giving added flexibility. The CPS have not had, hitherto, any power to administer a caution. A case had to go back to the police, in order for the caution to be formally given, normally by an inspector. The potentially wide definition of 'investigators' creates the possibility of cautions being administered by investigators other than the police. For example, the DSS deal with benefit fraud and already have powers under various Social Security Acts to deduct monies from fraudsters' benefit to make good any defalcations. A conditional caution here, for minor offences, would save considerable time preparing a case for court, and save attendant costs. Non-governmental bodies such as the RSPCA also investigate and prosecute – a conditional caution for a first-time offence where animal neglect was occasioned by inability to pay veterinary fees or through ignorance, with conditions, say, of not owning an animal for a set period of time, might save valuable time and money, protect animals and allow already scarce resources to be used elsewhere. The argument also extends to non-police prosecutions, such as truancy under the Education Acts, and offences under environmental health and pollution legislation. Conditions attached to the caution could assist in educating offenders to prevent repetition of unpleasant offences, yet bear the sanction of prosecution if the offender did not comply or failed to heed the lesson of the experience.

Requirements before a caution may be administered

3.18 Section 23 prescribes five requirements for a conditional caution.

(1) the 'cautioner' must have evidence that the suspect has committed the crime;
(2) the DPP must be satisfied there is sufficient evidence to charge that suspect with the offence and that a caution should be given. The DPP is unlikely to consider a caution appropriate in serious cases or where an offender has similar convictions, a poor record of offending or where the offence merits imprisonment;
(3) the suspect must admit the offence to the cautioner. A suspect may be content to accept a caution, even if he is not guilty of the offence, because it may be less risky than going to court and being involved in a trial. A caution represents a solved crime to a police officer, who is probably under constant pressure to increase his detection rate. A caution can therefore be a mutually convenient solution for all;
(4) the nature of the caution, and consequences of its breach, must be explained to the offender by the person administering it. It must be made clear that breach is likely to result in prosecution, but s 23 does not make prosecution automatic;
(5) the offender must sign a document which records the details of the offence and admission of it by him. This document is significant. In the case of a prosecution for breach, it will be admissible as evidence of the offence against the offender.

---

25 As defined by the Home Secretary in a Code of Practice to be issued under s 25 of the CJA 2003.

The offence prosecuted will not be the breach of the conditions, but, rather, the original offence. If A accepts a caution for criminal damage on condition he cleans up his graffiti within seven days, but then changes his mind, he could be prosecuted for the criminal damage offence. If he chose to plead not guilty, he would be faced with his signed admission to the offence as evidence against him (in law, a confession). Unless he had some compelling argument to exclude that evidence under s 76 or s 78 of PACE, he would be summarily convicted and could be sentenced accordingly. The fact of prosecution means the conditional caution ceases to have any effect, so there is no argument of double jeopardy.[26]

3.19 Cautioning does have its dangers (see **3.16**). These have always existed, but the new scheme adds the potential for criminal prosecution. Against that, the alternative in pre-existing law might well have been prosecution.

Legal advice may not necessarily be available. The Legal Services Commission (LSC) has already indicated that it intends to curb expenditure on police station advice and, as there is no risk of loss of liberty nor any need to interview under caution once the offer of a conditional caution is made, this would seem an area in which the LSC may feel that free legal advice need not be made available generally.[27] Cautions administered away from a police station or by a non-police officer may fall outside the duty solicitor free advice scheme because of the location of the cautioning or the identity of the cautioner. This would depend on the terms and conditions of an individual solicitor's contract with the Criminal Defence Service. In *R (on the application of Beale) v South Wiltshire Magistrates' Court*,[28] there was held to be no entitlement to free legal advice for a suspect at an interview at the DSS office. It may be thought that attending on the administering of one of these new cautions would be unnecessary, given the obligation in s 23 to explain everything. Further, if a person is prosecuted under s 24, it may be difficult to secure a representation order (legal aid) as the 'interests of justice' test may not in the circumstances be met.

Codes of practice

3.20 The new statutory provisions are skeletal in outline. However, a Code of Practice will be drawn up to deal with, among other things, when such cautions will be appropriate, the procedure to be followed, the types of conditions to be attached, who may administer cautions and at what type of premises, and how compliance with the conditions is to be monitored. Interested parties will have an opportunity to make representations about the Code at a draft stage.

The requirements in s 23 may be difficult to satisfy on an offender's first visit to a police station. He may therefore find he is bailed under the new s 37 of PACE and thus have conditions on his bail, while a decision is then taken as to whether to caution, prosecute or take no further action. Given that s 23(2) requires some input from the DPP (sufficiency of evidence and public interest test criteria), unless the CPS can be consulted while the offender is at the police station, bail seems inevitable while the CPS consider the police file.

---

26 See Chapter 11.

27 *Law Society Gazette* 100/38, 9 October 2003.

28 167 JP 41, DC.

The Code will need to deal with a whole range of issues, including the nature of any reparation (financial or non-financial), the extent to which the victim's agreement is necessary and the way conditions are defined. In this respect, s 25 is important. It involves the National Probation Service to assist cautioners in deciding whether conditional cautions should be given and if so, on what terms. The Service will also be responsible for supervising and rehabilitating cautionees and will presumably report non-compliance. Whether it will prosecute breaches (as it does with community orders which are not complied with) or whether this will be a CPS prosecution is unclear.

3.21   The position of the old cautioning system remains unclear. The Act does not formally abolish it – nor could it, for it was, in the context of adults, extra-statutory. No guidance was given during the passage of the Act. One can imagine cases of a relatively minor nature (perhaps, for example, the taking of a traffic cone by an over-exuberant student) where a caution would be appropriate, but where no necessity for conditions arises. A letter of apology for the probably unnoticed loss to the highway authority seems meaningless. If it is intended to end cautions without condition this would seem to create inflexibility and either force prosecution, which may be a disproportionate response by the police or CPS, or alternatively result in highly artificial conditions being imposed. Common sense might suggest that there will be times when a caution ought to be offered without conditions which would, presumably, be of an informal nature.

MODE OF INITIATING CRIMINAL PROCEEDINGS

3.22   Once ss 28 to 31 of the new Act are fully in force, the process of instituting criminal proceedings will change. The prosecutor (as defined by s 29(5)) will need to:

(1)   issue a written charge setting out the allegation;
(2)   issue a 'requisition' requiring the accused to appear before the magistrates' court at the same time as the charge is issued;
(3)   serve both documents upon the court and the accused.

3.23   The Auld Review pointed to the antiquated system of beginning the criminal process before the courts.[29] A prosecutor could charge, summons or lay an information against the proposed defendant. Only a charge usually brought with it an obligation to attend court. Many cases begun by summons were adjourned at the first hearing due to the non-appearance of the accused, whose attendance could thereafter only be compelled by warrant, and a further adjournment was often needed to give him the opportunity to attend, under threat of the issue of a warrant. This was because the mere fact of service of a summons did not place the offender on bail, and thus under an obligation to surrender. Many cases begun by summons could be dealt with in the offender's absence if he pleaded guilty by post or, if he failed to attend, his trial could be conducted in his absence provided he had been made aware of the date and time of the hearing. Such cases were dealt with under s 12 of the MCA 1980. Section 12 could be used where the offence was summary-only, and any term of

---

29   *Op cit*, Ch 10, 'Mechanics of Charging', paras 416–422.

imprisonment was limited to 3 months.[30] Section 308 of the new Act has removed that limit so that many more offences can be dealt with in the defendant's absence, although the court will require those whom it is considering dealing with in a manner more serious than a fine or absolute discharge to attend in person for sentencing.

The third method of commencing criminal proceedings – an information – required the attendance of someone at court to give brief evidence of the facts, eg a police officer (or probation officer in breach cases).

Sections 29 to 31 of the new Act create a new system of requisitions and written charge. These changes are intended to cut out wasted first and second appearances in motoring, local authority and breach of community penalty prosecutions. It should promote much faster resolution of these cases. The changes will necessitate alterations to the rules under s 144 of the MCA 1980, and the power to make new rules is conferred by s 30 of the new Act.

3.24   The power to issue an information as a means of obtaining a summons is abolished (s 29(4)). It remains an option for public prosecutors as a means of obtaining a warrant under s 1 of the MCA 1980 (issue of summons/warrant for arrest) to bring a charge against someone already in custody, and for a party other than a public prosecutor to obtain a summons or warrant under s 1 of the MCA 1980.

Consequential amendments are made to ensure that references to informations and Summonses henceforth read as if the words 'written charge' or requisition' had appeared in the original text. The Act also abolishes the practice of requiring evidence on oath to substantiate an information in order to obtain a warrant.

BAIL

3.25   Research conducted for the White Paper showed that 18% of adults offend on bail, and 38% of under-18s, and 12% of all those bailed subsequently fail to attend court.[31] The White Paper indicated the Government's commitment to preventing offending while on bail, as well as preventing trials from collapsing due to the non-attendance of a defendant. The Act makes considerable changes to the BA 1976, including the reduction of opportunities to challenge bail refusals or the imposition of conditions by a court.

3.26   Section 13 makes changes of emphasis in respect of non-imprisonable offences. Bail may be granted free of conditions, or with conditions, if it is not refused altogether. There must be a legitimate aim to a condition and any condition must be reasonable and proportionate to that aim. Conditions can be used to minimise a risk of, say, failure to attend, or of further offending, or to reduce the likelihood of contact with a witness. Section 13 amends ss 3 and 3A of, and Sch 1 to, the BA 1976, in that a court may now impose conditions upon an offender for his own protection or welfare. This extends to young defendants under the age of 18. Previously, a remand into custody often followed once the court felt satisfied there was a substantial risk to the

---

30   See Sch 26 for increase in penalties.

31   *Justice for All, op cit,* Ch 3.

welfare or protection of an accused: for example, where the suspect had suicidal tendencies, or where other people were hostile towards him, given the nature of the crime alleged to have been committed. A crime provoking serious public outrage (perhaps an assault against a child, or racially motivated offences) may cause some communities to seek out a defendant to dispense summary justice if the accused is bailed. Under the amended s 3(6), conditions may be imposed for the defendant's own welfare, perhaps requiring contact with the local mental health services, or requiring abstinence from alcohol. The existence of this power should prevent the keeping in custody until trial of some people who do not otherwise pose a risk of further trouble, thus freeing up prison or (in the case of mentally ill defendants) hospital spaces which might otherwise be occupied needlessly.

3.27   A change of emphasis concerning s 7 of the BA 1976 (absconding, etc) is introduced by s 13(4). Henceforth, the defendant should be granted bail if he has been arrested under s 7 and the court is satisfied that there is a no significant risk of his failing to surrender, commit further offences or interfere with witnesses, whether or not he was subject to conditions. Formerly, under Sch 1, para 5, Part II, to the BA 1976, the fact that a person had been arrested under s 7 meant that the court need not grant him bail again in those proceedings. Under the amended provision, the test for refusing bail is stiffened, in the defendant's favour at this stage, to bring it in to line with the recommendations of the Law Commission.[32] However, the commission of an offence on bail presents other problems as the climate hardens towards those who do not honour their obligations while on bail with the introduction of ss 14 and 15 of the Act.

Offending on bail

3.28   The distinction between indictable, either-way and summary-only offences maintained by s 26 of the CJPOA 1994 is abolished so far as the commission of an offence while on bail for an earlier crime is concerned. Being on bail for a summary-only offence is now treated in the same fashion as being on bail for the other two categories, so that all offenders on bail are treated in the same fashion if they commit a further offence while on bail.

Under pre-existing law, those who offended while on bail for a summary-only offence were much better positioned to obtain bail when subsequently brought before the court. The police, in particular, have expressed frustration that a suspect on bail re-offends but nonetheless is granted bail, sometimes with a relaxation of bail conditions. The Auld Review[33] reported police disenchantment at the lack of CPS vigour (as it perceived) that when an offender was arrested under s 7 of the BA 1976, the court frequently lessened the conditions and re-bailed that person. Some 25% of offenders re-offend while on bail.[34] The Attorney-General suggested that this could be as high as 40%.[35]

---

32   See *Guidance to Bail Decision-Takers and Their Advisers*, Law Com No 269 (2001).

33   *Op cit*, p 429, para 81.

34   Second Reading, HC Deb, 4 December 2002, col 991, per Stephen Hesford MP.

35   HL Committee, 7 July 2003, col 102.

The substitution made by the new Act, replacing the pre-existing Sch 1, para 2A to the BA 1976, now requires a court to 'give weight' to the fact that the defendant is already on bail when assessing whether there is a substantial risk that the defendant would commit further offences if released on bail. This obligation will be triggered where the defendant was on bail at the time of this new offence, and:

– the new offence is imprisonable; or
– the offence for which he was originally bailed was imprisonable; or
– both the old and new offences are imprisonable.

The 'giving particular weight' to the fact of offending while on bail seems destined in reality to lead to a presumption against bail. The prosecutor may well be more successful at securing a remand in custody by advancing this ground than by advancing the other grounds open to him, such as a danger of failure to surrender, or of interfering with a witness.

3.29   This new emphasis appears designed to make bail decision-takers think hard about the wisdom of re-bailing, given the behaviour of the accused since his last grant of bail, but, arguably, it nibbles away at the presumption of bail under s 4 of the 1976 Act, and raises issues under Art 5 ECHR because the court should now re-bail such a defendant only if it is *satisfied that there is no significant risk of committing an offence on bail*. Even then, if so satisfied, s 14 does not require that bail be granted.

Take, for example, the defendant (A) bailed for a public order offence at a football match, who returns to court charged with a common assault on his girlfriend. On this second occasion the CPS oppose bail. The court will be required to have regard to the alleged re-offending while on bail, and must be satisfied that there is no significant risk of any further offending before it can bail A. Even if it accepts that the fight with the girlfriend was a 'one-off' and the chances of him getting into trouble again while on bail are not great, A may well not be bailed because he must overcome the presumption against him. It effectively places the onus on the defendant to convince the court that he will not do anything criminal again in these proceedings, an inherently difficult task. During a bail application, the prosecution's version of the events is deemed to be correct, although the defence may comment on the strength of that evidence to expose weaknesses. The defendant must then convince the court that he should get bail, unlike the position under the pre-existing law where the prosecution had to show that there was a *substantial risk* that he would commit further offences, fail to surrender or interfere with witnesses.[36] If no such risk was proven, he could expect to be bailed with or without conditions.[37] Practitioners will need to be vigilant in challenging the strength of the evidence at bail hearings to try to offset the presumption that effectively flows from these changes.

---

36 See concerns of Lord Thomas of Gresford, HL Committee, 7 July 2003, cols 101–102.

37 Lord Borrie (and the Attorney-General) described the new law as ' … a well-justified tightening of the rules on bail both to ensure compliance with the ECHR and to prevent abuse and to retain the discretion of the court … '. Later, he added 'This is surely a very valid consideration that the court should take into account of [the fact a defendant had offended on bail] in determining whether there is a real risk of the defendant offending yet again while on bail. This is surely one of the key legitimate grounds for refusing bail, along with the other ones with which we are familiar such as the risk of absconding and the risk of interfering with witnesses': HL Committee, 7 July 2003, cols 102–104.

Article 5(1)(c) does permit detention in such circumstances. Normally, there is a presumption in favour of liberty. The onus is on the State to show that there are 'relevant and sufficient' reasons to justify continued detention. Such detention must be necessary and a proportionate deprivation of liberty. In *Letellier v France*[38] the European Court of Human Rights (ECtHR) held that the period of pre-trial detention must be limited to a reasonable period of time, and the court must examine all the circumstances for or against the public interest in detention, justifying any detention with due regard to the presumption of innocence. Decisions must be based on individual considerations and factors,[39] not upon abstract or stereotyped factors or reasons. Among the factors which might justify the withholding of bail are the risk of absconding, the risk of interference with the administration of justice, the prevention of crime, the preservation of public order, and the need to protect the defendant. The key test is whether, on the particular facts of the individual case, the restriction imposed by s 14 is proportionate to the risk posed and whether any risk can properly be contained by conditional bail, or not at all making custody pending trail inevitable.

3.30   The Joint Committee on Human Rights concluded that this provision, and that in s 15,[40] gave rise to an unacceptable risk of violating the right to liberty under Art 5(1), and other Convention rights (including the right to respect for private life under Art 8). The Committee expressed its concerns thus:

> '... the court would be prevented from granting bail in at least some cases even though it is not satisfied that there is a sufficient public interest in detaining the defendant pending trial. Instead, the court would have to detain him or her unless satisfied that there is no significant risk that he or she would abscond. In some cases (for example, where a minor offence has been committed and the defendant poses no real risk to the community) the court would be prevented from granting bail where detaining the defendant in custody would be self-evidently disproportionate to any purpose, and in other cases it might be clear that the public interest in detaining the defendant is outweighed by other considerations ... A court would be prevented from considering the other Convention rights of the defendant, members of his or her family, and other dependants. All factors relating to the circumstances of the offence (for example that it might be of a very minor character) and the defendant (apart from the likelihood of offending or failing to surrender to custody) would be excluded from the court's consideration. The defendant would be required to satisfy the court as to negative propositions ... This is notoriously difficult.'

Absconding by persons on bail

3.31   Section 15 broadly follows the ethos and wording of s 14, introducing what was described as 'creating a presumption against bail. It requires the court to refuse bail to an adult defendant who fails without reasonable cause to answer bail in the same proceedings unless the court is satisfied that there is no significant risk that he would again fail to surrender if released on bail.'[41] Bail can still be granted under the 1976 Act, but the fact of absconding will be a serious hindrance to re-bail unless the risk of repetition is insignificant. Whether bail is granted again in the proceedings will be a matter for the court's discretion.

---

38   (1991) 14 EHRR 83, ECtHR.

39   *Yagci and Sargan v Turkey* (1995) 20 EHRR 505, at para 52, ECtHR; *A v France* (1998).

40   See **3.31**.

41   Solicitor-General, HC Consideration of Amendments, 19 May 2003, col 719.

3.32 Section 15 also modifies the procedure for laying a charge for absconding contrary to s 6 of the BA 1976. When a person has absconded, the court commonly issues a warrant for his arrest, which the police then execute once the individual is found. Normally, he is brought to court in custody as soon as is practicable following the arrest and the question of bail has to be addressed. The prosecutor will often lay a charge of absconding at this stage, unless satisfied that there was a good reason for the failure to attend or that the charge would otherwise be unreasonable or unjust in some way. The charge had to be brought within six months of the date on which the person had absconded under s 127 of the MCA 1980. The defendant would then be expected to plead to the charge. A guilty plea would lead to this latest conviction appearing on his criminal record, if arrested again, whether in these or any other proceedings. It would flag him up as a bad risk for bail, enabling a prosecutor to argue for his remand in custody because the conviction plus any other relevant facts creates a 'substantial risk that he would fail to surrender' (BA 1976, s 4).

Under the new provisions, the prosecution can lay a charge of absconding anything up to three months from the date of the suspect's surrender (if he gives himself up voluntarily), or from the date of arrest (or attendance at the police station) or other appearance in court in connection with the original proceedings. The prosecution is not 'run out' because an accused manages to evade arrest for more than six months.

The defence of reasonable cause will be looked at in a different manner in some cases (BA 1976, Sch 1, Part 1, paras 3–6). In some instances there will be a two-fold test. First, did the defendant fail to surrender? Secondly, if the defendant did fail to surrender, did he have reasonable cause for that failure, having regard to when he could first have reasonably been expected to surrender? A defendant who hands himself in will need to show he did so as soon as was reasonably practicable from the time the failure occurred.

3.33 Two examples demonstrate the issues. A fails to surrender, being involved in a car crash and is kept in hospital until late that night, turning up at court first thing the following day. He has reasonable cause, and has surrendered as soon as he could have. B fails to surrender, because he visits a terminally ill relative in Ireland. Following the death, B stays on for a fortnight as he is having a better time there than in England, where he has no job or money and the prospect of court is not a tempting one. Although his initial failure might provide reasonable cause, that disappears as he chooses to remain rather than return to surrender to his bail. B will now have to persuade the court that he will turn up faithfully for the rest of the proceedings. But there is, perhaps, no significant risk of absconding in his case and the court ought therefore to exercise its discretion in his case to give him bail.

3.34 It was originally intended that these provisions would apply only to adult offenders,[42] but they were extended to juveniles by amendments in the House of Lords. Juveniles are not affected in the same way, because the presumption against bail unless there is no significant risk does not apply to them. Rather, the fact of failing to surrender will be looked at in the same way as it was before the new Act, as a potential impediment to bail if the prosecution can show there is a substantial risk that the accused would fail to surrender; but when looking at the existence of any

---

42 HC Committee, 19 May 2003, cols 719–720.

reasonable cause for the failure to surrender, the court should attach 'particular weight' to the reason for not coming to court and/or whether having failed to attend court, the accused then surrendered as soon as reasonably practicable.

The difference between adults and juveniles is that adults who abscond will not get bail unless there is no significant risk of further absconding and the court is willing to bail them, whereas with juveniles, the court will scrutinise the reasons for not attending court properly when deciding whether to re-bail. The difference can be explained by the application of the welfare principle to young defendants. Juveniles may also be remanded into local authority care under s 23 of the Children and Young Persons Act 1933 (CYPA 1933) to avoid detention in a young offenders' institute, and also to ensure there is supervision and support for the young person to reduce the risk of absconding, re-offending or interfering with witnesses, or to minimise self-harm. An adult can be required to live at a bail hostel but the supervision and support there is unlikely to be as intensive (if it is available at all) as that which a young person in local authority care would receive. A juvenile who has attained the age of 12 will only be remanded pre-conviction into custody (as opposed to local authority care) if the requirements of s 23(5A) of the CYPA 1933 are fulfilled.

Restrictions on bail for Class A drug-users

3.35   We noted at **2.42** the strategy of introducing a range of measures to address the issue of drug-taking and drug-related crime. Section 19 addresses the issue in the context of bail, s 19(4) amending Sch 1 to the BA 1976, to permit a court to deny the defendant bail altogether, unless the court is satisfied that there is no significant risk of offending whilst on bail, or the defendant declines to take up an offer of a 'relevant assessment', or, having agreed to one, fails to comply with such an assessment.

It is a precondition that:

- the defendant be aged 18 or over;
- the presence of Class A drugs has been detected in his body; and
- *either* he has been charged under s 5(2) or s 5(3) of the Misuse of Drugs Act 1971, *or* the court is satisfied that his misuse of Class A drugs caused or contributed to his behaviour, *or* his offending was wholly or partly motivated by his intended misuse of a Class A drug.

Given that Class A drug-users will usually have to engage in crime to fund their habit, the risk of offending whilst on bail is perceived to be a high risk, and thus a legitimate ground for refusal of bail. Arguably, this satisfies the Art 5 concerns identified at **3.30**, limiting bail in that situation being legitimate and proportionate. Those who refuse to agree to or honour arrangements to help them overcome their habit will find bail much harder to secure.

It is envisaged that s 19 will be introduced as a pilot, where relevant assessments and follow-ups by suitably qualified persons (as defined by s 19(2)) will be available.

Bail and appeals to the higher courts

3.36   The Crown Court may entertain an application for bail when such an application has been refused by the magistrates. Under ss 16 and 17, this power is extended to permit the Crown Court to entertain applications to vary conditions. The High Court loses most of its jurisdiction in this respect.

3.37 Bail conditions impose serious impositions on a person's liberty. A condition to protect witnesses may force a suspect to move out of the area for a period. A curfew has obvious restrictions, as do conditions not to attend football matches, not to enter off-licences, to hand in a passport, not to contact a named individual, or to report frequently to a police station. As already noted, Art 8 ECHR issues arise. Although a defendant will be pleased to be given conditional bail instead of being remanded into custody, the conditions may be onerous and the lower court not disposed to alter them. The new right of appeal to the Crown Court provides some remedy.[43] Appeals against conditions will be limited. The subject-matter of the appeal is limited to those conditions listed in s 16(3), to which detailed reference should be made. Such an appeal can only be brought if an application for bail was 'made and determined' by the lower court under s 3(8)(a) of the BA 1976 by the defendant or under either s 3(8)(b) or s 5(1)(b) of the BA 1976 by the prosecution or a constable.

Once the Crown Court has determined any appeal, no further appeal can be made by the party who originally initiated the appeal unless or until a fresh decision on a future adjournment is made after this appeal was heard (s 16(8)). Unless the conditions in this section are satisfied, an appeal against conditions may not be brought, so some conditions may not be appealed in practice because they fall outside s 16(3) or they do not attach to one of the hearings listed at s 16(1). This could cause injustice if an onerous condition is imposed, which restricts a person's liberty but falls outside of the conditions capable of appealing or is a post-conviction condition, because s 16(3) does not cater for this contingency.

In determining the appeal the Crown Court now has the power to vary a condition, a power previously belonging to the High Court. Although s 16 talks only of variation of conditions, the Crown Court must surely be capable of dispensing with conditions or even imposing new ones to ensure that the defendant does not abscond, commit further offences or interfere with witnesses, or for his own welfare or protection.

The High Court and bail appeals

3.38 Most of the High Court's powers relating to bail in other courts are abolished, ending the High Court judge in chambers applications beloved of optimistic defendants in custody.

Section 17 abolishes the defendant's right to apply to the High Court. The option to apply for judicial review or a writ of habeas corpus remains and the High Court will be able to bail (with or without conditions) or refuse bail to any person appearing before it in criminal proceedings initiated in the High Court (as opposed to proceedings

---

43 BA 1976, s 3(8) deals with committals for trial or sentence to the Crown Court.

before another court where redress in bail matters would, but for this section have been heard in the High Court). Such 'free-standing' criminal proceedings in front of the High Court are rare, but might include applications regarding tainted acquittals (s 54 of the CJPOA 1994) or judicial review of a Crown Court or magistrate's decision.

The High Court will not be able to entertain bail applications from the Crown Court in 'double jeopardy' cases (s 17(5)).[44] Such cases will commence in the Crown Court but the Court of Appeal will have powers to deal with bail, obviating any need for the High Court to become involved. Nor will the High Court have jurisdiction to deal with appeals against decisions under s 16.

Where a person has been refused bail by magistrates, generally there will no longer be a right to go before a High Court judge to seek bail. Defendants may well feel a sense of grievance at the removal of this final tier of appeal, particularly when the number of opportunities to apply afresh for bail are already scarce (unless an advocate can persuade the court of a true 'change in circumstances'). The Law Commission's Guidance to Bail Decision-Takers[45] indicates that passage of time of itself can amount to a change in circumstances, but those representing defendants will need to make full use of the right to trial within a reasonable time under Art 5(3) and Art 6 ECHR to try to minimise periods on remand.

Prosecution appeals against bail

3.39   The prosecution first was granted a right to appeal against grants of bail by the Bail (Amendment) Act 1993 (B(A)A 1993), in response to public outcry over 'bail bandits' (those who offend on bail where the offence carried a sentence of imprisonment of at least five years, especially those charged with so-called 'joy-riding' offences). By s 18(2), the requirement for the offence to carry a minimum term of five years has gone: the right of appeal will arise in respect of any imprisonable offence. There is nothing in the ECHR to render this state of affairs unfair and many European prosecutors have long possessed such a power. Its inclusion in this Act is a response to the fact that magistrates have granted bail to people who have re-offended – just as the prosecution had predicted – when they opposed bail.[46]

3.40   Section 18 is one response to the problem of mistaken grants of bail, lack of consistency and shortcomings in risk assessment.[47] Although ss 14 and 15[48] deal with obvious mistaken grants of bail to people who abscond or re-offend, this is with hindsight as the damage is done by that stage, as they have absconded or committed another offence. Section 18 may be seen by many as a sensible and justifiable

---

44   See CJA 2003, ss 87–91.

45   Law Com No 269 (2001).

46   See **3.25** and **3.28**.

47   Auld Review, Ch 10, paras 70–82.

48   See **3.28–3.35**.

balancing of power between the defence and prosecution.[49] But some will have concerns that the prosecution may choose to charge suspects with charges carrying imprisonment rather than non-imprisonable offences in cases where they hope to remand a defendant in custody. Over-charging is a short-term solution. It may allow the prosecutor to appeal a grant of bail but is likely to lead to an unnecessary trial as the accused has been wrongly charged, and runs counter to the attempts in the new Act to get the charge right at the outset. Deliberate overcharging (should it ever occur) may also amount to an abuse of process,[50] causing protracted legal arguments, delay, costs and anxiety for all parties to the process. Overcharging or charging with the wrong crime has been identified by the Auld Review as being one of the factors which causes so much delay in the criminal justice system: 22% of offences were incorrectly charged in 1999/2000 and 23% of indictments needed amending in the Crown Court.[51]

Furthermore, the Auld Review was keen to ensure the judicial workload was spread as efficiently as possible.[52] Although s 16 should soon reduce the number of appeals against bail which the Crown Court has been accustomed to hearing, little progress will have been made if the prosecution then fills the vacuum.

Repeals and other changes

3.41 Section 20 of the 2003 Act repeals and makes amendments to Sch 1, Part 1 to the BA 1976. Paragraphs of Sch 1, Part 1 are re-numbered, and Sch 2 to the 2003 Act facilitates the introduction of changes to pre-charge bail discussed at **3.8–3.12**.

DISCLOSURE

3.42 The provisions of the CPIA 1996 relating to disclosure, barely seven years old, are changed in significant ways. The subjective test governing primary prosecution disclosure gives way to an objective test. More controversially, the new Act imposes additional disclosure obligations on defendants, both in terms of what detail must be supplied in relation to the defence case, and to points of law which will be relied on. It requires details to be given of experts commissioned by the defence: the names and addresses of any such experts must be disclosed. A new s 11 in the CPIA 1996 deals with the consequences of faults in defence disclosure.

The Act does not change the position that defence disclosure in cases being tried summarily is voluntary. The provisions relating to defence disclosure therefore apply only to cases being tried summarily if the defence chooses to serve a defence

---

49   Auld Review, Ch 10, paras 70–82.

50   Eg *R v Rotherham JJ ex parte Brough* [1991] COD 89, DC and *R (Wardle) v Leeds Crown Court* [2002] 1 AC 754, HL.

51   Auld Review, Ch 10, para 34.

52   *Ibid*, paras 34–36.

statement. Nor does the new Act prevent prosecutors continuing the quite prevalent practice[53] of routinely disclosing certain types of documents.

The background

3.43 The new provisions modify what is, essentially, a three-stage process, introduced by the 1996 Act, which itself modified the pre-existing law.[54] The duty of the prosecutor to engage in 'primary disclosure' (now restyled as 'initial disclosure') requires the prosecutor (under s 3 of the CPIA 1996) to disclose to the accused any material which has not previously been disclosed and which in the prosecutor's opinion might undermine the case for the prosecution against the accused. Under s 5 of the CPIA 1996, the requirement (in cases to be tried on indictment) of defence disclosure was imposed, with the opportunity for voluntary defence disclosure in summary cases (s 6). The defence statement sets out the broad nature of the defence case. It was not intended to be a detailed statement of the defence case.[55] Following service of the defence statement, providing it contained enough detail to fulfil its purpose of putting the prosecution on notice of the issues, the prosecution is then under an obligation to engage in secondary prosecution disclosure, disclosing matters which might undermine the Crown's case or assist that of the defendant. Material could be withheld as sensitive material which a court permits to be withheld on the grounds of public interest immunity.[56]

In addition to obligations of disclosure under the statutory scheme, obligations to disclose might also arise under case-law,[57] or as a matter of professional ethics under the Bar Code of Conduct or those governing solicitors to disclose material to the defence.

3.44 Despite the youth of the disclosure provisions of the 1996 Act, the Auld Review[58] found them unsatisfactory in many respects. It pointed to the multiplicity of different sources and rules governing disclosure.[59] The Act does not address that issue, and a multiplicity of sources of rules remains. The Review found that the disclosure regime was not working as Parliament intended.[60] Unreliability of disclosure schedules, and undue reliance on them, the split of responsibilities between CPS and police and lack of consistency were all identified as failings or weaknesses in

---

53 See Auld Review, Ch 10, paras 135–136, citing Plotnikoff and Woolfson, *A Fair Balance?* (Home Office, 2001).

54 See *Keane* (1994) 99 Cr App R 1, CA; *Brown* [1995] 1 Cr App R 191, CA.

55 See **3.51**.

56 For a discussion of what might not be disclosable, see *Keane* (1994) 99 Cr App R 1, CA; *Reading Justices ex parte Berkshire CC* [1996] 1 Cr App R 239, DC.

57 See eg *DPP ex parte Leech* [1999] 2 All ER 737, DC.

58 *Op cit*, Ch 10, paras 115–197.

59 The 1996 Act; the disclosure rules contained in the Crown Court (Criminal Procedure and Investigations Act 1996) (Disclosure) Rules 1997 (SI 1997/696); the Attorney-General's Guidelines: Disclosure of Information in Criminal Proceedings (29 November 2000); the Code of Practice issued under the 1996 Act; rules issued under the Crime and Disorder Act 1998.

60 Auld Review, Ch 10, para 163, citing the review of disclosure rules carried out by the Crown Prosecution Service Inspectorate, and also Plotnikoff and Woolfson, *A Fair Balance?*, *op cit*, n 53.

the process of primary prosecution disclosure. So, too, were, lateness or incompleteness.

The Review also addressed concerns about the operation of defence disclosure. It considered that even after the 1996 Act the potential for 'trial by ambush' existed. The reduction or elimination of this was an aim set as far back as the Royal Commission on Criminal Justice,[61] although even then there was dispute as to how much of a problem this practice constituted.[62] The Auld Review observed:[63]

> 'I can understand why, as a matter of tactics, a defendant might wish to prefer to keep his case close to his chest. But that is not a valid reason for preventing a full and fair hearing on the issues canvassed at the trial. A criminal trial is not a game under which a defendant should be presented with a sporting chance. It is a search for the truth.'

Defence statements disclose little detail, and were not intended to do so, save in the context of alibi details.[64] In reality they often say very little. Judges often effectively fail to impose effective sanctions for non-compliance. The result is sometimes aborted trials, poorly prepared prosecution files, wasted witness or victim time through unnecessary attendance at court, and consequential knock-on costs to the courts, CPS and Criminal Defence Service.

The Auld Review proposals to remedy this,[65] in the context of disclosure, are the basis for the new provisions. Clearer guidance is set out as to when disclosure must be made by prosecution and defence, with greater obligations on the defence, and greater sanctions for when the law is ignored.

The Home Secretary explained[66] the new defence disclosure requirements in terms of parity between prosecution and defence:

> 'We are simply seeking to avoid any scope for abuse of the system, to ensure that information requirements for the defence are placed on a par with those of the prosecution, and to deal with the way in which witnesses can be protected, including ensuring that the development of knowledge about the list of expert witnesses on which the defence will draw will be available to the prosecution'.

Others, of course, view the proposals with concern.

The new law – prosecutor's initial duty of disclosure

3.45 Section 32 amends s 3 of the CPIA 1996. It does so by inserting an objective element for initial prosecution disclosure (as it is now to be known, replacing the term 'primary prosecution disclosure'). Instead of s 3 requiring prosecution disclosure in respect of evidence 'which in the prosecutor's opinion might undermine the case for

---

61 Cm 2263 (1993).

62 See Zander and Henderson, *Crown Court Study:* RCCJ Research Study, No 19 (HMSO, 1993); *The Right to Silence in Police Interviews*, RCCJ, No 10 (HMSO, 1993).

63 Auld Review, Ch 10, para 154, cited approvingly by Hilary Benn MP, HC Committee, 9 January 2003, col 230.

64 See White Paper *Justice For All, op cit*, paras 3.47–3.57.

65 Auld Review, paras 3.46–3.57.

66 David Blunkett MP, Second Reading, HC Deb, 4 December 2002, col 918.

the prosecution against the accused', it will now require prosecution disclosure in respect of evidence which has not previously been disclosed to the accused and which 'might reasonably be considered capable of undermining the case for the prosecution or of assisting the case for the accused'.

This more objective test, which substantially mirrors that for secondary prosecution disclosure contained in s 7 of the CPIA 1996, reflects the substance of the recommendations of the Auld Review[67] and provides the objective element the lack of which many criticised back in 1996. It does not return to a requirement of disclosure of all relevant material (although nothing prevents a prosecutor from doing that), but requires a prosecutor consider the effect of the material on the prosecution case or whether it assists the case for the defence. The prosecutor must be able to justify, on the basis of reasonableness, the judgment that is made. It is open to a court, in future, to entertain an argument that the prosecutor's opinion was unreasonable. No doubt such cases will be rare – it is not likely to be very often that the courts will wish to 'second guess' the prosecutor's judgment. Yet one of the perpetual problems in the context of prosecution disclosure is the difficult task of making judgments about the possible effect of material. The use of the word 'might' rather than the words 'likely to' confirms that it is the *possible effect* rather than the likely effect that matters. The fact that the amended s 3 does not identify the principle that any doubt ought to be resolved in favour of the defendant is, arguably, unimportant. If there is doubt, then it 'might' undermine or assist (as s 3 requires). However, such a statement within s 3 might have been useful in cementing attitudes and approaches to the use by prosecutors of s 3, and the compilation of schedules by disclosure officers.

Increased defence disclosure obligations

3.46 Sections 33 to 36 introduce additional disclosure requirements in respect of defendants. These are intended to add to the duties of defence disclosure where those arise. No such duties arise in summary trial, and thus the new provisions relating to disclosure of information will apply only if the defence chooses to make voluntary defence disclosure. The significantly expanded defence disclosure provisions may provide a further incentive not to engage in voluntary defence disclosure in cases to be tried summarily.

Service of defence statement on co-accused

3.47 Section 5 of the CPIA 1996 is amended by s 33(1). Where the court directs following an application by any party, or of its own motion, the accused must serve a copy of his defence statement on each co-accused specified by the court, within such period as the court specifies (s 5(5A)).

This is both logical and uncontroversial. If a defendant (A) gives a defence statement to the prosecutor (P) in a case where there is one or more co-accused (B), that statement is, under pre-existing law, material which has come into the prosecutor's possession in connection with the case for the prosecution against B for the purposes of the secondary prosecution disclosure provisions in s 7(2) and (3) of the 1996 Act.[68]

---

67   *Op cit*, Ch 10, para 171.

68   Confirmed by *Hillman and Knowles* (2001) 10 *Arch News* 4 (CC).

Nothing in the amended s 5 states that the court *must* order mutual disclosure but, rather, that it must occur if the court specifies. Nor does it prohibit the court from ordering sequential disclosure of a defence statement made by one co-accused after another. Any order must satisfy the standards of a fair trial required by Art 6 ECHR. It would surely be unfair to permit one co-accused to wait to see what another's defence was before committing himself to his version of events, particularly in a case where there was a 'cut-throat' defence. Sequential disclosure could, however, be appropriate, for example, if a co-accused absconds before trial. In such a case, mutual service of statements will not be possible unless the absconder's solicitors have a defence statement from their client. If one accused is to be tried separately, at the end of the trial of others, it may be appropriate for service of his statement to be delayed until the issues at the first trial have been aired.

The change is also inevitable given that the principle underpinning the disclosure changes is for greater and more detailed disclosure. What a co-accused may wish to present in his own case may depend in part what other accused parties are proposing to say, which pre-supposes knowledge that can only be acquired through the defence statement.

3.48 A court can make a direction of its own volition, or on the application of any party. Nothing prevents a prosecutor making an application that, say, A's defence statement be given to B. Indeed, fairness might suggest that it is important that all interested parties have the opportunity to be aware of the application and the right to make submissions. No such detailed provisions are contained in the Act, but doubtless will be dealt with by Rules.

The period for compliance will be that specified by the court. No doubt guidance will be issued. Clearly the widespread nature of electronic communication and photocopying (whether in the office or at court) makes long delays technically and logistically unnecessary, and by definition the defence statement already exists – it has already been served on the prosecutor.

Additional contents of the defence statement

3.49 A new s 6A is added to the 1996 Act by s 33(2). It re-defines the concept of a defence statement. Under s 6A, the following are required, on pain of adverse inference under s 11 (as re-cast by s 39 of the new Act).[69] The additional requirements are highlighted in italics.

The statement must be in writing and:

(a) set out the nature of the accused's defence *including any particular defences on which he intends to rely*;

(b) indicate the matters of *fact* on which he takes issue with the prosecution;

(c) set out, in the case of each matter, why he takes issue with the prosecution; and

(d) *indicate any point of law (including any point as to the admissibility of evidence) which he wishes to take, and any authority on which he intends to rely for that purpose.*

---

69 See **3.69**.

Section 6A(4) gives the Home Secretary the power to make provisions as to the details of the matters that are, by virtue of s 6A(1), to be included in a defence statement. Arguably, that does not mean the Home Secretary has the power to vary the terms of s 6A(1) itself – if it did, that would be a matter of considerable concern given the fundamental issues raised by defence disclosure in terms of the 'right to silence' and the principle against self-incrimination. Nonetheless, unpopular or unwelcome acquittals in cases where important information was not disclosed might prove to be the catalyst for further change. Moreover, unlike the earlier parts of this Act, relating to PACE Codes, s 6A does not create any legitimate expectation of consultation with interest groups when the Home Office chooses to use this power to vary. More likely, s 6A allows the Home Secretary to make regulations concerning the detailed disposal of those matters. The words 'by virtue of . . .' in s 6A(4) clearly suggest that the matters in s 6A(1) set the parameters within which the Home Secretary must keep. For some, that also might be a matter of concern. On the other hand, there is clearly a need for regulations dealing, as now, with defence disclosure procedures.

3.50   The pre-existing s 5(6)(a) spoke of 'setting out the general nature' of the defence. The new s 6A(1)(a) simply uses the term 'nature'. This, coupled with the new need to set out any 'particular' defence, requires a greater measure of specificity than hitherto.

A defendant who intends simply to put the prosecution to proof, calling no evidence himself, is not relying on a defence, unless the words 'nature of the defence' are interpreted to mean 'nature of the reasons why the defendant should not be convicted'. Nor is putting the prosecution to proof on aspects of the charge which it is its duty to prove a 'defence'. However, in reality the defence in such a case is 'I did not commit the acts' alleged to be criminal, or 'I did not have the requisite mental state' and thus there *is* a defence being put before the court. Where matters of fact are put to a prosecution witness which are at variance with those testified to by the witness, there are facts being relied upon, and thus a duty to set out in a defence statement the nature of that defence.[70] The defendant may raise the issue of fitness to plead, again, not technically a defence, but one which nevertheless determines how and in what form any trial will proceed, and thus possibly within the spirit (if not the letter) of the extended disclosure provisions. Arguably, this should be raised in a defence statement, although in this regard, as in many other matters, the reality will often be that the prosecution is aware of the issue, through disclosure of medical reports.

The difficulty with such cases is that if no defence statement, as defined, is served, then the obligation on the prosecution to engage in secondary disclosure does not arise and, indeed, the potentiality for a s 11 inference arises. The intent of the 1996 disclosure provisions is that the prosecution should be put into a position where it knows the matters to be canvassed at trial, and can judge what further needs to be disclosed. On this basis, s 5 and s 6 should be construed broadly, and require notification of an intention to raise the issue of unfitness to plead, or to disclose that the 'defence' of the accused is that the prosecution has not disclosed details that show that the accused has engaged in conduct which amounts to the crime charged.

---

70   See, by analogy, *Webber* [2004] All ER (D) 170.

Clearly, if the defence is as to specific matters – 'It wasn't me', 'I lacked the required mental state', or 'The charge should be reduced to manslaughter because of diminished responsibility' – those will be matters that have to be set out in a defence statement. This is, of course, irrespective of the fact that in many cases (in the Crown Court) the nature of the defence may be well known to the prosecutor because of statements made during the police investigation, or, in the case of diminished responsibility, because of disclosure of medical reports or because of discussions as to reduction of the charge to manslaughter.

3.51 The changes made by the new Act in respect of the level of detail required on defence disclosure are significant. The Royal Commission on Criminal Justice had recommended that disclosure should be of a relatively brief type.[71] When the 1996 Act was passed, there were clear limits as to the level of detail expected. The then Solicitor-General put it thus:[72]

> 'In providing a defence statement it is not intended that the accused should have to provide every last detail of the defence, such as the names and addresses of witnesses and so on ... We have decided that that is not necessary ... [Section 5(6)(c)] simply requires an accused to give a reason why he takes issue with a point. There is no suggestion that in giving the reason, details of the evidence to support the reason have to be given. So the fear ... that this might require the defence to set out its cross-examination is not well founded. That is not intended at all.'

The new Act marks a distinct change of approach, might be regarded as a move towards a more inquisitorial approach,[73] and is viewed by many as undesirable and dangerous. The changes also run counter to the view of the Auld Review:[74]

> 'As to the defence statement ... the present requirements, if observed, seem to be adequate to enable identification of the issues ... for the purpose of determining the scope and form of prosecution evidence required for trial. I have considered whether to recommend any additional requirements, for example a general obligation to identify defence witnesses and the content of their expected evidence similar to that where the defence is one of alibi or it is intended to call expert evidence for the defence. Whilst, as a matter of efficiency, there is much to be said for them, many more would find them objectionable as going beyond the definition of the issues and requiring a defendant to set out, in advance, an affirmative case. And they would be difficult to enforce.'

One may wonder whether efficiency alone is a sufficient justification for changes of this nature. Of course, the Review's finding was that the definition of 'defence statement' in the pre-existing s 5(6) required only what was disputed to be identified, not the nature of the defence. The changes could be justified on the basis of clarity in the meaning and application of the defence disclosure provisions.[75]

---

71 Royal Commission, *op cit*, para 68, p 99.

72 Sir Derek Spencer QC, MP, Criminal Procedure and Investigations Act 1996, HC Committee, col 68.

73 See eg Law Society Response Document to the White Paper, *Justice for All*.

74 *Op cit*, Ch 10, para 180.

75 See, eg, recognition by the Criminal Bar Association that the defence disclosure provisions were not working as well as they might. It recommended better guidance, education and use of the current law. See *Justice for All: Bar Council/CBA response to Criminal Justice White Paper*, www.barcouncil.org.uk.

3.52 Significant levels of detail will now be required. Not only must the nature of the defence be set out, but the matters of fact as to which issue is taken must be stated, with reasons. The practical difficulties should not be underestimated, with defence statements being drafted under pressure and within tight time-limits, at a time when not all prosecution material will necessarily have been discussed, or scrutinised and discussed with the defendant, and where the defence case may well not have been fully (or at all) investigated and prepared. Issues arise as to who will draft such statements (advocate, instructing solicitor, paralegal?) and how the work will be remunerated.

Some might answer these points by pointing to the terms of the new s 6B,[76] which requires a defendant to engage in updated defence disclosure. It is perfectly true that changes in the defence case can, and must, be reflected in an amended defence statement. The power contained in s 6E, relating to the disclosure of a defence statement to the jury (see **3.70**), extends only to the updated defence statement, not to the original (CPIA 1996, s 6(4), (6)). Nonetheless, the prospect of significantly different statements being supplied by the defendant to the prosecution, co-defendants and the court is not one that many will find attractive, and for that reason there is a real danger that the whole process will become self-defeating. Points may be taken for the purpose of protecting the defendant's position, or for completeness, and thus the purpose of clarifying the real issues in dispute may not be achieved.

Disputed facts

3.53 Under the new s 6A, a defendant who serves a defence statement must indicate which facts he disputes. But is this practical in all cases? What of the man accused of sexual offences which allegedly occurred 20 years earlier? Beyond a general denial, he may be unable to recall details which may be significant, or assume significance, during a trial. Secondary disclosure sometimes puts a new perspective on a set of events or jogs a witness's or suspect's memory, but a defendant must identify the details before he can get access to that material which may help him to recall what had happened at the time of a crime. Some of that material may be sensitive material requiring an application to a court (eg children's social services records). What of the case where the defendant was very drunk at the time of an offence and cannot remember? Such matters are, of course, habitual difficulties for defence lawyers, with or without the new provisions, but the obligation to disclose in detail, at a time when there has scarcely been an opportunity for adequate instruction or representation, is a matter of real concern.

Identity of witnesses

3.54 Section 34 inserts a new s 6C into the CPIA 1996. It requires a defendant to indicate whether he intends to call any persons (other than himself) as witnesses. This provision is not on its face limited to trial on indictment and can also be construed as applying to a case where voluntary defence disclosure has been made. A defendant facing summary trial need not declare his hand. However, while s 6A, s 6B and s 6E are each linked to the giving of a defence statement, neither s 6C nor s 6D are. They are free-standing, and not strictly part of the defence statement procedure. This would amount to a significant change, made without any great debate. Given that these

---

76 See **3.64**.

changes are introduced in the context of defence disclosure, it is arguable that the duty to advise as to witnesses or prior instruction of experts should be confined to trials where a defence statement was served.

3.55   The defendant does not have to give such notice if that detail has already been given as part of the details of an alibi under s 6A(2), although the cautious practitioner might wish to make it clear that what is required has already been supplied to put the matter beyond argument. Oddly, however, the drafting of s 6C(2) is such that the witness details for non-alibi must be disclosed in a s 6C notification even if they have already been disclosed in the defence statement or in any other way.

No detail as to the operation of this provision is contained in the Act, and regulations and Practice Directions will need to determine its mechanics. However, the time-limit for compliance will be the relevant period specified under s 12 of the CPIA 1996 for this purpose.

If there is an obligation to give details, the defendant must give to both the prosecutor and the court:

(a)   the name, address and date of birth of each witness, or such of those details as are known;

(b)   any information in the accused's possession which might be of material assistance in identifying or finding any such proposed witness in whose case any of the details set out in (a) above are not known to the accused.

3.56   Section 6C raises fundamental issues. It does not prevent a witness from being called. That would clearly infringe the right to a fair trial under Art 6 ECHR. It does, however, create the risk of comment under s 11, with the potential for inferences to be drawn. To that extent, therefore, it inhibits the taking of legitimate decisions by an advocate.

As noted above, there are practical difficulties in identifying a defence case, and in identifying possible or likely witnesses. Defence solicitors may only learn of the existence of potential witnesses after secondary disclosure has taken place, leaving them with a person to trace who may have little recollection of the events in question. Ought a person to face the potential for inference because the nature or quality of his witnesses makes them difficult to hunt down and prove? Further, deciding who is actually to be called at trial is a tactical decision for the defending advocate, based on considerations as varied as how well a witness may fare in cross-examination due to age, nerves, limited intelligence or simply how well or badly the trial has gone so far, whether they have previous convictions or an emotional involvement, and whether, depending on how the prosecution case has unfolded at trial, their evidence remains relevant or necessary. Few advocates (and still fewer non-advocates), would feel able to take such a decision about whom to call until the prosecution case is about to end. Of course, nothing in s 6C *requires* the defendant to call the specified witness, and nothing in s 6C permits the prosecution or court to comment on a failure to call a specified witness. The revised s 11 allows a court to comment on the calling of a witness who is not specified. Some might regard it as undesirable for a defendant to have to identify potential witnesses who may, or may not, be called.

3.57   The purpose of this additional detail is so that investigators can run checks on proposed defence witnesses to look at any criminal record or antecedents, or even to see if they were at the scene of a crime or with the defendant where the defence of alibi is raised. The White Paper[77] identified the need for an extension of disclosure in this way in order to prevent any 'surprise witnesses'. This is, in a sense, 'equality of arms'[78] operating in favour of the prosecution – after all, the defence must be told about the bad character of prosecution witnesses. However, such an approach is simplistic, for several reasons. The defence must give details of *potential* witnesses, if it is in a position to give details at all. By contrast few defendants have the resources or opportunity to investigate more widely than the police. Public funding is most unlikely to be available for such a purpose and many lawyers would be afraid to intrude on a person's private life for fear of being seen to intimidate a witness. State investigators have wide powers and authority to do this. In any event, the running of checks on witnesses is a task that can be undertaken during the trial itself.

Secondly, the intended purpose can only be to enable the prosecution to assess the veracity of what might be said by such witnesses. This raises concerns about the deterrence of potential witnesses coming forward for the defence, and of potential for interference and possible intimidation.

3.58 In its consideration of these proposed changes, the Criminal Bar Association observed[79] that:

'It is an unfortunate fact of life that potential defence witnesses are often those very people who harbour, rightly or wrongly, a deep distrust of authority in general and the police in particular. Knowing their details will be disclosed and that they may be investigated and interviewed by the police will provide a powerful incentive for them not to come forward and assist the defence, thereby depriving the defendant of relevant, truthful evidence that might exonerate him. It is not a sufficient answer to this objection that the defendant would have the option of taking out a witness summons against the recalcitrant witness.'

Such witnesses may be itinerant, illiterate, suffering from drink or substance abuse, in prison, dim-witted or feckless. Securing co-operation with them may be difficult. The provisions of s 6C take little regard of these realities.

Nor is it a sufficient answer to observe that a proof of evidence or witness statement taken from such a witness might be admissible under the revised provisions relating to hearsay contained in the new Act,[80] although the prudent defence lawyer will wish to take a proof of evidence at an early stage for possible use under those provisions. The danger is that potential witnesses will be deterred from coming forward in the first place.

3.59 Another danger is that of interference. A defence statement will be a valuable aid to a prosecutor in identifying gaps in the prosecution case, sometimes by re-visiting (or, equally likely, visiting for the first time) those who have been identified as actual or potential defence witnesses. One cannot ignore the possibility that over-zealous or unscrupulous investigators will interview, formally or informally, potential witnesses and persuade them to think again about their recollection, or even

---

77   See **3.51**.

78   See **3.58**.

79   Responses to the White Paper from the Criminal Bar Association/Bar Council.

80   See Chapter 6.

change it, or make the witness less willing to testify. The Auld Review considered that the defendant had to recognise that fairness cuts both ways and that a system cannot be built on the premise that police officers or anyone else involved in pursuing a case were dishonest.[81] However, a criminal justice system cannot automatically assume that powers will always be exercised fairly or properly or competently, and powers should be hedged with safeguards. There are none in s 6C.

Other dangers apply in respect of co-defendants. If s 6C statements are to be given to the court and to the prosecution, what of the co-defendant? Such statements are not defence statements and thus do not fall within the provisions in s 5 relating to service on co-defendants. Nonetheless they are information in the hands of the prosecution and, therefore, potentially unused material. In a case involving a cut-throat defence, perhaps where defendant A alleges that she was acting under duress from defendant B, the disclosure of witnesses who will testify on A's behalf creates a real risk of interference. It is unclear on what basis this information could be withheld.

Code of practice for police interviews of defence witnesses

3.60 The above discussion highlights real issues and concerns. Similar concerns were expressed by professional bodies, and heeded by the Government, which introduced (by s 40) what is a new s 21A into the CPIA 1996. The Home Secretary is charged with producing the Code and has a statutory obligation to consult with bodies representing the legal profession and the police in its preparation. It will be admissible in evidence in criminal and civil proceedings, but breach of the Code will not mean a police officer (or other investigator covered by it) will be liable in a civil or criminal capacity for the breach. A court may look at the provisions to determine whether there was any breach if matters connected to any alleged breach are relied upon by a party.

3.61 The Code will prescribe what information should be provided to both the witness and defendant about the interview; what notification is to be given to the defence solicitor; the right of that solicitor to attend any interview; the right of the solicitor to represent the interviewee's interest; and the presence of an appropriate adult (if necessary).

Defence lawyers will wish to know if attending an interview will be covered under the terms of a representation order. The police will, no doubt, be keen in many cases to interview prospective defence witnesses to test the weaknesses in the prosecution case, and to identify (were it to exist) potential false evidence, although should evidence of that nature arise during interview the police would have to terminate the interview. Material obtained during the interview will potentially be disclosable, unless it neither undermines the prosecution case nor assists the defence (a perhaps unlikely scenario given that the defence has indicated that it intends to call the witness). A statement which in fact implicates an accused would appear not to be disclosable. Further, r 5 of the Magistrates' Court (Advance Information) Rules 1985 permits a prosecutor to withhold statements where intimidation or interference with witnesses may occur. The statement would of course be revealed, with glee, by the prosecutor if the witness gave evidence inconsistent with it at trial to discredit him and thus the accused.

---

81 *Op cit*, Ch 10, para 154.

Will witnesses co-operate? The Bar Council was worried that they would not. Some people will be afraid of contact with the police despite having nothing to fear. Some may not have the time to meet the police or fear that speaking to the police tarnishes them in some way. Thus, an innocent suspect may find the people who can help him prove his innocence are deterred from doing so by the possibility or fact of the police wishing to interview them.

Advance warning of points of law

3.62   By the new s 6A a defence statement will now have to include details of:

–   any point of law the defence wishes to raise;
–   any point relating to admissibility;
–   and any authority upon which the defence proposes to rely.

It is difficult to argue against the principle that legal points should be identified in advance when it is possible to do so. Yet it is not entirely clear what mischief the new Act is seeking to address. Sometimes it will not be possible to identify points of law or issues relating to admissibility until investigations have occurred, or witnesses have been interviewed. It may be at a late stage, for example, that issues of police entrapment or issues relating to a confession emerge, perhaps not until the trial itself. In addition, arguably, the provision ignores the realities. Much of this information will have been included on the plea and directions form at arraignment. It is a well-recognised tenet of professional conduct that one must give copies of cases relied upon to one's opponent and the judge. Further, even unhelpful or opposing authorities must be supplied. A prosecutor, and certainly a judge, will or ought to anticipate any points relating to admissibility. In any event, even if no argument over the merits of a case took place before the judge at the plea and directions hearing, advocates are very good at telling each other when a point of law is coming up so that a case is not opened to a jury on the basis that something is admissible when there is going to be a dispute over its inclusion in the trial. Judges are equally good at anticipating points of law. Many advocates will serve skeleton arguments on one another, even if done on the morning of a case.

Should there be significant legal developments between any preparatory or preliminary hearing and the trial itself, updated details will have to be served under the new s 6B.

Section 6A(1)(d) of the CPIA 1996 also imposes a potential obligation upon defendants (through their lawyers) to give advance notification to the prosecutor to perfect the case by pointing out pitfalls. This is, of course, part of the trend towards regarding the criminal trial as a search for the truth. Nonetheless, the idea of the defence being obliged to tell the Crown the weaknesses of its case in this fashion sits uneasily with traditional notions of the adversarial system.

Alibi notices

3.63   The obligation to serve an alibi notice as part of the defence statement remains in force, but now greater details must be given to the prosecution under s 6A(2). The defendant must supply not only the names and addresses of alibi witnesses as was the pre-Act position, but, if he does not have that information, he must give as much of what he does know to the Crown, in order, presumably, that the police may trace those people and either interview them or at least carry out background checks on matters such as previous convictions. This is not new. There is no property in a witness. Investigators have often carried out inquiries in such cases, in order to discredit or disprove an alibi or those advancing it. Additionally, there is an ongoing duty now created under s 6A(2)(b) to update alibi witness details and pass them on to the prosecution as and when (or if) they are received, so that both sides know as much as each other about who may be called to give evidence probative of the alibi.

Updated defence disclosure

3.64 Section 33 inserts a new s 6B into the CPIA 1996. Section 6B imposes a duty upon defendants to provide updated disclosure within a time-limit to be laid down under s 12. The information which will need to be updated is that already specified in s 6A. This new statement must be served on the Crown and any co-accused upon whom the court orders service or where a party applies for such an order under ss 5A–5D. If there is nothing new to add, then the defence must certify so in writing under s 64(4). Presumably, updated disclosure will be triggered by the service of additional evidence by the Crown, perhaps by cross-service of the defence statements of the other defendants or where there are developments in the defence rendering the old statement out of date.

Expert evidence

3.65 The disclosure provision relating to expert witnesses is one of the most controversial aspects of the new Act. Section 35 inserts a new s 6D into the 1996 Act. Section 6D provides that if the accused instructs a person with a view to his providing any expert opinion for possible use as evidence at the trial of the accused, he must give to the court and the prosecutor a notice specifying the person's name and address, unless that has already been specified in the defence statement (s 6D(1), (2)). The notification must be during the period specified for the purpose by s 12 of the 1996 Act (s 6D(3)).

3.66 The duty that it imposes is in respect of any instruction with a view to 'providing any expert opinion for possible use as evidence at the trial of the accused'. Clearly, the only reason to instruct an expert in this context is to use the resulting report at trial, and, indeed the Criminal Defence Service would not otherwise extend a person's representation order to cover the cost of such a report. However, that leaves open the question as to the purpose of its use at trial. It must be for 'possible use as evidence'. A report may be commissioned to assist in cross-examination: nonetheless, it can scarcely be argued that it is not commissioned for 'possible' use in evidence. Thus, it will be caught. So, too, with the use of the report in any other context, for example a *Newton* hearing,[82] and, arguably, a medical report for use in sentencing or the report of a specialist risk assessment in respect of a sex offender. Assessments of risk are likely to be of increasing importance given the sentencing

---

82 A '*Newton* hearing' is a hearing to decide the extent of guilt, not guilt or innocence: *Newton* (1983) 77 Cr App R 13, CA.

provisions of the new Act.[83] There is nothing in the new s 6D to suggest that 'in evidence' is to be limited to evidence formally adduced by a witness as part of the trial.

3.67   The purpose of s 6D raises important issues. It cannot simply be to ensure that the prosecution is not caught unawares by defence expert evidence. The pre-existing rule that any expert evidence which is to be adduced must be served on the opposite party by the one relying upon it remains unaltered.[84] In any event, s 6D does not require overtly the disclosure of an expert report, which is itself privileged.[85] It does, however, ensure that the prosecution is aware of the fact that an expert has been consulted and his report is not being used. That could be because it is commissioned for background to assist in the preparation of the defence case, or in cross-examination, but more likely indicates that the opinion of the expert does not assist the defence. It is not clear that there is any adverse inference or other sanction under s 11 or elsewhere if the defendant fails to declare that he did approach an expert but does not intend to adduce any evidence from him. Section 11 is silent on non-compliance with s 6D, whereas sanctions for non-compliance under ss 6A, 6B, 6C and 6E are contained in the new s 11 of the CPIA 1996 and s 31 of the new Act. The lack of apparent sanction is surprising given the tenor of the other provisions in this part of the Act. Judicial comment would appear to be prevented by the fact that s 11 provides specific sanction in these other instances. It is hard to avoid the surprising conclusion that there is no sanction for breach. In those circumstances one wonders why practitioners will comply.

3.68   The prosecution is put on notice that the defence has sought expert opinion, and itself has the option of acquiring its own expert opinion or, indeed, of calling the expert consulted by the defence. There is no property in a witness, and some might see this provision as being fair. There are, however, very good reasons for concern. First, experts will frequently be sent legally privileged material. It can scarcely be otherwise if an expert is to give opinions that are properly grounded. Expert opinion which is not founded on a full factual and contextual background is severely open to question. If the prosecution wishes to interview, and if thought desirable, call the expert, there is the danger that the expert may, inadvertently, disclose privileged material, which could lead to applications for the proceedings to be stayed for abuse of process. There may be a temptation for the defence to instruct only 'tame' experts – ones who are known to take a view favourable to the defence. Alternatively, there may be an undesirable withholding of information from experts who are instructed, or worse, a chilling effect – with defence solicitors being increasingly circumspect as to when reports are sought. That can, of course, only be to the detriment of the defendant's interests, and create potential for a miscarriage of justice. Indeed, the effect may be to make it harder to persuade a client that acquittal is unlikely and that a guilty plea is in the accused's interest.

---

83   See **9.38** *et seq.*

84   Section 81 of PACE and the Crown Court (Advance Notice of Expert Evidence) Rules 1987 (SI 1987/716) and Magistrates' Court (Advance Notice of Expert Evidence) Rules 1997 (SI 1997/705).

85   *Davies (Keith)* (2002) *The Times*, 4 March, CA, which held that the contents of an expert's report were privileged against disclosure, being covered by legal professional privilege.

It is ironic that in civil litigation there is no duty to disclose the fact that an expert report has been commissioned.[86] A more stringent rule in criminal cases is not only odd, but unfair. The Art 6 fair trial provisions of the ECHR are capable of supporting a system which has distinctive inquisitorial approaches. A system which, for example, dealt with such matters by way of court-appointed specialist would be unlikely to be open to successful challenge. That, however, is not the position within the English system. To allow an adversarial approach while creating risks that a defendant cannot, or will not, preserve his legal professional privilege is to create the potential for unfairness.

Sanctions for non-compliance

3.69 By a new s 6E, a defence statement served by a solicitor[87] will be deemed to have been made on the instructions of an accused unless the opposite can be demonstrated, thus leading to difficulties for a defendant who attempts to resile from it. This perhaps codifies what many would have considered to be the pre-Act position, although it was never elevated to the status of a rebuttable presumption. There was criticism in some quarters[88] from the police and prosecutors that judges were not firm enough with those who tried to distance themselves from their defence statements nor were they often ready to permit previous inconsistent statements to be capitalised on in this area.

No doubt many judges felt an inquiry into what was *prima facie* privileged – between the accused and his lawyers – was unfair to the defendant, who could not really be expected to understand a lawyer's document. Some would have wondered about the need to have a *voir dire* to decide on who was factually responsible for the contents of the statement and how far it would advance the jury's understanding of the real trial issues. Others would have seen the likelihood of a conflict between solicitor and client leading to the end of a suspect's representation and probable discharge of the jury, all at great expense and with unwanted delay for all concerned – particularly the victim and witnesses. Section 6E may make it more likely that courts will be encouraged to draw inferences more often, as the issue, who is to blame for the defects in the statement, is less arguable.

3.70 Section 39 introduces a new s 11 into the CPIA 1996, which extends the pre-existing s 11 to accommodate the larger scope for non-compliance now that there are more details to include. First, the judge must warn the defendant of the risk of adverse comment by a party at trial or the drawing of an adverse inference by the trial judge in due course. This will no doubt have been done by a suspect's legal advisors before the plea and directions hearing and reiterated by the advocate in conference. At trial, the jury will be allowed sight of the statement at the discretion of the judge, who may also order editing of anything which is inadmissible. It should be noted that in some circumstances the defence statement might be admissible as evidence of its

---

86 See Civil Procedure Rules 1998, r 35(10). However, if the contents of a report remain privileged, the damage will probably have been done merely by showing who was used but not called.

87 There is no mention of counsel in s 6E, but the term 'solicitor' ought to be read as either of the defendant's representatives – solicitor or advocate.

88 Auld Review, *op cit.*

contents, because of the much-changed hearsay rule introduced by the new Act.[89] The judge may exercise these two powers either of his own volition or on the application of any other party, eg a co-accused or the prosecution. The orders can be made only where the judge believes that, by seeing the defence statement, it would be made easier for the jury to understand the case or decide an issue.

The term 'defence statement' at s 6E applies to statements furnished under s 5, s 6 or s 6B. This will include updated statements. Care will be needed to minimise inconsistencies between an old and an updated document.

Further prosecution obligations

3.71 Section 7 of the CPIA 1996 is repealed, and replaced by a new s 7A (CJA 2003, s 37). This obliges a prosecutor to keep the question of disclosure under review. It effectively replaces the old s 9 of the CPIA 1996 and requires the disclosure of prosecution material which *might reasonably be considered capable of undermining the case for the prosecution against the accused or of assisting the case for the accused'*. The prosecution is also required to consider the issue after the service of a defence statement, which also means updated defence statements in accordance with s 6E of the CPIA 1996. Material must still be disclosed as soon as practicable once the obligation to reveal it to the defendant has been identified. What is reasonably practicable is to be judged against the background of '*the state of affairs at that time (including the case for the prosecution as it stands at the time)*', thus precluding the benefits of hindsight, although the question as to whether a trial has been unfair is usually decided after the event, therefore with hindsight. This is not a change. It continues to allow an investigator to argue that he had not recognised the significance of an item at that time if material is disclosed late (or not at all). Otherwise s 7A simply repeats the pre-existing s 7, save that it caters for repeals of parts of ss 5, 6 and 7 made by the new Act.

Applications for disclosure by the defence

3.72 Section 38 ensures that there will still be a right for the accused to apply to the court of trial for further disclosure provided he has served his defence statement and the Crown has failed to comply, or has not adequately complied, with its obligations under s 7, or, again, that that compliance is not adequate for some reason. The pre-existing s 8 set a test of '*material which might reasonably be expected to assist the accused's defence as disclosed by the defence statement*'. That is replaced by the new objective test in s 7A discussed above. It is submitted that the objective test is to be preferred as a matter of procedural fairness. The former system created a risk of making investigators judge and jury in disclosure matters. It may also go some way to allowing those accused of crimes to challenge tardy disclosure which would otherwise have been justified by a prosecutor on the grounds that the investigator could not have been expected to reveal the material given the state of affairs existing at the time (s 7A(4)). Arguably, constructive knowledge, not actual knowledge, should be the test in future.

---

89 See Chapter 6.

Failure to comply by the defence

3.73 As already noted, a revised s 11 is introduced to the CPIA 1996. The expansion of defence duties under the new Act creates greater opportunities for non-compliance – and, to make the system work, these shortcomings will ordinarily be penalised by adverse comment or inference. The new 'failings' are as indicated below:

(1) section 11(2)(a) and (b) – failing to serve an initial defence statement as required by s 5 of the CPIA 1996 (as amended) or serving it out of time;
(2) section 11(2)(c) and (d) – not serving an updated statement when required to do so or serving it out of time;
(3) section 11(2)(e) – pleading inconsistent defences in the defence statement. The new Act uses the singular 'statement'. This could mean inconsistencies within the same document, for otherwise an accused would be at risk of an adverse inference if his defence statement was modified in the light of new investigations or information. However, a contrary, and arguably better, argument arises if one accepts that the singular includes the plural, and that the term 'statement' is simply a collective noun for all the documents emanating from an accused under the disclosure provisions;
(4) section 11(2)(f) – at his trial, the accused:
  (i) advances a defence not previously pleaded or which 'is different from' any previously pleaded one;
  (ii) advances something at trial which he failed to plead previously in breach of s 6A;
  (iii) relies on alibi evidence which has not previously been disclosed in the alibi notice. This is not new;
  (iv) calls a witness who was not identified in the defence statement (alibi section) or in the new 'advance notice of witnesses' section under s 6C.

In addition, failures with regard to late service of an initial defence statement under s 6 or behaviour thereafter covered by s 11(2)(c) to (f) will attract adverse comment, and service out of time of a s 6C witness notice or the failure to identify a witness adequately or at all will also be caught.

Comment/inferences

3.74 It will be open to any party or the court itself to make any comment about a failing here as is considered appropriate; thus a co-accused as well as a prosecutor or judge could use this tactic. Leave will be required for one party to comment where the failing touches:

– a failure to mention in the defence statement a matter which is then raised at trial, including alibi matters;
– failure to serve it within time;
– failure to indicate the matters of law relied upon;
– failure to give notification of a witness within time;
– the calling of a witness not previously identified.

Inferences can be drawn by judge or jury, but inferences alone will not be sufficient to found a conviction (s 11). Comment by parties as well as by the court is permitted.[90] What is the inference, if any, to be drawn? The case-law on ss 34–38 of the Criminal Justice and Public Order Act 1994 (CJPOA 1994) tends to suggest that an inference may be drawn if the failure to comply suggests that the defence as put to the court is manufactured. The same conclusion may be arrived at where an accused fails to produce a defence statement because he has no defence to put in it; or where details of witnesses or an alibi, etc, are suppressed, because his account of them would not withstand scrutiny by the police if they chose to investigate; or where an account shifts (for example, a defence statement pleads self-defence but a further draft pleads non-participation, thus showing inconsistencies which could also be viewed as 'previous inconsistent statements').

3.75   In deciding whether or not to grant leave to a party to make comment about a defendant's failure or in order to decide whether or not to direct a jury that they may draw inferences, or to examine the apparent non-compliance with the witness notice requirements, the court will want both to investigate the extent of any differences between versions of the defence statement and to determine if any justification exists (s 11(11)). This comes close to compelling a client to waive his legal professional privilege in some cases.

---

90   For a discussion of reasonableness in this context, see *Nickolson* [1999] Crim LR 61, CA; *Argent* [1997] 2 Cr App R 32, CA; *Condron v UK* (2001) 31 EHHR 679; *Gill* [2001] 1 Cr App R 11, CA.

Chapter 4

MODE OF TRIAL AND NON-JURY TRIAL

SUMMARY

4.1   The new Act does not generally limit jury trial. The arguments raised on the two Mode of Trial Bills in 1999 and 2000 were not, in that form, repeated. Yet the debate about jury trial continued in the light of significant changes. It provides for non-jury trial in some circumstances, discussed at **4.20**.

Schedule 3 makes radical procedural changes to the plea before venue (PBV) system. Committal hearings are abolished, and defendants will be able to seek an indication of the likely sentence which would follow after a plea of guilty in the magistrates' court. Committals for sentence to the Crown Court are greatly restricted. The changes affect both the adult and youth courts.

THE PROCEDURAL CHANGES

4.2   The main shape of the procedural changes is summarised in this chapter. Reference should be made to the extremely complex amendments made by Sch 3 to ss 17–25 of the Magistrates' Courts Act 1980 (MCA 1980) and ss 50–51 of the Crime and Disorder Act 1998 (CDA 1998). They form part of an overall package of measures designed to ensure that a greater number of cases are dealt with in the magistrates' court, with magistrates using extended sentencing powers, fewer cases being sent for trial, and committals for sentence being severely restricted,[1] and implement the clear direction set by the Auld Review and the White Paper *Justice for All*.[2] By contrast, s 288 makes certain firearms offences triable only on indictment, as part of a strategy to address gun crime (see **8.52**).

Limitation on either-way criminal damage offence

4.3   The new provisions do not apply to cases of serious or complex fraud, or those which involve children,[3] where the pre-existing transfer for trial provisions exist. Likewise, if there are allied summary-only or either-way offences, no PBV arises and they too will be transferred for trial (Sch 3, para 2).

4.4   A new s 17D of the MCA 1980 introduces revised maximum penalties for certain either-way offences triable summarily by virtue of s 22 of the MCA 1980 (Sch 3, para 3). Those offences are specified in Sch 2 to the 1980 Act and are, in

---

1   See Chapter 8.

2   At paras 4.23–4.26.

3   See CDA 1998, ss 51B and 51C.

essence, criminal damage offences where the amount involved does not exceed £5000.[4] The effect of the changes is to limit the maximum penalty to those specified in MCA 1980, s 33 (three months or a level 4 fine), keeping the case within magistrates' courts jurisdiction only and thus removing any power to commit to the Crown Court for sentence under s 3 of the Powers of Criminal Courts (Sentencing) Act 2000 (SA 2000). This does not apply in respect of the offence of aggravated vehicle-taking.

Note should also be taken of Schs 25 and 26 for changes to penalties for summary-only offences in certain instances.

Decision by single magistrate

4.5 Again, in a drive for efficiency recognised both by the White Paper[5] and by the *Auld Review*, ss 17A–17D of the MCA 1980 (which deal with the initial procedure to be followed where an adult is charged with an either-way offence) will be capable of being exercised by a single justice. For the conduct of summary trial or passing sentence, two justices will still be required. A single justice will also be empowered to deal with appearances under the re-cast ss 19–23 of the MCA 1980 (see **4.6**), subject to those same restrictions as above.

New mode of trial procedure

4.6 Schedule 3, paras 5–14 make major alterations as to how decisions as to allocation are taken, again for the purpose of efficiency, the encouragement of early guilty pleas and reduction of the numbers of cases reaching the Crown Court. They do so by inserting into the 1980 Act new ss 19–21. These sections do not replace their predecessors entirely, but simply add new considerations to the allocation of offences to venue. Both prosecution and defence retain the right to make representations as to venue and the defendant retains the right to elect trial by jury, but from now on, the court will invite the prosecutor to give details of the defendant's previous convictions (MCA 1980, s 19(2)).

This fits conceptually with the much greater use of bad character evidence generally[6] and is a change from the pre-existing position.[7] The court must also consider whether it is possessed of sufficient powers of sentence, bearing in mind its increased sentencing powers.[8] It must consider the views of the parties before it and have regard to allocation guidelines made by the Sentencing Guidelines Council.[9] Those Guidelines will be of particular importance as the court, having lost the general power to commit for sentence in many cases, must be careful not to commit unnecessarily nor to 'under-sentence' by wrongly retaining jurisdiction.

---

4   On value, see *R (DPP) v Prestatyn Magistrates' Court* (2002) LSG, 1 July, DC, which held, in the case of genetically modified maize, that it was impossible to give a value and thus the offence was either-way.

5   *Justice for All*, Cm 5563, paras 4.22–4.25.

6   See Chapter 5.

7   See *R v Colchester JJ, ex parte North Essex Building Co Ltd* [1977] 3 All ER 567, DC.

8   See **8.43–8.46**.

9   See **8.14–8.20**.

If the court has two or more offences before it, s 19(4) of the MCA 1980 applies. The effect is that, if the charges could be joined or arise out of the same or connected circumstances, the court should consider its potential sentencing powers in the light of the aggregate minimum sentence the magistrates could impose for all the offences taken together, unless notice of transfer is served by the prosecution under the CDA 1998.[10]

4.7 Where the court has decided to accept jurisdiction, it must, as before, give the defendant an opportunity to choose whether to agree to summary trial or to elect trial by jury. He will be warned of the risk of committal for sentence under the new s 3A of the SA 2000 if he is tried and found guilty of a 'specified offence' within the meaning of s 224 of the new Act (MCA 1980, s 20).[11] A significant change is that, before electing mode of trial, the defendant can ask for a broad indication as to sentence (MCA 1980, s 20(3)). The rationale for this important change is discussed at **8.44**. It forms part of a range of measures designed to keep cases which are within the increased sentencing powers of the magistrates in the magistrates' court.

The nature of an indication of likely sentence is not defined in the new provisions. Clearly, it addresses the question of whether he is likely to face custody. It is less clear as to whether the defendant can ask for an indication of the nature of requirements in any community sentence or licence period. The level of such requirements in a community sentence or custody-plus sentence may be a matter of importance to the defendant, but at this stage no pre-sentence report will exist and no proper information base will exist to justify any indication of such detail. In reality an indication will be an answer to the question: 'Am I likely to face custody if I plead guilty now?'. These same provisions will apply in the youth court (MCA 1980, s 24A).

The court will not be bound to give an indication (MCA 1980, s 20(8)), and many courts perhaps will be reluctant to do so, certainly in the initial stages of operation of these provisions. Indications in open court have been used frequently in the Crown Court for years, legitimately, where judges have been prepared to take a pragmatic approach to inject common sense in order to avoid a trial that they can see will not benefit anyone and where perhaps an advocate has needed a 'judicial nudge' in order to advise a client a little more confidently. Of course, there has been much criticism of the illegitimate practices of indications behind closed doors which undermine public confidence (victims in particular), and the Court of Appeal has deprecated such practices.[12] There are obvious benefits to the court and the parties, but defence lawyers will need to ensure that guilty pleas are entered for the right reasons. An indication is not considered to amount to the taking of a plea (MCA 1980, s 20A(4)) and the prosecutor will have to live with the occasional frustration of hearing hints of guilt then watching a party resile following no indication or an undesirable one.

An indication on sentence is binding. Section 20A of the MCA 1980 reflects common law by providing that no court[13] may go behind the indication by imposing a custodial sentence unless that option had been indicated by the previous court, or unless

---

10   See **4.2**.

11   See Chapter 9.

12   *A-G's Reference (No 44 of 2000) (Robin Prevett)* [2001] 1 Cr App R 416, CA.

13   See *Gillam* (1980) 2 Cr App R (S) 267, CA.

s 3A(4), s 4(8) or s 5(3) of the SA 2000 apply.[14] If any of the foregoing do apply, an indication will not bind the court, nor will any expectation thereby created in the mind of a defendant be relied upon by way of appeal against sentence (MCA 1980, s 20A(3)). The court record must contain a note of any indication given under s 20.

Where the court declines jurisdiction in an either-way offence, the case will be sent to the Crown Court.[15]

4.8   Having received the indication of likely sentence, the defendant can, if he wishes, reconsider any indication as he gave (or declined to give) under s 17A or s 17B at plea before venue (MCA 1980, s 20). If the defendant does wish to reconsider his indication, then he will be invited once more to give an indication as to plea (s 20(5), (6)) and the court will deal with mode of trial (not guilty/no indication) or sentence (guilty). Should the court decline to give an indication of sentence, or if the defendant either declines to reconsider his plea following one or, in the alternative, does not indicate that he wants to re-open PBV, then progress must be made by moving to mode of trial. The matter may be tried summarily, if both the bench and defendant agree, but if one or other nominates trial by jury, the case is then transferred under s 51(1) of the CDA 1998. Section 6 MCA 1980 committals are abolished.

Application to youth courts

4.9   These provisions apply equally in the youth courts, again in pursuit of efficiency so that the innocent are dealt with quickly, and the guilty convicted and their offending behaviour addressed before they have a chance to re-offend. It is anticipated that the new scheme will prevent unnecessary committals of young people to the Crown Court. The new ss 24A–24D of the MCA 1980 (Sch 3, para 10) bring youth courts into line with adult courts in so far as PBV and the indication of sentence are concerned. Young defendants will be sent to the Crown Court under s 51(1) of the CDA 1998 in the limited circumstances where trial on indictment can been ordered.

Those circumstances have themselves been amended by s 42 of the Act, which came into force on 22 January 2004 (see **1.3**). Section 42 amends s 24 of the MCA 1980, which provides for the circumstances in which a person under the age of 18 may be sent for trial to the Crown Court. Hitherto it was not possible for a juvenile to be tried summarily for homicide. The amendments insert a new subs (1B) into s 24, which includes in this absolute prohibition an offence where the requirements of s 51A(1) of the Firearms Act 1968 would apply to the offence and the person charged with it, and are transitory until such time as Sch 3 is brought into effect.

The new sections change the requirements for attendance. The young defendant is now to be required to be present at the PBV hearing unless his absence is due to his disorderly conduct such that it is impracticable to have him present in court. If he is so disorderly and the court is satisfied that proceedings should continue despite his absence, the matters will be put to his legal representative. If that representative indicates no plea, then the defendant is deemed to plead not guilty. If a guilty plea is indicated, the court can then consider sentence. Where there is an overt plea of not

---

14   The wording extends to any court taking an indication of a guilty plea under the MCA 1980, s 20(7) (MCA 1980, s 20A(1)).

15   See MCA 1980, s 21, as amended by Sch 3 to the CJA 2003.

guilty, then a determination as to whether to try the case in the youth court or Crown Court must be made. If the court chooses to send the case to the Crown Court in order that a sentence under s 91 of the SA 2000 may be passed, then the case will be transferred under s 51(1) of the CDA 1998. In cases where the youth is in court, the procedure is identical, save that he himself will respond to the court's questions, not his lawyer.

These matters are to be dealt with by a single justice in the youth court (MCA 1980, s 24D(1)). A further change to youth court procedure at allocation stage grants the court the power to switch from hearing a trial summarily to sitting as examining magistrates (MCA 1980, s 24D(11)). Amendments to s 25 of the MCA 1980 made by Sch 3, para 11 allow the prosecution to apply to re-open mode of trial to seek a trial on indictment, where the court had agreed otherwise under s 20(9) of the MCA 1980 to try the case summarily. If successful, the prosecutor may ask that the case be transferred to the Crown Court and tried on indictment. The prosecution will already have had some say on venue. Such an application can be granted if it is made before summary trial commences, and the court is satisfied that the sentence which it could impose would be inadequate. This change is one of several giving increased powers to prosecutors.[16] If the court accedes to the application, transfer is effected by s 51(1) of the CDA 1998. For the sake of clarity, the old MCA 1980, s 25(3)–(8) ceases to have effect.

Other detailed procedural matters

4.10   Schedule 3 makes a variety of detailed changes, to which reference should be made at the point indicated:

–   summons to appear following absence at allocation;
–   power of justices to sit after grant of bail. Previous convictions are now considered in an unqualified fashion during a bail application[17] and individuals from that bench will now enter a trial already aware of that record. This then goes beyond potential admissibility of previous convictions at trial. This is, however, unlikely to be challengeable under Art 6 ECHR.[18]

SENDING CASES TO THE CROWN COURT

4.11   Schedule 3, para 17 amends the CDA 1998 in respect of either-way offences (inserting a new s 50A of the CDA 1998) and in respect of the sending of indictable-only offences to the Crown Court (CDA 1998, ss 51–52D), all in the context of the recommendations of the Auld Review and White Paper *Justice for All* to achieve greater speed and efficiency in the handling of cases. The net effects of new s 51 and s 51A are to provide for common offenders and offences to be sent to the Crown Court automatically or, if parties appear on separate occasions, to allow for them to be sent to the Crown Court, no doubt to be joined on indictment.[19]

---

16   Schedule 3, para 11(2).
17   See Chapter 3.
18   See Chapter 5.
19   Indictments Act 1915, s 4.

The new provisions set out when a case will be transferred to the Crown Court, how this will take place, and what will happen to linked offences or the co-accused.[20] There will no longer be the need for an adjournment for committal papers to be prepared and served, nor any delay occasioned by 'read out' committals under s 6(1) of the MCA 1980. This ensures a speedy arrival in the Crown Court for a defendant as part of the Government's desire, expressed in the White Paper, to speed up trials, convictions and punishment of offenders. However, cases sent for trial under s 51 will not reach arraignment stage until the CPS has served its evidence on the defence, and normally the Crown has 42 days to achieve this,[21] although the authorities are at odds as to whether compliance is mandatory within that 42-day deadline.[22] Although sending matters to the Crown Court quickly is desirable, 42 days is not long for a prosecutor to gather witness statements and exhibits. Where no rapid progress can be made for that reason, the object of speedy disposal is defeated and that may mean longer remands in custody.

4.12 Section 51(1) of the CDA 1998 creates a mandatory obligation upon magistrates to send for trial *forthwith* any adult or child in respect of:

(a) any indictable-only offence, other than one where a notice has been served under s 51B (serious/complex frauds) or s 51C (cases concerning children);

(b) either-way offences where a defendant elects trial by jury, the court decides to commit for trial, or the magistrates sit as examining justices after the commencement of a summary trial, or cases of either-way offences which would be triable at the Crown Court but for their value which renders them summary-only;

(c) where a notice under s 51B or s 51C has been served.

In order to keep offences and offenders together, allied offences related to the offence(s) being transferred will accompany them so that the Crown Court is able to deal with everything connected (s 51(3)). This was previously the case except that s 51B and s 51C cases will be sent up in their own right. The result is that either-way offences must be related to the offence to be sent for trial, and summary-only ones must be punishable by imprisonment or carry an obligatory or discretionary driving disqualification (s 51(11)).

However, if the allied offence is one covered by s 51B or s 51C above, it must be sent up in its own right rather than as an allied or linked offence. If a defendant subsequently appears before the court charged with a fresh either-way offence related to an offence already sent for trial under s 51, then the new offence can be sent for trial, presumably to be joined to the indictment for that older offence.[23] Summary-only offences fitting the criteria at s 51(11) may also be dispatched to the Crown Court. However, fresh charges which would attract a notice under s 51B or s 51C should become the subject of such a notice and be sent for trial accordingly.

The benefits of linking the offences in one court will be that everything can be dealt with before the same judge, which will promote consistency and efficiency. Graver

---

20 CDA 1998, ss 51(5), 51A(6), as amended by Sch 3 to the CJA 2003.

21 Crime and Disorder Act (Service of Prosecution Evidence) Regulations 2000 (SI 2000/3305).

22 *Gallagher, White, Burke and Morris* (unreported) (2002) *Criminal Law Weekly* (CLW) 20/5, *R v Haynes* (unreported) (2002) CLW 25/6 and *Re Fehily* (2002) CLW 26/9.

23 See Indictment Rules 1971 (SI 1971/1253), r 9.

offences can be dealt with first, perhaps obviating the need to try lesser ones if the public interest will no longer be served by trying someone for lesser offences where he is now serving a substantial custodial sentence. Guilty pleas may be forthcoming after conviction for other offences once a defendant has experienced the reality of a trial and how his own credibility may have contributed to his conviction. On the other hand, proceedings may be discontinued where a witness upon whom the Crown wished to rely has fared badly in the credibility stakes. A defendant who has been convicted can be sentenced for the totality of his offending rather than piecemeal for individual offences, perhaps by two courts.

Linked defendants

4.13 By s 51(5), when an adult is sent for trial under s 51(1) or (3), any co-accused adult charged jointly with him for an either-way offence, or who is charged with an offence related to the one(s) for which the first accused was charged, 'shall' be sent to the Crown Court for trial providing they appear together. Where one is sent for trial and the other appears on a subsequent occasion (ie not at the same time) the court has a discretion to commit. That linkage in terms of offences will also extend to allied summary-only offences committed jointly where they carry imprisonment, or obligatory or discretionary disqualification from driving, and to either-way offences where jointly charged. Again, the benefit to the administration of justice is that the trial and/or sentencing judge has a complete overview of everyone's degree of criminality where convictions follow committal. The prosecution may have the attractive tactical opportunity to set defendant against defendant (especially where each is obliged to serve his defence statement upon the others). For the defendant, the risk of a disparate sentence should be minimised. The drawback for the Crown Court will be the possible increase in the volume of cases sent to it – but that may be offset by the abolition of committals for sentence.[24] Prosecutors will need to ensure that their administration system clearly identifies linked offences and defendants. The links between defendants and offences may not be obvious or may appear too late. There are also dangers of over-loaded indictments.

4.14 Under pre-existing law, it was possible for a young defendant to be committed to the Crown Court where he was jointly charged with an indictable-only offence with an adult, and any either-way offence the young person faced could be tried on the same indictment. Summary-only offences carrying imprisonment or obligatory or discretionary driving disqualification would also go to the Crown Court. Under s 51A of the CDA 1998, a linked child can be sent to the Crown Court to join an adult who faces an indictable-only offence where jointly charged and whether or not they appear at the same time. The magistrates must send the youth forthwith for trial providing it is in the interest of justice to do so. Any related indictable-only summary or summary offence (carrying a sentence of imprisonment or discretionary or obligatory driving disqualification) related to that indictable-only offence for which the youth has been jointly charged with the adult may also be sent for trial (s 51A(7), (8)).

First, the sending for trial must be 'in the interest of justice'. This can be considered from various perspectives. Following *V v UK*[25] and the subsequent Practice

---

24 See **8.43–8.46**.

25 (2001) 30 EHRR 121, ECtHR.

Direction,[26] it may be possible to argue that it would not be in a young person's interests to face trial by jury. Young defendants should be sent to the Crown Court only for grave crimes.[27] If a young person is unlikely to attract a sentence of detention, there is little point in sending the case to the Crown Court, and issues such as the need for speedy trial point in a different direction. Avoidance of disparate sentences is not an issue, given that youth and adult sentencing regimes are very different.

4.15 Sections 24A and 24B of the MCA 1980 will have the effect of possibly preventing sending for trial where a juvenile indicates his plea. If that plea were one of guilty then the court would be able to sentence him unless he faced a grave crime, and so no decision under s 51 need be made. Only if he was likely to receive a sentence under s 91 of the SA 2000, which should be reserved for grave crimes, would sending to the Crown Court be necessary.[28]

Further provisions relating to children and young persons

4.16 The new s 51A of the CDA 1998 now provides that cases sent to the Crown Court will take place under s 51, rather than under the MCA 1980. The sweeping-up exercise under s 51 provided for linked offences or offenders, or any related indictable-only or summary-only offences, being sent simultaneously (summary-only offences fulfilling the 'requisite conditions' including any under s 51(10), unless, as is the case for adults, they are sent by virtue of s 51B or s 51C). An offence coming to light after the sending up *may* also go forthwith to the Crown Court if related to one of the offences for which the accused was sent for trial originally or if it is a summary-only offence which falls within the description of 'requisite condition'. If the new offence falls within s 51A(3), then it merits its own committal.

Adults linked to children being sent for trial

4.17 Section 51A creates a power for a young defendant to take with him to the Crown Court a linked adult who is jointly charged with him in an either-way offence, or where the adult faces an either-way offence related to the one where he is jointly charged with the young defendant. For the preconditions, see s 51A(6). If the adult appears on another occasion, the court *may* direct he goes to the Crown Court.

Any other 'left-over' offences may be sent as long as they are either-way offences related to the subject matter of that offence sent up for trial or, if summary, they fulfil the requisite conditions.

Other provisions

4.18 A new s 51B prescribes the contents of the notices which are to be used to facilitate transfer of serious or complex fraud cases to the Crown Court. Once in the Crown Court there will be some procedural changes to proceedings. Reference should be made to these detailed provisions. Much of the detail is a re-enactment of existing law.

---

26 *Practice Direction (Crown Court; Young Defendants)* [2000] 1 WLR 659.

27 *R (C and another) v Sheffield Youth Court; R (N) v the Same* (2003) *The Times*, 3 February, DC.

28 See **4.9**.

Changes are likewise made to s 51C notices involving certain offences concerning children. The definition of 'child' has been expanded and now covers anyone under the age of 17 years or under 17 when a video recording of their examination-in-chief was made if that recording was made with a view to being admitted as such at trial. Until now 'child' carried different age limits in different circumstances.

Further notice requirements (s 51D)

4.19   When a case is sent for trial under s 51, s 51A or s 51B, the magistrates' court must issue a notice under s 51D setting out the following:

(a)   the offence(s) sent for trial;
(b)   the venue for trial (which in the case of a notice under s 51B must be the same venue as that notice has already specified);
(c)   how or why, in the case of a related offence, the court considers it to be related to the subject-matter of the s 51 notice.

NON-JURY TRIALS IN THE CROWN COURT

4.20   The proposed changes to availability of non-jury trial in the Crown Court were the most politically charged parts of the new Act, leading to disagreement between Commons and Lords right up to the last days of a long parliamentary process,[29] fuelled by the belief of opponents of the provisions (justified or not) that this was a further attempt to achieve limitations to jury trial which had been unsuccessfully attempted in the two Mode of Trial Bills in 1999 and 2000. The resulting legislation is the usual product of political give-and-take and horse-trading.

Part 7 of the Act enacts very controversial developments creating a system permitting trial without jury. At some future date, if both Houses of Parliament activate s 43 by affirmative resolution, suspected fraudsters will find their right to trial by jury removed by a judge in lengthy or complex cases. Of more immediate impact is likely to be s 44, which entitles the prosecution, in a case to be tried on indictment, to apply for non-jury trial where there is perceived to be a 'real and present danger' of jury interference.

Prosecution applications for a non-jury trial (s 43)

4.21   If and when brought into force, s 43 will confer a right on a prosecutor to apply for a judge-only trial where the subject-matter is likely to be complex, the trial long or both long and complex, and in consequence the trial would be too burdensome for a jury. Only cases sent to the Crown Court by s 51B of the CDA 1998 (serious or complex fraud) are involved (s 43(1)).This change was supported by the Auld Review,[30] which envisaged specialist fraud judges, trial by judge and experts, or trial by judge and lay assessors. The White Paper, *Justice for All*, identified the great strain

---

29   See HL Committee, 15 July 2003, cols 768–823; HC Consideration of Lords Amendments, 18 November 2003, cols 648–688.

30   Chapter 5, para 1097, pp 173–206. But see consideration of Roskill Committee on Serious Fraud Trials.

long trials in serious or complex fraud cases imposed on ordinary jurors. Such trials may last for many months. During this time, a juror is away from work, perhaps left with child-care problems, unable to talk to non-jurors about what he is doing in court all day, unable to make future plans or take time off unless the court agrees to adjournments.[31] The subject-matter of the trial may be dry and technical (perhaps even tedious). Some might regard some cases as involving 'victimless' frauds: a juror may be wholly disinterested and resentful of the burdens. However, the reality is that the conviction rate of the Serious Fraud Office (SFO) is now around 86%.[32] The problem might be a time problem, not one of lack of comprehension. Despite this, the Government concluded that such trials were so disproportionately burdensome to jurors to create the power to remove jurors from the trials where that burden is unacceptable.[33] The fact that the proposed change potentially affected few defendants was no answer to opponents, who feared this to be another assault on trial by jury.[34] As a last-minute compromise the Home Secretary agreed not to implement s 43 after he announced[35] that '... we are prepared to agree that we will not implement the proposals set out in [now s 43] ... while we seek an improved way forward that does not rely on a single judge sitting alone ...'.

4.22 A further safeguard, if s 43 is ever commenced, is that the approval of the Lord Chief Justice (or his nominee) must be given before any non-jury trial order can be made by a judge (s 43(4)). It is for the prosecutor to apply for the order. There is no power for a defendant to do so, even though some might wish to do so.

4.23 The provisions apply only to trial on indictment. If, due either to the length of the trial or its complexity or to both length and complexity, being a juror would be likely to be so burdensome to jury members, then serious consideration ought to be given, in the interests of justice, for the case to be conducted by a judge alone. There is no definition of the phrase 'so burdensome' nor of 'excessive burden', no doubt because it is difficult to define. A trial the length of that of the Maxwell brothers which ran on and on for months is an obvious example, but what of a four-week, multiple-defendant trial, where there are numerous exhibits, contested values of items, trade jargon, a collection of expert witnesses, charts showing who had what documents in their possession when raided by the police, diagrams and computer print-outs, credit card receipts showing who had travelled where and when to meet whom? Some jurors would find sitting through this scenario very burdensome even if, to a fraud specialist practitioner, it felt like a short case. Section 43 makes it clear that complexity and length are alternative, but not mutually exclusive grounds. What is relatively short may still fall within s 43. This section may be used by some prosecutors, urged on by investigators, to apply under s 43 to prevent the defendant exercising his right to trial by jury. Some defendants may thoroughly approve of the measure, others may fear the more critical attentions of a legally qualified tribunal,

---

31 *Op cit*, paras 4.26–4.31.

32 See, eg Simon Hughes MP, HC Committee, 14 January 2003, col 310.

33 See Hilary Benn MP, HC Committee, 14 January 2003, col 321. The Government expects s 43 to be applied to between 15 and 20 trials a year (*Justice for All*, para 4.30).

34 See, eg David Cameron MP, HC Committee, 14 January 2003, col 334.

35 David Blunkett MP, Disagreement to Lords' Amendments, 20 November 2003, col 1027.

which can understand the terminology of the trial, plough through the volumes of evidence and ask pertinent questions of witnesses.

When deciding on the merits of the application, s 43(6) obliges the judge to look at ways in which the trial could be simplified so that the length or complexity may be reduced. Those defending in potential s 43 cases will want to devise techniques for faster and easier assimilation of evidence by jurors to persuade the court that the trial is suitable for a jury to try. Although the judge is required to consider 'reasonable' steps to simplify matters, a step is not to be regarded as reasonable if it significantly disadvantages the prosecution (s 43(7)).

This is important for two reasons. First, efforts to make matters easier for the jury may be unfair to the Crown if they impact adversely on the presentation of the prosecution case, eg by cutting down on the counts to be tried so that only part of the criminality is on show or a false picture is given of the accused's dealings. Secondly, we now see one of several prosecution rights actively created and protected. Is this unfair to the defendant who cannot avail himself of the non-jury trial right? It can be argued that the emphasis should be on whether there is any significant disadvantage to the defendant, although Art 6 rights do not entitle a defendant to a particular mode of trial. There is a right under s 45(3) to make representations to the judge, who determines the question as a further protection.

The procedure to be followed is set out at s 45.

Removal of the right to trial by jury where there is danger of jury interference

4.24 Section 44 addresses the issue of jury 'nobbling',[36] allowing the prosecution to apply for trial by judge alone in cases where there is, first, a real and present danger of such interference, and secondly, a risk that notwithstanding that steps could be taken to protect jurors from these malign influences, the prospect of tampering occurring is so substantial that a non-jury trial is a necessity in the interests of justice.

These provisions are intended to prevent trials from collapsing due to jury nobbling. Judges find themselves compelled to discharge an entire jury for fear of contamination, necessitating a retrial, protracting the process for witnesses and victims who may have to give evidence all over again. The provisions are also intended to spare jurors the anxiety and inconvenience which accompanies police protection while they remain jurors and, perhaps, post-verdict. Should a jury be interfered with in future, the judge may discharge them and continue to sit alone (s 46(3)).[37]

The problem is apparently 'rife' in London.[38] The Metropolitan Police spend some £9 million each year on jury protection. Numerous examples were given by practising lawyers of collapsed trials, or difficulties faced. Opposition took two forms. The first

---

36 See *Justice for All, op cit*, paras 4.21–4.24.

37 Stephen Hesford MP, Second Reading, HC Deb, 4 December 2002, cols 912–1008.

38 HL Report, 19 November 2003, col 963.

was that there was little evidence of nobbling: *Justice for All*[39] stated that only 'a small number of trials are stopped each year because an attempt has been made to intimidate or influence the jury'. Indeed, no statistics were produced during the passage of the Act, the Government accepting that it is difficult to quantify such occurrences. Objections were also taken to the low threshold test, given that the Act requires that there need only be a 'danger' of tampering, and the police might use out-of-date or ill-founded intelligence to remove the right of the accused to a jury trial.[40]

Contaminating the trial judge by giving him information prejudicial to the accused, yet permitting him to continue to try the case as judge of both fact and law where there was to be no jury became a more pressing concern following the decision in *Edwards and Lewis v UK*.[41] Public interest in *Edwards*, an *ex parte* public interest immunity (PII) ruling made by the trial judge prevented the accused from seeing prosecution material which may have founded the basis for submissions of abuse of process following entrapment. The judge knew of the proposed submissions, and the failure to allow its revelation to the defendants in order that they may challenge it violated the defendant's Art 6 right to a fair trial. Further, and crucially, the court feared that the trial judge may have been influenced, albeit subconsciously, by his knowledge of what the PII material contained. This aspect of the decision does not appear to have been addressed in the subsequent decision in *H; C*.[42]

A judge will necessarily see similar material where the Crown applies for a non-jury trial; in some cases it may emanate from an informer who has alerted the police to a conspiracy to tamper with a jury. To reveal details of the informant may jeopardise life or limb or other investigations. Yet the defendant may have no ability to challenge what the Crown through its investigators tells a trial judge, who will then go on to judge the accused on the basis of the evidence called at trial but with the risk of subconscious influence. The Government has asked that the *Edwards* judgment be referred to the Grand Chamber of the ECtHR, and has undertaken to review the position once there is sufficient clarity to do so.

4.25 A typical s 44 application may be in chambers and, possibly, in the absence of the defence, if an application is based on material for which PII is claimed. The potential for losing the right to jury trial on an ill-founded or spurious basis cannot be discounted. One cannot automatically assume that powers will always be used properly.[43]

Grounds for an application under s 44

4.26 Section 44 allows a prosecutor to apply for trial by judge alone and, if the judge is satisfied that the grounds under s 44(4) and (5) are met, he must grant the

---

39 *Op cit*, paras 4.32–4.33.

40 Vera Baird MP, HC Committee, 14 January 2003, cols 347–348.

41 (2003) *The Times*, 29 July, ECtHR.

42 See *R v H; R v C* (2004) *The Times*, 6 February, HL. In that case the House of Lords set out guidelines on how PII applications should be dealt with, with the appointment of special counsel being a possible solution, but one of last resort.

43 For graphic support for this proposition, see *Early, Bawja, Vickers and Dowell*; *R v Patel (Rahul), Patel (Nilam) and Pearcy*; *R v Patel (Madhusudan Maganbhai)* (2002) *The Times*, 2 August, CA.

prosecutor's application. The first condition is that there be a 'real and present danger' of tampering; the second that protection will not alleviate the risk. Section 44(6) gives examples of when this situation may have been reached: where there is a retrial and the jury were discharged because of tampering; where there has been previous tampering with juries during a trial of the defendant(s) now on trial; and where there has been intimidation.

These examples raise interesting issues. The first (s 44(6)(a)) is unexceptionable – tampering has already occurred. The second (s 44(6)) is more problematic – the defendant may be being tried with co-accused who have been involved in the past, and for that reason may be deprived of his right. The third (s 44(6)(c)) stands to catch a wide variety of cases. Witness intimidation is, regrettably, a not uncommon event: there is a difference, perhaps, between intimidating a witness (perhaps trying to persuade a spouse to retract her statement in domestic violence cases or shouting abuse at a neighbour who witnessed a crime) and actually approaching jurors. This is a wide net to cast. If it is the concern that a witness may be intimidated alone, there seems no justification for denying a jury trial; it would be more appropriate that measures should be taken to adduce that witness's evidence, eg by special measures, or by use of the evidence procedures allowing hearsay evidence.[44]

4.27 The judge need merely be 'satisfied' that the grounds have been made out. Section 44(4) requires that there be a 'real and present danger' that the jury would be tampered with. Such a phrase is so broad as to fit many eventualities. 'Present danger' would seem to refer to the time of the application (s 45(2)). So what if the danger passes, for example where a gangster thought to be likely to nobble a jury goes to prison after a s 44 ruling has been made? Could the defence apply to the judge to review his ruling? Could the judge reconsider of his own volition or is an order under this section irrevocable? Much time can elapse between a preparatory hearing and the trial itself, and s 44 appears to permit a potentially adverse ruling to be made against a defendant on the basis of facts which may then disappear. The word 'danger' is imprecise and does not quantify the degree of risk alleged to be present. Here, although the word 'danger' is qualified only by the word 'real', it does not mean that there must be an actual attempt to tamper, an attempt or conspiracy to tamper. Presumably, a judge must give reasons for the order and some explanation of his findings of fact.

The second condition (s 44(5))

4.28 The Crown must persuade the judge that such is the danger of interference that nothing the police can offer by way of protection is going to reduce the substantial likelihood of tampering. This condition will not be difficult to make out. The police cannot protect jurors' families or friends who may be approached in lieu of the juror. The protection cannot last forever. The proximity of police officers to jurors would not necessarily prevent approaches by determined criminals – by telephone, letter, e-mail or other means. This may be convenient to the police working with resource constraints.

---

44 See **6.22**.

The judge's determination

4.29 If the Crown establishes the grounds, the judge must make an order for non-jury trial or dismiss the application (s 44(3)). There is nothing in the Act to prevent a second attempt, although in practice a judge would be unlikely to entertain another application unless new information came to light. As with s 43, the defendant may make representations about a non-jury trial under s 45(3) when the issue is determined at a preparatory hearing (s 45(2)) and may appeal the decision under s 45(5).

A non-jury trial

4.30 Having made a ruling under s 43 or s 44, the judge will then decide the facts and law himself in exactly the way a jury would have done. He will have all of the powers, duties and rights of the jury (s 48), save that if he convicts at the end of the trial he must give reasons for his decision under s 48(5). Those reasons must be given at the time or as soon as is possible thereafter, and the time-limit for appeals runs from the date on which the reasoned judgment is handed down for the purposes of s 18(2) of the Criminal Appeals Act 1968. Presumably, judges will be faced with the occasional need for protection in cases where they try the accused alone for fear of jury tampering, as they have been in Mafia trials in Italy. A defendant may wonder how much that, or the evidence heard at the preparatory hearing, will affect the judge's approach to the case. In some cases, Art 6(1) ECHR – right to trial by an independent and impartial tribunal – may be perceived to have failed, as with *Edwards and Lewis*.[45] The refusal of a jury trial is likely to lead to appeals based on the appearance of bias, whether or not a judge was influenced by what he had heard at the preparatory hearing. Interestingly, *The Times*, following the conviction of a Muslim cleric for soliciting murder, reported (on 25 February 2003) that there was to be an investigation after an attempt was made to bribe the trial judge with £50,000. Northern Irish judges have lived in a siege-like state for several decades, partly because they are ultimately responsible for trying serious, organised criminals. Is this the first allegation of many? And how will these sorts of pressures impact upon judges? Will they be less inclined to order a judge-only trial, feeling that the jury represents a real safeguard against the unwanted attentions which could otherwise dog a judge on his own?

Discharge of jury after tampering

4.31 Previously, a judge had the discretion to discharge jurors or the entire jury if there was 'nobbling' going on. Now s 46 permits him to discharge the jury and take over the trial as the tribunal of fact himself instead of having to empanel a fresh jury and start all over again if tampering appears to have occurred. It is to be hoped that organised criminals appreciate that s 46 is to be implemented and that there is little now to be gained by interference with jurors in such circumstances – provided their attentions are not turned to the judge instead.

Section 46(3) permits the judge to sit on his own, having discharged the jury, but providing he first:

---

45   (2003) *The Times*, 29 July, ECtHR. See also *R v H, R v C* (2004) *The Times*, 6 February, HL.

–   informs the parties that he is proposing to discharge the jury;
–   explains the basis upon which he proposes to discharge them; and
–   allows each party to make representations to him.

This would happen normally in any case where a judge intended to discharge a jury. However, the compulsion to explain his reasoning provides scope for an appeal by the defendant as a safeguard. The judge may sit on his own after discharging a jury only if (under s 46(3)) he is satisfied that tampering has occurred and it would not be unfair to the defendant(s) to continue the trial without a jury. If he believes it is in the interests of justice to terminate the trial at this stage, s 46(4) obliges him to do this.

This flexibility is advantageous – previously, the discharge of a jury could lead to delays of a few days to obtain a fresh panel or much longer if the Listing Office, judge or trial advocates had other commitments dependent on the original trial finishing by a certain date. This breathing space no doubt provided a good opportunity for the criminals to take stock of the evidence and plan the next stage, having seen some of the witnesses and become aware of how the prosecutor was putting the case. Some would have been banking on witnesses not being prepared to return to give evidence a second time. This can now be thwarted as the judge glides into the jury's role and the proceedings continue.

The termination of the trial under s 46(4) may be convenient to both sides if the trial had given rise to prejudicial publicity and any future jury might have preconceived ideas of guilt. If the retrial is to be a judge-only one, the criteria in s 46(5) are now fulfilled.[46] The prosecution is not faced with the argument that a retrial could not be fair, and the defence avoids a jury who may dislike the accused. Of course, it may be bad news for a defendant as the grounds in s 46(5) (a judge-only trial) now exist and the prosecution may seize the chance to prevent a jury trial. Sometimes defendants are not involved in nobbling, rather their well-meaning associates are responsible, or a trial is collapsed to prevent a defendant giving evidence. The case of *Chadwick and others*[47] demonstrates that defendants are sometimes afraid to give evidence. Tampering with a jury is occasionally a subtle way of warning a defendant to think carefully before giving evidence which may incriminate criminals who have yet to be apprehended. The invocation of s 46 following discharge may well be unfair to that type of defendant. But fairness now also applies to the witnesses and victims who will never see justice if trials can be 'thrown' by powerful criminals.

Appeals after discharge of jury

4.32   There is a right of appeal to the Court of Appeal against a decision taken under s 46(3) to order a non-jury trial after discharging the jury following a tampering allegation. Leave to appeal must be granted by the trial judge or Court of Appeal. Once the appeal is lodged, whatever the order made below under s 46(3) or (5), it is suspended until the appeal has been heard or abandoned. If no appeal is lodged, then the order takes effect once the deadline for the appeal to be lodged has expired. (The

---

46   There is now evidence of the 'real and present danger' of tampering.

47   [1998] 7 *Archbold News* 5.

section does not specify a time-limit for any such appeal but undoubtedly this will be effected by new rules of court for which s 49 provides.)

On hearing any appeal, the Court of Appeal may confirm or revoke the order. The defendant has an opportunity to appeal against a decision on appeal under s 46(3) or (5) thereafter to the House of Lords, with the leave of that House or if the Court of Appeal certifies that there is a point of law of general importance involved.[48]

On appeal, it is likely to be both the reasonableness and fairness of the judge's decision to discharge and or continue without a jury which would be scrutinised by the appellate court. The fairness of such a decision would be viewed as to how it had impacted on the overall fairness of the trial. Given that the judge exercised his judicial discretion in reaching a decision under one of these sections, for the reasons outlined earlier, the Court of Appeal is unlikely to alter it lightly. The mere fact someone was denied trial by jury will not be appealable by itself in any event – Parliament's will that some cases should be dealt with by judge alone is plain in the wording of the Act.

Delay between a s 47 ruling and any retrial or appeal may cause Art 5 ECHR issues to come to the fore. The Court of Appeal has a surfeit of pressing business. It is difficult to persuade the Listing Office to expedite hearings save in clear cases. People may spend long periods of time on remand in prison awaiting the outcome of an appeal before they know who is to try them at the retrial and when it will be. The type of character who is likely to be the accused in a trial which is nobbled is probably a bad risk for bail – especially when allied to the fact that jury tampering has occurred in his trial. The court will be concerned that witnesses may be interfered with or that the accused may abscond or he may commit further offences, eg by approaching and menacing witnesses. These are all grounds under the BA 1976 upon which the court may withhold bail, provided that it is satisfied that there is a significant risk that the defendant would do one or more of these things. The time spent on remand waiting for an appeal to be heard is counted as part of the 'reasonable time' in which trial must take place under Art 5(3) ECHR, as appeals are part of the trial process. Anyone whose rights are breached here has a right to compensation under Art 5(5). So appeals will need to be heard expeditiously to ensure the defendant is tried within a reasonable time.[49]

---

48   Section 33(1) of the Criminal Appeals Act 1968 (as amended by s 42 of the CJA 2003).

49   Also a requirement under Art 6(1) and so that the other participants – witnesses and victims – may know where they stand.

Chapter 5

EVIDENCE – BAD CHARACTER

5.1 The new Act contains major revisions to the law of evidence. It weakens the protections against the use of evidence of bad character. It recasts the hearsay rule and its exceptions, and modifies the law relating to expert evidence reports. It deals with the use of documents to refresh memory and adds a new s 76A to PACE, dealing with the use of confessions by a co-accused. It modifies the law relating to evidence by video recording and live TV link. All of the above, other than bad character, are discussed in Chapter 6.

SUMMARY

5.2 Evidence of a defendant's bad character has been admissible only in limited circumstances (see **5.3–5.8**). There has been relatively little protection for a non-defendant against being cross-examined about matters of bad character. The Act changes the position.[1] Section 100 defines the circumstances when the bad character of a non-defendant may be put in evidence, and s 101 substantially widens the circumstances in which the character of the defendant may be adduced. These changes draw on, but do not replicate, the recommendations of the Law Commission. The court has limited discretion in some (but not all) cases where admissibility arises to exclude evidence of a defendant's bad character, if it considers that to admit this would have such an adverse effect on the fairness of the proceedings that the court ought not to admit it (s 101(3)).

The common law rules governing the admissibility of evidence of bad character in criminal proceedings are abolished, except the rule relating to general reputation (s 99).[2]

These provisions will be supplemented by rules of court. Section 111 confers an enabling power for that purpose. No such rules had been made as at the date of going to press. The provisions apply in service courts in accordance with Sch 6.

---

1 Described by one commentator as 'pure strychnine' (Lord Kingsland, HL Committee, 15 September 2003, col 719) and by another as a 'disgrace ... [flying] in the face of principle ... ' (Baroness Kennedy, *ibid*, col 746). More measured language was used by Lord Woolf CJ in a Memorandum submitted to the House of Lords, when he observed: 'The provisions as a whole are extremely confusing and will prove very difficult to interpret' (cited by Lord Ackner at HL Committee, *ibid*, col 725).

2 See *Rowton* [1861–1873] All ER Rep 549.

THE PRE-EXISTING LAW

5.3   The pre-existing law remains relevant. It is based on the exclusionary principle that the prosecution may not, in general, adduce evidence of the accused's bad character (other than that relating to the offence charged) nor of the defendant's propensity to act in a particular way, even if that is relevant.[3] The justification for that exclusionary approach is lack of sufficient relevance, because the law accepts that the evidence may be logically relevant but have high prejudicial effect.[4] That does not mean that evidence of propensity is never relevant. Evidence of propensity is admissible if, but only if, it has strong probative force[5] in proving whether the crime was committed, or whether it was committed by this defendant.

5.4   Where the similar fact evidence rule applies, evidence of bad character, past acts or propensity is admissible as part of the prosecution case.[6] It permits evidence of disposition, propensity or previous acts (whether lawful or unlawful),[7] even including the facts of cases where the defendant was previously acquitted, if they have probative force.[8] Such evidence is admissible as relevant to the issue of guilt, and can be adduced by the prosecution, irrespective of the terms of s 1(3)(i) of the Criminal Evidence Act 1898 (CEA 1898),[9] which permits questions to be asked of the accused in cross-examination if they relate to the issue in the case.

Many misconceptions exist about the similar fact evidence rule. It has sometimes been thought that the rule requires 'striking similarity'.[10] Examples given by Lord Hailsham in *DPP v Boardman*[11] were couched in terms of unusual and striking similarity,[12] but the majority of the court couched their speeches in terms of probative force, and the courts on several occasions have stressed that 'positive probative force is what the law requires'.[13] Cases such as *Makin v Attorney-General for New South Wales*[14] and *Ball*[15] are not cases that depended for their result on 'striking similarities'.

---

3   *Evidence of Bad Character in Criminal Proceedings*, Law Com No 273 (October 2001), Cm 5257, at para 2.2.

4   See *Clarke* [1995] 2 Cr App R 485, CA, per Steyn LJ at 433; *DPP v Boardman* [1975] AC 421, HL.

5   See *DPP v P* [1991] 2 AC 447, HL, at 460, per Lord Mackay LC.

6   It is not confined to prosecution evidence. The rule can apply equally to evidence relating to a co-accused. This might open the defendant to cross-examination: see CEA 1898, s 1(3)(iii).

7   See, eg, *Ball* [1911] AC 47, HL, where the (then) lawful sexual relations between brother and sister showed a sexual disposition relevant when charged with incest (after that conduct had been criminalised). In *Butler* (1987) 84 Cr App R 12, CA, the lawful sexual acts of the defendant showed a sexual preference (disposition) that had probative force in confirming his identity on a charge of rape.

8   *Z* [2000] 2 AC 483, HL.

9   Formerly CEA 1898, s 1(f)(i).

10   See Lord Goddard CJ in *Sims* [1946] KB 531, CA.

11   [1975] AC 421, HL. See Lord Hoffmann, 'Similar Facts after Boardman' (1975) 91 LQR 193.

12   Examples including the leaving of humorous limericks scrawled in lipstick on mirrors, or the wearing of a ceremonial Red Indian headdress.

13   *Scarrott* [1978] QB 1016, CA, per Scarman LJ; *Rance and Herron* (1976) 62 Cr App R 118, CA.

14   [1894] AC 57, PC.

15   [1911] AC 47, HL.

The decision of the House of Lords in *P*[16] put beyond doubt that what was needed for the admission of similar fact evidence was strong probative force, although striking or unusual features might be one way of achieving that. That probative force may come from striking similarities, from the implausibility of coincidence or from being able to link cases together by virtue of common features, in order to establish identity. What has not been possible hitherto is for the prosecution to prove misconduct simply by showing disposition, without demonstrating that that disposition has probative force. The provisions in the Act do not, now, significantly depart from this approach.

Another misconception was about propensity and disposition. Evidence of propensity was thought of itself not to be admissible.[17] That statement is only partially true. Many cases do in fact depend upon reliance on propensity or disposition. The point is importance given the provisions of s 101(1)(d), which admits evidence of propensity.[18]

Background evidence

5.5 Another area of difficulty is background evidence. The distinction between similar fact evidence and background evidence is difficult to draw, and blurred. Evidence of past acts may be admitted, not as directly relevant to the issues and admissible as similar fact evidence rule, but to put into context the evidence that does relate to the issues.

In *Pettman*[19] Purchas LJ said:

'Where it is necessary to place before the jury evidence of part of a continual background of history relevant to the offence charged in the indictment and without the totality of which the account placed before the jury would be incomplete or incomprehensible, then the fact that the whole account involves including evidence establishing commission of an offence with which the accused is not charged is not of itself a ground for excluding the evidence.'

Examples include the existence of a pre-existing relationship between victim and accused, and evidence revealing a motive for the offence. In *Stevens*[20] evidence of previous assaults on the victim by the defendant was admitted as background evidence on a charge of murder. In *Sidhu*[21] the defendant was charged with conspiracy to possess explosives in England. A video showing the defendant apparently leading the activities of a group of armed rebels in Pakistan was admitted as evidence of a

---

16 [1991] 2 AC 447, HL: a multiplicity of allegation (lacking unusual or striking similarity) had probative force given (in the absence of collusion) the implausibility of coincidence. Cases such as *Inder* which required a repetition of unusual features no longer represented the law.

17 See HL Committee, 15 September 2003, cols 709–754. See the first limb of the statement of Lord Herschell in *Makin v Attorney-General for New South Wales* [1894] AC 57, PC: 'It is undoubtedly not competent for the prosecution to adduce evidence tending to show that the accused has been guilty of criminal acts other than those covered by the indictment, for the purpose of leading to the conclusion that the accused is a person likely from his criminal conduct or character to have committed the offence for which he is tried.'

18 See **5.32**.

19 2 May 1985, unreported, CA, cited with approval in *Stevens* [1995] Crim LR 649, CA.

20 [1995] Crim LR 649, CA.

21 (1994) 98 Cr App R 59, CA.

'continual background of history'. Again, in *Sawoniuk*,[22] where the charges included those of the murders of specified Jews by S, a police officer in Nazi Germany during World War II,[23] the court observed that evidence that he was a member of a police search and kill operation, and that he was also involved in a police operation to hunt down and execute any Jewish survivors of a massacre, was (quite apart from any other basis)[24] admissible as background evidence.[25]

The distinction between background evidence and evidence which had to satisfy the test for similar fact evidence rule has proved difficult to draw, with background evidence 'smuggling in'[26] otherwise inadmissible similar fact evidence.[27] The distinction between the two different types of evidence remains relevant under the new law, for the purpose in introducing the two types of evidence is itself different.

Statutory exceptions

5.6 Certain statutory provisions also permit evidence of bad character to be adduced as part of the prosecution's case, and go to issue. Section 27(3) of the Theft Act 1968 and s 1(2) of the Official Secrets Act 1911 are examples. These provisions remain in force.

Restrictions on cross-examination

5.7 Other restrictions relate to cross-examination. Section 1 of the CEA 1898[28] provides a shield protecting a defendant from being asked questions tending to show that he is of bad character. This presupposes that the defendant testifies, for it is a shield against being asked questions or being required to answer questions, matters that are applicable only if the defendant testifies.[29] Answers that establish or reveal, or elicit evidence of, bad character go only to the defendant's credit.

The shield can be lost in the circumstances set out in s 1(3)(i), (ii) or (iii). Of these, s 1(3)(i) relates to matters that go to issue, and chiefly relates to matters that could, in any event, be adduced under the similar fact evidence rule. Section 1(3)(ii) permits cross-examination as to bad character, where the accused has, personally or through his advocate, asserted good character, or sought to establish good character, or has

---

22 [2000] 2 Cr App R 220, CA.

23 Brought under the War Crimes Act 1991.

24 Such as providing evidence supporting identification.

25 See also *M and others* [2000] 1 All ER 148, CA: evidence of sexual abuse of the defendant and his sister, who was one of the alleged victims, admitted as background evidence, even though it showed the commission of an offence with which he had not been charged.

26 Law Com No 273, *op cit*, para 2.9, citing, with approval, *Cross & Tapper on Evidence* (Butterworths, 9th edn, 1999), p 343.

27 See, eg, *Mackie* (1973) 57 Cr App R 453, where, on a manslaughter charge, the court regarded the evidence of past incidents of violence as explanatory evidence, as explaining the boy's state of mind – and specifically directed that the jury should not use the evidence to show the accused's disposition to commit violence against the boy. See also *Underwood* [1999] Crim LR 227, CA; *Dolan* [2003] Crim LR 41, CA.

28 As amended by the Youth Justice and Criminal Evidence Act 1999 (YJCEA 1999).

29 *Butterwasser* [1948] 1 KB 4, CA.

cast imputations on the character of the prosecutor, a prosecution witness or the deceased victim of the alleged crime. The shield may also be lost under s 1(3)(iii), where the defendant has given evidence against any other person charged in the same proceedings.

The rationales for these exceptions varied. If evidence goes to the issue in the case, common sense dictates that it should be considered if it has probative force that outweighs the prejudice it will create. So, too, where the accused asserts his own good character: the prosecutor should have the right to correct a misleading impression. In relation to the casting of imputations (CEA 1898, s 1(3)(ii)), the rationale was less convincing: the 'tit for tat' principle (on which this exception is based) means that if the character of the prosecution witness is impugned, it is only right that the tribunal of fact should know the character of the person casting the imputation. It 'sets the record straight'.[30]

In short, except where evidence of bad character went directly to the issue in the case, there was only a limited set of circumstances where bad character was admissible as affecting the credit of the defendant when giving evidence. Bad character established in cross-examination under s 1(3)(ii) or (iii) went only to credit. This contrasts markedly with evidence of good character, admissible not only to bolster the credit of the defendant but also as relevant to the issues.[31] Of course, if the evidence of character goes neither to matters in issue, nor to credit,[32] it lacks the basic quality of relevance and ought not, for that reason, to be admitted.

This complex scheme applicable in the case of a defendant sought to strike a balance between the protection of the accused and fairness to the wider process. By contrast, few protections existed in respect of the bad character of a non-defendant witness. Subject to limited exceptions,[33] a witness could be asked any question if it was relevant to either issue or credit, and provided it was not offensive or oppressive.

INADEQUACIES OF PRE-EXISTING LAW

5.8 The Auld Review[34] did not make firm recommendations about character evidence, preferring to wait for the final report of the Law Commission,[35] but it considered the law highly unsatisfactory.[36] It invited the Government to have regard to the illogicality, ineffectiveness and complexity of any rule, whatever its form,

---

30 See Seabrooke, 'Closing the Credibility Gap: A New Approach to Section 1(f)(ii) of the Criminal Evidence Act 1898' [1987] Crim LR 231.

31 *Vye* [1993] 1 WLR 471, CA; *Bryant & Oxley* [1979] QB 108, CA.

32 The basic test as to whether a question was relevant in cross-examination was summarised by Lawton LJ in *Sweet-Escott* (1971) 55 Cr App R 316 at 320: 'Since the purpose of cross-examination as to credit is to show that the witness ought not to be believed on oath, the matters about which he is questioned must relate to his likely standing after cross-examination with the tribunal which is trying him or listening to his evidence'.

33 See, in particular, YJCEA 1999, s 41; Regulation of Investigatory Powers Act 2000, s 17.

34 HMSO, 2001.

35 Law Com No 273, *op cit.*

36 Auld Review, *op cit*, p 564, para 113.

which was directed to keeping a defendant's previous convictions from lay, but not professional, fact-finders. That prompt was not followed: neither the Law Commission nor the Government has adopted an approach based on the general admissibility of all bad character evidence.

The Law Commission considered that the pre-existing rules, as developed and applied in the multiplicity of case-law, constituted a:

> 'haphazard mixture of statute and common law rules, which produce inconsistent and unpredictable results, in crucial respects distort the trial process, make tactical considerations paramount and inhibit the defence in presenting its true case to the fact-finders whilst often exposing witnesses to gratuitous and humiliating exposure of long-forgotten misconduct.'[37]

The result was a series of recommendations which 'try to ... provide a clear, consistent and principled structure to support and guide parties, decision-takers and advisers whilst giving the courts the freedom to do justice in each case'.[38] Those guiding principles[39] are largely, though by no means entirely, reflected in the new law. The Law Commission considered, and rejected, a variety of different approaches, favouring an approach based on an exclusionary rule with a specified exception or exceptions,[40] underpinned by five fundamental considerations:[41]

(1)   No person who is involved in a criminal trial should be subject to a gratuitous and irrelevant public attack on his character.
(2)   To adduce evidence of a person's bad character is an invasion of his privacy and so prejudicial that it should not be adduced where any relevance it may have to the issues the fact-finder has to decide is of no real significance or is only marginal.
(3)   The fact-finders in any criminal trial must have all relevant material placed before them so as to enable them to perform their function, consistent with doing justice to the parties whose accounts they have to judge.
(4)   Wherever it is appropriate for aspects of a person's character to be adduced in evidence, it should only be permitted to the extent that it is relevant for the fact-finders to be aware of it for the performance of their task.
(5)   In the case of evidence of the bad character of the defendant, the probative value must be sufficient to outweigh the prejudicial effect of the evidence (except where the evidence is being adduced by one defendant about another).

The Law Commission's approach was exclusionary in nature and subject to exceptions, requiring the leave of the court in order for bad character evidence to be admitted. The Commission proposed a wide definition of the term 'bad character', to ensure that a wide range of conduct fell within the scope and safeguards of the leave requirements, and was defined by reference to objective criteria. That definition was adopted initially by the Bill, but within a different framework and finally abandoned.[42]

---

37   Law Comm No 273, *op cit*, para 1.7.

38   *Ibid*, para 4.83.

39   Set out at *ibid*, paras 5.2–5.25.

40   *Ibid*, para 6.67.

41   Taken from *ibid*, para 7.2.

42   See **5.10**.

The Government consciously chose an approach based on an inclusionary principle, subject to a discretion to exclude,[43] a philosophically important difference,[44] reflecting a 'search for the truth' philosophy inherent in the White Paper.[45]

The Human Rights Act dimension

5.9 The changes have to be measured against the right of an accused to a fair trial contained in Art 6 ECHR. The Law Commission noted that the admissibility of previous convictions *per se* did not infringe the right to a fair trial in Art 6,[46] but observed[47] that a rule which rendered evidence admissible or inadmissible and which thereby had the effect of preventing a defendant from achieving a fair trial might infringe Art 6. Its recommendations were designed to ensure that, throughout, procedures were in place to ensure that was no infringement of Art 6.

Prima facie, the admissibility of bad character evidence does not infringe Art 6. In *X v Denmark*[48] the European Commission on Human Rights observed:

'When interpreting such fundamental concepts as "fair hearing" … and "presumption of innocence" … the Commission finds it necessary to take into consideration the practice in different countries … [since it is] clear that in a number of countries information as to previous convictions is regularly given during the trial, before a court has reached a decision as to the guilt of the accused … [it] is not prepared to consider such a procedure as violating [Art 6], not even in cases where a jury is to decide on the guilt of an accused.'

Yet despite this, and despite the recognition by the ECtHR that rules of evidence are primarily matters for the signatory States,[49] the compliance of the new law in all aspects with the requirements of Art 6 cannot be taken for granted. In its Eleventh Report for 2002/2003,[50] the Joint Committee on Human Rights concluded that there were risks of human rights violations in the bad character evidence rules. The provisions of the new Act, which leave it to judicial discretion to safeguard a fair hearing by excluding evidence of general disposition, potentially compromise the right to a fair hearing. It also concluded that there was a significant risk of unfairness resulting from provisions which (in its view) were likely to indicate to the court that previous convictions should be admitted even if irrelevant.[51] This last concern has now been met by the deletion, at a late stage, of the provision that would routinely have rendered admissible previous convictions.[52]

---

43 HC Consideration of Amendments, 2 April 2003, col 1024.

44 Hilary Benn MP, HC Committee, 23 January 2003, col 544; Baroness Scotland, HL Committee, 15 September 2003, col 732.

45 White Paper *Justice for All, op cit.*

46 Law Com No 273, *op cit*, para 3.9.

47 *Ibid*, para 3.36.

48 (1965) 18 CD 44 at 45. See also *Asch v Austria* (1993) 15 EHRR 597, and, generally, Emmerson and Ashworth, *Human Rights and Criminal Justice* (Sweet & Maxwell, 2001), at para 15.141.

49 See *Schenk v Switzerland* (1988) 13 EHRR 242, ECtHR; *Khan (Sultan) v United Kingdom* 8 BHRC 310, ECtHR.

50 To be found at http://www.publications.parliament.uk/jt200203/.

51 *Ibid*, para 21.

52 See **5.26–5.27**.

THE NEW LAW

What is 'bad character'?

5.10   The definition of 'bad character' is crucial, because of the potential it creates for the adducing of evidence of matters that may be prejudicial.

The Bill originally proposed an extremely wide definition, namely, evidence that shows, or tends to show, that:

(a)   the person has committed an offence, or
(b)   he has behaved, or is disposed to behave, in a way that, in the opinion of the court, might be viewed with disapproval by a reasonable person.

The breadth of that definition was (despite the fact that it was that of the Law Commission) the subject of significant criticism.[53] The Joint Committee on Human Rights[54] considered it a threat to the Art 6 fair trial rights of a defendant, and, during the passage of the Act, fierce objection[55] was taken to that wording, with its vagueness and breadth. To meet such objections, at a late stage, amendments were introduced to define 'bad character' in the terms of what is now s 98. 'Bad character' is to mean evidence of, or a disposition towards, misconduct on the defendant's part, other than evidence which:

(a)   has to do with the alleged facts of the offence with which the defendant is charged, or
(b)   is evidence of misconduct in connection with the investigation or prosecution of that offence.

5.11   Under s 98, 'bad character' does not extend to evidence which (a) has to do with the alleged facts of the offence with which the defendant is charged, or (b) is evidence of misconduct in connection with the investigation or prosecution of that offence. Section 98 therefore preserves the admissibility of facts which relate to the offence itself. These must be distinguished from 'background evidence',[56] which places the facts themselves in context. This is apparent from the Law Commission Report itself,[57] and from the statutory provisions: s 101(1)(c) provides for the admissibility of important explanatory evidence, which is 'background evidence'[58] and which thus amounts to evidence of bad character. The rationale for s 98(a) is that fact-finders are entitled to have information relating to the actual offence put before them.

Thus, the fact that criminal damage was committed by the defendant during the commission of an alleged burglary, the fact that a car used in the robbery was stolen, and an allegation that the defendant lied to the police[59] are not to be regarded, for the

---

53   See, eg HC Committee, 23 January 2003; HL Committee, 15 September 2003.

54   Eleventh Report, *op cit*, para 9.

55   See HL Committee, 15 September 2003.

56   See **5.5**.

57   Law Com No 273, *op cit*, para 8.22.

58   See **5.20** and **5.29**.

59   All examples used by the Law Commission in its Report, *op cit*, para 8.26.

purposes of these provisions, as evidence of bad character, even if they reflect badly on the defendant. Evidence of previous conduct other than that relating to the actual commission of the offence does not fall within s 98, which would be 'misconduct' (s 98)(a); evidence of the facts of cases in which there were previous acquittals is not 'evidence relating to the alleged facts of the offence for which the accused is charged'. It is evidence of other facts, which may have probative force in respect of that offence, that fall within the definition of 'bad character'. Thus in Z^{60} the facts of complaints about previous allegations of rape (in respect of which the defendant was acquitted) were held to have potential probative force on the charge before the court, because of the similarity between the facts of the case before the court and those in the cases of which the defendant was acquitted, and could be admitted. That would be evidence that he had committed an offence, and thus amount to 'bad character'.[61]

Section 98(b) also removes from the ambit of the bad character provisions allegations by the defendant of malpractice by the police (by, for example, alleged fabrication of a confession), or allegations that an individual has behaved improperly during an investigation (perhaps by threatening or intimidating witnesses). The words 'in connection with' in s 98(b) restrict the ambit of the provision to misconduct during the investigation. In a case like *Edwards*,[62] where the allegation against the police officer was that he had engaged in wrong-doing in previous cases and been disbelieved by juries in the past, the allegation would not be of misconduct in connection with the investigation, and, again, the 'bad character' rules would apply. By contrast, the fact that a defendant absconds during the proceedings is misconduct during an investigation, and falls within the exception created by s 98(b).[63]

5.12 Although 'good character' has been considered on many occasions, no absolute definition of what constitutes 'bad character' under pre-existing law exists. The term 'character' has been described as 'the tendency of a person to act, think or feel in a particular way'.[64] Bad character is now defined in terms that relate to acts or behaviour that amount to misconduct, although that misconduct in no way is required to be unlawful.[65] Under pre-existing law, a non-defendant witness can be asked questions relating to the matters in issue, and, subject to a limited number of exceptions,[66] asked questions that reduce the standing of the witness in the eyes of the court (credit questions).[67] In respect of a defendant, a prosecutor can only adduce evidence which satisfied the tests under the similar fact evidence rule, and could only cross-examine about bad character in the circumstances set out in s 1(3) of the CEA 1898.[68] That was not confined to matters relating to the commission of offences, but also to other discreditable matters (whether involving past offences or not), such matters going to the credit of the defendant. That includes the facts of previous

---

60   [2000] 2 AC 483, HL.

61   Hilary Benn MP, HC Committee, 23 January 2003, col 545.

62   [1991] 2 All ER 266, CA.

63   See Law Com No 273, *op cit*, para 8.28.

64   *Cross & Tapper on Evidence* (Butterworths, 1999), p 324.

65   See **5.4**.

66   See **5.16**, and, in particular s 41 of the YJCEA 1999.

67   See **5.16**.

68   *Ibid*.

offences, evidence of reputation and of disposition.[69] In *Carter*,[70] the term 'bad character' was said to refer to any question whose 'purpose was to show [the accused] to be of a dishonest disposition'. The terms of s 98 potentially go beyond that, although matters that fall within s 98 would usually amount to evidence of bad character in pre-existing law.

5.13　Section 98 has to be read in combination with the provisions of s 100 or s 101. Ministers protested[71] that criticisms of the breadth of the original definition of bad character were misconceived, pointing out that, even if the definition of bad character in s 98 is satisfied, admissibility under s 100 or s 101 has to arise. The definition of 'bad character' is narrower in scope than that proposed by the Law Commission, which wanted a broad definition in order to create the widest scope for the protections conferred by the exclusionary approach that it favoured. It is also narrower than that in the original Bill, which is to be welcomed given the approach based on automatic admissibility of bad character evidence adopted by the new Act.

Nonetheless, issues arise. Its extent goes beyond unlawful conduct to include lawful conduct, although both can be 'misconduct'. Cheating at cards or engaging in domestic violence are each clearly misconduct. More discussion may centre around lawful, but immoral, sexual behaviour: the conducting of an illicit affair, the downloading of images of adult pornography, promiscuity or consensual deviant sexual behaviour which may not, of themselves, always amount to 'misconduct'. The use of the term 'disposition towards misconduct' in s 98 does, however, broaden the definition. 'Disposition' is not defined, but is a concept inherent in the pre-existing similar fact evidence rule.[72] Defined by the *Shorter Oxford English Dictionary* as including 'temperament, natural tendency, inclination to', we find identical terms used to define 'propensity'. The bad character provisions are clearly intended to include propensity, as does the pre-existing law on bad character,[73] provided that that propensity has probative value in relation to a matter in issue (see s 101(1)(d)). The middle-aged man who hangs around school gates, funfairs or children's playgrounds may not have engaged in 'misconduct', but if the totality of the evidence shows this to indicate a sexual interest in children it demonstrates a disposition towards misconduct. Evidence of preparations to embark on shoplifting expeditions might conceivably show pre-planning and thus misconduct, but in any event show a disposition to misconduct. So, too, with the possession of equipment or articles for the use in theft or robbery: possession will not necessarily amount to misconduct (unless one takes an extremely wide view of misconduct) but it may certainly show disposition. The down-loading of adult pornography may not of itself amount to misconduct, but it might, in combination with other evidence, show a disposition to misconduct.

To define bad character in terms of disposition to engage in misconduct is wide indeed, and in many ways wider than the definition proposed by the Law Commission or in the original Bill, which required the evidence to show, *inter alia*, that the defendant had committed an offence or other conduct which would meet with

---

69　See *Stirland v DPP* [1944] AC 315, per Viscount Simon.

70　(1996) 161 JP 207.

71　See **5.10**.

72　See **5.41**.

73　*Ibid*.

the disapproval of a reasonable person. The Government's claim that the definition of bad character was being tightened up is only true in one sense.[74] The breadth of the definition of bad character is mitigated only by the fact that s 98 is a threshold matter, and the specific criteria in s 100 or s 101 have to be satisfied before that evidence of bad character can be adduced.[75]

5.14 Further issues arise in respect of lawful conduct. This can amount, now, to evidence of probative force. The evidence of the women in Z[76] testifying as to the facts of the alleged rape (of which Z was acquitted) may nonetheless show, in the context of the current case, misconduct (ie that the women were in fact raped). Yet, not all matters which have probative force amount to misconduct in any shape or form. The defendants in *Ball*[77] engaged in sexual relations at a time when their incestuous conduct was not an offence, yet that conduct had strong probative force on the charge brought after a change in the law. The sexual preference of the defendant in *Butler*[78] was by no means misconduct, yet, in the overall factual context, had strong probative force in confirming the identity of the alleged rapist. It may be that we should recognise such cases as being conceptually different from misconduct cases, and determine the admissibility of such evidence on simple grounds of relevance and probative force in no way connected with the requirements and safeguards of the bad character provisions. None of these problems would, however, arise if the Law Commission's (and Government's) initial definition of evidence of bad character had been adopted. Arguably, what this part of the Act should be dealing with is the evidence of other conduct, unrelated directly to the facts of the case. That distinction has been blurred.

Non-defendant's bad character

5.15 The new provisions apply to non-defendant witnesses as well as defendants. Section 100 limits the circumstances when a non-defendant can be asked about bad character, or have evidence of it introduced, to those defined by s 100, and then only with leave of the court (unless all parties agree). The role of the court in granting or refusing leave will be to make judgments as to the matters set out in s 100(1)(a), (b) or (c). If the court grants leave at the instance of an accused, that defendant, as now, runs the risk of his own character being put in evidence, under s 101(1)(g).

5.16 This is a significant change of the law. At common law a witness could usually be asked about any matter which is relevant to the proceedings, provided that it was not offensive and fell within the proper bounds of cross-examination.[79] The question must be relevant to the issues in the case, or any of them, or to the credit of the witness. In *Sweet-Escott*[80] it was said that questions 'must relate to [the witness's]

---

74 See HC Consideration of Lords Amendments, 18 November 2003.

75 See **5.13**.

76 [2000] 2 AC 483, HL.

77 [1911] AC 47.

78 (1987) 84 Cr App R 12, CA.

79 Subject to limitations relating to cross-examination of complainants of a sexual offence (YJCEA 1999, s 41) or questions in relation to the interception of telecommunications (Regulation of Investigatory Powers Act 2000, s 17).

80 (1971) 55 Cr App R 316, CA, per Lawton LJ.

standing after cross-examination with the tribunal which is trying him or listening to his evidence'. A court could, at common law, prevent a witness from being asked, or required to answer, a question that had no bearing on the standing of the witness in the eyes of the court.[81] It might be thought that these general powers, if properly exercised by trial courts, were sufficient to prevent unfair questioning of non-defendant witnesses. Nonetheless, a significant body of respondents to the Law Commission Working Paper saw merit in looking for further ways to control unacceptable cross-examination, not only to prevent unnecessary, offensive or irrelevant embarrassing material being brought out at trial, but also to prevent potential witnesses from being deterred from giving evidence because of the fear of matters of marginal or no relevance being brought out.[82] The Law Commission based its conclusion that further limitations were needed on what may be asked of a non-defendant upon three reasons:[83]

(1) the special power of bad character evidence to distort the fact-finding process;
(2) the need to encourage witnesses to give evidence, by making it known that the witnesses will not have their past exposed publicly where it is at best of only minimal relevance to the questions in issue, such as whether they are telling the truth; and
(3) the need for the courts to have a 'clear and supportive framework to control gratuitous and offensive cross-examination which is of little or no purpose other than to intimidate or embarrass the witness or muddy the waters'.

It did recognise the need not to prejudice the fairness of the trial. This could, it concluded, best be achieved by a test expressed in terms of the degree of relevance that the evidence has to the issues in the case rather than a test based on the concept of the fairness of the trial. This test was intended to exclude bad character evidence of trivial relevance – the kind of evidence that cannot be said to be irrelevant, but which adds very little.[84] Its detailed recommendations form the basis for s 100.

5.17 Section 100(1) provides that evidence of the bad character of a person other than the defendant is admissible in criminal proceedings if, and only if:

(a) it is important explanatory evidence;[85]
(b) it has substantial probative value[86] in relation to a matter which:
    (i)   is a matter in issue in the proceedings, and
    (ii) is of substantial importance in the context of the case as a whole; or
(c) all parties to the proceedings agree to the evidence being admissible.

---

81 *Hobbs v Tinling* [1929] All ER Rep 33, CA.

82 Law Com No 273, *op cit*, paras 9.10–9.13. See 'Law Commission Dodges the Issue in Consultation Paper No 141' [1997] Crim LR 102. For an example of how the courts can prevent matters of marginal or no relevance coming out, under existing law, see *Eccleston* [2001] EWCA Crim 1626, where the Court of Appeal held that the past convictions of a non-defendant witness in a rape trial (not the complainant) for loitering as a prostitute, use of a controlled drug and theft were of marginal relevance and thus rightly not permitted to be adduced at trial.

83 Law Com No 273, *op cit*, para 9.35.

84 *Ibid*, para 9.36.

85 See **5.20**.

86 See **5.21**.

Nothing in s 100 is intended to prevent evidence being adduced which is probative of matters in issue (s 98(a)). That also is true in relation to matters that affect the witness's credibility,[87] although that will have to be within the framework of the provisions of s 98 and s 100.

Section 100 does not directly prohibit the asking of questions, but rather the adducing of evidence. In that respect it differs from provisions such as the pre-existing s 1 of the CEA 1898, or s 41 of the YJCEA 1999, each of which prohibits (or prohibits without leave) the asking of questions as well as the adducing of evidence. This difference is curious, given that the only purpose of the questions would be to adduce evidence for which the leave of the court is necessary. Section 111 (rules of court) clearly envisages limits on cross-examination without leave (see s 111(2)(b)), and the rules to be made thereunder will deal with the procedure to be followed. It will be the duty of the advocate who wishes to put questions about bad character to make the appropriate application, having given such notice as the rules may require. Such matters may be dealt with at trial or at a pre-trial ruling. Of course, to avoid questions of leave, the agreement of all parties can be secured (s 100(1)(c)). If this occurs, the court would appear to have no residual discretion to exclude it, except, perhaps, in the context of cross-examination, where it may be that the residual common-law power to restrict questions that are irrelevant or offensive still subsists. There is no provision in the new Act that explicitly restricts that power to control the trial in that way unless the terms of s 99 apply. Section 99(1) abolishes the common law rules governing the admissibility of evidence of bad character. That, surely, does not have the effect of restricting the right of the court to regulate questioning, which is, perhaps, a wider right than that simply to prevent evidence of bad character. After all, repetitive or unnecessary questions fall within the common-law power, yet do not relate to bad character. However, the issue is a theoretical rather than a practical one: it would indeed be odd if such a conclusion were justifiable given the clear parliamentary intent that if the parties agree the evidence should be admissible.

5.18   Even if one of these threshold conditions is satisfied, unless all parties agree, the leave of the court must be sought and given. For the advocate this may raise issues that are, on occasion, uncertain. Many matters will instantly be recognisable as amounting to evidence of 'bad character'. The leave of the court will be required (except where the parties agree) to ask (whether in chief or in cross-examination) a witness about, or to adduce evidence of, not only the commission of previous offences, but also anything that might be viewed as misconduct. Allegations of drug abuse, drunkenness, sexual immorality or deviance, previous false allegations of rape, dismissal from employment for dishonesty or misbehaviour could all fall within the definition of bad character (although they might not, in fact, do so in the particular case), as would allegations that the witness had fabricated part of his evidence. By contrast, no leave will be required to adduce evidence that, say, the witness is culpable, in whole or in part, for the offence charged, because such questions would go to the alleged facts of the offence and thus (because of s 98(a)) not amount to bad character.

5.19   Nothing in s 100 removes restrictions contained in other statutes. Thus the limitations contained in s 41 of the YJCEA 1999 remain in force and have to be

---

87   Baroness Scotland, HL Committee, 15 September 2003, cols 739–740.

complied with where appropriate (s 112(3)(b)).[88] That does not negate the need for leave under s 100. Even if leave is granted under s 41 of the YJCEA 1999, if what is being asked amounts to 'bad character' within the meaning of s 98, the need for leave to be obtained under s 100 arises. That raises the question about the circumstances when sexual behaviour might be regarded as 'misconduct'. It is, probably, inconceivable that a court would endow the reasonable person with attitudes to sexual behaviour different from those that they would apply under s 41, and, in that context, the circumstances in which sexual behaviour might be regarded as 'bad character' are, and should be, severely limited. Evidence of promiscuity (which would not be permitted generally under s 41 of the YJCEA 1999) will not be evidence of bad character. Indeed, since sexual behaviour which might be held relevant to the facts in issue will not fall foul of the bad character provisions (because of s 98(a)), it is difficult to see how, in a sexual case, s 100 has any significant operation (in respect of the sexual conduct of the non-defendant). If it is not relevant to issue, then it will fail to satisfy the criteria under s 41. If, by contrast, the matter which is to be put to the witness is a false allegation made in the past, it does not fall within the scope of s 41, because it is not about 'sexual behaviour'.[89] A false allegation would be regarded by most people as misconduct and would be likely to engage the bad character provisions in s 98.[90]

Nor does s 100 affect the operation of s 3, s 4 or s 5 of the Criminal Procedure Act 1865 (CPA 1865), relating to previous consistent or inconsistent statements, unless any such statement contains matters relating to the bad character of the maker of the statement, perhaps an implicit acknowledgement that credit questions remain legitimate. Schedules 25 and 37 to the new Act do amend s 6 of the 1865 Act to reflect the changes,[91] providing confirmation (if it were needed) that there is no intention to limit cross-examination of the type envisaged.

The threshold conditions

Important explanatory evidence

5.20 Section 100(1)(a) relates to 'important explanatory evidence'. By s 100(2), evidence is important explanatory evidence if:

(a) without it, the court or jury would find it impossible or difficult properly to understand other evidence in the case; and

(b) its value for understanding the case as a whole is substantial.

---

88 Section 41 of the YJCEA 1999 provides that if a person is charged with a sexual offence, then, without the leave of the court (a) no evidence may be adduced, and (b) no question may be asked in cross-examination, by or on behalf of any accused at the trial, about any sexual behaviour of the complainant.

89 See *BT and MH* [2002] 1 Cr App R 254, CA.

90 See **5.13**.

91 See Sch 25, para 36 and Sch 37, Part 5. Section 6(1) will now read: 'Upon a witness being lawfully questioned as to whether he has been convicted of any felony or misdemeanour he either denies or does not admit the fact, or refuses to answer, it shall be lawful for the cross-examining party to prove such conviction.'

Explanatory evidence will not of itself prove any fact in issue: it is 'background evidence', not evidence going to 'the central set of facts'.[92] Evidence which goes to that 'central set of facts' falls within s 98(b), and is not regarded for this purpose as evidence of bad character.[93] Under pre-existing law, evidence may relate to matters close in time, place or circumstance to the facts or circumstances of the charge. It may be necessary to complete the account of the circumstances of the offence charged, and thus make it comprehensible to the jury. That is evidence that 'has to do with the alleged facts of the offence' (s 98(b)). It is not, for this purpose, evidence of bad character. By contrast, there may be evidence of past conduct without which the prosecution's account would be 'incomplete or incoherent'.[94] For example, the defendant may have had a relationship with the victim of the offence charged, and the previous misconduct evidence may relate to this victim. [95] There is likely to be an 'explanatory purpose' if it shows a context which is valuable to the decision-maker in determining disputes on the facts in issue. That context must, however, be 'important': the fact that the evidence is explanatory is insufficient. The fact that it is helpful will not suffice. It must be evidence that leads the court to conclude that – without it – the court or jury would find it difficult or impossible to understand the matters it must decide (s 100(2)(a)). This echoes, in different language, the test adopted by Purchas LJ in *Pettman*.[96] The value of the explanatory evidence in understanding the case as a whole must be substantial (s 100(2)(b)). The term 'substantial' is vague, and intended to be contrasted with matters which are minor or trivial.[97] It does give the court complete freedom to decide the level of importance of the explanatory evidence to the trial overall. Section 100(2) does not require a court to take into account the level of probative force of that evidence, and the terms of s 100(3) (which deal with probative force) apply only to s 100(1)(b), not s 100(1)(a). It is, however, unlikely that a court would conclude that the value of background evidence which did not have significant probative force was substantial.

Substantial probative value

5.21 The second threshold condition (contained in s 100(1)(b)) relates to evidence of bad character of the non-defendant witness which has substantial probative value to any matter which:

(a) is a matter in issue in the proceedings, and
(b) is of substantial importance in the context of the case as a whole.

That probative value thus arises in the context of matters which have probative value relating to matters in issue, but which themselves may relate either to issue or to credit. 'Probative value' must be assessed on the basis that the evidence is true (s 109(1)),

---

92 See **5.5** and **5.11**.

93 See s 98 and **5.10**.

94 See Law Com No 273, *op cit*, para 9.13.

95 *Ibid*, paras 7.8–7.17, applied to this context by para 9.39.

96 (1985) (unreported) 2 May, per Purchas LJ. For discussion of what amounts to 'background evidence' see **5.5**.

97 Law Com No 273, *op cit*, para 9.1.

unless it appears to the court that no court or jury could reasonably find it to be true (s 109(2)).

The Law Commission specifically rejected approaches that would have confined this 'enhanced relevance' approach to matters going only to credibility,[98] and rightly so, given the difficulties that have arisen in the past in distinguishing matters relating to issue and credit.[99] Thus, s 100 will apply to allegations made against a police officer of past misconduct, false allegations of rape or whatever, no matter how central they are to the case before the court. The question that must be asked is whether there was an attempt to adduce evidence of bad character. If so, does the bad character evidence relate in a way that is substantially important to a matter in issue? If it does, the court should grant leave. If it does not, then the evidence of bad character should not be adduced.

5.22   Section 100(1)(b) requires the evidence to have 'substantial probative value', a requirement that does not formally apply to 'important explanatory evidence' under s 100(1)(a). The term 'substantial' eliminates probative value which is trivial or minor. There is still, however, the further threshold: even if the probative value on a matter in issue is high, if that matter is not of substantial importance to the proceedings as a whole it fails to satisfy the terms of s 100(1)(b).

The court must take a view as to the probative force of the bad character evidence. The purpose of s 100(1)(b) and (3) is to ensure that the defendant[100] has the opportunity to adduce evidence of bad character of a witness if it is sufficiently important to do so, but not to allow bad character evidence to be adduced if it has no, or limited, importance. Section 100(3) sets out the factors to which the court must have regard, although the list is not conclusive. Although the court must take the matters stated into account, it may have regard to any other matters it considers relevant.

The factors identified by s 100(3) are as follows.

(a) *The nature and number of the events, or other things, to which the evidence relates*
If, on charge of theft, there is evidence of dishonest conduct in the past by X, the crucial prosecution witness, the nature of that dishonesty and the number of instances of dishonesty must be taken into account by the court in determining whether evidence of that dishonesty should be adduced to weaken the credit of X on the matters in issue. Again, on a charge of rape, if the allegation against complainant Y is that she has made false allegations of rape in the past, and that the current case involves another such false allegation, the question should be asked by the court: how many false allegations were there, and were they in similar situations? If the complainant, Y, had a previous conviction for shoplifting some 20 years ago (unknown to her husband), and D alleges she is now lying, in determining whether leave to allow evidence of that conviction to be adduced the court must have regard to the fact that the conviction bears no relation to matters before the court, other than being an old instance of dishonesty.

---

98   Law Com No 273, *op cit*, para 9.1.

99   See, eg *Phillips* (1936) 26 Cr App R 17, CA; *Funderburk* [1990] 2 All ER 65, CA; *Busby* (1981) 75 Cr App R 79, CA; *Edwards* [1991] 2 All ER 266, CA.

100 Or any other party: s 100 is not confined to evidence wished to be adduced by defendants.

(b) *When those events or things are alleged to have happened or existed*
On the examples above, the court must take into account the question: how long ago?
A conviction for dishonesty 20 years ago may have less probative force in the case
before the court than several over the last 18 months.

(c) *The nature and extent of the similarities and dissimilarities between each of the
alleged instances of misconduct*
This applies only where:

(i)   the evidence is evidence of a person's misconduct, and
(ii)   it is suggested that the evidence has probative value by reason of similarity
       between that misconduct and other alleged misconduct.

Thus, in a case where D is charged with assault outside a nightclub, and claims he
acted in self-defence against an unprovoked attack by Z, the main prosecution witness
and alleged victim, the fact that Z has convictions for assault in highly similar
circumstances will be a matter to which the court must have regard. It must also have
regard to the lack of similarities, for example, of incidents of minor scuffles at football
matches, involving Z.

(d) *The extent to which the evidence shows or tends to show that the same person was
responsible each time*
This applies where:

(i)   the evidence is evidence of a person's misconduct,
(ii)   it is suggested that that person is also responsible for the misconduct charged,
       and
(iii) the identity of the person responsible for the misconduct charges is disputed.

Thus, in a case where D is charged with thefts of money from the workplace, D wishes
to allege that the thefts (the occurrence of which is not disputed) were committed by a
fellow-employee, X, who is a witness against D. D wishes to adduce evidence that the
witness was dismissed from his last job because of theft in the workplace. The court
must have regard to the extent to which the bad character evidence shows, or tends to
show, that these thefts may have been committed by X.

5.23   Section 100(1) requires an advocate directly to address the question: what is
the value to my case of the evidence I wish to adduce? How does it substantially
advance it? Why will it be unfair to my case not to allow the character evidence to be
adduced? As the Law Commission put it:[101]

> 'Applying the rigour of requiring the advocate to satisfy the court of the enhanced degree of
> relevance would mean that evidence going to the "specific credibility" of a witness (that is,
> evidence that suggests that the witness has an incentive to lie on this occasion) would be
> more likely to have the required level of relevance than evidence which merely suggests that
> the witness might lie if he or she did have an incentive to do so.'

---

101 Law Com No 273, *op cit*, para 9.26.

Bad character of the defendant

5.24 More controversial are the provisions that relate to the defendant's bad character. Section 101 in some (but not all) respects implements the Law Commission recommendations in its report on character evidence. It amounts to a significant extension of the law, for several reasons. First, because of the wide definition of 'bad character'.[102] Secondly, because the grounds for adducing evidence of a defendant's bad character are wider than those that have existed hitherto. Thirdly, because, unlike s 1(3) of the CEA 1898, s 101 is not confined to the asking of questions in cross-examination, but allows such evidence as part of the prosecution's case irrespective of whether the defendant testifies. Finally, s 101 does not define, or limit, the purpose for which the defendant's bad character may be adduced: the bad character is admissible irrespective of whether the defendant testifies and thus can be regarded as relevant to issue.

5.25 By s 101(1) evidence of the defendant's bad character is admissible if, but only if:

(a) all parties to the proceedings agree to the evidence being admissible;

(b) the evidence is adduced by the defendant himself or is given in answer to a question asked by him in cross-examination and intended to elicit it;

(c) it is important explanatory evidence;

(d) it is relevant to an important matter in issue between the defendant and prosecution (as defined by s 103). Only prosecution evidence is admissible under this category;

(e) it has substantial probative value in relation to an important matter in issue between the defendant and a co-defendant (as defined by s 104);

(f) it is evidence to correct a false impression given by the defendant (as defined by s 105); or

(g) the defendant has made an attack on another person's character.

These criteria are not mutually exclusive. In the light of the provisions of s 101(3) relating to the discretion to exclude,[103] it may be important under which provision a piece of evidence is admitted.

The court must not admit evidence under (d) or (g) above if, on an application by the defendant to exclude it, it appears to the court that the admission of the evidence would have such an adverse effect on the fairness of the proceedings that the court ought not to admit it (s 101(3)). On such an application the court must have regard, in particular, to the length of time between the matters to which that evidence relates and the matters which form the subject of the offence charged.

---

102 See **5.10**.

103 See **5.50**.

Grounds for admissibility – in detail

By agreement (s 101(1)(a))

5.26 A defendant has always been able to give evidence of his character, whether good or bad, and often there are tactical reasons why it is useful to do so.

There can be no objection to character evidence being adduced by agreement and this occurs now on a daily basis. Theoretically, s 101(1)(a) does not permit a defendant to adduce evidence of his bad character without the consent of all other parties, but that is unimportant because a defendant's bad character can be elicited without the consent of others under s 101(1)(b), either in his own testimony, or by the asking of questions of a witness in cross-examination. There is no question of a co-accused having a veto preventing an accused from eliciting evidence of bad character (if that is what he wants to do).

By the defendant (s 101(1)(b))

5.27 The defendant can testify as to his bad character. That is already the position. There will be cases where a defendant testifies not about previous offences, but about matters which show misconduct. The defendant who testifies about his racist beliefs, his membership of an unacceptable organisation, his bizarre or disgusting sexual *mores* or habits or practices, his drunkenness or anti-social behaviour, opens up that aspect of his character. No doubt most of these matters would have been regarded as bad character at common law in any event. The giving of testimony of bad character in this way has not hitherto opened up a defendant to cross-examination as to other aspects of his character.[104] That remains the case under s 101(1)(b), because of the words of the beginning of s 101(1)(b) ('the evidence is adduced by the defendant'). Clearly, 'the evidence' is the evidence of bad character. A prosecutor would be entitled to cross-examine as to other matters of bad character only if that other bad character fell within one of the other provisions under s 101(1). Thus, if the result of the defendant's testimony is to create a false impression, evidence of the whole of the defendant's bad character could go in under s 101(1)(g). That conclusion might have been reached under common law,[105] but a clear power existed at common law to exclude where fairness demanded. The position is now less clear. Because the exclusionary discretion contained in s 101(3) does not apply to s 101(1)(f), a defendant will need to take care to ensure that he is not painting a misleading picture. Of course, a defence advocate would not, other than out of choice, seek to adduce such matters, but the possibility of spontaneous answers that fit the wide definition of bad character should not be overlooked. Under pre-existing law, a court might choose to deal with this by the use of discretion, even though the 'shield' had technically been lost. That is more difficult under the new Act because the discretion to exclude contained in s 101(3) does not apply in that circumstance.[106] Arguably, nothing prevents a court from using its general discretion under s 78 of PACE, in this or any other circumstance: s 101(3) merely identifies circumstances when a court must

---

104 *Thompson* [1966] 1 All ER 505, CA.

105 See *dicta* in *Wattam* (1952) 36 Cr App R 72, CA.

106 See **5.50**.

exclude. Nothing in the Act indicates a clear parliamentary intention to limit the operation of s 78 of PACE.[107]

Of course, if a defendant has made such comments relative to the facts in issue in the proceedings then the evidence will not be that of 'bad character', because of s 98(a), which excludes from the definition of bad character matters that have to do with the alleged facts of the offences with which the defendant is charged.

5.28   In relation to the second part of s 101(1)(b), if questions are asked in cross-examination, they must be intended to elicit the bad character. That can only mean that the question must be framed in terms of seeking information about the character of the accused. The terms used by s 101(1)(b) are 'intended to elicit it'. 'It' can be related to the words 'evidence of the defendant's bad character', to be found at the beginning of s 101. A question intended to elicit 'good character' is not, in a literal sense, intended to elicit bad character, and yet it would be absurd if the response to a question posed by the defendant about his good character could not be considered by the court. Character is, after all, indivisible.[108] The answer could lie in the courts giving a wide meaning to the term 'about it'. In any event evidence of the defendant's bad character may well be admissible by virtue of s 101(1)(f): by the asking of such a question the defendant may well have been responsible for the creation of a false impression, and the wording of s 101(1)(f) (as defined by s 105(2)(a)) is wide enough to permit that conclusion.

Important explanatory evidence (s 101(1)(c))

5.29   This phrase is defined by s 102 in identical terms to s 100(2).[109] The evidence must have a role in putting the other evidence in context – in other words, amount to 'background evidence'. It is adduced not because of its probative force on the matters in issue in its own right, but because it provides the background to, and context of, the facts in issue.[110] If it does have probative force, there is nothing to stop that evidence being used under s 101(1)(d) (relevant to an important matter in issue).

Under s 101(1)(c) the value of the explanatory evidence must be substantial. There is no requirement in s 101(1)(c) to have regard to the risk of prejudice that may arise from admission.

The meaning of background evidence was seen at **5.5**. The examples seen of the application of the *Pettman* principle demonstrate the difficulties that have arisen in distinguishing between background that is explanatory and background that in reality is intended to be probative on the issues and thus falls to be considered as similar fact evidence.[111] Real problems of potential prejudice can sometimes arise.

5.30   If the terms of s 101(1)(c) are satisfied, the evidence can be adduced without leave, for s 101(3) does not apply. This is unfortunate. A trial judge or magistrate ought to be in the position of having to determine whether there are other ways of

---

107 See **5.50**.

108 *Winfield* [1939] 27 Cr App R 159, CA.

109 See **5.20**.

110 See **5.5**.

111 *Ibid.*

providing the explanatory context which s 101(1)(c) is seeking to permit.[112] Thus, on the facts of *Mackie*,[113] a trial judge might take the view that the evidence of past incidents, although admissible, was grossly and unnecessarily prejudicial. That is not an approach open to a court under the Act, although we may imply an overall exclusionary discretion to secure a fair trial.[114] It also places a defendant against whom 'background evidence' is being adduced at a disadvantage compared with the position he would be in if evidence was adduced to support probative force.

Relevant to an important matter in issue between the defendant and the prosecution (s 101(1)(d))

5.31 Evidence of bad character which is relevant to an important matter in issue between defence and prosecution is admissible. That obviously does not include evidence that relates to the alleged facts, because that would not be evidence of bad character (because of s 98(a)). But provided it has some relevance either to issue or credit, that is enough. The terms of s 101(1)(d) may, in this regard, be contrasted with those of s 101(1)(e). That latter subsection speaks of 'substantial probative force'. By implication, therefore, evidence of bad character which does not have substantial probative force is nonetheless admissible under s 101(1)(d). The notion that mere relevance suffices to render admissible evidence of bad character is one that will concern many, although the exclusionary discretion contained in s 101(3) provides some safeguard.

5.32 Section 103(1) provides some explanation as to whether, for the purpose of s 93(1)(e) a matter is 'in issue', but does not define when a matter is in issue, because the use of the word 'include' in s 103 confirms that it is illustrative rather than definitive.

Matters in issue between the defendant and the prosecution include:

(a) the question whether the defendant has a propensity to commit offences of the kind with which he is charged, except where his having such a propensity makes it no more likely that he is guilty of the offence;
(b) the question whether the defendant has a propensity to be untruthful, except where it is not suggested that the defendant's case is untruthful in any respect.

The principle underpinning s 101(1)(d) and s 103 is clear – that propensity to commit this type of offence can support, or confirm, guilt. However, the section raises as many questions as it answers.

5.33 Its phraseology is unhelpful. Propensity can, of course, show guilt, or support such a conclusion. That is one of the rationales under pre-existing law for the admission of similar fact evidence. But propensity is not 'a matter in issue' but, rather, how a 'matter in issue' can be proved. More importantly, the propensity that can be shown under s 103(1)(a) is a propensity to commit offences of the kind with which the accused is charged, except where that propensity makes it no more likely that he is

---

112 Vera Baird MP, HC Consideration of Amendments, col 1003.

113 (1973) 57 Cr App R 453.

114 See **5.50**.

guilty of the offence. Section 103(2) provides that that propensity may be proved by establishing, by evidence, that the defendant has been convicted of:

(a)   an offence of the same description as the one with which he is charged; or
(b)   an offence of the same category as the one with which he is charged.

The words 'may be proved' do not mean that previous convictions inevitably prove propensity, but this is an extension of the law. Although the original proposals would have admitted evidence of these previous convictions irrespective of propensity, this defines propensity by reference to the fact of conviction in such circumstances. Under pre-existing law, previous convictions were not of themselves admissible; it had to be shown that the facts of such cases had probative force on the issues. Now, such convictions will be admissible irrespective of whether they have probative force, the only safeguard being the exclusionary discretion under s 101(3).

5.34   By s 103(4):

(a)   two offences are of the same description as each other if the statement of the offence in an information or indictment would, in each case, be in the same terms;
(b)   two offences are of the same category as each other if they belong to the same category of offences prescribed for the purposes of this section by an order made by the Home Secretary.

Under pre-existing law, the mere repetition of multiple offences was insufficient to justify admission, unless probative force arose through striking similarity, or in some other way, for example because the bad character had probative force, by making the commission of the offence charged more likely or by rendering a defence improbable, or in some other way. On a charge of burglary, the fact that the defendant had convictions for other burglaries was not necessarily admissible, although it could be in the particular circumstances, because of the *modus operandi*, or because of the sheer implausibility of what the court was being asked to accept by way of defence. 'The defendant is a burglar, therefore he burgled' is precisely the 'forbidden chain of reasoning' referred to in *Boardman v DPP*[115] and against which the courts have always protected the accused.

In future, offences which have the same statement of offence will be admissible to show propensity, provided that that propensity makes it more likely that the defendant committed the offence. This clearly does not mean the same statement of facts. Indeed, some offences may be very different albeit that they have the same statement of the offence. Thus, a charge under s 4, s 4A or s 5 of the Public Order Act 1986 will have the same statement of facts even though these sections create offences that have different characteristics, and similarly with an offence of burglary under s 9(1) of the Theft Act 1968. Even where there are the same constituent elements of the offence, they may in reality vary quite markedly. A conviction for indecent assault on an adult female, because of an unwanted kiss and touching, while drunk, at a party would be admissible on a charge of indecent assault on a 15-year-old boy, yet the probative force is problematic. Again, on a charge of indecent assault on a female child, the fact that the accused has a conviction for indecent assault on an adult male will be admissible. On a charge of threatening, abusive or insulting behaviour under s 5 of the Public Order Act 1986, convictions for previous s 5 offences will be admissible

---

115 [1975] AC 421, (1975) 91 LQR 193, HL.

despite the fact that they may have been committed in totally different circumstances. In each of these cases, this conclusion can be avoided only if we conclude that the propensity does not make guilt more likely (s 103(1)(a)). Yet, if that be correct, one may ask what is the real purpose or point of s 103(2) and (4). And yet, a person charged with a Public Order Act 1986, s 5 offence outside a nightclub will not be liable to have his previous conviction for a racially aggravated offence outside the same nightclub adduced, at any rate under s 101(1)(d) (unless they were designated as falling into the same category by the Home Secretary).[116]

5.35 Difficult though s 103(4)(a) is, the terms of s 103(4)(b) are more concerning. It permits the Home Secretary to designate categories of offence for the purpose of s 101(1)(d).[117] The only limit on this power of prescription is that the offences must be of the same type (s 103(5)). What falls to be regarded as the 'same type' is, however, not specified by the Act. Clearly, the intent is to go beyond s 103(4)(a) and thus an offence falls within the same category even if it is not charged in identical terms.

Clearly, a racially aggravated assault is of the same type as a common assault. Common assault might be regarded as the same type of offence as actual bodily harm, or assault with intent to inflict grievous bodily harm. By contrast, arguably, murder is not of that same 'type' unless that phrase is construed widely to mean, in this example, 'offences against the person'. Murder is of the same 'type' as manslaughter, because both involve unlawful killing. But a conclusion that allows us to admit, on a trial on a charge of murder, in the home, evidence that the defendant was some years ago convicted of manslaughter for gross negligence in performing his work duties, and which led to the deaths of users of the service, is a very unattractive one. The fact that the prosecution is under no obligation to seek admission of that previous conviction, or that, if it did, a discretion to exclude would exist under s 103(3) should not obscure the fact that the new law changes a rule based on assessment of probative force to one potentially based on discretion.

Again, is a conviction for unlawful sexual intercourse, when aged 19, with a 15-year-old consenting girl, to be admissible when the man is charged many years later with the rape of a woman? The same answers apply.

This lack of definition is disturbing and gives rise to the potential for the law to be extended significantly beyond its current remit by ministerial prescription. That surely cannot be right.

5.36 Section 103(2) allows propensity to be proved by the previous conviction. But it does not say that previous convictions will automatically have the effect of showing propensity. Rather, it permits them to be used to so prove propensity if in fact they do. Nevertheless, the circumstances identified as creating probative force are wider than at common law. During the passage of the Act through Parliament, it was stated that:[118]

'We do not believe that that represents the correct approach. We do not think that juries cannot be trusted to assess that evidence in the context of the other evidence being presented

---

116 By order, to which the affirmative resolution procedure applies (s 330).

117 See **5.32**.

118 HL Committee, 15 September 2003, col 724.

in the case. No case will rest on evidence of previous misconduct alone. However, we do not believe that juries, when assessing all the evidence in the case, should be denied information that has a clear bearing on the issues, unless there is a good reason to do so.'

It is not difficult to conceive of a case where the main and crucial evidence is that of the previous conviction. Take the offence of 'meeting a child following sexual grooming' created by s 17 of the Sexual Offences Act 2003. It is an offence for a person aged 18 or over (a) having met or communicated with another person aged under 16, on at least two occasions, (b) to intentionally meet, or to travel with the intention of meeting, that individual under the age of 16, (c) intending to do anything to or in respect of that other person, during or after the meeting, that would involve the commission of a relevant offence. A previous conviction for a sexual offence may be admissible to prove the key element of intent. What is wrong with that? The fact of previous conviction is grossly prejudicial. Although the Government removed automatic admissibility of previous convictions from the Act, at a late stage,[119] to assume that previous convictions automatically show propensity would be to re-introduce that provision by the back door, and cannot be right. Section 103(1)(a) requires the previous convictions to be probative of propensity.

5.37   The matter in issue is: did this defendant commit this offence? When does propensity make it more likely that he is guilty of the offence? The reason why, under pre-existing law, evidence of previous convictions is prohibited is not because they are irrelevant to the question of likelihood of commission of the offence, but rather, because the weight of that evidence is far outweighed in most cases by the prejudicial effect that it creates. On this basis, the question a court will have to determine is the level of probative force of the evidence of bad character. A court, in this context, will have to determine the admissibility of the evidence of bad character by answering the question: if it is admitted, does it make it more likely the defendant is guilty of the offence charged?

Some examples are clear. In *Lewis*,[120] the evidence of bad character effectively killed off his defence. In that case the defence to an indecent assault charge was one of accidental touching. The prosecution was held entitled to adduce evidence of his paedophilic sexual propensity, this having strong probative force in rebutting the defence of accident. This would, under the new law, fall under s 101(1)(d). In Z[121] it was concluded that, on a charge of rape where the defence was one of consent, the prosecution was entitled to adduce evidence of the testimony of complainants of rape in a previous case to show a pattern of behaviour which was consistent with his guilt in the instant case and with him being wrongly acquitted in the previous case.[122] This would now fall within s 101(1)(d) and s 103(1). In a case of a racially aggravated assault, the fact that in the past the defendant has engaged in racist behaviour will relate to an important matter in issue (the racist motivation), and again fall within s 101(1)(d), although care must be taken to determine its true evidential value. After

---

119 See Consideration of Lords Amendments, HC Deb, 19 November 2003.

120 (1982) 76 Cr. App R 33, CA.

121 [2000] 3 All ER 385, CA.

122 It is perhaps odd to regard the testimony of the previous complainant as evidence of bad character, bearing in mind the defendant was acquitted, but that is the probable effect of the definition of bad character in s 90: see **5.11**.

all, a propensity towards anti-Irish thoughts or behaviour may or may not be relevant on a charge of assaults on Asian shopkeepers. A propensity to wreck or damage physical objects (furniture, crockery and the like) in fits of temper may not tell us very much about a defendant's propensity to use physical force against children if he is charged with the murder of a young baby.[123] Another example is that of *Randall*.[124] On a charge of murder, where a 'cut-throat defence' was run by the co-accused, the House of Lords held that the antecedent history of the co-accused was relevant not only in relation to the truthfulness of his evidence, but also because the imbalance of that antecedent history (convictions for theft and burglary, including one burglary where threats of violence were made) and the antecedent history of the defendant (minor driving and disorderly conduct offences) tended to show that the version of events put forward by the defendant was to be believed. This was evidence of propensity which was relevant to the facts in issue, and would be admissible, now, under s 101(1)(d). It might also be admissible under s 101(1)(e).[125]

The application of s 101(1)(d) may be wider than pre-existing law. In *Burrage*,[126] the charge was one of indecent assault on each of his two grandsons, aged 11 and 9. He denied the offences, and, at interview, stated that his sexual interests were in respect of adult women. The trial judge allowed questions to be put about the possession of homosexual pornography (not involving children). His conviction was quashed on appeal, the court concluding that, where the defence was one that the allegations were false, the evidence of possession of homosexual magazines should not have been admitted. The court relied on the earlier statement of Mustill LJ in *Wright*[127] that propensity evidence was not admissible to prove the commission of an offence when the accused denied that the offence ever occurred (ie that the whole allegation was a fabrication). Even if that was the right approach[128] that under the new law might well be different (although not inevitably so). The rationale underpinning *Wright* is that propensity of itself was insufficient. However, as noted above, propensity can on particular facts have probative force, and that is inherent in the provisions of s 101(1)(d) and s 103(1)(a). The possession of the magazines might (in some circumstances) be held to be bad character but, on the facts of *Burrage*, surely is not directly relevant to any issue before the court. Possession of adult homosexual pornography does not, on the same set of facts, have a propensity to show that the defendant has committed the offence (s 103(1)(a)). However, possession of such articles does put his claims of adult heterosexual preferences in a new light, and could be regarded as falling within s 101(1)(d) (as to which see **5.20**).

Even, however, if the possession of such articles was to be defined as bad character, and seemingly meets the standard set by s 101(1)(d), there are the concluding words of s 103(1)(a) 'except where his having such a propensity makes it no more likely that he is guilty of the offence'. This reinforces the conclusion that the test to be applied is

---

123 By analogy with *Dolan* [2003] Crim LR 41, CA.

124 [2004] All ER 479, HL. See also *Lowery v R* [1973] 3 All ER 662, PC; *Bracewell* [1978] 68 Cr App R 44, CA; *Murray* [1995] RTR 239, CA.

125 See **5.40**.

126 [1997] Crim LR 440.

127 (1990) 90 Cr App R 325, CA.

128 See the critical commentary at [1997] Crim LR 441.

simply: does the evidence of bad character make it more likely that he is guilty of an offence? If it does, it is admissible, subject only to the discretion to exclude under s 101(3).[129]

5.38   As noted above, a matter is in issue between defendant and prosecution if it is relevant to the question of whether the defendant has a propensity to be untruthful, except where it is not suggested that the defendant's case is untruthful in any respect (s 103(1)(b)). It is therefore open to the court to admit evidence of bad character (as defined by s 98) to establish a propensity to be untruthful in any case where the defendant's case (in whole or in part) is not true.

This is an extremely wide provision, which goes far wider than existing law. Under existing law, evidence of untruthfulness would be admissible only in cross-examination in the limited circumstances permitted by s 1(3) of the CEA 1898. Section 103(1)(b) relates to cases involving elements of 'untruthful' defence cases (either in whole or in part). A prosecutor is not suggesting that a simple plea of 'not guilty' is an 'untruthful defence case' – it is a plea putting the prosecution to proof. A defence of 'mistaken identity' is not, for this purpose, an 'untruthful' case, even though the prosecutor will seek to establish that the identification is correct. However, most cases involving a not guilty plea will be cases where a prosecutor is alleging that some aspect of the defence case is untruthful. On this basis, evidence of bad character involving untruthfulness will become admissible routinely.

In such circumstances, a court will need to determine the exact nature of the defence's 'case'. It is submitted that this is the defence case at trial. Thus, a defendant who makes statements to the police that the prosecution later wishes to show are untrue is not making an allegedly untruthful case if the allegedly untruthful statements are not relied on by the defendant at trial. Of course, in Crown Court cases there will be the details of the defence case disclosed under the extended provisions of the CPIA 1996.[130] It does not inevitably follow that those details will be in all respects followed at trial, and of course defence disclosure is not routine in summary trial in the magistrates' court.

5.39   The matter in issue does, however, have to be relevant to an important matter in issue. What is 'important' in this context will be for the court to determine – it is the 'matter in issue' that has to be important, and one might perhaps observe that all matters which are in issue are important in a criminal trial. Nor is 'important' intended to relate to concepts of probative force, or prejudice, for, as noted earlier, the differences between s 101(1)(d) and (e) could not be explained. It is simply a recognition that some things in issue are matters of more importance than others. In other words, the evidence of character must really be on an issue that matters, and not on matters of subsidiary detail. That will be for the trial judge or magistrates to determine. Arguably, what the court has to do is to ask itself the question: is the matter of such importance as to justify the admission of the evidence of propensity?

---

129 See **5.50**.

130 See **3.49** et seq.

'Substantial probative value in relation to a matter in issue between the defendant and a co-defendant' (s 101(1)(e))

5.40   This provision is the replacement for s 1(3)(iii) of the CEA 1898. Under s 1(3)(iii), the 'shield' against cross-examination about bad character was lost if a defendant gave 'evidence against' any other person charged in the same proceedings. Now, the question of bad character arises whenever that bad character has substantial probative value in relation to an important matter in issue. The term 'substantial probative value' is not defined, but, as noted earlier, is a higher threshold than that which applies in the context of s 101(1)(e) (which is simply the evidence being 'relevant to an important matter in issue'). Some may find it odd that different tests in this context apply to prosecution and defence, and arguments about a 'level playing-field' arise. Possible arguments in the context of Art 6 ECHR might reflect this, partly on the basis of an infringement of the principle of 'equality of arms',[131] although it should be noted that there is consistency of wording between this provision and that in relation to non-defendants in s 100(1). In that regard, there is a departure from the principle of treating matters of character equally no matter to whom they apply. A more obvious area of potential challenge under Art 6 is the fact that the section envisages that there may be relevant evidence that a co-defendant wishes to use, but which will not be admissible because it does not have the quality of 'substantial probative value'.

Only evidence adduced by a co-defendant, or adduced in response to a question put in cross-examination, is admissible under s 101(1)(e). There is no discretion to exclude evidence that satisfies the terms of s 101(1)(e): patently, to exclude evidence that had substantial probative value to a co-defendant would be unfair, and would infringe Art 6 of the ECHR.

5.41   When, however, is a matter in issue between a defendant and a co-defendant? The new requirement to serve on co-accused defence statements under s 6 of the CPIA 1996[132] will assist in determining the extent to which a matter is in issue between defendants, in advance of trial. A co-defendant may deny that he committed the offence, putting the blame on the defendant, either explicitly or, even, implicitly. Thus, in a case where D1 and D2 are accused of killing their young baby, where the circumstances are such that one or other (or both) must have killed the child, D1's defence may positively assert that D2 committed the murder, or simply deny involvement with the inference that it was D2 who killed the baby. Matters relating to the facts in issue do not amount to bad character (s 98(a)), but where such questions are before a court, a co-accused may seek to use evidence of bad character. That could be by the showing of propensity to act in the way the co-defendant claims. Thus, in the above example, D2 might wish to show that past deeds show D1 has a propensity to acts of violence, assuming, of course, that the prosecution has not itself adduced that evidence under s 101(1)(d). The case of *Randall*[133] is a good example of where s 101(1)(e) might now apply.

---

131 See *Funke v France* (1993) 16 EHRR 297, ECtHR.

132 See **3.49** et seq.

133 See **5.37**.

Alternatively, the evidence may show a propensity to be untruthful, thus making it more likely that the defendant's role was as claimed by the co-accused. However, s 104(1) states that evidence which is relevant to the question whether the defendant has a propensity to be untruthful is admissible under s 101(1)(e) only if the nature or conduct of his defence is such as to undermine the co-defendant's defence. This concept arguably bears the same meaning as was developed through the case-law under the old s 1(3)(iii). In that context, the words 'give evidence against' was held to mean evidence which either supports the prosecution case or which undermines the case for the co-accused.[134] That was refined, in *Bruce*,[135] to mean 'does the evidence make the acquittal of the co-accused less likely?'. Of course, s 104 refers only to evidence that 'undermines' the defence of the co-defendant. Yet for a defendant to support the prosecution case against a co-defendant can only, in plain language, undermine the co-defendant's case. It would, surely, be unfair, to deprive a co-defendant of the ability to adduce evidence of propensity for untruthfulness if the testimony or case of the defendant in fact supports the prosecution case.

'Evidence to correct a false impression' (s 101(1)(f))

5.42   The pre-existing s 1(3)(ii) had two distinct limbs. The first was where there was an assertion of good character. In that circumstance it was plainly right to permit a prosecutor to correct the misleading impression about his character created by the defendant. The second limb meant that the defendant lost his shield where an 'imputation' was cast on the character of a witness for the prosecution or on the deceased victim of a crime. Section 101(1)(f) addresses the first of these, s 101(1)(g) the second.

By s 101(1)(f), evidence of a defendant's bad character is admissible if it is evidence to correct a false impression given by the defendant. If the terms of s 101(1)(f) are satisfied, there is no discretion to exclude: s 101(3) does not apply to s 101(1)(f).

5.43   Section 103 contains lengthy provisions dealing with when a defendant gives a false impression. By s 103(1)(a), the defendant gives a false impression if he is responsible for the making of an express or implied assertion[136] which is apt to give the court or jury a false or misleading impression about the defendant.

Clearly, there can be no objection to a rule which allows false impressions to be corrected. The false impression must be about the defendant. Evidence to contradict false impressions about the facts in issue is admissible as such, irrespective of the Act, because evidence relating to facts in issue is not evidence of bad character (s 98(b)). The impression will be in respect of matters relating to his character, which is indivisible.[137] Thus, a defendant who asserts that he has never been convicted of an offence can expect s 101(1)(f) to be used to adduce evidence of his previous convictions (if not already adduced under s 101(1)(d)), or of him being cautioned for an offence. A defendant who admits previous convictions but claims that he would never use violence could expect details of previous convictions involving violence to

---

134 *Murdoch v Taylor* [1965] AC 574.

135 [1975] 1 WLR 1252.

136 See **5.46**.

137 *Winfield* (1939) 27 Cr App R 139, CCA.

be adduced, as well as other evidence of violent behaviour (such as incidence of domestic violence where the police were called but no formal action taken).

Self-evidently, however, s 101(1)(f) goes much further than correcting false impressions involving convictions. It extends to all matters relating to character – and, given the definition of 'bad character' in s 98, the scope for corrective material is wide indeed. The defendant who claims to be a faithful, happily married man could potentially have evidence adduced against him to show him to be a womaniser with a string of affairs; the defendant who claims to be a quiet, mild-mannered individual who would not cause violence at a nightclub might have evidence adduced of his explosive temper and his drunken binges on his last Greek island holiday. The defendant to a shop-lifting charge, who calls evidence of good character to bolster her defence that it was a memory lapse that caused her to leave the store without paying, could potentially face evidence that she was disciplined at work for using the work telephone for (unauthorised) calls to her international friends. The young City broker, who presents as an intelligent and mature individual and thus not prone to the making of racist chants at football matches, might expect to find his membership of the British National Party adduced. The examples are infinite in number.

5.44 In order for s 101(1)(f) to operate there must be an assertion, express or implied, which is apt to give the court or jury a false or misleading impression.

The term 'apt' is not one of precision. The *Concise Oxford Dictionary* (9th edn) defines 'apt', *inter alia*, as meaning 'having a tendency, prone, likely ... '. There are shades of meaning here. The use of the word 'likely' elsewhere in s 105 suggests that the shade of meaning to be applied veers towards 'tendency'. There is, perhaps, a danger here in over-analysis: the issue the court will have to determine is whether explicitly or implicitly it is being misled. It is clear from s 105(1)(a), s 105(2) and s 105(4) that there must be an intention to mislead.

5.45 The assertion must be either express or implied. No problems arise with express assertions. More difficulty arises with implied assertions. Clearly, there must be an intention to assert. But how? The witness who wears a regimental or old school tie is no doubt impliedly asserting his standing as a result of membership of that regiment or Old Boys' Association, and is making an implied assertion. The individual wearing a clerical 'dog-collar' is impliedly asserting religious beliefs and that he is a clergyman. But what of the prostitute who comes to court devoid of makeup, jewellery and dressed modestly? Or the alleged football thug who comes dressed for court in best pin-stripe suit (unless, of course, this is his normal garb)? In one sense an assertion is being made, yet these examples can scarcely be within the ambit of s 105. It is, we suggest, a matter for the common sense of the court, which is enjoined by s 105(4) to deal with this as an assertion only if it is just to do so.

Section 105(4) states that where it appears to the court that a defendant, by means of his conduct (other than the giving of evidence) in the proceedings, is seeking to give the court or jury an impression about himself that is false or misleading, the court may if it appears just to do so treat the defendant as being responsible for the making of an assertion which is apt to give that impression. 'Conduct' includes appearances or dress (s 105(5)). Thus, it would scarcely be just to apply s 101(1)(f) to a prostitute who comes to court demure and innocent-looking, but, arguably, entirely just to apply the section to the man who comes clothed in religious garb, or stands in the dock with crucifix in hand, when he has neither religious office or belief.

5.46   The defendant must be responsible for the making of the assertion. Section 105(2) states that a defendant is treated as being responsible for the making of an assertion if:

(a)   the assertion is made by the defendant in the proceedings (whether or not in evidence given by him). It will later be noted[138] that, under ss 116 and 117 of the new Act, some out-of-court statements may be admissible as proof of the truth of their contents. Any assertions made in such a statement adduced in court would be made 'in the proceedings';

(b)   the assertion was made by the defendant (i) on being questioned under caution, before charge, about the offence with which he is charged, or (ii) on being charged with the offence or officially informed that he might be prosecuted for it, and evidence of the assertion is given in the proceedings. Typically, the evidence of the assertion would be adduced by a police officer. In such circumstances there might be a temptation for that same officer to adduce evidence of the matters of bad character. That, however, raises issues about the operation of s 105(3) which presupposes that there may be an opportunity to withdraw the assertion;

(c)   the assertion is made by a witness called by the defendant;

(d)   the assertion is made by any witness in cross-examination in response to a question asked by the defendant that is intended to elicit it, or is likely to do so. Clearly a question that directly asks for information on the matter which creates the misleading impression is 'intended to elicit' that information. What is 'likely to do so' is more problematic. It will be a matter for the judge or magistrate to determine whether a question is likely to elicit the information;

(e)   the assertion was made by any person out of court, and the defendant adduces evidence of it in the proceedings.

However, a defendant who would otherwise be treated as responsible for the making of an assertion must not be so treated if, or to the extent that, he withdraws it or disassociates himself from it (s 105(3)). The purpose of this provision was explained by the Minister of State[139] in the following terms:

'... it should not be a foregone conclusion that the giving of a misleading impression should result in the admission of bad character evidence to correct it. Instead, the defendant should have the opportunity to correct the impression himself or to disassociate himself from it, thus ensuring that the jury are aware that he lays no claim to the impression. If that is so, there should be no question of evidence of his bad character being admitted ... [but] if the defendant allows a misleading impression to persist, it will be appropriate and fair to enable evidence of bad character to be given ... '

Evidence of bad character is admissible under s 101(1)(f) only to the extent necessary to correct the misleading impression (s 105(6)).

---

138   See **6.7** et seq.

139   Hilary Benn MP, HC Committee, 23 January 2003, col 592.

'*Attack on another person's character*' (*s 101(1)(g)*)

5.47 The second part of s 1(3)(ii) allowed cross-examination of an accused who cast imputations on the character of a prosecution witness or deceased victim. Section 101(1)(g) broadly, with important modifications, reflects that position. A defendant's bad character is admissible if the defendant makes an attack on another person's character. That other person does not have to be a victim or prosecution witness – it may be a third person. Thus, if on the trial of an individual for public order offences arising out of anti-Government demonstrations the defendant asserts that he regarded the war as immoral because of the falsification of evidence by leading named politicians, that would be sufficient to trigger s 101(1)(g).

Nor, unlike s 1(3)(ii), is the prosecution prevented from adducing matters of bad character if the defendant does not testify. Section 101(1)(g) allows the evidence to be tendered as part of the prosecution case, and clearly will enable the court to judge the credibility of what is being alleged by the defendant in the light of his own character.

5.48 A defendant makes an attack on another person's character if (a) he adduces evidence attacking the other person's character, (b) he asks questions in cross-examination that are intended to elicit such evidence, or are likely to do so, or (c) evidence is given of an imputation about the other person (as defined by s 106(2)) made by the defendant (i) on being questioned under caution, before charge, about the offence with which he is charged, or (ii) on being charged with the offence or officially informed that he might be prosecuted for it.

Issues arise as to when questions are 'likely' to elicit bad character evidence. The terms of s 101(3), however, allow a court to exclude bad character evidence, and it may be that a court should not allow cross-examination unless it was clearly the case that such bad character evidence was likely to be elicited.

5.49 There remains the question as to what amounts to 'evidence attacking the other person's character'. By s 106(2), this means evidence to the effect that the other person:

(a) has committed an offence (whether a different offence from the one with which the defendant is charged or the same one). The other person need not have been prosecuted for the offence, and there appears, on the face of the provisions, to be no requirement of proportionality between the offence that falls within s 106(2)(a) and the bad character of the defendant that might then be put into evidence. That, though, is a matter that can be dealt with by means of s 101(3);

(b) has behaved, or is disposed to behave in a reprehensible way. The term 'reprehensible' is not defined: in its original draft this provision related to conduct which 'might be viewed with disapproval by a reasonable person', which was the phrase which partially formed the originally proposed definition of bad character. Arguably, the original phrase sums up accurately what is meant by reprehensible, a word defined by the *Concise Oxford Dictionary* (9th edn) as meaning 'deserving censure or rebuke; blameworthy'. Lying, illegal or immoral conduct, or allegations of anti-social behaviour each appear to fall within the scope of reprehensibility, which will, arguably, be a matter for the tribunal of law, not the tribunal of fact to determine, it being a pre-condition to the admissibility of evidence.[140]

An 'imputation about the other person' means an assertion to that effect.[141]

Exclusion of admissible evidence

5.50 Section 101(3) creates a discretion to exclude in certain, but not all, of the circumstances set out in s 101(1). Those circumstances are where the evidence is admissible under s 101(1)(d) (propensity) and (g) (attack on another person's character).

Does s 78 of PACE provide an exclusionary route where s 101(3) does not apply? During the passage of the Act through Parliament, the Minister of State[142] observed that:

> '[s 101(3)] is central to the consideration of the clause. The test for the court to apply is designed to reflect the existing position under the common law as [PACE, s 78] does. Under that, the judge balances the probative value of the evidence against the prejudicial effect of admitting it and excludes the evidence where the prejudicial effect exceeds the probative value. The Government's intention is for the courts to apply the fairness test . . . in the same way . . . The trial judge has ultimate responsibility for ensuring that the proceedings are fair. Hon Members have expressed the concern that the test applied in [s 101(3)] does not apply across all the heads of admissibility set out in [s 101(1)]. That is because such a power is not appropriate in all the circumstances that we envisage in which evidence of a defendant's bad character should be admissible.'

This provides a key pointer that s 78 is not intended to provide a further exclusionary discretion. Indeed, why should s 101(3) specify certain circumstances as subject to an exclusionary discretion if the inference to be drawn was not that no such discretion existed in other cases? Indeed, the circumstances in which no such discretion is granted under s 101(3) are ones where there is unlikely to be a significant need for an exclusionary discretion. Yet, against all that, the common-law duty of a trial judge to ensure a fair trial remains. And the terms of s 101(4) are equally clear: nothing in Chapter 11 of the Act affects the exclusion of evidence on grounds other than the fact that it is evidence of the defendant's bad character. Exclusion, at common law or under s 78 of PACE, would not be because it is bad character evidence, but because the court considers that the admission of the evidence would cause unfairness to the proceedings, and might lead to the making of a terminating ruling.[143] The problem would not arise, of course, if the Government had accepted the model recommended by the Law Commission of requiring (in most circumstances) leave of the court before evidence of bad character should be admitted.

---

140 See **5.25** and **5.53**.

141 Thus the mass of case-law defining or applying the concept if 'imputation' within the meaning of the CEA 1898, s 1(3)(ii) will no longer be directly applicable, although it is difficult to conceive of any matter regarded as casting an imputation that would not be regarded as falling within the definition contained in s 106(2).

142 Hilary Benn MP, HC Committee, 23 January 2003, col 590.

143 As to which see **7.6** et seq.

5.51 There remains the question of how the court should exercise the discretion in s 101(3). It must weigh the probative value of the evidence against the prejudicial effect. It must consider whether the admission would have such an adverse effect on the fairness of the proceedings that the court ought not to admit it. When deciding the relevance or probative value of evidence, the court must assume that the evidence is true (s 109(1)). That general assumption is, however, subject to the important qualification that it need not make that assumption if it appears on the basis of any material before the court (including any evidence it decides to hear on the matter) that no court or jury could reasonably find it to be true. Among the matters to which a court must have regard are the length of time between the matters to which the evidence relates and the matters which form the subject-matter of the offence charged.

In determining the balance required by s 101(3), however, the intent of the legislation to make previous bad character evidence admissible on a much wider basis should not be overlooked. Critics of these provisions can point to aspects of their content (such as s 101(1)(d)) where, arguably, real dangers arise from the admission of such evidence. That, however, is the intent of the legislation.

Contaminated evidence – power to stop trial on indictment

5.52 Section 107 deals with the question of contaminated evidence. However, it only applies in respect of trial on indictment. No equivalent power exists in respect of summary trial.

It states that if evidence of bad character is admitted under s 101(1)(c)–(g) and the court is satisfied at any time after the close of the case for the prosecution that the evidence is contaminated, and that contamination is such that, considering the importance of the evidence to the case against the defendant his conviction of the offence would be unsafe, the court must either direct the jury to acquit the defendant or, if it considers that there ought to be a retrial, discharge the jury. The potential for a terminating ruling also should not be overlooked.[144]

Section 108(5) defines what is meant by 'contaminated'. A person's evidence is contaminated if:

(a) as a result of an agreement or understanding between that person and one or more others, or
(b) as a result of the person being aware of anything alleged by one or more others whose evidence may be, or has been, given in the proceedings,

the evidence is false or misleading in any respect, or is different from what it otherwise would have been.

Procedure to be adopted

5.53 Clearly, the provisions relating to admissibility of evidence of bad character are questions of law, to be determined in the normal way, whether at trial or through pre-trial rulings.

---

144 See **7.6** et seq.

When making such rulings, the court must state in open court (but in the absence of the jury, if there is one) the reasons for the ruling, and (in the case of a magistrates' court) must cause the ruling and the reasons for it to be entered in the register of court proceedings (s 110(1)).

Chapter 6

HEARSAY

SUMMARY

6.1 Section 114 provides that, in the circumstances identified in s 114(1), a court may admit evidence that amounts to hearsay, defined by s 114(1) as any 'statement not made in oral evidence in the proceedings ... '. Where the conditions of admissibility are met, a court can consider out-of-court statements, whether made orally or in a document, as evidence of any matter in those statements. Even where the criteria for admissibility are satisfied, a court retains a discretion to exclude the evidence (s 126). The changes are intended to promote greater certainty and clarity, by creating conditions of automatic admissibility.

6.2 Much time and effort have been spent in the past deciding whether out-of-court statements were being tendered for a non-hearsay purpose, and thus should not be caught by the exclusionary rule.[1] That case-law remains relevant, although less important. The circumstances in which hearsay evidence is permitted are:

(a) where the evidence is admissible by virtue of any statutory provision (s 114(1)(a)). The pre-existing statutory exceptions to the hearsay rule may permit the admission of hearsay.[2] Sections 23 to 26 of the CJA 1988 are repealed[3] and replaced by the general rule in s 114(1), by more specific provisions in s 116 relating to witnesses who are unavailable to give evidence, and by s 117, relating to business documents;

(b) where any preserved rule of law makes a statement admissible (s 114(1)(b)). Section 118 preserves many common-law exceptions;[4]

(c) by agreement (s 114(1)(c));

(d) where the court is satisfied that it is in the interests of justice for the statement to be admissible (s 114(1)(d)). This is new, and is referred to here as the 'safety valve'.

COMMENCEMENT AND APPLICATION

6.3 No commencement order had been made pursuant to s 336 at the date of going to press. The new law will apply only to criminal proceedings begun on or after the date of commencement (s 141).

---

1   See, eg, *Blastland* [1986] AC 41, HL; *Harry* (1986) 86 Cr App R 105, CA; *Woodhouse v Hall* (1980) 72 Cr App R 39, DC; *Kearley* [1992] 2 All ER 345, HL.

2   See **6.33–6.34**.

3   Schedule 37, Part 6.

4   See **6.35**.

These provisions relate to criminal proceedings, by which is meant criminal proceedings in relation to which the strict rules of evidence apply (s 140). They apply, subject to modifications, to proceedings before service courts (s 135 and Sch 7). Reference should be made to Sch 7 for those modifications.

BACKGROUND

6.4   Few rules of evidence cause more difficulty than the hearsay rule. The House of Lords in *Sharp*[5] endorsed the definition of hearsay given by *Cross on Evidence*: 'an assertion other than one made by a person while giving oral evidence in the proceedings is inadmissible as evidence of any fact stated'. That definition disguised a multitude of issues. What is meant by an assertion? When, if at all, should an assertion be implied? When is a statement being tendered to prove the truth of the fact asserted? So, too, in respect of the exceptions: the self-imposed limitation imposed by the House of Lords in *Myers v DPP*[6] (that it was not for the courts to develop new common-law exceptions) led to the courts avoiding the more unjust or absurd consequences of the rule through 'hearsay fiddles'.[7] The lack of a coherent statement of the hearsay rule, resulting in difficulties in application, and the piecemeal nature of statutory exceptions, sometimes incomplete and badly drafted (like s 24 of the Criminal Justice Act 1988 (CJA 1988)), were in striking contrast to the regime applicable in civil cases, which takes the position that hearsay evidence is generally admissible.[8]

6.5   More fundamental questions related to the question of why there was a need for an exclusionary rule. The traditional explanation is typified by that of Viscount Normand in *Teper v R*:[9]

'The rule against the admission of hearsay is fundamental. It is not the best evidence and it is not received on oath. The truthfulness and accuracy of the person whose words are spoken by another witness cannot be tested by cross-examination, and the light which his demeanour would throw on his evidence would be lost.'

The difficulty with this statement, and other similar explanations, is that while some or all of these justifications might be valid in some cases, it is not inevitable that hearsay evidence always suffers from these disadvantages. The pre-existing law amounted to a set of rules which excluded certain kinds of evidence, irrespective of the cogency of that evidence.

In its comprehensive review,[10] the Law Commission considered the rationale for the rule. It concluded that oral evidence was preferable to hearsay, principally because, with the former, the witness could be cross-examined. First-hand hearsay[11] was

---

5   [1988] 1 All ER 65, HL, at 68. *Cross on Evidence* (6th edn, Butterworths, 1985).

6   [1964] 2 All ER 881, HL.

7   A phrase coined by Professor Diane Birch in 'Hearsay-Logic and Hearsay Fiddles: Blastland Revisited' in *Criminal Law: Essays in Honour of JC Smith* (Butterworths, 1987), pp 28–29.

8   See, generally, the Civil Evidence Act 1995.

9   [1952] AC 480, PC.

10   *Evidence in Criminal Proceedings: Hearsay and Related Topics* Law Com No 245, Cm 3670.

11   Where what is sought to be adduced is the out-of-court statement of the person with knowledge of the matter to be adduced.

preferable to multiple hearsay, because, with multiple hearsay, the risk of manufacture and of error in repetition increases. It also was satisfied that the exceptions contained in the CJA 1988 had not worked well. It noted:

> 'Uncertainty as to the admissibility of evidence means that the prosecution cannot confidently assess the prospects of conviction in deciding whether or not to prosecute, and, if so, on what charges, and those advising the defendant cannot confidently advise on the pleas or the conduct of the defence.'

It concluded that there should continue to be an exclusionary rule to which there would be specified exceptions. In this regard the approach adopted by the Commission differs from that proposed by the Auld Commission,[12] which favoured an approach based on a presumption that all hearsay evidence should be admissible. The Law Commission recommended that its basic approach (that of exclusion subject to a range of exceptions) should be supplemented by a discretion to admit hearsay evidence which would otherwise be inadmissible, where that was in the interests of justice. The Commission considered, and rejected, a range of other alternatives, all of which had both advantages and disadvantages.[13] The Act broadly, but with some modifications, implements the recommendations of the Law Commission.

The Human Rights Act 1998 issues

6.6 Article 6 ECHR protects the right of an accused to a fair trial. In particular, Art 6(3)(d) confers the right on a defendant to examine or have examined witnesses against him and to obtain the attendance and examination of witnesses on his behalf under the same conditions as witnesses against him.

The exact impact of Art 6 in the context of the hearsay rule is open to argument, not least because Convention law looks at the fairness of the trial, not necessarily at the detailed content of rules of evidence, which is primarily for domestic law to determine.[14] The criticisms made of the Law Commission's own evaluation of Convention law[15] serve only to demonstrate the point. Nonetheless, certain aspects of the hearsay rule raise issues as to whether a fair trial has occurred.

(1)   The hearsay rule does not *intrinsically* infringe Art 6,[16] although its use in certain instances (such as excluding evidence relevant and helpful to an accused)[17] could perhaps be open to challenge, as could the terms or applicability of an exception to the hearsay rule.

---

12   Auld Review, *op cit*, see **1.4**.

13   Law Com No 245, Part VI, pp 69–81.

14   See *Saidi v France* (1994) 17 EHRR 251, ECtHR; *Schenk v Switzerland* (1991) 13 EHRR 242, ECtHR; *Doorson v Netherlands* (1996) 22 EHRR 330, ECtHR; *Khan (Sultan)* [1996] 3 All ER 289, HL, at 302–303, per Lord Nicholls.

15   Law Com No 245, *op cit*, paras 5.33–5.55.

16   *Blastland v United Kingdom* (1988) 10 EHRR 528, ECtHR.

17   See **6.42**.

(2)   An accused must have the right to challenge the evidence against him by putting
      questions about such evidence (although not necessarily directly).[18] The Special
      Measures Direction provisions of the YJCEA 1999, which relate to questioning
      taking place through an intermediary, or the taking of testimony by live link[19] or
      by video recording, do not infringe Art 6, because the defendant retains the right
      to be able to question or challenge the case against him.

(3)   Whether an accused *must* have a right to challenge the testimony of a witness is
      less clear. It is the substance, not the form, of the right to challenge that matters.
      The courts must look behind the appearances and investigate the realities of the
      procedure in question.[20] In *Unterpertinger v Austria*[21] the accused was charged
      with assault on his wife and step-daughter. The prosecutor sought to rely on their
      police statements, because they subsequently refused to testify, and were not
      compellable under Austrian law.[22] The ECtHR held that the use of their police
      statements infringed the accused's Art 6 rights, based on the inability of the
      accused to confront his accuser. Subsequent authorities point in a contrary
      direction. In *Bricmont v Belgium*[23] the Court accepted as legitimate the use of a
      witness statement, albeit one excused by the accused on the grounds of age and
      ill-health. In *Artner v Austria* [24] it was held not to be an infringement of Art 6 to
      utilise the witness statement of a witness who could not be found, given the
      existence of other incriminating evidence, together with the accused's avoidance
      of a confrontation at pre-trial stage. In *Asch v Austria* [25] the use by a prosecutor of
      witness statements made by members of the accused's family who subsequently
      declined to testify was held to comply with Art 6 rights. This case-law
      establishes that the context of each case must be considered, including the
      importance of the other evidence, the reason why it is not available at trial and the
      availability or otherwise of other evidence.

(4)   The defence must have the right to challenge the evidence. *Doorson v
      Netherlands*[26] shows that any limitation of the defendant's rights must be
      counterbalanced by measures to ensure that the defence can, in fact, effectively
      challenge that evidence. Even if that balance is achieved, evidence obtained from
      a witness where the rights of the defence cannot be secured to the extent normally
      required by the ECHR must be treated with extreme care, and certainly should
      not be used solely as the basis for a conviction, or to a decisive extent.

The hearsay provisions of the new Act are intended, and believed, to be
ECHR-compliant. Nonetheless, issues remain as to possible grounds of challenge
within the framework of the above principles. In particular, the Joint Committee on

---

18   *Kostovski v The Netherlands* (1990) 12 EHRR 434, ECtHR; *Saidi v France* (1994) 17 EHRR 251,
     ECtHR; *X, Y and Z v Austria* (1973) 43 Decisions 38, EHR Comm.

19   See **6.60**.

20   *Deweer v Belgium* [1980] 2 EHRR 439, ECtHR.

21   (1991) 13 EHRR 175, ECtHR. See also *Ludi v Switzerland* (1993) 15 EHRR 173, ECtHR; *Saidi v
     France* (1994) 17 EHRR 251, ECtHR.

22   In England and Wales they would in such circumstances be compellable: see PACE, s 80.

23   (1990) 12 EHRR 217, ECtHR.

24   (1992) Series A, No 242–A.

25   (1993) 15 EHRR 597, ECtHR.

26   (1996) 22 EHRR 330, ECtHR.

Human Rights[27] was of the view that compatibility of the new provisions may turn on a court's assessment of the adequacy of the safeguards to prevent a conviction being based, wholly or mainly, on unsafe or unfair use of hearsay evidence.

THE NEW LAW

Statements

6.7 The new provisions apply to 'statements'. Sections 114(1) and 116(1) each refer to 'a statement not made in oral evidence in the proceedings . . . ', while s 117(1) refers to 'a statement in a document'. The meaning of the term 'statement' is the starting point, and s 115(2) and (3) clarify and change the law in key respects.

Section 115 settles any confusion that might, conceptually, have existed between the hearsay rule and the rule against self-serving statements (which excludes the out-of-court statement of a witness who testifies). Although the justifications for these rules were different, commentators did not always clearly distinguish between the two, and the practical results were usually the same. Such distinctions are now redundant. The new Act governs 'statements' irrespective of whether they were made by a person who is available to testify, and even if he does so. The circumstances in which an out-of-court statement by a person who testifies is admissible are limited, and subject to the provisions of s 120.[28]

6.8 A 'statement' is any representation of fact or opinion made by a person by whatever means, including a representation made in a sketch, photofit or other pictorial form (s 115(2)). The use of the term 'person' means that this does not include a representation contained in a photograph, or arising as the direct result of the mechanical process.

At common law, sketches, photofits or other pictures were not regarded as falling within the hearsay rule, because they were not 'statements'. The rationale for that conclusion was not always either clear or convincing.[29] In *Taylor v Chief Constable of Cheshire*[30] police officers testified as to what they had seen on a video recording which allegedly showed the appellant stealing from a shop, and which had been accidentally erased. The tape itself would have been admissible as direct evidence, and the absence of the tape went only to the weight of the testimony, not its admissibility. Such a conclusion is unexceptionable: it was as if the officers were testifying as eye-witnesses.[31] However, in *Smith (Percy)*,[32] a sketch made by an officer from a description given by a witness was held to be direct evidence and not hearsay. The witness, by using her memory, had directed the sketching hand of the officer and it was in reality the sketch made by the witness. A written statement would have been caught by the hearsay rule, and, arguably, the decision owed as much to common

---

27 Second Report, Session 2002–2003, para 24 et seq.

28 See **6.51**.

29 See, eg, the critique by Andrews and Hirst *Criminal Evidence* (4th edn, Jordans, 2001), para 17.25.

30 [1987] 1 All ER 225, DC.

31 See also *Kajala* (1982) 75 Cr App R 149, CA; *Maqsud Ali* [1965] 2 All ER 464, CA.

32 [1976] Crim LR 511, CA.

sense as to logic, as indeed did its extension in *Cook*,[33] where a photofit picture compiled from a description given by a witness was regarded as 'the manifestation of the seeing eye' and no different from the compilation of a sketch, or, indeed, a photograph.[34] In each of these cases, 'common sense' demanded that the evidence be admitted. The new Act classifies these forms of representation as 'statements', and thus hearsay. This conceptual change is to be welcomed. The Law Commission wished to exclude direct evidence, not based on human input, from the operation of the hearsay rule. It had in mind evidence such as tapes, films or photographs which record a disputed incident, or documents produced by machines which automatically record an event or circumstance (such as the making of a telephone call from a particular number, or the level of alcohol in a person's breath).[35] If, and only if, we continue to accept sketches and photofits as akin to photographs could we continue to accept such documents as non-hearsay. That conclusion would be inconsistent with the wording of s 115(2).

6.9   The statement must contain a representation of fact or opinion 'made by a person' (s 115(2)). The Law Commission considered the problems that arise in respect of statements produced directly by machines, and recommended that the word 'statement' should be confined to a representation by a person. It considered that where a representation of fact is made otherwise than by a person, but depends for its accuracy on information supplied by a person, it should not be admissible as evidence of that fact unless it is proved that the information was accurate.[36]

Section 115(2) has the effect of confining the operation of the hearsay provisions to statements made by a person. That preserves the pre-existing common law: documents which were the direct product of the mechanical process are not hearsay.[37] Where, however, the document produced as part of the mechanical process is admitted because of the information contained therein, the common law characterised the document as hearsay if it was intended to use the statement to prove the truth of information supplied by a person. Thus a database which is used to store information currently falls within the hearsay rule if a print-out is being used to prove the data it contains. The Law Commission's analysis complicates the issue: it agreed that such evidence should be excluded, but considered that that should not be because of complicated hearsay provisions but because of the lack of probative value of statements produced where the accuracy of the information has not been established. It proposed that a special rule independent of the hearsay rule be created.[38] This approach is adopted by the new Act: the output of the mechanical process does not fall within the words of s 115, unless a strained interpretation is given to the words in s 115 ('any representation of fact or opinion made by a person by whatever means …'). This was not intended by the Law Commission to be the case: the representation of fact or opinion is not being made by the person who supplied the information, but is

---

33   [1987] QB 417, CA.

34   See *Dodson* (1984) 79 Cr App R 220, CA.

35   Law Com No 245, *op cit*, para 7.44.

36   See *Wood* (1982) 76 Cr App R 76, CA; *Coventry Justices ex parte Bullard* (1992) 95 Cr App R 175, DC.

37   See, eg, *Castle v Cross* (1982) 76 Cr App R 23, DC; *Spiby* (1990) 91 Cr App R 186.

38   Law Com No 245, *op cit*, paras 7.48–7.50.

the output of the machine or mechanical process. However, s 129(1) provides that where a representation of any fact:

(a)   is made otherwise than by a person, but
(b)   depends for its accuracy on information supplied (directly or indirectly) by a person,

the representation is not admissible in criminal proceedings as evidence of the fact unless it is proved that the information was accurate.

On this analysis, the statement adduced pursuant to s 129 is not hearsay. Section 129 requires the accuracy of the information to be established, working on the presumption that the mechanical device has been properly set and calibrated (s 129(2)). There is nothing to prevent the accuracy of the data or information being proved by any admissible means. Because the document produced by mechanical means is not hearsay, there is (for *that* reason) no need to regard any evidence establishing the accuracy of that data as multiple hearsay.[39]

6.10   By s 115(3), for the hearsay rule to apply there must be a statement intended to make a representation about the matter sought to be proved. The new statutory provisions apply if, and only if, the purpose, or one of the purposes of the person making the statement appears to the court to have been:

(a)   to cause another person to believe the matter, or
(b)   to cause another person to act or a machine to operate on the basis that the matter is as stated.

Thus, one looks at the intention of the maker of the statement, not the words used, although one could infer the latter from the former. The burden of proof is on the party seeking to adduce the statement – on the prosecution, beyond reasonable doubt; on the accused, on the balance of probabilities. If it is shown to the requisite standard that the maker of a statement does not intend to make a representation, or to cause another to believe the truth of what is stated, there is no 'statement' to be regarded as hearsay. If A states a fact and/or opinion to X, intending X to believe or act on that fact or opinion, that statement must be brought within a hearsay exception. If, by contrast, A states a fact or opinion, intending to joke, or not intending to be believed, or not intending to assert (eg the recitation of poetry) it is not hearsay, and admissibility depends on the relevance of the fact that the statement was made.

This is a change in the law. At common law – although debate often centred on whether a statement was making an assertion of fact, and if so, what – if it was asserting a fact, whether expressly or impliedly, then it was caught by the exclusionary rule. That is no longer the case. No longer do we have to consider whether a statement is *impliedly* asserting a fact.[40] Either it is intended to assert a fact or opinion or it is not. If it is, the hearsay rule applies, and the party seeking to adduce the statement must bring the statement within the terms of s 114. If it is not, then no

---

39   As to which, see **6.55**. The multiple hearsay rule might be infringed by the evidence called to establish accuracy, but not because the information was originally supplied by mechanical means.

40   For implied assertions, see *Wright v Doe d'Tatham* (1837) 132 ER 877, CCCR; *Kearley* [1992] 2 AC 228, HL; *Harry* (1986) 86 Cr App R 105, CA.

hearsay issue arises and the admissibility of the statement falls to be decided on simple questions of relevance.[41]

In *Kearley*[42] the House of Lords decided that evidence of telephone calls to the house of the appellant, and in respect of visitors to that house, asking for him and seeking to buy drugs, were inadmissible as hearsay in a prosecution for possession with intent to supply. These calls were irrelevant unless there was reliance on an implied assertion from these conversations (ie that K was a drug dealer). If there was reliance on that implied assertion, that would be hearsay. Now, the implied assertion aspect of a case is beside the point. No hearsay issue arises, unless it is established that the person making the statement intended to assert. Such a case depends purely and simply on the answer to the question: does the fact that these statements were made have circumstantial relevance? *Kearley* is, arguably, a case on relevance, and this change in the law confirms that, in the absence of intention, such cases should be decided without regard to the hearsay rule. That still leaves the court with the thorny question as to what a person intends to assert.

6.11 Section 115 also clarifies the position in respect of 'negative hearsay'. Sometimes the fact that a statement does *not* state a fact has evidential value in proving that the fact not mentioned did not exist or did not occur.[43] Only if it is the purpose of the person who fails to state or record that fact to cause another person to believe that that fact did not exist or occur will such a failure be caught by the hearsay provisions in the new Act. This raises difficult questions about matters of intent of the person making the statement. The individual keeping a log who records that A, B and C each visited premises will nonetheless be making a statement within the meaning of s 115(3) if the intent thereby is to cause another to believe that X did not visit those premises.

The general rule

6.12 The general rule contained in s 114(1) has already been stated.[44] Of the four categories of admissibility, no real comment is needed about admission by agreement. The parties can admit what they like if they all agree. The trial judge has, arguably, no direct say in the matter, and although the court retains the power to exclude admissible evidence under s 78 of PACE,[45] it is quite inconceivable that such exclusion would arise where all parties agree that the evidence should be admitted.

The admissibility under statutory or common-law rules set out by paras (a) and (b) is discussed later. Some further comment now is needed on the residual discretion in s 114(1)(d) to admit otherwise inadmissible hearsay (the 'safety valve'). Under s 114(1)(d), the court has to be satisfied that, despite the difficulties there may be in

---

41 For examples, see *Subramaniam v Public Prosecutor* [1956] 1 WLR 965, PC (words uttered showed mental state of appellant); *Woodhouse v Hall* (1980) 72 Cr App R 39, DC (offers of sexual services relevant irrespective of their truth to prove premises being used as a brothel); *Lydon* (1986) 85 Cr App R 221, CA (words themselves not adduced to prove the truth of any assertion, but to prove link with the appellant to establish identity of robber).

42 [1992] 2 AC 228, HL.

43 See, eg *Shone* (1983) 76 Cr App R 72, CA.

44 See **6.2**.

45 See s 114(3).

challenging the statement, it would not be contrary to the interests of justice for it to be admissible. In deciding that question, the court must have regard to the matters set out in s 114(2). This judgment[46] is not, however, the end of the matter. In this context, as in all others, the general discretion contained in s 126 exists, and allows a court to refuse to admit a statement notwithstanding that it has satisfied all other criteria. This and other discretionary exclusionary powers are discussed at **6.57**.

6.13 The main rule is supplemented by provisions relating to previous consistent and inconsistent statements of the witness (ss 119, 120).[47] In addition there are provisions relating to the use of confessions by an accused (s 128)[48] and expert evidence (s 129).[49]

6.14 There is a general discretion to exclude evidence that is nonetheless admissible. Section 126 provides that a court may refuse to admit evidence if the statement was made otherwise than in oral evidence in the proceedings and the case for excluding the statement, taking into account the danger that to admit it would result in an undue waste of time, substantially outweighs the case for admitting it, having regard to the value of the evidence. That is without prejudice to s 78 of PACE or any other power of exclusion (s 126(2)).

This is an important provision. Although it requires the court to take into account the lack of importance of the evidence (waste of time, etc), it essentially permits a court to have regard to the case for admitting the evidence. That is a potentially important safeguard, which should not be confined to situations where the evidence is of peripheral value but also extended to cases where the statement is important, but unreliable.

THE STATUTORY EXCEPTIONS

6.15 Section 114(1)(a) renders admissible any statement not made in oral evidence if any provision in the new Act or any other statutory provision makes it admissible. The Act contains new provisions (although not necessarily totally new exceptions) in cases where a witness is unavailable (s 116) and in respect of business and other documents (s 117). Previous statements are dealt with by ss 119 and 120, expert statements by s 127, and video recorded testimony by ss 137 and 138.

The witness is unavailable

6.16 By s 116(1), in criminal proceedings a statement not made in oral evidence in the proceedings is admissible as evidence of any matter stated in it if:

(a) oral evidence in the proceedings by the person who made the statement would be admissible of that matter;
(b) the person who made the statement (the relevant person) is identified to the court's satisfaction; and

---

46 Arguably a judgment and not a discretion. The practical implications are that an appeal court can substitute its judgment for that of the trial court: *Viola* [1982] 3 All ER 73, CA.

47 See **6.49–6.50**.

48 See **6.41–6.42**.

49 See **6.43–6.44**.

(c)   the five conditions mentioned in s 116(2) are satisfied.

The scope of s 116 is significantly wider than that of s 23 of the CJA 1988 to which s 116 bears some similarities. Although some of the preconditions for admissibility in s 23 were identical to, or substantially the same as, those in the new s 116, one key difference is that s 23 only applied to statements in documents. Section 116 applies to any statement whether oral or in a document, if the preconditions are satisfied. If A gives to X an oral description of the robber of a post office, A is the maker of the statement: that statement is potentially admissible under s 116 if A would have been a competent witness, and is not available to testify because of one of the five circumstances identified in s 116(2). That would not have been the case under s 23. If X is no longer available, but has written down what he had been told by A, he (X) would be the maker of the statement in the document. X did not have personal knowledge of the matters in the document, and thus the document would have been 'second-hand'. Although X (if available) could have testified as to what A said (if A satisfied the preconditions in s 116), whether the document is admissible would depend not only on s 116, but also the operation of the rules relating to multiple hearsay.[50]

6.17   The preconditions for admissibility of the out-of-court statement of a witness who is unavailable are set out at **6.18–6.27**. In this context, the terms of s 116(5) should be noted. Even if one of these preconditions is satisfied, if the circumstances which satisfy the precondition are caused:

(a)   by the person in support of whose case it is sought to give the statement in evidence, or

(b)   by a person acting on his behalf,

in order to prevent the relevant person giving oral evidence in the proceedings (whether at all or in connection with the subject-matter of the statement), then the precondition is not to be taken as having been satisfied.

The preconditions to be satisfied where the witness is unavailable

The relevant person is dead (s 116(2)(a))

6.18   This replicates the equivalent provision in s 23(2)(a) of the CJA 1988, and requires no further comment.

The relevant person is unfit to be a witness because of his bodily or mental condition (s 116(2)(b))

6.19   Again, this largely replicates the pre-existing provision relating to unfitness contained in s 23(2)(a) of the CJA 1988 , although the phrase 'unfit to be a witness' in s 116(2)(b) replaces the pre-existing 'unfit to attend as a witness'. This change serves to emphasise that the physical capacity to attend is insufficient. The witness must be able to give testimony that is meaningful. In *Setz-Dempsey*,[51] the main prosecution witness, in a case involving charges of theft or of handling stolen goods, was unable to recall any of the relevant events, due to mental illness. The fact that he was 'unfit to

---

50   See **6.55**.

51   (1994) 98 Cr App R 23. See also *Dragic* (1996, unreported), CA.

attend as a witness' was not doubted, although the conviction of the appellant was quashed on other grounds. The test in s 116(2)(b) goes further than an inability to give intelligible testimony. A witness who cannot give intelligible testimony is not a competent witness, and therefore would not fall within the terms of s 116 because he would not be able to give oral evidence in the proceedings (s 123). There would be no basis for seeking to rely on s 116.

The relevant person is outside the United Kingdom and it is not reasonably practicable to secure his attendance (s 116(2)(c))

6.20 This replicates the terms of s 23(2)(b) of the CJA 1988. As with s 23(2)(b), the court must look beyond questions of physical practicability, and consider what steps it is reasonable for a party to take, having regard to the nature of the charge and evidence, and the means and resources available to the parties.[52] In all these matters, an evidential base will need to be established,[53] through admissible evidence. The fact that it may be possible to take testimony by live TV link should also not be overlooked.[54] Cost will be a relevant factor: a live TV link might be practicable, but not *reasonably* practicable because of issues of cost.[55] Others factors might be the seriousness of the case and the importance of the information, or the availability of the witness on a different date.[56]

That the relevant person cannot be found although such steps as it is reasonably practicable to take have been taken (s 116(2)(d))

6.21 Subject to textual changes, this replicates s 23(2)(c) of the CJA 1988, although s 23(2)(c) applied only to statements in a document. It is a matter for the court to determine, on admissible evidence, whether it is established what steps have been taken and whether they are reasonable on the facts of the particular case.

What safeguards are there to ensure that unfairness does not arise because we do not know why the witness cannot be found?[57] How can we ensure that the reason he cannot be found is because of the actions of the party now seeking to adduce the out-of-court statement? The witness may be missing, of course, because he is dead, or because he is being kept out of the way, but often the reason why the witness cannot be found will not be known. The person seeking to adduce the statement will have to show what steps have been taken to find the witness, and, if the court is satisfied that the unavailability is at the instance of the party seeking to adduce the out-of-court statement, that party will have to negative this belief. For that reason, the Law Commission considered criticism of its proposal (on which s 116 is based) to be misconceived.[58] However, some might consider that unconvincing. First, the burden of proof of satisfying the court of one or other of the matters in s 116(5) lies on the

---

52 *Maloney* [1994] Crim LR 525, CA; *Hurst* [1995] 1 Cr App R 82, CA.

53 *Case* [1991] Crim LR 192, CA; *De Arango and others* (1993) 96 Cr App R 399, CA.

54 See **6.60**, and also the Criminal Justice (International Co-operation) Act 2003.

55 See Law Com No 245, *op cit*, para 8.38.

56 *French and Gardner* (1993) 97 Cr App R 421, CA.

57 See the criticisms of this proposal by Ormerod in 'The Hearsay Exceptions' [1996] Crim LR 16, at 20.

58 Law Com No 245, *op cit*, para 8.43.

party seeking to oppose admissibility: although the ultimate burden of proving the precondition is on the party seeking to adduce the statement, s 116(5) does not place any evidential burden on the party seeking admission. The wording of s 116(5) requires the court to be 'satisfied' that it is 'shown' that the circumstances 'are caused' by one or other of the stated matters. In the case of the prosecution that will, or should, be a significant hurdle to overcome. Although the terms of s 116(5) might appear to be relevant safeguards, they are not in reality likely to be so, because we will not know why the witness is unavailable, and thus it will be impossible for the party who seeks to oppose admissibility to satisfy the court of the matters in s 116(5)(a) or (b). The fact that a party can demonstrate that he has taken steps that appear on their face to be reasonable tells us nothing about where the witness is, how he got there and whether the party seeking to rely on the out-of-court statement had anything to do with the disappearance of the witness. In short, that party might sound convincing, and may be able to appear convincing as to what he had done. Indeed, elsewhere in its Report,[59] the Law Commission recognised that as a result of successful intimidation witnesses often disappear without any clear reason.

It is instructive to note that the requirement for leave under s 116(4) only applies in the context of admissibility under s 116(2)(e),[60] and not in the context of s 116(2)(d). This is of course intentional, and fits with the philosophy of these new provisions, which is to achieve automatic admissibility where the preconditions are satisfied. Yet the matters stated in s 116(4)(a) and (b) are, arguably, as important to the question of the testimony of a missing witness, of which no oral record may exist, as to the question to be determined under s 116(2)(e). Given that s 116 itself is a significant extension of hearsay admissibility (by extending admissibility to oral statements), some cause for concern arises.

Through fear the relevant person does not give (or does not continue to give) oral evidence in the proceedings, either at all or in connection with the subject-matter of the statement, and the court gives leave for the statement to be given in evidence (s 116(2)(e))

6.22   It is the provisions relating to 'fear' that have been subject to the greatest substantive change. The terms of s 23 of the CJA 1988 required a statement to be given in a document to a police officer or some other person charged with the duty of investigating offences by a person who does not testify through fear or because he is kept out of the way. Section 116(1)(e) is different. The statement does not to have to be documentary, and can have been made to any person. The words 'or because he is kept out of the way' form no part of s 116(1)(e). The effect of this is uncertain. The provisions in s 23(2)(b) of the CJA 1988 were read disjunctively, as alternatives.[61] A witness who has been kidnapped does not fall within s 116(2)(e), because his failure to testify is not due to fear, but due to his physical constraints. In most cases s 116(1)(d) would apply ('the ... person cannot be found ...'). Alternatively, the 'safety valve' in s 114(1)(d) might apply.[62]

---

59   At para 8.48.

60   See **6.22**.

61   *Acton Justices ex parte McMullen, R v Tower Bridge Magistrates' Court ex parte Lawlor* (1990) 92 Cr App R 98, DC.

62   See **6.48**.

6.23 Refusal to testify (or to continue to testify) on its own is not enough: it must be induced through 'fear'. What amounts to 'fear' is partially defined by s 116(3), which enjoins a court to construe that term 'widely', but by way of example *includes*[63] fear of the death or injury of another person or of financial loss.[64] Fear for one's own physical safety will be 'fear' in this context, but other examples might include fear of being exposed to public disgrace (an errant politician, perhaps), public ridicule or private disgrace (an adulterer, perhaps). Nor does s 116(3) prevent the fear being one induced by apprehension of the proceedings: one example is an alleged victim of rape, who fears the ordeal of testifying in person, with or without the benefit of special measures directions. Provided it is proved[65] that there is the failure of the type identified by s 116(2)(e), and that that failure was due to fear, the type of fear, and reason for it, appears to be irrelevant to the question of whether this threshold condition is satisfied, although not to the question of the grant or refusal of leave under s 116(4). Nor does, for the purpose of s 116(1)(e), the fear have to be objectively reasonable, provided it is genuinely felt.

6.24 The fear does not have to prevent totally the witness testifying: it suffices that the witness does not testify in connection with the subject-matter of the statement, or does not continue to give testimony on that subject-matter. This replicates the position under s 23: in *R v Ashford Magistrates' Courts ex parte Hilden*,[66] the witness took the oath and said that she had no comment to make on the injuries the defendant had allegedly caused her. The fact that she had given some evidence did not prevent the operation of the subsection. It was sufficient that the woman did not give any evidence of significant relevance to the case. That is rather different from the wording of s 116(1)(e), which extends to a failure to continue to testify in connection with the subject-matter of the statement. Of course, a literal interpretation of those words might suggest that a failure to 'continue' does not cover a situation where there was a failure to answer one or more specific questions, but a willingness to testify on other matters. However, s 116 is surely intended to encompass all situations where there is evidence in respect of a matter about which, because of fear, the witness is not prepared to testify orally.

6.25 Nothing in s 116 deals with the question of the proof of the fear. We can assume that the pre-existing approach holds good. In *Neil v North Antrim Magistrates' Court*,[67] the court stated that whether a witness is in fear must be proved by admissible evidence, and thus the testimony of a police officer as to what he had been told by the mother of the witness concerning the state of mind of the witness could not prove that the witness was in fact suffering fear, the evidence of the police officer being hearsay. However, fear can be proved in a variety of ways. The witness can be sworn to give

---

63 An illustrative and not a complete definition: see, in the context of PACE, s 76(8), *Fulling* [1987] 2 All ER 65, HL.

64 See *Acton JJ ex parte McMullen, Tower Bridge Magistrates' Court ex parte Lawlor* (1990) 92 Cr App R 98, DC; *Martin* (1996, unreported), CA.

65 See **6.25**.

66 (1992) 96 Cr App R 93, DC.

67 [1992] 4 All ER 846, DC.

reasons for not testifying;[68] a police officer or other witness can testify about what was said to them by the witness who is unwilling to testify.[69]

6.26   Admissibility under s 116(2)(e) differs from the other circumstances set out in s 116, in that leave of the court is required. The criteria for granting leave are set out in s 116(4). The court must be satisfied that the statements ought to be admitted in the interests of justice. Thus the starting point is that, despite the existence of the 'fear', the party seeking admission of the statement must convince the court that it is in the interests of justice to admit the statement. In this regard (although not necessarily in all others) it is like s 26 of the CJA 1988.[70] That section, which applied in rather different circumstances, required the court to be satisfied that it was in the interests of justice to admit the statement. Even then, of course, there is a residual discretion under s 123, although it is hard to conceive of how a court would seriously consider excluding under s 123, having considered the matters s 116(4) demands.

The matters to which a court must have regard under s 116(4) are as follows:

(a)   the statement's contents;
(b)   any risk that its admission or exclusion will result in unfairness to any party to the proceedings (and in particular to how difficult it will be to challenge the statement if the relevant person does not give oral evidence);
(c)   in appropriate cases, the fact that a special measure direction under s 19 of the YJCEA 1999 could be made in relation to the relevant person; and
(d)   any other relevant circumstances.

These factors are similar, although not the same, as those stated in s 26 of the CJA 1988.

6.27   How, then, should the court exercise its judgment in s 116(4), and why is there a special rule in respect of statements made by those who do not testify (or continue to testify) through fear?

The question as to whether there should be automatic admissibility was considered and rejected by the Law Commission. That raised the real danger that prospective witnesses could give statements to the police in the knowledge that at a later stage they could falsely claim to be frightened, thus being able to avoid going to court and being cross-examined.[71] It is for that reason that the Law Commission recommended, and s 116 creates, a requirement for the leave of the court.

The factors to be taken into account are at large. Clearly, any part played by a party to the proceedings in creating that fear is important, but should have been taken into account at an earlier stage (s 116(5)).

---

68   *Jennings and Miles* [1995] Crim LR 810, CA.

69   See, eg, *R v Tower Bridge Magistrates' Court ex parte Lawlor* (1990) 92 Cr App R 98, DC. This can be justified either because it is evidence of the fact that it was said, adduced to prove state of mind and thus not, at common law, hearsay, or alternatively as a statement of contemporaneous state of mind, now admissible by virtue of s 102(2) (preserved common-law exceptions, no 4).

70   See *Radak* [1999] 1 Cr App R 187, CA.

71   Law Com No 245, *op cit*, para 8.58.

Arguably if it could be shown that the accused's fear had nothing to do with the accused, to deprive the accused of the right to cross-examine may be unfair.[72] The fact that the potential witness can be protected by a special measures direction under s 19 of the YJCEA 1999 is relevant. The effect of s 19 is that, where the court concludes that the threshold conditions in either s 16 or s 17 of the 1999 Act are satisfied, it must determine which if any (and in what combination) of the available special measures would be likely to improve the quality of the witness's evidence. Specifically, s 17 of the 1999 Act makes a witness eligible for assistance if the court is satisfied that diminution of quality is by reason of fear or distress[73] on the part of the witness. Available special measures may potentially include the screening of the witness from the accused, evidence through live link or in private, or video-recorded evidence-in-chief. Clearly, evidence given with the assistance of special measures directions is better than reliance on an out-of-court statement with no possibility of cross-examination. This will also reflect the characteristics of the witness, which will be a relevant matter to consider.

The phrase 'interests of justice' is not defined, but will require a court to consider the interests of both prosecution and defence.[74] The court should take into account whether the evidence is important, or crucial,[75] whether it is undisputed or is supported by other evidence,[76] or is a particularly difficult form of evidence which should be carefully tested under cross-examination.[77] Arguably, the general principles that developed in respect of the use of s 26 of the 1988 Act[78] apply equally to the more limited discretion that has to be made under s 116. This balancing function will be key in ensuring that no potential for a successful Art 6 challenge exists.

Business documents

6.28 The pre-existing business documents exception in s 24 of the CJA 1988 is replaced by s 117. It, like s 24, deals with the admissibility of statements in a

---

72 Law Com No 245, *op cit*, para 8.60.

73 In determining the scope of s 116, note that, interestingly, s 17 of the 1999 Act draws a distinction between 'fear' and 'distress'.

74 *Patel* (1993) 97 Cr App R 294, CA.

75 *Kennedy* [1992] Crim LR 37, CA.

76 *Swindon* (1995, unreported), CA.

77 Such as identification evidence: see *Neil v North Antrim MC* [1992] 4 All ER 846; *cf Setz-Dempsey* (1994) 97 Cr App R 23, CA.

78 See *Cole* (1989) 90 Cr App R 478, CA. The Court of Appeal stated that the accused could contradict the witness statement by giving evidence himself, or by calling other evidence. The court had to consider the contents of the statement, and take into account the fact that the accused was unable to cross-examine the maker of the statement. A balance had to be struck between allowing a case to be properly presented and the interest of the accused in a fair trial – although s 26 was not (and s 116 is not) confined to the tendering of evidence by the prosecution. For the application of the principles, see, eg *Herbert* (1991, unreported), CA, where ID evidence was confirmed by other witnesses and could be controverted by testimony from the accused and his son; *Samuel* [1992] Crim LR 189, CA, where the evidence was crucial to the prosecution case; *Moore* [1992] Crim LR 882, CA; *Jennings and Miles* [1995] Crim LR 810, CA, where it was held unfair to admit a statement in a case based on flimsy evidence; *Lockley & Corah* [1995] Cr App R 554, CA, where it was held to be wrong to admit a statement where an opportunity to observe the demeanour of a witness claiming a cell confession was important.

document, unlike s 116 which extends to any out-of-court statements (whether in a document or oral).

6.29 The first precondition is that oral evidence given in the proceedings would be admissible in the proceedings as evidence of that matter (s 117(1)(a)). Thus, if oral evidence of the matter stated in the document could not be given, then the document is inadmissible under s 117. This replicates the provisions of s 24. Like the old s 24, provided oral evidence could be given by *somebody* of the matter, the fact that that might be a person other than the maker of the document is irrelevant.

6.30 The second precondition is that the terms of s 117(2) must each be satisfied. Section 117(2) states that its terms are satisfied if:

(a) the document or the part containing the statement was created or received by a person in the course of a trade, business, profession or other occupation, or as the holder of a paid or unpaid office;
(b) the person who supplied the information contained in the statement (the relevant person) had or may reasonably be supposed to have had personal knowledge of the matters dealt with; and
(c) each person (if any) through whom the information was supplied from the relevant person to the person mentioned in paragraph (a) received the information in the course of a trade, business, profession or other occupation, or as the holder of a paid or unpaid office.

The similarities with s 24 are clear. Both apply to statements in a 'document' defined by s 140(1) as 'anything in which any description is recorded'. Thus, it will include statements, and other written accounts. In each case the person creating or receiving the document must be acting as part of a trade, business, profession or as the holder of a paid or unpaid office. In each case the person who supplied the information contained in the statement may reasonably be supposed to have personal knowledge of the matters dealt with. In each case if the information came through an intermediary, the information must have been received by a person in the course of a trade, business or profession, or as part of an paid or unpaid office.

6.31 There is, however, a third set of preconditions (set out in s 117(5)) that need to be satisfied if s 117(4) applies. Section 117(4) applies if the statement:

(a) was prepared for the purposes of pending or contemplated criminal proceedings, or a criminal investigation, but
(b) was not prepared in accordance with s 3 of the Criminal Justice (International Co-operation) Act 1990, or an order under Sch 13, para 6 to the CJA 1988.

Thus, the old s 24(4) of the 1988 Act is replicated, but without some of the drafting and interpretive difficulties that arose with s 24(4). The effect of s 117(5) is that where a document falls within s 117(4) it is only admissible under this exception if:

(a) any of the five conditions mentioned in s 116(2) are satisfied (reasons for the unavailability of the witness: see **6.18–6.27**); or
(b) the relevant person cannot reasonably be expected to have any recollection of the matters dealt with in the statement (having regard to the length of time since he supplied the information and all other circumstances).

Under s 117, the 'relevant person' is the person who made the statement which is recorded in the document. That may, or may not, be the same person who made the document (s 117(3)). This was clearly the intention of the Law Commission, and is evident from the terms of s 117(2), which refers to the 'relevant person' as being 'the person who supplied the information contained in the statement ...'.[79] Thus, it is assumed that the recording of the information is accurate and that the key player is the person who supplied the information that has in fact been recorded. It is that person who has to be shown to be dead, unable to be found, etc, within the terms of s 116(2), or who, in the terms of s 117(5)(b), 'cannot reasonably be expected to have any recollection of the matters dealt with in the statement ...'.

6.32   Where, then, are the differences between s 24 and the new s 117? Section 24 was badly drafted, particularly in the context of the terms of s 24(4). The effect of the new s 117 is to remove such ambiguities. The thrust of the two sections remains the same, and the principles governing their application remain unchanged.

Even if the preconditions contained in s 117(2) and (5) are satisfied, nonetheless a court may, under s 117(6), direct that the statement not be admitted. Section 117(7) states that the court may make such a direction if satisfied that the statement's reliability as evidence for the purpose for which it is tendered is doubtful, in view of:

(a)   its contents;
(b)   the source of the information contained in it;
(c)   the way in which or the circumstances in which the information was supplied or received; or
(d)   the way in which or the circumstances in which the document concerned was created or received.

These are matters that go to reliability. The court may have concerns about reliability because of inherent doubts about the information contained in the document or, more likely, doubts about the way the information in the document was acquired, recorded or transmitted.

Other statutory provisions

6.33   Section 114(1)(a)[80] preserves the other statutory exceptions to the hearsay rule that are not repealed by the new Act. In some cases there may be overlap between the preserved statutory provision and the terms of either s 116 or s 117. Of particular importance are the provisions of s 9 of the Criminal Justice Act 1967 (CJA 1967) and of Sch 2 to the CPIA 1996.

6.34   Section 9(1) of the CJA 1967 provides that, in any criminal proceedings,[81] a written statement by any person shall, if any of the preconditions set out in s 9(2) are satisfied, be admissible evidence to the same extent as oral evidence to the like effect by that person. The preconditions effectively provide for non-contentious statements to be admitted if no objection is taken, and the various procedural steps satisfied.

---

79   Law Com No 245, *op cit*, at paras 8.78–8.83.

80   See **6.12**.

81   The words 'other than in committal proceedings' are deleted by Sch 37, Part 4.

Section 9 is preserved by the new Act. It does not apply to statements made overseas,[82] but in any event statements can be admitted if the parties agree. Since such statements are admitted by agreement, there is no issue about any exclusionary discretion.

Schedule 2 to the CPIA 1996 confers on a court a discretion to admit any statements and depositions already admitted in proceedings before magistrates. Such statements and depositions might have been admitted in evidence (and thus fall within para 1 of Sch 1) or have been taken as a deposition pursuant to s 97A of the MCA 1980 (in which case they fall within para 2 of Sch 1). These provisions survive the passage of the new Act. Paragraphs 1(4) and 2(4) of Sch 1 allow a court to overrule objections raised by any party if it considers it to be in the interests of justice to do so. The term 'interests of justice' is not defined, and therefore leaves the matter at large.[83] The objections of the Law Commission[84] to the broad discretion, where the witness might be available, were shared by the Home Affairs Committee in its Report.[85] Arguably, any concerns about this provision, on that basis, apply with equal, if not greater, force to the 'safety valve' under s 114(1)(d). Whether, in the light of the terms of s 114(1)(d), the Sch 1 powers are necessary or whether, alternatively, we should contemplate such provisions at all are completely different questions.

THE PRESERVED COMMON-LAW EXCEPTIONS

6.35　Section 114(1)(b) of the new Act preserves some eight different rules of law, which are part of the common law. It does so by reference to s 118(1), which identifies the rules of law in question. This is an unusually drafted section, containing both subsections and notes on subsections, and a numbering scheme no doubt well intentioned but likely to serve only to confuse. Reference should be made to s 118 for the full list. All common-law rules other than the ones specified below are abolished (s 118(2)). The main casualty is the quaint but practically anomalous and pointless rule relating to dying declarations.

The side-heading of s 118 is 'Preservation of certain common law categories of admissibility', which might suggest that the contents of the various paragraphs are merely descriptive. However, some of the rules described are ill-defined, and on occasion differences can be seen. In so far as the descriptions set out in s 118 differ from the understood position at common law, it is submitted that the scope of the exception is as set out in s 118.

Reputation as to character

6.36　Any rule of law under which in criminal proceedings evidence of a person's reputation is admissible for proving his good or bad character is preserved by s 118(1).

82　*Mullen* [1995] Crim LR 568, CA; Criminal Justice Act 1972, s 46(1).

83　Andrews and Hirst, *Criminal Evidence* (Jordans, 4th edn, 2001), at para 18.44 argue that this provision involves similar considerations as would be applicable when considering the exercise of the power in CJA 1988, s 26. While no authority supports the point, that conclusion seems correct as a matter of principle, and consistent with *dicta* in *Cole* [1990] 1 WLR 511, CA.

84　Law Com No 245, *op cit*, para 141.

85　Home Affairs Committee, Second Report 2002/2003, para 128.

However, confusingly, the note to that paragraph states that the rule is preserved only in so far as it allows the court to treat such evidence as proving the matter concerned.

The rules governing reputation are idiosyncratic and obscure. In *Rowton*[86] the court stated that, whilst evidence of general reputation was permissible, evidence of specific acts or deeds was not. Evidence of general reputation is, of course, inherently hearsay, because reputation, other than a judgment formed by an individual based on his own knowledge of specific deeds, must invariably take into account what one is told by others. Further, many would argue that evidence of specific deeds may have more cogency than testimony on generalised notions of 'reputation', although of course the danger of straying into too many collateral matters is real. However, the courts do not always apply the *Rowton* rule strictly: in *Redgrave*,[87] the court accepted that as a matter of judicial indulgence (rather than as of right) a court might be prepared to hear evidence about the state of the accused's marriage, in a sexual case where this might have had some legitimate bearing in the context of the issues the jury in that case had to decide. The question remains: what does the note qualifying the statement of the rule mean? The intention here is to confine the preservation of the rule to the extent of the decision in *Rowton*. To do so, however, perpetuates the difficult and arguably unworkable rule in that case, and is for that reason to be regretted.

Res gestae

6.37 Paragraph 4 of s 118(1) preserves the *res gestae* rule. This is defined as any rule of law under which in criminal proceedings a statement is admissible as evidence of any matter stated if:

(a) the statement was made by a person so emotionally overpowered by an event that the possibility of concoction or distortion can be disregarded;
(b) the statement accompanied an act which can properly be evaluated as evidence only if considered in conjunction with the statement; or
(c) the statement relates to a physical sensation or a mental state (such as intention or emotion).

The term *res gestae* has, at common law, a variety of meanings, broadly reflected by the terms of para 4. The test in para (a) mirrors that established by the House of Lords in *Andrews*,[88] the term 'emotionally overpowered' effectively reproducing the common law test of looking for circumstances of spontaneity and involvement in the event so as to enable the court to disregard the possibility of concoction. As Lord Ackner said in *Andrews*, the statement had to be so closely associated with the event that elicited the utterance that the victim's mind was still dominated by the event in question. If there were special features such as malice, the court must be satisfied that the possibility of concoction could be eliminated. The possibility of error, by contrast, went not to admissibility but to the weight to be given to the statement. A typical application of these principles is the case of *Harris*,[89] where a conviction was quashed in a case of threats to kill, because the trial judge had permitted a police officer to

---

86 [1861–73] All ER Rep 549, CA.

87 (1982) 74 Cr App R 10, CA. See also *Douglass* (1989) 89 Cr App R 264, CA.

88 [1987] 1 All ER 513, CA.

89 [2002] All ER (D) 376, CA.

testify as to what he had been told by a child of the alleged victim. The child had telephoned the police, but had not made the telephone call on her own initiative, and had spoken to three other people before in fact making that call. There had been an opportunity for the evidence to be influenced, whether intentionally or unintentionally, and it was not therefore possible to rule out the possibility of distortion.

6.38 The second aspect of the rule, stated in (b), reflects the existing common law that statements that accompany and explain an act are as much admissible as evidence as the act itself. Thus, in *McCay*[90] words accompanying an identification were held admissible. The wording of (b) in para 4 of s 118(1) is, however, curious in that it requires it to be necessary to admit the statement in order to 'properly evaluate' the statement. On one view no statement can be properly evaluated without considering the act in conjunction with the statement which accompanies it: on that basis all accompanying statements are admissible. On the other hand, that is not the wording of (b) in para 4, which suggests a more limited approach, and raises the question about what is 'proper evaluation'. Arguably, this provision is intended to apply in virtually all cases, for how else is the court to know of the context of the act, or have a complete picture as to what the maker of the statement actually did? The wording is perhaps unfortunate.

6.39 The third element of *res gestae* at common law is contemporaneous statement of feelings or state of health.[91] This formulation is rather wider than that of 'physical sensation'. A statement from an individual who stated that he was suffering from cancer would certainly be a statement as to state of health, but, on a literal view, not a statement of physical sensation. The point is unimportant because, in such circumstances, nearly always such a statement can be fitted within the alternative limb, that of 'mental state'.

6.40 Nothing in the new provisions clarifies some conceptual issues that have arisen as to whether the *res gestae* principle is describing non-hearsay, or whether it is an exception to the rule, although in the Act it is treated as an exception.[92] For practical purposes it does not matter. Of more practical import is the test to be applied to the different senses in which the *res gestae* rule operates. The differences in meaning have not always been maintained by the courts. In *Callender*,[93] an animal rights activist, who was charged with conspiracy to commit arson, claimed that his intention was to leave dummy devices. The trial judge ruled that the testimony of a witness, H, that the appellant had told her (H) that the devices were specifically designed not to ignite was inadmissible as hearsay. That conclusion was upheld on appeal, the court observing that this alleged *res gestae* statement (ie accompanying and explaining relevant acts) did not satisfy the requisite test of being made in circumstances where there was no possibility of concoction or distortion. It remains to be seen whether the courts will continue to utilise a test appropriate only to one form of *res gestae* (ie spontaneous utterances) in the context of the whole of para 4.

---

90   [1991] 1 All ER 232, CA.

91   *Gloster* (1868) 16 Cox CC 471, CA.

92   See *Ratten v R* [1972] AC 378, PC, and the judgment in *McCay* [1991] 1 All ER 232, CA.

93   [1998] Crim LR 337, CA.

Confessions

6.41   Nothing in the new Act removes the right of the court to consider a confession: indeed, para 5 to s 118(1) preserves the existing law. Thus, obviously the criteria in s 76 of PACE for admissibility remain, and s 76 is amended by the new Act. It is also possible to admit evidence of implied admissions, at common law. It will be recalled that statements may be admitted as an introduction to evidence of the accused's reaction when taxed with them.[94] Strictly speaking, the reaction of the accused is admissible evidence only if it shows acceptance of the allegation, and is made in circumstances where a denial might be expected.[95] This rule survives the passage of the new Act, although arguably, it is unimportant in the light of the silence provisions in ss 34 to 38 of the CJPOA 1994.

6.42   The new Act amends PACE: a new s 76A is added by s 128. The effect of this is that, subject to certain criteria and safeguards, a confession made by a co-accused may be given in evidence for another person charged in the same proceedings, but not unless the court is satisfied that it was not obtained through oppression or in circumstances likely to render it unreliable. It thus addresses issues left open by the House of Lords in *Myers*,[96] but is a matter to be regretted. If a confession has some relevance and probative force in relation to a defence that an accused wishes to put before a court, it can scarcely be right, or even fair within Art 6, to deprive him of the opportunity of adducing it because it does not satisfy criteria primarily designed to provide protections for those accused of crime. The matters in s 76A surely go to weight, not admissibility.

Expert evidence

6.43   Paragraph 8 preserves the rule of law under which, in criminal proceedings, an expert witness may draw on the body of expertise relevant to his field (s 118(1), para 8). Thus, the decision in *Abadon*[97] that an expert is 'entitled to draw on the works of others as part of the process of arriving at their conclusion' is upheld.

6.44   Note should also be taken of s 127. This new provision makes a statement prepared for the purposes of criminal proceedings admissible as evidence of what it states if the person who made it had personal knowledge of its contents, and if an expert is basing an opinion or inference on the statement. Thus, an expert who derives his own opinion from initial factual findings, or upon what was said, or how it was said, in another document, falls within s 127. The leave of the court is required.

The 'safety valve' – the discretion

6.45   The 'safety valve' provision in s 114(1)(d) marks a significant relaxation of the hearsay rule. It makes admissible a statement given otherwise than in testimony as evidence of any matter stated if the court is satisfied that, despite the difficulties there

---

94   *Christie* [1914] AC 545, HL.

95   *Hall v R* [1971] 1 All ER 322, PC; *cf Chandler* [1976] 3 All ER 105, CA. The parties must be 'on even terms': *Mitchell* (1892) 17 Cox CC 503, CCCR.

96   [1998] AC 124, HL. For criticism of this decision, see Hirst, 'Confessions on Proof of Innocence' [1998] CLJ 146.

97   (1983) 76 Cr App R 48.

may be in challenging the statement, it would not be contrary to the interests of justice for it to be admissible. The statement can be oral or documentary.

In deciding whether a statement should be admitted under s 114(1)(d) the court must have regard to the following factors (and to any others it considers relevant):

(a) how much probative value the statement has (assuming it to be true) in relation to a matter in issue in the proceedings, or how valuable it is for the understanding of other evidence in the case;
(b) what other evidence has been, or can be given, on the matter or evidence mentioned in para (a);
(c) how important the matter or evidence mentioned in para (a) is in the context of the case as a whole;
(d) the circumstances in which the statement was made;
(e) how reliable the maker of the statement appears to be;
(f) how reliable the evidence of the making of the statement appears to be;
(g) whether oral evidence of the matter can be given and, if not, why it cannot;
(h) the amount of difficulty involved in challenging the statement;
(i) the extent to which that difficulty would be likely to prejudice the party facing it.

Of all these new hearsay provisions, this is the most complex. The Law Commission considered that it would be used only exceptionally.[98] It identified some of the dangers of the rule:

> 'We recognise that we are introducing the risks of inconsistency and unpredictability which accompany judicial discretion, but believe that without such a discretion the proposed reforms would be too rigid: some limited flexibility must be incorporated ... Our purpose is to allow for the admission of reliable hearsay which could not otherwise be admitted, particularly to prevent a conviction which that evidence would render unsafe ... We remain convinced that a safety valve is needed.'

The 'safety valve' applies to multiple hearsay as well as to firsthand hearsay, subject to the specific provisions relating thereto.[99]

The wording of the new s 114(1)(d) differs from that in the draft Bill appended to the Law Commission's proposal, which was phrased in the following terms: 'probative value is such that the interests of justice require it to be admissible'. That wording was intended to encourage the court to consider certain factors such as the degree of relevance, the circumstances in which the statement was made, the extent to which it appears to supply evidence which would not otherwise be available and the creditworthiness of the declarant. These are all factors stated in s 114(2). The issues that go to probative value, however, are not the same as those which might relate to issues which affect the interests of justice. The Law Commission identified these latter issues as the fact that the declarant cannot give oral evidence, the inability of the accused sometimes to controvert the statement, and the risk of unfairness to the accused.[100]

6.46 A key question is whether a single test revolving around 'interests of justice' provides sufficient guidance as to its use and fairness. The Law Commission did not

---

98 See Law Com No 245, *op cit*, para 8.138.

99 See **6.55**.

100 Law Com No 245, *op cit*, para 8.142.

think so: '... this phrase is too vague, and would doubtless lead to widely differing practices in different courts followed by a rush of appeals'.[101] The provisions of s 114 do in part recognise this concern by identifying the factors that must be taken into account. Inherent in s 114(2) is a recognition that all of the factors set out therein are relevant in deciding what the interests of justice require, although some might argue that if the probative value of evidence is high it is in the interests of justice that it be admitted, and the other factors are ones in reality that affect the weight to be given to a particular piece of evidence. This is the reverse of the comment made to the Law Commissioner by one respondent who pointed out that '... it can't be in the interests of justice [to admit it] if the evidence is not trustworthy or cross-examination cannot safely be dispensed with'.[102]

Can it ever be in the interests of justice to admit evidence which does not have strong probative force in the absence of any opportunity in cross-examination to test it? The terms of s 114(2) were intended to satisfy the needs of Art 6.[103] Depending on how it is used, the potential for an Art 6 challenge remains.

6.47 The Law Commission saw admission of such evidence as exceptional, although the statutory formulation does not make this explicit: indeed, the Law Commission saw the potential need for Court of Appeal or Divisional Court guidance.[104] Such an application should be made at the pleas and direction hearing, or pre-trial review, but, again, no such limitation is contained in the legislation itself. No doubt rules made pursuant to s 132[105] will provide for this.

The Law Commission gave[106] examples of where such a direction might be used:

(1) D is prosecuted for indecent assault on a child. The child is too young to testify, but she initially described her assailant as 'a coloured boy' [*sic*]. The defence is identity and the defendant is white.[107]

(2) D is prosecuted for the murder of his girlfriend. He denies that it was he who killed her. Fixing the time of the murder is an essential part of proving that D must have done it. An eight-year-old child tells the police that he saw the victim leaving her home at a time after the prosecution says she was dead. By the time the case comes to trial the child can remember nothing about when he saw the victim.[108]

(3) D is charged with assault. X, who is not charged, admits to a friend that he, X, committed the assault. D and X are similar in appearance. X's confession is inadmissible hearsay.[109]

---

101 Law Com No 245, *op cit*, para 8.140.

102 *Ibid*, para 8.138.

103 See **6.6**.

104 Law Com No 245, *op cit*, para 8.143.

105 Section 132 empowers the making of rules deemed to be necessary or expedient.

106 Law Com No 245, *op cit*, para 8.147.

107 The facts of *Sparks* [1964] AC 964, PC.

108 The facts of *Thomas* [1994] Crim LR 745, CA.

109 The facts of *Cooper* [1969] 1 All ER 32, CA.

In each of these examples it is in the interests of the accused that the statement is admitted. Some respondents to the Law Commission argued that the 'safety valve' should be available only in favour of the accused, an argument it rejected on the basis that it was consistent with principle that the same rules of evidence should apply to both prosecution and defence alike.[110] The issues of principle identified by the Law Commission make interesting reading. First, because if all the defendant has to do is raise a reasonable doubt, then it would be easy to achieve this by the use of manufactured or very low-quality hearsay. A rule which assists only the defence protects the innocent and guilty alike. In other words, to ensure parity we must accept that some evidence tendered, or sought to be tendered, by the prosecution will likewise be manufactured or of low quality. This surely cannot be right. Such evidence should not pass the threshold of admissibility under s 114(2) and it will often not do so. Secondly, the defendant will not be precluded from adducing reliable hearsay evidence under the 'safety valve'. That is true, but begs the question as to whether the safety valve itself should apply equally to prosecution and defence. Finally, one party may be able to cross-examine on matters in respect of which it would not have been allowed itself to adduce evidence: an accused might be entitled to elicit from a defence witness hearsay evidence implicating a co-accused which the prosecution would not have been able to lead. That again is true, although one might wonder why that should be wrong.

6.48   The prosecution and defence are in different positions. The fact that the burden of proof lies on the prosecution, and that other rules of evidence may differ, is recognition of that fact. There is one further unresolved question: how is s 114(2) to be applied? Can it ever be right, now that we have recognised the need for a 'safety valve', for an accused to be denied the right under s 114(2) to adduce evidence which has some probative force? Will not courts be more willing to allow evidence to be adduced pursuant to s 114(2) for the accused rather than the prosecution? In relation to the prosecution, wider considerations surely apply, including the inability of an accused to be able to challenge the testimony. It of course should be borne in mind that, by definition, the witness in question is available (for otherwise, save in the context of incompetence, or loss of memory, the case should be dealt with under s 116) and a written statement has not been given to the police or other investigating agency, for otherwise it should be dealt with under s 117.

Previous inconsistent statements

6.49   Under pre-existing law, if a witness makes a statement inconsistent with his previous statements, he may be asked about them. If he does not admit the making of such a statement, the statement may be put to him under the terms of s 3, s 4 or s 5 of the Criminal Procedure Act 1865.[111] The statement proved in this way is, under the new Act, evidence of any fact of which direct oral evidence by him would be admissible (s 119(1)).

This is a clear change in the law: hitherto, a previous inconsistent statement went only to weaken, or cancel out, the credibility of the witness, with the contents of that statement only evidence as to their truth if accepted in oral testimony (in which case,

---

110 See Law Com No 245, *op cit*, paras 12.0–12.8.

111 Amended by the new Act: see Sch 36, Part 5, para 79.

conceptually, it was the acceptance in oral testimony and not the statement that amounted to the proof of the matter). Alternatively, the out-of-court statement might have been admissible under one of the pre-existing exceptions (a rare event). The Law Commission took the view[112] that a court should be permitted to treat the earlier statement as the true one where it was possible to do so, on the basis of other evidence or the witness's response under cross-examination. As it states:

'... if jurors or magistrates are trusted to decide that a witness has lied throughout, and to disregard that witness's testimony, why should they not be free to decide that the witness's previous testimony was correct, and to take as reliable the parts of the testimony that they find convincing?'

6.50 It is possible that a witness may be subject to cross-examination on only part of a previous statement. To overcome that problem, s 122(2) prohibits (in cases of jury trial) the jury having a copy of any out-of-court statement which becomes an exhibit, unless the court considers it appropriate, or all parties agree. This also overcomes the danger that a written statement may be accorded more weight than oral testimony. That said, s 122 does not apply to cases of summary trial: those sitting at summary trial will see matters that go beyond the inconsistencies established in cross-examination.

A statement may incriminate others. Thus an accused may incriminate a co-accused in his out-of-court statement and not do so in testimony at trial (or, of course, vice versa). The result is an important change in the law, and has the result of allowing the statement to be evidence against the co-accused. The Law Commission observed that:

'Given that the co-accused can cross-examine the accused on the incriminating statement, and the fact that it will be obvious to the fact-finders that the accused has not been consistent, we believe that there is no danger in permitting the fact-finders to decide for themselves whether to believe the oral testimony, the previous statement or neither.' (para 10.96)

If the accused originally exculpated a co-accused in his out-of-court statement, but incriminates that co-accused during testimony at trial, the co-accused will be able to use the exculpatory statement as part of his case that he is not guilty of the offence. Arguably, however, in such circumstances the failure to mention the co-accused at the pre-trial stage would significantly weaken the testimony of the accused in any event. More significantly, where an accused incriminates a co-accused in his statement, but then withdraws that when testifying at trial, the contents of the out-of-court statement could be used by the prosecution to prove the case against the co-accused. Important issues arise. Should a prosecutor be entitled to adduce evidence of the out-of-court statement of the accused as part of the prosecutor's case against the co-accused? The terms of s 119 clearly indicate that the answer to that question is 'No': there can be an inconsistency only if there is testimony with which to be inconsistent – and that will not be until the accused determines whether or not to testify. The Law Commission clearly envisaged that the statement would become evidence only if admitted to contradict inconsistent testimony.[113] If the accused is consistent in testimony, the matter will be before the court; if he is not, the matter is admissible by virtue of s 119(1). Logically, the prosecution ought to be able to adduce that as part of its case, but practically this would be fraught with difficulty and is not permitted.

---

112 Law Com No 245, *op cit*, para 10.89.

113 *Ibid*, paras 10.95–10.96.

However, further issues arise. Suppose that the out-of-court statement was made in circumstances which would render that statement inadmissible in the hands of the prosecutor, for example because of a breach of s 76(2) of PACE, or of the Codes of Practice. Exclusion under s 78 of PACE is of no assistance, because it applies only to testimony tendered by the prosecution. The answer lies in the discretion conferred by s 126,[114] which permits a court to exclude otherwise admissible evidence given other than in the proceedings orally, if the court is satisfied that the case for excluding the statement, taking into account of the danger that to admit it would result in undue waste of time, substantially outweighs the case for admitting it, taking account of the value of the evidence.[115]

Section 126 might also provide a solution to another problem, namely the accused of bad character who, in an out-of-court statement, makes statements attacking the character of another person. If that statement is admitted as evidence of its truth by virtue of s 122, then this could in some circumstances allow the character of the accused to be admissible,[116] pursuant to s 104(1)(f). Section 104 defines what is meant by 'attack on another person's character'. Although the terms of s 104(1)(a), or (b), will not apply, because the accused will not himself have adduced evidence or asked questions, s 104(1)(c) might.

Other out-of-court statements

6.51 The previous consistent statements of a witness have not generally been admissible. The rule against self-serving statements ruled them out as a matter of principle (even if they were not to be regarded as hearsay), and their use was confined to certain limited situations: principally, for refreshing memory, to rebut allegations of recent fabrication, as recent complaints in sexual cases, previous consistent identification, and the reaction of an accused when first taxed with the accusation.

The general scheme of the hearsay reform is to permit relevant evidence which may have probative force to be admitted. As with previous inconsistent statements, the Act permits consistent statements to be admitted as evidence of their truth in the circumstances set out in s 120. In summary these are:

– to rebut allegation of fabrication (s 120(2));
– documents used to refresh memory on which the witness is cross-examined (s 120(3));
– certain out-of-court statements that fall within s 120(4)–(7) (identity, facts fresh in the memory, complaint by alleged victim).

The out-of-court statement should add to the testimony, not replace it. In each of the instances in s 120, the witness will testify and be available for cross-examination. In providing for a previous statement to be admissible as to its truth, the difficult and sometimes illogical distinctions previously drawn as to what a statement could be used for, with the confusion which that engendered,[117] are overcome.

---

114 See **6.57**.
115 See **6.50**.
116 See **5.47**.
117 See Law Com No 245, *op cit*, para 10.39.

6.52   Section 136 applies to both oral statements and statements in a document, but, in either case, the witness must have the required capacity at the time of making the statement sought to be adduced (s139(1)). The 'required capacity' is defined by s 139(3) as meaning a person who is capable of (a) understanding questions put to him about the matter stated, and (b) giving answers which can be understood. Any issue about capability must be determined in accordance with s 139(3), with the burden of proof on the party seeking to adduce the document. The standard of proof, whether for prosecution or defence, is the balance of probabilities. Expert evidence may be adduced.

Fabrication

6.53   Section 120 provides that if a statement is admitted to rebut an allegation that his oral testimony has been fabricated, that statement is admissible as evidence on any matter of which oral evidence by the witness would be admissible.

The admission of the statement is to be determined in accordance with common law principles: the Act does not extend the scope of the exception in any way. The Law Commission considered, but rejected, the extension of the rule.[118] Thus, the statement will be admissible to rebut allegations that the witness has fabricated his testimony at a later point of time. In *Oyesiku*[119] the statement of W to her solicitor at a time when she had not had an opportunity to talk to her husband about the relevant matters was admissible to negate the allegation that it was a story concocted by her and the accused. The allegation must not simply be one of inconsistency with present testimony: in that circumstance, of course, s 119 will potentially allow the previous inconsistent statement to be evidence of its truth, and to be weighed against the testimony given in court.

Refreshing memory documents

6.54   By s 120(3), a statement made by the witness in a document:

(a)   which is used by him to refresh memory while giving evidence;
(b)   on which he is cross-examined; and
(c)   which as a consequence is received in evidence in the proceedings,

is admissible as evidence of any matter stated of which oral evidence by him would be admissible.

Again, this does not affect the substance of the rule but provides for the refreshing memory document to be admissible as to the truth of its contents. The witness may refresh his memory from a document which is made contemporaneously with the matters it concerns, and, in some circumstances and purposes, from a non-contemporaneous document.[120] A witness may be cross-examined on the basis of the document used to refresh memory if it is relevant to do so.[121] However, the terms of s 120(3)(c) should be noted. The effect of that section is that only in respect of matters

---

118 Law Com No 245, *op cit*, para 10.45.

119 (1971) 56 Cr App R 240, CA.

120 See generally *Da Silva* [1990] 1 WLR 31, CA; *South Ribble Justices ex parte Cochrane* [1996] Crim LR 74, DC.

121 *Sekhon* (1986) 85 Cr App R 19, CA.

the subject of cross-examination that go beyond the matters on which the witness refreshed his memory will statements be admissible as to their truth.[122]

If the document is admissible as to its truth under s 120, that will include all parts of the document – not simply in respect of matters on which the witness has refreshed his memory, and include matters which are inconsistent with current testimony.

Multiple hearsay

6.55   The dangers inherent in hearsay increase when the hearsay is not first-hand, but multiple in nature. In the case of first-hand hearsay it is possible to question or challenge the person who heard the relevant statement being made. With multiple hearsay there is an increased risk that unreliable or manufactured evidence might be admitted. The Law Commission also identified problems in how juries (in a trial on indictment) might be directed, and the possibly significant expenditure of time in dealing with submissions as to the origins and weight of multiple hearsay. Those factors led the Law Commission to the recommendation (at para 8.17) that the 'unavailability' exception proposed should not extend to a statement of any fact of which the declarant could not have given evidence when the statement was made. The basis of that recommendation, and its implications, led to a complex set of provisions being introduced in the original Bill. Persistent criticism during the Act's parliamentary passage, however, convinced the Government that the dangers were such that stronger provisions were needed if unfairness was to be avoided. The revised provisions are to be found in s 121.

Section 121 states that hearsay is not admissible to prove that an earlier hearsay statement was made, unless:

(a)   either of the statements is admissible under s 117 (business documents), s 119 (inconsistent statements) or s 120 (other statements);
(b)   all parties agree; or
(c)   the court is satisfied that the value of the evidence in question, taking into account how reliable the statements appear to be, is so high that the interests of justice require the later statement to be admissible for that purpose.

These provisions are significantly stricter than those originally introduced. The preconditions are alternatives. The provisions of s 121(1)(c) leave it open to the court to admit evidence in the interest of justice. The phrase 'so high', however, is incapable of definition: at the end of the day it will be for the court to determine whether the admission of the evidence is fair. That may satisfy Art 6 ECHR. It is, arguably, an extremely high standard and should not routinely be used. The presumption should be that this is exceptional.

The effect of admission – credibility

6.56   If a statement is admitted as evidence of any matter stated, and the maker of the statement does not give oral evidence in connection with the subject-matter of the statement, s 124(2) applies. It provides that:

---

122 *Fenlon* (1980) 71 Cr App R 307, CA; *Virgo* (1978) 67 Cr App R 323, CA.

(a) any evidence which (if he had given such evidence) would have been admissible as relevant to his credibility as a witness is so admissible in the proceedings;

(b) evidence may, with the court's leave, be given of any matter which (if he had given such evidence) could have been put to him in cross-examination as relevant to his credibility as a witness but of which evidence could not have been adduced by the cross-examining party;

(c) evidence tending to prove that he made (at whatever time) any other statement inconsistent with the statement as evidence is admissible for the purpose of showing that he contradicted himself.

For these purposes, and for those in s 124(3), the 'maker of the statement' in a document admitted under s 117 is each person who, for the document to be admissible, supplied or received the information, or created or received the document (s 124(4)). If evidence is admitted under s 124, and as a result an allegation is made against the maker of the statement, the court may (but is not required to) permit a party to lead additional evidence of such description as the court may specify for the purpose of denying or answering the allegation (s 124(3)).

Discretion to exclude

6.57 Section 126 confers on a court a discretion to exclude otherwise admissible hearsay. It provides (s 126(1)) that a court may refuse to admit a statement as evidence of a matter stated if:

(a) the statement was made otherwise than in oral evidence in the proceedings, and

(b) the court is satisfied that the case for excluding the statement, taking account of the danger that to admit it would result in undue waste of time, substantially outweighs the case for admitting it, taking account of the value of the evidence.

A court may thus exclude evidence which it perceives to be of low evidential importance in the context of the case as a whole, a conclusion confirmed by the use of the phrase 'waste of time'. Evidence which has substantial evidential importance can scarcely be described as the 'waste of time' of a trial court.

The discretion under s 78 of PACE is preserved by s 126(2).

The power to stop an unconvincing case

6.58 Section 125 confers a power on a Crown Court (but not a magistrates' or youth court) to stop a case. This power does not remove any other power of a Crown Court trying a case on indictment to acquit a person or to discharge a jury (s 125(4)). Section 125(1) provides that if the court is satisfied at any time after the close of the prosecution case that:

(a) the case against the defendant is based wholly or partly on a statement not made in oral evidence in the proceedings, and

(b) the evidence provided by the statement is so unconvincing that, considering its importance to the case against the defendant, his conviction of the offence would be unsafe,

the court must either direct the jury to acquit the defendant of the offence, or if it considers that there ought to be a retrial, discharge the jury. An equivalent provision is contained in s 124(3) in respect of the situation where a jury is required to determine an issue under s 4A(2) of the Criminal Procedure (Insanity) Act 1964 (s 109(3)).

EVIDENCE BY VIDEO-RECORDING

6.59 The problem of ensuring that eye-witness descriptions of events are available, and as accurate as possible, is a key issue. That is also a key issue in the interests of justice. Accounts are more likely to be accurate at an early date rather than later. That is a principle that has been accepted in the context of children's evidence, and is now extended to eye-witness testimony. There will also be advantages in securing the testimony of those who are subsequently put under pressure not to testify or who have to testify in a hostile environment.

Section 137 now allows a video-recording of the account of an eye-witness, given while the events were fresh in the mind of the witness to amount to the evidence-in-chief of that witness, with the leave of the court.

The court must be satisfied that the witness's recollection of the events is likely to be significantly better when he gave the recorded account than when he gives oral evidence (s 137(3)). Given the length of time that will elapse in a serious case, that is often likely, presumptively, to be the case. It must also be in the interests of justice for the recording to be admitted, having regard to matters identified by s 137(4). Section 138 contains consequential provisions.

LIVE LINKS

6.60 Part 8 of the Act deals with live links. It confers a general power to give evidence through a live TV link in the proceedings defined by s 51. That includes all trials, whether summary or on indictment (s 51(2)). The court must so direct.

The power to testify through live TV link is not new. Section 32 of the CJA 1988 permitted children, or a witness outside the United Kingdom, to testify by means of live TV link. Following the passage of s 24 of the YJCEA 1999, s 32 was confined to the testimony of those outside the United Kingdom, the testimony of children being subsumed within the special measures directions of the 1999 Act. Those provisions remain in force. The provisions of the Crime (International Co-operation) Act 2003, which provide for the hearing of witnesses through a live television link, or by telephone, should also be noted.

6.61 The capacity to make a special measures direction is governed by the eligibility provisions of s 16 (age or incapacity) or s 17 (fear or distress about testifying). Section 21 made special assumptions about children. Nothing in the new Act deals with the relationship between those provisions and those in s 19 of the new Act, which is a much more general provision.

Section 51(4) states that a direction by a court to permit live TV testimony may not be given unless:

(a) the court is satisfied that it is in the interests of the efficient or effective administration of justice for the person to give evidence through a live TV link; and

(b)   suitable facilities are in place.

No guidance currently exists as to how such powers should be used: the court must look at all the circumstances, which include the availability of the witness, the need to attend in person, the importance of testimony in person, the views of the witness, the suitability of the link arrangements, and whether a direction might tend to inhibit any party from effectively testing the witness's evidence. This last provision is key if Art 6 ECHR is to be satisfied. There appears to be no limitation on this, general, provision effectively superseding the provisions of the 1999 Act.

The principle of permitting live TV link arrangements is long accepted. The question is whether the general applicability is a step too far. Some may regret the lack of procedural safeguards, but it can scarcely be argued successfully that live testimony is inferior in any way to the alternative hearsay evidence provisions permitted by the Act. The crucial question will be whether the courts will recognise that, in an appropriate case, it is important to have the witness's demeanour and presentation assessed in court.

Chapter 7

PROSECUTION RIGHTS OF APPEAL

SUMMARY

7.1 Defendants in a criminal case have many rights of appeal against a variety of adverse outcomes in a criminal court. By contrast, the prosecutor has enjoyed only limited rights of appeal against certain outcomes, but not against conviction or other matters which are capable of ending the trial. The new Act extends those rights to include rights of appeal against judicial rulings which result in the termination of a trial, in addition to the major extension of rights of appeal against bail grants conferred on prosecutors by s 18 of the new Act.[1]

Section 57 provides a prosecution right of appeal against certain types of judicial ruling ('terminating rulings'), save against a ruling that a jury be discharged or where there is already a right of appeal under another Act, eg s 9(11) of the CJA 1987.[2] Section 62 also confers rights of appeal against qualifying evidentiary rulings.

BACKGROUND

7.2 Under pre-existing law, prosecution rights of appeal have been limited. The power to apply under s 111 of the MCA 1980 to the High Court by way of 'case stated' for a review of a decision from the magistrates' court is not, technically, an appeal, but a review on certain grounds;[3] but nonetheless, in reality, the remedies at the High Court's disposal to redress the grievance of either prosecutor or defence amount to much the same. Both prosecution and defence may make such an application following an adverse verdict. Section 28(1) of the Supreme Court Act 1981 (SCA 1981) creates the opportunity to challenge the decision of a Crown Court by way of case stated, but there are limits on which determinations may be challenged in this fashion. In particular, s 29(3) of the SCA 1981 excludes review of any 'matter relating to trial on indictment', a phrase which the courts decline to define comprehensively.[4]

The prosecution also has a power to challenge certain grants of bail (s 18); to challenge 'unduly lenient sentences' under s 36 of the CJA 1988; in some

---

1   See **3.39**.

2   Interlocutory appeals form preparatory hearings in serious fraud cases.

3   Section 28 of the SCA 1981 permits the High Court, *inter alia*, to reverse or affirm a lower court's decision or to remit the case to the lower court with the opinion of the High Court, which may include a direction to the lower court to convict.

4   *Smalley v Crown Court at Warwick* [1985] AC 622, HL, and *R v Manchester Crown Court ex parte DPP* (1994) 94 Cr App R 461, HL; *R v Central Criminal Court ex parte Serious Fraud Office* [1993] 2 All ER 399, DC; *R v Crown Court at Southwark* [1993] 1 WLR 764, DC JA.

circumstances to challenge a mode of trial decision;[5] and to 'appeal' against a ruling on a point of law following an acquittal, although (until now) leaving the acquittal unaffected.[6] There are opportunities also to appeal against interlocutory orders made in preparatory hearings [7] and to challenge tainted acquittals under s 54 of the CPIA 1996.

7.3   In 2001 the Law Commission produced its Report on Double Jeopardy.[8] It concluded:

> 'If a case is to fall on a legal argument, it is better for public confidence in the criminal justice system that it should be susceptible to the second opinion of a higher court, than it be unappealable.'

The Auld Review[9] had proposed three new prosecution rights:

(1)   allowing appeals from preparatory hearings against potentially terminating rulings such as the quashing, joinder or severing of counts from an indictment or against stays for abuse of process;

(2)   creating a prosecution right of appeal against an acquittal borne of a terminating ruling right up to the close of the prosecution case; and

(3)   creating a right of appeal against a *Galbraith* 'no case to answer'.[10]

Auld's proposals later found approval in the White Paper *Justice for All*, particularly as defendants already had considerable rights of appeals in such cases. The Law Commission thereafter concluded[11] that the Crown should be given a right of appeal against terminating rulings which arose in advance of the trial, but this should not be limited to rulings made at a preparatory hearing or rulings made up to the conclusion of the Crown's case (except where the ruling was made under the first limb of *Galbraith*),[12] nor against rulings which would not result in an immediate acquittal or an acquittal because the jury had been misdirected. It recommended[13] that appeals be limited to certain categories of offence only.

The recommendations of Auld and of the Law Commission form the basis for the approach of the new Act, if not reflected always in the detail. In particular, the White Paper pledged to introduce appeals so that rulings made wrongly by trial judges, which would otherwise cost the Crown its case, could be put right.

7.4   In its original form the Bill created rights of appeal against 'terminating' and 'non-terminating' rulings arising from any trial on indictment. By the end of the parliamentary process, the Government had retreated from its initial position here for fear of creating too many appeals, and because of the practicalities of identifying

---

5   *R v Northampton Justices ex parte Commissioners of Customs and Excise* [1994] Crim LR 598, DC.

6   Section 36 of the CJA 1972.

7   Section 9(11) of the CJA 1987; ss 35–36 of the CPIA 1996.

8   *Double Jeopardy and Prosecution Appeals*, Law Com No 267 (2001).

9   *Op cit*, Ch 12, paras 47–65.

10   *R v Galbraith* (1981) 73 Cr App R 124, CA.

11   Law Com No 267, *op cit*, Summary, paras 5–7.

12   *Ibid*, para 7.

13   *Ibid*, para 8.

terminating and non-terminating rulings and distinguishing between them. Some 100 to 150 such appeals are expected per year, perhaps one fifth of which would be 'expedited' appeals. The provisions were subject to some criticisms during their passage, but late amendments led to safeguards being introduced which met some of the concerns expressed.

COMMENCEMENT

7.5 These provisions had not been brought into force as at the date of going to press. Appeals against evidentiary rulings will not be introduced until the impact of appeals against terminating rulings have been evaluated[14] and rules of court under s 73 will need to be made to make the system workable.

NEW PROSECUTION RIGHTS OF APPEAL AGAINST TERMINATING RULINGS

7.6 Two categories of appeal are created in the Crown Court. The first is a general right of appeal against appeals to which Part 9 relates (s 58). The second operates in respect of appeals against evidentiary rulings, defined by s 62(2) as those which significantly weaken the prosecution case.[15] The Crown cannot appeal the discharge of a jury, or appeal where statute already provides for a prosecution appeal (s 57(2)). Depending upon the category of ruling,[16] either s 58 or s 62 sets out the procedure to be followed by the Crown and sets out the judge's powers and duties.

7.7 The explicit phrase 'terminating ruling' was dropped from the Bill on its Third Reading in the House of Lords, but the Attorney-General nevertheless continued to use it[17] in debate and it remains an apt description of what these provisions are about. The new Act does not list examples of what type of ruling would fall into each category. It will depend upon the facts of the case, the nature of the ruling and, most importantly, its impact upon the trial. This permits flexibility. A 'terminating ruling' is defined only by its effect. The Solicitor-General was moved to observe:[18]

> 'A terminating ruling is like an elephant. One can recognise it when it comes lumbering through the doors or the court. If it looks like a terminal ruling, it is appealable.'

In reality, it is a ruling which collapses the prosecution case, so that unless the prosecution successfully appeals, the issues of guilt or innocence will not go to the jury. It is the ruling which is appealable, not the verdict as is the case on defence appeals where the defence appealed. Parts of the trial may continue undisturbed by the fact of an appeal by the prosecution where that ruling does not affect that part (s 60). If the Court of Appeal reverses or varies that judge's ruling, the proceedings may resume or start afresh (s 61).

---

14 See **7.26**.

15 See **7.23**.

16 'Ruling' includes a decision, determination, direction, finding, notice, order, refusal, rejection or requirement (s 74(1)).

17 HL Report, 17 November 2003, cols 1781–1789.

18 HC Committee, 25 February 2003, col 1114.

What may amount to such a ruling?

7.8 The new Act does not list examples of terminating rulings. The Explanatory Notes to the Bill[19] described the Government's intention that they be:

'... rulings that are terminating in themselves and those that are so fatal to the prosecution case that it proposes to treat them as terminating, and in the absence of a right of appeal, would offer no or no further evidence.'

7.9 Section 57(2) excludes rulings that a jury be discharged, and any ruling for which there is already provision under statute to appeal, for example rulings in preparatory hearings under s 9(11) of the CJA 1987. The Bill initially precluded appeals against rulings in fitness to plead cases, but an amendment removed this ground as part of a major redrafting exercise to achieve workability and clarity.[20]

7.10 The Act does not extend to the use of the Attorney-General's termination of a prosecution (*nolle prosequi*), jury decisions (such as a decision, of their own volition, to acquit part way through a trial) and the discharge of a jury. Applications that counts should 'lie on file' under s 17 of the Criminal Appeals Act 1968 (CAA 1968) prevent a trial of the count to which the order made relates but, being consensual and capable of being undone on the Crown's application, do not need the mechanics of Part 9. Defects in the indictment and invalid committals[21] (or sending for trial) would seem to be capable of rescue by normal process and are thus not appealable – the Crown may begin the process again by charging the defendant afresh, providing there was no verdict to which *autrefois acquit* would provide a bar. However, in a trial of several defendants, the loss of a defendant who had played a major role – perhaps in a conspiracy – might place the Crown in considerable difficulties if it is forced to seek to charge that one individual again and he has become separated permanently from his co-conspirators; again, in theory, the Crown could still proceed, since the admission of any conviction of the others on the indictment may be admissible under s 74 of PACE to prove a conspiracy, for example. However, in practice, the prosecution may find itself compelled to offer no evidence in some cases where such a defendant has become separated from the others.

7.11 The following *may* be considered appealable under the Act depending upon their impact on the viability of the prosecution case:

– a ruling that the indictment be stayed, eg for abuse of process,[22] because the trial of that count – or even of the whole indictment – can go no further. The evidence will not be heard, and there can be no conviction;
– a successful argument of *autrefois acquit* or *convict*[23] preventing a trial of the facts the Crown now seeks to prove;
– a successful submission of no case to answer;[24]

19 HL Explanatory Notes, para 36.
20 HL Report, 17 November 2003, col 1784.
21 *Archbold: Criminal Pleading, Evidence and Practice* (Sweet & Maxwell, looseleaf), 1–209 et seq.
22 *R v Croydon Crown Court ex parte Dean* (1994) 98 Cr App R 76, DC; *R v Horseferry Road Magistrates' Court ex parte Bennett* [1994] 1 AC 42, HL.
23 See **11.4**.
24 See *R v Galbraith* (1981) 73 Cr App R 124, CA.

– an adverse PII ruling where, for example, the Crown unsuccessfully seeks anonymity for an informant. The effect is terminal because the Crown is not able to go on with the case if the ruling is made. While in this example the Crown could lead evidence, compromising the informer in the process, the reality is that either it jeopardises the informer or allows the defendant to be acquitted without the evidence being tested even though he may be guilty of a serious offence. It is this sense of being hamstrung by the ruling that elevates a ruling into a terminating one, although the Court of Appeal may refuse leave and conclude that the ruling is not a terminating one because the possibility of a trial continues to exist. It is the Crown's choice, not the ruling *per se*, that prevents progress. Given that with non-evidentiary rulings s 58(8) obliges the Crown to consent to an acquittal if it does not succeed on appeal, prosecutors will wish to choose carefully between appealing and proceeding in the trial despite the ruling if at all possible;

– a ruling that the indictment discloses no offence punishable in English law;[25]

– applications regarding joinder or severance of indictments, or counts upon them, may be terminating, depending upon the circumstances and what is at stake for the Crown where an adverse ruling is made amount to appealable rulings. Counts may be severed where the Crown depends vitally upon the cumulative support each count provides.

7.12 The ruling is one made by a Crown Court judge *in relation* to a trial on indictment (s 57(1)). It will therefore include rulings in a pre-trial review or preparatory hearing. The phrase 'in relation to a trial on indictment' arguably bears the same meaning as ascribed to s 29(3) of the SCA 1981, and thus may also include a stay for abuse of process[26] or the quashing of an indictment for lack of jurisdiction.[27] One test, although not all-embracing, is to ask whether the decision arises in the issue between the Crown and the defendant formulated by the indictment.[28] An appeal may be brought against a ruling affecting more than one count on the indictment (s 58(1)).

7.13 The appeal goes direct to the Court of Appeal (s 57(3)), either with the leave of the trial judge or with the leave of the Court of Appeal (s 57(4)). Plainly, it will be quicker to obtain the leave of the trial judge as this can be done once the terminating ruling has been announced and the Crown has elected to appeal. To seek the leave of the Court of Appeal is normally a paper exercise, although oral leave may be sought where leave has been refused after submitting a written application. The exact details of the procedure will be contained in rules of court made under s 73. Whichever route is used, there will be facilities to seek an expedited hearing for the substantive matter of whether the ruling was proper or not under s 59 or s 64. Again, rules of court will set out the finer procedural points, but there will be a choice of an expedited hearing or a non-expedited one. The choice is that of the judge who made the ruling and once the Crown announces its intentions, he must decide whether or not to expedite matters. The Court of Appeal may reverse his decision to expedite, as may the judge himself (s 59(4)). Where either court rules that a hearing should be non-expedited, two

---

25 *Yates* (1872) 12 Cox 233.

26 *R v Manchester Crown Court ex parte DPP* [1994] AC 9, HL.

27 *DPP v Crown Court at Manchester and Huckfield* [1993] NLJR 1711, DC.

28 *R v Manchester Crown Court ex parte DPP* (above).

additional powers come into play under s 59(3) – to order an adjournment of the trial from which the ruling emanated or to discharge the jury where one had been sworn.

7.14 Section 59(3) (and s 64(3)) confirms that the automatic discharge of any jury is not required. Proceedings may be continued in respect of any offence which is not the subject of the appeal. The trial can continue, providing the issues being appealed against can in practice be divorced from the remainder of the trial. Where that is not the case the whole trial will have to be held in abeyance, but where, say, there is a clear issue relating to one minor count, or an accused playing a minor role where there are others on indictment, it may be practical to continue without that count or individual. Both prosecution and defence will want to make representations if the judge indicates that he is minded to continue the trial, as each may have its own perceptions as to whether or not the absence of part of the issues may prejudice the conduct of the trial pending appeal. MPs were perplexed by the potential for chaos in such a situation. The idea of some pieces of the case being split off to go to the Court of Appeal, thus 'on hold' in the Crown Court, yet the unaffected part of the trial continuing (if a trial has commenced) bemused some. Issues that might arise include: what happens to the jury (if one has been sworn) if all of the defendants or all of the counts on the indictment are being appealed against, the proceedings cannot proceed because of s 58(10) and a Court of Appeal ruling is awaited? How are conflicting commitments of judge or advocate to be managed if a delay in a complex case (or one that goes to the House of Lords) is substantial? Crown Court or Court of Appeal rules will need to be drawn up, or judicial protocols created, as to what is to be regarded as 'expedited' and 'non-expedited'.[29] It may well be that, in an effort to avoid delay and uncertainty occasioned by any appeal, the prosecution and defence may see their way to offering or accepting pleas of guilty with which both are content.

Further procedural considerations

7.15 Sections 58 to 60 and ss 64 to 66 govern the time when an appeal may be launched, the effect of a pending appeal upon a Part 9 ruling, the prosecution obligations in connection with any appeal and the limits upon the judge once notice of appeal has been given.

The Crown may appeal a ruling made at 'an applicable time', defined by s 58(13) as ' ... in relation to a trial on indictment, ... any time (whether before or after the commencement of the trial) before the start of the judge's summing-up to the jury'. Given the far greater proposed use of preparatory hearings at ss 309 to 310, Part 9 brings the new prosecution rights of appeal into line with those it already possessed in serious fraud preparatory hearings under the CJA 1987. Rulings made during the judge's summing-up are immune from appeal by the Crown. The wording of the Act might have extended to the taking of any verdict or, in the event no verdict is reached, the discharge of the jury, because there might be situations where a ruling or direction is given after a summing-up has commenced or, even, during a retirement. That said, it is clearly the intention not to provide an opportunity for disruption of the final stage of jury trial, the summing-up and consideration of verdict.

---

29 The Solicitor-General indicated that rules would set out the procedure to be followed: see HC Committee, 25 February 2003.

7.16   There is a discretion on the part of a judge to grant an adjournment which the Crown may well wish to request while it considers whether or not to appeal. The danger of appealing is that in some cases where the appeal is unsuccessful, the Crown must 'throw in its hand' under s 58(8) and accept that the defendant should be found not guilty, thus appeals are not a step to undertake lightly. However, there is no equivalent obligation for appeals against evidentiary rulings (s 66(3)). The Bill originally provided an immediate right to an adjournment,[30] but this was fraught with uncertainties about how long the Crown would take to make a decision.[31] The Solicitor-General observed:

> 'It is envisaged that on day one the judge will say he or she is minded to give the ruling. Things will then swing into action. Overnight, the CPS will have to make high-level decisions. On day two it will become clear whether an appeal will happen, and the court of Appeal will decide whether it is expedited. In an expedited case, the intention is that it will take place within a few days.'

A prudent prosecutor may come to a view in advance as to whether or not to appeal if a particular ruling is made. Nevertheless, no advocate will wish to rush into an appeal. Once a decision to appeal has been reached, the Crown must announce its intention by informing the court of it or by asking for an adjournment to consider the position (s 58(4)). When giving notice of its intention to appeal where there are two or more offences affected by the ruling, the prosecution must state which offences will be the subject of the appeal as it may appeal all or only some of the offences.[32]

7.17   Section 58(7) provides details of how rulings of no case to answer under *Galbraith* will be dealt with, in order to limit appeals. Where the judge accedes to a submission of no case, the prosecution must inform the court of its intention to appeal under s 58(7), and it may also nominate other rulings made during the currency of the case against which it wishes to appeal. This creates, in effect, a retrospective right of appeal. This would prevent premature appeals against individual rulings, and the prosecution is able to take stock of their cumulative effect where such a submission is made and succeeds. The rationale for this was explained as follows:[33]

> ' . . . a ruling of no case to answer is a special case. It may well be preceded by a number of earlier rulings, each of them incrementally weakening the prosecution case. The effect of some or all of those earlier rulings might contribute significantly to the judge's eventual decision to make the ruling of no case to answer . . . In that way the Court of Appeal will have a better grasp of the case and . . . will be able to review more effectively the judge's terminating ruling.'

Any other rulings allied to the fatal no case ruling need to be identified as such by the Crown when giving notice of its intention to appeal. It is also incumbent on the prosecution at this stage to indicate under s 58(8) and (9) that, in the event that leave to appeal is not granted, or it abandons any appeal, it will agree that the defendant should be acquitted in relation to each offence whose terminating ruling had given rise to an appeal under this part. This is an incentive to choose only the most meritorious

---

30   Clause 51.

31   HC Committee, 25 February 2003, col 1125.

32   Sections 58(6), 62(5).

33   HL Committee, 30 October 2003, col 444.

grounds of appeal rather than acting out of frustration after an adverse ruling. To ensure this result, s 58(12) requires the judge, if leave is not granted or the appeal is abandoned, to acquit the defendant in respect of each offence which has been the subject of an appeal. The Court of Appeal has the same power.

Effect of the terminating ruling on the trial

7.18 Once the intention to appeal has been indicated, the part of the trial affected is frozen because of s 58(11), as the judge's ruling can have no effect on the offence(s) to which it relates. Nor may any consequences which would normally flow from such a ruling come into effect and the judge cannot take any actions based on the ruling as he would have been able to do had no appeal been initiated. Any such actions do not take effect pending appeal.

DETERMINATION BY THE COURT OF APPEAL

7.19 Rules made under s 73 will cover such matters as procedure and time-limits. Significant pre-Act discussion and liaison has already occurred to achieve these.[34]

Powers on appeal under s 61 or s 62 – single rulings

7.20 The Court of Appeal has the power under s 61(1) to confirm, reverse or vary any ruling to which an appeal under s 58 relates. Where the prosecution's appeal is dismissed, if the appeal relates to a single ruling (but not necessarily a single offence), s 61(3) requires the Court, when confirming the trial judge's terminating ruling, to acquit the defendant on each count which was the subject of the unsuccessful appeal, or to vary the ruling, perhaps removing any unlawful part or re-drafting it or perhaps by limiting its effect to particular offences or defendants.

The Court must set out, when confirming, reversing or varying a terminating ruling, which of the offences are covered by its decision (s 61(4)). Further, when reversing or varying a ruling the Court must make one of the following three orders under s 61(4):

- that the proceedings resume;
- that a fresh trial takes place; or
- that the defendant be acquitted,

but the first or second order may be made only where it considers it necessary in the interests of justice to do so (s 61(5)).

Rulings of no case to answer and allied terminating rulings

7.21 Where the appeal consists of an appeal against such a ruling, plus others made en route[35] to the submission of no case to answer being made, s 61(7)–(8) applies.

Section 61(6) makes it plain that these clauses apply to no case rulings *and* one or more other rulings. The Court of Appeal in such an instance must, if it confirms the

---

34   Harriet Harman, Solicitor-General, HC Committee, 25 February 2003, cols 1125–1126.

35   See **7.17**.

trial judge's ruling of no case, order an acquittal in respect of the offence(s) which were the subject of the appeal. However, if the ruling of no case is varied or reversed, then one of the orders under s 61(4) must be made providing that order will be in the interests of justice. Given that it is not mandatory to make a particular order on varying or reversing a ruling under s 61, the Court of Appeal has some discretion as to how it can act following a prosecution appeal. It seems that it is possible to find for the prosecution, yet order an acquittal, although this is scarcely likely.

Appeals in the House of Lords

7.22 These should be rare and will tail off as judges and advocates become familiar with the new legislation and how it is being interpreted by the Court of Appeal. Section 68 gives the Lords power to deal with appeals from the Court of Appeal by amending the CJA 1988 to take into account this new kind of appeal. That is the extent of the change. The House of Lords has the same powers as the Court of Appeal.

Appeals in respect of evidentiary rulings

7.23 As noted earlier,[36] the Act creates a second type of appeal, those against evidentiary rulings. The regime is different, and governed by ss 62 to 67, introduced at a late stage. The Attorney-General explained[37] that the right of appeal (against a terminating ruling) will not always be enough. There will be situations in criminal trials where an evidentiary ruling has a significant impact for the worse on a prosecution case, but is not fatal to it. In such cases there was a need for review by the Court of Appeal.[38] Accordingly, these provisons were introduced in place of wider provisions relating to non-terminating rulings that were widely drawn and likely to give rise to too many appeals.

What may be appealed?

7.24 A 'qualifying evidentiary ruling' may be appealed. Section 62(9) defines an evidentiary ruling as one made by a judge on trial on indictment at any time (whether before or after the commencement of the trial) before the opening of the case for the defence.

'Evidentiary' means a ruling relating to admissibility and the exclusion of prosecution evidence (s 62(9)) and 'qualifying offence' refers to those offences listed in Sch 4, Part 1 (certain grave offences). Section 62(10) permits the Home Secretary to add, remove or modify the descriptions of those offences.

7.25 A ruling excluding a confession under s 76 of PACE may deprive the Crown of vital evidence, significantly weakening its case. It removes evidence central to the Crown's case from the trial, and will amount to an evidentiary ruling provided it relates to a qualifying offence. So, too, with the exclusion of a confession under s 78 of PACE. A ruling to exclude because the evidence has become contaminated (s 107) may give rise to the right for a retrial, but in any event is arguably an evidentiary

---

36 See **7.6**.

37 Lord Goldsmith, HL Committee, 30 October 2003, col 441.

38 Lord Goldsmith, HL Committee, 17 November 2003, col 1787.

ruling, at any rate if its exclusion significantly weakened the prosecution case at that trial. A refusal to rule a witness hostile and thus available for cross-examination could prevent the Crown at least damaging that witness's credibility to stop him supporting the defendant, but often a ruling that a witness is hostile does little to advance the prosecution case once the jury have been properly directed.[39] A denial of an application for a witness summons may prevent a witness from being compelled to give important evidence, leaving the Crown significantly weakened. Likewise, a refusal to permit hearsay to be adduced, say, from a dead witness or one abroad under s 116 may weaken the prosecution case. As with terminating rulings, it is the impact on the prosecution case which will identify whether an appeal may lie against the adverse ruling once the ruling has been identified as an evidentiary one.

An evidentiary ruling leading to a refusal to direct a jury that they may draw an adverse inference against the defendant's silence in interview under s 34 of the CJPOA 1994 might well not be appealable under this provision, given that the courts are reluctant to permit the drawing of inferences except where a case is strong.

Conditions to be met before an appeal may be made

7.26 The Crown may appeal a single evidentiary ruling, but only where it relates to two or more qualifying offences (s 62(3)). Where more than one such ruling is made, no appeal is permitted (s 62(4)) unless each ruling relates to one or more qualifying offence. Under both s 62(3) and (4), the fact that the ruling may relate to a non-qualifying offence is immaterial. There must be the requisite number of qualifying offences to attract the correct combination of rulings for the appeal to satisfy s 62(3).

Section 62(6) reinforces these conditions precedent by stating that the subject of the appeal must be a qualifying offence to which the ruling relates, and permits any other offence to be part of the appeal provided it is joined to a qualifying offence. It would be perverse to allow only qualifying rulings to be appealed. The necessity of the offence being 'qualifying' means that the appeal can only be used in serious cases, preventing it being debased, but if an indictment came back from the Court of Appeal with the prosecution victorious only in relation to the qualifying offences, it could mean that the non-qualifying offences were deemed to have been acquitted by lack of challenge to the ruling terminating them.

Procedural obligations on the prosecution

7.27 Section 62(7) obliges the Crown to give notice of its intention to appeal to the court before the defence case begins and to specify which ruling(s) it intends to appeal and in respect of which offences.

Leave of the trial judge or the Court of Appeal is needed. This is dealt with by s 63, to which reference should be made. Section 64 deals with the expedition of appeals.

---

39 Judicial Studies Board Specimen Direction No 28.

The Court of Appeal's powers

7.28 Section 66 provides for the determination of appeals against qualifying evidentiary rulings. The Court of Appeal retains the power to confirm, vary or reverse the trial judge's ruling(s) and may order:

- resumption of proceedings in the Crown Court;
- a fresh trial – so the jury are discharged and the parties start again; or
- an acquittal in respect of the offence(s) for which the appeal was brought, but only if the prosecution indicates that it does not intend to continue with the prosecution of an offence which has given rise to an appeal (s 66(3)). This may mean that the defendant faces no more charges, but if only some of the indictment was being appealed against, the rest of the offences await resolution either by retrial or resumption of the old trial, depending on what order under s 66 was made before the appeal was heard.

Grounds for reversal of trial judge's ruling

7.29 By s 67, the Court of Appeal is only permitted to reverse a ruling if it is satisfied that it was: wrong in law; involved an error of law or principle; or was one that it was not reasonable for the judge to have made.[40]

Bail or custody pending appeal

7.30 Section 70 amends the custody time-limits under the Prosecution of Offences Act 1985 (POA 1985) so as to read that time spent in custody pending appeal under Part 9 does not count towards those limits, which were originally devised to prevent undue lengths of time being spent on prison remand prior to the trial. However, it is important to note that this applies to appeals made before the trial starts, ie when the jury are empanelled. Once the trial is under way, the custody time-limits under s 22 of the POA 1985 cease to apply. Section 70 is drafted to include pre-trial rulings which generate appeals under this Part. Excepting an application to the Court of Appeal for bail pending the prosecution appeal against the trial judge's ruling, the defendant has little prospect of bail unless he was already on bail during the trial.

---

40 Presumably following the *Wednesbury* principles in *Associated Provincial Picture Houses v Wednesbury Corporation* [1948] 1 KB 223.

Chapter 8

SENTENCING – GENERAL ISSUES

OVERVIEW

8.1 The Act makes major changes to the sentencing process, to the substantive rules relating to custodial and non-custodial sentences, and to the release on licence of life prisoners. In so doing, it gives effect to many of the recommendations of the Halliday Report.[1] In the Government's words: 'It . . . aims to bring sense into sentencing, so that offenders are adequately and appropriately punished and re-offending is reduced'.[2]

In particular:

- it sets out the purposes of sentencing – punishment, public protection, crime reduction, reform and rehabilitation, and reparation;
- it establishes a Sentencing Guidelines Council;
- previous convictions, where recent and relevant, are to be treated as an aggravating factor in determining offence seriousness;
- the sentencing power of magistrates' courts is increased to 12 months in respect of any one summary or either-way offence, and 15 months in respect of two or more such offences in which the terms are to be served consecutively;
- new arrangements are introduced in respect of suspended sentences;
- the current range of community sentences is replaced by a single sentence, which can be tailored to meet the needs of the offence and of the offender;
- prison sentences of less than 12 months are replaced by 'custody plus' – a short period served in custody followed by a longer period under supervision in the community;
- intermittent custody is introduced;
- new arrangements are introduced for extended sentences for dangerous, violent or sexual offenders;
- there is a simplification of the rules for release of prisoners serving more than 12 months;
- there is a new scheme for the setting of the tariff for life prisoners in murder cases;
- a mandatory minimum term is introduced for firearms offences.

The new Act also contains a whole range of other detailed measures. These include widespread changes to maximum penalties, and also repeals of some significant provisions. General principles and issues, fines and increases in maximum terms of imprisonment are dealt with in this chapter. The major changes to the arrangements

---

1 · See **1.4**.

2   Government Response to Second Report of the Home Affairs Committee, Cm 5787 (March 2003).

relating to custodial and community sentences are dealt with in Chapters 9 and 10 respectively.

COMMENCEMENT

8.2   The sentencing provisions will come into force on a day or days to be appointed. It is likely that some of the provisions will take a period of years to be brought into force, given the resource enhancement needs prior to the implementation of new disposals such as 'custody plus'.

The provisions relating to the minimum term to be served for a mandatory life sentence came into effect on 18 December 2003.[3]

The provisions relating to intermittent custody came into force on 26 January 2004,[4] and are to be piloted in two areas as from that date. These will be in two purpose-built sites in Derbyshire and Lancashire.[5] The new provisions relating to suspended sentences ('custody minus') are likely to be fully implemented during the financial year 2005/06. The implementation of 'custody plus' is likely to begin during 2006/07.

The provisions relating to sentences for firearms offences came into force on 22 January 2004. Those relating to sentencing and allocation guidelines, and increases in penalties for certain driving-related offences, came into force on 27 February 2004.

REPEALS

8.3   Key features of the current sentencing landscape are repealed. Section 303 repeals the provisions in the CJA 1991 relating to early release of prisoners, ss 80 to 82 of the CDA 1998 relating to sentencing guidelines, ss 29, 33, 35 and 40 of the Crime (Sentences) Act 1997 (CSA 1997), and certain provisions in the Powers of Criminal Courts (Sentencing) Act 2000 (SA 2000):

-   ss 41 to 59 (community orders available only where the offender is aged 16 or over – community rehabilitation orders, community punishment orders, community punishment and rehabilitation orders, drug treatment and testing orders, drug abstinence orders, orders for persistent petty offenders). The provisions of the new Act replace these (see Chapter 10);
-   s 85 (extended licence for sexual or violent offence) (see **9.38** et seq);
-   ss 87 and 88 (credit for periods of remand in custody) (see **9.75**);
-   s 109 (mandatory life sentence for second serious offence, first introduced by s 2 of the CSA 1997); and
-   ss 188 to 125 (the provisions relating to suspended sentences).

Schedule 37 makes further repeals. These are consequential upon provisions contained in the new Act. Of these, the repeal of ss 80 and 81 of the Crime and Disorder Act 1998 came into effect on 27 February 2004. In particular, note should be

---

3   Section 336(2): see **9.78**.

4   See **1.4**.

5   Baroness Scotland, HL Report, 5 November 2003, col 863.

taken of the repeal of the provisions relating to longer than commensurate sentences contained in s 80 of the SA 2000.

BACKGROUND – THE HALLIDAY REPORT

8.4 The Halliday Report was the conclusion of a review 'born out of a belief that the present sentencing structure suffers from serious deficiencies that reduce its contributions to crime reduction and public confidence'.[6] Among the deficiencies of the pre-existing law which it believed 'cried out' for change were the lack of any clear message about the effect of persistent offending on severity of sentence; the absence of reality in the second half of sentences; and the continued unexploited opportunities for non-custodial sentences, including reparation for victims. It saw both limitations and opportunities, considering that the pre-existing statutory framework had a narrow sense of purpose.[7]

The effect of the changes made by the CJA 1991 was to require sentencers to concentrate primarily on the offences committed and the level of punishment commensurate with those offences. Despite the fact that inroads were made into that principle by allowances for previous convictions, permitted by the swift amendment of the 1991 Act by the CJA 1993 and, more recently, by the mandatory and minimum sentences introduced by the CSA 1997,[8] the concepts of proportionality and just deserts form the corner-stones of sentencing principle in the pre-existing law.[9]

Proportionality requires the court to weigh the seriousness of the offence, together with any associated offences, both in relation to other offences and in relation to the range of punishments available to it. It addresses issues relating to the impact of the offence and the degree of culpability. Sentencers, the Report observed,[10] are not encouraged to consider crime reduction or reparation. Nor does statutory guidance exist on how offence seriousness was to be measured, a matter left to guideline judgments from the Court of Appeal, latterly in partnership with the Sentencing Advisory Panel, or to the Magistrates' Courts Sentencing Guidelines drawn up by the Magistrates' Association (most recently in January 2004).

8.5 The attempt to establish a regime based on just deserts was not consistently applied. The taking into account of previous convictions, the reinstatement of deterrence as an aim of sentencing, the power (in s 59 of the SA 2000) to impose a community sentence in place of a fine even where the offence for which the fine was imposed was not serious enough to justify such a sentence, and the power (introduced by s 53 of the CJCSA 2000)[11] to impose a prison sentence for non-compliance with a

---

6 *Making Punishments Work: Report of a Review of the Sentencing Framework for England and Wales* (Home Office, July 2001) ('the Halliday Report'), Introduction (available at www.homeoffice.gov.uk/docs/halliday.html).

7 *Ibid*, para 1.8.

8 Mandatory life sentence for second serious offence (s 109 of the SA 2000, repealed by s 303); minimum term of seven years for third Class A drug offence (s 110 of the SA 2000); minimum term of three years for third domestic burglary (s 111 of the SA 2000).

9 For offence seriousness, see in particular *Howells* [1999] 1 Cr App R 98, CA. See, generally, **8.33**.

10 At para 1.9.

11 See, now, **8.43**.

community sentence illustrate how principles of just deserts were diluted or not fully observed. The 1991 attempt to construct a new framework for sentencing, said Halliday, failed to achieve its purpose, with no 'new vision' being put in place. The result was a 'muddle, which is not good for consistency, public understanding, or a sense amongst the various agencies involved in sentencing. Practitioners complain bitterly about the consequent complexities and inconsistencies', which were seen as a drag both on efficiency and effectiveness.[12]

8.6 Despite the work done through guideline judgments given by the Court of Appeal, in tandem with the Sentencing Advisory Panel, Halliday regarded the sentencing framework as inaccessible, with a mass of often difficult and obscurely worded statutory provision and case-law. That might be partly the product of incessant legislative intervention, the repeal of provisions scarcely brought into force (if at all[13]), ongoing and frequent changes in policy direction, and even the ongoing amendment of the consolidating legislation (the SA 2000).[14] Whatever the reasons, the Report identified the need for the framework to be more accessible.[15]

The result of this lack of a clear framework was considered to be inconsistency and lack of public confidence, particularly in the context of the sentencing of persistent offenders. The role of previous convictions was far from clear, even though s 151 of the SA 2000 permitted a court to take them into account in determining offence seriousness[16] and through the doctrine of progressive loss of mitigation – the doctrine where the reduction in the severity of sentence that may be made on account of an offender's good character is progressively lost as the number of previous convictions increases.[17] Of course, in some circumstances even good character was of marginal relevance.[18]

8.7 Halliday concluded that the case for change was clear. As well as there being a need for a more accessible framework, decisions in individual cases need to be clearly understood. The legal framework needed to do more to require decisions to be explained, to ensure that sentences mean what they say, and are understood. Further, the use of short prison sentences served limited purposes.[19] The sentencing framework needed to address more directly the purposes of crime reduction and reparation, as well as punishment.[20] Prison sentences of less than 12 months were of limited value, while longer sentences had limited supervision after release. There was also uncertain and unpredictable treatment of persistent offenders.

Community sentences were not seen as sufficiently punitive or protective of the general public. Little guidance existed on how to measure the relative severity of the

---

12   Halliday Report, *op cit*, para 1.36.

13   See the provisions relating to dangerous offenders discussed at **9.38**.

14   The CJCSA 2000 amended the SA 2000 before the latter was even in force.

15   *Op cit*, para 1.39.

16   For the role of previous convictions in PBV, see **4.6**.

17   See, eg, *Queen* (1981) 3 Cr App R (S) 245, CA.

18   See, eg, *Billam* [1986] 1 WLR 349, CA.

19   See *Kefford* [2002] Crim LR 432, CA; *Mills* [2002] 2 Cr App R (S) 51, CA.

20   Halliday Report, *op cit*, para 1.71.

various non-custodial orders, despite the passage of s 53 of the CJCSA 2000, which provided that, if a community sentence breaks down as a result of non-compliance by the offender, a prison sentence should normally be substituted.[21] The requirement to consider some crime reduction purposes is present for some orders but not others. Reparation (other than financial) is notably absent for adults, although now a key area of aspects of provisions relating to young offenders.[22]

Current arrangements for enforcement of sentences are inconsistent and unclear, with varying mechanisms for dealing with breach of licence or community sentence. The pre-existing law did not encourage 'continuous review' of offenders' progress, except in the context of drug treatment and testing orders (DTTOs).[23]

8.8 The Report considered that the new, and more integrated, national leadership and management of the prison and probation services, with a strategy of 'What Works' involving sophisticated risk assessment systems, and the development of accredited programmes, provided real opportunities. It could enable case-workers to develop programmes most likely to work for the individual offender. These programmes might include developing the offenders' thinking and understanding, to address attitudes and likelihood of re-offending; reducing drug or alcohol addiction or dependency; improving literacy and numeracy levels, or other aspects of their education; or by improving job-related skills.[24] Research studies indicated that, with development, such programmes could reduce re-conviction rates to, perhaps, 40% from the present level of 56%. An appropriate sentencing framework was needed to help these decisions, and to maximise the chances of success.

It also considered that a sentencing framework can secure specific changes in sentencing behaviour by courts.[25] It can encourage public confidence, encourage the deterrent effect of sentences in appropriate cases, place added value on the incapacitation of persistent offenders and provide greater opportunities for reform and rehabilitation, and for reparation. In these ways it can make an important contribution to crime reduction and public confidence. The Report considered that the available evidence supported the following conclusions:

– public confidence could be improved through changes which improve awareness of sentencing practices;

– changing present levels of punishment as an end in itself, or exclusively to enhance deterrence or incapacitative effects on crime, would not be justified;

– improvements in the present state of knowledge about deterrence and incapacitation are desirable;

– outcomes are more likely to be improved by targeting resources on the offenders most likely to re-offend, and who commit offences serious enough to cause concern to local communities;

---

21 Now repealed.

22 See, eg, supervision order with requirement for reparation: SA 2000, ss 63–68, Sch 6, para 2(d).

23 Halliday Report, *op cit*, para 1.29. DTTOs, dealt with by SA 2000, s 62, are repealed by the new Act: see now **10.23**.

24 Halliday Report, *op cit*, para 1.48.

25 *Ibid*, para 1.57.

– if targeting persistent offenders reduced crime through additional deterrence, incapacitation or both, that would be a bonus. Changes in the framework aimed at promoting effective work with offenders during their sentences are most likely to improve outcomes; and

– there is greater scope for general attention to reparation.

In that context, the Report addressed, first, the principles of sentencing, and then the detailed issues which formed the bulk of the Report's recommendations. The Act is intended to implement the Halliday recommendations. The provisions of the Act in turn form the basis of a further raft of far-reaching reforms recommended by the Carter Review[26] in December 2003. These include the establishment of a new National Offender Management Service (NOMS) and the setting of sentencing guidelines on the new sentences within two years.

PRINCIPLES OF SENTENCING

8.9 Mixed messages have sometimes been sent about the objectives which sentencers are trying to achieve, with a consequent lack of consideration of opportunities such as reparation and rehabilitation. There has been, in the context of adults, no statutory statement of the principles a court should adopt, although, in the context of young offenders, s 37 of the CDA 1998 states that the principal aim of the youth justice system is to prevent re-offending by children and young persons.

The new Act will now require a court, when passing a sentence, to have regard to the purposes of sentencing identified in s 142. A 'sentence' for this purpose includes any order made by a court when dealing with the offender in respect of his offence, and will thus include orders such as compensation orders, or orders for deportation (s 142(3)).

The purposes of sentencing identified by s 142 are:

(a) the punishment of offenders;
(b) the reduction of crime (including its reduction by deterrence);
(c) the reform and rehabilitation of offenders;
(d) the protection of the public; and
(e) the making of reparation by offenders to persons affected by their offences.

This reparation may be either financial or non-financial.[27] The term 'persons affected' means not only an individual who might be affected but also the wider community.[28] Thus, the thief of eggs from an endangered bird species might properly be required to make reparation by working in a bird sanctuary, despite the fact that there may be no *individual* affected (only the birds themselves).[29]

The provision does not apply to certain types of offender (s 142(2)). Young offenders fall within the provisions of s 37(1) of the CDA 1998. The provision is clearly

---

26 *Correctional Services Review*, 11 December 2003 (available at www.homeoffice.gov.uk).

27 Hilary Benn MP, HC Committee, 30 January 2003, cols 715–716.

28 *Ibid*, col 732.

29 The colourful example given David Heath MP, and adopted by the Minister of State, HC Committee, 30 January 2003, col 718.

inapplicable to those being sentenced for an offence the sentence for which is fixed by law, or for an offence that falls under s 110 or s 111 of the SA 2000. Nor is it applicable to any order in respect of dangerous offenders under ss 225 to 228 of the Act, or where one of the orders under Part 3 of the Mental Health Act 1983 (MHA 1983)[30] is made.

Nothing in s 142 specifically requires the new Sentencing Guidelines Council[31] to have regard to these matters. It is inconceivable that it would not.[32]

8.10 Some consider that this statement of purposes should include the need to maintain public confidence, and the prevalence of the offence in the community.[33] This is, in pre-existing law, a matter relevant to offence seriousness.[34] There can be, it was argued, good reasons for differential sentencing practice that reflect the priorities of sentencers in different localities. This is clearly an area of some difficulty, because lack of consistency in sentencing practice was one of the failings of the sentencing system identified by the Halliday Report and the Government in *Justice for All*. There is nothing in s 142 that prevents 'well-justified' local variations, and is likely to be one of the factors to which the Sentencing Guidelines Council will have regard when issuing sentencing guidelines.[35] Yet, in the House of Lords, Baroness Scotland observed:[36]

> 'Nor do we think that the maintenance of public confidence and the prevalence of the offence in the locality should feature on the list of purposes of sentencing. While we agree that sentencing and the framework within which it operates need to earn and merit public confidence, this is a complex relationship and not one in which sentencers can simply be "driven by the wind of public mood". Public understanding of sentencing is regrettably low ... We need to do much more to improve this but we should not make public confidence – or the prevalence of local offending – an aim of sentencing. This could lead to very inconsistent sentencing around different parts of the country. Creating an effective sentencing framework in which sentences and the treatment of offenders promote public confidence is certainly a necessary goal. We believe that there is sufficient flexibility in [the wording of s 142] to allow local expression of issues which are pressing and difficult in a particular area'.

This serves only to demonstrate the difficulty with general statements of purpose. Local sentencing responses to local problems are seeking to achieve a 'reduction in crime', or 'the protection of the public'. A sentencer will not often have difficulty in having regard to any of the matters stated. The crucial question is the weight to be given to each such matter. Further, the wording of s 142 is 'must have regard', not 'must have regard only ... ', and s 142 does not appear to prevent a court from having

---

30 A hospital order (with or without a restriction order), an interim hospital order or a limitation direction.

31 See **8.13**.

32 Hilary Benn MP, HC Committee, 30 January 2003, col 722.

33 See, eg, Dominic Grieve MP, HC Committee, 30 January 2003, col 730.

34 *Cunningham* (1993) Cr App R (S) 444, CA; *Cox* (1993) 96 Cr App R 464, CA.

35 Hilary Benn MP, HC Committee, 30 January 2003, col 733.

36 Baroness Scotland, HL Committee, 6 October 2003, col 50.

regard to any other matter. The Government consistently denied any intention to limit the discretion of sentencers. That said, the passage cited above, and other expressions of governmental policy, all point towards the matters identified in s 142 as being the only purposes to which it is intended a court should have regard. The view of the Sentencing Guidelines Council will be key.

8.11   Section 142 gives no guidance as to which of these matters is to be given priority in sentencing and, for that reason, may end up being of little value. The priorities will be for the sentencing court to determine within the framework of sentencing principles and guidelines developed by the courts and the new Sentencing Guidelines Council. This may in fact lead to a 'pick 'n' mix' approach to sentencing,[37] lacking the coherent philosophy that Halliday sought. The statutory statement of purposes may not change the existing practice of the courts, although one objective of such a statement, perhaps, is to require a court to have regard to a wider range of matters than simply the proportionality of the sentence to the offence and to issues of deterrence. Matters of punishment, rehabilitation of offenders and reparation are all matters of equal relevance, as is public protection through deterrence or the nature of the offence. It will also set out clearly, for the wider public, the purposes of sentencing.

Section 142 does not eliminate the need to have regard to the proportionality of the offence: the term used by s 142 is '*must* have regard to', not '*must* have regard *only* to'. The Halliday Report specifically stated that the principle of proportionate punishment needs to be sustained.[38] That raises the question: proportionate to what? The Halliday Report related the sentence to what the offender had done. That leads to the detailed recommendations about matters which affect the seriousness of the offence, for example antecedent criminal behaviour, or persistent offending.[39]

8.12   There remains the question of why these general principles do not apply to certain types of offence which attract minimum or mandatory sentences. Logically, they should apply to all offences. The reality is that Parliament has chosen in some cases to remove the sentencing discretion of the court, either because it considers that, for wider reasons such as public perceptions or opinions, a mandatory sentence is required (murder being an example), or that, because of recidivism, and the perceived need to address it through deterrence or incapacitation, one particular sentencing aim should be pursued (through the minimum sentence) to the exclusion of others.

SENTENCING AND ALLOCATION GUIDELINES

8.13   Section 167 establishes a Sentencing Guidelines Council, and s 169 provides for the continuation of the Sentencing Advisory Panel created by the Crime and Disorder Act 1998. It came into force on 27 February 2004, as did s 168(3)–(5) and ss 169 to 173.[40]

---

37   The phrase of Lord Dholakia, HL Report, 4 November 2003, col 762.

38   Halliday Report, *op cit*, para 2.6. See also Baroness Scotland, HL Report, 4 November 2003, col 765.

39   See **8.32–8.40**.

40   See **1.3**.

The Sentencing Guidelines Council will be chaired by the Lord Chief Justice and comprise others appointed by the Lord Chancellor after consultation with the Home Secretary and Lord Chief Justice (s 167(2), (3)). The composition of the Council is to include seven judicial members (s 167(1)). The judicial membership must include a circuit judge, district judge (magistrates' courts) and a lay justice (s 167(3)). As the Bill was originally drafted, the Council was to have had an exclusively judicial composition, but during its passage this was amended to include a non-judicial element (s 167(1), (4)). It will have four non-judicial members with experience in policing, criminal prosecution, criminal defence or the welfare of victims. This change proved highly controversial, and was deprecated by Lord Woolf, the Lord Chief Justice, as a significant incursion into judicial discretion.[41] He complained of 'the legislature taking over what has been accepted to be the proper role of the judiciary'.[42]

The response of the Government was to stress the desirability of non-judicial input. The Minister of State observed that 'All of society has an interest in sentencing. [The proposal] is intended to bring in that wider interest', although the Minister did not explain how that wider non-judicial input was not reflected by the non-legally qualified membership of the Sentencing Advisory Panel that currently exists. The Minister also attempted to provide reassurance in relation to membership of the Council by civil servants: one out of the five non-judicial members will be there by virtue of their office – the Director of Public Prosecutions.[43] Some might consider it more appropriate for the Act to have clearly stated this, and who might not be appointed, given the importance in ensuring independence of sentencing from the Executive.

8.14   The purpose of the Council is to continue and develop the work currently done by the Court of Appeal through guideline judgments and the Magistrates' Association Sentencing Guidelines, but with a wider input.[44] It is intended to enable the judiciary, practitioners and Parliament to work together, although it is not entirely clear what it achieves that is not currently being achieved by the Court of Appeal and Sentencing Advisory Panel.[46] Sections 80 and 81 of the CDA 1998 (sentencing guidelines from the Court of Appeal) are repealed, but with that repeal goes the requirement that the Court of Appeal must consult the Sentencing Advisory Panel before issuing guideline judgments. Some see that as entitling the Court of Appeal on its own to issue guideline

---

41   HL, 2nd Reading, 16 June 2003, col 574.

42   Lord Woolf, *op cit*, col 997.

43   See s 167(5).

44   HL Committee, 6 October 2003, col 30.

45   The Court of Appeal has given significant numbers of guideline judgments on the advice of the Sentencing Advisory Panel, including in respect of offences of rape: *Millberry, Morgan and Lackenby* [2003] Crim LR 561, CA; child pornography: *Oliver, Hartley and Baldwin* [2003] Crim LR 127, CA; possession of offensive weapons: *Celaire and Poulton* [2003] Crim LR 124, CA; domestic burglary: *McInerney and Keating* [2002] EWCA Crim 3003, [2003] Crim LR 209, CA; street robbery: *R* [2003] Crim LR 898, CA; causing death by dangerous driving: *Cooksley* [2003] Crim LR 564, CA. The Lord Chief Justice's *Practice Direction on Life Sentences for Murder*, in May 2002, was issued after consultation with the Panel: see [2002] 4 All ER 1089, CA. The Panel is unhappy at the new Council's non-judicial composition: see Lord Ackner, HL Committee, 6 October 2003, col 317.

judgments (as it did before the creation of the Sentencing Advisory Panel),[46] but that is not the view of the Lord Chief Justice.[47] The Panel remains in being (s 169), but the Act does not regulate the powers of the Panel other than as to how it must interact with the Council. Nothing in the new Act theoretically prevents the Court of Appeal from developing its own guidelines independently, although that would scarcely fall within the overall scheme of the legislation, nor, unsurprisingly, is there any provision *preventing* the Court from continuing to seek the views of the Panel, because it is the clear intention that guidelines be developed through the *Council*. Arguably, the Panel *must* follow the route through the Council identified by s 170(2).

8.15   Section 170 deals with the making of guidelines relating either to the sentencing of offenders ('sentencing guidelines') or to decisions by a magistrates' court (under s 19 of the MCA 1980) as to mode of trial ('allocation guidelines').

The Sentencing Guidelines Council may decide to frame or revise guidelines, or may be required to *consider* doing so by the Home Secretary (s 170(2)), although it is not obliged to do more than consider such a request. The Home Secretary has no power to require the Council to formulate guidelines. Guidelines may be general in nature, or limited to a particular category of offence or type of offender.

8.16   When framing or revising 'sentencing guidelines', the Council must have regard to the need to promote consistency in sentencing, the sentences imposed by courts, the cost of different sentences and their relative effectiveness in preventing re-offending, the need to promote public confidence in the criminal justice system and the views communicated to it by the Sentencing Advisory Panel. The Council is not required to address the purposes of sentencing.[49] Although the purposes of sentencing are for sentencers, the guidelines formulated will in fact address the types and levels of sentence for particular offences, and it is odd that the Council is not equally required to have regard to the statutory statement of purpose. It is inconceivable that it would not do so. The Carter Review[49] also envisages that the Council will stabilise sentencing practice, and look to rebuilding the use of fines. Within five years it is proposed that the Council would be issuing annual guidelines informed by Government priorities to manage the demand for prison and probation [sic], ensuring the cost-effective use of capacity.[50]

8.17   The matters to which the Council must have regard in respect of allocation guidelines are set out in s 170(5) and include the need for consistency in allocation decisions, and any views of the Panel.

8.18   Sentencing guidelines in respect of an offence or category of offences must include criteria for the determining the seriousness of the offence, including (where appropriate) criteria for determining the weight to be given to any previous

---

46   See the submission of Professor David Thomas to the Constitution Committee of the House of Lords.

47   See HL Report, 5 November 2003, col 842.

48   See **8.9**.

49   *Ibid.*

50   *Op cit*, p 41.

convictions of offenders (s 170(7)). This effectively re-enacts the provisions of s 80(4) of the CDA 1998 (in relation to the pre-existing sentencing guidelines) and invites the question of why existing approaches to previous convictions in sentencing were inadequate. The answer is not that the attitudes of the courts to previous convictions were unclear but, rather, that the Government did not agree with them.

8.19   A sentencing court has a duty to have regard to any guidelines which are relevant to the offender's case, and have regard to them in exercising any other function relating to the sentencing of offenders (s 172(1)). The court must also *have regard* to the purposes of sentencing. Nothing binds a court to follow a specific position slavishly without regard to the facts of the individual case. Within the scope of the guidelines, sentencers retain discretion. However, it will not be open for a sentencer to disagree with the guidelines, and if a court fails to apply any applicable guidelines it faces being varied on appeal either at the instance of the offender or, in the case of an over-lenient sentence, at the instance of the Attorney-General.

PRE-SENTENCE REPORTS AND MEDICAL REPORTS

Definition and copies

8.20   Section 158 re-enacts the definition of a pre-sentence report (PSR),[51] with the most minor of textual amendments in respect of who must prepare such a report. Section 159 re-enacts the terms of s 156 of the SA 2000 with a slight amendment. The Bill originally proposed that a copy of the report must be given to the offender (unless he is under 17 and unrepresented, in which case it must be given to his parent or guardian), to his counsel or solicitor, and to the prosecutor. Following criticism of this provision by the Joint Committee on Human Rights,[52] s 159 now provides that a juvenile should receive a full copy of the PSR or other report, irrespective of whether the juvenile is represented, or accompanied by a parent or guardian, unless the court considers that to do so would place the juvenile at risk of significant harm.[53] The court must also provide the parent or guardian with a full copy of the report unless it considers that to do so would place the juvenile at risk of significant harm. This is in line with existing Youth Justice Board and Department of Health good practice.[54] Section 160 makes similar provision in respect of other reports.

Procedural requirements

8.21   Section 156 re-enacts, with amendments to reflect the changes in formulation of the new preconditions for the making of a custodial or community sentence, the provisions in s 36 and s 81 of the SA 2000 which cover pre-sentence reports for community and custodial sentences. The general thrust of the PSR requirements remains unchanged.

---

51   Formerly s 162 of the SA 2000.

52   Second Report, Session 2002–2003.

53   'Significant harm' is defined at s 31 of the Children Act 1989, and means ill-treatment or the impairment of health or development.

54   Baroness Scotland, HL Committee, 8 October 2003, col 299.

The circumstances where a PSR will generally be obtained are where one or more of the following questions or issues is being determined:

- in the case of a custodial sentence, whether the offence (with associated offences) is so serious that neither a fine alone nor a community sentence can be justified for the offence;
- where the court is imposing a custodial sentence, the length which is commensurate with its seriousness;
- in the case of life sentences for dangerous offenders aged 18 or over, under s 225, or in the case of detention for life of offenders aged under 18, under s 226, whether there is a significant risk to members of the public of serious harm occasioned by commission of further specified offences, or whether the seriousness of the offence, or the offence and associated offences, justifies life imprisonment or detention for life;
- in the case of extended sentences for certain violent or sexual offences, under s 227 or s 228, whether there is a significant risk to members of the public of serious harm caused by the commission by the offender of further specified offences;
- in the case of community sentences, whether the offence (with any associated offences) is serious enough to warrant such a sentence;
- in the case of a community sentence, whether the restrictions on liberty are commensurate with the seriousness of the offence; and
- in the case of a community sentence, any opinion as to the suitability for the offender of the particular requirements to be imposed in the order.

In respect of a young offender, it was the case that where the offence is not triable on indictment only, and there is no associated offence which is triable only on indictment, the court is not permitted to regard a PSR as unnecessary unless there is a previous PSR and the court has had regard to that report. By s 156(8), a court must now obtain a PSR even if the offence is indictable-only. It is often those cases that require an offence and offender analysis, a risk assessment and details of sentencing options.[56] Nothing in the Act alters the basic principle that in cases where a sentencer is contemplating sending an offender to prison for the first time, he should obtain a PSR.[57]

8.22 Section 157, which deals with requirements for medical reports in the case of a mentally disordered offender, re-enacts with the most minor of textual changes the terms of s 82 of the SA 2000.

It imposes a requirement on a court considering the imposition of a custodial sentence (other than one fixed by law) on a person who is, or appears to be, mentally disordered, to obtain and consider a medical report, unless in the circumstances of the case the court considers it unnecessary to do so. This provision links in to s 157(3), which requires a court in such circumstances to consider any information before it which relates to the offender's mental condition before imposing a custodial sentence, and to

---

55 Baroness Scotland, HL Report, 5 November 2003, col 829.

56 See *Gillette* (1999) *The Times*, 3 December, CA; cf *Armsaramah* [2001] 1 Cr App R (S) 323, CA; *ILCC ex parte Matash* [2001] Crim App R (S) 467, DC.

consider the likely effect of such a sentence on that condition and on any treatment which may be available for it.

The obligatory nature of the provision might appear to be at odds with the residual discretion not to obtain such a report.[57] The exception is intended to deal with situations where such a report already exists, for example, where a court has remanded the person to hospital for treatment under s 36 of the MHA 1983.[58] The Minister of State made it clear that:[59]

> 'we expect the court to have the kind of evidence upon which it can make a properly informed judgment. We believe that any opportunity to exercise this discretion should be used very judiciously. It should be reserved for the exception and should by no means become the rule.'

Pre-sentence drug testing

8.23 The theme of reducing drug-related crime has already been noted.[60] In that context, s 161 introduces a wider power to test, post-conviction but pre-sentence, for Class A drugs. It is intended that this provision be introduced initially in limited areas for evaluative purposes.[61]

Limited drug-testing powers already exist. Section 52 of the SA 2000 contained the power to make a DTTO. This is repealed, and replaced by the new drug rehabilitation requirement provisions.[62] Section 161 goes further, extending the power to order a pre-sentence drug test to anyone aged 14 or over, where the court is considering passing a community sentence. It also amends provisions relating to adults by enabling a pre-sentence drug-testing order to be made where the court is considering passing a suspended sentence.

A community sentence is an order comprising one or more community orders, or one or more youth community orders.[63] The power to order a pre-sentence drug test is not conditional upon the court considering a drug rehabilitation requirement – nor can it do so in the case of 14- to 18-year-olds. The minimum age of 14[64] brings within the ambit of this power 14- to 16-year-olds the subject of a supervision order. The extension of this power to those in the 14 to 17 age group proved controversial, perhaps raising human rights issues. A requirement (on pain of criminal penalty) to undergo a pre-sentence drug test for a Class A drug raises Art 8 ECHR issues, and it will have to be shown that the requirement is necessary and proportionate. The younger the juvenile, arguably the harder that is to do. Where a test is taken in respect of an offender aged under 17, it must be taken in the presence of an appropriate adult (s 161(3), (8)).

---

57   See, eg, Baroness Anelay of St Johns, HL Committee, 8 October 2003, col 300 *et seq*.

58   Baroness Scotland, HL Committee, 8 October 2003, col 302.

59   Baroness Scotland, HL Report, 5 November 2003, col 833.

60   See **2.42**.

61   Baroness Scotland, HL Report, 5 November 2003, col 828.

62   See **10.23**.

63   See **10.5**.

64   This age may be amended by order: s 161(7).

The change is intended to ensure that younger offenders who may be misusing specified Class A drugs are identified and actions taken to address their needs. It is intended to be part of a package of interventions.[65] It will complement assessments by Youth Offending Teams (YOTs), and following arrest referrals. Examples of its possible use are where the offender had not previously been tested or, where despite previous negative tests, the court has reason to believe that the offender is misusing Class A drugs, or where the offender had not co-operated with the YOT and the supervising officer believes the offender has a specified Class A drugs problem. Other examples might be where the offender claims to be no longer using drugs, having tested positive on charge. The matter will be within the discretion of the court: clearly, it must not be used routinely and an order without any basis for believing that there was a Class A drug problem would be open to challenge on Art 8 principles.

8.24   The consent of the offender is not needed before a court makes a s 161 order. Clearly, forcible taking of samples is not envisaged. If it is proved to the satisfaction of the court that the offender has, without reasonable excuse, failed to comply with the order, he may be fined a sum not exceeding level 4 (s 161(5)). If the offender does not agree to give a sample, a court may draw its own conclusions about what is the appropriate disposal for the offender, or what requirements should be imposed as part of a community sentence, or licence conditions on 'custody plus'.[66]

The offence for which the offender has been convicted does not have to be a drugs offence or a drugs-related offence. Nor is there any need for there to be any evidence to justify a conclusion that the offender *might* be a user of Class A drugs. This may lead to a routine use of the testing power which, in the context of restrictions on bail,[67] may have a significant impact.

Fines – power to order financial circumstances statement

8.25   Section 162 re-enacts, in identical terms, what was s 126 of the SA 2000. In some cases a court may wish to know the financial circumstances of the offender and, if it does, it can make a financial circumstances order. Section 162 sets out the preconditions and consequences of failure to comply.

OFFENCE SERIOUSNESS

8.26   The sentencing scheme in the SA 2000 was introduced by the CJA 1991, with thresholds of offence seriousness being set which, in most circumstances, had to be reached before either a community sentence or a custodial sentence could be imposed. By s 79(2) of the SA 2000, a court could not generally pass a custodial sentence unless it was of the opinion that the offence or the combination of the offence, together with any associated offences, was *so serious* that only such a sentence could be justified for such an offence, or, in the case of a violent or sexual offence, that only such a sentence

---

65   Baroness Scotland, HL Report, 5 November 2003, col 826.

66   See **9.2**.

67   See **3.35**.

would be adequate to protect the public from serious harm from the offender.[68] Section 79 is repealed by s 332 and Sch 37.

Further, under s 35(1) of the SA 2000, a court could not pass a community sentence on an offender unless it was of the opinion that the offence, or the combination of the offence and any associated offences, was *serious enough* to warrant such a sentence. That is also repealed.

Section 143 sets out, in some detail, how the seriousness of an offence is to be determined. Sections 148 to 153 set out the thresholds for community sentences and custodial sentences.

8.27   The changes made by the Act stem from the Halliday Report, which concluded[69] that sentence severity should be commensurate with the seriousness of the criminal conduct, in respect of the seriousness of the offence and the offender's criminal history. The seriousness of the offence should also reflect its degree of harm, or risk of harm, and the offender's culpability in committing the offence.[70] The severity of the sentence should also increase to reflect previous convictions, taking into account how recent and relevant they were.

8.28   By s 143(1), a court must, in considering the seriousness of any offence, consider the offender's culpability in committing the offence and the harm, or risk of harm, which the offence caused or was intended to cause. This amounts to a restatement, in more specific terms, of the 'just deserts' principle, of the fact that the punishment should be commensurate with the offence, and relates the punishment to what the offender has actually done. It spells out that culpability – the level of blameworthiness – is a matter to which regard should be had. Despite long semantic debates during the passage of the new Act, the provisions of s 143 do not limit the matters which the court may take into account as aggravating or mitigating factors. In this context, the circumstances of the offence are important,[71] although this should not be misunderstood. Section 143 requires the court to look at issues of individual culpability. This will include the harm caused, or the risk of harm, because the fact that the risk does not translate into actual harm is not within the control of the offender and does not render the culpability of the offender any less great. The circumstances of the offence itself – culpability, harm, risk of harm – are relevant to that.[72] But matters relating to the *surrounding circumstances* do not relate to offence seriousness; rather, these are aggravating or mitigating factors. The Minister of State observed:[73]

'[Section 143] concerns how the court should determine the seriousness of the offence. The circumstances of the offence are an important factor when considering, for example, whether there are any aggravating or mitigating factors. However, here it is the seriousness of the offence that the court is being required to consider in order to determine what sentence to impose. The sentencing principles set out ... are to guide the sentencer in reaching a

68   See Ashworth and von Hirsch, 'Recognising Elephants: The Problem of the Custody Threshold' [1997] Crim LR 187.

69   Halliday Report, *op cit*, para 2.7.

70   *Ibid*, para 2.8.

71   Hilary Benn MP, HC Committee, 30 January 2003, cols 741–742.

72   Baroness Scotland, HL Committee, 6 October 2003, col 51.

73   Baroness Scotland, *ibid*, col 61.

decision on the seriousness of the offence ... The surrounding circumstances are not relevant to that ... '

Previous convictions

8.29   In determining the seriousness of an offence, the court may at present take into account any previous convictions (SA 2000, s 151(1)). Previous repeat offending may lead to progressive loss of mitigation. The new Act develops that further. By s 143(2), if the offender has one or more previous convictions in a court in Great Britain,[74] the court must treat each previous conviction as an aggravating factor if (in the case of that conviction) the court considers that it can reasonably be so treated having regard, in particular, to:

(a) the nature of the offence to which the conviction relates and its relevance to the current offence, and

(b) the time that has elapsed since the conviction.

These convictions include convictions from any court in the United Kingdom or service court (s 143(4)). Convictions from a court outside the United Kingdom must also be taken into account where the court considers that such an offence can reasonably be regarded as an aggravating factor (s 143(5)). A conviction for an assault at a Cypriot nightclub might well be an aggravating factor in respect of an offender being sentenced for a similar offence in England. The term 'convictions' includes spent convictions,[75] but does not include matters in respect of which a caution was administered.

8.30   This strengthens the rules relating to character. The pre-existing s 151 of the SA 2000 allowed a court to take into account previous convictions, and no doubt courts invariably did so.[76] The new s 143 *requires* a court not only to do this, but, equally importantly, also to treat each previous conviction as an aggravating factor to offence seriousness if it can reasonably be so treated. Some might consider that previous convictions should not, normally, be regarded as relevant to offence seriousness, but rather to the question of aggravating or mitigating factors that determine the nature and length of the sentence.[77] Previous convictions, but not cautions, are intended to aggravate offence seriousness, which (as s 143 requires) is heightened by previous offending. The expectation is that persistent offenders should be treated progressively more severely. Those convictions, however, should be relevant and recent, and s 143 operates within the principle of sentence proportionality.[78]

A court should have regard to matters such as whether the previous convictions are of the same type, committed in similar circumstances, show recidivism, are drug- or

---

74   Convictions in Northern Ireland are therefore excluded.

75   Hilary Benn MP, HC Committee, 30 January 2003, cols 748–749.

76   See eg, *Bernard* (1997) 18 Cr App R (S) 135, CA; *Marriott* (1995) 16 Cr App R (S) 428; *Nunn* [1996] 2 Cr App R (S) 136; *W (Sentencing: Age of Defendant)* (2000) *The Times*, 26 October, CA; *Ollerenshaw* [1998] Crim LR 515, CA.

77   See, eg, Lord Goodhart, HL Committee, 8 October 2003, col 53: he deprecated the lengthening effect that previous convictions were likely to have on sentence length, citing the views of the Penal Affairs Consortium.

78   Halliday Report, *op cit*, para 2.

alcohol-related or can be regarded as showing a pattern of offending behaviour. A continued pattern of behaviour may cause a court to treat them more robustly, or in a different way that addresses the root causes of this pattern of behaviour. An increase in the size of the prison population is not intended. It remains to be seen whether previous convictions will simply, as some fear, lead to such an increase. The guidelines issued by the Sentencing Guidelines Council will be important in identifying the principles to be applied. These guidelines will govern the extent to which the severity of sentence could increase, in relation to what sort of previous convictions. The more recent, frequent and serious they were, the greater the effect. All crimes will be potentially relevant, but the extent of relevance is important in order to guard against disproportionate effects. Halliday considered that the 'most relevant would be offences showing a continuing course of criminal conduct, even when the types of offence committed were various (as they commonly are)'.

There are dangers in this approach. One is of a general increase in the severity of sentences. Another, in the context of juveniles, is whether a pattern of adolescent offending which might die out will in fact be perpetuated by treating repeat offending as an aggravating feature of offence seriousness, taking the juvenile further into the criminal justice system than might be necessary or appropriate.

A still further unresolved issue is the relationship with the doctrine of proportionality. Paragraphs D1 and D2 of the Council of Europe recommendations on consistency in sentencing[79] state that previous convictions should not be used mechanically as a factor working against a defendant. The sentence should be kept proportionate to the seriousness of the current offence. The fact that previous convictions might be relevant to offence seriousness was of course recognised by the changes made in 1993.[80] It is not intended that 'wholly disproportionate sentences'[81] should result. Yet the section is intended to modify the proportionality principle.[82] It requires the Sentencing Guidelines Council to set out the exact extent to which severity of sentence should increase (if at all) in relation to the kind of previous convictions and the nature of the current offence. If this is not intended to increase sentence length or level, one may wonder as to the purpose of the change in the law.

Offending while on bail

8.31   The commission of an offence whilst on bail is also an aggravating factor (SA 2000, s 151(2)), and remains so by virtue of s 143(3), which re-enacts the repealed s 151(2) in almost identical terms: the commission of an offence while on bail *must* be regarded as an aggravating factor. What weight is to be given to it remains a matter for the court, but, again, will be the subject of sentencing guidelines. The change in wording (from 'shall' to 'must') serves only to remind the court of what courts no doubt routinely do, namely, have regard to the fact that the alleged offence was committed (if in fact it was) while on bail.

---

79   Cited by Lord Goodhart, HL Committee, 8 October 2003, col 56.

80   By the Criminal Justice Act 1983.

81   Baroness Scotland, HL Committee, 8 October 2003, col 61.

82   See **8.4**.

Racial or religious aggravation, sexual orientation and disability

8.32   Section 145 deals with matters hitherto covered by the repealed s 153 of the SA 2000. It does so in similar terms. The court *must* apply s 145 where it is considering offence seriousness in respect of any offence other than one under ss 29 to 32 of the CDA 1998 (racially aggravated assaults, racially aggravated criminal damage, racially aggravated public order offences and racially aggravated harassment, etc). If the offence is racially or religiously aggravated, the court must treat that fact as an aggravating factor (that is to say, a factor which increases the seriousness of the offence) and must state in open court that the offence was so aggravated.

The term 'racially aggravated' bears the same meaning as in s 28 of the CDA 1998. Of course, the racial or religious aggravation must be proved, either by the evidence adduced at trial, or, if not, by other evidence adduced, if necessary, in a *Newton* hearing.[83] It is not open to the prosecution to seek a *Newton* hearing for this purpose where the offender was convicted of a non-aggravated version of the same offence.[84]

8.33   At a late stage, what is now s 146 was introduced. It provides for disability or sexual orientation to be aggravating factors. Section 146(1) and (3) provide that, in considering offence seriousness, the court must treat the fact that the offence was committed in any of the circumstances identified by s 146(2) as an aggravating factor. It is immaterial whether the offence had any other aggravating factor.

The circumstances identified by s 146(2) are:

(a)   at the time of committing the offence, or immediately before or after doing so, the offender demonstrates towards the victim of the offence hostility based on the sexual orientation (or presumed sexual orientation) of the victim, or a disability (or presumed disability) of the victim, or

(b)   that the offence is wholly or partly motivated by hostility towards persons who are of a particular sexual orientation, or who have a disability or particular disability.

As with racial or religious aggravation, these matters must be proved either at trial or in a *Newton* hearing.

The problem of harassment and assaults against individuals because of their disability or sexual orientation is significant, and growing. It was explained thus:[85]

> 'The Disability Awareness survey of 2001 found that a quarter of disabled people surveyed had suffered harassment. A Mencap survey found that 90% of people with a learning disability suffer from bullying on a regular basis, and a quarter reported physical assault. Many of these offences are not reported because of a lack of confidence that the criminal justice system can deal with them. ACPO is aware of the problem. In most parts of the country, lesbian and gay police liaison groups work with the police to encourage reporting, respond to physical incidents, support victims and often also cover issues such as homophobic bullying. We believe that legislating will send a very clear message to offenders, victims and witnesses that these very serious offences will not be tolerated.'

---

83   *Finch* (1992) 14 Cr App R (S) 226, CA; *Robinson* (1969) 53 Cr App R 314, CA.

84   *Druce* (1993) 14 Cr App R (S) 691, CA.

85   Baroness Scotland, HL Report, 5 November 2003, col 819.

Of course, nothing prevents a court from regarding such matters as aggravating, irrespective of s 146. Nonetheless, it is intended to make a clear statement which may, in due course, be followed by further legislation on 'hate crime'.[86]

8.34 'Disability' means any physical or mental impairment (s 146(5)). The term 'mental impairment' is not defined but surely has the same meaning as is ascribed under the MHA 1983, and does not extend to those who lack intelligence. An assault against an 'idiot', 'blockhead' or 'dimwit' is to be condemned, but does not fall within s 146. 'Sexual orientation' is not defined, but clearly applies to gays and lesbians, and, presumably, bi-sexuals. Whether it can be extended to others is more doubtful: paedophilia might, possibly, be regarded as a sexual orientation, showing a sexual interest in, and preference for, pre-pubescent children. Revenge assaults on released sex offenders against children literally fall within the ambit of s 146, although there is no evidence that that was the Government's intention.

Reduction for guilty plea

8.35 Section 144 re-enacts the pre-existing s 152(1) and (3) of the SA 2000. The provisions of s 152(2), which required a court to state in open court if it had reduced the otherwise appropriate sentence, are not re-enacted.

The new s 144 does not formally enact that those offenders who fulfil its terms must be given lower sentences, but requires a court, when determining the appropriate sentence, to take into account:

(a)   the stage in the proceedings for the offence at which the offender indicated his intention to plead guilty, and
(b)   the circumstances in which the indication was given.

If a sentence falls to be imposed under s 110(2) or s 111 of the SA 2000,[87] a court may, having taken into account matters relating to a guilty plea, impose a sentence which is not less than 80% of that specified in those provisions.

SENTENCE THRESHOLDS

8.36 A court must have regard to sentencing guidelines in determining the levels of seriousness within s 143, and how they are dealt with in terms of type and length of sentence (s 172). The new Act states, at s 148, the seriousness threshold for the making of a community sentence.[88] A community sentence must not be passed unless the court is of the opinion that the offence, or the combination of the offence with one or more associated offence, is serious enough to warrant such a sentence. Note should be taken of the new s 151, which creates a power to impose a community sentence on a persistent offender fined on at least three previous occasions.

---

86   Following forthcoming Home Office response to the Report of the Select Committee on Religious Offences.

87   Minimum sentence for repeat Class A drug offence, or for third domestic burglary respectively.

88   Defined by s 130; see **10.7**.

Financial penalties are valuable, whether on their own or in association with other non-custodial sentences. A new s 163 allows a Crown Court in certain circumstances to impose a fine instead of, or as well as, dealing with the offender in any other way. The effect of the changes is to remove the pre-existing distinction between community sentences and fines in terms of the threshold which the offence must cross.

Custody

8.37 Section 152 sets the threshold for a custodial sentence, and replaces (with amendments) s 79 of the SA 2000. It applies where a person is convicted by a custodial sentence other than one fixed by law or falling to be imposed under s 110(2) or s 111(2) of the SA 2000, or under ss 225 to 228 of the new Act.

By s 152(2), the court must not pass a custodial sentence unless it is of the opinion that the offence, or the combination of the offence and one or more offences associated with it, *was so serious that neither a fine alone nor a community sentence can be justified* for the offence. The words in italics above mark a change from those in the pre-existing s 79 ('so serious that only such a sentence can be justified for the offence'), a change that caused some consternation during the passage of the new Act.[89] The new wording is intended to provide emphasis to the sentencer to the fact that a custodial sentence should be a sentence of last resort.[90] The court must address in its own mind, if not necessarily in its explanation to the offender,[91] the possibility of a fine. In addition, the provisions in the pre-existing s 79 relating to violent or sexual offences, and only a custodial sentence being adequate to protect the public from serious harm, have not been replicated. That is not a fundamental change, given that public protection is one of the purposes of sentencing set out in s 142, and of the provisions for life imprisonment for public protection for serious offences or extended sentences contained in ss 225 to 227. Nothing in s 152 prevents the imposition of a custodial sentence on the offender if:

(a) he fails to express his willingness to comply with a requirement which is proposed by the court to be included in a community order and which requires an expression of such willingness, or

(b) he fails to comply with an order under s 161(2) (pre-sentence drug testing).

8.38 The general principle to be applied when determining the length of a discretionary custodial sentence is set out in s 153(2), which replaces s 80 of the SA 2000, with some changes. 'Longer than commensurate sentences' are no longer part of the law, but, for the same reasons as set out above, that is not a significant issue. Any custodial sentence must be commensurate, except in the cases identified by s 136(2), the custodial sentence must be for the shortest term (not exceeding the permitted maximum) that in the opinion of the court is commensurate with the seriousness of the offence, or of that offence and any associated offences.

The words italicised in **8.37** above are new, and might appear to suggest that offence seriousness is the only criterion to be considered by the court when sentencing, a

---

89   See, eg, Humphrey Malins MP, HC Committee, 4 February 2003, col 776.

90   Hilary Benn MP, HC Committee, 4 February 2003, col 780.

91   Hilary Benn MP, *ibid*.

conclusion that would be at odds not only with the wider purposes of sentencing stated in s 142 but also with pre-existing authority. In *Cunningham*[92] the court said that the provisions of s 80 of the SA 2000 did not prevent a sentence being imposed for deterrence, so long as the sentence was commensurate with the seriousness of the relevant offence. Lord Taylor CJ observed:

> 'the sentence commensurate with the seriousness of an offence of this kind will be substantial to reflect the need both for punishment and deterrence. What [s 80(2)(a)] does prohibit is adding any extra length to the sentence by which those criteria is commensurate with the seriousness of the offence simply to make a special example of the defendant.'

It is not the intention of s 153 to change the approach taken by the Court of Appeal. During consideration at Committee stage, it was said:[93]

> ' ... we have already agreed [section 143], which sets out general purposes of sentencing, and punishment is one of those purposes. It will certainly almost always be the case that if a sentencer considers a custodial sentence to be appropriate, the need to punish the offender or to protect the public will influence their decision. The [section] sets out a principle ... it is not our wish to change the interpretation of the law; we have no intention of departing from the Court of Appeal's interpretation of the *Cunningham* case ... '

So much is clear. What is less clear is the meaning, or purpose, of those words italicised ('the shortest term'), which find their way into the length of sentence provision. It may be that this is, in effect, a parliamentary exhortation to keep sentences to the minimum necessary but, of course, that begs the question: necessary for what sentencing purpose?

8.39 New arrangements governing release of prisoners sentenced to a term of 12 months or more (subject to limited exceptions) are introduced by the new Act. One consequence is that generally one-half of the sentence will be served in the community, on licence. A new power is given to a sentencing court, in respect of an offender who is being sentenced to a term of 12 months or more, except where the sentence is detention under s 91 of the SA 2000 or under s 228 of the new Act. Section 238 provides that, in those circumstances, a court may, when passing sentence, recommend to the Home Secretary particular conditions which, in its view, should be included in any licence granted to the offender on his release from prison. The recommendation does not form part of the sentence (s 238(3)) and thus the recommendation cannot be appealed. The Home Secretary must have regard to the recommendation, but is not bound by it (s 238(2)).

LIMITS ON POWERS OF MAGISTRATES' COURTS

8.40 Section 154 changes the limits on the power of a magistrates' court to impose imprisonment. Under pre-existing law, magistrates' courts do not have the power to impose imprisonment for more than six months in respect of any one summary or either-way offence, and 12 months in total respect of any such offences. The new Act changes that: once s 154 is brought into effect, magistrates' courts will have the power to impose a sentence of no more than 51 weeks in respect of any one such offence, and

---

92   (1993) 14 Cr App R (S) 444, CA.

93   Hilary Benn MP, HC Committee, 4 February 2003, col 781.

a maximum (for more than one such offence) of 65 weeks. The Act confers on the Home Secretary the power to amend these limits to maxima of 18 months and 24 months respectively. At the same time it limits the circumstances when a magistrates' court may commit an offender to the Crown Court for sentence.

Rationale

8.41 The sentencing powers of magistrates' courts are inextricably linked with issues relating to mode of trial.[94] This is explicitly recognised by the Explanatory Notes which accompanied the Act, which stated that it 'aims to improve the management of cases through the courts ... by increasing magistrates' sentencing powers so that fewer cases have to go to the Crown Court'.[95]

Whether in fact any changes to maximum sentencing powers will have that effect is arguable. The Royal Commission on Criminal Justice in 1993[96] observed that an allocation system based on sentencing powers was not working as well as it might because the Crown Court was passing sentences which in many cases the magistrates themselves could have imposed. It was for that reason that the PBV procedure was introduced, to encourage early guilty pleas and to facilitate the completion of more cases by magistrates, by giving them the opportunity to consider all offence and offender information and take account of credit for early guilty plea, before considering whether their sentencing powers were sufficient. The perceived inadequacy of prosecution disclosure, subsequent offence negotiation, the fact that in reality decisions about mode of trial are often negotiated by the parties and the belief, justified or not, that the quality of Crown Court process is superior have all been cited as contributing factors to this position.[97] In his research study, Herbert cites one sample court where magistrates declined jurisdiction in 11 cases of violent disorder. He observes: 'Yet not one of these defendants was ultimately convicted of that offence, and all those who admitted lesser offences of violence at the Crown Court received community orders. Increased sentencing powers will not influence this predicament'.[98]

Some of these issues are addressed by provisions in the Act encouraging more accurate offence charging, with the greater role of the CPS,[99] and with opportunities to give indications of likely sentence.[100] But there are potential dangers and difficulties. Extended powers of sentencing may simply result not in magistrates retaining more cases, but in them being more severe in terms of the length of

---

94   For discussion of mode of trial procedures, see Chapter 4.

95   At para 4.

96   Royal Commission, 1993, para 6.12, relying on research conducted by Hedderman and Moxon, *Magistrates Court or Crown Court? Mode of Trial Decisions and Sentencing?* Home Office Research Study No 125 (HMSO, 1992).

97   Herbert, 'Mode of Trial and Magistrates' Sentencing Powers' [2003] Crim LR 315.

98   *Ibid*, at 321. The particular example may reflect the cost–benefit analysis of proceeding with such charges, and the difficulties of the law in this area. For the changes in charging procedure, see **3.1**.

99   See **3.1** et seq.

100 See **4.7**.

sentence,[101] defeating the whole purpose. The introduction of custody plus[102] (where only an element of the term is served in custody) may remove the worst effects of any such 'sentence-creep', but that will not inevitably be brought in at the same time as the commencement of increased sentencing powers. Alternatively, if magistrates retain cases they would otherwise have committed, that may only be because they consider the offence to merit a custodial sentence, leading to, perhaps, more defendants electing for trial in the Crown Court.

Implementation

8.42   The extension of magistrates' courts powers is clearly controversial, but the new Act increases the sentencing powers in the context of the new custody plus sentence. Custodial sentences of less than 12 months must be in the form of a custodial sentence where the maximum period an offender can serve in custody is 13 weeks for any single offence. This effectively means that the actual period to be served in custody is no greater than the offender would have served had he been sentenced to a six-month term under pre-existing powers. If a magistrates' court wanted to impose a longer term it would have to impose a 12-month term. If that, however, was the appropriate length, reduction for early guilty plea might require a reduction into the range of custody plus.

This might mollify some, although by no means all, critics of the provision. However, the likely implementation date of custody plus is not likely to be before 2005/2006. It requires a long lead-in time, both for training and resources. The concerns expressed during the passage of the Act were such as to cause some to seek confirmation from the Government that it would not implement the new custody length provisions until custody plus is introduced. The Government declined to give such assurances.[103] Indeed, it was stressed that the Government wished to introduce the new sentencing provisions at the same time as the changes to the allocation of offences. Some might argue that the extended sentencing powers are inextricably linked to the introduction of custody plus. In the House of Lords, amendments were made which would have had the effect of postponing the commencement of the extended sentence powers until the national 'roll-out' of custody plus. Those amendments were overturned in the final scramble that marked the passage of the Act. Arguments that seek legally to require the postponement of the commencement of the new sentencing powers are doomed to failure. Section 336 permits the commencement of provisions on such date or dates as are appointed. That is a discretion that is entirely within the power of the Home Secretary. While it is true that the discretion must not be used to thwart the intention of Parliament,[104] the clear statements of the Minister and the actions of Parliament in rejecting the amendment are such as to make any argument of abuse of power impossible to sustain. Nonetheless, there are indications that, in fact, ss 154 and 155 will not in fact be commenced until 2005/2006.

---

101 See the survey comments quoted by Herbert, *op cit*, p 322.

102 See **9.2–9.20**.

103 Baroness Scotland, HL Committee, 6 October 2003, cols 75–76.

104 *R v Secretary of State for the Home Department ex parte Fire Brigades Union* [1995] 2 AC 513, HL.

Committals for sentence

8.43 It follows from an increase in magistrates' courts powers that the powers to commit for sentence should be limited. That is the effect of the new Act. In pre-existing law, the power to commit for sentence was contained in s 3 of the SA 2000. That permits the committal for sentence to the Crown Court where the offender is convicted of an offence if the court is of the opinion that the offence (together with any associated offence) is so serious that greater punishment should be inflicted for the offence than the court has power to impose. The fact that the court retained jurisdiction at mode of trial does not prohibit the offender being committed for sentence at a later stage.[105] There is also the power contained in s 4 of the SA 2000 which enables magistrates to commit for sentence in respect of an either-way offence in respect of which there has been an indication of a guilty plea, and the court has already committed the defendant for trial in respect of one or more related offences.

8.44 Schedule 3, para 22 inserts a new s 3 into the 2000 Act, replicated by a new s 3B in respect of young offenders. Under the new s 3 the power to commit for sentence applies in respect of a person aged at least 18 who has indicated he would plead guilty to it, and the court convicts him of the offence by virtue of s 9 of the MCA 1980. If, in that situation, the court is of the opinion that the offence together with any associated offences is so serious that the Crown Court should have the power to deal with the offender in any way it could have done if the offender had been convicted on indictment, the court may (but is not required to) commit for sentence. Of course, a court may, under the new PBV provisions, have already given an indication of sentence, therefore this power may be used rather less than the pre-existing s 3. There is no power to commit for sentence if jurisdiction is accepted, a not-guilty plea is entered and the defendant is convicted, unless the powers of committal for sentence of dangerous offenders apply.

8.45 A new s 3A of the SA 2000 is created by Sch 3, para 23, replicated by a new s 3C in respect of children and young persons.

The new s 3A applies where a person aged at least 18 is convicted, and it appears that either the criteria for the imposition of a sentence of life for public protection[106] or the criteria for the imposition of an extended sentence[107] are met the court must commit for sentence on that offence, together with certain other offences (as to which see s 6 of the 2000 Act). In taking that step, the court is not bound by any indication of sentence or challengeable on that basis (SA 2000, s 3A(4)).

8.46 If a case is committed for sentence, a new s 5 and s 5A are inserted into the SA 2000, and confer powers on the Crown Court to deal with the offender in any way in which it could have dealt with him if he had just been convicted of the offence on indictment before the court. The Crown Court is also protected against any challenge founded on the indication of sentence given by the magistrates' court (SA 2000, ss 5(3), 5A(3)).

---

105 *R v North Sefton Magistrates' Court ex parte Marsh* (1994) 16 Cr App R (S) 401, DC.

106 See **9.41**.

107 See **9.50**.

DEFERMENT OF SENTENCE

8.47   Section 278 and Sch 23 insert new provisions about deferment of sentence into the SA 2000. In most cases, a court will pass sentence on an offender immediately after his conviction for the offence or offences for which he is before the court. The court also has the power to defer sentencing. The existing provisions in ss 1 and 2 of the SA 2000 are replaced by a new s 1 and ss 1A to 1F.

The pre-existing s 1 allows the court to defer sentencing for the purpose of enabling the court to have regard to the conduct of the offender and any change in his circumstances, for a period of up to six months. That remains the case (s 1(1), (3)), although a court may not remand an offender on the same occasion as it defers sentence on him (s 1(6)).

The new s 1 extends the power to defer further by allowing it to set such requirements relating to his behaviour as the court thinks it appropriate to impose, and a court may take into account the making of reparation for the offence after conviction.

To this end, a court can defer under s 1 only if:

(a)   the offender consents;
(b)   the offender undertakes to comply with any requirements as to his conduct during the period of deferment that the court considers it appropriate to impose; and
(c)   the court is satisfied, having regard to the nature of the offence and the character and circumstances of the offender, that it would be in the interests of justice to exercise the power.

8.48   Section 1(2) extends the meaning of 'conduct' within s 1(1) to include reference to how well the offender complies with such requirements. The offender must consent to giving such undertakings and there can be no question of compulsion. It is a matter for the offender whether he wishes to accept the proposed requirements of the court and, for that reason, any challenge to the nature or proportionality of the requirements should inevitably fail. The requirements can include requirements as to the residence of the offender during the whole or part of the deferment (SA 2000, s 1A(1)), and the court may appoint a supervisor (s 1A(2)).

A court will, if sentence is deferred, measure the offender's progress against these requirements. Progress will continue to act as a mitigating factor in the final sentence passed, including imposing a community sentence in lieu of a custodial one when clear progress against undertakings has been made.

The court has the power to issue a summons or a warrant to arrest the offender if he does not appear on the date for sentencing specified by the court (SA 2000, s 1(7)). Section 1(5) prescribes who should receive a copy of the order deferring the passing of sentence.

8.49   The new s 1B provides for the return of the offender to court. Under the pre-existing s 1 the offender can only be returned to court early for sentencing if he commits another offence. By s 1B(2) the offender could, when it is in force, be returned to court if the supervisor has reported to the court that the offender has failed to comply with one or more requirements in respect of which the offender gave an undertaking (s 1B(2)(c)). Section 1B(2) clearly sets out the circumstances in which he can be returned to court early, and s 1B(3) gives the court the power to issue a summons or warrant for the offender to appear before it.

Under s 1C the court may deal with an offender before the end of the period of deferment if he commits another offence. Subsections (2) and (3) set out the powers of the Crown Court and magistrates' courts in these cases. If the offender is convicted of another offence during the period of deferment, the court may deal with the original deferred sentence at the same time as sentencing him for the new offence. If the original sentence was deferred by a Crown Court, it must be a Crown Court that passes sentence for both the offences. If the original sentence was deferred by a magistrates' court, and the offender is brought before a Crown Court to be sentenced for the two offences, the court cannot pass a sentence greater than that which a magistrates' court could have passed. Thus, it cannot pass a sentence of greater than 12 months. The court has the power to issue a summons or a warrant for the offender to appear before it.

A new s 1D clarifies some of the legal detail surrounding the deferment of sentences. Deferment of sentence is to be regarded as an adjournment, and if the offender does not appear before the court when required to, he is to be dealt with accordingly. When the court deals with an offender at the end of the period of deferment (or earlier if he does not comply with the requirements or commits another offence) it has the same powers as if the offence had just been committed. This includes committing him for sentence to the Crown Court. The court may issue a summons to someone appointed as a supervisor if that person refuses to appear before the court when the court wants to consider an offender's failure to comply with the requirements of the deferment or anything to do with the original offence.

MINIMUM SENTENCE FOR CERTAIN FIREARMS OFFENCES

8.50   Considerable concern has arisen in respect of the widespread possession and use of firearms. In some areas, gun crime is a major cause of fear and distress. A significant rise in the number of young people carrying firearms has occurred, either to boost their image or from a misguided idea about self-protection.[108] In 2002, 97 lives were lost to gun crime. A gun amnesty in six months in 2003 led to some 43,908 guns and 1,039,358 rounds of ammunition being handed in.

As is not unusual, the response of Government was to seek to add additional sentencing and other powers, and it did so by inserting new provisions into the Bill. These are contained in s 287, which creates a new s 51A of the Firearms Act 1968, and form part of the overall package which includes the provisions of s 288, which make certain firearms offences triable only on indictment,[109] as provisions which, at least in part, bind the hands of the judiciary. They are another example of how the sentencing provisions of the new Act seek to curtail the discretion of judges when sentencing.

---

108 See Home Office Crime and Policing Note: www.homeoffice.gov.uk/crimpol/firearms/.

109 See **4.1**. These are: possession, or distributing prohibited weapons or ammunition or firearms disguised as another object.

Note should also be taken of increases in penalty for importation or exportation of certain firearms (s 293). These provisions were brought into effect on 22 January 2004.

8.51 The court must, when sentencing an offender for one of the relevant offences, committed after commencement (a provision which avoids any complaints of retrospectivity) and at a time when the offender was aged at least 16, impose a custodial sentence of at least the minimum term, unless it is of the opinion that there are exceptional circumstances relating to the offence or the offender which justify its not doing so. Reference should be made to s 287 for the offences to which it applies.

The 'exceptional circumstance' proviso mirrors that contained in s 109 of the SA 2000 in respect of automatic life sentences for a second serious offence. The case-law in that context may provide some guidance as to how 'exceptional circumstances' is to be applied here. In *Kelly*[110] Lord Bingham CJ observed that 'exceptional' was to be construed as an ordinary familiar English adjective, and not as a term of art. By contrast, in *Offen*[111] Lord Woolf CJ looked at the legislative purpose, observing that if too restrictive an approach were taken to the meaning of 'exceptional circumstances' the life sentence might turn out to be arbitrary and disproportionate, thereby contravening Art 5 ECHR. It is submitted that the same approach will be taken to the new provision. Courts should be mindful of the need to protect the public from gun crime or gun-supported crime. If, however, a sentence would be totally disproportionate a court would appear to have the freedom to conclude that 'exceptional circumstances' exist. The burden of proof will be on the offender to show that exceptional circumstances exist.[112]

ALTERATION OF PENALTIES

8.52 Section 280 and Sch 25 remove powers of imprisonment in respect of the offences set out in Sch 25. These are all summary offences thought no longer to justify imprisonment as a penalty. The change applies in respect of an offence committed after the commencement of this change.

8.53 Section 281(2) and Sch 26 increase the maximum term of imprisonment for certain summary offences stated in Sch 26 from four months to 51 weeks. Section 245 confers an enabling power on the Home Secretary to amend legislation to remove the power of imprisonment or to extend it to 51 weeks. The effect of this change is to bring within the ambit of custody plus[113] a wide range of offences punishable hitherto only with short custodial terms. A similar change is made by s 282 of the new Act to s 32 of the MCA 1980 (maximum term that can be imposed on summary conviction of either-way offences).

8.54 Section 284 and Sch 28 increase the penalties for certain drug-related offences specified in Sch 27. The maximum terms are increased from five years to 14 years and

---

110 [1999] 2 Cr App R (S) 176, CA.

111 [2001] 1 WLR 253, CA.

112 *Kelly (No 2)* [2002] 1 Cr App R (S) 360, CA.

113 See **9.2**.

reflect the emphasis in the new Act of seeking to address drug-related crime. These came into force on 29 January 2004.

8.55   Section 286 increases the penalties for offences under s 174 of the Road Traffic Act 1988 (false statements, etc) (in force 29 January 2004).

8.56   Section 285 increases the penalties for certain drug-related offences. These came into force on 27 February 2004.

AMENDMENTS

8.57   Schedule 32 makes a great many detailed amendments to sentencing provisions. Where the amendment is anything other than consequential, the amendment has been dealt with at the appropriate part of this text.

Chapter 9

SENTENCING – CUSTODIAL SENTENCES

9.1 The new Act makes significant changes to custodial sentences. We have already noted the wider issues of sentencing principles and thresholds,[1] and the widespread increases in terms of imprisonment made by the new Act.[2] In respect of new, or amended, custodial sentences, and the new provisions as to how long a period of custody will in fact be served, the Act makes the following changes:

–   introduction of a new 'custody plus' sentence, for prison sentences of less than 12 months, involving a period of custody in prison (a maximum of three months) and a period of compulsory supervision;
–   introduction of intermittent custody;
–   revised provision in respect of suspended sentences;
–   additional sentencing powers in respect of dangerous offenders;
–   new provisions relating to the minimum terms to be served by life prisoners; and
–   new arrangements for the release of prisoners on licence.

These provisions and the other detailed changes that accompany them are intended to implement the recommendations of the Halliday Report.[3]

CUSTODY PLUS – SENTENCES OF LESS THAN 12 MONTHS

Introduction

9.2 The general approach and the case for change identified by the Halliday Report has already been discussed.[4] It highlighted the lack of utility in short prison sentences as one of the most important deficiencies of the current sentencing framework.[5] Only half of any sentence under 12 months is in fact served, because of automatic release (CJA 1991, s 33(1)(a)). No power exists to impose conditions on the second six-month period. Further, home detention curfew permits release even before the expiration of the first six-month period. The Report observed:[6]

'With Home Detention Curfew, for many the period in custody is shorter than it would otherwise have been. The sentence is nevertheless used for large numbers of persistent

---

1   See, generally, Chapter 8.
2   See **8.53–8.56**.
3   Halliday Report, *op cit*. See, generally, **8.4–8.8**.
4   See **8.4**.
5   Halliday Report, *op cit*, para 3.1.
6   *Ibid*, para 3.1.

offenders, with multiple problems and high risks of re-offending, whose offences and record are serious enough to justify a custodial sentence, but not so serious that longer prison sentences would be justified. A more effective recipe for failure could hardly be conceived.'

The statistics cited by the Report highlight the significance of this view. Between 1989 and 1999, a 67% increase occurred in sentences of less than 12 months in respect of those aged 18 or above, to some 45,000.[7] The bulk of that increase was in the shorter sentences – an increase of 176% in sentences of under three months, and of 89% in those of between three and six months. No clear reason for this increase was identified by the Report except, perhaps, the suspicion that sentencers feel that repeated offending following non-custodial sentences leaves no alternative.[8] Yet risks of re-offending by short-term prisoners are broadly similar to those on probation or combination orders.[9]

9.3   Few could be happy with this growth in the number of sentences of too little value to permit meaningful work in prison, and with the probation service effectively powerless on release. Halliday considered that a greater use of community sentences could be justified, and noted the possibility that a greater use of such sentences had occurred before 1995.[10] Other measures, such as intermittent custody, might also have a role to play. Above all, Halliday saw the main need to provide a framework for work with the large numbers of offenders who persist in criminality, but not at a level of seriousness such as to require longer prison sentences.[11] That framework could be created by requiring those who serve short sentences to undertake programmes under supervision in the community, under conditions which, if breached, could lead to return to custody. This is the context in which s 181 provides a framework for a new scheme for sentences of less than 12 months – 'custody plus'.

The new provision

9.4   Section 181 applies in respect of offenders aged 18 or above. It provides that unless an intermittent custody order is made, a sentence of imprisonment of less than 12 months must be made in accordance with s 181, irrespective of the type of offence, whether in the magistrates' court or the Crown Court. The term of the sentence, which must be expressed in weeks, must be a minimum of 28 weeks, and not more than 51 weeks, in respect of any one offence (s 181(2)). The length of the sentence must be within the permitted maximum for the offence (s 181(2)(d)). If two or more periods of imprisonment are imposed to run consecutively, the aggregate terms of imprisonment must not exceed 65 weeks (s 181(7)).

Commencement

9.5   The custody plus provisions are not likely to be brought into effect for some time, probably the financial year 2006/07. The sentencing reforms will be introduced in phases over several years to allow the system to absorb new measures gradually

---

7   Halliday Report, *op cit*, para 3.3.

8   *Ibid*, para 3.5.

9   *Ibid*, para 3.7.

10   *Ibid*.

11   *Ibid*, para 3.8.

without too much disruption, and to allow the correctional services, particularly probation, to reach the capacity necessary to implement them successfully.[12]

This clearly has effects in the context of the extension of magistrates' court sentencing powers.[13] Until custody plus is brought into effect, a court will have the pre-existing power to impose a 'normal' term of imprisonment.

9.6 Within the total length of the sentence, the court, when passing sentence must:

(a) specify a *custodial period* – the length of time to be served in prison. That period must be a minimum of two weeks, and, in respect of any one offence, must not be more than 13 weeks (s 181(5)). Where there are two or more terms of imprisonment to be served consecutively, the aggregate length of the custodial period must not exceed 26 weeks (s 181(7)(b));

(b) specify a *licence period* – the period of licence, granted subject to conditions. The length of this period is the remainder of the custodial term (ie the number of weeks that result if the custodial period is subtracted from the total length of the sentence imposed) (s 181(3)(b)), but this must be at least 26 weeks in length (s 181(6)). This licence period requirement does not apply to a term of imprisonment which is a suspended sentence (s 181(9)).[14]

Within this framework it is for the court to determine the length of the custodial period and the length of the sentence.

9.7 This minimum licence period is intended to ensure that sufficient time exists to achieve an impact on the risk of a persistent offender re-offending.[15] There is no power to dispense with the post-release supervision. Halliday concluded that there should be a discretion to dispense with the 'custody plus' element, for example in cases of contempt of court, or where the case involved a foreign national who intended to return to his own country on release from custody, or in the case of those who commit a serious offence but where there is a low risk of re-offending.[16] Of offenders sentenced to a term of six or fewer months' imprisonment during the survey period, some 14% were first-time offenders, 50% of males had their own accommodation (whether owned or rented), and 28% were in employment, all factors that reduce the likelihood of re-offending.[17] There was, therefore, a good case for not making the requirement mandatory. That approach did not find favour with the Government, and in all cases there must be a period of licence. The same effect can be achieved by revoking a requirement in a custody plus order or by using intermittent custody as an alternative disposal.[18]

9.8 The operation of the new sentence can be seen from the following examples:

---

12 Baroness Scotland, HL Committee, 6 October 2003, col 75.

13 See **8.42**.

14 See **9.29**.

15 Halliday Report, *op cit*, para 3.10.

16 *Ibid*, para 3.24.

17 *Ibid*, para 3.22.

18 See **9.17** and **9.21**.

Example 1: The court imposes a term of imprisonment of 28 weeks, the minimum possible (s 181(2)(b)). The custodial period is two weeks, because of the 26-week minimum licence period.

Example 2: The court imposes a term of imprisonment of 51 weeks. The custody period can be no less than two weeks and no greater than 25 weeks, the maximum possible custody period for a single offence because of the 26-week minimum licence period. It approximates to the reality of what would occur under the pre-existing law.

Example 3: The court imposes consecutive terms of imprisonment amounting in total to 65 weeks, the maximum that can be imposed by consecutive sentences. The custody period must be no less than two weeks for each offence, and no more in total than 26 weeks. Thus the licence period will be at least 39 weeks (the total term less the maximum permitted cumulative custodial period).

Example 4: A court sentencing on a single offence wishes the offender to serve a longer period than custody plus will permit. It can impose a 12-month sentence, of which the offender will serve six months, subject to any earlier release on home detention curfew. If the court wishes the offender to serve longer, it must impose a longer term, a course of action not within the power of a magistrates' court.

9.9   The sentence will mean what it says, because the court, when passing sentence, will specify the length of the custody period. This is in comparison with the current position where typically the offender serves one-half of the term imposed. It will also allow sentence severity to reflect distinctions between co-defendants, by varying the length of the custodial and supervisory periods.[19]

9.10   Care will need to be taken when a court wishes to impose sentences that are consecutive, in whole or in part. In respect of each there will need to be a total sentence length. In respect of consecutive custody plus orders, that aggregate length must not exceed 65 weeks, and the custody periods for each order must be two weeks or more, but not exceed 13. Thus, if the court wished to impose two orders of 40 and 50 weeks respectively, these would have to be at least partially concurrent, because of the 65-week maximum.

Nothing in s 181 prevents a court from imposing a custody plus sentence consecutive to a longer term (say of 18 months) that does not require a custody plus sentence. That is because the restriction on consecutive terms in excess of 65 weeks speaks of ' ... terms of imprisonment in accordance with this section ... ' (s 181(7)). It would be an unusual case that might justify that course. For the release position in such a case, see **9.61**.

9.11   Section 181(3) permits the sentencing court to impose conditions requiring the compliance of the offender with one or more requirements during the whole or part of the licence period. Those requirements will be determined by the sentencing court on the basis of the PSR. The order may specify during which parts of the licence period particular requirements are to be complied with, and, indeed, one of the purposes of

---

19   Halliday Report, *op cit*, para 3.13.

requirements may be to follow on from work begun during the period of custody, for example, treatment for drug or alcohol abuse.[20]

A court may impose different requirements consecutively (eg a programme requirement requiring attendance on an accredited programme to address behavioural problems followed by an unpaid work requirement). Requirements may overlap. The court must, where it is imposing two or more different requirements, consider whether the requirements are compatible with each other (s 182(5)).

The only restriction is that the totality of the requirements must not be disproportionate to their aim. That is not explicit, but clearly is the case both by analogy with other statutory provisions and in the light of the decisions of the European Court of Human Rights. In relation to the former, s 35(3) of the SA 2000 states that the particular orders comprising a community sentence must not comprise a restriction on liberty which is not commensurate with the seriousness of the offence taken together with any associated offences. The case-law on Art 8 ECHR[21] confirms that restrictions on this right to private and family life (which is what requirements will often amount to) must be both necessary in a democratic society and proportionate to a pressing social need.

9.12   Section 182 deals with licence conditions. These can include an unpaid work requirement (s 199),[22] an activity requirement (s 201),[23] a programme requirement (s 202),[24] a prohibited activity requirement (s 203),[25] a curfew requirement (s 204),[26] an exclusion requirement (s 205),[27] a supervision requirement (s 213)[28] and (in the case of an offender aged under 21) an attendance centre requirement (s 214).[29]

There may be preconditions to be fulfilled before such a requirement can be imposed, as part of the custody plus licence. These are dealt with in Chapter 10.[30]

9.13   In some cases there is an obligation on the court to impose an electronic monitoring requirement under s 215.[31] It must do so where it imposes a curfew requirement (s 204)[32] or an exclusion requirement (s 205),[33] unless prevented from

---

20   Halliday Report, *op cit*, para 3.5.

21   *Handyside v United Kingdom* (1979) 1 EHRR 737, ECtHR; *Arrowsmith v United Kingdom* (1978) 19 DR 5, ECtHR; *Laskey and others v United Kingdom* (1997) 24 EHRR 9, ECtHR; *Hoare v United Kingdom* [1997] EHRLR 678, ECtHR.

22   See **10.14**.

23   See **10.16**.

24   See **10.17**.

25   See **10.18**.

26   See **10.19**.

27   See **10.20**.

28   See **10.27**.

29   See **10.28**.

30   Some of these contain different detailed requirements in respect of an offender aged under 18 years. They are not dealt with here because custody plus is not available to such offenders.

31   See **10.29**.

32   See **10.24**.

33   See **10.20**.

doing so by s 205(2) (lack of practicability) or s 205(4) (no available arrangements) or, alternatively, because it is inappropriate in the particular circumstances of the case (s 205(3)).

By contrast, there is a power, but not an obligation, to impose an electronic monitoring requirement where the court imposes an activity requirement, unpaid work requirement, programme requirement, prohibited activity requirement, residence requirement, supervision requirement or attendance centre requirement, subject only to the limitations in s 205(2) or s 205(4) mentioned above. Guidelines will be issued by the Sentencing Guidelines Council as to the use of these powers.

A court must decide whether electronic monitoring is a necessary or proportionate response. It may not be justified because there is a low risk of breach of licence requirements. Unpaid work and prohibited activity requirements are likely to be imposed on a substantial number of offenders, but in many cases there will be no evidence to suggest that the offender presents a high degree of risk of failure to comply. In such circumstances, mandatory monitoring would be disproportionate, unnecessary and a waste of resources.[34]

9.14   The Home Secretary may in some circumstances impose licence conditions (s 182). This will be in situations where the need for additional conditions becomes necessary for the purposes of public protection. For example, the offender's relationship may break down and he may have made threats against his former partner. An exclusion requirement might then be appropriate.[35] The Home Secretary can, under this power and for the purpose of public protection, choose only from the list of licence conditions available to the court. There appear to be no other limits on this power, and it would, theoretically, be open to the Home Secretary to impose conditions considered and rejected by the sentencing court, although that would be an executive act that would be judicially reviewable on normal *Wednesbury* principles.[36] There is no requirement in s 182 that the need for an additional condition has arisen subsequent to the imposition of the sentence, yet that is probably what is intended and how s 182 should be interpreted. Nor does there appear to be any right of appeal, although the power of amendment or revocation exists, and it is not clear why that should not be the appropriate route for adding additional conditions onto a licence.[37] That surely would have been preferable to what amounts to a power to alter by executive action a sentence of the court.

9.15   The offender must be released from imprisonment at the end of the custody period (s 244(3)(b)). That release is on licence, and governed by the provisions relating to release of prisoners in Chapter 6 of the new Act.[38] If the offender is in breach of the conditions imposed as part of the licence part of the custody plus order, the licence may be revoked and the offender recalled to prison (s 254). The effect of that in fact may be to increase the length of time an offender serves in custody under the original order, compared with that which would be served in pre-existing law

---

34   Baroness Scotland, HL Committee, 8 October 2003, col 380.

35   *Ibid*, col 387.

36   *Associated Provincial Picture Houses v Wednesbury Corporation* [1948] 1 KB 223, CA.

37   See **9.16**.

38   See **9.57–9.74**.

under a comparable sentence. If an offender was sentenced, under pre-existing law, to a term of six months, he would serve no longer than three months. Under s 254, an offender sentenced to a term of 28 weeks (the minimum length of a custody plus order) would be released after two weeks but, if recalled for breach of licence conditions shortly after release, might potentially serve up to something approaching six months, not exceeding the total length of the sentence.

The procedures set out at s 254 must be complied with. The offender will then serve the remaining part of his sentence in prison, subject only to the operation of the powers for further release after recall contained in s 254(4) and s 256. The term cannot be extended by the imposition of additional days.

Revocation and amendment of order

9.16 Section 187 of, and Sch 10 to, the new Act deal with the revocation and amendment of custody plus orders (and also intermittent custody orders).[39] They provide for the amendment or revocation of an order by the 'appropriate court' which is, in respect of an order made by the Crown Court, or one made on appeal, the Crown Court, and, in any other case, the magistrates' court for the petty sessions division specified in the order (Sch 10, paras 1, 2).

An application cannot be made while an appeal against the sentence is pending (Sch 10, para 7) except, where the application is one requesting the cancellation of a requirement, if the application is made by the responsible officer. The offender must be summonsed, and a warrant for arrest may be issued if the offender fails to attend (Sch 10, para 8). The court making the amendment or revocation must comply with the procedural requirements of Sch 10, para 9.

Revocation

9.17 If it appears to the appropriate court on the application of the offender or responsible officer[40] that, having regard to the circumstances that have arisen since the order was made, it would be in the interests of justice to do so, it may revoke the custody plus order (Sch 10, para 3(1)). That revocation does not affect the sentence of imprisonment to which the order related: in other words, the offender must serve the custody period specified in the order (Sch 10, para 3(2)). The powers of amendment of the order do not include the power to vary that custody period. Subject to that, this power of revocation will be the appropriate vehicle for cases of the type which the Halliday Report identified as ones where no licence period was necessary.[41]

Amendment because of change of residence

9.18 Where the appropriate court is satisfied that the offender proposes to change, or has changed, his residence during the licence period, it may (and must if the responsible officer makes an application) substitute another petty sessions area for that specified in the order (Sch 10, para 4(2)). It may be that a requirement cannot be complied with in the new petty sessions area: in such circumstances, that requirement

---

39 See **9.21**.

40 Defined by s 197.

41 See **9.7**.

must either be cancelled, or another (which can be complied with) imposed in substitution (Sch 10, para 4(3)).

There is one exception to this general power to amend, contained in Sch 10, para 4(4). This states that the court may not, under para 4, amend an order imposing a programme requirement unless it appears to the court that the accredited programme is available in the other petty sessions area. This seems to mean that, irrespective of the offender's change of circumstances, if the accredited programme is not available in the new petty sessions area, then the original requirement stands. This seemingly inconvenient result, which might perhaps in an extreme case raise Art 8 ECHR issues, can be avoided by using, instead, the powers of amendment in Sch 10, para 5.

Amendment of requirements

9.19 At any time during the term of imprisonment (ie the custody period) the appropriate court may, on the application of the offender or responsible officer, amend any requirement, either by cancelling it, or by imposing a requirement of the same kind imposing different obligations in substitution of the original requirement (Sch 10, para 5(1)). A requirement is of the same kind for this purpose if it falls within the list set out at s 177(1) (Sch 10, paras 1, 2).[42] The restrictions on any of those requirements identified by s 164(2) continue to apply (Sch 10, para 5(3)).

Residence in Scotland or Northern Ireland

9.20 Schedule 11 provides for the transfer of custody plus orders (and intermittent custody orders) to Scotland or Northern Ireland. Where the court making the order is satisfied that the offender resides in Scotland or Northern Ireland, or will reside there during the licence period, it may impose requirements that are to be complied with and supervised in that jurisdiction. Detailed provisions apply as to when an order can be made (Sch 11, paras 2(2), 9(2)), and Part 4 of the Schedule deals with the enforcement of the order in an appropriate court in that jurisdiction.

INTERMITTENT CUSTODY

9.21 Section 183 permits a court to impose a sentence of at least 28 weeks but not exceeding 51 weeks, to be served during intermittent periods. Consecutive orders must not exceed 65 weeks in total. The order will specify periods during which the offender is to be released temporarily on licence before he has served the appropriate number of days in custody (s 183(1)).

The intermittent custody provisions are being piloted. To enable that to occur, the Criminal Justice Act 2003 (Commencement No 1) Order 2003 (SI 2003/3282) brought certain provisions into force, as from 26 January 2004. These are s 183 (other than s 183(8), which deals with powers of the Home Secretary), ss 184–186, s 187 and Sch 10. A range of other provisions is brought into effect to enable the imposition and administration of sentences of intermittent custody.

---

42 See **10.5**.

One of those provisions is s 250, which deals with the imposition of licence conditions prescribed by the Home Secretary. The Criminal Justice (Sentencing) (Licence Conditions) Order 2003 (SI 2003/3337) came into force on 26 January 2004 and sets out the standard and other conditions that may be imposed when a prisoner is released from prison on licence under s 250 and s 251 of the new Act. These provisions apply only to those released on licence under intermittent custody, and do not have (for the moment) wider effect, although in due course when the Act is fully in force, s 250 and s 251 will have wider impact in respect of custody plus. They are discussed at **9.27**. Because the extended powers of sentencing conferred on magistrates' courts are not yet in force, transitory arrangements are required. These are specified by the Intermittent Custody (Transitory Provisions) Order 2003 (SI 2003/3283) which, again, came into force on 26 January 2004. This modifies s 183, pending the commencement of the extended magistrates' courts sentencing powers, and s 241, pending the commencement of s 240 (credit for days spent on remand). These are discussed at **9.26**.

Background

9.22 Imprisonment can have negative aspects: loss of job or home, or damage to family or other relationships. In some instances it may be possible to mark the seriousness of the offence by requiring a period of incarceration without depriving the prisoner totally of his liberty for the full custodial term. The Halliday Report identified the benefits of 'partial' or 'weekend' or 'intermittent' custody. It pointed to the pre-existing power to release prisoners on temporary licence in support of their rehabilitation – some 256,179 instances during 1999.[43] It also noted the difficulties – whether in fact it would spread the net wider, encouraging the court to consider custody when it might not otherwise have done so, and increasing the prison population. There are also issues as to whether the prison stock is suitable for a 'floating' population, whether having prison accommodation unoccupied is a waste of precious resource, and whether public confidence would suffer if re-offending occurred during the periods when the offender is released on licence. A further consideration is whether the aims of intermittent custody can be achieved by other means, for example by appropriately constructed community sentences.

The Government's response[44] was to propose the intermittent custody provisions which now are contained in s 183, and which apply to terms of imprisonment not exceeding 51 weeks (ie the same group of sentences that will attract custody plus if intermittent custody is not used). It explained its thinking thus:[45]

> '[The] section is . . . aimed at offenders who have crossed the custodial threshold but who have strong links with the community, such as employment, educational or caring responsibilities. Serving the custodial part of the sentence round these responsibilities should reduce the chance that [the offender] will re-offend as these are all factors associated with [a reduced likelihood of] re-offending.'

---

43 Halliday Report, *op cit*, para 5.4.

44 *Justice for All*, *op cit*, para 4.28. See Government response to Home Affairs Committee, 1997–1998, HC 486, *Alternatives to Prison Sentences*, Cm 4174.

45 Baroness Scotland, HL Committee, 8 October 2003, cols 381–382.

The pilot schemes will show whether the potential difficulties are outweighed by the benefits. It is not, however, intended for serious offences. Typically, offences of fraud, theft, forgery and less serious driving offences are envisaged as falling within its ambit.[46] Care will need to be taken to ensure that where the custody threshold is in fact crossed, 'net widening' does not occur, with intermittent custody being used in place of non-custodial alternatives.

The order

9.23 No order can be made unless a probation officer has been consulted. The process will commence with a recommendation in a PSR, containing an assessment of the offender's personal circumstances and a risk assessment.

The offender must consent to the making of the order. If he does not, then ordinary custody will result. That must be the case, because by proposing intermittent custody the court has accepted that a custodial sentence is necessary. That 'ordinary' custodial sentence will be in the form of custody plus, assuming that the custody plus provisions have been brought into effect.

The intermittent custody order will specify the number of days that the offender must serve in prison before being released on licence for the remainder of the term (s 183(1)(a)). These must be at least 14, and must not (in respect of any one offence) exceed 90. Where the sentence constitutes consecutive terms, the aggregate number of custodial days must not exceed 180.[47]

The effect of this may be seen as follows:

Offence	Minimum length of order	Maximum length of order	Days in custody	Remaining period of licence
Single offence	28 weeks	51 weeks	Not less than 14 days or more than 90 days	The period following service of days in custody until expiration of maximum length of order
Multiple offences – orders concurrent	28 weeks	51 weeks in respect of any one of the offences	Not less than 14 days or more than 90 days for the longest of any of the offences	The period following service of days in custody until expiration of maximum length of order
Multiple offences – orders consecutive	28 weeks for any one offence	No more than 65 weeks in total	No less than 14 days for each offence to be served consecutively (or partially consecutively), and no more than 180 days in aggregate	The period following service of days in custody until expiration of maximum length of order

---

46   Baroness Scotland, *ibid.*

47   But see **9.26**.

9.24   The intermittent custody order is an alternative to custody plus. The effect of s 181 is that a court is not obliged to make a custody plus order if it makes an intermittent custody order (s 181(1)). The court will need to consider carefully which order is preferable, having decided to impose a custodial sentence. The court will have to consider a variety of factors including sentencing guidelines, the particular needs of the supervision requirements and how they will impact on the offender and a whole range of factors which relate to the offender, his family and circumstances, the length and type of requirements to be imposed. The following tables show the minimum and maximum periods[48] spent in custody under the custody plus and intermittent custody order:

	Custody Plus	Intermittent Custody
Total length of order	28 weeks	28 weeks
Minimum period of custody to be served	2 weeks	14 days
Maximum period of custody to be served	13 weeks	90 days

	Custody Plus	Intermittent Custody
Total length of order	36 weeks	36 weeks
Minimum period of custody to be served	2 weeks	14 days
Maximum period of custody to be served	10 weeks	90 days

	Custody Plus	Intermittent Custody
Total length of order	51 weeks	51 weeks
Minimum period of custody to be served	2 weeks	14 days
Maximum period of custody to be served	13 weeks	90 days

While broadly comparable periods in custody result, in the middle range the custody period may be significantly less under custody plus than under intermittent custody. This result is inevitable given that, for custody plus, the licence period must be a minimum of 26 weeks.

9.25   If the custody plus provisions are not brought into effect until after intermittent custody, the appropriate comparison will be with ordinary custody, but within the extended sentencing powers of the magistrates' court. Under pre-existing provision, automatic release occurs after service of half the sentence. Release can be earlier under home detention curfew. Under that provision, the minimum custody period is 30 days, and the maximum of 50% of the sentence. In respect of a sentence of more than three months but less than eight, there are minima and maxima of 25% and 50% respectively, and for eight to 12 months, a minimum of 60 days less than 50%. The comparisons below show the result.

	Imprisonment	Intermittent Custody
Total length of order	7 months	28 weeks
Minimum period of custody to be served	14 weeks	14 days
Maximum period of custody to be served	14 weeks	90 days

---

48   But see **9.26**.

	Imprisonment	Intermittent Custody
Total length of order	9 months	36 weeks
Minimum period of custody to be served	18 weeks	14 days
Maximum period of custody to be served	18 weeks	90 days

	Custody Plus	Intermittent Custody
Total length of order	51 weeks	51 weeks
Minimum period of custody to be served	6 months	14 days
Maximum period of custody to be served	6 months	90 days

The commencement arrangements for the different provisions are thus crucial.

Transitory arrangements

9.26   As noted at **9.21**, transitory arrangements apply until such time as the extended powers of imprisonment given to magistrates' courts are commenced. The effect of the Intermittent Custody (Transitory Provisions) Order 2003 (SI 2003/3283) is to introduce these. The effect of these is that the minimum and maximum lengths of order are, for the moment, 14 and 26 (not 28 or 52) weeks. The maximum period to be served in custody is 45 (not 90) days. In respect of consecutive orders, the maximum total period is 52 (not 65) weeks, and the total aggregate of days to be served must not exceed 90 days (not 180).

Licence

9.27   Those serving a sentence of intermittent custody will be released for periods of time on licence. That licence (like that applicable in custody plus) can be subject to requirements.

The Home Secretary may require courts to specify particular periods or particular parts of the week when making intermittent custody orders. It is likely to be introduced in two forms – service of custody at weekends, or during the week. It is likely to specify that custodial periods must be between two and four days, or require custodial periods at weekends. It might, for example, require a custodial period to include a Friday if heavy binge drinking on Friday nights has been an underlying cause of offending. The order will specify prescribed durations for licence periods, at what times of the day licence periods should begin or end, or may prohibit licence on prescribed days. The effect of this level of regulation is intended to be consistency, with broadly similar intermittent custody licences. It will prevent offenders serving custodial blocks of a single day, which would be impossible for prison and probation services to manage.[49]

The Criminal Justice (Sentencing) (Licence Conditions) Order 2003 (SI 2003/3337) sets out the standard conditions to be imposed on a prisoner released on licence as part of an intermittent custody order.

Article 2 of the Order provides that a prisoner must:

(a)   keep in touch with the responsible officer in accordance with instructions;
(b)   receive visits from the responsible officer in accordance with instructions;

---

49   White Paper, *op cit*, para 5.33.

(c)   permanently reside at an approved address, and obtain the prior permission of the responsible officer for any stay of one or more nights at a different address;

(d)   undertake work (including voluntary work) only with the approval of the responsible officer, and obtain prior approval in relation to any change in the nature of that work;

(e)   not travel outside the United Kingdom without the prior permission of the responsible officer;

(f)   be of good behaviour, and not behave in a way which undermines the purposes of the release on licence, which are to protect the public, prevent re-offending and promote successful re-integration into the community;

(g)   not to commit any offence.

These are the 'Standard Conditions'. In addition, the Home Secretary has specified conditions that may (under s 250(2)(b)(ii)) be included in an order if the court chooses to do so. These are that the prisoner must:

(a)   attend appointments arranged with a named psychologist or medical practitioner, and co-operate fully with any recommended care or treatment;

(b)   not take work (including voluntary work) or participate in any organised activity which will involve a person below an age specified by the responsible officer;

(c)   not spend one or more nights in the same household as any person below an age specified by the responsible officer;

(d)   not seek to approach or communicate with any person specified by the responsible officer without his prior approval or (in the case of a person aged under 18, that of a relevant social services department);

(e)   not enter a place (including an area) specified by the responsible officer except with the prior permission of the responsible officer;

(f)   remain at specified place for specified periods.

9.28   Intermittent custody depends on an offender being able to get to and from the place of detention. An offender may not wish, or be in a position, to consent if he has to pay significant travel costs. For that reason, s 186 provides a power, in effect, for the Home Office to subsidise the costs of travel to and from the place of imprisonment.

An offender who does not return to custody following a licence period will be regarded as unlawfully at large (s 186). He may then be returned to custody. The effect of s 186 is that the offender does not have to be released again for the intermittent licence period: the offender may be kept in custody while an application is made to the court to vary the order to full-time custody (s 186). The Home Secretary is not required to make such an application, but the option is there and, if he chooses to use it, the application must be made within 24 hours.

SUSPENDED SENTENCES

9.29   Section 189 enables prison sentences of less than 12 months to be suspended for a period between six months and two years. Part of the sentence is classified as the supervision period, and must be for at least six months. One or more of the requirements specified in s 189 can be imposed.

Background

9.30   Prison sentences may currently be suspended in the circumstances identified by s 118 of the SA 2000, which restricts the imposition of a suspended sentence to exceptional circumstances (SA 2000, s 118(4)).[50] The term of imprisonment cannot be for more than two years (SA 2000, s 118(1)) and a court cannot impose a community sentence on the same occasion as this sentence (s 118(6)). The operational period of suspension can be for no less than one year and no more than three years.

The Halliday Report considered that these restrictions were justified and should generally remain in place, for otherwise an offender might regard a suspended sentence as escaping punishment. Further, the new custody plus provisions and punishments for breach of community sentences 'should make a significant difference to the perceived "toughness" of the different community penalties'.[51] The Report noted, however, that in many jurisdictions community sentences have developed into 'conditional' prison sentences. It recommended that a sentencing court should have the power, when passing a community sentence, to indicate the length of prison service that would be a starting point for re-sentencing. It would concentrate the mind of the offender on the need to comply with the requirements of the community sentence.

The new Act does not follow that route, but, instead, creates a new system of intermediate sanctions – custody minus. A court can in some circumstances impose a suspended sentence of imprisonment which contains a supervision period during which the offending behaviour of the offender can be addressed.

The order

9.31   Section 189 applies where a court passes a sentence of imprisonment of at least 28 weeks but no more than 51 weeks, for a single offence. Where consecutive terms are imposed (wholly or partially consecutive) the aggregate must not exceed 65 weeks if the provisions of s 189 are to apply (s 189(2)). It thus mirrors the custody plus provisions.

Where s 189 applies the court may:

(a)   order the offender to comply during the *supervision period* with one or more requirements falling within s 189(1). The supervision period must be a period of not less than six months or no longer than the 'operational period' or two years, whichever is shorter, calculated from the commencement of the sentence (s 189(3), (4));

(b)   specify an *operational period*, again of not less than six months or more than two years, similarly calculated (s 189(3)).

The sentence of imprisonment does not take effect unless, during that operational period, the offender either fails to comply with a requirement in the order, or commits

---

50   See *Morrish* [1996] 1 Cr App R(S) 215, CA; *Snelling* [1996] 2 Cr App R (S) 56, CA; *Bellikli* [1998] 1 Cr App R(S) 135, CA.

51   Halliday Report, *op cit*, paras 5.16–5.17.

another offence, and a court having the power to do so orders the sentence to have effect (s 189(1)).

9.32 A suspended sentence under s 189 is a sentence of imprisonment for all purposes (s 189(6)), and the threshold for a custodial sentence applies. A court cannot impose a community sentence at the same time (s 189(5)).

Except where the order contains a drug rehabilitation order[52] (in respect of which separate review provisions exist), when making the order the court may provide that it be reviewed at specified intervals. Nothing in the Act limits the discretion of the court as to what those specified intervals might be. Those intervals may themselves be amended at a review hearing (s 191(7)).

The review will be by the court specified in the order as responsible for it. Despite the curious wording of s 191(3) and (4), it is clear that this will usually be the court which makes the order, but that court can specify another court. The section refers to 'the area' but nowhere states what the 'area' is meant to be. It presumably is intended to reflect the petty sessions area applicable to the place of residence of the offender. It is open to a sentencing court to specify the home court as the reviewing court. An order made by the Crown Court or the Court of Appeal when dealing with an appeal is deemed for these purposes to be made by that court (s 189(5)).

Requirements that may be imposed

9.33 These are specified by s 190(1), to which reference should be made. The available orders are rather wider than those available on custody plus, because the custodial nature of custody plus obviously restricts the range of appropriate requirements. Any particular provisions relating to specific requirements must be complied with (s 190(2)).[53]

Review

9.34 The order can provide for periodic review. It will provide for the responsible officer to report to the court responsible for the order. That report will deal with the offender's progress in complying with the community requirements of the order (s 191(1)(d)). At the review hearing, which, by s 191(1)(c), the offender must attend, the court must consider that report, and, subject to certain preconditions, amend the community requirements or any part of the order that relates to those requirements (s 192(1)). This power to amend the order presumably does not include the power to remove a requirement entirely, although s 192 does not say so explicitly. That conclusion necessarily follows, however, from the fact that Sch 12, para 12 contains powers to apply for the 'cancellation' of a requirement, and thus distinguishes cancellation from amendment. Provided the procedural requirements of Sch 12 are met there will not be any significant difference in practice.

The preconditions contained in s 192(2) are as follows:

---

52 The successor to the DTTO made under SA 2000, s 6. See **10.23**.

53 See generally Chapter 10, and **9.11**.

(a)   the court cannot impose a requirement of a different kind[54] unless the offender expresses his willingness to comply with the requirement;

(b)   it may not amend a mental health treatment requirement, a drug rehabilitation requirement or an alcohol treatment requirement unless the offender expresses his willingness to comply with the requirement as amended. If the view expressed above as to removal is not correct, then presumably removal of such a requirement (not being an amendment of such a requirement) does not require the consent of the offender;

(c)   the court may amend the supervision period only within the overall permitted time parameters of the order;

(d)   it cannot amend the operational period;

(e)   except with the consent of the offender, the court cannot amend the order while an appeal against the order is pending.

9.35   On review under s 192 the court can, if there is satisfactory progress, order that no further review hearing is to be held, or it may decide at the hearing, or before it, that the subsequent review be conducted without a hearing (s 192(4)), in accordance with s 192(8). The wording of s 192(4) is not entirely clear: the use of the words 'if before a review hearing is held at any review' might suggest that it is open to a court to dispense with the first review hearing. Yet the words ' ... so as to provide for each subsequent review ...' suggest that at any rate the first hearing must be held, with the offender in attendance. It would be a pity if a court was required to hold a hearing where nobody saw any need for one, but probably those subsequent words in fact require at least one hearing.

If there is a review without a hearing and the court considers that the offender's progress is not satisfactory, it can require the offender to attend at a specified time and place (s 192(5)). That is a permissive rather than a mandatory provision, yet it is difficult to envisage circumstances when it would not be appropriate for the court to require attendance of the offender. The court cannot proceed to breach the offender without first finding out whether reasonable excuse for non-compliance exists and, arguably, this can normally be established only with the offender present.

Failure to comply with a requirement without reasonable excuse entitles a court to adjourn for the purposes of dealing with the case under Sch 12, para 8.[55]

Breach of the order

9.36   An offender will be in breach of the order if he fails to comply with the requirement (s 189(1)(b)(i)), or if he commits another offence. That offence does not have to be punishable with imprisonment (s 189(1)(b)(ii)). Technically, it is the commission of, rather than conviction for, the offence that triggers breach, but it is difficult to envisage when it would in fact not be proved by evidence of conviction. Theoretically, an admission to an offence which, for whatever reason, is not proceeded with could trigger s 189(1)(b)(ii). The nature of the offence that triggers breach is not limited in any way: it could be the most minor of motoring offences and completely unrelated to the type of offence for which the suspended sentence order

---

54   Defined by s 192(3).

55   See **9.37**.

was imposed. All such matters will be relevant when considering the application of Sch 12.

9.37 Breach or amendment of a suspended sentence order is dealt with by Sch 12, to which detailed reference should be made. In broad terms its provisions are as follows:

- a duty is imposed on the responsible officer to warn the offender in respect of failure to comply without reasonable excuse with a requirement, unless one warning has already been given within 12 months, or proceedings are commenced in relation to the failure (para 3(1)). The content of the warning is specified by para 3(2);
- if there is failure to comply without reasonable excuse within 12 months following such a warning, proceedings must be commenced (para 4);
- the offender will be summonsed by the relevant magistrates' court or Crown Court (paras 5, 6);
- if the offender is found to be in breach of community requirement or by *conviction* for an offence, then in respect of an order imposed by a magistrates' court, the offender may be dealt with by any Crown Court or any magistrates' court before which he appears. In respect of a Crown Court order, only the Crown Court may deal with him (paras 7, 10);
- the court may bring into effect the original term, or a lesser term, or amend the order (para 7). If it brings the sentence into effect, it must make a custody plus order;
- on application by the offender or responsible officer, the court can cancel the community requirements (which presumably includes cancelling some of them) (para 12);
- the court can amend the petty sessions area following change of address (para 13);
- the court can amend the community requirements of the order (para 14);
- it can amend the treatment requirements in a mental health treatment requirement, drug rehabilitation requirement or an alcohol treatment requirement (para 15);
- the court can amend the review arrangements for drug rehabilitation requirement (para 16);
- it can extend an unpaid work requirement (para 17).

Paragraphs 18 to 21 of Sch 12 deal with detailed matters of procedure.

DANGEROUS OFFENDERS

9.38 Sections 225 to 236 create new indeterminate sentences in respect of dangerous offenders, whether adults or juveniles. Where a person aged 18 or over is convicted of a serious offence as defined by s 224, and the court is of the view that there is a significant risk to members of the public of serious harm occasioned by the commission of further specified offences, it must either impose a life sentence or a sentence of imprisonment for public protection (s 225). Equivalent provisions in respect of detention for life or a sentence of detention for public protection of an offender aged under 18 are contained in s 226. Sections 227 and 228 provide for extended sentences in respect of certain violent or sexual offences not falling within the serious offence indeterminate provisions.

Background

9.39   The need has long been recognised to create a regime whereby sex offenders and violent offenders, who may pose an ongoing risk to the public at large, are subject to restraint or supervision. Section 2 of the CJA 1991 provided for longer than commensurate sentences for violent or sexual offences. In addition, the arrangement for the release of prisoners contained in the CJA 1991 was based on special release provisions for sex offenders, with the licence period on release extending throughout the whole of the sentence period. No power existed to extend the period of supervision beyond the term of the sentence. That regime was considered inadequate and was tackled, first, by provisions in the C(S)A 1997 relating to sex offenders and violent offenders, which created extended supervision periods which could last beyond the end of the custodial term imposed. These provisions were never brought into force, and were repealed by the CDA 1998. The 1998 Act left in place the regime established by the 1991 Act, but subject to significant modification. The 'extended sentence' provisions are now to be found at s 85 of the SA 2000. These are repealed by the new Act. Other provisions enable a court to impose a custodial sentence when it would not otherwise be permitted to do so, when the court considers that there is a need to protect the public from serious harm from an offender.[56]

The Halliday Report recommended the replacement of these provisions. It considered[57] that where an offender does not fall within the MHA 1983 provisions, but a life sentence was available, it should always be considered. Where, however, the current offence, the risks of re-offending and the risks of resulting harm are not so serious as to justify imposing a life sentence, but when the risk of serious harm is clearly established, there should be a new indeterminate sentence, to be available where there were high risks of re-offending and serious harm. The new Act implements the Halliday recommendations.

The offences to which the provisions apply

9.40   A precondition for the imposition of the new sentences is that the offence is a '*serious offence*', although that alone does not suffice. The Act defines 'serious' offences by reference to '*specified*' offences (defined in turn by s 224(3) and Sch 15). Specified violent and specified sexual offences are identified by Parts 1 and 2 of Sch 15, to which detailed reference should be made. This Schedule contains more than 60 violent and more than 40 sexual offences. These offences cover a wide range of activities and of levels of seriousness, ranging, in the case of violent offences, from manslaughter, soliciting murder and wounding with intent to cause grievous bodily harm, to causing death by careless driving while under the influence of drink or drugs, carrying a firearm with criminal intent, racially aggravated assaults or public order offences. In respect of sexual offences, the net is again cast widely, from rape,

---

56   SA 2000, ss 79–80.

57   Halliday Report, *op cit*, paras 4.26–4.27.

unlawful sexual intercourse, incest, indecent assault, the offence of causing prostitution of women, to possession of indecent photographs of children, among others.

A 'serious offence' is defined by s 224(2) as a specified violent or sexual offence, which is (apart from s 224) punishable in the case of a person aged 18 or over by either a life sentence or imprisonment for a determinate term of ten years or more. Not all offences within Sch 12 are punishable with life imprisonment or a minimum of 10 years, and thus not all specified offences are serious offences. The new indeterminate power to detain for public protection (or its under-18 equivalent) applies only to serious offences.

Life sentence or imprisonment for public protection for serious offences – persons aged 18 or over

9.41   Section 225(1) provides that if:

(a)   a person aged 18 or over is convicted of a serious offence committed after the commencement of s 225; and
(b)   the court is of the opinion that there is a significant risk to members of the public of serious harm occasioned by the commission by him of further specified offences,

then the court must impose one or other of these sentences.

The wording of this provision was the subject of debate at a late stage. It was originally proposed that the court must be satisfied as to a significant risk of significant harm. That, however, was considered too vague[58] and the wording of s 225 now requires a court to look at the level of risk of serious harm occasioned by the commission of further specified offences. Those specified offences do not have to be of the same type as that for which the offender is before the court.

If the offence is punishable by imprisonment for life, and the court considers that the seriousness of the offence and any associated offence justifies a life sentence, it *must* impose such a sentence (s 225(2)). If that is not the case, but it considers a term of imprisonment other than under s 225 would not be adequate for the purpose of protecting the public from serious harm occasioned by the commission of further specified offences, it *must* impose a sentence of imprisonment for public protection. Both are to be regarded as indeterminate sentences (s 225(4)), but the licence arrangements differ in respect of each.[59]

Risk – assessment of dangerousness

9.42   As noted above, the risk of harm to members of the public must be 'significant', a term that seeks to distinguish minimal risks. The court must then determine whether those specified offences involve a significant degree of risk of serious harm to members of the public. In determining that question, s 229 applies.

---

58   See the debate at HL Committee, 14 October 2003, cols 780–794.

59   See **9.55** and **9.61**.

If, at the date of commission of the offence,[60] the offender had not been convicted in the United Kingdom of any 'relevant offence' (a term different from 'specified' or 'serious' offence), or was under the age of 18, the court must take into account all such information as is available to it about the nature and circumstances of the offence, and may take into account any information which is before it about any pattern of behaviour of which the offence forms part, and any information about the offender that is before it (s 229(2)).

If, at that date, the offender was aged 18 or over and had been convicted in any part of the United Kingdom of one or more relevant offences, the court must *assume* that the 'significant risk' exists, unless it decides that it would be unreasonable to conclude that there was such a risk. In deciding whether it would be unreasonable so to conclude, the court must take into account all such information as is available to it about the nature and circumstances of each of the offences, any information about any pattern of behaviour of which any of the offences forms part, and any information about the offender which is before it (s 229(3)).

The term 'relevant offence' is defined by s 229(4). It means a 'specified offence' committed in England and Wales, offences in Scotland or Northern Ireland falling within Schs 12 or 13 to the new Act, and an offence specified by Schs 15, 16 or 17 or constituted by an act or omission outside the United Kingdom. Thus, if an offender has been convicted of a serious violent offence, and has, say, a prior conviction for an indecent assault in adolescence many years previously the court *must assume* that the requisite risk exists unless it concludes that it would be unreasonable to assume so. It is not entirely clear why the assessment of risk should not be left at large for the court to decide. Interestingly, the Minister of State observed:[61]

> ' ... we think that any offender who appears before a court for a second sexual or violent offence must be considered a threat to the public, regardless of whether the offences were of a serious nature. Restricting the provisions to offences of a serious sexual and violent nature could result in dangerous offenders being sentenced to a determinate rather than an indeterminate sentence, thus causing an unnecessary risk of harm to the public ... The [Act] provides a valuable safety net, to ensure that all offenders convicted of two relevant offences are assumed to be dangerous ...'

No such presumption arises in the context of those aged under 18, suggesting that, with young offenders, courts are, rightly, expected to look at the issue on a case-by-case basis. That may well be the reality of what the courts do, given the proviso that no presumption arises if it is unreasonable so to assume. That would effectively make s 229 a dead letter. By contrast, if the courts rely on the presumption to any great extent there is a danger of indeterminate or extended sentences being imposed inappropriately and in a disproportionate way, thus inviting challenge.

9.43 Section 229 identifies the matters that must and those that may be taken into account. It is unclear as to whether these are the only matters to which a court may, or must, have regard. Take, for example, conduct which has not led to a conviction, such as, in the case of a man convicted of a sex offence against a child, evidence of hanging

---

60 If an offence was committed over two or more days, it must be taken to have been committed on the last of those days (s 234).

61 Baroness Scotland, HL Committee, 14 October 2003, col 776.

round school gates or children's playgrounds, or the taking of children to a burger bar or funfair.[62] That conduct, although not having led to a conviction for an offence within the meaning of s 229(3), is relevant to risk, and is information about a 'pattern of behaviour' (if we can construe the concept of 'pattern' broadly) or, alternatively, is 'information about the offender'.

In assessing risk, arrangements should be in place in each area for assessing and managing the risks posed in that area by relevant sexual or violent offenders, and other persons who by reason of offences committed by them (wherever committed) are considered by the responsible authority to be persons who may cause serious harm to the public. The detail of that is set out in ss 325 to 327.

9.44 What amounts to a 'significant risk' will be a matter for the court. The concept of risk should not be confused with that of 'danger'. Risk relates to the probability that a harmful event or behaviour will occur. 'Danger' describes the actual exposure to harm, or the propensity of certain individuals or circumstances to present harm.[63] The use of the word 'significant' is therefore designed to ensure that risks that are remote or slight do not form a basis of the making of a s 225 order. The element of risk must be 'important'.[64]

This 'significant risk' must be one of serious harm to the public. 'Serious harm' is defined in the same way as was the case in s 31(3) of the CJA 1991, namely death or serious personal injury, whether physical or psychological (s 224(3)). In this context the decision in *Bowler*[65] is relevant, despite the fact that it was dealing with the power contained in the 1991 Act to impose a longer than commensurate sentence. This power was not limited to exceptional cases where the danger of serious harm was obvious and had actually been caused in the past. A judge could reasonably form the opinion that there was a danger that serious harm might occur in the future. An indecent assault on a young girl might well lead to serious psychological injury, and some adult women might be severely disturbed by a relatively minor indecent assault.[66] The purpose of that section included the protection of those women, less robust than average, who might be vulnerable to that kind of conduct.[67] It should not be overlooked that a precondition for the exercise of the s 225 power is that the offence is punishable with either life, or a maximum determinate term of at least ten years. If a sexual or violent offence does not attract such a sentence, then a court will need to consider the imposition of an extended sentence under s 227.[68]

9.45 The risk must be that of serious harm to the public. The 'public' is not defined. Unlike some statutory provisions there is no reference to 'section of the public', but

---

62 In some circumstances that conduct may amount to an offence under Sexual Offences Act 2003, s 17.

63 See Kemshall, *Reviewing Risk* (Home Office, 1997).

64 Baroness Scotland, HL Committee, 14 October 2003, col 788.

65 (1994) 15 Cr App R (S) 78, CA.

66 See *Att-Gen's References (Nos 37, 38, 44, 54, 51, 35, 40, 43, 45, 41 and 42 of 2003)* (2003) *The Times*, 29 October, CA.

67 *Apelt* (1994) 15 Cr App R (S) 532, CA; *Williams* (1994) 15 Cr App R (S) 330, CA; see also *Creasy* (1994) 15 Cr App R 671, CA, for a case involving a minor assault on a boy.

68 See **9.50**.

that is unimportant. An offence against an individual, or even the targeting of an individual, potentially gives rise to a risk in respect of members of the public generally. Whether in fact it does so, and the level of that risk, is for the court to decide, taking into account the conclusions of the agencies which know of the offender.

Clearly, the perpetrator of sexual offences against women or children poses a risk of serious harm to the public, ie to other potential victims. More difficulty arises in the context of marital rape or other domestic violence. The offender may be unlikely to offend sexually against other women. Although it might be argued that he posed a danger only to his wife, and thus there was no danger to the public, his conduct shows a propensity to engage in inappropriate and unlawful sexual behaviour. The fact that the sexual offence was against his wife is relevant to the level of risk of future harm, but a risk of harm to the public nonetheless exists. An offender who has targeted only one child has nonetheless caused concerns to arise not only for that child, but for other children, because he has shown, by his conduct, that he has a sexual attraction to children. The man who downloads indecent images of children may not, in a narrow sense, have caused 'harm' to anybody, but nonetheless by providing a 'market' for such material may cause a significant risk of serious harm to those who, as a result, may be forced to be photographed and misused in that way – and may, of course, show a sexual interest and predilection that in itself gives rise to an assessment of a significant risk of serious harm.

9.46   The risk must be one of serious harm occasioned by the commission of 'further specified offences'. Those do not have to be the same offences, or even of the same type, as the one for which the offender is being sentenced. Thus, if a court is sentencing an offender for assault and the court concludes that there is a significant risk that he will cause serious harm to the public by the commission of sex offences, this will suffice.

9.47   Where the preconditions for s 225 are satisfied, the court will have to determine:

–   whether the specified offence is punishable by life or by a maximum term of at least ten years. If it is not, the court must look to the extended sentence provisions in s 227 and s 228;
–   whether this is an offence for which a life sentence is appropriate. That will be answered on normal sentencing principles. If it is, such a sentence must be imposed. That has to be determined on the basis of the seriousness of the offence, and any associated offences. Other factors relating to matters other than offence seriousness are not relevant for this purpose;
–   if the offence seriousness is not such as to justify a life sentence, the court must pass a sentence for public protection, if the court is of the view that a determinate term would not be adequate for the purposes of protecting the public from serious harm occasioned by the commission of further specified offences. The court will need to consider the alternative courses of action. In particular, it will need to consider whether an extended sentence is a realistic alternative.

9.48   The life sentence or sentence of imprisonment for public protection is an indeterminate sentence, and s 230 and Sch 18 apply in respect of release on licence. The fact remains that a number of offenders will remain in detention for perhaps indefinite periods justified not by what they have in fact done but in respect of what it is believed they may do in the future. The legality of that will be determined by the proportionality of the detention to the level of risk posed.

Detention for life or for public protection for serious offences – persons aged under 18

9.49   Section 226 replicates the provisions of s 225 in the context of offenders aged under 18. With the substitution of the terms 'detention for life' and 'detention for public protection' for 'life imprisonment' and 'imprisonment for public protection', the provisions are identical, and the issues that arise are the same. The use of this power must be considered in the context of s 37 of the CDA 1998, which states that the principal aim of the youth justice system is to prevent offending by children and young persons. The fact that s 44 of the CYPA 1933 requires a court, in fulfilling its duties, to take account of the welfare of the child or young person does not disentitle Parliament and the courts from taking steps in the name of public protection.

Section 226 applies, where the offender has committed a serious offence. The definition of 'serious offence' in s 224 defines offences by the possible punishment for a person aged 18 or over. Thus, the fact that special arrangements exist limiting punishment in respect of young offenders does not deprive the offence of the characteristic of being a 'serious offence'.

Extended sentence for violent or sexual offences – persons aged 18 or over

9.50   Section 227 provides for the imposition of an extended sentence in respect of specified offences which do not fall within the definition of 'serious offence' in s 224(2).

If a person aged 18 or over is convicted of such an offence after the commencement of s 227, and the court considers that:

(a)   there is a significant risk to members of the public of serious harm occasioned by the commission by the offender of further specified offences, and

(b)   the term of imprisonment which it would pass if it passed a term of imprisonment otherwise than under s 227 would not be adequate for the purpose of protecting the public from serious harm occasioned by the commission by the offender of further specified offences,

it must impose an extended sentence of imprisonment.

An extended sentence of imprisonment is a term equal to the aggregate of the 'appropriate custodial term', and a further period ('the extension period') for which the offender is to be subject to a licence and which is of such length as the court considers necessary for the purpose of protecting members of the public from serious harm occasioned by the commission by him of further specified offences (s 227(2)). The total length of the extended sentence must not exceed the maximum term permitted for the offence (s 227(5)).

9.51   The extended sentence thus comprises two elements. The first, 'the appropriate custodial term', is the term of imprisonment that would otherwise be imposed, unless that term would be less than 12 months, in which case it is to be 12 months (s 227(3)). The effect of that is to avoid the effect of the custody plus provisions[69] that would otherwise result in a much shorter custodial period.

The second is the 'extension period'. This is a period of licence, which must not exceed five years in the case of a specified violent offence, and nine years in the case of a specified sexual offence (s 227(4)). There is no minimum extension period.

9.52   An offender may be being sentenced for two or more offences, only some of which are specified offences. In that situation the rules will apply appropriately to each aspect of the sentence.

9.53   The period served will be determined by the licence provisions contained in s 247.[70] The prisoner is eligible for release having served one-half of the appropriate custodial term, of whatever length, if recommended by the Parole Board. He must be released on licence at the expiration of the appropriate custodial sentence unless previously recalled under s 254 (s 249(2)).

Extended sentence for violent or sexual offence – persons aged under 18

9.54   Section 228 contains similar, but not identical, provisions to those created by s 227 in respect of offenders aged 18 or over. The detention provisions contained in s 91 of the SA 2000 are repealed.

The preconditions in s 228(1) are exactly the same, and the nature of the order and the extension periods mirror those in s 227. The one significant difference is in respect of the custodial term. It must be at least 12 months, but must not exceed 24 months, or the maximum term of imprisonment permitted for commission of the offence by an adult. The 24-month maximum reflects the maximum period for a detention and training order (the normal custodial disposal for those aged under 18).

Release on licence

9.55   Those who are subject to a sentence of imprisonment, or detention, for public protection are subject to the licence regime applicable to life prisoners and contained in ss 28 to 31 of the 1997 Act, set out in Sch 18 to the new Act. Schedule 18 amends s 31 of the C(S)A 1997, and inserts a new s 31A. Where a prisoner has been released on licence, and the 'qualifying period' has expired, the prisoner can make an application to the Parole Board that the licence is to cease to have effect. The 'qualifying period' is the period of ten years beginning with the date of his release.

The prisoner cannot make an application to the Parole Board within 12 months of any previous application. When considering the application, the Parole Board can direct the Home Secretary to terminate the licence period only if it is satisfied that it is no longer necessary for the protection of the public that the licence should remain in force. If a direction is made, the Home Secretary is under a duty to terminate that licence (s 31A(2)).

---

69   See **9.2**.

70   See **9.61**.

Conversion of sentences of detention into sentences of imprisonment

9.56   Section 99 of the SA 2000 provided for the case of an offender sentenced to detention in a young offender institution, detention during Her Majesty's pleasure, detention under s 91 of the SA 2000, or custody for life, who attained the age of 21 during the period of detention. That provision is repealed and re-enacted by s 236 of the new Act.

The new s 99 simply replicates the pre-existing s 99. Where a direction has been made in respect of a detainee under s 226 or s 228, he is then to be regarded as having been sentenced to a term of imprisonment under s 225 or s 227. A further change is the repeal without re-enactment of s 99(2). The effect of this is that when the prisoner is released, following a direction, he is subject to the supervision arrangements appropriate to a term of imprisonment, not those applicable to the supervision of young offenders after release.[71]

FIXED-TERM SENTENCES – PERIOD TO BE SERVED AND RELEASE ON LICENCE

9.57   The new Act repeals the provisions of Part 2 of the CJA 1991, which deal with the early release of prisoners. They are replaced by the provisions of Chapter 6 (ss 237 to 268). The effect is to alter significantly the rules relating to those sentenced to a term of imprisonment greater than 12 months. A standard pattern that one-half of the sentence is served in prison, subject only to earlier release on home detention curfew, is introduced. The distinction between long-term and short-term prisoners is abolished. The new provisions ensure the release on licence at the half-way mark of a fixed-term sentence, subject to early release on home detention curfew up to 135 days early, not hitherto available for long-term prisoners. The period of 135 days is also an increase from the pre-existing 60 days applicable hitherto only to short-term prisoners. The period of licence following release will extend throughout the term of the whole sentence, not, as now, terminating at the two-thirds point.

Section 239 re-enacts s 32 of the 1991 Act. The effect is to continue in being the Parole Board, although with the abolition of parole for long-term prisoners under the new arrangements its focus will change towards looking at issues of risk in respect of dangerous offenders and life prisoners. Section 239 also provides for its constitution and is supplemented by Sch 16.

9.58   A new power is vested in the court in respect of an offender who is being sentenced to a term of 12 months or more (except where the sentence is detention under s 91 of the SA 2000 – detention for certain serious offences – or under s 228 of the new Act – see **9.54**). Section 238 provides that, in those circumstances, a court may, when passing sentence, recommend to the Home Secretary particular conditions which, in its view, should be included in any licence granted to the offender on his release from prison. The recommendation does not form part of the sentence (s 238(3)) and thus the recommendation cannot be appealed. The Home Secretary

---

71   See **9.64**.

must have regard to the recommendation, but is not bound by it when determining what conditions are to be applied to the licence on release (s 238(2)).

Background

9.59 The Halliday Report considered that current sentencing provisions lack clarity, are not well understood, and do not fully engage with the need to work with offenders to reduce offending behaviour.[72] Nowhere is that more true than in the context of sentence length. Despite its relatively recent origin, the body of law relating to calculation of sentence length and early release is complex, confusing, in some aspects difficult to apply and not transparent, in the sense of it not being clear to the public what a sentence actually means in terms of the period of time actually served. Back in 1996 the then Government observed that 'the public, and sometimes even the courts, are frequently confused and increasingly cynical about what prison sentences mean'.[73] Some clarity might have been achieved had the provisions of the C(S)A 1997 been implemented, but those provisions were viewed as excessively complicated and unsatisfactory and were repealed by the CDA 1998 which, instead, made significant amendment to the 1991 Act, including the introduction of home detention curfew. In the light of this background, the need for further review and change is, perhaps, unsurprising.

Under the pre-existing provisions contained in the CJA 1991, a distinction is drawn between short-term and long-term prisoners. In relation to the former (persons serving a term of up to four years or more), the prisoner served half of the sentence, and the remainder on licence, subject also to early release under the home detention curfew provisions, which permit early release up to 90 days. Thus, it was possible for a prisoner sentenced to a 12-month term in fact to serve little more than four months. In respect of long-term prisoners (those sentenced to a term of four years or more), the prisoner served half of the sentence before being eligible for release on licence following a decision of the Parole Board. Automatic release occurred at the two-thirds of sentence point, and the licence continues until the three-quarters of sentence point. This difference in the treatment of long- and short-term prisoners could be explained on the basis that those serving longer sentences were likely to include prisoners who might be a danger to the public and thus different release and supervision arrangements needed to be in place.[74]

9.60 The Halliday Report identified key issues in, and problems with, the existing arrangements, in particular the illogicality of the distinction between different types of prisoner, the end of supervision arrangements at the three-quarters point, and the difficulty (and embarrassment) the current arrangements cause to sentencers who have to try to explain them in open court.[75] It concluded as follows:[76]

'... prison sentences should be served partly in prison and partly in the community, so that resettlement and behaviour after release can be steered and monitored under conditions

---

72 See **8.4–8.9**.

73 *Protecting the Public*, Cm 3190 (1996), at para 9.3.

74 See Lord Filkin, HL Committee, 14 October 2003, col 803.

75 Halliday Report, *op cit*, paras 4.1–4.10.

76 *Ibid*, para 4.15.

whose breach may necessitate return to prison. But to make prison sentences more meaningful they should be served in full. The first half should always be in prison. Whether any part of the second half needs to be in prison should depend on the offender's compliance with conditions imposed on release. Those conditions should be based on up to date assessments of risks, and of needs for continuing work to prevent re-offending and protect the public.'

The new Act builds on this approach.

The duty to release prisoners

9.61 By s 244, the Home Secretary must release a fixed-term prisoner[77] on licence,[78] once the prisoner has served the 'requisite custodial period'. The one exception to that is a prisoner who is serving an intermittent custody order.[79] Such a prisoner is released on licence between periods of time spent in custody. If the prisoner is recalled from licence, then the obligation to release at the end of the requisite custodial period does not exist – although the Home Secretary might choose to do so (s 244(2)).

The requisite custody period is defined by s 244. The potential for release earlier than at the end of this period exists under s 246 (home detention curfew – see **9.67**). The requisite custody period is 50% of a term of 12 months or more. To that must be added any additional days imposed for disciplinary offences under s 257.[80]

Single sentence
In respect of a term of 12 months or more the custodial period will be one-half of the term imposed. The requisite custody period for a sentence of less than 12 months or of intermittent custody is the custody period calculated under the requirements of those orders.[81] In respect of a custody plus order there must be a minimum licence period of 26 weeks. In all cases the actual time served after date of the imposition of the sentence may be affected by credit for time spent in custody.[82]

Concurrent sentences
Where a court makes orders that are wholly or partly concurrent, the length of the requisite custody period is calculated by reference to the longest sentence (s 263(1)). The offender is not entitled to be released until eligible for release in respect of each of the sentences. If the sentences were passed on different occasions, the offender must not have been released under these provisions at any time during the period beginning with the first sentence and ending with the date of sentence for the last offence.

The effect of this is that if one of the sentences is for 12 months or more, his release and licence provisions will be in accordance with such a sentence, and not under custody plus or intermittent custody arrangements (s 263(3)).

---

77 See s 237 for the definition of fixed-term prisoner.

78 Except for fine defaulters and contemnors: see **9.61**.

79 As to which, see **9.21**. Section 244 only applies to fixed-term prisoners, defined to exclude these by s 237.

80 See **9.62**.

81 See **9.2** and **9.21**.

82 See **9.75**.

Consecutive sentences
Where consecutive sentences are passed on the same occasion or, alternatively, the offender has not been released from one sentence before being sentenced to another to be served consecutively, the length of the requisite period is the aggregate of the custodial periods of the component sentences.

The licence provisions that are applicable will depend on whether the sentences which are consecutive are of less than 12 months, or include at least one term of 12 months or more (s 264).

Extended sentences
In relation to extended sentences, the custodial period is the appropriate custodial term determined either under s 227 or s 228. At this point the offender may be released on licence at the one-half point of the custodial term if the Parole Board so recommends (s 247(2)).

Additional days

9.62   Section 257 re-enacts pre-existing provisions that allow for additional days to be added to the period to be served. Prison rules can make provision for these. The effect is that any period which must be served before becoming entitled to or eligible for release is increased, and any licence period is extended by the aggregate of the additional days. Thus, if seven extra days are awarded to a prisoner serving 12 months, he will serve 12 months plus seven days, and then be subject to licence for a further period ending six months after his actual date of release.

Release on licence

9.63   A period of licence follows release on service of the custodial term, except in the case of those committed to prison in default of a sum adjudged to be paid by a conviction, or for contempt of court or any kindred offence (s 258). Such individuals must be released unconditionally once they have served one-half of the term imposed.

Release on licence at the end of the custodial term is automatic. There may be discretionary release on licence on home detention curfew where the terms of s 246 are satisfied. The power to release on compassionate grounds is re-enacted (s 248).

Length

9.64   The licence period continues until the expiration of the total length of the term imposed (s 249(1)), subject to the provisions relating to recall under s 254, and subject to the special arrangements that apply in the context of intermittent custody orders (s 245(2)). The potential for earlier release under home detention curfew should not be overlooked.

Where there are concurrent sentences, the licence period will be the period that is applicable to the longest sentence (s 263(2)(c)). Where one or more of those custodial sentences is a term of 12 months or more, the relevant licence period will be in respect of that sentence.

Where there are consecutive terms of imprisonment, all individually of less than 12 months in length, the licence continues up to the 'relevant time' (s 264(4)). The 'relevant time' is calculated as the sum total of all the custodial periods and the longest of any of the licence periods. Thus, if the offender is sentenced to two terms of 28 weeks and 32 weeks, the maximum custody period that can be imposed for any one offence is 13 weeks, and together a maximum custody period of 26 weeks. If, therefore, the custody period for each of the two terms was 13 weeks, the offender would serve eight weeks in custody (the aggregate of the sum total of adding together the product of taking each term and deducting 26) because of the rule that the licence period for any one offence must be a minimum of 26 weeks. The licence period in respect of each offence is 26 weeks. Thus, the sentence length comprises 34 weeks in total, 26 of which are on licence.

If one of the consecutive sentences is of 12 months or greater, s 264(3) applies. The offender serves a period on licence so that, by the end of the licence period, the total length of the sentence served, whether in custody or on licence, is equal to the aggregate of the terms. If the sentences are respectively 48 weeks and 18 months, consecutive, the custody periods may be 13 weeks and nine months. The offender will thus serve approximately[83] 49 weeks in custody, with the licence period being approximately 70 weeks in length.

Conditions on sentence less than 12 months

9.65 The licence will be subject to conditions. These conditions will be those specified in the court order, and 'the standard conditions'. The court, when making a custody plus, intermittent custody or suspended sentence order, has the power to impose requirements in the order, and will do so in the light of the detailed assessments in the PSR. Those will be part of the licence conditions. If it specifies a prohibited activity requirement, exclusion requirement, residence requirement or supervision requirement, those requirements will apply to any licence period, including home detention curfew or compassionate release (s 240(3)). The licence may also include an electronic monitoring condition[84] or a condition in respect of a drug-testing requirement[85] (s 240(2)(b)). The standard conditions are conditions that may be prescribed by order made by the Home Secretary (s 240(1)). When making an order specifying standard conditions, the Home Secretary must have regard to the need for protection of the public, the prevention of re-offending, and of securing the successful re-integration of the prisoner into the community (s 240(8)).

Conditions on sentence of 12 months or greater

9.66 In respect of these sentences, conditions will be the standard conditions, and those other conditions specified, of a kind prescribed by the Home Secretary. A

---

83   The arithmetic is not exact because of the difficulty in an example (and probably in real life) of combining weeks and months in the same calculation.

84   Section 62 of the CJCSA 2000 permits the imposition of conditions on release on licence for securing the electronic monitoring of the offender's compliance with any other conditions of his release, and for securing the electronic monitoring of his whereabouts (otherwise than for the purpose of securing his compliance with other conditions of his release).

85   Section 64 of the CJCSA 2000 permits the imposition of conditions on a person aged 14 or over in respect of drug-testing requirements. It is amended by the new Act: see s 161.

sentencing court can recommend the imposition of conditions: those will be borne in mind, but the recommendations of the court are not binding.[86]

Conditions on home detention curfew

9.67   Section 246 re-enacts, with amendments, the home detention curfew provisions. Where early release on licence is granted under these provisions, a curfew condition will apply, and is dealt with by s 252.[87]

Compliance with conditions

9.68   The offender is under a duty to comply with the licence conditions (s 251). If he fails to do so, he may be dealt with under the recall provisions of ss 254 to 256.[88]

Drug-testing requirements on release on licence

9.69   Section 64 of the CJCSA 2000 introduced a power to impose drug-testing requirements on a person aged 18 or over. For the purpose of determining whether the person is complying with any conditions of a licence issued to a person being released from a term of imprisonment imposed for a trigger offence, a drug-testing requirement could be imposed. This is a requirement that the person must provide, when instructed to do so by an officer of a local probation board or other authorised person, any sample mentioned in the instruction for the purposes of ascertaining whether he has any specified Class A drug in his body.

As part of the series of changes made by the new Act to strengthen powers to deal with drug misuse, s 266 amends s 64. It does so, first, by extending its ambit to those aged 14 or over. This extension to persons under 18 is a significant extension. A sample may not be required from a person aged under 17 except in the presence of an appropriate adult (CJCSA 2000, s 64(4A)), defined by a new s 64(6).

The preconditions for the requirement are also amended. References to 'trigger offences' have disappeared. The amended s 64(1) will now provide that the responsible officer must be of the opinion that the offender has a propensity to misuse specified Class A drugs, and that the misuse by the offender of any specified Class A drug caused or contributed to any offence of which he has been convicted, or is likely to cause or contribute to the commission of further offences.

The opinion that the offender 'has a propensity to misuse' drugs does not mean that it must be shown that there is evidence of presence of a drug at any particular time. It may be that it is the offence itself rather than the offender's physical or mental state that gives rise to that opinion. Nor do the offences which the misuse caused or to which it contributed have to be drugs offences. They may be burglaries, to fund the drug habit, or public order offences caused by drug-induced lack of inhibition.

---

86   See **9.11**.

87   See **9.70**.

88   See **9.74**.

Home detention curfew

9.70 The CDA 1998 amended the CJA 1991 to introduce a power for the Home Secretary to release some, although not all, short-term prisoners on licence, and for a curfew to be imposed on that licence. Persons granted early release in this way would thus serve part of their sentence at home which would otherwise be served in custody. Section 246 of the new Act re-enacts that power, with significant amendment. In particular, it extends the power to most fixed-term sentences, departing from the principle that it ought not to apply to those serving longer sentences. It also extends the period of licence, by increasing the number of days left to be served (one of the criteria for the granting of early release) to 135 days.

9.71 The power to release on licence under s 246 does not apply to all offenders. The list of those who are not eligible is set out in s 246.

9.72 Alongside the power to release early is the power to impose a curfew condition, contained in s 253. The curfew condition may specify different places or periods for different days, but may not specify periods which amount to less than nine hours in any one day (excluding the first and last days) (s 253(2)). The curfew condition continues in force until the date when the released prisoner would (but for this early release) be entitled to release under s 244. Detailed provisions apply in the case of intermittent custody: in essence, s 252(4) provides that one calculates how many custodial days remained to be served when the prisoner was released. The curfew condition remains in force until the number of days that it has been in force equals that first number.

Licence for extended sentences

9.73 The changes discussed above bring many prisoners serving long sentences for serious offences within the ambit of automatic licence. The main exception to that is in respect of prisoners serving extended sentences. Because, by definition, these offenders are considered dangerous, the concept of automatic release does not apply. Instead, the Parole Board retains its decision-making role.

By s 247, as soon as a prisoner who is serving an extended sentence has served one-half of the custodial term, and the Parole Board has directed his release, the Home Secretary must release him on licence. The licence will last through the remainder of the sentence (s 259).

The Parole Board may not give a direction for release unless it is satisfied that it is no longer necessary for the protection of the public that the prisoner should be confined (s 247(2)).

Recall from licence

9.74 Sections 254 to 256 re-enact, with necessary amendments, the provisions relating to recall of prisoners while on licence. Such a case must be referred to the Parole Board (s 254(3)). Reference should be made to these provisions for the detail.

Sentence length – crediting of periods in custody on remand

9.75   Section 240 re-enacts, with amendments, s 87 of the SA 2000, which was never brought into force because of the difficulties of calculating police detention and court custody time. The Halliday Report recommended the amendment of s 87 to remove references to police detention.[89] It explained its view thus:

'The reasons ... are to do with both reasons of principle and practicability. There is a qualitative difference between time spent on remand and time spent in police custody. The former is preventative and imposed by the courts, whereas the latter is an unavoidable feature of the investigation of crime ... There are also administrative difficulties.'

The new provision adopts the Halliday approach.

9.76   Section 241 applies where:

(a)   a court sentences an offender to imprisonment for a term in respect of an offence committed after the commencement of s 240; and

(b)   the offender has been remanded in custody in connection with the offence for a related offence, that is to say, any other offence the charge for which was founded on the same facts or evidence.

Subject to the exceptions contained in s 240(4), the sentencing court must direct that the number of days for which the offender was remanded in custody in connection with an offence or a related offence shall count as time served by the offender as part of the sentence imposed (s 240(3)). Despite the seemingly clear words of s 240(3) that the court must specify the number of days the offender was remanded in custody, in fact a court may give a direction in respect of a lesser number of days if the test in s 240(4)(b) is satisfied ('where in the opinion of the court it is just in all the circumstances not to give a direction'). That is not expressly stated, but clearly flows from the terms of s 240(5)(b) and from s 240(6), which speaks of 'a number of days less than that for which the offender was remanded in custody ... '. In giving a direction, the court must state in open court the number of days for which the offender was remanded in custody, and the number of days in relation to which the direction is given (s 240(5)).

9.77   Section 240(4) deals with the power not to give a direction, where it is just not to do so. This addresses the issue of whether credit should be given for periods of time spent on remand concurrently with the service of imprisonment for other offences. The wording of s 240(4) is such that the presumption will be that such a period can potentially count, for otherwise there would be no need for the exception to the general rule in s 240(4)(a). The exception will be contained in rules made by the Home Secretary.

DETERMINATION OF MINIMUM TERM IN RELATION TO MANDATORY LIFE SENTENCE

9.78   During the passage of the Act, new provisions were added to set out minimum periods of imprisonment to be served by prisoners sentenced to life imprisonment for

---

89   Halliday Report, *op cit*, para 7.12.

murder. These changes have proved some of the most controversial of all the changes in the new Act.

9.79 Prior to December 2002, guidance as to the minimum period to be served by a mandatory life prisoner was given by the judiciary to the Home Secretary. Since 1983 the setting of the tariff governing the period to be served by a mandatory life prisoner has been in the hands of the Home Secretary, in the light of the recommendation of the trial judge and Lord Chief Justice. The Home Secretary's role has been the subject of repeated challenge, both in domestic courts and at the European Court of Human Rights (ECtHR).[90] In 1991, following the decision of the ECtHR in *Thynne v United Kingdom*,[91] to the effect that the setting of a tariff in the case of a discretionary life sentence was a judicial function that should be independent of the Executive, Parliament passed what is now s 28 of the C(S)A 1997, which requires the trial judge to set the tariff. Subsequent challenges have been made in respect of the sentence of young offenders to detention during Her Majesty's pleasure: in *V v United Kingdom*[92] the ECtHR held that the Home Secretary had acted in breach of Art 6 in setting the tariff for V, a convicted young person. In *R v Secretary of State for the Home Department ex parte Venables*,[93] the majority of the House of Lords found that a sentence of detention during Her Majesty's pleasure was not the same as a mandatory life sentence, and that it was unfair for the Home Secretary to set the tariff. Other cases, however, drew a distinction between these situations and mandatory life sentences for adults.[94]

9.80 This distinction between mandatory and discretionary life sentences was called into question by the ruling of the ECtHR in *Stafford v United Kingdom*[95] where the Court observed (at para 79) that it was now established that there is no distinction between mandatory life prisoners, life prisoners and juvenile murderers as regards the nature of tariff-fixing, it being regarded as a sentencing exercise. This rejection of these distinctions, which involved a rejection of the principle inherent in *Wynne v United Kingdom*[96] that the mandatory life sentence constituted punishment for life, was the cornerstone of the decision of the House of Lords in *R (Anderson) v Secretary of State*,[97] which concluded that the Home Secretary should not play a part in fixing the tariff of a convicted murderer, even if he did no more than confirm what the judge had recommended. The fixing of the tariff was a sentencing exercise, involving an assessment of the quantum of punishment. The role of the Home Secretary was open to objection because it infringed the right to a fair trial under Art 6: the Home Secretary was not independent of the Executive. Section 29 of the C(S)A 1997 could

---

90 For a detailed chronology of events, see the speech of Lord Bingham in *R (Anderson) v Secretary of State for Home Affairs* [2002] 4 All ER 1089 at 1097b–1098b.

91 13 EHRR 666, ECtHR.

92 Reported, with its companion case *T v United Kingdom*, at [2000] 2 All ER 1024, ECtHR.

93 [1997] 3 All ER 97, HL.

94 See *Doody v Secretary of State for the Home Department* [1993] 3 All ER 92, HL; *R v Secretary of State for Home Affairs ex parte Venables* [1997] 3 All ER 97, HL.

95 (2002) 13 BHRC 260.

96 (1995) 19 EHRR 333.

97 [2002] 4 All ER 1089.

not be read in a way that was compatible with the Convention right.[98] The House therefore made a declaration on incompatibility under s 4 of the Human Rights Act 1998, a conclusion confirmed as correct by the decision in 2003 by the ECtHR in *Easterbrook v United Kingdom*[99] that the fundamental principle of the separation of judicial and executive powers was breached when the Home Secretary, albeit guided by judicial opinion, fixed a tariff for a life prisoner.

This decision was the catalyst for interim changes brought in during 2002, when the Lord Chief Justice issued sentencing guidelines as to minimum terms following consultation with the Sentencing Advisory Panel.[100] This was the reason, perhaps, why the provisions relating to determination of minimum term for mandatory life sentences were not part of the original Bill when published in December 2002.

9.81 Section 269 makes provision for the setting of a mandatory term to be served for cases where the court passes a life sentence in circumstances where the sentence is fixed by law (ie murder). It provides that, unless an order is made under s 269(4), s 28(5)–(8) of the 1997 Act (the 'early release provisions') is to apply to the offender as soon as he has served the part of his sentence which is specified in the order.

The effect of this is that the sentencing court must, in most cases, specify a minimum period of sentence. It must do so in open court, setting out its reasons for the making of the order (s 270(1)). It must state which of the starting points in Sch 21 it has chosen, and its reasons for doing so, and the reasons for any departure from that starting point (s 270(2)). As soon as the life prisoner has served the part of his sentence specified in the order, and the Parole Board has directed his release under s 28 of the 1997 Act, the Home Secretary must release him on licence (C(S)A 1997, s 28(5)). Section 28(6) to (8) deals with the questions as to when, and by whom, a case may be referred to the Parole Board, and its operation is now extended to mandatory life prisoners (s 275(2)). Where a life prisoner is transferred to England and Wales and has been the subject of an indeterminate sentence of imprisonment or detention, special rules apply.

9.82 The length of time to be specified in the order will be that which the court thinks appropriate, taking into account the seriousness of the offence, or the combination of the offence and any offences associated with it (s 269(3)(a)). It must also take into account the effect of any direction it would have made in respect of credit for periods of time on remand[101] in custody had it been a sentence to a term of imprisonment (s 269(3)(b)).

Section 269(4) applies to an offender who was aged 21 or over when he committed the offence. If the court is of the opinion that, because of the seriousness of the offence, or of the offence and any associated offences, no order should be made, it must order that the early release provisions are not to apply.

9.83 At the heart of these provisions is the question of the determination of offence seriousness. The court must have regard to the general principles set out in Sch 21, and

---

98 Section 29(1) of the C(S)A 1997.

99 (2003) *The Times*, 18 June, ECtHR.

100 *Practice Statement (Crime: Life Sentences)* [2002] 1 WLR 1789.

101 See **9.75**.

to any guidelines relating to offences in general which are relevant to the case and not incompatible with Sch 21 (s 271(5)).

Schedule 21 sets out the starting points, and identifies aggravating and mitigating factors. The following Table sets out the starting points identified by Sch 21. These provisions do not restrict the application of s 128(2) of the new Act (relating to previous convictions being an aggravating feature), of s 128(3) (relating to offences while on bail),[102] or of s 129 (credit for guilty plea).[103]

Criteria	Examples	Starting Point
High seriousness, offender aged 21 or over on commission	Murder of two or more people where each involved one or more of: (i) substantial premeditation or planning; (ii) abduction of victim; (iii) sexual or sadistic conduct	Whole life (Sch 21, para 4(1), (2)(a))
	Murder of a child if involves abduction of the child, or sexual or sadistic motivation	Whole life (Sch 21, para 4(1), (2)(b))
	Murder for the advancing of political, religious or ideological cause	Whole life (Sch 21, para 4(1), (2)(c))
	Murder by person previously convicted of murder	Whole life (Sch 21, para 4(1), (2)(d)
High seriousness, offender aged over 18 but under 21 on commission	Case would fall within Sch 21, para 4 examples above but for age	30 years (Sch 21, para 5(1), (2)(h))
Offender aged 18 or over when committed the offence (not within para 4)	Murder of police officer or prison officer in course of duty	30 years (Sch 21, para 5(1), (2)(a))
High seriousness		
Sch 21, para 5	Murder involving firearm or explosive	30 years (Sch 21, para 5(1), (2)(b))
Sch 21, para 5	Murder done for gain (eg in furtherance of robbery or burglary, done for payment or in expectation of gain flowing from death)	30 years (Sch 21, para 5(1), (2)(c))
Sch 21, para 5	Murder intended to obstruct or interfere with course of justice	30 years (Sch 21, para 5(1), (2)(d))
Sch 21, para 5	Murder involving sexual or sadistic conduct	30 years (Sch 21, para 5(1), (2)(e))
Sch 21, para 5	Murder of two or more persons	30 years (Sch 21, para 5(1), (2)(f))

---

102 See **8.31**.

103 See **8.35**.

Criteria	Examples	Starting Point
Sch 21, para 5	Racially or religiously aggravated murder or aggravated by sexual orientation	30 years (Sch 21, para 5(1), (2)(g))
Sch 21, para 6	Cases not falling within the above examples	15 years (Sch 21, para 6)

Aggravating and mitigating factors

9.84 The matters that are aggravating and mitigating factors are set out in the following Table.

Aggravating	Mitigating
Significant degree of planning or premeditation	Intention to cause serious bodily harm rather than to kill
Victim particularly vulnerable because of age or disability	Lack of premeditation
Mental or physical suffering inflicted on the victim before death	Fact that offender suffered from mental disorder or mental disability which lowered his degree of culpability
Abuse of position of trust	Fact that offender provoked (for example) by prolonged stress in a way not amounting to a defence of provocation
Use of duress or threats against another person to facilitate the commission of the offence	Fact that offender to any extent acted in self-defence
Fact that victim was providing public service or performing a public duty	Belief by offender that the murder was an act of mercy
Concealment, destruction or dismemberment of the body	The age of the offender

Appeals

9.85 Section 9 of the Criminal Appeal Act 1968 does not include an order made under s 270. However, it is open to the Attorney-General to seek a review of the minimum term on a reference made under s 36 of the CJA 1988. The Court of Appeal in such a case must not make any allowance for the fact that the person to whom the order relates is being sentenced for a second time.

Transitional arrangements

9.86 Section 276 and Sch 21 deal with transitional arrangements. Complex provisions are put in place to deal with the cases of prisoners serving mandatory indeterminate sentences before the commencement of s 269, and which permit application to the High Court. Schedule 22, paras 11 to 12 deal with procedure and the requirement to give reasons, and paras 14 and 15 deal with matters relating to appeal and review.

The position varies, depending on whether the prisoner has been notified of a minimum period which, in the view of the Home Secretary, should be served before the prisoner is released on licence, or that the Home Secretary does not intend that the prisoner should ever be released on licence (referred to here as 'notification').

In this situation, the prisoner may, before the end of the notified term, make an application to the High Court. That court may either direct that the early release provisions are to apply to him at the end of the period specified in the order (which must not be longer than the notified period), or (in the case where no release is intended) order that the early release provisions are not to apply. In dealing with the application, the court must have regard to the seriousness of the offence, and associated offences, the effect of s 67 of the CJA 1967 had the prisoner been sentenced to a term of imprisonment, and the length of the notified minimum term. The court must have regard to the general principles in Sch 21, and any recommendation made by the trial judge or Lord Chief Justice to the Home Secretary.

One important transitional arrangement should be noted. It applies after the commencement of s 269, but where the life sentence is in respect of an offence which was committed before that date. In those circumstances, the court may not make an order specifying a part of the sentence which, in the opinion of the court, is greater than that which would have been notified by the Home Secretary under the practice followed by the Home Secretary before December 2002, and may not order that the early release provisions are not to apply to him unless, unless pre-December 2002, the Home Secretary would have notified the prisoner of his intention never to release.

Where no notification

9.87   Schedule 22, para 6 requires the Home Secretary to refer the prisoner's case to the High Court. The powers of the High Court are the same as outlined above, save only that Sch 22, para 8 contains certain restrictions designed to ensure that a prisoner is not subject to an order which is greater in length than that which would have been made by the Home Secretary prior to December 2002.

Chapter 10

COMMUNITY SENTENCES

10.1 The new Act re-casts the range of pre-existing community orders into one 'community sentence', to permit a court to impose one community sentence which comprises one or more community orders (s 147). This will permit a sentencing court to construct a package of orders, and requirements within orders, that best reflects the need of the court to achieve the various purposes of sentencing – punishment, deterrence, rehabilitation, public protection and reparation.[1] It largely implements the recommendations of the Halliday Report.[2] It sets out the range of requirements available, and the detailed conditions that apply to each, re-enacting, with amendments, changes and repeals, the statutory framework contained in the SA 2000. It sets out general procedural requirements for community orders, and provides a new scheme for their enforcement (Sch 8).

BACKGROUND

10.2 The recommendation by the Halliday Report of non-custodial powers was in the context of the major re-casting of community sentences in the CJA 1991, and, since then, the proliferation of new orders. The 1991 Act created a framework where community sentences were seen as alternatives to custody. The sentencing court has to be satisfied that the offence, with any associated offences, was 'serious enough' to justify a community sentence but not 'so serious' that a custodial disposal was required.[3] If the community sentence threshold was reached a court, under pre-existing law, had a range of orders, some of long standing, others introduced by the 1991 Act, and a third group of orders introduced by recent legislation. The range of orders available to a court in respect of an offender aged at least 16 was as follows:

– community rehabilitation order (SA 2000, s 41);
– community punishment order (SA 2000, s 46);
– community punishment and rehabilitation order (SA 2000, s 51);
– curfew order (SA 2000, s 37);
– drug treatment and testing order (s 52);
– drug abstinence order (SA 2000, s 58A) available in respect of an offender aged at least 18;

---

1   See **8.2**.

2   See **8.4**.

3   See **8.27**.

–   attendance centre order (SA 2000, s 60), available generally in respect of an offender aged under 21.[4]

Other community orders are limited to juveniles: supervision orders (SA 2000, s 63) and action plan orders (SA 2000, s 69) are only available in respect of a person under 18. Curfew orders (SA 2000, s 37) are available in respect of juveniles and adults alike. Exclusion orders (SA 2000, s 40A) have not yet been brought into effect.

10.3   These orders were seen very much as alternatives to custody, with the courts regarding the combination of a community order and custodial term in the same sentence as wrong in principle.[5] The court does have, under pre-existing law, the power to re-sentence for breach of the order (SA 2000, Sch 3, paras 4 and 5). The CJCSA 2000 created a new regime for the enforcement of such sentences by providing for a prison sentence to be substituted if a community sentence fails through non-compliance. Halliday viewed this, together with the greater intensity of such sentences through the greater use of requirements in orders, as amounting to a redefinition of the nature of community sentences, 'making them more akin to "conditional sentences" '.[6] The Report noted, however, that little guidance existed as to the punitive value to be ascribed to the various non-custodial orders, while the purpose of each order often differed. Rehabilitation and prevention of harm were stated aims for community rehabilitation orders, but not for curfew orders, community punishment orders and DTTOs. Mention of reparation as an aim in the context of adults is conspicuous by its absence. There was, concluded the Report,[7] a need to clarify the purposes of the various community orders and how they should be used. That is one of the objectives of the new statement of sentencing purposes in s 142.[8]

This lack of clarity also extended to the sentencing threshold, which might have unintentionally created the impression that fines should be used for the least serious cases. There was a case, Halliday argued, for a more flexible sentencing framework in which community sentences could be imposed instead of financial penalties where there was a history of failure to pay fines, or where the offender was of limited means.[9]

10.4   Halliday recommended that the existing sentences should be replaced by a new generic community punishment order, whose punitive weight would be proportionate to the current offence (and associated offences), with any additional severity for previous convictions. The sentence would comprise the ingredients best suited to meeting the needs of crime reduction, and exploiting opportunities for reparation, within 'an appropriately punitive "envelope" '.[10] That requires a court to be aware of

---

4   SA 2000, s 60 permits an attendance centre order in respect of a person aged at least 21 but under 25 committed to prison in default of any sum of money.

5   *Evans (No 3)* (1959) 43 Cr App R 66, CA; *Duporte* (1989) 11 Cr App R (S) 116, CA; *Carr-Thompson* [2000] Crim LR 401, CA.

6   Halliday Report, *op cit*, para 6.3.

7   *Ibid*, para 6.4.

8   See **8.10**.

9   Halliday Report, *op cit*, para 6.5. For sentence threshold, see **8.27**. For community sentences in cases of history of non-payment, see **10.9**.

10 See Halliday Report, *op cit*, paras 6.6–6.21.

the purposes, content and impact of the various requirements at its disposal. Probation services would indicate to the courts the nature and content of different programmes and the element of loss of liberty they involved. By way of example, the Report set out an outline 'tariff' for the making up of the new community sentence:[11]

'*Bottom Tier*   Financial penalty, appropriate reparation, supervision towards practical but non-intensive efforts to prevent re-offending (singly or in combination);

Middle Tier   Higher financial penalty, more substantial reparation, compulsory work, programme of moderate intensity to prevent re-offending, disqualification from driving (singly or in combination);

Top Tier   Hefty financial penalty, substantial reparation activity, enforced work (for a longer number of hours), intensive programmes to prevent re-offending, with enforced attendance at designated centres, residence requirements, curfew/exclusion (with tag where appropriate) (singly or in combination).'

Such examples were given simply to illustrate the suggested approach. The new statutory framework builds on this. Clearly, the mix of constituent elements of a community sentence will be for the court to consider on an individual basis, having regard to the PSR and the recommendations of the probation service. New systems available to the probation service, such as OASys assessment,[12] will allow that service better to identify offender risk and needs. Nonetheless, there are four general considerations: first, the purposes of sentencing;[13] secondly, the sentencing thresholds;[14] thirdly, the guidelines issued by the Sentencing Guidelines Council;[15] and lastly, the extent to which the impact of the total package is necessary and proportionate: clearly, a package which goes beyond this is liable to challenge under Art 8 ECHR.

THE GENERIC ORDER

Community sentence

10.5   The pre-existing provisions in s 33 of the SA 2000 defined a 'community order' as one or more of certain specified orders.[16] A 'community sentence' was a sentence comprising one or more of those orders. Section 147 of the new Act creates one single, unified, community sentence, which comprises either a 'community order', as defined by s 177, or one or more youth community sentences, as defined by s 147(2).

The community order which may form part of a community sentence imposed on a person aged 16 or over who is convicted of an offence can by s 177(1) include one or more of the requirements set out in the following Table, which also identifies the pre-existing provision re-enacted with or without amendment.

---

11   Halliday Report, *op cit*, para 6.8.

12   The risk assessment tool and programme of the Probation Service.

13   See **8.10**.

14   See **8.27**.

15   See **8.14**.

16   See **10.2**.

Requirement	New	Pre-existing
An unpaid work requirement	s 198	SA 2000, s 46
An activity requirement	s 201	SA 2000, Sch 2, para 2
A programme requirement, aimed at changing offending behaviour	s 202	SA 2000, s 42
A prohibited activity requirement, prohibiting the offender from certain activities	s 203	SA 2000, Sch 2
A curfew requirement	s 204	SA 2000, s 42, Sch 2, para 7
An exclusion requirement, excluding the offender from certain areas	s 205	
A residence requirement	s 206	
With the consent of the offender, a mental health treatment requirement	s 207	SA 2000 Act, s 42, Sch 2, para 5
With the consent of the offender, a drug rehabilitation requirement	s 209	SA 2000, s 42, Sch 2, para 6
With the consent of the offender, an alcohol treatment requirement	s 212	SA 2000, s 42, Sch 2, para 6
A supervision requirement	s 213	SA 2000, s 63, Sch 6, para 1
In respect of an offender aged under 21, an attendance centre requirement	s 214	SA 2000, s 60

10.6 Section 177(2) defines a 'youth community order' as one or more of the following orders, defined by reference to the SA 2000:

(a) curfew order (2000 Act, s 37);
(b) exclusion order (2000 Act, s 40A(1));
(c) attendance centre order (2000 Act, s 60);
(d) supervision order (2000 Act, s 63);
(e) action plan order (2000 Act, s 69(1)).

There is, under the new Act, no power to make a community rehabilitation and punishment order (the old 'combination order'). Section 51 of the SA 2000 is repealed. That is a natural result of the main change of substance made by these provisions, which is that the list of community orders is a 'menu' from which combinations can be chosen, and incorporated into one community sentence to meet the needs of the particular offence and offender.

Restrictions on imposing community sentence

10.7 Section 150 re-enacts s 34 of the SA 2000, which prohibited the imposition of a community order in respect of an offence the sentence for which is fixed by law, or for certain other offences. It does so by extending the list of offences to which it applies, reflecting the new provisions relating to dangerous offenders. A community sentence is not now to be available in respect of offences for which the sentence is fixed by law, or in respect of any of the sentences for dangerous offenders contained in ss 225 to 228 of the new Act[17] or in respect of an offence that falls under ss 110 and 111 of the SA 2000,[18] or under s 51A of the Firearms Act 1968.[19]

10.8 Section 148(1) re-enacts s 35(1) of the SA 2000. A court must not pass a community sentence unless it is of the opinion that the offence, or the combination of the offence with any associated offences, is serious enough to warrant such a sentence. This is, however, subject to s 151.[20] Section 148(2) re-enacts s 35(3) of the 2000 Act with textual changes to reflect the reformulation of the community sentence provisions. It requires the particular orders which form part of the community sentence to be, in the opinion of the court, those most suitable for the offender, and the restrictions on liberty imposed by the orders to be, in the opinion of the court, commensurate with the seriousness of the offence and any associated offences.

Section 148(3) sets out the principles that are to apply where a youth community order is made, and in that context replicates s 148(2).

10.9 If the sentence threshold for the imposition of a community sentence is not reached, the court will have to consider the alternatives: a fine, conditional discharge or absolute discharge. However, s 151 permits a community order to be made in respect of a persistent offender who has been previously fined, even if, apart from s 143(2), the offence, of itself or together with any associated offences, would not be serious enough to warrant such a sentence. It replaces the pre-existing s 59 of the SA 2000, which allowed a curfew order or community punishment order to be imposed in respect of offenders who had unpaid fines, and where the offender would not have sufficient means to pay a fine for the current offence (if imposed). The new provision is of general application and allows a community sentence comprising any of the community orders to be imposed in these circumstances.

The new provisions, in s 151, are a means of dealing with persistent petty offenders. Section 151 applies where an offender aged at least 16 has been convicted on three or more occasions of an offence committed after attaining the age of 16, and on each occasion the sentence has consisted only of a fine (s 151(1)). A compensation order is not for this purpose to be regarded as part of the sentence (s 151(5)), and thus s 151 will apply to cases where compensation orders and fines have been made and imposed on previous occasions. Care should be taken to have regard to the *number* of occasions, which refers to the number of appearances and not the number of offences, in respect of which he has been sentenced. It is immaterial that on other occasions the offender has been before the court and has had imposed on him a sentence other than imprisonment (s 151(6)).[21] Of course, the previous offences may of themselves increase the level of offence seriousness and nothing in s 151 prevents that (s 151(7)).

Where it applies, s 151 permits a court to impose a community sentence even if the current offence is one which would on its own warrant a fine, if it is in the interests of justice to do so (s 151(2)). In deciding that, the court must consider the nature of the

---

17 See **9.38** et seq.

18 Mandatory life sentence provision.

19 See **8.52**.

20 See **10.9**.

21 See **8.30**.

previous offences, and how recent and relevant they are to the current offence (s 151(3)).

10.10   If an offender has been remanded in custody, and then receives a custodial sentence, the time spent on remand counts towards his sentence.[22] It is difficult to reflect time on remand if a community sentence is passed. Section 149 introduces a new duty, by requiring a sentencing court, in deciding what restrictions on liberty are to be imposed by a community sentence or a youth community sentence, to have regard to any period of remand in custody in respect of that offence or any other offence the charge for which was founded on the same facts or evidence.

Information to be given to offender

10.11   Under pre-existing law, the various statutory powers set out the detail as to what the offender must be told when the order is imposed. Those individual statements are redundant in the light of the terms of the new s 174, which sets out the duty to give reasons for, and explain the effect of, the sentence. Specifically, in respect of community sentences, the court will need to explain the effects of non-compliance with any order or part of the order, and the power of the court to vary or review the order. It is also under an obligation to explain why the offence is serious enough to warrant the imposition of a community sentence (s 174(2)(c)).

Court review of community orders

10.12   The Halliday Report saw that supervision of a community order is the means of managing sentence content, ensuring compliance and monitoring outcomes, while providing additional support against re-offending.[23] Clearly, ongoing review is crucial. The Report envisaged the development of ongoing review, not only by supervisors, but by the court.[24] Section 178 paves the way for such a 'sentence review' capacity. It confers an enabling power on the Home Secretary to make orders which will either enable or require a court making a community order to provide for that order to be reviewed periodically by the court, or another court, to amend community orders to provide for (or remove a requirement for) a review, and as to the timing on any such review.

REQUIREMENTS IN ORDERS

10.13   Part 12, Chapter 4 of the Act makes provision in respect of requirements that may be part of either a community sentence, a custody plus order,[25] a suspended sentence order,[26] or an intermittent custody order. For ease of reference these provisions are dealt with in the context of community orders, but they apply equally to the other orders stated above.

---

22   See **9.75**.

23   Halliday Report, *op cit*, para 6.8.

24   *Ibid*, para 7.26.

25   See **9.2**.

26   See **9.29**.

Any requirements imposed are subject to the provisions of s 217 which replicates pre-existing provisions. The court must ensure, so far as practicable, that any requirement imposed is such as to avoid:

(a) any conflict with the offender's religious beliefs or with the requirements of any other relevant order to which he may be subject, and
(b) any interference with the times, if any, at which he normally works or attends school or any other educational establishment.

Similar obligations are placed on the responsible officer.[27]

Unpaid work requirement

10.14   Section 199 re-enacts, with modifications, s 46 of the SA 2000. That provision dealt with community punishment orders, the successor to community service. Under s 46, an offender aged at least 16 could be required to undertake unpaid work in the community for not less than 40 hours and not more than 240 hours. Section 199 increases the maximum number of hours to 300, implementing Halliday's suggestion that the maximum hours for unpaid work requirements be raised, to increase the extent of the punitive element.[28]

The provisions of s 46 dealing with the information to be given to the offender are not re-enacted, because the information to be given generally to offenders is dealt with by the wider s 174.[29] Under s 199(3), the court must not impose an unpaid work requirement unless it is satisfied that the offender is a suitable person to perform work under such a requirement. If the court thinks that it is necessary to do so, it will first hear from an appropriate officer.[30] Where the court is sentencing an offender for two or more offences, and imposes unpaid work requirements in respect of each of them, it can, as under s 46, decide whether the hours of unpaid work should be served concurrently or consecutively. However, the total number of hours must not exceed 300.

10.15   Under s 199, the offender must perform work as and when required by his responsible officer. Section 199(2) applies where an unpaid work requirement is imposed as part of a community order or a suspended sentence order. In these cases, as now, the work must be completed within 12 months, although powers exist to extend that period.[31] The order remains in force until the number of hours ordered have in fact been worked. That is equally true in respect of both a community order and a suspended sentence order,[32] but the latter order cannot be extended beyond the end of the 'operational period' (s 199(4)).

---

27   Defined by s 197.

28   Halliday Report, *op cit*, para 6.8.

29   See **10.11**.

30   Defined by s 197(2) as an officer of a local probation board, or in the case of an offender aged under 18 such a local probation board officer, a local authority social worker or a member of a youth offending team.

31   See Sch 7, para 20 (unpaid work activity); Sch 10, para 17 (suspended sentence order).

32   See **9.29**.

Activity requirement

10.16 Section 201 of the new Act permits the making of an order containing a requirement that the offender must do either or both of the following:

(a) present himself to a specified person or persons at a specified place or places, on a specified day or days;

(b) participate in specified activities in the order on such days as may be specified.

Such powers are not new. In respect of those aged 10 to 17 inclusive, similar powers exist in the context of a supervision order[33] or action plan orders.[34] In respect of offenders aged 16 or above, the power to impose requirements regarding activities is contained in Sch 2, paras 2–4 to the SA 2000. It is the powers in Sch 2 that are broadly replicated.

The new s 201 makes it clear that the total period of reporting and activities must not in the aggregate exceed 60 days, reflecting the pre-existing provision but removing any ambiguity or doubt. The one exception to the 60-day limit contained in the pre-existing Sch 2, para 4, which related to a person who has been convicted of a sexual offence, has not been re-enacted, which should not be a surprise, given the new provisions relating to dangerous offenders.[35]

The specified activities may include activities involving reparation, such as those involving contact between offenders and persons affected by their offences, provided that any such person consents (s 201(2), (4)).

Section 201 specifies procedural requirements (s 201(4)) and obliges the offender to present himself at designated places[36] as instructed to do so by the responsible officer,[37] to comply with instructions generally given by such officer (s 201(6)).

Programme requirement

10.17 Section 202 states that a 'programme requirement' is a requirement that the offender must participate in an accredited programme specified in the order at a specified place and on specified days. It defines 'programme' as a systematic programme of activities (s 202(2)(a)) and relates 'accredited' to those programmes (for example, sex offender treatment programmes) which have been designated by the Home Office (s 202(2)(b)).

No specific similar power existed under pre-existing law in the context of adult offenders, although the power to require participation in activities at a specified place and on specified days falls within the generality of the pre-existing s 42(1) of the SA 2000 and Sch 2 to that Act. The power to impose such requirements in a supervision order can likewise be found in the SA 2000, at Sch 6. The new s 202(4) requires the court to be satisfied that the accredited programme is recommended by a probation

---

33 SA 2000, Sch 6, para 3.

34 CDA 1998, s 70(1).

35 See **9.38**.

36 See s 200(7), (8), (10).

37 Defined by s 197.

officer or, in the case of an offender under 18, by an officer of the local probation board or a member of a youth offending team, as suitable for the offender, and that a place is available for the offender. If the co-operation of another person is required, that other person must consent.

The requirement is particularly suitable for addressing behavioural causes of offending – sex offending, anger management and other similar programmes. The Act does not provide any limits on the length of attendance. The order will specify the number of days and the place, but detailed implementation (for example, as to when to attend) is left to the responsible officer.[38] Care will need to be taken that the totality of the requirement is one which is not disproportionate given the characteristics of the offence and offender (eg age), and, of course, that the requirements of either the requirement or the responsible officer do not infringe s 217.[39]

Prohibited activity requirement

10.18   Section 203 introduces a power to impose a requirement that the offender refrain from participating in activities specified in the order on a day or days specified or during a specified period. This may include a requirement that the offender does not possess, use or carry a firearm within the meaning of the Firearms Act 1968. The court cannot impose such a requirement without first consulting a probation officer or, if the offender is under 18, a probation officer or member of a youth offending team (s 203).

The scope for specifying prohibited activities is endless, but must be viewed in the context also of curfew requirements and exclusion requirements.[40] If the court wishes to prohibit an offender from going to a particular place, it should make an exclusion order under s 205, for example prohibiting the offender from visiting the home of his girlfriend or of the victim of crime, or a particular nightclub or public house. Prohibited activities are wider: examples might include driving motor vehicles, attending football matches generally, or drinking alcohol. Care will, however, need to be taken to ensure that any prohibitions (which are, by definition, restrictions on liberty) are reasonable, relate to the level of offence seriousness, and do not have a disproportionate effect on the private life of the offender. The factors in s 217 should be borne in mind.

Curfew requirement

10.19   Section 204 re-enacts, with some textual modification, s 37 of the SA 2000. It defines a curfew requirement as a requirement that the offender must remain at a place specified by the court for certain periods of time. By s 204(2), as under s 37 of the 2000 Act, the periods of time must not be less than two hours nor more than 12 hours in any given day. The order might, for example, require the offender to stay at home during the evening and night hours. Section 207(3) to (5) limits the curfew periods for community orders or suspended sentence orders (no specified periods more than six months from the date of the order), custody plus orders (no specified periods more than six months from the commencement of the licence period), and intermittent

---

38   Defined by s 197.

39   See **10.4**.

40   See **10.19** and **10.20**.

custody orders (no specified period which would take the number of days to which the offender is subject to the restriction to more than 182 (ie six months)).

The court must obtain and consider information about the place specified in the order and the attitude of persons likely to be affected by the presence of the offender (s 203(6)).

As with all of these provisions, restrictions on liberty of this type must be necessary and proportionate.

Exclusion requirement

10.20   Section 205 re-enacts, with some modification, s 40A of the SA 2000, an example of the repeal of a provision not yet in force. It defines an exclusion requirement as a requirement prohibiting the offender from entering a place during a period specified in the order (s 205(1)). That specified period may not, in the case of a community order, exceed two years (s 205(2)). There is no need for such provision in the case of suspended sentence orders, custody plus or intermittent custody because the total length of the licence period by definition cannot exceed that period.

The requirement may provide that prohibition operates only for certain periods of time and may specify different places for different periods (s 205(3)). 'Place' in this context includes not only specific locations but extends to include an 'area' (s 205(4)). The term 'area' is not defined, but could include, say, a district of a town, city or village – a city centre, village green, or the area round a nightclub or football ground.[41] Whether it could legally include a large city or county is more arguable: the larger the 'area' defined, the harder it will be for the requirement to be justifiable in law as a necessary and proportionate restriction on the liberty of the offender. There will also be a need for clear definition, both to provide clarity for the offender and to give the necessary exactitude to provide a means to determine whether there has been a breach.

Residence requirement

10.21   Existing residence requirement provisions are to be fond in Sch 2 to the SA 2000. Section 206 re-enacts, with modifications, those provisions, defining a residence requirement as a requirement that the offender must reside at a place specified in the order for a specified period (s 206(1)). The new s 206(2) for the first time permits a court to allow the offender to live at an alternative address, with the approval of his responsible officer, thus providing flexibility in the requirement and obviating the need for variation orders. The order of the court must state specifically that this is to apply, although it will not need to specify the alternative address or addresses. Before making a residence requirement the court must consider the home surroundings of the offender (s 206(3)). The court must place the offender in a hostel or similar accommodation only with the recommendation of a probation officer (s 206(4)).

---

41   Examples given by the Explanatory Notes to the Bill.

Mental health treatment requirement

10.22 Section 207 deals with mental health treatment requirements, broadly re-enacting the provisions to be found in Sch 2, para 5 to the SA 2000. It is defined as a requirement that the offender must submit, during a specified period, to treatment by or under the direction of a registered medical practitioner or chartered psychologist[42] (or both, for different periods) with a view to the improvement of the offender's medical condition. A requirement cannot specify a non-medically qualified individual as part of such a requirement, unlike the provisions that relate to a drug rehabilitation requirement.[43]

That treatment may be provided in an independent hospital or care home[44] or a hospital,[45] or as a non-resident patient at a place specified in the order, or as treatment under the direction of such registered medical practitioner or chartered psychologist as specified in the order (s 207(2)). Section 207 also permits that mental health treatment to occur at an institution or place not specified by the order, provided that the offender consents and that the procedures set out in s 207(3) are satisfied.

The court must be satisfied that the mental condition of the offender requires treatment and may be helped by treatment, but is not such that it warrants making a hospital or guardianship order. The court must also be satisfied that arrangements can be made for the offender to receive treatment as specified in the order, and that the offender consents.

The responsible officer will supervise the offender only to the extent necessary for revoking or amending the order.

DRUG REHABILITATION REQUIREMENT

10.23 The provisions of ss 209 to 211 of the new Act provide for a new drug rehabilitation requirement, which replaces the drug treatment and testing order (DTTO). It forms part of a raft of measures which place emphasis on addressing drug abuse. The provisions of s 209 mirror, with necessary amendments to reflect the new scheme, the provisions of the pre-existing DTTO.

As part of a community sentence or suspended sentence, but not custody plus or intermittent custody, a court may impose a drug rehabilitation requirement, which includes drug treatment and testing. The court must be satisfied that the offender is dependent on or has a propensity to misuse any controlled drug and as such requires and would benefit from treatment. The offence for which the offender is being sentenced does not have to be a drug-related offence. In addition, the court must be satisfied that the necessary arrangements are or can be made for the treatment and that the offender has expressed a willingness to comply with the drug rehabilitation requirement. The treatment provided may not be for a period of less than six months or for more than three years.

---

42 For definition, see s 198(6).

43 See **10.23**.

44 Within the meaning of the Care Standards Act 2000.

45 Within the meaning of the MHA 1983.

A suitably qualified or experienced individual supervises the treatment. It is for the court to decide whether treatment should be residential or non-residential. The Home Secretary may provide guidance as to the arrangements for testing (s 211).

10.24   Section 210(1) provides that the court may provide for the review of any drug treatment and testing requirement. Such a review must be part of any order lasting more than 12 months. The reviews cannot take place more frequently than once a month. The review occurs at a 'review hearing', at which the offender is present. The responsible officer[46] must provide to the court a written report on the offender's progress before each hearing, which is to include the results of the offender's drug tests. A review hearing takes place before the court responsible for the order, which will be the court which made the order, unless that court has specified a court in the area in which the offender lives. Where the drug treatment and testing requirement was made on appeal from the Crown Court, the Crown Court will be the responsible court (s 210(4)).

10.25   On a review, and having considered the report of the responsible officer, the court may amend the requirement, provided the offender consents. It cannot reduce the term of treatment and testing below the minimum permitted period of six months. Nor can it amend the order while an appeal against the making of the order is pending. If the offender does not consent, the court has the power to revoke and re-sentence (s 211(3)).

Under s 211(3), if the offender does not consent to amending the order, the court may revoke the order and re-sentence the offender as if he had just been convicted, taking into account the extent to which the offender had complied with the requirements of the order. If the court wishes, it may sentence the offender to a custodial sentence, providing the offence was punishable with imprisonment.

If the offender's progress is satisfactory, the court can state that for future reviews the offender need not be present (s 211(6)), but retains the power in future to require him to attend (s 211(7)).

Alcohol treatment requirement

10.26   The power to impose an alcohol treatment requirement as part of a community rehabilitation order is currently to be found at Sch 2, para 6 to the SA 2000. Section 212 replicates that provision, with necessary amendments to reflect the new legislative scheme.

By s 212(1), a court can require the offender to undergo alcohol treatment by, or under the direction of, a person who is qualified or experienced to reduce or eliminate the offender's dependency on alcohol, provided the offender consents. The order must specify that person. The precondition for the making of an order is that the court must be satisfied that the offender is dependent on alcohol, that his dependency requires and is susceptible to treatment, and that arrangements can be made for treatment. It does not, however, have to be made in respect of an offence directly related to alcohol misuse, although a court is likely to make such an order if it is of the opinion that alcohol plays a part in the offending behaviour.

---

46   See s 197.

An alcohol treatment requirement must last at least six months. It may be residential or non-residential treatment in a place the court decides, or by or under a qualified or experienced person whom the court identifies in the order.

Supervision requirements

10.27 Supervision is an integral component of both a community rehabilitation order and a supervision order. Section 213 replaces with appropriate textual amendments the relevant supervision requirements, and the obligations of the offender.

Attendance centre orders

10.28 Under pre-existing law, a court may make an attendance centre order in respect of an offender aged under 21 (SA 2000, s 60). Section 214 replaces this free-standing order with an order that can form part of a community sentence. The detailed provisions of the pre-existing law are replicated by the new Act, with only textual amendments. Section 221 re-enacts s 62 of the SA 2000, which empowers the Home Secretary to provide attendance centres and make arrangements with local authorities and police authorities regarding premises to be used.

Electronic monitoring requirement

10.29 Section 215 replicates, with amendment, the provisions of the pre-existing s 36B of the SA 2000 in respect of electronic monitoring requirements in community orders. As originally introduced, electronic monitoring was available in respect of all community orders, but was confined to home detention curfew, curfew orders, bail of young defendants and detention and training orders. The effect of the new s 215 is to make the power to engage in electronic monitoring available in the context of any requirement in an order.

Section 215(3) and (4) deal with administrative arrangements surrounding electronic monitoring, and in particular deal with the notification of the requirement by the responsible officer to the relevant parties. The Home Secretary has the power to specify a description of a person responsible for electronic monitoring. This is left to delegated legislation, since changes in the description of electronic monitoring providers will be required from time to time as the technology changes and develops.

BREACH, AMENDMENT AND REVOCATION OF A COMMUNITY ORDER

10.30 The current scheme is set out in some detail by Sch 3 to the SA 2000. Schedule 8 to the new Act replicates that, but with amendments. This detailed scheme creates a new regime for the enforcement of community orders designed to improve the effectiveness of enforcement. In summary, it provides for:

- the issue of a warning, except in certain limited situations;
- the return of the offender to court if the warning system is exhausted;

–   powers for a court to make a finding of breach to amend the order, deal with the offender in any way it could have dealt with him initially, or impose (in the case of a person aged at least 18) imprisonment of 51 weeks in the case of an otherwise non-imprisonable offence, provided that the offender has persistently and wilfully failed to comply with the order. Of course, a term of imprisonment of up to 51 weeks will be custody plus, when in force.

YOUNG OFFENDERS

10.31   The provisions discussed above apply to offenders aged 16 or above. The new Act does not address young offender provisions in a fundamental way. However, Sch 24 amends s 70 of the SA 2000, which deals with requirements that may be included in action plan orders. These orders, made under s 69 of the SA 2000, can be made in respect of an offender aged under 18.

The amendment introduces drug treatment, which may include testing, as a requirement available for inclusion in an action plan order. The Schedule also amends Sch 6 to the SA 2000 to allow drug treatment, which may include testing, as a requirement available for inclusion in a supervision order.

The new requirement is available where the court is satisfied that the young offender is dependent on, or has a propensity to misuse, drugs and that this dependency or propensity may be susceptible to treatment. This mirrors provisions relating to adult offenders. The Schedule strengthens the existing interventions available to the court to assist young offenders with a drug misuse problem to address both their drug misuse and offending behaviour. The testing element of the requirement can only apply to those aged 14 years and over and can be included in an action plan order or supervision order only if the offender consents and the court has been notified by the Home Secretary that arrangements are in place for implementation.

Chapter 11

RETRIAL FOR SERIOUS OFFENCES

SUMMARY

11.1 Sections 75 to 97 restrict the operation of the double jeopardy rule, which prevents the prosecution of an individual for an offence in respect of which he has been acquitted. It does so in respect of certain 'qualifying offences'. The rule continues to apply in other circumstances, as does the statutory exception contained in s 54 of the CPIA 1996 relating to tainted acquittals.

The Act confers new police powers, normally exercisable only with the prior consent of the DPP, to investigate offences which resulted in an acquittal, but where it is believed that new and compelling evidence has or is likely to come to light (s 78). An application must be made to the Court of Appeal for an order that the acquittal[1] be quashed and a retrial ordered. Preconditions for the DPP's consent are created by s 76(4).

Sections 87–91 set out new provisions relating to bail, custody, and the procedure in the Crown Court. Magistrates' courts have no role at any stage. Sections 76 and 77 set out the powers of the Court of Appeal in respect of an application for retrial.

COMMENCEMENT AND OPERATION

11.2 When these provisions are in force, they will apply to acquittals prior to the commencement date. These provisions are not in force at the date of going to press. This was described retrospectively as 'profoundly shocking' and as creating 'conditional acquittals'.[2] When they are in force, they will apply in England and Wales, and Northern Ireland, but not Scotland. It will be open to the Home Secretary to amend the list of offences to which these provisions apply (s 75).

---

1   In England and Wales only. It applies in some circumstances to acquittals in other jurisdictions: see **11.9**.

2   Lord Berwick; Baroness Kennedy, HL Committee, 30 October 2003, cols 462–463.

BACKGROUND

11.3 The principle of double jeopardy is long standing.[3] It exists to protect the citizen from being harassed by an omnipotent, well-resourced State and was well-explained by Justice Black in the US case of *Green v US*:[4]

> 'The underlying idea, one that is deeply ingrained in at least the Anglo-American system of jurisprudence, is that the State with all its resources and power should not be allowed to make repeated attempts to convict an individual for an alleged offence, thereby subjecting him to embarrassment, expense and ordeal and compelling him to live in a continuing state of anxiety and insecurity, as well as enhancing the possibility that even though innocent he may be found guilty.'

The rule prohibits the prosecution of a person for an offence of which he has been acquitted (*autrefois acquit*), or one which arises out of the same, or substantially the same set of facts.[5] It also prevents the prosecution once again of someone already convicted (*autrefois convict*). The new Act affects only previous acquittals, but issues may arise where an individual is convicted of an alternative offence.[6] Where there is an application to stay for breach of *autrefois acquit*, the court must determine whether the new proceedings are based on the same or substantially the same facts or offence, bearing in mind that a criminal act (such as an assault) can frequently be defined by reference to one or more of several offences.

11.4 In *Connelly v DPP* Lord Morris identified nine 'governing principles' of *autrefois acquit*:

(1) a person should not be tried for a crime in respect of which he has already been acquitted or convicted;

(2) nor should he be convicted of an offence in respect of which he could lawfully have been convicted on the first indictment;

(3) *autrefois* extends to cases where the offence charged is the same or substantially the same in practical terms as one for which he was previously acquitted, convicted or could have been convicted on an earlier indictment;

(4) the test to be applied is whether the evidence relied upon or facts constituting the later offence would have been enough to lead to conviction, lawfully, for the offence charged on the earlier indictment or another one on which he could have been convicted;[7]

---

3   See Corns, 'Retrial of acquitted persons: Time for Reform of the Double Jeopardy rule?' (2003) 27 Crim LJ 80; Kirby, 'Carroll, double jeopardy and international human rights law' (2003) 27 Crim LJ 231.

4   355 US 184 (1957), 2 Led 2nd, 199 at 201.

5   *Elrington* (1861) 1 B & S 688, CCCR; *Connolly v DPP* [1964] AC 1254, HL.

6   See **11.8**.

7   Lords Pearce and Devlin disagreed, identifying the fourth principle as abuse of process, not *autrefois*. See, in support, *Beedie* [1997] 2 Cr App R 167, CA, adding that both the third and fourth principle amounted to abuses of process, the difference being that *autrefois* is a complete answer to the prosecution case, whereas an abuse of process argument is launched to persuade the judge that it is unfair to try the defendant in these circumstances and the quashing of an indictment which follows if an abuse application is successful is a discretionary remedy, not a right.

(5) the principle would not apply in the case of murder where the accused had been tried for an assault, dealt with, then the victim had died as a consequence of his injuries – given that the death (and thus the *actus reus* of murder) had not occurred at the time of the assault trial. A new event (the death) had occurred after the first trial, and which justified further proceedings;

(6) the accused is not confined to arguments based on a comparison of the later and earlier indictment to assert *autrefois*: he may also call evidence of the facts, personages, material dates, court records to support his argument. A submission of *autrefois* was not limited to a pure legal argument about the nature and similarity or otherwise of the old and new charge;

(7) the fact that both trials featured common witnesses or facts is immaterial;[8]

(8) the verdict in the earlier proceedings must have arisen out of a lawful trial and before a competent court. A verdict which was a nullity could not be relied upon to found an *autrefois* argument because it was never a verdict at all;

(9) the fundamental rule is that no person should be prosecuted twice for the same offence.

Lord Devlin emphasised that the rule was not absolute. There can be exceptional circumstances which give rise to a second trial arising out of the same set of facts, providing that a second trial was not oppressive. Examples given by Lord Devlin included sequential trials where an indictment had been severed so that counts were tried separately; a murder trial if death resulted after the trial for the original offence which caused injury; the trial of an offence which could have been included on an earlier indictment as part of a series of offences but was not in fact included (perhaps because the evidence had not yet come to light or the arrest for the later offence came too late to join that new offence to the existing indictment).

11.5   In 1999 the Law Commission reported on the rule.[9] It concluded that the law should exempt some offences from the effects of the rule and that the High Court should be empowered to quash an acquittal on the grounds of new evidence subject to certain conditions. The Government, impelled in part by various high-profile cases that caused public disquiet,[10] was of the view that:

> 'The double jeopardy rule . . . is an important safeguard to acquitted defendants, but there is an important general public interest in ensuring that those who have committed serious crimes are convicted of them.'[11]

It believed that the double jeopardy rule was not serving the public interest[12] and largely, although not entirely, adopted those recommendations which are reflected in the new Act.

---

8   See, now, *Z* [2000] 2 AC 483, HL.

9   *Double Jeopardy*, Law Com No 156 (1999).

10 See, eg, *The Stephen Lawrence Inquiry – Report of an Inquiry by Sir William MacPherson of Cluny*, Cm 4262 (1999).

11 *Justice for All, op cit*, para 4.63.

12 *Ibid.*

THE NEW LAW

Acquittal

11.6   The new rules apply to acquittals in respect of qualifying offences (s 75). The acquittal may have occurred at trial, or been ordered on appeal (s 75(1)). Only if the power exists will the new powers of investigation apply, and the right to make application to the court come into being.

The term 'acquittal' is self-explanatory. It can amount to a verdict of not guilty entered by a jury following a trial, after deliberation on the facts or on the direction of the judge. An acquittal will result from a conviction being quashed or may occur if there are alternative counts, and a conviction is achieved only on the lesser offence. Thus, if a defendant is indicted on counts of rape and unlawful sexual intercourse arising out of the same facts, but convicted only of the latter, there is an acquittal on the former. They are different offences, and the new provisions will, if the preconditions are satisfied, permit retrial on the former. Of course, nothing in the new Act takes away the right of a court to stay for abuse of process, but it is difficult to conceive of that argument being successful given that the legislation specifically allows acquittals to be re-opened in the specified circumstances.

11.7   Only cases where the acquittal followed trial on indictment fall within the scope of the new provisions. That applies irrespective of whether the acquittal came immediately after trial, or following appeal against conviction on indictment, whether by the Court of Appeal or the House of Lords (s 75(1)(c)). Appeals against conviction also include appeals against findings on fitness to plead.

11.8   A person may be acquitted of an offence impliedly. An acquittal of a particular offence may by implication acquit that person also of a lesser offence.[13] Section 75(2) paves the way for retrials for offences where the accused is acquitted by implication in earlier proceedings. Section 75(2) provides that a person acquitted of one of the qualifying offences in Part 1 of Sch 5 is also to be considered as having been acquitted of a lesser offence for which he could have faced proceedings on the same indictment which gave rise to the original offence. Some of the offences in Sch 5 are alternatives or lesser offences to others upon the same indictment: murder or manslaughter; rape or attempted rape. Ordinarily, an attempt to prosecute for the lesser offence would be caught by *autrefois acquit*. Under the new law, the prosecution may convince the Court of Appeal under s 76 that the implied acquittal should be quashed and a retrial ordered. For example, if D is acquitted of murder on the grounds of self-defence, the killing is lawful and by implication he is acquitted of manslaughter. Were new and compelling evidence to come to light supporting a charge of manslaughter, Part 10 permits the prosecution to apply under s 75 for the acquittal to be quashed.

11.9   Section 76 confers the power to quash acquittals from foreign courts, in order to cover qualifying offences committed abroad or where the domestic court had jurisdiction over the citizen although his crime was committed abroad.[14]

---

13   See s 6(3), (4) of the CLA 1967 (conviction for alternative offence on indictment).

14   Sections 75(4), (5) and 76(2).

There are two sets of circumstances in which a person might be acquitted of a qualifying offence in a foreign court, but now face retrial in England or Wales. First, if the offence of which he was acquitted abroad would amount to the commission of one of the qualifying offences in England or Wales, the prosecution is entitled to try to secure a retrial. Secondly, if the facts of the case were such as to involve the commission of a qualifying offence in England and Wales, again, the potential for retrial arises. A drug dealer who exports heroin from London to Paris commits a qualifying offence in England (exportation) and commits an offence under French law (importation). The disillusioned wife who conspires to murder her husband, and later assists the hit-man in committing the murder on a remote Greek island, potentially commits the offence of murder in Greece and conspiracy in England. If the defendant were acquitted in the foreign jurisdiction, he could nonetheless potentially face retrial in the United Kingdom. On the first, exportation would be a qualifying offence. On the second both murder and conspiracy would amount to qualifying offences. The question as to what is a qualifying offence is discussed at **11.12**.

11.10   The new Act permits the re-opening of acquittals. Clearly, no issue arises directly with regard to convictions. In a case where, for example, D had been acquitted of murder but convicted of manslaughter, there appears to be nothing in s 76 to prevent the prosecution from applying to quash the murder acquittal to retry him for the graver crime. The power to quash the acquittal is there, but D has been sentenced for an offence arising out of substantially the same facts. Similar issues arise in cases where a conviction for unlawful sexual intercourse arises on a charge of rape. Nothing in s 76 appears to prevent an application for retrial on the more serious offence if new evidence comes to light. Yet the defendant will have been convicted of, and punished for, the lesser offence.

At common law, such prosecution for the graver offence would have fallen foul of the *autrefois* principle.[15] In *Beedie*[16] an attempt to prosecute B for manslaughter foundered on the bar of *autrefois convict*, B having pleaded guilty to lesser offences arising out of the same facts. The crimes of which he had been convicted were in effect the same or substantially the same as that on the indictment in the Crown Court, and thus authority barred the manslaughter charge. Where the facts of the acquitted offence were not the same, or substantially the same, as the ones on which the conviction was based, no problem arises, and a prosecutor may seek a declaration to that effect under s 76(2)).

Nor does a problem arise if the elements of the two offences are different. The wording of s 76 speaks of 'acquittals' and nowhere does it limit the reason why an acquittal has been made. Some might argue that clear and unambiguous words should be used before a court concludes that the principle of *autrefois acquit* has been limited, and that in some cases the acquitted and convicted offences are substantially the same. In that case, one wonders why an alternative or lesser verdict was entered, and the new Act talks of neither *autrefois acquit* nor *autrefois convict*. The answer to potential unfairness may lie in the use of the discretion under s 79 that it would not be

---

15   *Elrington* (1861) 1 B & S 688.

16   [1997] 2 Cr App R 167, CA.

in the interests of justice for the previous acquittal to be quashed.[17] The pre-Act case-law would be relevant in persuading a court how this discretion should be used.

Qualifying offences

11.11   The choice of offences – as well as the removal of the double jeopardy protection was described as ' ... a populist measure. It is being introduced because some murderer has been acquitted and thereafter boasted of what he has done. It is limited, in the hope of making it palatable, but it is unprincipled, being partial'.[18] Attempts to limit the operation of the new provisions to murder, limited sex offences and war crimes offences, were resisted, the Government having:

> ' ... therefore sought to identify offences considered to have a particularly serious impact on the victims, their family or on society more widely, which, for the most part, carry a maximum penalty of life imprisonment.'[19]

11.12   Schedule 5 to the Act defines offences that amount to 'qualifying offences' and reference should be made thereto. All of these offences are serious but most are also happily very rare. Predictions for CPS budgets to fund second trials are estimated at £0.4 million for the financial year 2005/06.[20] If accurate, those figures suggest only a tiny minority of criminals are likely to be affected and this in turn suggests overall crime detection and convictions will scarcely be affected.

In most cases, identifying the qualifying offence will be straightforward. The offence will not normally have changed its character between the acquittal and the date of the s 75 application. In the case of foreign acquittals the court will need to compare the foreign crime with the offence in Sch 5 which the prosecution says is the same. Section 75(4) states that where a person has been acquitted in proceedings other than in England and Wales or Scotland, of an offence under the law of the place where the proceedings which led to the acquittal were held, the provisions of s 75 apply if the commission of the offence as alleged, no matter how described in that other jurisdiction (s 75(5)) would have amounted to or included the commission in the United Kingdom of a qualifying offence. Of course, if there is no counterpart, then no issues arise under the new Act.

Where there is an implied acquittal, the court will want to look at the facts of the old proceedings, and the content of the old indictment, to determine the offence(s) for which the defendant was at risk of conviction, other than the counts on which he was acquitted. If there is an offence in Sch 5 which matches one for which he could have been acquitted, the potential for a s 75 application exists. Some prosecutors may wish to apply under s 75 not only in respect of the actual counts on which the defendant was acquitted, but also in respect of any alternatives for which he was at risk of conviction at the original trial.

---

17   See **11.18**.

18   Lord Neill, HL Committee 30 October 2003, cols 480–481.

19   Lord Goldsmith, *ibid*, cols 1078–1079.

20   HC Explanatory Notes, para 669.

PROCEDURAL STEPS TO SECURE A RETRIAL

11.13   Sections 76 to 80 set out the steps the prosecution must take to persuade the Court of Appeal that the previous acquittal is no bar to a second trial and that there is evidence of such quality and relevance as to create a very real chance of conviction. That Court needs also to be satisfied that it is in the interests of justice to order such a trial (s 79). Once the Court of Appeal is satisfied as to these matters, there is no discretion. There must be a retrial (s 77(1)), unless the prosecution neglects to prefer the new indictment within time (s 84(2), (4)).

11.14   A retrial will be governed by the procedure then in force for a Crown Court trial. It will have the appearance of an ordinary trial, but to those aware of the history of the case it is unlikely to feel like a normal trial. Reporting restrictions under s 82 will prevent reporting of the proceedings in the Court of Appeal to prevent prejudice to the accused: a jury might (if it knew) feel that the fact that a court of the standing of the Court of Appeal had ruled there was enough evidence for a retrial was in itself a strong indicator of guilt. It is to be hoped that reporting restrictions will minimise any prior knowledge on the part of a juror who may otherwise assume that if the case is good enough to be retried, the defendant must be guilty. The Act contains no guidance on what jurors may be told about the previous trial.[21] It may be that rules of court or Judicial Studies Board directions may accommodate any necessary explanation. Both sides will occasionally want to make reference to evidence given previously – perhaps to show inconsistency, or even lies, on the part of the other side's witnesses and reference to a previous trial for this purpose is acceptable. Previous statements might, in some circumstances, be admissible in evidence.[22] Care will need to be taken to ensure a jury is not influenced adversely by the fact it is an unusual retrial.

Basis of application to Court of Appeal

11.15   A prosecutor must obtain an order under s 77(1) from the Court of Appeal to quash the acquittal as a preliminary matter to clear the way for a retrial. A second order, requiring a retrial, needs to be made at the same time. If the acquittal occurred abroad an additional determination under s 77(2) needs to be made as to whether or not the offence is a qualifying one and the acquittal is a bar.

An application is made direct to the Court of Appeal, and a right of appeal to the House of Lords is available to the parties. The prosecutor can only make an application with the express and personal written consent of the DPP (s 76(3)), although the power can be delegated to a limited category of people in the DPP's absence. It is this personal power which marks the entrance to the Home Secretary's 'double-locked gateway'.[23] The DPP can also reopen private prosecutions such as that in the Stephen Lawrence case,[24] but a private prosecutor cannot deploy the Act,

---

21   See *Sambasivam v Public Prosecutor, Federation of Malaya* [1950] AC 458, PC; *Binham* [1991] Crim LR 774, CA.

22   See **6.15**.

23   David Blunkett MP, Second Reading, HC Deb, 4 December 2002, col 924.

24   Section 79(4). See also **11.27**.

although he can lobby the CPS, and undoubtedly will do so once the legislation comes into force.

Basis of DPP's decision to make application to Court of Appeal

11.16   The DPP can only give his consent if, first, he is satisfied that there is new and compelling evidence (as defined by s 78) and, secondly, that it is in the public interest to proceed under s 79. Section 78(3) defines 'new and compelling': it is a matter to be determined by the court, based on the totality of the evidence collected during the investigations. No doubt scientific evidence will be particularly important.[25]

The DPP will have only one chance to make the application as s 76(5) permits only one application. Multiple opportunities would certainly cause tremendous harassment of a citizen, be oppressive and, arguably, infringe international protections.[26] Those investigating and taking decisions will need to perfect their application to minimise the risk of losing it and thus the prospect of any future remedy.

To meet some concerns of the Eleventh Report of the Joint Committee on Human Rights, safeguards were added to these provisions during the passage of the Act. Section 76(4)(c) requires the DPP to be satisfied that ss 78 and 79 will be made out. He must also be satisfied that any trial would not be inconsistent with the United Kingdom's obligations under Arts 31 and 34 of the Treaty of Rome where the principle of *ne bis in idem* (double jeopardy) is a component of EU law. Article 31 requires EU members to take common action to secure judicial co-operation between Member States and Art 34 to pursue, *inter alia*, the approximation of laws between members. Lord Goldsmith told the House of Lords that the provision was aimed at:

> ' ... preventing the re-opening of cases where there has already been an acquittal, except in exceptional circumstances ... the DPP will have to consider any obligations [negotiations between EU members to provide mutual recognition of acquittals in other Member States] that arise as an outcome of those negotiations before making an application ... '[27]

Section 76(4)(c) suggests that the Court of Appeal should measure the DPP's application against EU human rights standards to ensure the obligation here is not about to be broken.[28]

New and compelling evidence

11.17   Section 78(1) defines what amounts to new and compelling evidence. 'New' means that it was not adduced in the proceedings in which the person was acquitted (nor, if those were appeal proceedings, in earlier proceedings to which the appeal

---

25   See Second Reading, HC Deb, 4 December 2002, col 922; HC Committee, 21 January 2003, cols 446–467.

26   HL Report, 4 November 2003, col 703.

27   HL Committee, 4 November 2003, col 703.

28   See [2000] OJ C346/1; Doc ref 32000Y1218 (01). Indeed, the United Kingdom is expected shortly to ratify the Charter of Fundamental Rights of the European Union of 7 December 2000, Art 50 of which states:
'Right not to be tried or punished twice in criminal proceedings for the same criminal offence. No one shall be liable to be tried or punished again in criminal proceedings for an offence for which he or she has already been finally acquitted or convicted within the Union in accordance with the law.'

related). Evidence will be considered 'compelling' under s 78(3) and (4) if it is reliable, substantial and, when looked at against the background of the issues in the case, makes that evidence 'highly probative of the case against the acquitted person'. The court will need to identify facts in dispute in the first trial in order to identify whether the evidence on which the prosecution now relies is new and compelling and to determine what difference it would have made to the verdict had it been adduced at the first trial. Naturally, the factual issues may take on an added dimension now that there is new evidence, and the court will need to measure the probative value of the new evidence against the facts in dispute between the parties to gauge its novelty or compelling nature.

As well as questions of fact, there may have been questions of law. Those may be decided differently in the future because of changes in the substantive law or in rules of evidence. In particular, changes to the rules relating to bad character and to out-of-court statements may make a range of evidence available that was not admissible at the first trial. Section 78(5) makes it plain that it is legitimate for the court to disregard the old legal position if it has changed between the date of the acquittal and the s 75 application for retrial. It is irrelevant whether any evidence would have been admissible in earlier proceedings against the acquitted person.

Part 10 will also apply to newly discovered evidence as technology develops, and there have been several examples of criminal proceedings brought years after the crime,[29] due to the continued compilation of a database with which samples at a crime scene may be compared in the hope of a match which then leads to identification of the perpetrator. New evidence could also come from other sources, including, perhaps, a confession.[30]

11.18 In order to evaluate whether evidence is reliable, substantial and highly probative, the Court of Appeal will need to examine the evidence presented in the earlier proceedings, together with any information which was not admissible at that time to identify what was in dispute. Providing that the transcripts, witness statements and exhibits have been preserved, the Court can embark upon what will probably be a lengthy task. Where the documents were not kept, it is difficult to see how the issues can be accurately dissected. Police documentation may be destroyed or deteriorate; exhibits may also diminish in quality or (in the case of tissue) decompose. Witnesses – including the accused – are unlikely to remember with objectivity what was said and will be susceptible to the influence of new information which will have emerged in order that the application for a fresh trial can be made.

The Court will need to assess what is new about the evidence upon which the Crown now wishes to rely and what effect it would have had if adduced at the trial. Given that one of the main functions of the Court of Appeal is to consider how wrongly admitted evidence (or the refusal to admit evidence at trial) impacted on a conviction which is now challenged by the defendant as being unsafe, this anticipatory task will be one to which the Court is well suited. What is substantial for the purpose of s 78 can be

---

29 See Home Office Press Release 091/2003 'Extending the use of fingerprints and DNA samples to combat crime' (27 March 2003) for a list of successes achieved through the preservation of samples taken from the scene.

30 See the Julie Hogg case cited at HC Committee, 21 January 2003, where the former accused has confessed that he *did* kill his victim despite denials at his trial, which led to his acquittal.

identified by carrying out the exercise of assessing to what extent the new material would have influenced the previous outcome. The more likely a jury would have been to convict had they been in possession of the new material, the more substantial it is likely to be.

How can reliability be assessed? If the new evidence is capable of corroborating an old piece of evidence or vice versa then it might be considered to be reliable. If it is scientific, then the integrity of the scientist's methods will assist, as will the scope for errors, alternative theories or how well advanced that field is. But how, for example, would an alleged confession with no supporting evidence be assessed as reliable? The Court of Appeal could examine the witness for itself – the power to call witnesses or for other evidence has been created by s 80(6) – and decide whether the witness was credible and honest or unworthy of belief.

Identical powers exist under s 23 of the CAA 1995 to facilitate the hearings of appeals against conviction where new evidence has become available to the appellant, although the Court has to 'vet' that evidence under s 23(2). Section 78(5) allows the pre-existing rules of evidence to be ignored when deciding whether there is new evidence in a double jeopardy case, creating a seeming inequality between an accused who wishes to appeal his conviction and a prosecutor who wishes to appeal an acquittal, which causes some to reflect (in such an appeal by an accused) whether an Art 6 challenge might stand any chance of success on the principle of equality of arms.

The interests of justice test

11.19　The Court of Appeal must answer the four questions posed by s 79(2) in determining whether it is in the interests of justice to permit a retrial. Section 79(2)(a) requires the Court to consider whether a second trial can be fair. That will be looked at in the context of the time which has passed since the original trial concluded. The Court must inquire into whether or not the evidence could have been discovered earlier had the investigator or prosecutor acted with due diligence (s 79(2)(c)). It will then need to decide how expeditiously the authorities acted when it became apparent that there was new evidence and whether there was any failure to act (s 79(2)(d)).

Procedure on an application under s 80

11.20　As the Court of Appeal is the only court empowered to deal with applications at first instance, the prosecutor will need to give notice of its intention under s 80. From the moment that notice is given, the Crown has two days to serve proceedings upon the new defendant (s 80(2)). Rules of court will no doubt deal with questions of service. In some cases an arrest will have been made as part of the re-investigation process, so the accused will already be in the hands of the police. Considerable problems may arise where a person flees abroad – the notice needs to be served in order to trigger the s 76 hearing – there does not appear to be provision for a hearing of which the accused is unaware.

Where a person absents himself deliberately the court may be reluctant to deal with the application in his absence because of Art 6 considerations,[31] but this stage is not

---

31　*Colozza v Italy* (1985) 7 EHRR 516.

the actual trial and if the defendant has legal representation the matter could be heard in his, but not his lawyers', absence, provided they are properly instructed.[32] The Court will not wish to allow a suspect to prevent proceedings being reopened by absconding.

Extradition from a foreign jurisdiction may be an option – the Government is also working on new legislation to make extradition simpler. If a person were served with notice then failed to attend, this would not present a problem (providing he was eventually caught) as a warrant could be issued to secure his arrest. If a person does flee from service there is power under s 80 (3) to extend the time for service, including the situation where a suspect is abroad.

Where the defendant is served, then he has the right to attend the hearing or he may decline. If he is in custody (the Crown Court may have remanded him in custody at the conclusion of the investigation stage) and wishes to be produced at court, then that is his right.

11.21 Where there were defendants tried together on the same indictment in the earlier Crown Court proceedings, the discovery of new and compelling evidence may affect some or all of them. Section 80(7) permits the Court of Appeal to deal with applications for the quashing of acquittals and retrials for several people or several offences where there was more than one count on the indictment.

Court of Appeal's powers on hearing an application

11.22 Under s 77, the Court must rule whether or not the tests under ss 78 and 79 are met. If they are, then the Crown is entitled to its order (which cannot in such circumstances be refused). If the tests are not made out, the Court must dismiss the Crown's application, ending any risk of retrial for the accused as s 76(5) only permits one application. In the case of a conviction in England and Wales, if the Court holds that the previous acquittal is a bar to retrial, it must say so and indicate whether or not it found the tests at ss 78 and 79 satisfied. Equally, if it is decided that the acquittal is no bar, this must be stated by the Court. In this way, the parties know how and why the Court arrived at its decision (an essential prerequisite of determining whether an appeal may lie).

Bail and custody during and after the Court of Appeal hearing

11.23 The Act makes provision in respect of the grant of bail, or remand in custody. Reference should be made to s 90. Bail will need to be decided against the background of the BA 1976, including the changes made by the new Act.[33] The major worry for those representing an accused posed by the sections of this Act covering bail will be the length of time involved in bringing a case before the Court of Appeal or waiting for the outcome of any appeal to the House of Lords. Although the Crown must normally prefer the indictment within two months of obtaining the Court of Appeal's authority for a new trial (s 84), arraignment is not the same as commencing the trial. Defendants will still have to spend time in custody for what may be very substantial

---

32 See *Karatas and Sari v France* 35 EHHR 1253.

33 See **3.3–3.4** and **3.27–3.33**.

periods of time, on charges where not only are they still presumed innocent but have once been tried and acquitted. The custody time-limit provisions[34] apply, but this protection is of little use if the prosecution complies with the Act by acting with due diligence and expedition and there is good cause to keep a person on remand in prison.

Appeals from the Court of Appeal

11.24 A right to appeal any decision to the House of Lords exists, and the CAA 1968 is amended to reflect this. Either party will be able to appeal with the leave of the Court of Appeal or by petition to the Law Lords.

Reporting restrictions

11.25 Sections 82 and 83 create reporting restrictions and sanctions to prevent a trial being rendered unfair by adverse media coverage.

Retrials

11.26 Once the Court of Appeal has decided that a fresh trial should take place, a fresh indictment must be preferred on the direction of the Court (s 84(1)), not by the prosecutor, as would normally occur in the Crown Court. This ensures that the Court of Appeal can control the content of the indictment. Presumably, as with voluntary bills of indictment, only the Court of Appeal will have power to add any counts beyond those directed at the conclusion of proceedings under s 84.[35] This will protect an accused whose retrial will only be limited to allegations which the Court of Appeal considers acceptable under the new Act in that particular case. Of course, offences may have been committed in connection with the original trial and it is difficult to see how the Court of Appeal would decline to add those, if the prosecutor applied for joinder of new counts to the old as part and parcel of the s 76 application. A draft indictment may become a common document for a prosecutor to include in his application under these provisions or be ordered when rules of court are drawn up to set out more details of the procedure to be used under Part 10 of the Act.

11.27 Section 84(5) gives the Court the scope to include other counts and other defendants and is widely enough drawn to incorporate people who are not the subject of double jeopardy proceedings, so a hitherto unknown accomplice could now be sucked into the retrial.

To ensure that a sense of urgency is maintained in retrials, the Crown has two months to have the accused arraigned on the new indictment and, if this deadline lapses, the prosecutor risks losing his opportunity to try the accused again unless he can satisfy the Court of Appeal (not the Crown Court or High Court judge at the Crown Court where the trial is listed to be heard) that he acted with 'due expedition' and there is 'good and sufficient cause' for an arraignment out of time.[36] However, if the two months elapse without action from the Crown, the defendant may take the initiative under s 84(4) by applying for his earlier acquittal to be restored or to seek a declaration

---

34 Section 88(6), (7).

35 *Thompson and Clein* 61 Cr App R 108, CA.

36 The same wording as used under s 22 of the POA 1985 (custody time-limits).

that his acquittal from another jurisdiction is now a bar to retrial. If he is successful, no further attempts to try him for the old offence can be made by virtue of s 76(5).

Evidence at the fresh trial

11.28 If the evidence at the original trial was given orally, then it must be given in the same fashion at the fresh proceedings under s 84(6) unless s 114 applies. This should deal with problems such as the death, disappearance, illness, intimidation or absence abroad of a material witness, subject only to the discretion in s 116. Depositions read under Sch 3 to the CDA 1998 will not be read at the retrial (s 84(7)), although presumably, they could be read if all parties agreed (under s 9 of the CJA 1967). That provision allows an acquitted person facing retrial to require witnesses to attend once more so that he may cross-examine them in furtherance of his right to do so under Art 6(3)(d) ECHR.

INVESTIGATIONS OF MATTERS WITH A VIEW TO A RETRIAL

11.29 Little point exists in having retrial powers based on new evidence without permitting the police or other investigators to reinvestigate the case to ensure that the evidence will fit the 'new and compelling' test prescribed at s 78. The prosecution must gather what they need under s 78 to maximise their prospect of success under s 76, because they are permitted only one opportunity and presenting a case under s 76 which is too weak for lack of investigation would rule out any retrial now and forever. There may be a good explanation for the fresh evidence which is not commensurate with guilt on the part of the previously acquitted suspect. Perhaps the fresh evidence is capable of pointing in another direction, at someone other than the acquitted person. The fresh evidence may need legitimately 'firming up' to pass the threshold in ss 78 and 79.

Statutory authority to investigate is essential, for without it there would be no basis for the police to exercise the coercive powers of arrest and search and so forth in fact conferred by s 85 or s 86, and there would be no safeguards for individuals who in law are innocent (and have been adjudged to be so) against ongoing police investigation. Until the Court of Appeal has ruled whether the acquittal can be quashed and or a retrial ordered, whether the acquittal is a bar and whether it should be quashed and a retrial held, the accused has the benefit of a not guilty verdict.

11.30 Sections 85 to 87 contain police powers to facilitate all aspects of a new investigation but contain also restrictions on the timing and scope of those powers, thus striking a balance between society's interests in the investigation and the suspect's rights to respect for his private and family life, home and correspondence arising under Art 8 ECHR. During the passage of the Act considerable reservations were expressed about empowering the police to reinvestigate, engaging the whole 'paraphernalia of an oppressive process'[37] against an individual who had already been tried and acquitted. For that reason prior authorisation is generally required under s 85 to prevent officers investigating on a personal or organisational whim. However, s 86

---

37 Dominic Grieve MP, HC Committee, 21 January 2003, col 498.

permits retrospective authorisation of emergency steps. That is not intended to be the usual process.[38]

11.31 So that police powers are not extended beyond the scope of double jeopardy enquiries, s 78 of the CJA 2003 is only to apply to the investigation of qualifying offences which are suspected of having taken place, and which resulted in an acquittal. A fresh offence, such as perjury, where the accused apparently lied about his guilt at the earlier trial of a qualifying offence securing an acquittal in consequence, would have to be investigated under the normal powers under PACE, and would not need the DPP's consent.

Senior officers and prosecutors will need to ensure that investigators are aware of the ambit of their powers and that the appropriate consent is granted in 'mixed' investigations. The spectre also arises of multiple suspects being treated throughout a reinvestigation in different ways. Those once acquitted and now being reinvestigated will be treated differently from those who, for whatever reason, were never tried. Someone suspected of a crime for the first time can be arrested under PACE without a warrant and be interviewed or have samples taken, subject to compliance with PACE. If charged, following the decision of a custody officer, he will appear in the magistrates' court to be sent for trial to the Crown Court, subject only to the custody time-limits under s 22 of the POA 1985.

The CPS or counsel will prepare the indictment. A person arrested under these provisions can only be arrested on a warrant issued by a magistrate, can only be questioned or have samples, etc, taken with the DPP's consent (or that of a superintendent – s 86), cannot be charged without the consent of a superintendent unconnected to the inquiry, and proceedings begin in the Crown Court and the indictment is preferred by the Court of Appeal. Arraignment must normally occur within two months. The existence of this two-tiered system creates a risk that if a police officer acts without lawful authority, for example by confusing the issues pertinent to each offender, he creates the danger that the trial judge may accede to an application to exclude evidence unlawfully, ie under the wrong power or without the right consent at the right time obtained under s 78 of PACE.

DPP's prior authority for a reinvestigation

11.32 Section 85 provides that the DPP must personally give written consent for a reinvestigation. This must be given prospectively unless there is an emergency, in which case s 86 will apply. If the acquittal occurred abroad, he can only give that authority once he has certified that he believes the acquittal would not be a bar to a retrial in this jurisdiction. The DPP will be approached by the police (or other investigator). That consent can only be applied for by a senior officer (s 85(4)). That officer will not be able to seek the DPP's consent unless new evidence is known or available to him or he has reasonable grounds for believing that new evidence is likely to become available or known to him. The evidence known to the high-ranking officer must be relevant to the Crown's application for a fresh trial.

By s 85(6), the DPP can only give authorisation if he is satisfied that either there is already, or there is likely to become available through this investigation, *sufficient*

---

38   Hilary Benn MP, HC Committee, 21 January 2003, col 506.

new evidence to justify its launch *and* that it is in the public interest to embark on that investigation. The police force which made the application will not necessarily be the one which investigates, as the DPP has the power to recommend investigation by another force. For example, if there had been criticisms of one force's handling of the original case, another force might be felt to be better able to conduct a new inquiry with greater impartiality.

11.33 The statute does not create a right of appeal for a suspect to challenge the granting of consent by the DPP, nor did an attempt to require scrutiny by a circuit judge succeed.[39] While no one would suggest that the DPP would succumb to wider political pressures, or those created by public opinion, it does not mean he is immune from making unmeritorious decisions from which an appeal ought to be capable of arising. Decisions of the DPP are challengeable by way of judicial review on the normal basis governing the review of discretionary powers.[40] That said, the suspect often will not know of the application to, and decision of, the DPP until the inquiry is under way. Further, the Administrative Court will be loath to interfere with the exercise of a discretion in this area, provided it was a reasonable exercise.

11.34 A further protection for a person under investigation for a qualifying offence is contained in s 85(3), whereby a suspect may not, without that permission, be arrested, questioned, searched personally, have his vehicle or home or premises owned or occupied by him searched; nor may anything in his possession be seized, his fingerprints or any other samples be taken (even with consent). Of course, the police may well have taken fingerprints and samples from the earlier investigation, or from other investigations.

Investigations falling outside these categories do not need the DPP's consent, although until the acquittal is quashed, attempts to investigate a suspect, for example through questioning a suspect's wife, family, friends or workmates, attempting covert identification, or looking at his bank account, may legitimately be considered a breach of privacy by the suspect and thus invasive under Art 8 ECHR as the law regards him as an innocent man. Repeat testing of scientific samples already held may not impinge on a person's privacy, and thus such inquiries do not need advance consent, but there will sometimes be a fine line – or even no distinction – between the invasive *per se* and arguably non-invasive investigations. A failure to identify where consent is needed and where it is not could lead to arguments at trial to exclude evidence under s 78 of PACE.[41]

In addition, there is nothing to stop an investigation of the suspect under PACE for any new offence connected to the qualifying one, as long as an officer takes care to keep the two matters and the police powers in each investigation distinct in his mind.

11.35 Solicitors advising a suspect facing reinvestigation will have to make a quick judgment about whether to advise the suspect to answer questions in interview,

---

39 Lady Anelay, HL Committee, 15 September 2003, cols 698 and 706.

40 See, by analogy, *Chief Constable of Kent ex parte L* [1995] 1 All ER 756, DC; *R v Commissioner of Police for the Metropolis ex parte P* (1996) 5 Admin LR 6, DC.

41 See, by analogy, *Veneroso* [2002] Crim LR 307 – an unlawful search made in good faith leading to the discovery of Class A drugs which were later excluded under s 78 of PACE on appeal. Also see *Chalkley v UK* (2003) 37 EHHR 680(30).

without perhaps knowing in detail what happened at the last trial, or to advise an initial 'no comment' interview and risk an adverse inference being drawn if the client unreasonably fails to mention a fact he later relies upon at trial. The Crown can refer to previous trials to establish facts or lies by the defendant.[42]

If the suspect voluntarily comments on an issue relating to the old trial, he may find it can be used against him at trial by way of previous inconsistent statement if it appears that he said something different at the last trial.[43]

Emergency investigations

11.36   The Act confers investigatory powers in emergencies where there is not time to seek consent under s 85. Reference should be made to s 86. Such a power may be needed to stop someone disposing of evidence. Section 86(3) thus permits 'urgent investigative steps' to be pursued where: (a) the action is necessary as a matter of urgency to prevent the investigation being substantially and irrevocably prejudiced; or (b) to prevent death or serious personal injury.

Section 85 procedure is intended to be the normal route to relaunching an investigation;[44] it is not suitable for emergency use. Section 86 will be used where otherwise an investigation may be prejudiced while all the key players in the s 85 process are contacted and consent obtained.

Arrest and charge

11.37   At some point in the investigation the police will wish to question or charge the suspect. If he will not attend the police station voluntarily, questioning is unlikely to be possible and he will have to be served under s 80 with the notice of the application to the Court of Appeal.

An arrest can only take place if an arrest warrant has been issued by a magistrate under s 87(1). The magistrate need only be satisfied that there is new evidence *of relevance* to an application to quash the acquittal. There are some differences over charging compared to investigations outside the Act. Normally, the custody officer would hear from the investigating officer and perhaps from the suspect or his solicitor as to their views on charge. He would charge the suspect if he felt there was sufficient evidence for a prosecution to succeed under s 37 of PACE. Under the regime relating to double jeopardy, the custody officer can charge only if a superintendent (or above) believes there is sufficient evidence either available or known to that individual officer to send the file to the CPS for the prosecution to decide whether to apply to quash the acquittal by s 87(4). The superintendent (or above) must be unconnected with the investigation. The suspect can be charged only with the offence for which he was arrested – which differs from the usual position on charge, where he could be charged with any offence disclosed (s 87(3)). It is not inevitable that someone who is arrested

---

42   *Sambasivam v Public Prosecutor, Federation of Malaya* [1950] AC 458; *R v Binham* [1991] Crim LR 774, CA.

43   See **6.52–6.53**.

44   See Hilary Benn, HC Committee, 21 January 2003, cols 503–517. See also criticisms of Dominic Grieve MP, *ibid*, col 504, and David Heath MP, *ibid*, col 510.

will be charged, nor that the CPS will decide to seek a fresh trial. To ensure that the superintendent is fully acquainted with the facts, there is a statutory obligation imposed by s 87(5) on the custody officer to furnish his senior officer with the new evidence as soon as practicable following the arrest, or as soon as it becomes apparent to him personally that there is new evidence which may be relevant to an application under s 76. A suspect's detention following arrest under the magistrate's warrant or, if arrested for failing to answer bail, is governed by s 34 of PACE and thus is an identical regime to the one for other arrestees. However, someone arrested in a normal PACE investigation has the express benefit of the detention clock – he can only be detained for up to 36 hours. Arguably, the same principles implicitly apply *ab initio* to a suspect being reinvestigated.

Post-charge matters – bail or custody?

11.38   Once a person has been charged but before the s 76 application can be heard, he must either be bailed, remanded to the care of the local authority[45] or produced in custody at the Crown Court as soon as practicable and certainly within 24 hours. The magistrates' court has no involvement beyond granting the arrest warrant under s 87. Bail can be granted by the police under s 88(1) or by a Crown Court judge under s 88(4). A judge may also remand a person in custody under s 88(4).

The judge will then deal with any representations regarding bail and decide whether to grant bail unconditionally, with conditions or remand the defendant in custody. The statutory presumption of bail under s 4 of the BA 1976 is preserved, but in the case of a retrial for murder, manslaughter, rape or an attempted murder or rape, and where the defendant has a previous conviction for one of these offences, s 25 of the CJPOA 1994 bites to remove the right, subject to exceptional circumstances. The case will then be adjourned to permit the Crown to apply to the Court of Appeal under s 75 to quash the acquittal. If notice of that application has already been served, the case will be adjourned to the date fixed for the hearing of that s 76 application. It should be noted that the Crown Court has the power to revoke bail under s 91, although there would need to be a substantial risk of absconding, interference with witnesses or the course of justice, or commission of further offences demonstrated for the court to revoke.[46]

The merits of any quashing application, if not already determined, will need to be considered by a prosecutor who, if satisfied that there is sufficient new evidence and it is in the public interest to proceed, will have to draft the documents, serve them upon the defence and have the case listed before the Court of Appeal. To minimise time spent in custody, s 88(6) limits any remand in custody by the Crown Court post-charge to 42 days unless an advance application to extend those custody time-limits is granted. An application to extend them will be only be granted if the Crown can show good and sufficient cause and that it has acted with due diligence and expedition (s 88(8)).[47] If the time-limits lapse with no application having been served upon him, the defendant will be released from any obligations imposed upon him by a grant of bail or, if in custody, he will be released unconditionally under s 88(7).

---

45   Section 38(6) of PACE is limited to juveniles although juveniles are not specifically mentioned anywhere in Part 10.

46   See the BA 1976.

47   For case-law on s 22 of the POA 1985 see *Archbold* (Sweet & Maxwell, looseleaf) 1–272 to 276.

Section 88 therefore allows the Crown Court to oversee the progress of the application and adjust the bail or remand status of the suspect as and when necessary. These protections are necessary to preserve the suspect's rights under Art 5 ECHR so far is possible by reviewing the Crown's efforts.

Bail or custody before the Court of Appeal hearing

11.39   Reference should be made to s 89 for the position in respect of bail or custody prior to the Court of Appeal hearing. Section 89 applies to cases where notice under s 80(1) has been given[48] and governs bail and custody from the date of application to the hearing. For someone in custody, this means being produced in the Crown Court within the next 48 hours or as soon as practicable (s 89(2)). The time runs from when notice is given (s 89(2)). A defendant on bail will be notified of the obligation to attend the Court of Appeal by summons, or the Court may grant an application by the prosecutor for the issue of an arrest warrant, for example if the accused cannot be found or is believed unlikely to attend voluntarily. Anyone who is arrested on warrant must be produced in the Crown Court as soon as is reasonably practicable and in any event within 48 hours. The court will then have to decide whether to grant bail or remand in custody to the Court of Appeal. Bail, once granted, can be revoked by the Crown Court by virtue of s 89(8).

Where a court does revoke bail under these new provisions and the accused is not present, he will be ordered to surrender forthwith. On surrender he will be remanded into custody (s 89(8)), so there is no discretion to re-bail. If the individual fails to comply, without reasonable excuse, he can be arrested without warrant (s 89(3)). Anyone who is arrested must be produced before the Crown Court as soon as practicable or, at the latest, within 48 hours. The case will then be adjourned to permit the Crown to apply to the Court of Appeal to quash the acquittal or, if the notice has been served, the case will be adjourned.

Bail or custody after the Court of Appeal hearing

11.40   After the application under s 76 has been granted or pending its determination, ss 90 and 91 govern the accused's bail position and broadly mirror the pre-application provisions, save that s 91 provides for the revocation of an accused's bail. This permits his arrest without warrant and requires that he be produced before the Crown Court within 24 hours.

Where a court does revoke bail under these new provisions and the accused is not present, he will be ordered to surrender forthwith. On surrender he will be remanded into custody (s 91(2)). There is no discretion to re-bail. If the individual fails to comply, without reasonable excuse, he can be arrested without a warrant in this situation by s 91(3). Anyone who is arrested must be produced before the Crown Court as soon as practicable, or, under s 91(4) within 24 hours of arrest at the latest – not 48 hours as in the other sections under Part 10.

---

48   See **11.20**.

The human rights context

11.41 These provisions raise human rights issues. The Joint Committee on Human Rights[49] initially considered that the proposals that Part 10 would raise were compatible with human rights,[50] but expressed concerns about aspects of the changes made during the passage of the Act.

Article 7 ECHR deals with retrospectivity.[51] The new provisions concerning retrial are unlikely to infringe this principle, because no one is being prosecuted for a newly created offence or given a harsher penalty than existed at the time of offending:[52] they are being re-prosecuted for an offence which already existed at the time they were first accused. No greater punishment than the maximum sentence open to the court in the earlier trial can be imposed under Art 7, but the Sch 4 qualifying offences under Part 10 of the new Act have always carried maximum life sentences. Nor are any issues in respect of Art 7(2) raised. By definition, the fact that the defendant was acquitted means that the conduct complained of was criminal, unless the acquittal was on the uncommon grounds that the facts alleged disclosed no offence known to the criminal law.

11.42 Of more likely import is Art 4 of the Seventh Protocol. This Article has not yet been ratified but it is intended to ratify in the future, when it will be part of domestic law by reason of the Human Rights Act 1998. Article 4 states:

'(1) No one shall be liable to be tried or punished again in criminal proceedings under the jurisdiction of the same State for an offence for which he has already been finally acquitted or convicted in accordance with the law and penal procedure of that State.

(2) The provisions of the preceding paragraph shall not prevent the re-opening of the case in accordance with the law and penal procedure of the State concerned, if there is evidence of new or newly discovered facts, or if there has been a fundamental defect in the previous proceedings, which could affect the outcome of the case.'

The vital words in Art 4(1) are 'finally acquitted or convicted'. Finality is defined as the stage reached whereby time-limits to seek any remedies against any judicial decision have expired or when any available remedies have run out. Many European States give their prosecutors rights of appeal against conviction or sentence.

The remedies during or after a trial refer to those available to any of the parties involved, normally by the appellate route. The delivery of a verdict in an English trial is not the end of the process, because finality has not yet been achieved. An appeal against sentence or conviction may be pursued by the defence, an appeal against an unduly lenient sentence may follow, or an appeal against conviction, if it be a tainted

---

49 See Second Report, 2002–03, *op cit*.

50 Eleventh Report, 2002–03, *op cit*, para 27.

51 '1. No person shall be held guilty of any criminal offence on account of any act or omission which did not constitute a criminal offence under national or international law at the time when it was committed. Nor shall a heavier penalty be imposed than the one that was applicable at the time the offence was committed. 2. This Article shall not prejudice the trial and punishment of any person for any act or omission which, at the time when it was committed, was criminal according to the general principles of law recognised by civilised nations.'

52 See, by contrast, the removal of marital rape exemption *SW and CR v UK* (1996) 21 EHRR 363, ECtHR, and increased penalties in *Welch v UK* (1995) 20 EHRR 247, ECtHR.

one, may be initiated by the prosecution under s 54 of the CPIA 1996. Article 4(1) therefore prevents retrial following acquittal or conviction only once the last possible decision has been taken. But what if a case has reached this stage and then the prosecution decides to prosecute for another offence based on the same facts?

11.43   In *Oliviera v Switzerland*,[53] the Court had to decide whether or not Art 4(1) had been infringed where O was fined for failing to control her vehicle following a traffic accident. The case had erroneously been listed before a court empowered only to deal with minor infractions. The accident had led to another party suffering injuries, a crime if caused by negligence in Switzerland. The court should have notified the Swiss prosecution service of the second offence of negligently inflicting serious injury but failed to do so, thus the prosecutor took matters into his own hands and fined O a much greater sum by means of a penal order.

O argued that she had been convicted on two different occasions on the same facts, in breach of Art 4(1). The ECtHR ruled that her conduct *did* arise from one set of facts, but that those facts gave rise to two different offences. Thus there was no breach of Art 4, which prohibits retrial for the same offence.

This mirrors the approach in *Connolly*.[54] In *Hartnett*,[55] H (who was convicted of driving with excess blood alcohol levels) was subsequently tried for dangerous driving, the conviction for excess alcohol aiding in proving the driving element of the second offence. H appealed against the conviction for dangerous driving, arguing abuse of process. His appeal was dismissed. The two offences arose out of the same circumstances, but were for different offences.

A different approach was taken in *Gradinger v Austria*,[56] where G was found guilty of the equivalent of causing death by careless driving. He was acquitted of the more serious charge of causing death by drink driving because the prosecution had no evidence to rebut that of the defendant, which demonstrated that he was below the legal limit. Only later, after the trial, did it obtain an expert report which revealed in fact the contrary. The prosecutor then pursued G for an offence of driving with excess alcohol levels by way of imposing a fine upon him. This was done administratively, and not through court proceedings. G argued that this conviction was in breach of Art 4(1) because he had been acquitted of being over the limit – the meaning, he argued, of the first verdict. The ECtHR accepted that argument. Although the two offences were different, the blood alcohol level required for the two offences was the same. The offences were, in reality, based on the same conduct.[57]

11.44   A distinction therefore arises between prosecution for multiple offences arising out of the same facts (*Oliviera*) and multiple prosecution for the same facts.[58] The Law Commission concluded:

---

53   ECtHR, 1998-V– p1990.

54   [1964] AC 1254, HL, at para 26.

55   [2003] Crim LR 719, CA.

56   A 328 C (1995).

57   Paragraphs 3.20–3.21a.

58   Emmerson and Ashworth, *Human Rights and Criminal Justice, op cit*, at para 12.26.

'The decision [in *Gradinger*] suggests that Article 4(1) is triggered only where the offence with which the defendant is charged is, in law, the same offence as that of which he or she was previously acquitted or convicted.'[59]

It could see no justification for the different outcomes in the two cases.

11.45 The Law Commission[60] considered that the defendant in *Connolly* would not have been protected under Art 4(1) because, like Oliviera, C was not being tried for the same offence twice. But Gradinger succeeded in preventing a second trial because the court held that a further trial, where the offences were based on the same facts and were essentially the same charge, could only occur in the special circumstances under Art 4(2).[61] Had Connolly's case been decided on *Gradinger* principles, he could not have been retried. If the more generous *Gradinger* interpretation prevailed, it would widen the principle in *Connolly* to offences arising out of the same facts, absent Art 4(2) considerations, thereby limiting the prosecution's ability to bring further charges.

11.46 Article 4(2) permits a retrial where there is 'evidence of new or newly-discovered facts, or there has been a fundamental defect in the previous proceedings which could affect the outcome of the case'. It permits double jeopardy in limited circumstances, where there is new evidence suggesting that the earlier acquittal was wrong. The s 79 requirements arguably strengthen the test the prosecutor has to meet, thus safeguarding an accused from undue risk of retrial. The Court of Appeal must satisfy itself that s 79 is satisfied before ordering a retrial. Indeed, Part 10 imposes a 'double-locked gateway' – the sanctioning of any new investigation by the DPP and then the Court of Appeal,[62] preventing anyone from being sent back to the Crown Court for trial on a whim. This accords with the underlying aim of Part 10 of the Act, to convict criminals who 'got away with it' where new and compelling evidence comes to light, eg forensic evidence like DNA, perhaps through technological advances, or where the former accused was foolish enough to confess his crime after his acquittal.

11.47 The Joint Committee had concerns about amendments to the Bill now contained in s 78. That defines 'new and compelling' so that what was new became that which had not been adduced in the proceedings in which the person was acquitted, whether at trial or on appeal. The Committee felt that this changed the human rights perspective. This new approach now may both conflict with Art 4(2), and fall short of the standards set down at Art 14.7 of the International Covenant on Civil and Political Rights (ICCPR),[63] binding on the United Kingdom in international law, although not part of domestic law. The conflict comes because the definition of 'new' has changed, and it was now a matter for judicial discretion under s 78 as to what amounted to new evidence or as the Committee put it:[64]

59 *Double Jeopardy – A Consultation Paper*, Law Com No 156 of 1999, para 3.27.

60 *Op cit*, para 10.67.

61 *Op cit*, para 3.41.

62 David Blunkett MP, Second Reading, 4 December 2002, col 924.

63 Second Report of the Joint Committee on Human Rights, 2002–03, *op cit*, para 29.

64 *Ibid*, para 28.

'However, the Court of Appeal would still have power to order a new trial where evidence was available at the time of the original acquittal, even if there has been a lack of due diligence or expedition, taking account of other factors'.

Article 14.7 of the ICCPR states:

'No one shall be liable to be retried or punished again for an offence for which he has finally been convicted or acquitted in accordance with the law and penal procedure of each country.'

Noting[65] that the UN recognised a need to reopen trials in exceptional circumstances, the Committee expressed its reservations thus:

'if the evidence in question is not new, this [that newly available evidence can justify a fresh trial following acquittal] is very doubtful.'

The Government argued that it was impossible to come up with a test to fulfil the aim of s 78[66] and that the new test obviated the need for the court to judge whether the 'new' evidence had been known to the police or prosecutor at the time of the acquittal when looking at an acquittal many years ago. The insertion of the word 'compelling' also added to the test the Crown had to meet.[67] The Committee was unimpressed and gave three examples of what it saw as unsatisfactory uses to which Part 10 could be put:[68]

– allowing evidence not formerly admissible to be put forward under s 78 – a possibility given Part 11 of the CJA 2003;
– where the Crown had kept its powder dry and not adduced admissible evidence at the trial for good tactical reasons;
– where lack of due diligence resulted in the non-adducing of evidence but the court exercised its discretion under s 79(2)(c) to order a trial in the interests of justice.

Concerns remain, therefore, as to how human rights-compliant ss 78 and 79 are in terms of Art 4(7) ECHR and Art 14.7 ICCPR.

---

65 Joint Committee Report, *op cit*, para 29.

66 *Ibid*, para 32.

67 *Ibid*, para 32.

68 *Ibid*, para 34.

Appendix

CRIMINAL JUSTICE ACT 2003

CONTENTS

PART 4

CHARGING ETC

PART 5

DISCLOSURE

PART 6

ALLOCATION AND SENDING OF OFFENCES

PART 7

TRIALS ON INDICTMENT WITHOUT A JURY

PART 8

LIVE LINKS

PART 9

PROSECUTION APPEALS

Introduction

General right of appeal in respect of rulings

Right of appeal in respect of evidentiary rulings

Miscellaneous and supplemental

PART 10

RETRIAL FOR SERIOUS OFFENCES

Cases that may be retried

Application for retrial

PART 11

EVIDENCE

CHAPTER 1

EVIDENCE OF BAD CHARACTER

Introductory

CHAPTER 2

HEARSAY EVIDENCE

Hearsay: main provisions

Principal categories of admissibility

Supplementary

Miscellaneous

General

CHAPTER 2

COMMUNITY ORDERS: OFFENDERS AGED 16 OR OVER

CHAPTER 3

PRISON SENTENCES OF LESS THAN 12 MONTHS

Prison sentences of less than twelve months

Intermittent custody

Further provision about custody plus orders and intermittent custody orders

Suspended sentences

Interpretation of Chapter

CHAPTER 4

FURTHER PROVISIONS ABOUT ORDERS UNDER CHAPTERS 2 AND 3

Introductory

Requirements available in case of all offenders

CHAPTER 5

DANGEROUS OFFENDERS

CHAPTER 6

RELEASE ON LICENCE

Preliminary

CHAPTER 7

EFFECT OF LIFE SENTENCE

CHAPTER 8

OTHER PROVISIONS ABOUT SENTENCING

Deferment of sentence

Power to include drug treatment and testing requirement in certain orders in respect of young offenders

CHAPTER 9

SUPPLEMENTARY

PART 13

MISCELLANEOUS

Detention of suspected terrorists

Enforcement of legislation on endangered species

Miscellaneous provisions about criminal proceedings

Outraging public decency

Jury service

Individual support orders

PART 1

AMENDMENTS OF POLICE AND CRIMINAL EVIDENCE ACT 1984

1 Extension of powers to stop and search

(1) In this Part, 'the 1984 Act' means the Police and Criminal Evidence Act 1984 (c. 60).

(2) In section 1(8) of the 1984 Act (offences for purpose of definition of prohibited article), at the end of paragraph (d) there is inserted '; and

(e) offences under section 1 of the Criminal Damage Act 1971 (destroying or damaging property).'

2 Warrants to enter and search

In section 16 of the 1984 Act (execution of warrants), after subsection (2) there is inserted –

'(2A) A person so authorised has the same powers as the constable whom he accompanies in respect of –

(a) the execution of the warrant, and

(b) the seizure of anything to which the warrant relates.

(2B) But he may exercise those powers only in the company, and under the supervision, of a constable.'

3 Arrestable offences

(1) Schedule 1A to the 1984 Act (specific offences which are arrestable offences) is amended as follows.

(2) After paragraph 2 there is inserted –

'Criminal Justice Act 1925

2ZA An offence under section 36 of the Criminal Justice Act 1925 (untrue statement for procuring a passport).'

(3) After paragraph 6 there is inserted –

'Misuse of Drugs Act 1971

6A An offence under section 5(2) of the Misuse of Drugs Act 1971 (having possession of a controlled drug) in respect of cannabis or cannabis resin (within the meaning of that Act).'

(4) After paragraph 17 there is inserted –

'17A An offence under section 174 of the Road Traffic Act 1988 (false statements and withholding material information).'

4 Bail elsewhere than at police station

(1) Section 30 of the 1984 Act (arrest elsewhere than at police station) is amended as follows.

(2) For subsection (1) there is substituted –

'(1) Subsection (1A) applies where a person is, at any place other than a police station –

(a) arrested by a constable for an offence, or

(b) taken into custody by a constable after being arrested for an offence by a person other than a constable.

(1A) The person must be taken by a constable to a police station as soon as practicable after the arrest.

(1B) Subsection (1A) has effect subject to section 30A (release on bail) and subsection (7) (release without bail).'

(3) In subsection (2) for 'subsection (1)' there is substituted 'subsection (1A)'.

(4) For subsection (7) there is substituted –

'(7) A person arrested by a constable at any place other than a police station must be released without bail if the condition in subsection (7A) is satisfied.

(7A) The condition is that, at any time before the person arrested reaches a police station, a constable is satisfied that there are no grounds for keeping him under arrest or releasing him on bail under section 30A.'

(5) For subsections (10) and (11) there is substituted –

'(10) Nothing in subsection (1A) or in section 30A prevents a constable delaying taking a person to a police station or releasing him on bail if the condition in subsection (10A) is satisfied.

(10A) The condition is that the presence of the person at a place (other than a police station) is necessary in order to carry out such investigations as it is reasonable to carry out immediately.

(11) Where there is any such delay the reasons for the delay must be recorded when the person first arrives at the police station or (as the case may be) is released on bail.'

(6) In subsection (12) for 'subsection (1)' there is substituted 'subsection (1A) or section 30A'.

(7) After section 30 there is inserted –

'30A Bail elsewhere than at police station

(1) A constable may release on bail a person who is arrested or taken into custody in the circumstances mentioned in section 30(1).

(2) A person may be released on bail under subsection (1) at any time before he arrives at a police station.

(3) A person released on bail under subsection (1) must be required to attend a police station.

(4) No other requirement may be imposed on the person as a condition of bail.

(5) The police station which the person is required to attend may be any police station.

30B Bail under section 30A: notices

(1) Where a constable grants bail to a person under section 30A, he must give that person a notice in writing before he is released.

(2) The notice must state –

    (a)   the offence for which he was arrested, and
    (b)   the ground on which he was arrested.

(3) The notice must inform him that he is required to attend a police station.

(4) It may also specify the police station which he is required to attend and the time when he is required to attend.

(5) If the notice does not include the information mentioned in subsection (4), the person must subsequently be given a further notice in writing which contains that information.

(6) The person may be required to attend a different police station from that specified in the notice under subsection (1) or (5) or to attend at a different time.

(7) He must be given notice in writing of any such change as is mentioned in subsection (6) but more than one such notice may be given to him.

30C Bail under section 30A: supplemental

(1) A person who has been required to attend a police station is not required to do so if he is given notice in writing that his attendance is no longer required.

(2) If a person is required to attend a police station which is not a designated police station he must be –

(a) released, or

(b) taken to a designated police station,

not more than six hours after his arrival.

(3) Nothing in the Bail Act 1976 applies in relation to bail under section 30A.

(4) Nothing in section 30A or 30B or in this section prevents the re-arrest without a warrant of a person released on bail under section 30A if new evidence justifying a further arrest has come to light since his release.

30D Failure to answer to bail under section 30A

(1) A constable may arrest without a warrant a person who –

(a) has been released on bail under section 30A subject to a requirement to attend a specified police station, but

(b) fails to attend the police station at the specified time.

(2) A person arrested under subsection (1) must be taken to a police station (which may be the specified police station or any other police station) as soon as practicable after the arrest.

(3) In subsection (1), 'specified' means specified in a notice under subsection (1) or (5) of section 30B or, if notice of change has been given under subsection (7) of that section, in that notice.

(4) For the purposes of –

(a) section 30 (subject to the obligation in subsection (2)), and

(b) section 31,

an arrest under this section is to be treated as an arrest for an offence.'

5 Drug testing for under-eighteens

(1) The 1984 Act is amended as follows.

(2) In section 38 (duties of custody officer after charge) –

(a) in subsection (1) –

(i) for sub-paragraph (iiia) of paragraph (a) there is substituted –

'(iiia) except in a case where (by virtue of subsection (9) of section 63B below) that section does not apply, the custody officer has reasonable grounds for believing that the detention of the person is necessary to enable a sample to be taken from him under that section;',

(ii) in sub-paragraph (i) of paragraph (b), after 'satisfied' there is inserted '(but, in the case of paragraph (a)(iiia) above, only if the arrested juvenile has attained the minimum age)',

(b) in subsection (6A), after the definition of 'local authority accommodation' there is inserted –

"minimum age' means the age specified in section 63B(3) below;'.

(3) In section 63B (testing for presence of Class A drugs) –

(a) in subsection (3), for '18' there is substituted '14',
(b) after subsection (5) there is inserted –

'(5A) In the case of a person who has not attained the age of 17 –

(a) the making of the request under subsection (4) above;
(b) the giving of the warning and (where applicable) the information under subsection (5) above; and
(c) the taking of the sample,

may not take place except in the presence of an appropriate adult.',

(c) after subsection (6) there is inserted –

'(6A) The Secretary of State may by order made by statutory instrument amend subsection (3) above by substituting for the age for the time being specified a different age specified in the order.

(6B) A statutory instrument containing an order under subsection (6A) above shall not be made unless a draft of the instrument has been laid before, and approved by a resolution of, each House of Parliament.',

(d) after subsection (8) there is inserted –

'(9) In relation to a person who has not attained the age of 18, this section applies only where –

(a) the relevant chief officer has been notified by the Secretary of State that arrangements for the taking of samples under this section from persons who have not attained the age of 18 have been made for the police area as a whole, or for the particular police station, in which the person is in police detention; and
(b) the notice has not been withdrawn.

(10) In this section –

'appropriate adult', in relation to a person who has not attained the age of 17, means –

(a) his parent or guardian or, if he is in the care of a local authority or voluntary organisation, a person representing that authority or organisation; or
(b) a social worker of a local authority social services department; or
(c) if no person falling within paragraph (a) or (b) is available, any responsible person aged 18 or over who is not a police officer or a person employed by the police;

'relevant chief officer' means –

(a) in relation to a police area, the chief officer of police of the police force for that police area; or
(b) in relation to a police station, the chief officer of police of the police force for the police area in which the police station is situated.'

6 Use of telephones for review of police detention

For section 40A(1) and (2) of the 1984 Act (use of telephone for review under s.40) there is substituted –

'(1) A review under section 40(1)(b) may be carried out by means of a discussion, conducted by telephone, with one or more persons at the police station where the arrested person is held.

(2) But subsection (1) does not apply if –

    (a) the review is of a kind authorised by regulations under section 45A to be carried out using video-conferencing facilities; and

    (b) it is reasonably practicable to carry it out in accordance with those regulations.'

7 Limits on period of detention without charge

In section 42(1) of the 1984 Act (conditions to be satisfied before detention without charge may be extended from 24 to 36 hours), for paragraph (b) there is substituted –

'(b) an offence for which he is under arrest is an arrestable offence; and'.

8 Property of detained persons

(1) In subsection (1) of section 54 of the 1984 Act (which requires the custody officer at a police station to ascertain and record everything which a detained person has with him), there is omitted 'and record or cause to be recorded'.

(2) For subsection (2) of that section (record of arrested person to be made as part of custody record) there is substituted –

'(2) The custody officer may record or cause to be recorded all or any of the things which he ascertains under subsection (1).

(2A) In the case of an arrested person, any such record may be made as part of his custody record.'

9 Taking fingerprints without consent

(1) Section 61 of the 1984 Act (fingerprinting) is amended as follows.

(2) For subsections (3) and (4) (taking of fingerprints without appropriate consent) there is substituted –

'(3) The fingerprints of a person detained at a police station may be taken without the appropriate consent if –

    (a) he is detained in consequence of his arrest for a recordable offence; and

    (b) he has not had his fingerprints taken in the course of the investigation of the offence by the police.

(4) The fingerprints of a person detained at a police station may be taken without the appropriate consent if –

    (a) he has been charged with a recordable offence or informed that he will be reported for such an offence; and

    (b) he has not had his fingerprints taken in the course of the investigation of the offence by the police.'

(3) In subsection (3A) (disregard of incomplete or unsatisfactory fingerprints) for the words from the beginning to 'subsection (3) above' there is substituted 'Where a person mentioned in paragraph (a) of subsection (3) or (4) has already had his fingerprints taken in the course of the investigation of the offence by the police'.

(4) In subsection (5) (authorisation to be given or confirmed in writing) for 'subsection (3)(a) or (4A)' there is substituted 'subsection (4A)'.

(5) In subsection (7) (reasons for taking of fingerprints without consent) for 'subsection (3) or (6)' there is substituted 'subsection (3), (4) or (6)'.

10 Taking non-intimate samples without consent

(1) Section 63 of the 1984 Act (other samples) is amended as follows.

(2) After subsection (2) (consent to be given in writing) there is inserted –

    '(2A) A non-intimate sample may be taken from a person without the appropriate consent if two conditions are satisfied.

    (2B) The first is that the person is in police detention in consequence of his arrest for a recordable offence.

    (2C) The second is that –

        (a) he has not had a non-intimate sample of the same type and from the same part of the body taken in the course of the investigation of the offence by the police, or
        (b) he has had such a sample taken but it proved insufficient.'

(3) In subsection (3)(a) (taking of samples without appropriate consent) the words 'is in police detention or' are omitted.

(4) In subsection (3A) (taking of samples without appropriate consent after charge) for '(whether or not he falls within subsection (3)(a) above)' there is substituted '(whether or not he is in police detention or held in custody by the police on the authority of a court)'.

(5) In subsection (8A) (reasons for taking of samples without consent) for 'subsection (3A)' there is substituted 'subsection (2A), (3A)'.

11 Codes of practice

(1) In section 67 of the 1984 Act (supplementary provisions about codes), for subsections (1) to (7C) there is substituted –

    '(1) In this section, 'code' means a code of practice under section 60, 60A or 66.

    (2) The Secretary of State may at any time revise the whole or any part of a code.

    (3) A code may be made, or revised, so as to –

        (a) apply only in relation to one or more specified areas,
        (b) have effect only for a specified period,

(c) apply only in relation to specified offences or descriptions of offender.

(4) Before issuing a code, or any revision of a code, the Secretary of State must consult –

(a) persons whom he considers to represent the interests of police authorities,
(b) persons whom he considers to represent the interests of chief officers of police,
(c) the General Council of the Bar,
(d) the Law Society of England and Wales,
(e) the Institute of Legal Executives, and
(f) such other persons as he thinks fit.

(5) A code, or a revision of a code, does not come into operation until the Secretary of State by order so provides.

(6) The power conferred by subsection (5) is exercisable by statutory instrument.

(7) An order bringing a code into operation may not be made unless a draft of the order has been laid before Parliament and approved by a resolution of each House.

(7A) An order bringing a revision of a code into operation must be laid before Parliament if the order has been made without a draft having been so laid and approved by a resolution of each House.

(7B) When an order or draft of an order is laid, the code or revision of a code to which it relates must also be laid.

(7C) No order or draft of an order may be laid until the consultation required by subsection (4) has taken place.

(7D) An order bringing a code, or a revision of a code, into operation may include transitional or saving provisions.'

(2) Section 113 of the 1984 Act (application of Act to armed forces) is amended as follows.

(3) After subsection (3) there is inserted –

'(3A) In subsections (4) to (10), 'code' means a code of practice under subsection (3).'

(4) For subsections (5) to (7) there is substituted –

'(5) The Secretary of State may at any time revise the whole or any part of a code.

(6) A code may be made, or revised, so as to –

(a) apply only in relation to one or more specified areas,
(b) have effect only for a specified period,
(c) apply only in relation to specified offences or descriptions of offender.

(7) The Secretary of State must lay a code, or any revision of a code, before Parliament.'

12 Amendments related to Part 1

Schedule 1 (which makes amendments related to the provisions of this Part) has effect.

PART 2

BAIL

13 Grant and conditions of bail

(1) In section 3(6) of the 1976 Act (which sets out cases where bail conditions may be imposed) –

    (a) the words 'to secure that' are omitted,

    (b) the words 'to secure that' are inserted at the beginning of each of paragraphs (a) to (e),

    (c) after paragraph (c) there is inserted –
        '(ca) for his own protection or, if he is a child or young person, for his own welfare or in his own interests,',

    (d) for 'or (c)' there is substituted ', (c) or (ca)'.

(2) In section 3A(5) of the 1976 Act (no conditions may be imposed under section 3(4), (5), (6) or (7) unless necessary for certain purposes) –

    (a) the words 'for the purpose of preventing that person from' are omitted,

    (b) the words 'for the purpose of preventing that person from' are inserted at the beginning of each of paragraphs (a) to (c),

    (c) after paragraph (c) there is inserted 'or
        (d) for that person's own protection or, if he is a child or young person, for his own welfare or in his own interests.'

(3) In paragraph 8(1) of Part 1 of Schedule 1 to the 1976 Act (no conditions may be imposed under section 3(4) to (7) unless necessary to do so for certain purposes) for the words from 'that it is necessary to do so' onwards there is substituted 'that it is necessary to do so –

    (a) for the purpose of preventing the occurrence of any of the events mentioned in paragraph 2(1) of this Part of this Schedule, or

    (b) for the defendant's own protection or, if he is a child or young person, for his own welfare or in his own interests.'

(4) For paragraph 5 of Part 2 of that Schedule (defendant need not be granted bail if having been released on bail he has been arrested in pursuance of section 7) there is substituted –

    '5 The defendant need not be granted bail if –
      (a) having been released on bail in or in connection with the proceedings for the offence, he has been arrested in pursuance of section 7 of this Act; and
      (b) the court is satisfied that there are substantial grounds for believing that the defendant, if released on bail (whether subject to conditions or not) would fail to surrender to custody, commit an offence on bail or interfere with witnesses or otherwise obstruct the course of justice (whether in relation to himself or any other person).'

14 Offences committed on bail

(1) For paragraph 2A of Part 1 of Schedule 1 to the 1976 Act (defendant need not be granted bail where he was on bail on date of offence) there is substituted –

    '2A(1) If the defendant falls within this paragraph he may not be granted bail unless the court is satisfied that there is no significant risk of his committing an offence while on bail (whether subject to conditions or not).

(2) The defendant falls within this paragraph if –

(a)   he is aged 18 or over, and
(b)   it appears to the court that he was on bail in criminal proceedings on the date of the offence.'

(2) After paragraph 9 of that Part there is inserted –

'9AA (1) This paragraph applies if –

(a)   the defendant is under the age of 18, and
(b)   it appears to the court that he was on bail in criminal proceedings on the date of the offence.

(2) In deciding for the purposes of paragraph 2(1) of this Part of this Schedule whether it is satisfied that there are substantial grounds for believing that the defendant, if released on bail (whether subject to conditions or not), would commit an offence while on bail, the court shall give particular weight to the fact that the defendant was on bail in criminal proceedings on the date of the offence.'

15 Absconding by persons released on bail

(1) For paragraph 6 of Part 1 of Schedule 1 to the 1976 Act (defendant need not be granted bail if having been released on bail he has been arrested in pursuance of section 7) there is substituted –

'6(1) If the defendant falls within this paragraph, he may not be granted bail unless the court is satisfied that there is no significant risk that, if released on bail (whether subject to conditions or not), he would fail to surrender to custody.

(2) Subject to sub-paragraph (3) below, the defendant falls within this paragraph if –

(a)   he is aged 18 or over, and
(b)   it appears to the court that, having been released on bail in or in connection with the proceedings for the offence, he failed to surrender to custody.

(3) Where it appears to the court that the defendant had reasonable cause for his failure to surrender to custody, he does not fall within this paragraph unless it also appears to the court that he failed to surrender to custody at the appointed place as soon as reasonably practicable after the appointed time.

(4) For the purposes of sub-paragraph (3) above, a failure to give to the defendant a copy of the record of the decision to grant him bail shall not constitute a reasonable cause for his failure to surrender to custody.'

(2) After paragraph 9AA of that Part (inserted by section 14(2)) there is inserted –

'9AB(1) Subject to sub-paragraph (2) below, this paragraph applies if –
(a)   the defendant is under the age of 18, and
(b)   it appears to the court that, having been released on bail in or in connection with the proceedings for the offence, he failed to surrender to custody.

(2) Where it appears to the court that the defendant had reasonable cause for his failure to surrender to custody, this paragraph does not apply unless it also appears to the court that he failed to surrender to custody at the appointed place as soon as reasonably practicable after the appointed time.

(3) In deciding for the purposes of paragraph 2(1) of this Part of this Schedule whether it is satisfied that there are substantial grounds for believing that the defendant, if released on bail (whether subject to conditions or not), would fail to surrender to custody, the court shall give particular weight to –

   (a) where the defendant did not have reasonable cause for his failure to surrender to custody, the fact that he failed to surrender to custody, or
   (b) where he did have reasonable cause for his failure to surrender to custody, the fact that he failed to surrender to custody at the appointed place as soon as reasonably practicable after the appointed time.

(4) For the purposes of this paragraph, a failure to give to the defendant a copy of the record of the decision to grant him bail shall not constitute a reasonable cause for his failure to surrender to custody.'

(3) In section 6 of the 1976 Act (offence of absconding by person released on bail) after subsection (9) there is inserted –

'(10) Section 127 of the Magistrates' Courts Act 1980 shall not apply in relation to an offence under subsection (1) or (2) above.

(11) Where a person has been released on bail in criminal proceedings and that bail was granted by a constable, a magistrates' court shall not try that person for an offence under subsection (1) or (2) above in relation to that bail (the "relevant offence") unless either or both of subsections (12) and (13) below applies.

(12) This subsection applies if an information is laid for the relevant offence within 6 months from the time of the commission of the relevant offence.

(13) This subsection applies if an information is laid for the relevant offence no later than 3 months from the time of the occurrence of the first of the events mentioned in subsection (14) below to occur after the commission of the relevant offence.

(14) Those events are –

   (a) the person surrenders to custody at the appointed place;
   (b) the person is arrested, or attends at a police station, in connection with the relevant offence or the offence for which he was granted bail;
   (c) the person appears or is brought before a court in connection with the relevant offence or the offence for which he was granted bail.'

16 Appeal to Crown Court

(1) This section applies where a magistrates' court grants bail to a person ('the person concerned') on adjourning a case under –

   (a) section 10 of the Magistrates' Courts Act 1980 (c. 43) (adjournment of trial),
   (b) section 17C of that Act (intention as to plea: adjournment),
   (c) section 18 of that Act (initial procedure on information against adult for offence triable either way),
   (d) section 24C of that Act (intention as to plea by child or young person: adjournment),
   (e) section 52(5) of the Crime and Disorder Act 1998 (c. 37) (adjournment of proceedings under section 51 etc), or
   (f) section 11 of the Powers of Criminal Courts (Sentencing) Act 2000 (c. 6) (remand for medical examination).

(2) Subject to the following provisions of this section, the person concerned may appeal to the Crown Court against any condition of bail falling within subsection (3).

(3) A condition of bail falls within this subsection if it is a requirement –

    (a) that the person concerned resides away from a particular place or area,

    (b) that the person concerned resides at a particular place other than a bail hostel,

    (c) for the provision of a surety or sureties or the giving of a security,

    (d) that the person concerned remains indoors between certain hours,

    (e) imposed under section 3(6ZAA) of the 1976 Act (requirements with respect to electronic monitoring), or

    (f) that the person concerned makes no contact with another person.

(4) An appeal under this section may not be brought unless subsection (5) or (6) applies.

(5) This subsection applies if an application to the magistrates' court under section 3(8)(a) of the 1976 Act (application by or on behalf of person granted bail) was made and determined before the appeal was brought.

(6) This subsection applies if an application to the magistrates' court –

    (a) under section 3(8)(b) of the 1976 Act (application by constable or prosecutor), or

    (b) under section 5B(1) of that Act (application by prosecutor),

was made and determined before the appeal was brought.

(7) On an appeal under this section the Crown Court may vary the conditions of bail.

(8) Where the Crown Court determines an appeal under this section, the person concerned may not bring any further appeal under this section in respect of the conditions of bail unless an application or a further application to the magistrates' court under section 3(8)(a) of the 1976 Act is made and determined after the appeal.

17 Appeals to High Court

(1) In section 22(1) of the Criminal Justice Act 1967 (c. 80) (extension of power of High Court to grant, or vary conditions of, bail) –

    (a) after 'Where' there is inserted '(a)', and

    (b) after 'proceedings,', in the second place where it occurs, there is inserted 'and

        (b) it does so where an application to the court to state a case for the opinion of the High Court is made,'.

(2) The inherent power of the High Court to entertain an application in relation to bail where a magistrates' court –

    (a) has granted or withheld bail, or

    (b) has varied the conditions of bail,

is abolished.

(3) The inherent power of the High Court to entertain an application in relation to bail where the Crown Court has determined –

    (a) an application under section 3(8) of the 1976 Act, or

    (b) an application under section 81(1)(a), (b), (c) or (g) of the Supreme Court Act 1981 (c. 54), is abolished.

(4) The High Court is to have no power to entertain an application in relation to bail where the Crown Court has determined an appeal under section 16 of this Act.

(5) The High Court is to have no power to entertain an application in relation to bail where the Crown Court has granted or withheld bail under section 88 or 89 of this Act.

(6) Nothing in this section affects –

   (a) any other power of the High Court to grant or withhold bail or to vary the conditions of bail, or
   (b) any right of a person to apply for a writ of habeas corpus or any other prerogative remedy.

(7) Any reference in this section to an application in relation to bail is to be read as including –

   (a) an application for bail to be granted,
   (b) an application for bail to be withheld,
   (c) an application for the conditions of bail to be varied.

(8) Any reference in this section to the withholding of bail is to be read as including a reference to the revocation of bail.

18 Appeal by prosecution

(1) Section 1 of the Bail (Amendment) Act 1993 (c. 26) (prosecution right of appeal) is amended as follows.

(2) For subsection (1) (prosecution may appeal to Crown Court judge against bail in case of offence punishable by imprisonment for five years or more etc) there is substituted –

   '(1) Where a magistrates' court grants bail to a person who is charged with, or convicted of, an offence punishable by imprisonment, the prosecution may appeal to a judge of the Crown Court against the granting of bail.'

(3) In subsection (10)(a) for 'punishable by a term of imprisonment' there is substituted 'punishable by imprisonment'.

19 Drug users: restriction on bail

(1) The 1976 Act is amended as follows.

(2) In section 3 (general provisions), after subsection (6B) there is inserted –

   '(6C) Subsection (6D) below applies where –

   (a) the court has been notified by the Secretary of State that arrangements for conducting a relevant assessment or, as the case may be, providing relevant follow-up have been made for the petty sessions area in which it appears to the court that the person referred to in subsection (6D) would reside if granted bail; and
   (b) the notice has not been withdrawn.

   (6D) In the case of a person ('P') –

(a) in relation to whom paragraphs (a) to (c) of paragraph 6B(1) of Part 1 of Schedule 1 to this Act apply;

(b) who, after analysis of the sample referred to in paragraph (b) of that paragraph, has been offered a relevant assessment or, if a relevant assessment has been carried out, has had relevant follow-up proposed to him; and

(c) who has agreed to undergo the relevant assessment or, as the case may be, to participate in the relevant follow-up,

the court, if it grants bail, shall impose as a condition of bail that P both undergo the relevant assessment and participate in any relevant follow-up proposed to him or, if a relevant assessment has been carried out, that P participate in the relevant follow-up.

(6E) In subsections (6C) and (6D) above –

(a) 'relevant assessment' means an assessment conducted by a suitably qualified person of whether P is dependent upon or has a propensity to misuse any specified Class A drugs;

(b) 'relevant follow-up' means, in a case where the person who conducted the relevant assessment believes P to have such a dependency or propensity, such further assessment, and such assistance or treatment (or both) in connection with the dependency or propensity, as the person who conducted the relevant assessment (or conducts any later assessment) considers to be appropriate in P's case,

and in paragraph (a) above 'Class A drug' and 'misuse' have the same meaning as in the Misuse of Drugs Act 1971, and 'specified' (in relation to a Class A drug) has the same meaning as in Part 3 of the Criminal Justice and Court Services Act 2000.

(6F) In subsection (6E)(a) above, 'suitably qualified person' means a person who has such qualifications or experience as are from time to time specified by the Secretary of State for the purposes of this subsection.'

(3) In section 3A(3) (conditions of bail in case of police bail), for ', (6A) and (6B)' there is substituted 'and (6A) to (6F)'.

(4) In Schedule 1 (which contains supplementary provisions about bail), in Part 1 (imprisonable offences) –

(a) after paragraph 6 there is inserted –

'Exception applicable to drug users in certain areas

6A Subject to paragraph 6C below, a defendant who falls within paragraph 6B below may not be granted bail unless the court is satisfied that there is no significant risk of his committing an offence while on bail (whether subject to conditions or not).

6B(1) A defendant falls within this paragraph if –

(a) he is aged 18 or over;

(b) a sample taken –

(i) under section 63B of the Police and Criminal Evidence Act 1984 (testing for presence of Class A drugs) in connection with the offence; or

(ii) under section 161 of the Criminal Justice Act 2003 (drug testing after conviction of an offence but before sentence), has revealed the presence in his body of a specified Class A drug;

(c) either the offence is one under section 5(2) or (3) of the Misuse of Drugs Act 1971 and relates to a specified Class A drug, or the court is satisfied that there are substantial grounds for believing –

    (i) that misuse by him of any specified Class A drug caused or contributed to the offence; or

    (ii) (even if it did not) that the offence was motivated wholly or partly by his intended misuse of such a drug; and

(d) the condition set out in sub-paragraph (2) below is satisfied or (if the court is considering on a second or subsequent occasion whether or not to grant bail) has been, and continues to be, satisfied.

(2) The condition referred to is that after the taking and analysis of the sample –

    (a) a relevant assessment has been offered to the defendant but he does not agree to undergo it; or

    (b) he has undergone a relevant assessment, and relevant follow-up has been proposed to him, but he does not agree to participate in it.

(3) In this paragraph and paragraph 6C below –

    (a) 'Class A drug' and 'misuse' have the same meaning as in the Misuse of Drugs Act 1971;

    (b) 'relevant assessment' and 'relevant follow-up' have the meaning given by section 3(6E) of this Act;

    (c) 'specified' (in relation to a Class A drug) has the same meaning as in Part 3 of the Criminal Justice and Court Services Act 2000.

6C Paragraph 6A above does not apply unless –

    (a) the court has been notified by the Secretary of State that arrangements for conducting a relevant assessment or, as the case may be, providing relevant follow-up have been made for the petty sessions area in which it appears to the court that the defendant would reside if granted bail; and

    (b) the notice has not been withdrawn.',

(b) in paragraph 8(1), for '(4) to (7)' there is substituted '(4) to (6B) or (7)'.

20 Supplementary amendments to the Bail Act 1976

(1) In Part 1 of Schedule 1 to the 1976 Act (supplementary provisions relating to bail of defendant accused or convicted of imprisonable offence) the existing text of paragraph 2 is to be sub-paragraph (1) of that paragraph, and after that sub-paragraph (as so re-numbered) there is inserted –

'(2) Where the defendant falls within one or more of paragraphs 2A, 6 and 6B of this Part of this Schedule, this paragraph shall not apply unless –

    (a) where the defendant falls within paragraph 2A, the court is satisfied as mentioned in sub-paragraph (1) of that paragraph;

    (b) where the defendant falls within paragraph 6, the court is satisfied as mentioned in sub-paragraph (1) of that paragraph;

    (c) where the defendant falls within paragraph 6B, the court is satisfied as mentioned in paragraph 6A of this Part of this Schedule or paragraph 6A does not apply by virtue of paragraph 6C of this Part of this Schedule.'

(2) In paragraph 9 of that Part (matters to be taken into account in making decisions under paragraph 2 or 2A of that Part) for '2 or 2A' there is substituted '2(1), or in deciding whether it is satisfied as mentioned in paragraph 2A(1), 6(1) or 6A,'.

21 Interpretation of Part 2

In this Part –

'bail' means bail in criminal proceedings (within the meaning of the 1976 Act),
'bail hostel' has the meaning given by section 2(2) of the 1976 Act,
'the 1976 Act' means the Bail Act 1976 (c. 63),
'vary' has the same meaning as in the 1976 Act.

PART 3

CONDITIONAL CAUTIONS

22 Conditional cautions

(1) An authorised person may give a conditional caution to a person aged 18 or over ('the offender') if each of the five requirements in section 23 is satisfied.

(2) In this Part 'conditional caution' means a caution which is given in respect of an offence committed by the offender and which has conditions attached to it with which the offender must comply.

(3) The conditions which may be attached to such a caution are those which have either or both of the following objects –

(a) facilitating the rehabilitation of the offender,
(b) ensuring that he makes reparation for the offence.

(4) In this Part 'authorised person' means –

(a) a constable,
(b) an investigating officer, or
(c) a person authorised by a relevant prosecutor for the purposes of this section.

23 The five requirements

(1) The first requirement is that the authorised person has evidence that the offender has committed an offence.

(2) The second requirement is that a relevant prosecutor decides –

(a) that there is sufficient evidence to charge the offender with the offence, and
(b) that a conditional caution should be given to the offender in respect of the offence.

(3) The third requirement is that the offender admits to the authorised person that he committed the offence.

(4) The fourth requirement is that the authorised person explains the effect of the conditional caution to the offender and warns him that failure to comply with any of the conditions attached to the caution may result in his being prosecuted for the offence.

(5) The fifth requirement is that the offender signs a document which contains –

(a) details of the offence,

    (b)   an admission by him that he committed the offence,

    (c)   his consent to being given the conditional caution, and

    (d)   the conditions attached to the caution.

24 Failure to comply with conditions

(1) If the offender fails, without reasonable excuse, to comply with any of the conditions attached to the conditional caution, criminal proceedings may be instituted against the person for the offence in question.

(2) The document mentioned in section 23(5) is to be admissible in such proceedings.

(3) Where such proceedings are instituted, the conditional caution is to cease to have effect.

25 Code of practice

(1) The Secretary of State must prepare a code of practice in relation to conditional cautions.

(2) The code may, in particular, include provision as to –

    (a)   the circumstances in which conditional cautions may be given,

    (b)   the procedure to be followed in connection with the giving of such cautions,

    (c)   the conditions which may be attached to such cautions and the time for which they may have effect,

    (d)   the category of constable or investigating officer by whom such cautions may be given,

    (e)   the persons who may be authorised by a relevant prosecutor for the purposes of section 22,

    (f)   the form which such cautions are to take and the manner in which they are to be given and recorded,

    (g)   the places where such cautions may be given, and

    (h)   the monitoring of compliance with conditions attached to such cautions.

(3) After preparing a draft of the code the Secretary of State –

    (a)   must publish the draft,

    (b)   must consider any representations made to him about the draft, and

    (c)   may amend the draft accordingly,

but he may not publish or amend the draft without the consent of the Attorney General.

(4) After the Secretary of State has proceeded under subsection (3) he must lay the code before each House of Parliament.

(5) When he has done so he may bring the code into force by order.

(6) The Secretary of State may from time to time revise a code of practice brought into force under this section.

(7) Subsections (3) to (6) are to apply (with appropriate modifications) to a revised code as they apply to an original code.

26 Assistance of National Probation Service

(1) Section 1 of the Criminal Justice and Court Services Act 2000 (c. 43) (purposes of Chapter 1) is amended as follows.

(2) After subsection (1) there is inserted –

'(1A) This Chapter also has effect for the purposes of providing for –

(a) authorised persons to be given assistance in determining whether conditional cautions should be given and which conditions to attach to conditional cautions, and

(b) the supervision and rehabilitation of persons to whom conditional cautions are given.'

(3) After subsection (3) there is inserted –

'(4) In this section 'authorised person' and 'conditional caution' have the same meaning as in Part 3 of the Criminal Justice Act 2003.'

27 Interpretation of Part 3

In this Part –

'authorised person' has the meaning given by section 22(4),

'conditional caution' has the meaning given by section 22(2),

'investigating officer' means a person designated as an investigating officer under section 38 of the Police Reform Act 2002 (c. 30),

'the offender' has the meaning given by section 22(1),

'relevant prosecutor' means –

(a) the Attorney General,

(b) the Director of the Serious Fraud Office,

(c) the Director of Public Prosecutions,

(d) a Secretary of State,

(e) the Commissioners of Inland Revenue,

(f) the Commissioners of Customs and Excise, or

(g) a person who is specified in an order made by the Secretary of State as being a relevant prosecutor for the purposes of this Part.

PART 4

CHARGING ETC

28 Charging or release of persons in police detention

Schedule 2 (which makes provision in relation to the charging or release of persons in police detention) shall have effect.

29 New method of instituting proceedings

(1) A public prosecutor may institute criminal proceedings against a person by issuing a document (a 'written charge') which charges the person with an offence.

(2) Where a public prosecutor issues a written charge, it must at the same time issue a document (a 'requisition') which requires the person to appear before a magistrates' court to answer the written charge.

(3) The written charge and requisition must be served on the person concerned, and a copy of both must be served on the court named in the requisition.

(4) In consequence of subsections (1) to (3), a public prosecutor is not to have the power to lay an information for the purpose of obtaining the issue of a summons under section 1 of the Magistrates' Courts Act 1980 (c. 43).

(5) In this section 'public prosecutor' means –

(a) a police force or a person authorised by a police force to institute criminal proceedings,

(b) the Director of the Serious Fraud Office or a person authorised by him to institute criminal proceedings,

(c) the Director of Public Prosecutions or a person authorised by him to institute criminal proceedings,

(d) the Attorney General or a person authorised by him to institute criminal proceedings,

(e) a Secretary of State or a person authorised by a Secretary of State to institute criminal proceedings,

(f) the Commissioners of Inland Revenue or a person authorised by them to institute criminal proceedings,

(g) the Commissioners of Customs and Excise or a person authorised by them to institute criminal proceedings, or

(h) a person specified in an order made by the Secretary of State for the purposes of this section or a person authorised by such a person to institute criminal proceedings.

(6) In subsection (5) 'police force' has the meaning given by section 3(3) of the Prosecution of Offences Act 1985 (c. 23).

30 Further provision about new method

(1) Rules under section 144 of the Magistrates' Courts Act 1980 may make –

(a) provision as to the form, content, recording, authentication and service of written charges or requisitions, and

(b) such other provision in relation to written charges or requisitions as appears to the Lord Chancellor to be necessary or expedient.

(2) Without limiting subsection (1), the provision which may be made by virtue of that subsection includes provision –

(a) which applies (with or without modifications), or which disapplies, the provision of any enactment relating to the service of documents,

(b) for or in connection with the issue of further requisitions.

(3) Nothing in subsection (1) or (2) is to be taken as affecting the generality of section 144(1) of that Act.

(4) Nothing in section 29 affects –

(a) the power of a public prosecutor to lay an information for the purpose of obtaining the issue of a warrant under section 1 of the Magistrates' Courts Act 1980 (c. 43),

(b) the power of a person who is not a public prosecutor to lay an information for the purpose of obtaining the issue of a summons or warrant under section 1 of that Act, or

(c) any power to charge a person with an offence whilst he is in custody.

(5) Except where the context otherwise requires, in any enactment contained in an Act passed before this Act –

(a) any reference (however expressed) which is or includes a reference to an information within the meaning of section 1 of the Magistrates' Courts Act 1980 (c.43) (or to the laying of such an information) is to be read as including a reference to a written charge (or to the issue of a written charge),

(b) any reference (however expressed) which is or includes a reference to a summons under section 1 of the Magistrates' Courts Act 1980 (or to a justice of the peace issuing such a summons) is to be read as including a reference to a requisition (or to a public prosecutor issuing a requisition).

(6) Subsection (5) does not apply to section 1 of the Magistrates' Courts Act 1980.

(7) The reference in subsection (5) to an enactment contained in an Act passed before this Act includes a reference to an enactment contained in that Act as a result of an amendment to that Act made by this Act or by any other Act passed in the same Session as this Act.

(8) In this section 'public prosecutor', 'requisition' and 'written charge' have the same meaning as in section 29.

31 Removal of requirement to substantiate information on oath

(1) In section 1(3) of the Magistrates' Courts Act 1980 (warrant may not be issued unless information substantiated on oath) the words 'and substantiated on oath' are omitted.

(2) In section 13 of that Act (non-appearance of defendant: issue of warrant) in subsection (3)(a) the words 'the information has been substantiated on oath and' are omitted.

(3) For subsection (3A)(a) of that section there is substituted –

'(a) the offence to which the warrant relates is punishable, in the case of a person who has attained the age of 18, with imprisonment, or'.

PART 5

DISCLOSURE

32 Initial duty of disclosure by prosecutor

In the Criminal Procedure and Investigations Act 1996 (c. 25) (in this Part referred to as 'the 1996 Act'), in subsection (1)(a) of section 3 (primary disclosure by prosecutor) –

(a) for 'in the prosecutor's opinion might undermine' there is substituted 'might reasonably be considered capable of undermining';

(b) after 'against the accused' there is inserted 'or of assisting the case for the accused'.

33 Defence disclosure

(1) In section 5 of the 1996 Act (compulsory disclosure by accused), after subsection (5) there is inserted –

'(5A) Where there are other accused in the proceedings and the court so orders, the accused must also give a defence statement to each other accused specified by the court.

(5B) The court may make an order under subsection (5A) either of its own motion or on the application of any party.

(5C) A defence statement that has to be given to the court and the prosecutor (under subsection (5)) must be given during the period which, by virtue of section 12, is the relevant period for this section.

(5D) A defence statement that has to be given to a co-accused (under subsection (5A)) must be given within such period as the court may specify.'

(2) After section 6 of that Act there is inserted –

'6A Contents of defence statement

(1) For the purposes of this Part a defence statement is a written statement –

- (a) setting out the nature of the accused's defence, including any particular defences on which he intends to rely,
- (b) indicating the matters of fact on which he takes issue with the prosecution,
- (c) setting out, in the case of each such matter, why he takes issue with the prosecution, and
- (d) indicating any point of law (including any point as to the admissibility of evidence or an abuse of process) which he wishes to take, and any authority on which he intends to rely for that purpose.

(2) A defence statement that discloses an alibi must give particulars of it, including –

- (a) the name, address and date of birth of any witness the accused believes is able to give evidence in support of the alibi, or as many of those details as are known to the accused when the statement is given;
- (b) any information in the accused's possession which might be of material assistance in identifying or finding any such witness in whose case any of the details mentioned in paragraph (a) are not known to the accused when the statement is given.

(3) For the purposes of this section evidence in support of an alibi is evidence tending to show that by reason of the presence of the accused at a particular place or in a particular area at a particular time he was not, or was unlikely to have been, at the place where the offence is alleged to have been committed at the time of its alleged commission.

(4) The Secretary of State may by regulations make provision as to the details of the matters that, by virtue of subsection (1), are to be included in defence statements.'

(3) After section 6A of that Act (inserted by subsection (2) above) there is inserted –

'6B Updated disclosure by accused

(1) Where the accused has, before the beginning of the relevant period for this section, given a defence statement under section 5 or 6, he must during that period give to the court and the prosecutor either –

- (a) a defence statement under this section (an "updated defence statement"), or
- (b) a statement of the kind mentioned in subsection (4).

(2) The relevant period for this section is determined under section 12.

(3) An updated defence statement must comply with the requirements imposed by or under section 6A by reference to the state of affairs at the time when the statement is given.

(4) Instead of an updated defence statement, the accused may give a written statement stating that he has no changes to make to the defence statement which was given under section 5 or 6.

(5) Where there are other accused in the proceedings and the court so orders, the accused must also give either an updated defence statement or a statement of the kind mentioned in subsection (4), within such period as may be specified by the court, to each other accused so specified.

(6) The court may make an order under subsection (5) either of its own motion or on the application of any party.'

34 Notification of intention to call defence witnesses

After section 6B of the 1996 Act (inserted by section 33 above) there is inserted –

'6C Notification of intention to call defence witnesses

(1) The accused must give to the court and the prosecutor a notice indicating whether he intends to call any persons (other than himself) as witnesses at his trial and, if so –

    (a) giving the name, address and date of birth of each such proposed witness, or as many of those details as are known to the accused when the notice is given;

    (b) providing any information in the accused's possession which might be of material assistance in identifying or finding any such proposed witness in whose case any of the details mentioned in paragraph (a) are not known to the accused when the notice is given.

(2) Details do not have to be given under this section to the extent that they have already been given under section 6A(2).

(3) The accused must give a notice under this section during the period which, by virtue of section 12, is the relevant period for this section.

(4) If, following the giving of a notice under this section, the accused –

    (a) decides to call a person (other than himself) who is not included in the notice as a proposed witness, or decides not to call a person who is so included, or

    (b) discovers any information which, under subsection (1), he would have had to include in the notice if he had been aware of it when giving the notice,

he must give an appropriately amended notice to the court and the prosecutor.'

35 Notification of names of experts instructed by defendant

After section 6C of the 1996 Act (inserted by section 34 above) there is inserted –

'6D Notification of names of experts instructed by accused

(1) If the accused instructs a person with a view to his providing any expert opinion for possible use as evidence at the trial of the accused, he must give to the court and the prosecutor a notice specifying the person's name and address.

(2) A notice does not have to be given under this section specifying the name and address of a person whose name and address have already been given under section 6C.

(3) A notice under this section must be given during the period which, by virtue of section 12, is the relevant period for this section.'

36 Further provisions about defence disclosure

After section 6D of the 1996 Act (inserted by section 35 above) there is inserted –

'6E Disclosure by accused: further provisions

(1) Where an accused's solicitor purports to give on behalf of the accused –

    (a)   a defence statement under section 5, 6 or 6B, or

    (b)   a statement of the kind mentioned in section 6B(4),

the statement shall, unless the contrary is proved, be deemed to be given with the authority of the accused.

(2) If it appears to the judge at a pre-trial hearing that an accused has failed to comply fully with section 5, 6B or 6C, so that there is a possibility of comment being made or inferences drawn under section 11(5), he shall warn the accused accordingly.

(3) In subsection (2) "pre-trial hearing" has the same meaning as in Part 4 (see section 39).

(4) The judge in a trial before a judge and jury –

    (a)   may direct that the jury be given a copy of any defence statement, and

    (b)   if he does so, may direct that it be edited so as not to include references to matters evidence of which would be inadmissible.

(5) A direction under subsection (4) –

    (a)   may be made either of the judge's own motion or on the application of any party;

    (b)   may be made only if the judge is of the opinion that seeing a copy of the defence statement would help the jury to understand the case or to resolve any issue in the case.

(6) The reference in subsection (4) to a defence statement is a reference –

    (a)   where the accused has given only an initial defence statement (that is, a defence statement given under section 5 or 6), to that statement;

    (b)   where he has given both an initial defence statement and an updated defence statement (that is, a defence statement given under section 6B), to the updated defence statement;

    (c)   where he has given both an initial defence statement and a statement of the kind mentioned in section 6B(4), to the initial defence statement.'

37 Continuing duty of disclosure by prosecutor

Before section 8 of the 1996 Act there is inserted –

'7A Continuing duty of prosecutor to disclose

(1) This section applies at all times –

    (a)   after the prosecutor has complied with section 3 or purported to comply with it, and

    (b)   before the accused is acquitted or convicted or the prosecutor decides not to proceed with the case concerned.

(2) The prosecutor must keep under review the question whether at any given time (and, in particular, following the giving of a defence statement) there is prosecution material which –

(a) might reasonably be considered capable of undermining the case for the prosecution against the accused or of assisting the case for the accused, and

(b) has not been disclosed to the accused.

(3) If at any time there is any such material as is mentioned in subsection (2) the prosecutor must disclose it to the accused as soon as is reasonably practicable (or within the period mentioned in subsection (5)(a), where that applies).

(4) In applying subsection (2) by reference to any given time the state of affairs at that time (including the case for the prosecution as it stands at that time) must be taken into account.

(5) Where the accused gives a defence statement under section 5, 6 or 6B –

(a) if as a result of that statement the prosecutor is required by this section to make any disclosure, or further disclosure, he must do so during the period which, by virtue of section 12, is the relevant period for this section;

(b) if the prosecutor considers that he is not so required, he must during that period give to the accused a written statement to that effect.

(6) For the purposes of this section prosecution material is material –

(a) which is in the prosecutor's possession and came into his possession in connection with the case for the prosecution against the accused, or

(b) which, in pursuance of a code operative under Part 2, he has inspected in connection with the case for the prosecution against the accused.

(7) Subsections (3) to (5) of section 3 (method by which prosecutor discloses) apply for the purposes of this section as they apply for the purposes of that.

(8) Material must not be disclosed under this section to the extent that the court, on an application by the prosecutor, concludes it is not in the public interest to disclose it and orders accordingly.

(9) Material must not be disclosed under this section to the extent that it is material the disclosure of which is prohibited by section 17 of the Regulation of Investigatory Powers Act 2000 (c. 23).'

38 Application by defence for disclosure

In section 8 of the 1996 Act (application by accused for disclosure), for subsections (1) and (2) there is substituted –

'(1) This section applies where the accused has given a defence statement under section 5, 6 or 6B and the prosecutor has complied with section 7A(5) or has purported to comply with it or has failed to comply with it.

(2) If the accused has at any time reasonable cause to believe that there is prosecution material which is required by section 7A to be disclosed to him and has not been, he may apply to the court for an order requiring the prosecutor to disclose it to him.'

39 Faults in defence disclosure

For section 11 of the 1996 Act there is substituted –

'11 Faults in disclosure by accused

(1) This section applies in the three cases set out in subsections (2), (3) and (4).

(2) The first case is where section 5 applies and the accused –

    (a) fails to give an initial defence statement,

    (b) gives an initial defence statement but does so after the end of the period which, by virtue of section 12, is the relevant period for section 5,

    (c) is required by section 6B to give either an updated defence statement or a statement of the kind mentioned in subsection (4) of that section but fails to do so,

    (d) gives an updated defence statement or a statement of the kind mentioned in section 6B(4) but does so after the end of the period which, by virtue of section 12, is the relevant period for section 6B,

    (e) sets out inconsistent defences in his defence statement, or

    (f) at his trial –

        (i)   puts forward a defence which was not mentioned in his defence statement or is different from any defence set out in that statement,

        (ii)   relies on a matter which, in breach of the requirements imposed by or under section 6A, was not mentioned in his defence statement,

        (iii) adduces evidence in support of an alibi without having given particulars of the alibi in his defence statement, or

        (iv) calls a witness to give evidence in support of an alibi without having complied with section 6A(2)(a) or (b) as regards the witness in his defence statement.

(3) The second case is where section 6 applies, the accused gives an initial defence statement, and the accused –

    (a) gives the initial defence statement after the end of the period which, by virtue of section 12, is the relevant period for section 6, or

    (b) does any of the things mentioned in paragraphs (c) to (f) of subsection (2).

(4) The third case is where the accused –

    (a) gives a witness notice but does so after the end of the period which, by virtue of section 12, is the relevant period for section 6C, or

    (b) at his trial calls a witness (other than himself) not included, or not adequately identified, in a witness notice.

(5) Where this section applies –

    (a) the court or any other party may make such comment as appears appropriate;

    (b) the court or jury may draw such inferences as appear proper in deciding whether the accused is guilty of the offence concerned.

(6) Where –

    (a) this section applies by virtue of subsection (2)(f)(ii) (including that provision as it applies by virtue of subsection (3)(b)), and

    (b) the matter which was not mentioned is a point of law (including any point as to the admissibility of evidence or an abuse of process) or an authority,

comment by another party under subsection (5)(a) may be made only with the leave of the court.

(7) Where this section applies by virtue of subsection (4), comment by another party under subsection (5)(a) may be made only with the leave of the court.

(8) Where the accused puts forward a defence which is different from any defence set out in his defence statement, in doing anything under subsection (5) or in deciding whether to do anything under it the court shall have regard –

(a) to the extent of the differences in the defences, and
(b) to whether there is any justification for it.

(9) Where the accused calls a witness whom he has failed to include, or to identify adequately, in a witness notice, in doing anything under subsection (5) or in deciding whether to do anything under it the court shall have regard to whether there is any justification for the failure.

(10) A person shall not be convicted of an offence solely on an inference drawn under subsection (5).

(11) Where the accused has given a statement of the kind mentioned in section 6B(4), then, for the purposes of subsections (2)(f)(ii) and (iv), the question as to whether there has been a breach of the requirements imposed by or under section 6A or a failure to comply with section 6A(2)(a) or (b) shall be determined –

(a) by reference to the state of affairs at the time when that statement was given, and
(b) as if the defence statement was given at the same time as that statement.

(12) In this section –

(a) "initial defence statement" means a defence statement given under section 5 or 6;
(b) "updated defence statement" means a defence statement given under section 6B;
(c) a reference simply to an accused's "defence statement" is a reference –
    (i) where he has given only an initial defence statement, to that statement;
    (ii) where he has given both an initial and an updated defence statement, to the updated defence statement;
    (iii) where he has given both an initial defence statement and a statement of the kind mentioned in section 6B(4), to the initial defence statement;
(d) a reference to evidence in support of an alibi shall be construed in accordance with section 6A(3);
(e) "witness notice" means a notice given under section 6C.'

40 Code of practice for police interviews of witnesses notified by accused

In Part 1 of the 1996 Act after section 21 there is inserted –

'21A Code of practice for police interviews of witnesses notified by accused

(1) The Secretary of State shall prepare a code of practice which gives guidance to police officers, and other persons charged with the duty of investigating offences, in relation to the arranging and conducting of interviews of persons –

(a) particulars of whom are given in a defence statement in accordance with section 6A(2), or
(b) who are included as proposed witnesses in a notice given under section 6C.

(2) The code must include (in particular) guidance in relation to –

(a) information that should be provided to the interviewee and the accused in relation to such an interview;
(b) the notification of the accused's solicitor of such an interview;

   (c)   the attendance of the interviewee's solicitor at such an interview;

   (d)   the attendance of the accused's solicitor at such an interview;

   (e)   the attendance of any other appropriate person at such an interview taking into account the interviewee's age or any disability of the interviewee.

(3) Any police officer or other person charged with the duty of investigating offences who arranges or conducts such an interview shall have regard to the code.

(4) In preparing the code, the Secretary of State shall consult –

   (a)   to the extent the code applies to England and Wales –
      (i)   any person who he considers to represent the interests of chief officers of police;
      (ii)   the General Council of the Bar;
      (iii)   the Law Society of England and Wales;
      (iv)   the Institute of Legal Executives;
   (b)   to the extent the code applies to Northern Ireland –
      (i)   the Chief Constable of the Police Service of Northern Ireland;
      (ii)   the General Council of the Bar of Northern Ireland;
      (iii)   the Law Society of Northern Ireland;
   (c)   such other persons as he thinks fit.

(5) The code shall not come into operation until the Secretary of State by order so provides.

(6) The Secretary of State may from time to time revise the code and subsections (4) and (5) shall apply to a revised code as they apply to the code as first prepared.

(7) An order bringing the code into operation may not be made unless a draft of the order has been laid before each House of Parliament and approved by a resolution of each House.

(8) An order bringing a revised code into operation shall be laid before each House of Parliament if the order has been made without a draft having been so laid and approved by a resolution of each House.

(9) When an order or a draft of an order is laid in accordance with subsection (7) or (8), the code to which it relates shall also be laid.

(10) No order or draft of an order may be laid until the consultation required by subsection (4) has taken place.

(11) A failure by a person mentioned in subsection (3) to have regard to any provision of a code for the time being in operation by virtue of an order under this section shall not in itself render him liable to any criminal or civil proceedings.

(12) In all criminal and civil proceedings a code in operation at any time by virtue of an order under this section shall be admissible in evidence.

(13) If it appears to a court or tribunal conducting criminal or civil proceedings that –

   (a)   any provision of a code in operation at any time by virtue of an order under this section, or
   (b)   any failure mentioned in subsection (11),

is relevant to any question arising in the proceedings, the provision or failure shall be taken into account in deciding the question.'

PART 6

ALLOCATION AND SENDING OF OFFENCES

41 Allocation of offences triable either way, and sending cases to Crown Court

Schedule 3 (which makes provision in relation to the allocation and other treatment of offences triable either way, and the sending of cases to the Crown Court) shall have effect.

42 Mode of trial for certain firearms offences: transitory arrangements

(1) The Magistrates' Courts Act 1980 is amended as follows.

(2) In section 24 (summary trial of information against child or young person for indictable offence) –

    (a) in subsection (1), for 'homicide' there is substituted 'one falling within subsection (1B) below',
    (b) in subsection (1A)(a), for 'of homicide' there is substituted 'falling within subsection (1B) below',
    (c) after subsection (1A), there is inserted –

    '(1B) An offence falls within this subsection if –

        (a) it is an offence of homicide; or
        (b) each of the requirements of section 51A(1) of the Firearms Act 1968 would be satisfied with respect to –
            (i)   the offence; and
            (ii)   the person charged with it,
        if he were convicted of the offence.'

(3) In section 25 (power to change from summary trial to committal proceedings and vice versa), in subsection (5), for 'homicide' there is substituted 'one falling within section 24(1B) above'.

PART 7

TRIALS ON INDICTMENT WITHOUT A JURY

43 Applications by prosecution for certain fraud cases to be conducted without a jury

(1) This section applies where –

    (a) one or more defendants are to be tried on indictment for one or more offences, and
    (b) notice has been given under section 51B of the Crime and Disorder Act 1998 (c. 37) (notices in serious or complex fraud cases) in respect of that offence or those offences.

(2) The prosecution may apply to a judge of the Crown Court for the trial to be conducted without a jury.

(3) If an application under subsection (2) is made and the judge is satisfied that the condition in subsection (5) is fulfilled, he may make an order that the trial is to be conducted without a jury; but if he is not so satisfied he must refuse the application.

(4) The judge may not make such an order without the approval of the Lord Chief Justice or a judge nominated by him.

(5) The condition is that the complexity of the trial or the length of the trial (or both) is likely to make the trial so burdensome to the members of a jury hearing the trial that the interests of justice require that serious consideration should be given to the question of whether the trial should be conducted without a jury.

(6) In deciding whether or not he is satisfied that that condition is fulfilled, the judge must have regard to any steps which might reasonably be taken to reduce the complexity or length of the trial.

(7) But a step is not to be regarded as reasonable if it would significantly disadvantage the prosecution.

44 Application by prosecution for trial to be conducted without a jury where danger of jury tampering

(1) This section applies where one or more defendants are to be tried on indictment for one or more offences.

(2) The prosecution may apply to a judge of the Crown Court for the trial to be conducted without a jury.

(3) If an application under subsection (2) is made and the judge is satisfied that both of the following two conditions are fulfilled, he must make an order that the trial is to be conducted without a jury; but if he is not so satisfied he must refuse the application.

(4) The first condition is that there is evidence of a real and present danger that jury tampering would take place.

(5) The second condition is that, notwithstanding any steps (including the provision of police protection) which might reasonably be taken to prevent jury tampering, the likelihood that it would take place would be so substantial as to make it necessary in the interests of justice for the trial to be conducted without a jury.

(6) The following are examples of cases where there may be evidence of a real and present danger that jury tampering would take place –

  (a) a case where the trial is a retrial and the jury in the previous trial was discharged because jury tampering had taken place,
  (b) a case where jury tampering has taken place in previous criminal proceedings involving the defendant or any of the defendants,
  (c) a case where there has been intimidation, or attempted intimidation, of any person who is likely to be a witness in the trial.

45 Procedure for applications under sections 43 and 44

(1) This section applies –

  (a) to an application under section 43, and
  (b) to an application under section 44.

(2) An application to which this section applies must be determined at a preparatory hearing (within the meaning of the 1987 Act or Part 3 of the 1996 Act).

(3) The parties to a preparatory hearing at which an application to which this section applies is to be determined must be given an opportunity to make representations with respect to the application.

(4) In section 7(1) of the 1987 Act (which sets out the purposes of preparatory hearings) for paragraphs (a) to (c) there is substituted –

'(a) identifying issues which are likely to be material to the determinations and findings which are likely to be required during the trial,
(b) if there is to be a jury, assisting their comprehension of those issues and expediting the proceedings before them,
(c) determining an application to which section 45 of the Criminal Justice Act 2003 applies,'.

(5) In section 9(11) of that Act (appeal to Court of Appeal) after 'above,' there is inserted 'from the refusal by a judge of an application to which section 45 of the Criminal Justice Act 2003 applies or from an order of a judge under section 43 or 44 of that Act which is made on the determination of such an application,'.

(6) In section 29 of the 1996 Act (power to order preparatory hearing) after subsection (1) there is inserted –

'(1A) A judge of the Crown Court may also order that a preparatory hearing shall be held if an application to which section 45 of the Criminal Justice Act 2003 applies (application for trial without jury) is made.'

(7) In subsection (2) of that section (which sets out the purposes of preparatory hearings) for paragraphs (a) to (c) there is substituted –

'(a) identifying issues which are likely to be material to the determinations and findings which are likely to be required during the trial,
(b) if there is to be a jury, assisting their comprehension of those issues and expediting the proceedings before them,
(c) determining an application to which section 45 of the Criminal Justice Act 2003 applies,'.

(8) In subsections (3) and (4) of that section for 'subsection (1)' there is substituted 'this section'.

(9) In section 35(1) of that Act (appeal to Court of Appeal) after '31(3),' there is inserted 'from the refusal by a judge of an application to which section 45 of the Criminal Justice Act 2003 applies or from an order of a judge under section 43 or 44 of that Act which is made on the determination of such an application,'.

(10) In this section –

'the 1987 Act' means the Criminal Justice Act 1987 (c. 38),
'the 1996 Act' means the Criminal Procedure and Investigations Act 1996 (c. 25).

46 Discharge of jury because of jury tampering

(1) This section applies where –

(a) a judge is minded during a trial on indictment to discharge the jury, and
(b) he is so minded because jury tampering appears to have taken place.

(2) Before taking any steps to discharge the jury, the judge must –

(a) inform the parties that he is minded to discharge the jury,

(b) inform the parties of the grounds on which he is so minded, and

(c) allow the parties an opportunity to make representations.

(3) Where the judge, after considering any such representations, discharges the jury, he may make an order that the trial is to continue without a jury if, but only if, he is satisfied –

(a) that jury tampering has taken place, and

(b) that to continue the trial without a jury would be fair to the defendant or defendants;

but this is subject to subsection (4).

(4) If the judge considers that it is necessary in the interests of justice for the trial to be terminated, he must terminate the trial.

(5) Where the judge terminates the trial under subsection (4), he may make an order that any new trial which is to take place must be conducted without a jury if he is satisfied in respect of the new trial that both of the conditions set out in section 44 are likely to be fulfilled.

(6) Subsection (5) is without prejudice to any other power that the judge may have on terminating the trial.

(7) Subject to subsection (5), nothing in this section affects the application of section 43 or 44 in relation to any new trial which takes place following the termination of the trial.

47 Appeals

(1) An appeal shall lie to the Court of Appeal from an order under section 46(3) or (5).

(2) Such an appeal may be brought only with the leave of the judge or the Court of Appeal.

(3) An order from which an appeal under this section lies is not to take effect –

(a) before the expiration of the period for bringing an appeal under this section, or

(b) if such an appeal is brought, before the appeal is finally disposed of or abandoned.

(4) On the termination of the hearing of an appeal under this section, the Court of Appeal may confirm or revoke the order.

(5) Subject to rules of court made under section 53(1) of the Supreme Court Act 1981 (c. 54) (power by rules to distribute business of Court of Appeal between its civil and criminal divisions) –

(a) the jurisdiction of the Court of Appeal under this section is to be exercised by the criminal division of that court, and

(b) references in this section to the Court of Appeal are to be construed as references to that division.

(6) In section 33(1) of the Criminal Appeal Act 1968 (c. 19) (right of appeal to House of Lords) after '1996' there is inserted 'or section 47 of the Criminal Justice Act 2003'.

(7) In section 36 of that Act (bail on appeal by defendant) after 'hearings)' there is inserted 'or section 47 of the Criminal Justice Act 2003'.

(8) The Secretary of State may make an order containing provision, in relation to proceedings before the Court of Appeal under this section, which corresponds to any provision, in relation to appeals or other proceedings before that court, which is contained in the Criminal Appeal Act 1968 (subject to any specified modifications).

48 Further provision about trials without a jury

(1) The effect of an order under section 43, 44 or 46(5) is that the trial to which the order relates is to be conducted without a jury.

(2) The effect of an order under section 46(3) is that the trial to which the order relates is to be continued without a jury.

(3) Where a trial is conducted or continued without a jury, the court is to have all the powers, authorities and jurisdiction which the court would have had if the trial had been conducted or continued with a jury (including power to determine any question and to make any finding which would be required to be determined or made by a jury).

(4) Except where the context otherwise requires, any reference in an enactment to a jury, the verdict of a jury or the finding of a jury is to be read, in relation to a trial conducted or continued without a jury, as a reference to the court, the verdict of the court or the finding of the court.

(5) Where a trial is conducted or continued without a jury and the court convicts a defendant –

    (a) the court must give a judgment which states the reasons for the conviction at, or as soon as reasonably practicable after, the time of the conviction, and

    (b) the reference in section 18(2) of the Criminal Appeal Act 1968 (c. 19) (notice of appeal or of application for leave to appeal to be given within 28 days from date of conviction etc) to the date of the conviction is to be read as a reference to the date of the judgment mentioned in paragraph (a).

(6) Nothing in this Part affects –

    (a) the requirement under section 4 of the Criminal Procedure (Insanity) Act 1964 (c. 84) that a question of fitness to be tried be determined by a jury, or

    (b) the requirement under section 4A of that Act that any question, finding or verdict mentioned in that section be determined, made or returned by a jury.

49 Rules of court

(1) Rules of court may make such provision as appears to the authority making them to be necessary or expedient for the purposes of this Part.

(2) Without limiting subsection (1), rules of court may in particular make provision for time limits within which applications under this Part must be made or within which other things in connection with this Part must be done.

(3) Nothing in this section is to be taken as affecting the generality of any enactment conferring powers to make rules of court.

50 Application of Part 7 to Northern Ireland

(1) In its application to Northern Ireland this Part is to have effect –

    (a) subject to subsection (2), and

(b)   subject to the modifications in subsections (3) to (16).

(2) This Part does not apply in relation to a trial to which section 75 of the Terrorism Act 2000 (c. 11) (trial without jury for certain offences) applies.

(3) For section 45 substitute –

'45 Procedure for applications under sections 43 and 44

(1) This section applies –

(a)   to an application under section 43, and
(b)   to an application under section 44.

(2) An application to which this section applies must be determined –

(a)   at a preparatory hearing (within the meaning of the 1988 Order), or
(b)   at a hearing specified in, or for which provision is made by, Crown Court rules.

(3) The parties to a hearing mentioned in subsection (2) at which an application to which this section applies is to be determined must be given an opportunity to make representations with respect to the application.

(4) In Article 6(1) of the 1988 Order (which sets out the purposes of preparatory hearings) for sub-paragraphs (a) to (c) there is substituted –

"(a)   identifying issues which are likely to be material to the determinations and findings which are likely to be required during the trial;
(b)   if there is to be a jury, assisting their comprehension of those issues and expediting the proceedings before them;
(c)   determining an application to which section 45 of the Criminal Justice Act 2003 applies; or".

(5) In Article 8(11) of the 1988 Order (appeal to Court of Appeal) after "(3)," there is inserted "from the refusal by a judge of an application to which section 45 of the Criminal Justice Act 2003 applies or from an order of a judge under section 43 or 44 of that Act which is made on the determination of such an application,".

(6) In this section "the 1988 Order" means the Criminal Justice (Serious Fraud) (Northern Ireland) Order 1988.'

(4) For section 47(1) substitute –

'(1) An appeal shall lie to the Court of Appeal –

(a)   from the refusal by a judge at a hearing mentioned in section 45(2)(b) of an application to which section 45 applies or from an order of a judge at such a hearing under section 43 or 44 which is made on the determination of such an application,
(b)   from an order under section 46(3) or (5).'

(5) In section 47(3) after 'order' insert 'or a refusal of an application'.

(6) In section 47(4) for 'confirm or revoke the order' substitute –

'(a)   where the appeal is from an order, confirm or revoke the order, or
(b)   where the appeal is from a refusal of an application, confirm the refusal or make the order which is the subject of the application'.

(7) Omit section 47(5).

(8) For section 47(6) substitute –

'(6) In section 31(1) of the Criminal Appeal (Northern Ireland) Act 1980 (right of appeal to House of Lords) after "1988" there is inserted "or section 47 of the Criminal Justice Act 2003".'

(9) For section 47(7) substitute –

'(7) In section 35 of that Act (bail) after "hearings)" there is inserted "or section 47 of the Criminal Justice Act 2003".'

(10) In section 47(8) for 'Criminal Appeal Act 1968' substitute 'Criminal Appeal (Northern Ireland) Act 1980'.

(11) In section 48(4) after 'enactment' insert '(including any provision of Northern Ireland legislation)'.

(12) For section 48(5)(b) substitute –

'(b) the reference in section 16(1) of the Criminal Appeal (Northern Ireland) Act 1980 (c. 47) (notice of appeal or application for leave) to the date of the conviction is to be read as a reference to the date of the judgment mentioned in paragraph (a).'

(13) In section 48(6) –

(a) for 'section 4 of the Criminal Procedure (Insanity) Act 1964 (c. 84)' substitute 'Article 49 of the Mental Health (Northern Ireland) Order 1986',
(b) for 'section 4A of that Act' substitute 'Article 49A of that Order', and
(c) for 'that section' substitute 'that Article'.

(14) After section 48 insert –

'48A   Reporting restrictions

(1) Sections 41 and 42 of the Criminal Procedure and Investigations Act 1996 (c. 25) are to apply in relation to –

(a) a hearing of the kind mentioned in section 45(2)(b), and
(b) any appeal or application for leave to appeal relating to such a hearing,

as they apply in relation to a ruling under section 40 of that Act, but subject to the following modifications.

(2) Section 41(2) of that Act is to have effect as if for paragraphs (a) to (d) there were substituted –

"(a) a hearing of the kind mentioned in section 45(2)(b) of the Criminal Justice Act 2003;
(b) any appeal or application for leave to appeal relating to such a hearing."

(3) Section 41(3) of that Act is to have effect as if –

(a) for "(2)" there were substituted "(2)(a) or an application to that judge for leave to appeal to the Court of Appeal", and
(b) after "matter" in the second place where it occurs there were inserted "or application".

(4) Section 41 of that Act is to have effect as if after subsection (3) there were inserted –

"(3A) The Court of Appeal may order that subsection (1) shall not apply, or shall not apply to a specified extent, to a report of –

(a) an appeal to that Court, or

(b) an application to that Court for leave to appeal.

(3B) The House of Lords may order that subsection (1) shall not apply, or shall not apply to a specified extent, to a report of –

(a) an appeal to that House, or

(b) an application to that House for leave to appeal."

(5) Section 41(4) of that Act is to have effect as if for "(3) the judge" there were substituted "(3), (3A) or (3B), the judge, the Court of Appeal or the House of Lords".

(6) Section 41(5) of that Act is to have effect as if for "(3) the judge" there were substituted "(3), (3A) or (3B), the judge, the Court of Appeal or the House of Lords".'

(15) For section 49(2) substitute –

'(2) Without limiting subsection (1), rules of court may in particular make provision –

(a) for time limits within which applications under this Part must be made or within which other things in connection with this Part must be done;

(b) in relation to hearings of the kind mentioned in section 45(2)(b) and appeals under section 47.'

(16) In section 49(3) –

(a) after 'section' insert 'or section 45(2)(b)', and

(b) after 'enactment' insert '(including any provision of Northern Ireland legislation)'.

PART 8

LIVE LINKS

51 Live links in criminal proceedings

(1) A witness (other than the defendant) may, if the court so directs, give evidence through a live link in the following criminal proceedings.

(2) They are –
(a) a summary trial,
(b) an appeal to the Crown Court arising out of such a trial,
(c) a trial on indictment,
(d) an appeal to the criminal division of the Court of Appeal,
(e) the hearing of a reference under section 9 or 11 of the Criminal Appeal Act 1995 (c. 35),
(f) a hearing before a magistrates' court or the Crown Court which is held after the defendant has entered a plea of guilty, and
(g) a hearing before the Court of Appeal under section 80 of this Act.

(3) A direction may be given under this section –

(a) on an application by a party to the proceedings, or

(b) of the court's own motion.

(4) But a direction may not be given under this section unless –

(a) the court is satisfied that it is in the interests of the efficient or effective administration of justice for the person concerned to give evidence in the proceedings through a live link,

(b) it has been notified by the Secretary of State that suitable facilities for receiving evidence through a live link are available in the area in which it appears to the court that the proceedings will take place, and

(c) that notification has not been withdrawn.

(5) The withdrawal of such a notification is not to affect a direction given under this section before that withdrawal.

(6) In deciding whether to give a direction under this section the court must consider all the circumstances of the case.

(7) Those circumstances include in particular –

(a) the availability of the witness,

(b) the need for the witness to attend in person,

(c) the importance of the witness's evidence to the proceedings,

(d) the views of the witness,

(e) the suitability of the facilities at the place where the witness would give evidence through a live link,

(f) whether a direction might tend to inhibit any party to the proceedings from effectively testing the witness's evidence.

(8) The court must state in open court its reasons for refusing an application for a direction under this section and, if it is a magistrates' court, must cause them to be entered in the register of its proceedings.

52 Effect of, and rescission of, direction

(1) Subsection (2) applies where the court gives a direction under section 51 for a person to give evidence through a live link in particular proceedings.

(2) The person concerned may not give evidence in those proceedings after the direction is given otherwise than through a live link (but this is subject to the following provisions of this section).

(3) The court may rescind a direction under section 51 if it appears to the court to be in the interests of justice to do so.

(4) Where it does so, the person concerned shall cease to be able to give evidence in the proceedings through a live link, but this does not prevent the court from giving a further direction under section 51 in relation to him.

(5) A direction under section 51 may be rescinded under subsection (3) –

(a) on an application by a party to the proceedings, or

(b) of the court's own motion.

(6) But an application may not be made under subsection (5)(a) unless there has been a material change of circumstances since the direction was given.

(7) The court must state in open court its reasons –

(a) for rescinding a direction under section 51, or

(b) for refusing an application to rescind such a direction,

and, if it is a magistrates' court, must cause them to be entered in the register of its proceedings.

53 Magistrates' courts permitted to sit at other locations

(1) This section applies where –

    (a) a magistrates' court is minded to give a direction under section 51 for evidence to be given through a live link in proceedings before the court, and

    (b) suitable facilities for receiving such evidence are not available at any petty-sessional court-house in which the court can (apart from subsection (2)) lawfully sit.

(2) The court may sit for the purposes of the whole or any part of the proceedings at any place at which such facilities are available and which has been appointed for the purposes of this section by the justices acting for the petty sessions area for which the court acts.

(3) A place appointed under subsection (2) may be outside the petty sessions area for which it is appointed; but (if so) it shall be deemed to be in that area for the purpose of the jurisdiction of the justices acting for that area.

54 Warning to jury

(1) This section applies where, as a result of a direction under section 51, evidence has been given through a live link in proceedings before the Crown Court.

(2) The judge may give the jury (if there is one) such direction as he thinks necessary to ensure that the jury gives the same weight to the evidence as if it had been given by the witness in the courtroom or other place where the proceedings are held.

55 Rules of court

(1) Rules of court may make such provision as appears to the authority making them to be necessary or expedient for the purposes of this Part.

(2) Rules of court may in particular make provision –

    (a) as to the procedure to be followed in connection with applications under section 51 or 52, and

    (b) as to the arrangements or safeguards to be put in place in connection with the operation of live links.

(3) The provision which may be made by virtue of subsection (2)(a) includes provision –

    (a) for uncontested applications to be determined by the court without a hearing,

    (b) for preventing the renewal of an unsuccessful application under section 51 unless there has been a material change of circumstances,

    (c) for the manner in which confidential or sensitive information is to be treated in connection with an application under section 51 or 52 and in particular as to its being disclosed to, or withheld from, a party to the proceedings.

(4) Nothing in this section is to be taken as affecting the generality of any enactment conferring power to make rules of court.

56 Interpretation of Part 8

(1) In this Part –

    'legal representative' means an authorised advocate or authorised litigator (as defined by section 119(1) of the Courts and Legal Services Act 1990 (c. 41)), 'petty-sessional court-house' has the same meaning as in the Magistrates' Courts Act 1980 (c. 43),

'petty sessions area' has the same meaning as in the Justices of the Peace Act 1997 (c. 25),

'rules of court' means Magistrates' Courts Rules, Crown Court Rules or Criminal Appeal Rules,

'witness', in relation to any criminal proceedings, means a person called, or proposed to be called, to give evidence in the proceedings.

(2) In this Part 'live link' means a live television link or other arrangement by which a witness, while at a place in the United Kingdom which is outside the building where the proceedings are being held, is able to see and hear a person at the place where the proceedings are being held and to be seen and heard by the following persons.

(3) They are –

(a) the defendant or defendants,
(b) the judge or justices (or both) and the jury (if there is one),
(c) legal representatives acting in the proceedings, and
(d) any interpreter or other person appointed by the court to assist the witness.

(4) The extent (if any) to which a person is unable to see or hear by reason of any impairment of eyesight or hearing is to be disregarded for the purposes of subsection (2).

(5) Nothing in this Part is to be regarded as affecting any power of a court –

(a) to make an order, give directions or give leave of any description in relation to any witness (including the defendant or defendants), or
(b) to exclude evidence at its discretion (whether by preventing questions being put or otherwise).

PART 9

PROSECUTION APPEALS

Introduction

57 Introduction

(1) In relation to a trial on indictment, the prosecution is to have the rights of appeal for which provision is made by this Part.

(2) But the prosecution is to have no right of appeal under this Part in respect of –

(a) a ruling that a jury be discharged, or
(b) a ruling from which an appeal lies to the Court of Appeal by virtue of any other enactment.

(3) An appeal under this Part is to lie to the Court of Appeal.

(4) Such an appeal may be brought only with the leave of the judge or the Court of Appeal.

General right of appeal in respect of rulings

58 General right of appeal in respect of rulings

(1) This section applies where a judge makes a ruling in relation to a trial on indictment at an applicable time and the ruling relates to one or more offences included in the indictment.

(2) The prosecution may appeal in respect of the ruling in accordance with this section.

(3) The ruling is to have no effect whilst the prosecution is able to take any steps under subsection (4).

(4) The prosecution may not appeal in respect of the ruling unless –

    (a) following the making of the ruling, it –
        (i)   informs the court that it intends to appeal, or
        (ii)   requests an adjournment to consider whether to appeal, and
    (b) if such an adjournment is granted, it informs the court following the adjournment that it intends to appeal.

(5) If the prosecution requests an adjournment under subsection (4)(a)(ii), the judge may grant such an adjournment.

(6) Where the ruling relates to two or more offences –

    (a) any one or more of those offences may be the subject of the appeal, and
    (b) if the prosecution informs the court in accordance with subsection (4) that it intends to appeal, it must at the same time inform the court of the offence or offences which are the subject of the appeal.

(7) Where –

    (a) the ruling is a ruling that there is no case to answer, and
    (b) the prosecution, at the same time that it informs the court in accordance with subsection (4) that it intends to appeal, nominates one or more other rulings which have been made by a judge in relation to the trial on indictment at an applicable time and which relate to the offence or offences which are the subject of the appeal,

that other ruling, or those other rulings, are also to be treated as the subject of the appeal.

(8) The prosecution may not inform the court in accordance with subsection (4) that it intends to appeal, unless, at or before that time, it informs the court that it agrees that, in respect of the offence or each offence which is the subject of the appeal, the defendant in relation to that offence should be acquitted of that offence if either of the conditions mentioned in subsection (9) is fulfilled.

(9) Those conditions are –

    (a) that leave to appeal to the Court of Appeal is not obtained, and
    (b) that the appeal is abandoned before it is determined by the Court of Appeal.

(10) If the prosecution informs the court in accordance with subsection (4) that it intends to appeal, the ruling mentioned in subsection (1) is to continue to have no effect in relation to the offence or offences which are the subject of the appeal whilst the appeal is pursued.

(11) If and to the extent that a ruling has no effect in accordance with this section –

    (a)   any consequences of the ruling are also to have no effect,
    (b)   the judge may not take any steps in consequence of the ruling, and
    (c)   if he does so, any such steps are also to have no effect.

(12) Where the prosecution has informed the court of its agreement under subsection (8) and either of the conditions mentioned in subsection (9) is fulfilled, the judge or the Court of Appeal must order that the defendant in relation to the offence or each offence concerned be acquitted of that offence.

(13) In this section 'applicable time', in relation to a trial on indictment, means any time (whether before or after the commencement of the trial) before the start of the judge's summing-up to the jury.

59 Expedited and non-expedited appeals

(1) Where the prosecution informs the court in accordance with section 58(4) that it intends to appeal, the judge must decide whether or not the appeal should be expedited.

(2) If the judge decides that the appeal should be expedited, he may order an adjournment.

(3) If the judge decides that the appeal should not be expedited, he may –

    (a)   order an adjournment, or
    (b)   discharge the jury (if one has been sworn).

(4) If he decides that the appeal should be expedited, he or the Court of Appeal may subsequently reverse that decision and, if it is reversed, the judge may act as mentioned in subsection (3)(a) or (b).

60 Continuation of proceedings for offences not affected by ruling

(1) This section applies where the prosecution informs the court in accordance with section 58(4) that it intends to appeal.

(2) Proceedings may be continued in respect of any offence which is not the subject of the appeal.

61 Determination of appeal by Court of Appeal

(1) On an appeal under section 58, the Court of Appeal may confirm, reverse or vary any ruling to which the appeal relates.

(2) Subsections (3) to (5) apply where the appeal relates to a single ruling.

(3) Where the Court of Appeal confirms the ruling, it must, in respect of the offence or each offence which is the subject of the appeal, order that the defendant in relation to that offence be acquitted of that offence.

(4) Where the Court of Appeal reverses or varies the ruling, it must, in respect of the offence or each offence which is the subject of the appeal, do any of the following –

    (a)   order that proceedings for that offence may be resumed in the Crown Court,
    (b)   order that a fresh trial may take place in the Crown Court for that offence,
    (c)   order that the defendant in relation to that offence be acquitted of that offence.

(5) But the Court of Appeal may not make an order under subsection (4)(a) or (b) in respect of an offence unless it considers it necessary in the interests of justice to do so.

(6) Subsections (7) and (8) apply where the appeal relates to a ruling that there is no case to answer and one or more other rulings.

(7) Where the Court of Appeal confirms the ruling that there is no case to answer, it must, in respect of the offence or each offence which is the subject of the appeal, order that the defendant in relation to that offence be acquitted of that offence.

(8) Where the Court of Appeal reverses or varies the ruling that there is no case to answer, it must in respect of the offence or each offence which is the subject of the appeal, make any of the orders mentioned in subsection (4)(a) to (c) (but subject to subsection (5)).

Right of appeal in respect of evidentiary rulings

62 Right of appeal in respect of evidentiary rulings

(1) The prosecution may, in accordance with this section and section 63, appeal in respect of –

   (a) a single qualifying evidentiary ruling, or
   (b) two or more qualifying evidentiary rulings.

(2) A 'qualifying evidentiary ruling' is an evidentiary ruling of a judge in relation to a trial on indictment which is made at any time (whether before or after the commencement of the trial) before the opening of the case for the defence.

(3) The prosecution may not appeal in respect of a single qualifying evidentiary ruling unless the ruling relates to one or more qualifying offences (whether or not it relates to any other offence).

(4) The prosecution may not appeal in respect of two or more qualifying evidentiary rulings unless each ruling relates to one or more qualifying offences (whether or not it relates to any other offence).

(5) If the prosecution intends to appeal under this section, it must before the opening of the case for the defence inform the court –

   (a) of its intention to do so, and
   (b) of the ruling or rulings to which the appeal relates.

(6) In respect of the ruling, or each ruling, to which the appeal relates –

   (a) the qualifying offence, or at least one of the qualifying offences, to which the ruling relates must be the subject of the appeal, and
   (b) any other offence to which the ruling relates may, but need not, be the subject of the appeal.

(7) The prosecution must, at the same time that it informs the court in accordance with subsection (5), inform the court of the offence or offences which are the subject of the appeal.

(8) For the purposes of this section, the case for the defence opens when, after the conclusion of the prosecution evidence, the earliest of the following events occurs –

   (a) evidence begins to be adduced by or on behalf of a defendant,

(b) it is indicated to the court that no evidence will be adduced by or on behalf of a defendant,

(c) a defendant's case is opened, as permitted by section 2 of the Criminal Procedure Act 1865 (c. 18).

(9) In this section –

'evidentiary ruling' means a ruling which relates to the admissibility or exclusion of any prosecution evidence,

'qualifying offence' means an offence described in Part 1 of Schedule 4.

(10) The Secretary of State may by order amend that Part by doing any one or more of the following –

(a) adding a description of offence,

(b) removing a description of offence for the time being included,

(c) modifying a description of offence for the time being included.

(11) Nothing in this section affects the right of the prosecution to appeal in respect of an evidentiary ruling under section 58.

63 Condition that evidentiary ruling significantly weakens prosecution case

(1) Leave to appeal may not be given in relation to an appeal under section 62 unless the judge or, as the case may be, the Court of Appeal is satisfied that the relevant condition is fulfilled.

(2) In relation to an appeal in respect of a single qualifying evidentiary ruling, the relevant condition is that the ruling significantly weakens the prosecution's case in relation to the offence or offences which are the subject of the appeal.

(3) In relation to an appeal in respect of two or more qualifying evidentiary rulings, the relevant condition is that the rulings taken together significantly weaken the prosecution's case in relation to the offence or offences which are the subject of the appeal.

64 Expedited and non-expedited appeals

(1) Where the prosecution informs the court in accordance with section 62(5), the judge must decide whether or not the appeal should be expedited.

(2) If the judge decides that the appeal should be expedited, he may order an adjournment.

(3) If the judge decides that the appeal should not be expedited, he may –

(a) order an adjournment, or

(b) discharge the jury (if one has been sworn).

(4) If he decides that the appeal should be expedited, he or the Court of Appeal may subsequently reverse that decision and, if it is reversed, the judge may act as mentioned in subsection (3)(a) or (b).

65 Continuation of proceedings for offences not affected by ruling

(1) This section applies where the prosecution informs the court in accordance with section 62(5).

(2) Proceedings may be continued in respect of any offence which is not the subject of the appeal.

66 Determination of appeal by Court of Appeal

(1) On an appeal under section 62, the Court of Appeal may confirm, reverse or vary any ruling to which the appeal relates.

(2) In addition, the Court of Appeal must, in respect of the offence or each offence which is the subject of the appeal, do any of the following –

(a) order that proceedings for that offence be resumed in the Crown Court,
(b) order that a fresh trial may take place in the Crown Court for that offence,
(c) order that the defendant in relation to that offence be acquitted of that offence.

(3) But no order may be made under subsection (2)(c) in respect of an offence unless the prosecution has indicated that it does not intend to continue with the prosecution of that offence.

67 Reversal of rulings

The Court of Appeal may not reverse a ruling on an appeal under this Part unless it is satisfied –

(a) that the ruling was wrong in law,
(b) that the ruling involved an error of law or principle, or
(c) that the ruling was a ruling that it was not reasonable for the judge to have made.

Miscellaneous and supplemental

68 Appeals to the House of Lords

(1) In section 33(1) of the 1968 Act (right of appeal to House of Lords) after 'this Act' there is inserted 'or Part 9 of the Criminal Justice Act 2003'.

(2) In section 36 of the 1968 Act (bail on appeal by defendant) after 'under' there is inserted 'Part 9 of the Criminal Justice Act 2003 or'.

(3) In this Part 'the 1968 Act' means the Criminal Appeal Act 1968 (c. 19).

69 Costs

(1) The Prosecution of Offences Act 1985 (c. 23) is amended as follows.

(2) In section 16(4A) (defence costs on an appeal under section 9(11) of Criminal Justice Act 1987 may be met out of central funds) after 'hearings)' there is inserted 'or under Part 9 of the Criminal Justice Act 2003'.

(3) In section 18 (award of costs against accused) after subsection (2) there is inserted –

'(2A) Where the Court of Appeal reverses or varies a ruling on an appeal under Part 9 of the Criminal Justice Act 2003, it may make such order as to the costs to be paid by the accused, to such person as may be named in the order, as it considers just and reasonable.'

(4) In subsection (6) after 'subsection (2)' there is inserted 'or (2A)'.

70 Effect on time limits in relation to preliminary stages

(1) Section 22 of the Prosecution of Offences Act 1985 (c. 23) (power of Secretary of State to set time limits in relation to preliminary stages of criminal proceedings) is amended as follows.

(2) After subsection (6A) there is inserted –

'(6B) Any period during which proceedings for an offence are adjourned pending the determination of an appeal under Part 9 of the Criminal Justice Act 2003 shall be disregarded, so far as the offence is concerned, for the purposes of the overall time limit and the custody time limit which applies to the stage which the proceedings have reached when they are adjourned.'

71 Restrictions on reporting

(1) Except as provided by this section no publication shall include a report of –

(a) anything done under section 58, 59, 62, 63 or 64,
(b) an appeal under this Part,
(c) an appeal under Part 2 of the 1968 Act in relation to an appeal under this Part, or
(d) an application for leave to appeal in relation to an appeal mentioned in paragraph (b) or (c).

(2) The judge may order that subsection (1) is not to apply, or is not to apply to a specified extent, to a report of –

(a) anything done under section 58, 59, 62, 63 or 64, or
(b) an application to the judge for leave to appeal to the Court of Appeal under this Part.

(3) The Court of Appeal may order that subsection (1) is not to apply, or is not to apply to a specified extent, to a report of –

(a) an appeal to the Court of Appeal under this Part,
(b) an application to that Court for leave to appeal to it under this Part, or
(c) an application to that Court for leave to appeal to the House of Lords under Part 2 of the 1968 Act.

(4) The House of Lords may order that subsection (1) is not to apply, or is not to apply to a specified extent, to a report of –

(a) an appeal to that House under Part 2 of the 1968 Act, or
(b) an application to that House for leave to appeal to it under Part 2 of that Act.

(5) Where there is only one defendant and he objects to the making of an order under subsection (2), (3) or (4) –

(a) the judge, the Court of Appeal or the House of Lords are to make the order if (and only if) satisfied, after hearing the representations of the defendant, that it is in the interests of justice to do so, and
(b) the order (if made) is not to apply to the extent that a report deals with any such objection or representations.

(6) Where there are two or more defendants and one or more of them object to the making of an order under subsection (2), (3) or (4) –

   (a) the judge, the Court of Appeal or the House of Lords are to make the order if (and only if) satisfied, after hearing the representations of each of the defendants, that it is in the interests of justice to do so, and

   (b) the order (if made) is not to apply to the extent that a report deals with any such objection or representations.

(7) Subsection (1) does not apply to the inclusion in a publication of a report of –

   (a) anything done under section 58, 59, 62, 63 or 64,

   (b) an appeal under this Part,

   (c) an appeal under Part 2 of the 1968 Act in relation to an appeal under this Part, or

   (d) an application for leave to appeal in relation to an appeal mentioned in paragraph (b) or (c),

at the conclusion of the trial of the defendant or the last of the defendants to be tried.

(8) Subsection (1) does not apply to a report which contains only one or more of the following matters –

   (a) the identity of the court and the name of the judge,

   (b) the names, ages, home addresses and occupations of the defendant or defendants and witnesses,

   (c) the offence or offences, or a summary of them, with which the defendant or defendants are charged,

   (d) the names of counsel and solicitors in the proceedings,

   (e) where the proceedings are adjourned, the date and place to which they are adjourned,

   (f) any arrangements as to bail,

   (g) whether a right to representation funded by the Legal Services Commission as part of the Criminal Defence Service was granted to the defendant or any of the defendants.

(9) The addresses that may be included in a report by virtue of subsection (8) are addresses –

   (a) at any relevant time, and

   (b) at the time of their inclusion in the publication.

(10) Nothing in this section affects any prohibition or restriction by virtue of any other enactment on the inclusion of any matter in a publication.

(11) In this section –

   'programme service' has the same meaning as in the Broadcasting Act 1990 (c. 42),

   'publication' includes any speech, writing, relevant programme or other communication in whatever form, which is addressed to the public at large or any section of the public (and for this purpose every relevant programme is to be taken to be so addressed), but does not include an indictment or other document prepared for use in particular legal proceedings,

   'relevant time' means a time when events giving rise to the charges to which the proceedings relate are alleged to have occurred,

   'relevant programme' means a programme included in a programme service.

     (b) as to procedures to be applied in connection with this Part,

     (c) enabling a single judge of the Court of Appeal to give leave to appeal under this Part or to exercise the power of the Court of Appeal under section 58(12).

(3) Nothing in this section is to be taken as affecting the generality of any enactment conferring powers to make rules of court.

74 Interpretation of Part 9

(1) In this Part –

'programme service' has the meaning given by section 71(11),
'publication' has the meaning given by section 71(11),
'qualifying evidentiary ruling' is to be construed in accordance with section 62(2),
'the relevant condition' is to be construed in accordance with section 63(2) and (3),
'relevant programme' has the meaning given by section 71(11),
'ruling' includes a decision, determination, direction, finding, notice, order, refusal, rejection or requirement,
'the 1968 Act' means the Criminal Appeal Act 1968 (c. 19).

(2) Any reference in this Part (other than section 73(2)(c)) to a judge is a reference to a judge of the Crown Court.

(3) There is to be no right of appeal under this Part in respect of a ruling in relation to which the prosecution has previously informed the court of its intention to appeal under either section 58(4) or 62(5).

(4) Where a ruling relates to two or more offences but not all of those offences are the subject of an appeal under this Part, nothing in this Part is to be regarded as affecting the ruling so far as it relates to any offence which is not the subject of the appeal.

(5) Where two or more defendants are charged jointly with the same offence, the provisions of this Part are to apply as if the offence, so far as relating to each defendant, were a separate offence (so that, for example, any reference in this Part to a ruling which relates to one or more offences includes a ruling which relates to one or more of those separate offences).

(6) Subject to rules of court made under section 53(1) of the Supreme Court Act 1981 (c. 54) (power by rules to distribute business of Court of Appeal between its civil and criminal divisions) –

(a) the jurisdiction of the Court of Appeal under this Part is to be exercised by the criminal division of that court, and

(b) references in this Part to the Court of Appeal are to be construed as references to that division.

PART 10

RETRIAL FOR SERIOUS OFFENCES

Cases that may be retried

75 Cases that may be retried

(1) This Part applies where a person has been acquitted of a qualifying offence in proceedings –

(a) on indictment in England and Wales,

(b) on appeal against a conviction, verdict or finding in proceedings on indictment in England and Wales, or

(c) on appeal from a decision on such an appeal.

(2) A person acquitted of an offence in proceedings mentioned in subsection (1) is treated for the purposes of that subsection as also acquitted of any qualifying offence of which he could have been convicted in the proceedings because of the first-mentioned offence being charged in the indictment, except an offence –

    (a) of which he has been convicted,

    (b) of which he has been found not guilty by reason of insanity, or

    (c) in respect of which, in proceedings where he has been found to be under a disability (as defined by section 4 of the Criminal Procedure (Insanity) Act 1964 (c. 84)), a finding has been made that he did the act or made the omission charged against him.

(3) References in subsections (1) and (2) to a qualifying offence do not include references to an offence which, at the time of the acquittal, was the subject of an order under section 77(1) or (3).

(4) This Part also applies where a person has been acquitted, in proceedings elsewhere than in the United Kingdom, of an offence under the law of the place where the proceedings were held, if the commission of the offence as alleged would have amounted to or included the commission (in the United Kingdom or elsewhere) of a qualifying offence.

(5) Conduct punishable under the law in force elsewhere than in the United Kingdom is an offence under that law for the purposes of subsection (4), however it is described in that law.

(6) This Part applies whether the acquittal was before or after the passing of this Act.

(7) References in this Part to acquittal are to acquittal in circumstances within subsection (1) or (4).

(8) In this Part 'qualifying offence' means an offence listed in Part 1 of Schedule 5.

Application for retrial

76 Application to Court of Appeal

(1) A prosecutor may apply to the Court of Appeal for an order –

    (a) quashing a person's acquittal in proceedings within section 75(1), and

    (b) ordering him to be retried for the qualifying offence.

(2) A prosecutor may apply to the Court of Appeal, in the case of a person acquitted elsewhere than in the United Kingdom, for –

    (a) a determination whether the acquittal is a bar to the person being tried in England and Wales for the qualifying offence, and

    (b) if it is, an order that the acquittal is not to be a bar.

(3) A prosecutor may make an application under subsection (1) or (2) only with the written consent of the Director of Public Prosecutions.

72 Offences in connection with reporting

(1) This section applies if a publication includes a report in contravention of section 71.

(2) Where the publication is a newspaper or periodical, any proprietor, editor or publisher of the newspaper or periodical is guilty of an offence.

(3) Where the publication is a relevant programme –

    (a) any body corporate or Scottish partnership engaged in providing the programme service in which the programme is included, and

    (b) any person having functions in relation to the programme corresponding to those of an editor of a newspaper,

is guilty of an offence.

(4) In the case of any other publication, any person publishing it is guilty of an offence.

(5) If an offence under this section committed by a body corporate is proved –

    (a) to have been committed with the consent or connivance of, or

    (b) to be attributable to any neglect on the part of,

an officer, the officer as well as the body corporate is guilty of the offence and liable to be proceeded against and punished accordingly.

(6) In subsection (5), 'officer' means a director, manager, secretary or other similar officer of the body, or a person purporting to act in any such capacity.

(7) If the affairs of a body corporate are managed by its members, 'director' in subsection (6) means a member of that body.

(8) Where an offence under this section is committed by a Scottish partnership and is proved to have been committed with the consent or connivance of a partner, he as well as the partnership shall be guilty of the offence and shall be liable to be proceeded against and punished accordingly.

(9) A person guilty of an offence under this section is liable on summary conviction to a fine not exceeding level 5 on the standard scale.

(10) Proceedings for an offence under this section may not be instituted –

    (a) in England and Wales otherwise than by or with the consent of the Attorney General, or

    (b) in Northern Ireland otherwise than by or with the consent of –

        (i)   before the relevant date, the Attorney General for Northern Ireland, or

        (ii)   on or after the relevant date, the Director of Public Prosecutions for Northern Ireland.

(11) In subsection (10) 'the relevant date' means the date on which section 22(1) of the Justice (Northern Ireland) Act 2002 (c. 26) comes into force.

73 Rules of court

(1) Rules of court may make such provision as appears to the authority making them to be necessary or expedient for the purposes of this Part.

(2) Without limiting subsection (1), rules of court may in particular make provision –

    (a) for time limits which are to apply in connection with any provisions of this Part,

(4) The Director of Public Prosecutions may give his consent only if satisfied that –

    (a) there is evidence as respects which the requirements of section 78 appear to be met,

    (b) it is in the public interest for the application to proceed, and

(c) any trial pursuant to an order on the application would not be inconsistent with obligations of the United Kingdom under Article 31 or 34 of the Treaty on European Union relating to the principle of *ne bis in idem*.

(5) Not more than one application may be made under subsection (1) or (2) in relation to an acquittal.

77 Determination by Court of Appeal

(1) On an application under section 76(1), the Court of Appeal –

(a) if satisfied that the requirements of sections 78 and 79 are met, must make the order applied for;
(b) otherwise, must dismiss the application.

(2) Subsections (3) and (4) apply to an application under section 76(2).

(3) Where the Court of Appeal determines that the acquittal is a bar to the person being tried for the qualifying offence, the court –

(a) if satisfied that the requirements of sections 78 and 79 are met, must make the order applied for;
(b) otherwise, must make a declaration to the effect that the acquittal is a bar to the person being tried for the offence.

(4) Where the Court of Appeal determines that the acquittal is not a bar to the person being tried for the qualifying offence, it must make a declaration to that effect.

78 New and compelling evidence

(1) The requirements of this section are met if there is new and compelling evidence against the acquitted person in relation to the qualifying offence.

(2) Evidence is new if it was not adduced in the proceedings in which the person was acquitted (nor, if those were appeal proceedings, in earlier proceedings to which the appeal related).

(3) Evidence is compelling if –

(a) it is reliable,
(b) it is substantial, and
(c) in the context of the outstanding issues, it appears highly probative of the case against the acquitted person.

(4) The outstanding issues are the issues in dispute in the proceedings in which the person was acquitted and, if those were appeal proceedings, any other issues remaining in dispute from earlier proceedings to which the appeal related.

(5) For the purposes of this section, it is irrelevant whether any evidence would have been admissible in earlier proceedings against the acquitted person.

79 Interests of justice

(1) The requirements of this section are met if in all the circumstances it is in the interests of justice for the court to make the order under section 77.

(2) That question is to be determined having regard in particular to –

(a) whether existing circumstances make a fair trial unlikely;

(b) for the purposes of that question and otherwise, the length of time since the qualifying offence was allegedly committed;

(c) whether it is likely that the new evidence would have been adduced in the earlier proceedings against the acquitted person but for a failure by an officer or by a prosecutor to act with due diligence or expedition;

(d) whether, since those proceedings or, if later, since the commencement of this Part, any officer or prosecutor has failed to act with due diligence or expedition.

(3) In subsection (2) references to an officer or prosecutor include references to a person charged with corresponding duties under the law in force elsewhere than in England and Wales.

(4) Where the earlier prosecution was conducted by a person other than a prosecutor, subsection (2)(c) applies in relation to that person as well as in relation to a prosecutor.

80 Procedure and evidence

(1) A prosecutor who wishes to make an application under section 76(1) or (2) must give notice of the application to the Court of Appeal.

(2) Within two days beginning with the day on which any such notice is given, notice of the application must be served by the prosecutor on the person to whom the application relates, charging him with the offence to which it relates or, if he has been charged with it in accordance with section 87(4), stating that he has been so charged.

(3) Subsection (2) applies whether the person to whom the application relates is in the United Kingdom or elsewhere, but the Court of Appeal may, on application by the prosecutor, extend the time for service under that subsection if it considers it necessary to do so because of that person's absence from the United Kingdom.

(4) The Court of Appeal must consider the application at a hearing.

(5) The person to whom the application relates –

(a) is entitled to be present at the hearing, although he may be in custody, unless he is in custody elsewhere than in England and Wales or Northern Ireland, and

(b) is entitled to be represented at the hearing, whether he is present or not.

(6) For the purposes of the application, the Court of Appeal may, if it thinks it necessary or expedient in the interests of justice –

(a) order the production of any document, exhibit or other thing, the production of which appears to the court to be necessary for the determination of the application, and

(b) order any witness who would be a compellable witness in proceedings pursuant to an order or declaration made on the application to attend for examination and be examined before the court.

(7) The Court of Appeal may at one hearing consider more than one application (whether or not relating to the same person), but only if the offences concerned could be tried on the same indictment.

81 Appeals

(1) The Criminal Appeal Act 1968 (c. 19) is amended as follows.

(2) In section 33 (right of appeal to House of Lords), after subsection (1A) there is inserted –

'(1B) An appeal lies to the House of Lords, at the instance of the acquitted person or the prosecutor, from any decision of the Court of Appeal on an application under section 76(1) or (2) of the Criminal Justice Act 2003 (retrial for serious offences).'

(3) At the end of that section there is inserted –

'(4) In relation to an appeal under subsection (1B), references in this Part to a defendant are references to the acquitted person.'

(4) In section 34(2) (extension of time for leave to appeal), after 'defendant' there is inserted 'or, in the case of an appeal under section 33(1B), by the prosecutor'.

(5) In section 38 (presence of defendant at hearing), for 'has been convicted of an offence and' substitute 'has been convicted of an offence, or in whose case an order under section 77 of the Criminal Justice Act 2003 or a declaration under section 77(4) of that Act has been made, and who'.

82 Restrictions on publication in the interests of justice

(1) Where it appears to the Court of Appeal that the inclusion of any matter in a publication would give rise to a substantial risk of prejudice to the administration of justice in a retrial, the court may order that the matter is not to be included in any publication while the order has effect.

(2) In subsection (1) 'retrial' means the trial of an acquitted person for a qualifying offence pursuant to any order made or that may be made under section 77.

(3) The court may make an order under this section only if it appears to it necessary in the interests of justice to do so.

(4) An order under this section may apply to a matter which has been included in a publication published before the order takes effect, but such an order –

  (a) applies only to the later inclusion of the matter in a publication (whether directly or by inclusion of the earlier publication), and

  (b) does not otherwise affect the earlier publication.

(5) After notice of an application has been given under section 80(1) relating to the acquitted person and the qualifying offence, the court may make an order under this section only –

  (a) of its own motion, or

  (b) on the application of the Director of Public Prosecutions.

(6) Before such notice has been given, an order under this section –

  (a) may be made only on the application of the Director of Public Prosecutions, and

  (b) may not be made unless, since the acquittal concerned, an investigation of the commission by the acquitted person of the qualifying offence has been commenced by officers.

(7) The court may at any time, of its own motion or on an application made by the Director of Public Prosecutions or the acquitted person, vary or revoke an order under this section.

(8) Any order made under this section before notice of an application has been given under section 80(1) relating to the acquitted person and the qualifying offence must specify the time when it ceases to have effect.

(9) An order under this section which is made or has effect after such notice has been given ceases to have effect, unless it specifies an earlier time –

   (a) when there is no longer any step that could be taken which would lead to the acquitted person being tried pursuant to an order made on the application, or

   (b) if he is tried pursuant to such an order, at the conclusion of the trial.

(10) Nothing in this section affects any prohibition or restriction by virtue of any other enactment on the inclusion of any matter in a publication or any power, under an enactment or otherwise, to impose such a prohibition or restriction.

(11) In this section –

   'programme service' has the same meaning as in the Broadcasting Act 1990 (c. 42),
   'publication' includes any speech, writing, relevant programme or other communication in whatever form, which is addressed to the public at large or any section of the public (and for this purpose every relevant programme is to be taken to be so addressed), but does not include an indictment or other document prepared for use in particular legal proceedings,
   'relevant programme' means a programme included in a programme service.

83 Offences in connection with publication restrictions

(1) This section applies if –

   (a) an order under section 82 is made, whether in England and Wales or Northern Ireland, and

   (b) while the order has effect, any matter is included in a publication, in any part of the United Kingdom, in contravention of the order.

(2) Where the publication is a newspaper or periodical, any proprietor, editor or publisher of the newspaper or periodical is guilty of an offence.

(3) Where the publication is a relevant programme –

   (a) any body corporate or Scottish partnership engaged in providing the programme service in which the programme is included, and

   (b) any person having functions in relation to the programme corresponding to those of an editor of a newspaper,

is guilty of an offence.

(4) In the case of any other publication, any person publishing it is guilty of an offence.

(5) If an offence under this section committed by a body corporate is proved –

   (a) to have been committed with the consent or connivance of, or

   (b) to be attributable to any neglect on the part of,

an officer, the officer as well as the body corporate is guilty of the offence and liable to be proceeded against and punished accordingly.

(6) In subsection (5), 'officer' means a director, manager, secretary or other similar officer of the body, or a person purporting to act in any such capacity.

(7) If the affairs of a body corporate are managed by its members, 'director' in subsection (6) means a member of that body.

(8) Where an offence under this section is committed by a Scottish partnership and is proved to have been committed with the consent or connivance of a partner, he as well

as the partnership shall be guilty of the offence and shall be liable to be proceeded against and punished accordingly.

(9) A person guilty of an offence under this section is liable on summary conviction to a fine not exceeding level 5 on the standard scale.

(10) Proceedings for an offence under this section may not be instituted –

    (a) in England and Wales otherwise than by or with the consent of the Attorney General, or

    (b) in Northern Ireland otherwise than by or with the consent of –
        (i)   before the relevant date, the Attorney General for Northern Ireland, or
        (ii) on or after the relevant date, the Director of Public Prosecutions for Northern Ireland.

(11) In subsection (10) 'the relevant date' means the date on which section 22(1) of the Justice (Northern Ireland) Act 2002 (c. 26) comes into force.

Retrial

84 Retrial

(1) Where a person –

    (a) is tried pursuant to an order under section 77(1), or
    (b) is tried on indictment pursuant to an order under section 77(3),

the trial must be on an indictment preferred by direction of the Court of Appeal.

(2) After the end of 2 months after the date of the order, the person may not be arraigned on an indictment preferred in pursuance of such a direction unless the Court of Appeal gives leave.

(3) The Court of Appeal must not give leave unless satisfied that –

    (a) the prosecutor has acted with due expedition, and
    (b) there is a good and sufficient cause for trial despite the lapse of time since the order under section 77.

(4) Where the person may not be arraigned without leave, he may apply to the Court of Appeal to set aside the order and –

    (a) for any direction required for restoring an earlier judgment and verdict of acquittal of the qualifying offence, or
    (b) in the case of a person acquitted elsewhere than in the United Kingdom, for a declaration to the effect that the acquittal is a bar to his being tried for the qualifying offence.

(5) An indictment under subsection (1) may relate to more than one offence, or more than one person, and may relate to an offence which, or a person who, is not the subject of an order or declaration under section 77.

(6) Evidence given at a trial pursuant to an order under section 77(1) or (3) must be given orally if it was given orally at the original trial, unless –

    (a) all the parties to the trial agree otherwise,
    (b) section 116 applies, or

    (c) the witness is unavailable to give evidence, otherwise than as mentioned in subsection (2) of that section, and section 114(1)(d) applies.

(7) At a trial pursuant to an order under section 77(1), paragraph 5 of Schedule 3 to the Crime and Disorder Act 1998 (c. 37) (use of depositions) does not apply to a deposition read as evidence at the original trial.

Investigations

85 Authorisation of investigations

(1) This section applies to the investigation of the commission of a qualifying offence by a person –

    (a) acquitted in proceedings within section 75(1) of the qualifying offence, or
    (b) acquitted elsewhere than in the United Kingdom of an offence the commission of which as alleged would have amounted to or included the commission (in the United Kingdom or elsewhere) of the qualifying offence.

(2) Subject to section 86, an officer may not do anything within subsection (3) for the purposes of such an investigation unless the Director of Public Prosecutions –

    (a) has certified that in his opinion the acquittal would not be a bar to the trial of the acquitted person in England and Wales for the qualifying offence, or
    (b) has given his written consent to the investigation (whether before or after the start of the investigation).

(3) The officer may not, either with or without the consent of the acquitted person –

    (a) arrest or question him,
    (b) search him or premises owned or occupied by him,
    (c) search a vehicle owned by him or anything in or on such a vehicle,
    (d) seize anything in his possession, or
    (e) take his fingerprints or take a sample from him.

(4) The Director of Public Prosecutions may only give his consent on a written application, and such an application may be made only by an officer who –

    (a) if he is an officer of the metropolitan police force or the City of London police force, is of the rank of commander or above, or
    (b) in any other case, is of the rank of assistant chief constable or above.

(5) An officer may make an application under subsection (4) only if –

    (a) he is satisfied that new evidence has been obtained which would be relevant to an application under section 76(1) or (2) in respect of the qualifying offence to which the investigation relates, or
    (b) he has reasonable grounds for believing that such new evidence is likely to be obtained as a result of the investigation.

(6) The Director of Public Prosecutions may not give his consent unless satisfied that –

    (a) there is, or there is likely as a result of the investigation to be, sufficient new evidence to warrant the conduct of the investigation, and
    (b) it is in the public interest for the investigation to proceed.

(7) In giving his consent, the Director of Public Prosecutions may recommend that the investigation be conducted otherwise than by officers of a specified police force or specified team of customs and excise officers.

86 Urgent investigative steps

(1) Section 85 does not prevent an officer from taking any action for the purposes of an investigation if –

- (a) the action is necessary as a matter of urgency to prevent the investigation being substantially and irrevocably prejudiced,
- (b) the requirements of subsection (2) are met, and
- (c) either –
  - (i)   the action is authorised under subsection (3), or
  - (ii) the requirements of subsection (5) are met.

(2) The requirements of this subsection are met if –

- (a) there has been no undue delay in applying for consent under section 85(2),
- (b) that consent has not been refused, and
- (c) taking into account the urgency of the situation, it is not reasonably practicable to obtain that consent before taking the action.

(3) An officer of the rank of superintendent or above may authorise the action if –

- (a) he is satisfied that new evidence has been obtained which would be relevant to an application under section 76(1) or (2) in respect of the qualifying offence to which the investigation relates, or
- (b) he has reasonable grounds for believing that such new evidence is likely to be obtained as a result of the investigation.

(4) An authorisation under subsection (3) must –

- (a) if reasonably practicable, be given in writing;
- (b) otherwise, be recorded in writing by the officer giving it as soon as is reasonably practicable.

(5) The requirements of this subsection are met if –

- (a) there has been no undue delay in applying for authorisation under subsection (3),
- (b) that authorisation has not been refused, and
- (c) taking into account the urgency of the situation, it is not reasonably practicable to obtain that authorisation before taking the action.

(6) Where the requirements of subsection (5) are met, the action is nevertheless to be treated as having been unlawful unless, as soon as reasonably practicable after the action is taken, an officer of the rank of superintendent or above certifies in writing that he is satisfied that, when the action was taken –

- (a) new evidence had been obtained which would be relevant to an application under section 76(1) or (2) in respect of the qualifying offence to which the investigation relates, or
- (b) the officer who took the action had reasonable grounds for believing that such new evidence was likely to be obtained as a result of the investigation.

Arrest, custody and bail

87 Arrest and charge

(1) Where section 85 applies to the investigation of the commission of an offence by any person and no certification has been given under subsection (2) of that section –

(a) a justice of the peace may issue a warrant to arrest that person for that offence only if satisfied by written information that new evidence has been obtained which would be relevant to an application under section 76(1) or (2) in respect of the commission by that person of that offence, and

(b) that person may not be arrested for that offence except under a warrant so issued.

(2) Subsection (1) does not affect section 89(3)(b) or 91(3), or any other power to arrest a person, or to issue a warrant for the arrest of a person, otherwise than for an offence.

(3) Part 4 of the 1984 Act (detention) applies as follows where a person –

(a) is arrested for an offence under a warrant issued in accordance with subsection (1)(a), or

(b) having been so arrested, is subsequently treated under section 34(7) of that Act as arrested for that offence.

(4) For the purposes of that Part there is sufficient evidence to charge the person with the offence for which he has been arrested if, and only if, an officer of the rank of superintendent or above (who has not been directly involved in the investigation) is of the opinion that the evidence available or known to him is sufficient for the case to be referred to a prosecutor to consider whether consent should be sought for an application in respect of that person under section 76.

(5) For the purposes of that Part it is the duty of the custody officer at each police station where the person is detained to make available or known to an officer at that police station of the rank of superintendent or above any evidence which it appears to him may be relevant to an application under section 76(1) or (2) in respect of the offence for which the person has been arrested, and to do so as soon as practicable –

(a) after the evidence becomes available or known to him, or

(b) if later, after he forms that view.

(6) Section 37 of that Act (including any provision of that section as applied by section 40(8) of that Act) has effect subject to the following modifications –

(a) in subsection (1) –
  (i) for 'determine whether he has before him' there is substituted 'request an officer of the rank of superintendent or above (who has not been directly involved in the investigation) to determine, in accordance with section 87(4) of the Criminal Justice Act 2003, whether there is';
  (ii) for 'him to do so' there is substituted 'that determination to be made';
(b) in subsection (2) –
  (i) for the words from 'custody officer determines' to 'before him' there is substituted 'officer determines that there is not such sufficient evidence';
  (ii) the word 'custody' is omitted from the second place where it occurs;
(c) in subsection (3) –
  (i) the word 'custody' is omitted;
  (ii) after 'may' there is inserted 'direct the custody officer to';
(d) in subsection (7) for the words from 'the custody officer' to the end of that subsection there is substituted 'an officer of the rank of superintendent or above (who has not been directly involved in the investigation) determines, in accordance with section 87(4) of the Criminal Justice Act 2003, that there is sufficient evidence to charge the person arrested with the offence for which he was arrested, the person arrested shall be charged.';
(e) subsections (7A), (7B) and (8) do not apply;

(f)   after subsection (10) there is inserted –

'(10A) The officer who is requested by the custody officer to make a determination under subsection (1) above shall make that determination as soon as practicable after the request is made.'.

(7) Section 40 of that Act has effect as if in subsections (8) and (9) of that section after '(6)' there were inserted 'and (10A)'.

(8) Section 42 of that Act has effect as if in subsection (1) of that section for the words from 'who' to 'detained' there were substituted '(who has not been directly involved in the investigation)'.

88 Bail and custody before application

(1) In relation to a person charged in accordance with section 87(4) –

(a)   section 38 of the 1984 Act (including any provision of that section as applied by section 40(10) of that Act) has effect as if, in subsection (1), for 'either on bail or without bail' there were substituted 'on bail',

(b)   section 47(3) of that Act does not apply and references in section 38 of that Act to bail are references to bail subject to a duty to appear before the Crown Court at such place as the custody officer may appoint and at such time, not later than 24 hours after the person is released, as that officer may appoint, and

(c)   section 43B of the Magistrates' Courts Act 1980 (c. 43) does not apply.

(2) Where such a person is, after being charged –

(a)   kept in police detention, or

(b)   detained by a local authority in pursuance of arrangements made under section 38(6) of the 1984 Act,

he must be brought before the Crown Court as soon as practicable and, in any event, not more than 24 hours after he is charged, and section 46 of the 1984 Act does not apply.

(3) For the purpose of calculating the period referred to in subsection (1) or (2), the following are to be disregarded –

(a)   Sunday,

(b)   Christmas Day,

(c)   Good Friday, and

(d)   any day which is a bank holiday under the Banking and Financial Dealings Act 1971 (c. 80) in the part of the United Kingdom where the person is to appear before the Crown Court as mentioned in subsection (1) or, where subsection (2) applies, is for the time being detained.

(4) Where a person appears or is brought before the Crown Court in accordance with subsection (1) or (2), the Crown Court may either –

(a)   grant bail for the person to appear, if notice of an application is served on him under section 80(2), before the Court of Appeal at the hearing of that application, or

(b)   remand the person in custody to be brought before the Crown Court under section 89(2).

(5) If the Crown Court grants bail under subsection (4), it may revoke bail and remand the person in custody as referred to in subsection (4)(b).

(6) In subsection (7) the 'relevant period', in relation to a person granted bail or remanded in custody under subsection (4), means –

    (a) the period of 42 days beginning with the day on which he is granted bail or remanded in custody under that subsection, or

    (b) that period as extended or further extended under subsection (8).

(7) If at the end of the relevant period no notice of an application under section 76(1) or (2) in relation to the person has been given under section 80(1), the person –

    (a) if on bail subject to a duty to appear as mentioned in subsection (4)(a), ceases to be subject to that duty and to any conditions of that bail, and

    (b) if in custody on remand under subsection (4)(b) or (5), must be released immediately without bail.

(8) The Crown Court may, on the application of a prosecutor, extend or further extend the period mentioned in subsection (6)(a) until a specified date, but only if satisfied that –

    (a) the need for the extension is due to some good and sufficient cause, and

    (b) the prosecutor has acted with all due diligence and expedition.

89 Bail and custody before hearing

(1) This section applies where notice of an application is given under section 80(1).

(2) If the person to whom the application relates is in custody under section 88(4)(b) or (5), he must be brought before the Crown Court as soon as practicable and, in any event, within 48 hours after the notice is given.

(3) If that person is not in custody under section 88(4)(b) or (5), the Crown Court may, on application by the prosecutor –

    (a) issue a summons requiring the person to appear before the Court of Appeal at the hearing of the application, or

    (b) issue a warrant for the person's arrest,

and a warrant under paragraph (b) may be issued at any time even though a summons has previously been issued.

(4) Where a summons is issued under subsection (3)(a), the time and place at which the person must appear may be specified either –

    (a) in the summons, or

    (b) in a subsequent direction of the Crown Court.

(5) The time or place specified may be varied from time to time by a direction of the Crown Court.

(6) A person arrested under a warrant under subsection (3)(b) must be brought before the Crown Court as soon as practicable and in any event within 48 hours after his arrest, and section 81(5) of the Supreme Court Act 1981 (c. 54) does not apply.

(7) If a person is brought before the Crown Court under subsection (2) or (6) the court must either –

    (a) remand him in custody to be brought before the Court of Appeal at the hearing of the application, or

    (b) grant bail for him to appear before the Court of Appeal at the hearing.

(8) If bail is granted under subsection (7)(b), the Crown Court may revoke the bail and remand the person in custody as referred to in subsection (7)(a).

(9) For the purpose of calculating the period referred to in subsection (2) or (6), the following are to be disregarded –

    (a) Sunday,
    (b) Christmas Day,
    (c) Good Friday, and
    (d) any day which is a bank holiday under the Banking and Financial Dealings Act 1971 (c. 80) in the part of the United Kingdom where the person is for the time being detained.

90 Bail and custody during and after hearing

(1) The Court of Appeal may, at any adjournment of the hearing of an application under section 76(1) or (2) –

    (a) remand the person to whom the application relates on bail, or
    (b) remand him in custody.

(2) At a hearing at which the Court of Appeal –

    (a) makes an order under section 77,
    (b) makes a declaration under subsection (4) of that section, or
    (c) dismisses the application or makes a declaration under subsection (3) of that section, if it also gives the prosecutor leave to appeal against its decision or the prosecutor gives notice that he intends to apply for such leave,

the court may make such order as it sees fit for the custody or bail of the acquitted person pending trial pursuant to the order or declaration, or pending determination of the appeal.

(3) For the purpose of subsection (2), the determination of an appeal is pending –

    (a) until any application for leave to appeal is disposed of, or the time within which it must be made expires;
    (b) if leave to appeal is granted, until the appeal is disposed of.

(4) Section 4 of the Bail Act 1976 (c. 63) applies in relation to the grant of bail under this section as if in subsection (2) the reference to the Crown Court included a reference to the Court of Appeal.

(5) The court may at any time, as it sees fit –

    (a) revoke bail granted under this section and remand the person in custody, or
    (b) vary an order under subsection (2).

91 Revocation of bail

(1) Where –

    (a) a court revokes a person's bail under this Part, and
    (b) that person is not before the court when his bail is revoked,
the court must order him to surrender himself forthwith to the custody of the court.

(2) Where a person surrenders himself into the custody of the court in compliance with an order under subsection (1), the court must remand him in custody.

(3) A person who has been ordered to surrender to custody under subsection (1) may be arrested without a warrant by an officer if he fails without reasonable cause to surrender to custody in accordance with the order.

(4) A person arrested under subsection (3) must be brought as soon as practicable, and, in any event, not more than 24 hours after he is arrested, before the court and the court must remand him in custody.

(5) For the purpose of calculating the period referred to in subsection (4), the following are to be disregarded –

    (a) Sunday,
    (b) Christmas Day,
    (c) Good Friday,
    (d) any day which is a bank holiday under the Banking and Financial Dealings Act 1971 (c. 80) in the part of the United Kingdom where the person is for the time being detained.

Part 10: supplementary

92 Functions of the DPP

(1) Section 1(7) of the Prosecution of Offences Act 1985 (c. 23) (DPP's functions exercisable by Crown Prosecutor) does not apply to the provisions of this Part other than section 85(2)(a).

(2) In the absence of the Director of Public Prosecutions, his functions under those provisions may be exercised by a person authorised by him.

(3) An authorisation under subsection (2) –

    (a) may relate to a specified person or to persons of a specified description, and
    (b) may be general or relate to a specified function or specified circumstances.

93 Rules of court

(1) Rules of court may make such provision as appears to the authority making them to be necessary or expedient for the purposes of this Part.

(2) Without limiting subsection (1), rules of court may in particular make provision as to procedures to be applied in connection with sections 76 to 82, 84 and 88 to 90.

(3) Nothing in this section is to be taken as affecting the generality of any enactment conferring power to make rules of court.

94 Armed Forces: Part 10

(1) Section 31 of the Armed Forces Act 2001 (c. 19) (provision in consequence of enactments relating to criminal justice) applies to an enactment contained in this Part so far as relating to matters not specified in subsection (2) of that section as it applies to a criminal justice enactment.

(2) The power under that section to make provision equivalent to that made in relation to qualifying offences by an enactment contained in this Part (with or without modifications) includes power to make such provision in relation to such service offences as the Secretary of State thinks fit.

(3) In subsection (2) 'service offence' means an offence under the Army Act 1955 (3 & 4 Eliz. 2 c. 18), the Air Force Act 1955 (3 & 4 Eliz. 2 c. 19) or the Naval Discipline Act 1957 (c. 53).

95 Interpretation of Part 10

(1) In this Part –

'the 1984 Act' means the Police and Criminal Evidence Act 1984 (c. 60),
'acquittal' and related expressions are to be read in accordance with section 75(7),
'customs and excise officer' means an officer as defined by section 1(1) of the Customs and Excise Management Act 1979 (c. 2), or a person to whom section 8(2) of that Act applies,
'new evidence' is to be read in accordance with section 78(2),
'officer', except in section 83, means an officer of a police force or a customs and excise officer,
'police force' has the meaning given by section 3(3) of the Prosecution of Offences Act 1985 (c. 23),
'prosecutor' means an individual or body charged with duties to conduct criminal prosecutions,
'qualifying offence' has the meaning given by section 75(8).

(2) Subject to rules of court made under section 53(1) of the Supreme Court Act 1981 (c. 54) (power by rules to distribute business of Court of Appeal between its civil and criminal divisions) –

(a) the jurisdiction of the Court of Appeal under this Part is to be exercised by the criminal division of that court, and
(b) references in this Part to the Court of Appeal are to be construed as references to that division.

(3) References in this Part to an officer of a specified rank or above are, in the case of a customs and excise officer, references to an officer of such description as –

(a) appears to the Commissioners of Customs and Excise to comprise officers of equivalent rank or above, and
(b) is specified by the Commissioners for the purposes of the provision concerned.

96 Application of Part 10 to Northern Ireland

(1) In its application to Northern Ireland this Part is to have effect subject to the modifications in this section.

(2) In sections 75(1)(a) and (b), 76(2)(a), 79(3) and 85(2)(a) for 'England and Wales' substitute 'Northern Ireland'.

(3) For section 75(2)(c) substitute –
'(c) in respect of which, in proceedings where he has been found to be unfit to be tried in accordance with Article 49 of the Mental Health (Northern Ireland) Order 1986 (S.I. 1986/595 (N.I. 4)), a finding has been made that he did the act or made the omission charged against him.'

(4) In section 75(8) for 'Part 1' substitute 'Part 2'.

(5) In section 81(1) for 'Criminal Appeal Act 1968 (c. 19)' substitute 'Criminal Appeal (Northern Ireland) Act 1980 (c. 47)'.

(6) In section 81(2) –

    (a) for '33' substitute '31', and

    (b) for 'An' substitute 'Subject to the provisions of this Part of this Act, an'.

(7) In section 81(4) –

    (a) for '34(2)' substitute '32(2)', and

    (b) for '33(1B)' substitute '31(1B)'.

(8) In section 82(10) after 'enactment' in each place insert '(including any provision of Northern Ireland legislation)'.

(9) In section 84(1) and (2) for 'preferred' substitute 'presented'.

(10) Section 84(6) has effect –

    (a) as if any reference to a provision of Part 11 were a reference to any corresponding provision contained in an Order in Council to which section 334(1) applies, at any time when such corresponding provision is in force;

    (b) at any other time, with the omission of paragraphs (b) and (c).

(11) After section 84(6) insert –

    '(6A) Article 29 of the Legal Aid, Advice and Assistance (Northern Ireland) Order 1981 (S.I. 1981/228 (N.I. 8)) applies in the case of a person who is to be tried in accordance with subsection (1) as if –

        (a) he had been returned for trial for the offence in question, and

        (b) the reference in paragraph (2)(a) of that Article to a magistrates' court included a reference to the Court of Appeal.'

(12) In section 87 –

    (a) in subsection (3), for 'Part 4 of the 1984 Act' substitute 'Part 5 of the Police and Criminal Evidence (Northern Ireland) Order 1989 (S.I. 1989/1341 (N.I. 12)) ('the 1989 Order')',

    (b) in paragraph (b) of that subsection, for 'section 34(7) of that Act' substitute 'Article 35(8) of that Order',

    (c) in subsection (6) –

        (i)   for the words from the beginning to '40(8) of that Act)' substitute 'Article 38 of that Order (including any provision of that Article as applied by Article 41(8) of that Order)',

        (ii)   for 'subsection' in each place substitute 'paragraph',

        (iii) in paragraph (e), for 'subsections (7A), (7B) and (8)' substitute 'paragraph (8)', and

        (iv) in paragraph (f), in the inserted paragraph (10A) omit 'above',

    (d) for subsection (7) substitute –

        '(7) Article 41 of that Order has effect as if in paragraphs (8) and (9) of that Article after "(6)" there were inserted "and (10A)".',

    (e) in subsection (8) –

        (i)   for 'Section 42 of that Act' substitute 'Article 43 of that Order', and

        (ii)   for 'subsection (1) of that section' substitute 'paragraph (1) of that Article'.

(13) For section 88(1) substitute –

    '(1) In relation to a person charged in accordance with section 87(4) –

Article 39 of the 1989 Order (including any provision of that Article as applied by Article 41(10) of that Order) has effect as if, in paragraph (1), for "either on bail or without bail" there were substituted "on bail",

(b) Article 48 of that Order has effect as if for paragraphs (1) to (11) there were substituted –

"(1) A person who is released on bail shall be subject to a duty to appear before the Crown Court at such place as the custody officer may appoint and at such time, not later than 24 hours after the person is released, as that officer may appoint.

(2) The custody officer may require a person who is to be released on bail to enter into a recognisance conditioned upon his subsequent appearance before the Crown Court in accordance with paragraph (1).

(3) A recognisance under paragraph (2) may be taken before the custody officer.", and

(c) Article 132A of the Magistrates' Courts (Northern Ireland) Order 1981 (S.I. 1981/1675 (N.I. 26)) does not apply.'

(14) In section 88(2) –

(a) for paragraph (b) substitute –

'(b) detained in a place of safety in pursuance of arrangements made under Article 39(6) of the 1989 Order,', and

(b) for 'section 46 of the 1984 Act' substitute 'Article 47 of the 1989 Order'.

(15) In section 89(6) for 'section 81(5) of the Supreme Court Act 1981 (c. 54)' substitute 'section 51(8) of the Judicature (Northern Ireland) Act 1978 (c. 23)'.

(16) For section 90(4) substitute –

'(4) The court may at any time, as it sees fit, vary the conditions of bail granted under this section.'

(17) In section 92(1) for the words from the beginning to 'does' substitute 'Sections 30(4) and 36 of the Justice (Northern Ireland) Act 2002 (c. 26) do'.

(18) Until the coming into force of section 36 of that Act of 2002 the reference to that section in subsection (17) is to be read as a reference to Article 4(8) of the Prosecution of Offences (Northern Ireland) Order 1972 (S.I. 1972/538 (N.I. 1)).

(19) In section 93(2) for 'the Criminal Appeal Rules and the Crown Court Rules' substitute 'rules under section 55 of the Judicature (Northern Ireland) Act 1978 and Crown Court Rules'.

(20) In section 93(3) after 'enactment' insert '(including any provision of Northern Ireland legislation)'.

(21) In section 95(1) for the definition of 'police force' substitute –

'"police force" means –

(a) the Police Service of Northern Ireland or the Police Service of Northern Ireland Reserve,

    (b) the Ministry of Defence Police,

    (c) any body of constables appointed under Article 19 of the Airports (Northern Ireland) Order 1994 (S.I. 1994/426 (N.I. 1)), or

    (d) any body of special constables appointed in Northern Ireland under section 79 of the Harbours, Docks and Piers Clauses Act 1847 (c. 27) or section 57 of the Civil Aviation Act 1982 (c. 16),'.

(22) Omit section 95(2).

97 Application of Criminal Appeal Acts to proceedings under Part 10

Subject to the provisions of this Part, the Secretary of State may make an order containing provision, in relation to proceedings before the Court of Appeal under this Part, which corresponds to any provision, in relation to appeals or other proceedings before that court, which is contained in the Criminal Appeal Act 1968 (c. 19) or the Criminal Appeal (Northern Ireland) Act 1980 (c. 47) (subject to any specified modifications).

PART 11

EVIDENCE

CHAPTER 1

EVIDENCE OF BAD CHARACTER

Introductory

98 'Bad character'

References in this Chapter to evidence of a person's 'bad character' are to evidence of, or of a disposition towards, misconduct on his part, other than evidence which –

    (a) has to do with the alleged facts of the offence with which the defendant is charged, or

    (b) is evidence of misconduct in connection with the investigation or prosecution of that offence.

99 Abolition of common law rules

(1) The common law rules governing the admissibility of evidence of bad character in criminal proceedings are abolished.

(2) Subsection (1) is subject to section 118(1) in so far as it preserves the rule under which in criminal proceedings a person's reputation is admissible for the purposes of proving his bad character.

Persons other than defendants

100 Non-defendant's bad character

(1) In criminal proceedings evidence of the bad character of a person other than the defendant is admissible if and only if –

    (a) it is important explanatory evidence,

    (b) it has substantial probative value in relation to a matter which –

        (i)   is a matter in issue in the proceedings, and

        (ii)   is of substantial importance in the context of the case as a whole, or

(c) all parties to the proceedings agree to the evidence being admissible.

(2) For the purposes of subsection (1)(a) evidence is important explanatory evidence if –

(a) without it, the court or jury would find it impossible or difficult properly to understand other evidence in the case, and
(b) its value for understanding the case as a whole is substantial.

(3) In assessing the probative value of evidence for the purposes of subsection (1)(b) the court must have regard to the following factors (and to any others it considers relevant) –

(a) the nature and number of the events, or other things, to which the evidence relates;
(b) when those events or things are alleged to have happened or existed;
(c) where –
  (i) the evidence is evidence of a person's misconduct, and
  (ii) it is suggested that the evidence has probative value by reason of similarity between that misconduct and other alleged misconduct,
  the nature and extent of the similarities and the dissimilarities between each of the alleged instances of misconduct;
(d) where –
  (i) the evidence is evidence of a person's misconduct,
  (ii) it is suggested that that person is also responsible for the misconduct charged, and
  (iii) the identity of the person responsible for the misconduct charged is disputed,
  the extent to which the evidence shows or tends to show that the same person was responsible each time.

(4) Except where subsection (1)(c) applies, evidence of the bad character of a person other than the defendant must not be given without leave of the court.

Defendants

101 Defendant's bad character

(1) In criminal proceedings evidence of the defendant's bad character is admissible if, but only if –

(a) all parties to the proceedings agree to the evidence being admissible,
(b) the evidence is adduced by the defendant himself or is given in answer to a question asked by him in cross-examination and intended to elicit it,
(c) it is important explanatory evidence,
(d) it is relevant to an important matter in issue between the defendant and the prosecution,
(e) it has substantial probative value in relation to an important matter in issue between the defendant and a co-defendant,
(f) it is evidence to correct a false impression given by the defendant, or
(g) the defendant has made an attack on another person's character.

(2) Sections 102 to 106 contain provision supplementing subsection (1).

(3) The court must not admit evidence under subsection (1)(d) or (g) if, on an application by the defendant to exclude it, it appears to the court that the admission of

the evidence would have such an adverse effect on the fairness of the proceedings that the court ought not to admit it.

(4) On an application to exclude evidence under subsection (3) the court must have regard, in particular, to the length of time between the matters to which that evidence relates and the matters which form the subject of the offence charged.

102 'Important explanatory evidence'

For the purposes of section 101(1)(c) evidence is important explanatory evidence if –

(a) without it, the court or jury would find it impossible or difficult properly to understand other evidence in the case, and

(b) its value for understanding the case as a whole is substantial.

103 'Matter in issue between the defendant and the prosecution'

(1) For the purposes of section 101(1)(d) the matters in issue between the defendant and the prosecution include –

(a) the question whether the defendant has a propensity to commit offences of the kind with which he is charged, except where his having such a propensity makes it no more likely that he is guilty of the offence;

(b) the question whether the defendant has a propensity to be untruthful, except where it is not suggested that the defendant's case is untruthful in any respect.

(2) Where subsection (1)(a) applies, a defendant's propensity to commit offences of the kind with which he is charged may (without prejudice to any other way of doing so) be established by evidence that he has been convicted of –

(a) an offence of the same description as the one with which he is charged, or

(b) an offence of the same category as the one with which he is charged.

(3) Subsection (2) does not apply in the case of a particular defendant if the court is satisfied, by reason of the length of time since the conviction or for any other reason, that it would be unjust for it to apply in his case.

(4) For the purposes of subsection (2) –

(a) two offences are of the same description as each other if the statement of the offence in a written charge or indictment would, in each case, be in the same terms;

(b) two offences are of the same category as each other if they belong to the same category of offences prescribed for the purposes of this section by an order made by the Secretary of State.

(5) A category prescribed by an order under subsection (4)(b) must consist of offences of the same type.

(6) Only prosecution evidence is admissible under section 101(1)(d).

104 'Matter in issue between the defendant and a co-defendant'

(1) Evidence which is relevant to the question whether the defendant has a propensity to be untruthful is admissible on that basis under section 101(1)(e) only if the nature or conduct of his defence is such as to undermine the co-defendant's defence.

(2) Only evidence –

(a) which is to be (or has been) adduced by the co-defendant, or

(b) which a witness is to be invited to give (or has given) in cross-examination by the co-defendant,

is admissible under section 101(1)(e).

105 'Evidence to correct a false impression'

(1) For the purposes of section 101(1)(f) –

(a) the defendant gives a false impression if he is responsible for the making of an express or implied assertion which is apt to give the court or jury a false or misleading impression about the defendant;

(b) evidence to correct such an impression is evidence which has probative value in correcting it.

(2) A defendant is treated as being responsible for the making of an assertion if –

(a) the assertion is made by the defendant in the proceedings (whether or not in evidence given by him),

(b) the assertion was made by the defendant –

    (i)   on being questioned under caution, before charge, about the offence with which he is charged, or

    (ii) on being charged with the offence or officially informed that he might be prosecuted for it,

and evidence of the assertion is given in the proceedings,

(c) the assertion is made by a witness called by the defendant,

(d) the assertion is made by any witness in cross-examination in response to a question asked by the defendant that is intended to elicit it, or is likely to do so, or

(e) the assertion was made by any person out of court, and the defendant adduces evidence of it in the proceedings.

(3) A defendant who would otherwise be treated as responsible for the making of an assertion shall not be so treated if, or to the extent that, he withdraws it or disassociates himself from it.

(4) Where it appears to the court that a defendant, by means of his conduct (other than the giving of evidence) in the proceedings, is seeking to give the court or jury an impression about himself that is false or misleading, the court may if it appears just to do so treat the defendant as being responsible for the making of an assertion which is apt to give that impression.

(5) In subsection (4) 'conduct' includes appearance or dress.

(6) Evidence is admissible under section 101(1)(f) only if it goes no further than is necessary to correct the false impression.

(7) Only prosecution evidence is admissible under section 101(1)(f).

106 'Attack on another person's character'

(1) For the purposes of section 101(1)(g) a defendant makes an attack on another person's character if –

(a) he adduces evidence attacking the other person's character,

(b) he (or any legal representative appointed under section 38(4) of the Youth Justice and Criminal Evidence Act 1999 (c. 23) to cross-examine a witness in his interests) asks questions in cross-examination that are intended to elicit such evidence, or are likely to do so, or

(c) evidence is given of an imputation about the other person made by the defendant –

    (i) on being questioned under caution, before charge, about the offence with which he is charged, or

    (ii) on being charged with the offence or officially informed that he might be prosecuted for it.

(2) In subsection (1) 'evidence attacking the other person's character' means evidence to the effect that the other person –

(a) has committed an offence (whether a different offence from the one with which the defendant is charged or the same one), or

(b) has behaved, or is disposed to behave, in a reprehensible way;

and 'imputation about the other person' means an assertion to that effect.

(3) Only prosecution evidence is admissible under section 101(1)(g).

107 Stopping the case where evidence contaminated

(1) If on a defendant's trial before a judge and jury for an offence –

(a) evidence of his bad character has been admitted under any of paragraphs (c) to (g) of section 101(1), and

(b) the court is satisfied at any time after the close of the case for the prosecution that –

    (i) the evidence is contaminated, and

    (ii) the contamination is such that, considering the importance of the evidence to the case against the defendant, his conviction of the offence would be unsafe,

the court must either direct the jury to acquit the defendant of the offence or, if it considers that there ought to be a retrial, discharge the jury.

(2) Where –

(a) a jury is directed under subsection (1) to acquit a defendant of an offence, and

(b) the circumstances are such that, apart from this subsection, the defendant could if acquitted of that offence be found guilty of another offence,

the defendant may not be found guilty of that other offence if the court is satisfied as mentioned in subsection (1)(b) in respect of it.

(3) If –

(a) a jury is required to determine under section 4A(2) of the Criminal Procedure (Insanity) Act 1964 (c. 84) whether a person charged on an indictment with an offence did the act or made the omission charged,

(b) evidence of the person's bad character has been admitted under any of paragraphs (c) to (g) of section 101(1), and

(c) the court is satisfied at any time after the close of the case for the prosecution that –

     (i)   the evidence is contaminated, and

     (ii)   the contamination is such that, considering the importance of the evidence to the case against the person, a finding that he did the act or made the omission would be unsafe,

the court must either direct the jury to acquit the defendant of the offence or, if it considers that there ought to be a rehearing, discharge the jury.

(4) This section does not prejudice any other power a court may have to direct a jury to acquit a person of an offence or to discharge a jury.

(5) For the purposes of this section a person's evidence is contaminated where –

    (a)   as a result of an agreement or understanding between the person and one or more others, or

    (b)   as a result of the person being aware of anything alleged by one or more others whose evidence may be, or has been, given in the proceedings,

the evidence is false or misleading in any respect, or is different from what it would otherwise have been.

108 Offences committed by defendant when a child

(1) Section 16(2) and (3) of the Children and Young Persons Act 1963 (c. 37) (offences committed by person under 14 disregarded for purposes of evidence relating to previous convictions) shall cease to have effect.

(2) In proceedings for an offence committed or alleged to have been committed by the defendant when aged 21 or over, evidence of his conviction for an offence when under the age of 14 is not admissible unless –

    (a)   both of the offences are triable only on indictment, and

    (b)   the court is satisfied that the interests of justice require the evidence to be admissible.

(3) Subsection (2) applies in addition to section 101.

109 Assumption of truth in assessment of relevance or probative value

(1) Subject to subsection (2), a reference in this Chapter to the relevance or probative value of evidence is a reference to its relevance or probative value on the assumption that it is true.

(2) In assessing the relevance or probative value of an item of evidence for any purpose of this Chapter, a court need not assume that the evidence is true if it appears, on the basis of any material before the court (including any evidence it decides to hear on the matter), that no court or jury could reasonably find it to be true.

110 Court's duty to give reasons for rulings

(1) Where the court makes a relevant ruling –

    (a)   it must state in open court (but in the absence of the jury, if there is one) its reasons for the ruling;

    (b)   if it is a magistrates' court, it must cause the ruling and the reasons for it to be entered in the register of the court's proceedings.

(2) In this section 'relevant ruling' means –

(a) a ruling on whether an item of evidence is evidence of a person's bad character;

(b) a ruling on whether an item of such evidence is admissible under section 100 or 101 (including a ruling on an application under section 101(3));

(c) a ruling under section 107.

111 Rules of court

(1) Rules of court may make such provision as appears to the appropriate authority to be necessary or expedient for the purposes of this Act; and the appropriate authority is the authority entitled to make the rules.

(2) The rules may, and, where the party in question is the prosecution, must, contain provision requiring a party who –

(a) proposes to adduce evidence of a defendant's bad character, or

(b) proposes to cross-examine a witness with a view to eliciting such evidence,

to serve on the defendant such notice, and such particulars of or relating to the evidence, as may be prescribed.

(3) The rules may provide that the court or the defendant may, in such circumstances as may be prescribed, dispense with a requirement imposed by virtue of subsection (2).

(4) In considering the exercise of its powers with respect to costs, the court may take into account any failure by a party to comply with a requirement imposed by virtue of subsection (2) and not dispensed with by virtue of subsection (3).

(5) The rules may –

(a) limit the application of any provision of the rules to prescribed circumstances;

(b) subject any provision of the rules to prescribed exceptions;

(c) make different provision for different cases or circumstances.

(6) Nothing in this section prejudices the generality of any enactment conferring power to make rules of court; and no particular provision of this section prejudices any general provision of it.

(7) In this section –

'prescribed' means prescribed by rules of court;
'rules of court' means –

(a) Crown Court Rules;

(b) Criminal Appeal Rules;

(c) rules under section 144 of the Magistrates' Courts Act 1980 (c. 43).

112 Interpretation of Chapter 1

(1) In this Chapter –

'bad character' is to be read in accordance with section 98;
'criminal proceedings' means criminal proceedings in relation to which the strict rules of evidence apply;
'defendant', in relation to criminal proceedings, means a person charged with an offence in those proceedings; and 'co-defendant', in relation to a defendant, means a person charged with an offence in the same proceedings;
'important matter' means a matter of substantial importance in the context of the case as a whole;

'misconduct' means the commission of an offence or other reprehensible behaviour;

'offence' includes a service offence;

'probative value', and 'relevant' (in relation to an item of evidence), are to be read in accordance with section 109;

'prosecution evidence' means evidence which is to be (or has been) adduced by the prosecution, or which a witness is to be invited to give (or has given) in cross-examination by the prosecution;

'service offence' means an offence under the Army Act 1955 (3 & 4 Eliz. 2 c. 18), the Air Force Act 1955 (3 & 4 Eliz. 2 c. 19) or the Naval Discipline Act 1957 (c. 53);

'written charge' has the same meaning as in section 29 and also includes an information.

(2) Where a defendant is charged with two or more offences in the same criminal proceedings, this Chapter (except section 101(3)) has effect as if each offence were charged in separate proceedings; and references to the offence with which the defendant is charged are to be read accordingly.

(3) Nothing in this Chapter affects the exclusion of evidence –

(a) under the rule in section 3 of the Criminal Procedure Act 1865 (c. 18) against a party impeaching the credit of his own witness by general evidence of bad character,

(b) under section 41 of the Youth Justice and Criminal Evidence Act 1999 (c. 23) (restriction on evidence or questions about complainant's sexual history), or

(c) on grounds other than the fact that it is evidence of a person's bad character.

113 Armed forces

Schedule 6 (armed forces) has effect.

CHAPTER 2

HEARSAY EVIDENCE

Hearsay: main provisions

114 Admissibility of hearsay evidence

(1) In criminal proceedings a statement not made in oral evidence in the proceedings is admissible as evidence of any matter stated if, but only if –

(a) any provision of this Chapter or any other statutory provision makes it admissible,

(b) any rule of law preserved by section 118 makes it admissible,

(c) all parties to the proceedings agree to it being admissible, or

(d) the court is satisfied that it is in the interests of justice for it to be admissible.

(2) In deciding whether a statement not made in oral evidence should be admitted under subsection (1)(d), the court must have regard to the following factors (and to any others it considers relevant) –

(a) how much probative value the statement has (assuming it to be true) in relation to a matter in issue in the proceedings, or how valuable it is for the understanding of other evidence in the case;

(b) what other evidence has been, or can be, given on the matter or evidence mentioned in paragraph (a);
(c) how important the matter or evidence mentioned in paragraph (a) is in the context of the case as a whole;
(d) the circumstances in which the statement was made;
(e) how reliable the maker of the statement appears to be;
(f) how reliable the evidence of the making of the statement appears to be;
(g) whether oral evidence of the matter stated can be given and, if not, why it cannot;
(h) the amount of difficulty involved in challenging the statement;
(i) the extent to which that difficulty would be likely to prejudice the party facing it.

(3) Nothing in this Chapter affects the exclusion of evidence of a statement on grounds other than the fact that it is a statement not made in oral evidence in the proceedings.

115 Statements and matters stated

(1) In this Chapter references to a statement or to a matter stated are to be read as follows.

(2) A statement is any representation of fact or opinion made by a person by whatever means; and it includes a representation made in a sketch, photofit or other pictorial form.

(3) A matter stated is one to which this Chapter applies if (and only if) the purpose, or one of the purposes, of the person making the statement appears to the court to have been –

(a) to cause another person to believe the matter, or
(b) to cause another person to act or a machine to operate on the basis that the matter is as stated.

Principal categories of admissibility

116 Cases where a witness is unavailable

(1) In criminal proceedings a statement not made in oral evidence in the proceedings is admissible as evidence of any matter stated if –

(a) oral evidence given in the proceedings by the person who made the statement would be admissible as evidence of that matter,
(b) the person who made the statement (the relevant person) is identified to the court's satisfaction, and
(c) any of the five conditions mentioned in subsection (2) is satisfied.

(2) The conditions are –

(a) that the relevant person is dead;
(b) that the relevant person is unfit to be a witness because of his bodily or mental condition;
(c) that the relevant person is outside the United Kingdom and it is not reasonably practicable to secure his attendance;
(d) that the relevant person cannot be found although such steps as it is reasonably practicable to take to find him have been taken;
(e) that through fear the relevant person does not give (or does not continue to give) oral evidence in the proceedings, either at all or in connection with the subject matter of the statement, and the court gives leave for the statement to be given in evidence.

(3) For the purposes of subsection (2)(e) 'fear' is to be widely construed and (for example) includes fear of the death or injury of another person or of financial loss.

(4) Leave may be given under subsection (2)(e) only if the court considers that the statement ought to be admitted in the interests of justice, having regard –

    (a) to the statement's contents,

    (b) to any risk that its admission or exclusion will result in unfairness to any party to the proceedings (and in particular to how difficult it will be to challenge the statement if the relevant person does not give oral evidence),

    (c) in appropriate cases, to the fact that a direction under section 19 of the Youth Justice and Criminal Evidence Act 1999 (c. 23) (special measures for the giving of evidence by fearful witnesses etc) could be made in relation to the relevant person, and

    (d) to any other relevant circumstances.

(5) A condition set out in any paragraph of subsection (2) which is in fact satisfied is to be treated as not satisfied if it is shown that the circumstances described in that paragraph are caused –

    (a) by the person in support of whose case it is sought to give the statement in evidence, or

    (b) by a person acting on his behalf,

in order to prevent the relevant person giving oral evidence in the proceedings (whether at all or in connection with the subject matter of the statement).

117 Business and other documents

(1) In criminal proceedings a statement contained in a document is admissible as evidence of any matter stated if –

    (a) oral evidence given in the proceedings would be admissible as evidence of that matter,

    (b) the requirements of subsection (2) are satisfied, and

    (c) the requirements of subsection (5) are satisfied, in a case where subsection (4) requires them to be.

(2) The requirements of this subsection are satisfied if –

    (a) the document or the part containing the statement was created or received by a person in the course of a trade, business, profession or other occupation, or as the holder of a paid or unpaid office,

    (b) the person who supplied the information contained in the statement (the relevant person) had or may reasonably be supposed to have had personal knowledge of the matters dealt with, and

    (c) each person (if any) through whom the information was supplied from the relevant person to the person mentioned in paragraph (a) received the information in the course of a trade, business, profession or other occupation, or as the holder of a paid or unpaid office.

(3) The persons mentioned in paragraphs (a) and (b) of subsection (2) may be the same person.

(4) The additional requirements of subsection (5) must be satisfied if the statement –

    (a) was prepared for the purposes of pending or contemplated criminal proceedings, or for a criminal investigation, but

(b) was not obtained pursuant to a request under section 7 of the Crime (International Co-operation) Act 2003 (c. 32) or an order under paragraph 6 of Schedule 13 to the Criminal Justice Act 1988 (c. 33) (which relate to overseas evidence).

(5) The requirements of this subsection are satisfied if –

(a) any of the five conditions mentioned in section 116(2) is satisfied (absence of relevant person etc), or
(b) the relevant person cannot reasonably be expected to have any recollection of the matters dealt with in the statement (having regard to the length of time since he supplied the information and all other circumstances).

(6) A statement is not admissible under this section if the court makes a direction to that effect under subsection (7).

(7) The court may make a direction under this subsection if satisfied that the statement's reliability as evidence for the purpose for which it is tendered is doubtful in view of –

(a) its contents,
(b) the source of the information contained in it,
(c) the way in which or the circumstances in which the information was supplied or received, or
(d) the way in which or the circumstances in which the document concerned was created or received.

118 Preservation of certain common law categories of admissibility

(1) The following rules of law are preserved.

Public information etc

1 Any rule of law under which in criminal proceedings –

(a) published works dealing with matters of a public nature (such as histories, scientific works, dictionaries and maps) are admissible as evidence of facts of a public nature stated in them,
(b) public documents (such as public registers, and returns made under public authority with respect to matters of public interest) are admissible as evidence of facts stated in them,
(c) records (such as the records of certain courts, treaties, Crown grants, pardons and commissions) are admissible as evidence of facts stated in them, or
(d) evidence relating to a person's age or date or place of birth may be given by a person without personal knowledge of the matter.

Reputation as to character

2 Any rule of law under which in criminal proceedings evidence of a person's reputation is admissible for the purpose of proving his good or bad character.

Note
The rule is preserved only so far as it allows the court to treat such evidence as proving the matter concerned.

Reputation or family tradition

3 Any rule of law under which in criminal proceedings evidence of reputation or family tradition is admissible for the purpose of proving or disproving –

(a) pedigree or the existence of a marriage,

    (b)   the existence of any public or general right, or

    (c)   the identity of any person or thing.

> *Note*
>
> The rule is preserved only so far as it allows the court to treat such evidence as proving or disproving the matter concerned.

Res gestae

4 Any rule of law under which in criminal proceedings a statement is admissible as evidence of any matter stated if –

    (a)   the statement was made by a person so emotionally overpowered by an event that the possibility of concoction or distortion can be disregarded,

    (b)   the statement accompanied an act which can be properly evaluated as evidence only if considered in conjunction with the statement, or

    (c)   the statement relates to a physical sensation or a mental state (such as intention or emotion).

Confessions etc

5 Any rule of law relating to the admissibility of confessions or mixed statements in criminal proceedings.

Admissions by agents etc

6 Any rule of law under which in criminal proceedings –

    (a)   an admission made by an agent of a defendant is admissible against the defendant as evidence of any matter stated, or

    (b)   a statement made by a person to whom a defendant refers a person for information is admissible against the defendant as evidence of any matter stated.

Common enterprise

7 Any rule of law under which in criminal proceedings a statement made by a party to a common enterprise is admissible against another party to the enterprise as evidence of any matter stated.

Expert evidence

8 Any rule of law under which in criminal proceedings an expert witness may draw on the body of expertise relevant to his field.

(2) With the exception of the rules preserved by this section, the common law rules governing the admissibility of hearsay evidence in criminal proceedings are abolished.

119 Inconsistent statements

(1) If in criminal proceedings a person gives oral evidence and –

    (a)   he admits making a previous inconsistent statement, or

    (b)   a previous inconsistent statement made by him is proved by virtue of section 3, 4 or 5 of the Criminal Procedure Act 1865 (c. 18),

the statement is admissible as evidence of any matter stated of which oral evidence by him would be admissible.

(2) If in criminal proceedings evidence of an inconsistent statement by any person is given under section 124(2)(c), the statement is admissible as evidence of any matter stated in it of which oral evidence by that person would be admissible.

120 Other previous statements of witnesses

(1) This section applies where a person (the witness) is called to give evidence in criminal proceedings.

(2) If a previous statement by the witness is admitted as evidence to rebut a suggestion that his oral evidence has been fabricated, that statement is admissible as evidence of any matter stated of which oral evidence by the witness would be admissible.

(3) A statement made by the witness in a document –

- (a) which is used by him to refresh his memory while giving evidence,
- (b) on which he is cross-examined, and
- (c) which as a consequence is received in evidence in the proceedings,

is admissible as evidence of any matter stated of which oral evidence by him would be admissible.

(4) A previous statement by the witness is admissible as evidence of any matter stated of which oral evidence by him would be admissible, if –

- (a) any of the following three conditions is satisfied, and
- (b) while giving evidence the witness indicates that to the best of his belief he made the statement, and that to the best of his belief it states the truth.

(5) The first condition is that the statement identifies or describes a person, object or place.

(6) The second condition is that the statement was made by the witness when the matters stated were fresh in his memory but he does not remember them, and cannot reasonably be expected to remember them, well enough to give oral evidence of them in the proceedings.

(7) The third condition is that –

- (a) the witness claims to be a person against whom an offence has been committed,
- (b) the offence is one to which the proceedings relate,
- (c) the statement consists of a complaint made by the witness (whether to a person in authority or not) about conduct which would, if proved, constitute the offence or part of the offence,
- (d) the complaint was made as soon as could reasonably be expected after the alleged conduct,
- (e) the complaint was not made as a result of a threat or a promise, and
- (f) before the statement is adduced the witness gives oral evidence in connection with its subject matter.

(8) For the purposes of subsection (7) the fact that the complaint was elicited (for example, by a leading question) is irrelevant unless a threat or a promise was involved.

Supplementary

121 Additional requirement for admissibility of multiple hearsay

(1) A hearsay statement is not admissible to prove the fact that an earlier hearsay statement was made unless –

- (a) either of the statements is admissible under section 117, 119 or 120,
- (b) all parties to the proceedings so agree, or

(c)   the court is satisfied that the value of the evidence in question, taking into account how reliable the statements appear to be, is so high that the interests of justice require the later statement to be admissible for that purpose.

(2) In this section 'hearsay statement' means a statement, not made in oral evidence, that is relied on as evidence of a matter stated in it.

122 Documents produced as exhibits

(1) This section applies if on a trial before a judge and jury for an offence –

(a)   a statement made in a document is admitted in evidence under section 119 or 120, and
(b)   the document or a copy of it is produced as an exhibit.

(2) The exhibit must not accompany the jury when they retire to consider their verdict unless –

(a)   the court considers it appropriate, or
(b)   all the parties to the proceedings agree that it should accompany the jury.

123 Capability to make statement

(1) Nothing in section 116, 119 or 120 makes a statement admissible as evidence if it was made by a person who did not have the required capability at the time when he made the statement.

(2) Nothing in section 117 makes a statement admissible as evidence if any person who, in order for the requirements of section 117(2) to be satisfied, must at any time have supplied or received the information concerned or created or received the document or part concerned –

(a)   did not have the required capability at that time, or
(b)   cannot be identified but cannot reasonably be assumed to have had the required capability at that time.

(3) For the purposes of this section a person has the required capability if he is capable of –

(a)   understanding questions put to him about the matters stated, and
(b)   giving answers to such questions which can be understood.

(4) Where by reason of this section there is an issue as to whether a person had the required capability when he made a statement –

(a)   proceedings held for the determination of the issue must take place in the absence of the jury (if there is one);
(b)   in determining the issue the court may receive expert evidence and evidence from any person to whom the statement in question was made;
(c)   the burden of proof on the issue lies on the party seeking to adduce the statement, and the standard of proof is the balance of probabilities.

124 Credibility

(1) This section applies if in criminal proceedings –

(a)   a statement not made in oral evidence in the proceedings is admitted as evidence of a matter stated, and

(b)   the maker of the statement does not give oral evidence in connection with the subject matter of the statement.

(2) In such a case –

(a)   any evidence which (if he had given such evidence) would have been admissible as relevant to his credibility as a witness is so admissible in the proceedings;

(b)   evidence may with the court's leave be given of any matter which (if he had given such evidence) could have been put to him in cross-examination as relevant to his credibility as a witness but of which evidence could not have been adduced by the cross-examining party;

(c)   evidence tending to prove that he made (at whatever time) any other statement inconsistent with the statement admitted as evidence is admissible for the purpose of showing that he contradicted himself.

(3) If as a result of evidence admitted under this section an allegation is made against the maker of a statement, the court may permit a party to lead additional evidence of such description as the court may specify for the purposes of denying or answering the allegation.

(4) In the case of a statement in a document which is admitted as evidence under section 117 each person who, in order for the statement to be admissible, must have supplied or received the information concerned or created or received the document or part concerned is to be treated as the maker of the statement for the purposes of subsections (1) to (3) above.

125 Stopping the case where evidence is unconvincing

(1) If on a defendant's trial before a judge and jury for an offence the court is satisfied at any time after the close of the case for the prosecution that –

(a)   the case against the defendant is based wholly or partly on a statement not made in oral evidence in the proceedings, and

(b)   the evidence provided by the statement is so unconvincing that, considering its importance to the case against the defendant, his conviction of the offence would be unsafe,

the court must either direct the jury to acquit the defendant of the offence or, if it considers that there ought to be a retrial, discharge the jury.

(2) Where –

(a)   a jury is directed under subsection (1) to acquit a defendant of an offence, and

(b)   the circumstances are such that, apart from this subsection, the defendant could if acquitted of that offence be found guilty of another offence,

the defendant may not be found guilty of that other offence if the court is satisfied as mentioned in subsection (1) in respect of it.

(3) If –

(a)   a jury is required to determine under section 4A(2) of the Criminal Procedure (Insanity) Act 1964 (c. 84) whether a person charged on an indictment with an offence did the act or made the omission charged, and

(b)   the court is satisfied as mentioned in subsection (1) above at any time after the close of the case for the prosecution that –

(i)   the case against the defendant is based wholly or partly on a statement not made in oral evidence in the proceedings, and

(ii)   the evidence provided by the statement is so unconvincing that, considering its importance to the case against the person, a finding that he did the act or made the omission would be unsafe,

the court must either direct the jury to acquit the defendant of the offence or, if it considers that there ought to be a rehearing, discharge the jury.

(4) This section does not prejudice any other power a court may have to direct a jury to acquit a person of an offence or to discharge a jury.

126 Court's general discretion to exclude evidence

(1) In criminal proceedings the court may refuse to admit a statement as evidence of a matter stated if –

(a)   the statement was made otherwise than in oral evidence in the proceedings, and
(b)   the court is satisfied that the case for excluding the statement, taking account of the danger that to admit it would result in undue waste of time, substantially outweighs the case for admitting it, taking account of the value of the evidence.

(2) Nothing in this Chapter prejudices –

(a)   any power of a court to exclude evidence under section 78 of the Police and Criminal Evidence Act 1984 (c. 60) (exclusion of unfair evidence), or
(b)   any other power of a court to exclude evidence at its discretion (whether by preventing questions from being put or otherwise).

Miscellaneous

127 Expert evidence: preparatory work

(1) This section applies if –

(a)   a statement has been prepared for the purposes of criminal proceedings,
(b)   the person who prepared the statement had or may reasonably be supposed to have had personal knowledge of the matters stated,
(c)   notice is given under the appropriate rules that another person (the expert) will in evidence given in the proceedings orally or under section 9 of the Criminal Justice Act 1967 (c. 80) base an opinion or inference on the statement, and
(d)   the notice gives the name of the person who prepared the statement and the nature of the matters stated.

(2) In evidence given in the proceedings the expert may base an opinion or inference on the statement.

(3) If evidence based on the statement is given under subsection (2) the statement is to be treated as evidence of what it states.

(4) This section does not apply if the court, on an application by a party to the proceedings, orders that it is not in the interests of justice that it should apply.

(5) The matters to be considered by the court in deciding whether to make an order under subsection (4) include –

(a)   the expense of calling as a witness the person who prepared the statement;
(b)   whether relevant evidence could be given by that person which could not be given by the expert;

(c)   whether that person can reasonably be expected to remember the matters stated well enough to give oral evidence of them.

(6) Subsections (1) to (5) apply to a statement prepared for the purposes of a criminal investigation as they apply to a statement prepared for the purposes of criminal proceedings, and in such a case references to the proceedings are to criminal proceedings arising from the investigation.

(7) The appropriate rules are rules made –

(a)   under section 81 of the Police and Criminal Evidence Act 1984 (advance notice of expert evidence in Crown Court), or

(b)   under section 144 of the Magistrates' Courts Act 1980 (c. 43) by virtue of section 20(3) of the Criminal Procedure and Investigations Act 1996 (c. 25) (advance notice of expert evidence in magistrates' courts).

128 Confessions

(1) In the Police and Criminal Evidence Act 1984 (c. 60) the following section is inserted after section 76 –

'76A Confessions may be given in evidence for co-accused

(1) In any proceedings a confession made by an accused person may be given in evidence for another person charged in the same proceedings (a co-accused) in so far as it is relevant to any matter in issue in the proceedings and is not excluded by the court in pursuance of this section.

(2) If, in any proceedings where a co-accused proposes to give in evidence a confession made by an accused person, it is represented to the court that the confession was or may have been obtained –

(a)   by oppression of the person who made it; or

(b)   in consequence of anything said or done which was likely, in the circumstances existing at the time, to render unreliable any confession which might be made by him in consequence thereof,

the court shall not allow the confession to be given in evidence for the co-accused except in so far as it is proved to the court on the balance of probabilities that the confession (notwithstanding that it may be true) was not so obtained.

(3) Before allowing a confession made by an accused person to be given in evidence for a co-accused in any proceedings, the court may of its own motion require the fact that the confession was not obtained as mentioned in subsection (2) above to be proved in the proceedings on the balance of probabilities.

(4) The fact that a confession is wholly or partly excluded in pursuance of this section shall not affect the admissibility in evidence –

(a)   of any facts discovered as a result of the confession; or

(b)   where the confession is relevant as showing that the accused speaks, writes or expresses himself in a particular way, of so much of the confession as is necessary to show that he does so.

(5) Evidence that a fact to which this subsection applies was discovered as a result of a statement made by an accused person shall not be admissible unless evidence of how it was discovered is given by him or on his behalf.

(6) Subsection (5) above applies –

   (a) to any fact discovered as a result of a confession which is wholly excluded in pursuance of this section; and

   (b) to any fact discovered as a result of a confession which is partly so excluded, if the fact is discovered as a result of the excluded part of the confession.

(7) In this section "oppression" includes torture, inhuman or degrading treatment, and the use or threat of violence (whether or not amounting to torture).'

(2) Subject to subsection (1), nothing in this Chapter makes a confession by a defendant admissible if it would not be admissible under section 76 of the Police and Criminal Evidence Act 1984 (c. 60).

(3) In subsection (2) 'confession' has the meaning given by section 82 of that Act.

129 Representations other than by a person

(1) Where a representation of any fact –

   (a) is made otherwise than by a person, but

   (b) depends for its accuracy on information supplied (directly or indirectly) by a person,

the representation is not admissible in criminal proceedings as evidence of the fact unless it is proved that the information was accurate.

(2) Subsection (1) does not affect the operation of the presumption that a mechanical device has been properly set or calibrated.

130 Depositions

In Schedule 3 to the Crime and Disorder Act 1998 (c. 37), sub-paragraph (4) of paragraph 5 is omitted (power of the court to overrule an objection to a deposition being read as evidence by virtue of that paragraph).

131 Evidence at retrial

For paragraphs 1 and 1A of Schedule 2 to the Criminal Appeal Act 1968 (c. 19) (oral evidence and use of transcripts etc at retrials under that Act) there is substituted –

'Evidence

1(1) Evidence given at a retrial must be given orally if it was given orally at the original trial, unless –

   (a) all the parties to the retrial agree otherwise;

   (b) section 116 of the Criminal Justice Act 2003 applies (admissibility of hearsay evidence where a witness is unavailable); or

   (c) the witness is unavailable to give evidence, otherwise than as mentioned in subsection (2) of that section, and section 114(1)(d) of that Act applies (admission of hearsay evidence under residual discretion).

(2) Paragraph 5 of Schedule 3 to the Crime and Disorder Act 1998 (use of depositions) does not apply at a retrial to a deposition read as evidence at the original trial.'

General

132 Rules of court

(1) Rules of court may make such provision as appears to the appropriate authority to be necessary or expedient for the purposes of this Chapter; and the appropriate authority is the authority entitled to make the rules.

(2) The rules may make provision about the procedure to be followed and other conditions to be fulfilled by a party proposing to tender a statement in evidence under any provision of this Chapter.

(3) The rules may require a party proposing to tender the evidence to serve on each party to the proceedings such notice, and such particulars of or relating to the evidence, as may be prescribed.

(4) The rules may provide that the evidence is to be treated as admissible by agreement of the parties if –

(a) a notice has been served in accordance with provision made under subsection (3), and
(b) no counter-notice in the prescribed form objecting to the admission of the evidence has been served by a party.

(5) If a party proposing to tender evidence fails to comply with a prescribed requirement applicable to it –

(a) the evidence is not admissible except with the court's leave;
(b) where leave is given the court or jury may draw such inferences from the failure as appear proper;
(c) the failure may be taken into account by the court in considering the exercise of its powers with respect to costs.

(6) In considering whether or how to exercise any of its powers under subsection (5) the court shall have regard to whether there is any justification for the failure to comply with the requirement.

(7) A person shall not be convicted of an offence solely on an inference drawn under subsection (5)(b).

(8) Rules under this section may –

(a) limit the application of any provision of the rules to prescribed circumstances;
(b) subject any provision of the rules to prescribed exceptions;
(c) make different provision for different cases or circumstances.

(9) Nothing in this section prejudices the generality of any enactment conferring power to make rules of court; and no particular provision of this section prejudices any general provision of it.

(10) In this section –

'prescribed' means prescribed by rules of court;
'rules of court' means –

(a) Crown Court Rules;
(b) Criminal Appeal Rules;

    (c) rules under section 144 of the Magistrates' Courts Act 1980 (c. 43).

133 Proof of statements in documents

Where a statement in a document is admissible as evidence in criminal proceedings, the statement may be proved by producing either –

    (a) the document, or
    (b) (whether or not the document exists) a copy of the document or of the material part of it,

authenticated in whatever way the court may approve.

134 Interpretation of Chapter 2

(1) In this Chapter –

    'copy', in relation to a document, means anything on to which information recorded in the document has been copied, by whatever means and whether directly or indirectly;
    'criminal proceedings' means criminal proceedings in relation to which the strict rules of evidence apply;
    'defendant', in relation to criminal proceedings, means a person charged with an offence in those proceedings;
    'document' means anything in which information of any description is recorded;
    'oral evidence' includes evidence which, by reason of any disability, disorder or other impairment, a person called as a witness gives in writing or by signs or by way of any device;
    'statutory provision' means any provision contained in, or in an instrument made under, this or any other Act, including any Act passed after this Act.

(2) Section 115 (statements and matters stated) contains other general interpretative provisions.

(3) Where a defendant is charged with two or more offences in the same criminal proceedings, this Chapter has effect as if each offence were charged in separate proceedings.

135 Armed forces

Schedule 7 (hearsay evidence: armed forces) has effect.

136 Repeals etc

In the Criminal Justice Act 1988 (c. 33), the following provisions (which are to some extent superseded by provisions of this Chapter) are repealed –

    (a) Part 2 and Schedule 2 (which relate to documentary evidence);
    (b) in Schedule 13, paragraphs 2 to 5 (which relate to documentary evidence in service courts etc).

CHAPTER 3

MISCELLANEOUS AND SUPPLEMENTAL

137 Evidence by video recording

(1) This section applies where –

  (a) a person is called as a witness in proceedings for an offence triable only on indictment, or for a prescribed offence triable either way,
  (b) the person claims to have witnessed (whether visually or in any other way) –
    (i)   events alleged by the prosecution to include conduct constituting the offence or part of the offence, or
    (ii) events closely connected with such events,
  (c) he has previously given an account of the events in question (whether in response to questions asked or otherwise),
  (d) the account was given at a time when those events were fresh in the person's memory (or would have been, assuming the truth of the claim mentioned in paragraph (b)),
  (e) a video recording was made of the account,
  (f) the court has made a direction that the recording should be admitted as evidence in chief of the witness, and the direction has not been rescinded, and
  (g) the recording is played in the proceedings in accordance with the direction.

(2) If, or to the extent that, the witness in his oral evidence in the proceedings asserts the truth of the statements made by him in the recorded account, they shall be treated as if made by him in that evidence.

(3) A direction under subsection (1)(f) –

  (a) may not be made in relation to a recorded account given by the defendant;
  (b) may be made only if it appears to the court that –
    (i)   the witness's recollection of the events in question is likely to have been significantly better when he gave the recorded account than it will be when he gives oral evidence in the proceedings, and
    (ii) it is in the interests of justice for the recording to be admitted, having regard in particular to the matters mentioned in subsection (4).

(4) Those matters are –

  (a) the interval between the time of the events in question and the time when the recorded account was made;
  (b) any other factors that might affect the reliability of what the witness said in that account;
  (c) the quality of the recording;
  (d) any views of the witness as to whether his evidence in chief should be given orally or by means of the recording.

(5) For the purposes of subsection (2) it does not matter if the statements in the recorded account were not made on oath.

(6) In this section 'prescribed' means of a description specified in an order made by the Secretary of State.

138 Video evidence: further provisions

(1) Where a video recording is admitted under section 137, the witness may not give evidence in chief otherwise than by means of the recording as to any matter which, in the opinion of the court, has been dealt with adequately in the recorded account.

(2) The reference in subsection (1)(f) of section 137 to the admission of a recording includes a reference to the admission of part of the recording; and references in that section and this one to the video recording or to the witness's recorded account shall, where appropriate, be read accordingly.

(3) In considering whether any part of a recording should be not admitted under section 137, the court must consider –

  (a) whether admitting that part would carry a risk of prejudice to the defendant, and
  (b) if so, whether the interests of justice nevertheless require it to be admitted in view of the desirability of showing the whole, or substantially the whole, of the recorded interview.

(4) A court may not make a direction under section 137(1)(f) in relation to any proceedings unless –

  (a) the Secretary of State has notified the court that arrangements can be made, in the area in which it appears to the court that the proceedings will take place, for implementing directions under that section, and
  (b) the notice has not been withdrawn.

(5) Nothing in section 137 affects the admissibility of any video recording which would be admissible apart from that section.

139 Use of documents to refresh memory

(1) A person giving oral evidence in criminal proceedings about any matter may, at any stage in the course of doing so, refresh his memory of it from a document made or verified by him at an earlier time if –

  (a) he states in his oral evidence that the document records his recollection of the matter at that earlier time, and
  (b) his recollection of the matter is likely to have been significantly better at that time than it is at the time of his oral evidence.

(2) Where –

  (a) a person giving oral evidence in criminal proceedings about any matter has previously given an oral account, of which a sound recording was made, and he states in that evidence that the account represented his recollection of the matter at that time,
  (b) his recollection of the matter is likely to have been significantly better at the time of the previous account than it is at the time of his oral evidence, and
  (c) a transcript has been made of the sound recording,

he may, at any stage in the course of giving his evidence, refresh his memory of the matter from that transcript.

140 Interpretation of Chapter 3

In this Chapter –

'criminal proceedings' means criminal proceedings in relation to which the strict rules of evidence apply;

'defendant', in relation to criminal proceedings, means a person charged with an offence in those proceedings;

'document' means anything in which information of any description is recorded, but not including any recording of sounds or moving images;

'oral evidence' includes evidence which, by reason of any disability, disorder or other impairment, a person called as a witness gives in writing or by signs or by way of any device;

'video recording' means any recording, on any medium, from which a moving image may by any means be produced, and includes the accompanying sound-track.

141 Saving

No provision of this Part has effect in relation to criminal proceedings begun before the commencement of that provision.

PART 12

SENTENCING

CHAPTER 1

GENERAL PROVISIONS ABOUT SENTENCING

Matters to be taken into account in sentencing

142 Purposes of sentencing

(1) Any court dealing with an offender in respect of his offence must have regard to the following purposes of sentencing –

   (a)   the punishment of offenders,
   (b)   the reduction of crime (including its reduction by deterrence),
   (c)   the reform and rehabilitation of offenders,
   (d)   the protection of the public, and
   (e)   the making of reparation by offenders to persons affected by their offences.

(2) Subsection (1) does not apply –

   (a)   in relation to an offender who is aged under 18 at the time of conviction,
   (b)   to an offence the sentence for which is fixed by law,
   (c)   to an offence the sentence for which falls to be imposed under section 51A(2) of the Firearms Act 1968 (c. 27) (minimum sentence for certain firearms offences), under subsection (2) of section 110 or 111 of the Sentencing Act (required custodial sentences) or under any of sections 225 to 228 of this Act (dangerous offenders), or
   (d)   in relation to the making under Part 3 of the Mental Health Act 1983 (c. 20) of a hospital order (with or without a restriction order), an interim hospital order, a hospital direction or a limitation direction.

(3) In this Chapter 'sentence', in relation to an offence, includes any order made by a court when dealing with the offender in respect of his offence; and 'sentencing' is to be construed accordingly.

143 Determining the seriousness of an offence

(1) In considering the seriousness of any offence, the court must consider the offender's culpability in committing the offence and any harm which the offence caused, was intended to cause or might forseeably have caused.

(2) In considering the seriousness of an offence ('the current offence') committed by an offender who has one or more previous convictions, the court must treat each previous conviction as an aggravating factor if (in the case of that conviction) the court considers that it can reasonably be so treated having regard, in particular, to –

(a) the nature of the offence to which the conviction relates and its relevance to the current offence, and
(b) the time that has elapsed since the conviction.

(3) In considering the seriousness of any offence committed while the offender was on bail, the court must treat the fact that it was committed in those circumstances as an aggravating factor.

(4) Any reference in subsection (2) to a previous conviction is to be read as a reference to –

(a) a previous conviction by a court in the United Kingdom, or
(b) a previous finding of guilt in service disciplinary proceedings.

(5) Subsections (2) and (4) do not prevent the court from treating a previous conviction by a court outside the United Kingdom as an aggravating factor in any case where the court considers it appropriate to do so.

144 Reduction in sentences for guilty pleas

(1) In determining what sentence to pass on an offender who has pleaded guilty to an offence in proceedings before that or another court, a court must take into account –

(a) the stage in the proceedings for the offence at which the offender indicated his intention to plead guilty, and
(b) the circumstances in which this indication was given.

(2) In the case of an offence the sentence for which falls to be imposed under subsection (2) of section 110 or 111 of the Sentencing Act, nothing in that subsection prevents the court, after taking into account any matter referred to in subsection (1) of this section, from imposing any sentence which is not less than 80 per cent of that specified in that subsection.

145 Increase in sentences for racial or religious aggravation

(1) This section applies where a court is considering the seriousness of an offence other than one under sections 29 to 32 of the Crime and Disorder Act 1998 (c. 37) (racially or religiously aggravated assaults, criminal damage, public order offences and harassment etc).

(2) If the offence was racially or religiously aggravated, the court –

(a) must treat that fact as an aggravating factor, and
(b) must state in open court that the offence was so aggravated.

(3) Section 28 of the Crime and Disorder Act 1998 (meaning of 'racially or religiously aggravated') applies for the purposes of this section as it applies for the purposes of sections 29 to 32 of that Act.

146 Increase in sentences for aggravation related to disability or sexual orientation

(1) This section applies where the court is considering the seriousness of an offence committed in any of the circumstances mentioned in subsection (2).

(2) Those circumstances are –

  (a) that, at the time of committing the offence, or immediately before or after doing so, the offender demonstrated towards the victim of the offence hostility based on –
  (i)   the sexual orientation (or presumed sexual orientation) of the victim, or
  (ii)   a disability (or presumed disability) of the victim, or
  (b) that the offence is motivated (wholly or partly) –
  (i)   by hostility towards persons who are of a particular sexual orientation, or
  (ii)   by hostility towards persons who have a disability or a particular disability.

(3) The court –

  (a) must treat the fact that the offence was committed in any of those circumstances as an aggravating factor, and
  (b) must state in open court that the offence was committed in such circumstances.

(4) It is immaterial for the purposes of paragraph (a) or (b) of subsection (2) whether or not the offender's hostility is also based, to any extent, on any other factor not mentioned in that paragraph.

(5) In this section 'disability' means any physical or mental impairment.

General restrictions on community sentences

147 Meaning of 'community sentence' etc

(1) In this Part 'community sentence' means a sentence which consists of or includes –

  (a) a community order (as defined by section 177), or
  (b) one or more youth community orders.

(2) In this Chapter 'youth community order' means –

  (a) a curfew order as defined by section 163 of the Sentencing Act,
  (b) an exclusion order under section 40A(1) of that Act,
  (c) an attendance centre order as defined by section 163 of that Act,
  (d) a supervision order under section 63(1) of that Act, or
  (e) an action plan order under section 69(1) of that Act.

148 Restrictions on imposing community sentences

(1) A court must not pass a community sentence on an offender unless it is of the opinion that the offence, or the combination of the offence and one or more offences associated with it, was serious enough to warrant such a sentence.

(2) Where a court passes a community sentence which consists of or includes a community order –

(a) the particular requirement or requirements forming part of the community order must be such as, in the opinion of the court, is, or taken together are, the most suitable for the offender, and

(b) the restrictions on liberty imposed by the order must be such as in the opinion of the court are commensurate with the seriousness of the offence, or the combination of the offence and one or more offences associated with it.

(3) Where a court passes a community sentence which consists of or includes one or more youth community orders –

(a) the particular order or orders forming part of the sentence must be such as, in the opinion of the court, is, or taken together are, the most suitable for the offender, and

(b) the restrictions on liberty imposed by the order or orders must be such as in the opinion of the court are commensurate with the seriousness of the offence, or the combination of the offence and one or more offences associated with it.

(4) Subsections (1) and (2)(b) have effect subject to section 151(2).

149 Passing of community sentence on offender remanded in custody

(1) In determining the restrictions on liberty to be imposed by a community order or youth community order in respect of an offence, the court may have regard to any period for which the offender has been remanded in custody in connection with the offence or any other offence the charge for which was founded on the same facts or evidence.

(2) In subsection (1) 'remanded in custody' has the meaning given by section 242(2).

150 Community sentence not available where sentence fixed by law etc.

The power to make a community order or youth community order is not exercisable in respect of an offence for which the sentence –

(a) is fixed by law,

(b) falls to be imposed under section 51A(2) of the Firearms Act 1968 (c. 27) (required custodial sentence for certain firearms offences),

(c) falls to be imposed under section 110(2) or 111(2) of the Sentencing Act (requirement to impose custodial sentences for certain repeated offences committed by offenders aged 18 or over), or

(d) falls to be imposed under any of sections 225 to 228 of this Act (requirement to impose custodial sentences for certain offences committed by offenders posing risk to public).

151 Community order for persistent offender previously fined

(1) Subsection (2) applies where –

(a) a person aged 16 or over is convicted of an offence ('the current offence'),

(b) on three or more previous occasions he has, on conviction by a court in the United Kingdom of any offence committed by him after attaining the age of 16, had passed on him a sentence consisting only of a fine, and

(c) despite the effect of section 143(2), the court would not (apart from this section) regard the current offence, or the combination of the current offence and one or more offences associated with it, as being serious enough to warrant a community sentence.

(2) The court may make a community order in respect of the current offence instead of imposing a fine if it considers that, having regard to all the circumstances including the matters mentioned in subsection (3), it would be in the interests of justice to make such an order.

(3) The matters referred to in subsection (2) are –

    (a) the nature of the offences to which the previous convictions mentioned in subsection (1)(b) relate and their relevance to the current offence, and

    (b) the time that has elapsed since the offender's conviction of each of those offences.

(4) In subsection (1)(b), the reference to conviction by a court in the United Kingdom includes a reference to the finding of guilt in service disciplinary proceedings; and, in relation to any such finding of guilt, the reference to the sentence passed is a reference to the punishment awarded.

(5) For the purposes of subsection (1)(b), a compensation order does not form part of an offender's sentence.

(6) For the purposes of subsection (1)(b), it is immaterial whether on other previous occasions a court has passed on the offender a sentence not consisting only of a fine.

(7) This section does not limit the extent to which a court may, in accordance with section 143(2), treat any previous convictions of the offender as increasing the seriousness of an offence.

General restrictions on discretionary custodial sentences

152 General restrictions on imposing discretionary custodial sentences

(1) This section applies where a person is convicted of an offence punishable with a custodial sentence other than one –

    (a) fixed by law, or

    (b) falling to be imposed under section 51A(2) of the Firearms Act 1968 (c. 27), under 110(2) or 111(2) of the Sentencing Act or under any of sections 225 to 228 of this Act.

(2) The court must not pass a custodial sentence unless it is of the opinion that the offence, or the combination of the offence and one or more offences associated with it, was so serious that neither a fine alone nor a community sentence can be justified for the offence.

(3) Nothing in subsection (2) prevents the court from passing a custodial sentence on the offender if –

    (a) he fails to express his willingness to comply with a requirement which is proposed by the court to be included in a community order and which requires an expression of such willingness, or

    (b) he fails to comply with an order under section 161(2) (pre-sentence drug testing).

153 Length of discretionary custodial sentences: general provision

(1) This section applies where a court passes a custodial sentence other than one fixed by law or falling to be imposed under section 225 or 226.

(2) Subject to section 51A(2) of the Firearms Act 1968 (c. 27), sections 110(2) and 111(2) of the Sentencing Act and sections 227(2) and 228(2) of this Act, the custodial sentence must be for the shortest term (not exceeding the permitted maximum) that in the opinion of the court is commensurate with the seriousness of the offence, or the combination of the offence and one or more offences associated with it.

General limit on magistrates' court's power to impose imprisonment

154 General limit on magistrates' court's power to impose imprisonment

(1) A magistrates' court does not have power to impose imprisonment for more than 12 months in respect of any one offence.

(2) Unless expressly excluded, subsection (1) applies even if the offence in question is one for which a person would otherwise be liable on summary conviction to imprisonment for more than 12 months.

(3) Subsection (1) is without prejudice to section 133 of the Magistrates' Courts Act 1980 (c. 43) (consecutive terms of imprisonment).

(4) Any power of a magistrates' court to impose a term of imprisonment for non-payment of a fine, or for want of sufficient distress to satisfy a fine, is not limited by virtue of subsection (1).

(5) In subsection (4) 'fine' includes a pecuniary penalty but does not include a pecuniary forfeiture or pecuniary compensation.

(6) In this section 'impose imprisonment' means pass a sentence of imprisonment or fix a term of imprisonment for failure to pay any sum of money, or for want of sufficient distress to satisfy any sum of money, or for failure to do or abstain from doing anything required to be done or left undone.

(7) Section 132 of the Magistrates' Courts Act 1980 contains provisions about the minimum term of imprisonment which may be imposed by a magistrates' court.

155 Consecutive terms of imprisonment

(1) Section 133 of the Magistrates' Courts Act 1980 (consecutive terms of imprisonment) is amended as follows.

(2) In subsection (1), for '6 months' there is substituted '65 weeks'.

(3) Subsection (2) is omitted.

(4) In subsection (3) for 'the preceding subsections' there is substituted 'subsection (1) above'.

156 Pre-sentence reports and other requirements

(1) In forming any such opinion as is mentioned in section 148(1), (2)(b) or (3)(b), section 152(2) or section 153(2), a court must take into account all such information as is available to it about the circumstances of the offence or (as the case may be) of the offence and the offence or offences associated with it, including any aggravating or mitigating factors.

(2) In forming any such opinion as is mentioned in section 148(2)(a) or (3)(a), the court may take into account any information about the offender which is before it.

(3) Subject to subsection (4), a court must obtain and consider a pre-sentence report before –

    (a) in the case of a custodial sentence, forming any such opinion as is mentioned in section 152(2), section 153(2), section 225(1)(b), section 226(1)(b), section 227(1)(b) or section 228(1)(b)(i), or

    (b) in the case of a community sentence, forming any such opinion as is mentioned in section 148(1), (2)(b) or (3)(b) or any opinion as to the suitability for the offender of the particular requirement or requirements to be imposed by the community order.

(4) Subsection (3) does not apply if, in the circumstances of the case, the court is of the opinion that it is unnecessary to obtain a pre-sentence report.

(5) In a case where the offender is aged under 18, the court must not form the opinion mentioned in subsection (4) unless –

    (a) there exists a previous pre-sentence report obtained in respect of the offender, and

    (b) the court has had regard to the information contained in that report, or, if there is more than one such report, the most recent report.

(6) No custodial sentence or community sentence is invalidated by the failure of a court to obtain and consider a pre-sentence report before forming an opinion referred to in subsection (3), but any court on an appeal against such a sentence –

    (a) must, subject to subsection (7), obtain a pre-sentence report if none was obtained by the court below, and

    (b) must consider any such report obtained by it or by that court.

(7) Subsection (6)(a) does not apply if the court is of the opinion –

    (a) that the court below was justified in forming an opinion that it was unnecessary to obtain a pre-sentence report, or

    (b) that, although the court below was not justified in forming that opinion, in the circumstances of the case at the time it is before the court, it is unnecessary to obtain a pre-sentence report.

(8) In a case where the offender is aged under 18, the court must not form the opinion mentioned in subsection (7) unless –

    (a) there exists a previous pre-sentence report obtained in respect of the offender, and

    (b) the court has had regard to the information contained in that report, or, if there is more than one such report, the most recent report.

157 Additional requirements in case of mentally disordered offender

(1) Subject to subsection (2), in any case where the offender is or appears to be mentally disordered, the court must obtain and consider a medical report before passing a custodial sentence other than one fixed by law.

(2) Subsection (1) does not apply if, in the circumstances of the case, the court is of the opinion that it is unnecessary to obtain a medical report.

(3) Before passing a custodial sentence other than one fixed by law on an offender who is or appears to be mentally disordered, a court must consider –

(a) any information before it which relates to his mental condition (whether given in a medical report, a pre-sentence report or otherwise), and

(b) the likely effect of such a sentence on that condition and on any treatment which may be available for it.

(4) No custodial sentence which is passed in a case to which subsection (1) applies is invalidated by the failure of a court to comply with that subsection, but any court on an appeal against such a sentence –

(a) must obtain a medical report if none was obtained by the court below, and

(b) must consider any such report obtained by it or by that court.

(5) In this section 'mentally disordered', in relation to any person, means suffering from a mental disorder within the meaning of the Mental Health Act 1983 (c. 20).

(6) In this section 'medical report' means a report as to an offender's mental condition made or submitted orally or in writing by a registered medical practitioner who is approved for the purposes of section 12 of the Mental Health Act 1983 by the Secretary of State as having special experience in the diagnosis or treatment of mental disorder.

(7) Nothing in this section is to be taken to limit the generality of section 156.

158 Meaning of 'pre-sentence report'

(1) In this Part 'pre-sentence report' means a report which –

(a) with a view to assisting the court in determining the most suitable method of dealing with an offender, is made or submitted by an appropriate officer, and

(b) contains information as to such matters, presented in such manner, as may be prescribed by rules made by the Secretary of State.

(2) In subsection (1) 'an appropriate officer' means –

(a) where the offender is aged 18 or over, an officer of a local probation board, and

(b) where the offender is aged under 18, an officer of a local probation board, a social worker of a local authority social services department or a member of a youth offending team.

Disclosure of pre-sentence reports etc

159 Disclosure of pre-sentence reports

(1) This section applies where the court obtains a pre-sentence report, other than a report given orally in open court.

(2) Subject to subsections (3) and (4), the court must give a copy of the report –

(a) to the offender or his counsel or solicitor,

(b) if the offender is aged under 18, to any parent or guardian of his who is present in court, and

(c) to the prosecutor, that is to say, the person having the conduct of the proceedings in respect of the offence.

(3) If the offender is aged under 18 and it appears to the court that the disclosure to the offender or to any parent or guardian of his of any information contained in the report would be likely to create a risk of significant harm to the offender, a complete copy of the

report need not be given to the offender or, as the case may be, to that parent or guardian.

(4) If the prosecutor is not of a description prescribed by order made by the Secretary of State, a copy of the report need not be given to the prosecutor if the court considers that it would be inappropriate for him to be given it.

(5) No information obtained by virtue of subsection (2)(c) may be used or disclosed otherwise than for the purpose of –

(a)   determining whether representations as to matters contained in the report need to be made to the court, or
(b)   making such representations to the court.

(6) In relation to an offender aged under 18 for whom a local authority have parental responsibility and who –

(a)   is in their care, or
(b)   is provided with accommodation by them in the exercise of any social services functions,

references in this section to his parent or guardian are to be read as references to that authority.

(7) In this section and section 160 –

'harm' has the same meaning as in section 31 of the Children Act 1989 (c. 41);
'local authority' and 'parental responsibility' have the same meanings as in that Act;
'social services functions', in relation to a local authority, has the meaning given by section 1A of the Local Authority Social Services Act 1970 (c. 42).

160 Other reports of local probation boards and members of youth offending teams

(1) This section applies where –

(a)   a report by an officer of a local probation board or a member of a youth offending team is made to any court (other than a youth court) with a view to assisting the court in determining the most suitable method of dealing with any person in respect of an offence, and
(b)   the report is not a pre-sentence report.

(2) Subject to subsection (3), the court must give a copy of the report –

(a)   to the offender or his counsel or solicitor, and
(b)   if the offender is aged under 18, to any parent or guardian of his who is present in court.

(3) If the offender is aged under 18 and it appears to the court that the disclosure to the offender or to any parent or guardian of his of any information contained in the report would be likely to create a risk of significant harm to the offender, a complete copy of the report need not be given to the offender, or as the case may be, to that parent or guardian.

(4) In relation to an offender aged under 18 for whom a local authority have parental responsibility and who –

(a)   is in their care, or

(b) is provided with accommodation by them in the exercise of any social services functions,

references in this section to his parent or guardian are to be read as references to that authority.

161 Pre-sentence drug testing

(1) Where a person aged 14 or over is convicted of an offence and the court is considering passing a community sentence or a suspended sentence, it may make an order under subsection (2) for the purpose of ascertaining whether the offender has any specified Class A drug in his body.

(2) The order requires the offender to provide, in accordance with the order, samples of any description specified in the order.

(3) Where the offender has not attained the age of 17, the order must provide for the samples to be provided in the presence of an appropriate adult.

(4) If it is proved to the satisfaction of the court that the offender has, without reasonable excuse, failed to comply with the order it may impose on him a fine of an amount not exceeding level 4.

(5) In subsection (4) 'level 4' means the amount which, in relation to a fine for a summary offence, is level 4 on the standard scale.

(6) The court may not make an order under subsection (2) unless it has been notified by the Secretary of State that the power to make such orders is exercisable by the court and the notice has not been withdrawn.

(7) The Secretary of State may by order amend subsection (1) by substituting for the age for the time being specified there a different age specified in the order.

(8) In this section –

'appropriate adult', in relation to a person under the age of 17, means –

(a) his parent or guardian or, if he is in the care of a local authority or voluntary organisation, a person representing that authority or organisation,
(b) a social worker of a local authority social services department, or
(c) if no person falling within paragraph (a) or (b) is available, any responsible person aged 18 or over who is not a police officer or a person employed by the police;

'specified Class A drug' has the same meaning as in Part 3 of the Criminal Justice and Court Services Act 2000 (c. 43).

Fines

162 Powers to order statement as to offender's financial circumstances

(1) Where an individual has been convicted of an offence, the court may, before sentencing him, make a financial circumstances order with respect to him.

(2) Where a magistrates' court has been notified in accordance with section 12(4) of the Magistrates' Courts Act 1980 (c. 43) that an individual desires to plead guilty without

appearing before the court, the court may make a financial circumstances order with respect to him.

(3) In this section 'a financial circumstances order' means, in relation to any individual, an order requiring him to give to the court, within such period as may be specified in the order, such a statement of his financial circumstances as the court may require.

(4) An individual who without reasonable excuse fails to comply with a financial circumstances order is liable on summary conviction to a fine not exceeding level 3 on the standard scale.

(5) If an individual, in furnishing any statement in pursuance of a financial circumstances order –

  (a) makes a statement which he knows to be false in a material particular,
  (b) recklessly furnishes a statement which is false in a material particular, or
  (c) knowingly fails to disclose any material fact,

he is liable on summary conviction to a fine not exceeding level 4 on the standard scale.

(6) Proceedings in respect of an offence under subsection (5) may, notwithstanding anything in section 127(1) of the Magistrates' Courts Act 1980 (c. 43) (limitation of time), be commenced at any time within two years from the date of the commission of the offence or within six months from its first discovery by the prosecutor, whichever period expires the earlier.

163 General power of Crown Court to fine offender convicted on indictment

Where a person is convicted on indictment of any offence, other than an offence for which the sentence is fixed by law or falls to be imposed under section 110(2) or 111(2) of the Sentencing Act or under any of sections 225 to 228 of this Act, the court, if not precluded from sentencing an offender by its exercise of some other power, may impose a fine instead of or in addition to dealing with him in any other way in which the court has power to deal with him, subject however to any enactment requiring the offender to be dealt with in a particular way.

164 Fixing of fines

(1) Before fixing the amount of any fine to be imposed on an offender who is an individual, a court must inquire into his financial circumstances.

(2) The amount of any fine fixed by a court must be such as, in the opinion of the court, reflects the seriousness of the offence.

(3) In fixing the amount of any fine to be imposed on an offender (whether an individual or other person), a court must take into account the circumstances of the case including, among other things, the financial circumstances of the offender so far as they are known, or appear, to the court.

(4) Subsection (3) applies whether taking into account the financial circumstances of the offender has the effect of increasing or reducing the amount of the fine.

(5) Where –

  (a) an offender has been convicted in his absence in pursuance of section 11 or 12 of the Magistrates' Courts Act 1980 (c. 43) (non-appearance of accused), or

    (b) an offender –
        (i) has failed to furnish a statement of his financial circumstances in response to a request which is an official request for the purposes of section 20A of the Criminal Justice Act 1991 (c.53) (offence of making false statement as to financial circumstances),
        (ii) has failed to comply with an order under section 162(1), or
        (iii) has otherwise failed to co-operate with the court in its inquiry into his financial circumstances,

and the court considers that it has insufficient information to make a proper determination of the financial circumstances of the offender, it may make such determination as it thinks fit.

165 Remission of fines

(1) This section applies where a court has, in fixing the amount of a fine, determined the offender's financial circumstances under section 164(5).

(2) If, on subsequently inquiring into the offender's financial circumstances, the court is satisfied that had it had the results of that inquiry when sentencing the offender it would –

    (a) have fixed a smaller amount, or
    (b) not have fined him,

it may remit the whole or part of the fine.

(3) Where under this section the court remits the whole or part of a fine after a term of imprisonment has been fixed under section 139 of the Sentencing Act (powers of Crown Court in relation to fines) or section 82(5) of the Magistrates' Courts Act 1980 (magistrates' powers in relation to default) it must reduce the term by the corresponding proportion.

(4) In calculating any reduction required by subsection (3), any fraction of a day is to be ignored.

Savings for power to mitigate etc

166 Savings for powers to mitigate sentences and deal appropriately with mentally disordered offenders

(1) Nothing in –

    (a) section 148 (imposing community sentences),
    (b) section 152, 153 or 157 (imposing custodial sentences),
    (c) section 156 (pre-sentence reports and other requirements),
    (d) section 164 (fixing of fines),

prevents a court from mitigating an offender's sentence by taking into account any such matters as, in the opinion of the court, are relevant in mitigation of sentence.

(2) Section 152(2) does not prevent a court, after taking into account such matters, from passing a community sentence even though it is of the opinion that the offence, or the combination of the offence and one or more offences associated with it, was so serious that a community sentence could not normally be justified for the offence.

(3) Nothing in the sections mentioned in subsection (1)(a) to (d) prevents a court –

    (a) from mitigating any penalty included in an offender's sentence by taking into account any other penalty included in that sentence, and

    (b) in the case of an offender who is convicted of one or more other offences, from mitigating his sentence by applying any rule of law as to the totality of sentences.

(4) Subsections (2) and (3) are without prejudice to the generality of subsection (1).

(5) Nothing in the sections mentioned in subsection (1)(a) to (d) is to be taken –

    (a) as requiring a court to pass a custodial sentence, or any particular custodial sentence, on a mentally disordered offender, or

    (b) as restricting any power (whether under the Mental Health Act 1983 (c. 20) or otherwise) which enables a court to deal with such an offender in the manner it considers to be most appropriate in all the circumstances.

(6) In subsection (5) 'mentally disordered', in relation to a person, means suffering from a mental disorder within the meaning of the Mental Health Act 1983.

Sentencing and allocation guidelines

167 The Sentencing Guidelines Council

(1) There shall be a Sentencing Guidelines Council (in this Chapter referred to as the Council) consisting of –

    (a) the Lord Chief Justice, who is to be chairman of the Council,

    (b) seven members (in this section and section 168 referred to as 'judicial members') appointed by the Lord Chancellor after consultation with the Secretary of State and the Lord Chief Justice, and

    (c) four members (in this section and section 168 referred to as 'non-judicial members') appointed by the Secretary of State after consultation with the Lord Chancellor and the Lord Chief Justice.

(2) A person is eligible to be appointed as a judicial member if he is –

    (a) a Lord Justice of Appeal,

    (b) a judge of the High Court,

    (c) a Circuit judge,

    (d) a District Judge (Magistrates' Courts), or

    (e) a lay justice.

(3) The judicial members must include a Circuit judge, a District Judge (Magistrates' Courts) and a lay justice.

(4) A person is eligible for appointment as a non-judicial member if he appears to the Secretary of State to have experience in one or more of the following areas –

    (a) policing,

    (b) criminal prosecution,

    (c) criminal defence, and

    (d) the promotion of the welfare of victims of crime.

(5) The persons eligible for appointment as a non-judicial member by virtue of experience of criminal prosecution include the Director of Public Prosecutions.

(6) The non-judicial members must include at least one person appearing to the Secretary of State to have experience in each area.

(7) The Lord Chief Justice must appoint one of the judicial members or non-judicial members to be deputy chairman of the Council.

(8) In relation to any meeting of the Council from which the Lord Chief Justice is to be absent, he may nominate any person eligible for appointment as a judicial member to act as a member on his behalf at the meeting.

(9) The Secretary of State may appoint a person appearing to him to have experience of sentencing policy and the administration of sentences to attend and speak at any meeting of the Council.

(10) In this section and section 168 'lay justice' means a justice of the peace who is not a District Judge (Magistrates' Courts).

168 Sentencing Guidelines Council: supplementary provisions

(1) In relation to the Council, the Lord Chancellor may by order make provision –

  (a)   as to the term of office, resignation and re-appointment of judicial members and non-judicial members,
  (b)   enabling the appropriate Minister to remove a judicial member or non-judicial member from office on grounds of incapacity or misbehaviour, and
  (c)   as to the proceedings of the Council.

(2) In subsection (1)(b) 'the appropriate Minister' means –

  (a)   in relation to a judicial member, the Lord Chancellor, and
  (b)   in relation to a non-judicial member, the Secretary of State.

(3) The validity of anything done by the Council is not affected by any vacancy among its members, by any defect in the appointment of a member or by any failure to comply with section 167(3), (6) or (7).

(4) The Lord Chancellor may pay –

  (a)   to any judicial member who is appointed by virtue of being a lay justice, such remuneration or expenses as he may determine, and
  (b)   to any other judicial member or the Lord Chief Justice, such expenses as he may determine.

(5) The Secretary of State may pay to any non-judicial member such remuneration or expenses as he may determine.

169 The Sentencing Advisory Panel

(1) There shall continue to be a Sentencing Advisory Panel (in this Chapter referred to as 'the Panel') constituted by the Lord Chancellor after consultation with the Secretary of State and the Lord Chief Justice.

(2) The Lord Chancellor must, after consultation with the Secretary of State and the Lord Chief Justice, appoint one of the members of the Panel to be its chairman.

(3) The Lord Chancellor may pay to any member of the Panel such remuneration or expenses as he may determine.

170 Guidelines relating to sentencing and allocation

(1) In this Chapter –

  (a) 'sentencing guidelines' means guidelines relating to the sentencing of offenders, which may be general in nature or limited to a particular category of offence or offender, and
  (b) 'allocation guidelines' means guidelines relating to decisions by a magistrates' court under section 19 of the Magistrates' Courts Act 1980 (c. 43) as to whether an offence is more suitable for summary trial or trial on indictment.

(2) The Secretary of State may at any time propose to the Council –

  (a) that sentencing guidelines be framed or revised by the Council –
    (i)   in respect of offences or offenders of a particular category, or
    (ii) in respect of a particular matter affecting sentencing, or
  (b) that allocation guidelines be framed or revised by the Council.

(3) The Council may from time to time consider whether to frame sentencing guidelines or allocation guidelines and, if it receives –

  (a) a proposal under section 171(2) from the Panel, or
  (b) a proposal under subsection (2) from the Secretary of State,

must consider whether to do so.

(4) Where sentencing guidelines or allocation guidelines have been issued by the Council as definitive guidelines, the Council must from time to time (and, in particular, if it receives a proposal under section 171(2) from the Panel or under subsection (2) from the Secretary of State) consider whether to revise them.

(5) Where the Council decides to frame or revise sentencing guidelines, the matters to which the Council must have regard include –

  (a) the need to promote consistency in sentencing,
  (b) the sentences imposed by courts in England and Wales for offences to which the guidelines relate,
  (c) the cost of different sentences and their relative effectiveness in preventing re-offending,
  (d) the need to promote public confidence in the criminal justice system, and
  (e) the views communicated to the Council, in accordance with section 171(3)(b), by the Panel.

(6) Where the Council decides to frame or revise allocation guidelines, the matters to which the Council must have regard include –

  (a) the need to promote consistency in decisions under section 19 of the Magistrates' Courts Act 1980 (c. 43), and
  (b) the views communicated to the Council, in accordance with section 171(3)(b), by the Panel.

(7) Sentencing guidelines in respect of an offence or category of offences must include criteria for determining the seriousness of the offence or offences, including (where appropriate) criteria for determining the weight to be given to any previous convictions of offenders.

(8) Where the Council has prepared or revised any sentencing guidelines or allocation guidelines, it must –

(a) publish them as draft guidelines, and
(b) consult about the draft guidelines –
      (i)   the Secretary of State,
      (ii)   such persons as the Lord Chancellor, after consultation with the Secretary of State, may direct, and
      (iii) such other persons as the Council considers appropriate.

(9) The Council may, after making any amendment of the draft guidelines which it considers appropriate, issue the guidelines as definitive guidelines.

171 Functions of Sentencing Advisory Panel in relation to guidelines

(1) Where the Council decides to frame or revise any sentencing guidelines or allocation guidelines, otherwise than in response to a proposal from the Panel under subsection (2), the Council must notify the Panel.

(2) The Panel may at any time propose to the Council –

(a) that sentencing guidelines be framed or revised by the Council –
      (i)   in respect of offences or offenders of a particular category, or
      (ii)   in respect of a particular matter affecting sentencing, or
(b) that allocation guidelines be framed or revised by the Council.

(3) Where the Panel receives a notification under subsection (1) or makes a proposal under subsection (2), the Panel must –

(a) obtain and consider the views on the matters in issue of such persons or bodies as may be determined, after consultation with the Secretary of State and the Lord Chancellor, by the Council, and
(b) formulate its own views on those matters and communicate them to the Council.

(4) Paragraph (a) of subsection (3) does not apply where the Council notifies the Panel of the Council's view that the urgency of the case makes it impracticable for the Panel to comply with that paragraph.

172 Duty of court to have regard to sentencing guidelines

(1) Every court must –

(a) in sentencing an offender, have regard to any guidelines which are relevant to the offender's case, and
(b) in exercising any other function relating to the sentencing of offenders, have regard to any guidelines which are relevant to the exercise of the function.

(2) In subsection (1) 'guidelines' means sentencing guidelines issued by the Council under section 170(9) as definitive guidelines, as revised by subsequent guidelines so issued.

173 Annual report by Council

(1) The Council must as soon as practicable after the end of each financial year make to the Ministers a report on the exercise of the Council's functions during the year.

(2) If section 167 comes into force after the beginning of a financial year, the first report may relate to a period beginning with the day on which that section comes into force and ending with the end of the next financial year.

(3) The Ministers must lay a copy of the report before each House of Parliament.

(4) The Council must publish the report once the copy has been so laid.

(5) In this section –

'financial year' means a period of 12 months ending with 31st March;
'the Ministers' means the Secretary of State and the Lord Chancellor.

Duty of court to explain sentence

174 Duty to give reasons for, and explain effect of, sentence

(1) Subject to subsections (3) and (4), any court passing sentence on an offender –

(a) must state in open court, in ordinary language and in general terms, its reasons for deciding on the sentence passed, and
(b) must explain to the offender in ordinary language –
   (i) the effect of the sentence,
   (ii) where the offender is required to comply with any order of the court forming part of the sentence, the effects of non-compliance with the order,
   (iii) any power of the court, on the application of the offender or any other person, to vary or review any order of the court forming part of the sentence, and
   (iv) where the sentence consists of or includes a fine, the effects of failure to pay the fine.

(2) In complying with subsection (1)(a), the court must –

(a) where guidelines indicate that a sentence of a particular kind, or within a particular range, would normally be appropriate for the offence and the sentence is of a different kind, or is outside that range, state the court's reasons for deciding on a sentence of a different kind or outside that range,
(b) where the sentence is a custodial sentence and the duty in subsection (2) of section 152 is not excluded by subsection (1)(a) or (b) or (3) of that section, state that it is of the opinion referred to in section 152(2) and why it is of that opinion,
(c) where the sentence is a community sentence and the case does not fall within section 151(2), state that it is of the opinion that section 148(1) applies and why it is of that opinion,
(d) where as a result of taking into account any matter referred to in section 144(1), the court imposes a punishment on the offender which is less severe than the punishment it would otherwise have imposed, state that fact, and
(e) in any case, mention any aggravating or mitigating factors which the court has regarded as being of particular importance.

(3) Subsection (1)(a) does not apply –

(a) to an offence the sentence for which is fixed by law (provision relating to sentencing for such an offence being made by section 270), or
(b) to an offence the sentence for which falls to be imposed under section 51A(2) of the Firearms Act 1968 (c. 27) or under subsection (2) of section 110 or 111 of the Sentencing Act (required custodial sentences).

(4) The Secretary of State may by order –

(a) prescribe cases in which subsection (1)(a) or (b) does not apply, and

  (b) prescribe cases in which the statement referred to in subsection (1)(a) or the explanation referred to in subsection (1)(b) may be made in the absence of the offender, or may be provided in written form.

(5) Where a magistrates' court passes a custodial sentence, it must cause any reason stated by virtue of subsection (2)(b) to be specified in the warrant of commitment and entered on the register.

(6) In this section –

> 'guidelines' has the same meaning as in section 172;
> 'the register' has the meaning given by section 163 of the Sentencing Act.

Publication of information about sentencing

175 Duty to publish information about sentencing

In section 95 of the Criminal Justice Act 1991 (c. 53) (information for financial and other purposes) in subsection (1) before the 'or' at the end of paragraph (a) there is inserted –

> '(aa) enabling such persons to become aware of the relative effectiveness of different sentences –
>
> > (i) in preventing re-offending, and
> > (ii) in promoting public confidence in the criminal justice system;'.

Interpretation of Chapter

176 Interpretation of Chapter 1

In this Chapter –

> 'allocation guidelines' has the meaning given by section 170(1)(b);
> 'the Council' means the Sentencing Guidelines Council;
> 'the Panel' means the Sentencing Advisory Panel;
> 'sentence' and 'sentencing' are to be read in accordance with section 142(3);
> 'sentencing guidelines' has the meaning given by section 170(1)(a);
> 'youth community order' has the meaning given by section 147(2).

CHAPTER 2

COMMUNITY ORDERS: OFFENDERS AGED 16 OR OVER

177 Community orders

(1) Where a person aged 16 or over is convicted of an offence, the court by or before which he is convicted may make an order (in this Part referred to as a 'community order') imposing on him any one or more of the following requirements –

  (a) an unpaid work requirement (as defined by section 199),
  (b) an activity requirement (as defined by section 201),
  (c) a programme requirement (as defined by section 202),
  (d) a prohibited activity requirement (as defined by section 203),
  (e) a curfew requirement (as defined by section 204),
  (f) an exclusion requirement (as defined by section 205),
  (g) a residence requirement (as defined by section 206),

(h) a mental health treatment requirement (as defined by section 207),

(i) a drug rehabilitation requirement (as defined by section 209),

(j) an alcohol treatment requirement (as defined by section 212),

(k) a supervision requirement (as defined by section 213), and

(l) in a case where the offender is aged under 25, an attendance centre requirement (as defined by section 214).

(2) Subsection (1) has effect subject to sections 150 and 218 and to the following provisions of Chapter 4 relating to particular requirements –

(a) section 199(3) (unpaid work requirement),

(b) section 201(3) and (4) (activity requirement),

(c) section 202(4) and (5) (programme requirement),

(d) section 203(2) (prohibited activity requirement),

(e) section 207(3) (mental health treatment requirement),

(f) section 209(2) (drug rehabilitation requirement), and

(g) section 212(2) and (3) (alcohol treatment requirement).

(3) Where the court makes a community order imposing a curfew requirement or an exclusion requirement, the court must also impose an electronic monitoring requirement (as defined by section 215) unless –

(a) it is prevented from doing so by section 215(2) or 218(4), or

(b) in the particular circumstances of the case, it considers it inappropriate to do so.

(4) Where the court makes a community order imposing an unpaid work requirement, an activity requirement, a programme requirement, a prohibited activity requirement, a residence requirement, a mental health treatment requirement, a drug rehabilitation requirement, an alcohol treatment requirement, a supervision requirement or an attendance centre requirement, the court may also impose an electronic monitoring requirement unless prevented from doing so by section 215(2) or 218(4).

(5) A community order must specify a date, not more than three years after the date of the order, by which all the requirements in it must have been complied with; and a community order which imposes two or more different requirements falling within subsection (1) may also specify an earlier date or dates in relation to compliance with any one or more of them.

(6) Before making a community order imposing two or more different requirements falling within subsection (1), the court must consider whether, in the circumstances of the case, the requirements are compatible with each other.

178 Power to provide for court review of community orders

(1) The Secretary of State may by order –

(a) enable or require a court making a community order to provide for the community order to be reviewed periodically by that or another court,

(b) enable a court to amend a community order so as to include or remove a provision for review by a court, and

(c) make provision as to the timing and conduct of reviews and as to the powers of the court on a review.

(2) An order under this section may, in particular, make provision in relation to community orders corresponding to any provision made by sections 191 and 192 in relation to suspended sentence orders.

(3) An order under this section may repeal or amend any provision of this Part.

179 Breach, revocation or amendment of community order

Schedule 8 (which relates to failures to comply with the requirements of community orders and to the revocation or amendment of such orders) shall have effect.

180 Transfer of community orders to Scotland or Northern Ireland

Schedule 9 (transfer of community orders to Scotland or Northern Ireland) shall have effect.

CHAPTER 3

PRISON SENTENCES OF LESS THAN 12 MONTHS

Prison sentences of less than twelve months

181 Prison sentences of less than 12 months

(1) Any power of a court to impose a sentence of imprisonment for a term of less than 12 months on an offender may be exercised only in accordance with the following provisions of this section unless the court makes an intermittent custody order (as defined by section 183).

(2) The term of the sentence –

  (a)   must be expressed in weeks,
  (b)   must be at least 28 weeks,
  (c)   must not be more than 51 weeks in respect of any one offence, and
  (d)   must not exceed the maximum term permitted for the offence.

(3) The court, when passing sentence, must –

  (a)   specify a period (in this Chapter referred to as 'the custodial period') at the end of which the offender is to be released on a licence, and
  (b)   by order require the licence to be granted subject to conditions requiring the offender's compliance during the remainder of the term (in this Chapter referred to as 'the licence period') or any part of it with one or more requirements falling within section 182(1) and specified in the order.

(4) In this Part 'custody plus order' means an order under subsection (3)(b).

(5) The custodial period –

  (a)   must be at least 2 weeks, and
  (b)   in respect of any one offence, must not be more than 13 weeks.

(6) In determining the term of the sentence and the length of the custodial period, the court must ensure that the licence period is at least 26 weeks in length.

(7) Where a court imposes two or more terms of imprisonment in accordance with this section to be served consecutively –

  (a)   the aggregate length of the terms of imprisonment must not be more than 65 weeks, and
  (b)   the aggregate length of the custodial periods must not be more than 26 weeks.

(8) A custody plus order which specifies two or more requirements may, in relation to any requirement, refer to compliance within such part of the licence period as is specified in the order.

(9) Subsection (3)(b) does not apply where the sentence is a suspended sentence.

182 Licence conditions

(1) The requirements falling within this subsection are –

    (a) an unpaid work requirement (as defined by section 199),
    (b) an activity requirement (as defined by section 201),
    (c) a programme requirement (as defined by section 202),
    (d) a prohibited activity requirement (as defined by section 203),
    (e) a curfew requirement (as defined by section 204),
    (f) an exclusion requirement (as defined by section 205),
    (g) a supervision requirement (as defined by section 213), and
    (h) in a case where the offender is aged under 25, an attendance centre requirement (as defined by section 214).

(2) The power under section 181(3)(b) to determine the conditions of the licence has effect subject to section 218 and to the following provisions of Chapter 4 relating to particular requirements –

    (a) section 199(3) (unpaid work requirement),
    (b) section 201(3) and (4) (activity requirement),
    (c) section 202(4) and (5) (programme requirement), and
    (d) section 203(2) (prohibited activity requirement).

(3) Where the court makes a custody plus order requiring a licence to contain a curfew requirement or an exclusion requirement, the court must also require the licence to contain an electronic monitoring requirement (as defined by section 215) unless –

    (a) the court is prevented from doing so by section 215(2) or 218(4), or
    (b) in the particular circumstances of the case, it considers it inappropriate to do so.

(4) Where the court makes a custody plus order requiring a licence to contain an unpaid work requirement, an activity requirement, a programme requirement, a prohibited activity requirement, a supervision requirement or an attendance centre requirement, the court may also require the licence to contain an electronic monitoring requirement unless the court is prevented from doing so by section 215(2) or 218(4).

(5) Before making a custody plus order requiring a licence to contain two or more different requirements falling within subsection (1), the court must consider whether, in the circumstances of the case, the requirements are compatible with each other.

Intermittent custody

183 Intermittent custody

(1) A court may, when passing a sentence of imprisonment for a term complying with subsection (4) –

    (a) specify the number of days that the offender must serve in prison under the sentence before being released on licence for the remainder of the term, and

(b) by order –
    (i)   specify periods during which the offender is to be released temporarily on licence before he has served that number of days in prison, and
    (ii)   require any licence to be granted subject to conditions requiring the offender's compliance during the licence periods with one or more requirements falling within section 182(1) and specified in the order.

(2) In this Part 'intermittent custody order' means an order under subsection (1)(b).

(3) In this Chapter –

'licence period', in relation to a term of imprisonment to which an intermittent custody order relates, means any period during which the offender is released on licence by virtue of subsection (1)(a) or (b)(i);
'the number of custodial days', in relation to a term of imprisonment to which an intermittent custody order relates, means the number of days specified under subsection (1)(a).

(4) The term of the sentence –

(a)   must be expressed in weeks,
(b)   must be at least 28 weeks,
(c)   must not be more than 51 weeks in respect of any one offence, and
(d)   must not exceed the maximum term permitted for the offence.

(5) The number of custodial days –

(a)   must be at least 14, and
(b)   in respect of any one offence, must not be more than 90.

(6) A court may not exercise its powers under subsection (1) unless the offender has expressed his willingness to serve the custodial part of the proposed sentence intermittently, during the parts of the sentence that are not to be licence periods.

(7) Where a court exercises its powers under subsection (1) in respect of two or more terms of imprisonment that are to be served consecutively –

(a)   the aggregate length of the terms of imprisonment must not be more than 65 weeks, and
(b)   the aggregate of the numbers of custodial days must not be more than 180.

(8) The Secretary of State may by order require a court, in specifying licence periods under subsection (1)(b)(i), to specify only –

(a)   periods of a prescribed duration,
(b)   periods beginning or ending at prescribed times, or
(c)   periods including, or not including, specified parts of the week.

(9) An intermittent custody order which specifies two or more requirements may, in relation to any requirement, refer to compliance within such licence period or periods, or part of a licence period, as is specified in the order.

184 Restrictions on power to make intermittent custody order

(1) A court may not make an intermittent custody order unless it has been notified by the Secretary of State that arrangements for implementing such orders are available in the area proposed to be specified in the intermittent custody order and the notice has not been withdrawn.

(2) The court may not make an intermittent custody order in respect of any offender unless –

(a) it has consulted an officer of a local probation board,
(b) it has received from the Secretary of State notification that suitable prison accommodation is available for the offender during the custodial periods, and
(c) it appears to the court that the offender will have suitable accommodation available to him during the licence periods.

(3) In this section 'custodial period', in relation to a sentence to which an intermittent custody order relates, means any part of the sentence that is not a licence period.

185 Intermittent custody: licence conditions

(1) Section 183(1)(b) has effect subject to section 218 and to the following provisions of Chapter 4 limiting the power to require the licence to contain particular requirements –

(a) section 199(3) (unpaid work requirement),
(b) section 201(3) and (4) (activity requirement),
(c) section 202(4) and (5) (programme requirement), and
(d) section 203(2) (prohibited activity requirement).

(2) Subsections (3) to (5) of section 182 have effect in relation to an intermittent custody order as they have effect in relation to a custody plus order.

186 Further provisions relating to intermittent custody

(1) Section 21 of the 1952 Act (expenses of conveyance to prison) does not apply in relation to the conveyance to prison at the end of any licence period of an offender to whom an intermittent custody order relates.

(2) The Secretary of State may pay to any offender to whom an intermittent custody order relates the whole or part of any expenses incurred by the offender in travelling to and from prison during licence periods.

(3) In section 49 of the 1952 Act (persons unlawfully at large) after subsection (4) there is inserted –

'(4A) For the purposes of this section a person shall also be deemed to be unlawfully at large if, having been temporarily released in pursuance of an intermittent custody order made under section 183 of the Criminal Justice Act 2003, he remains at large at a time when, by reason of the expiry of the period for which he was temporarily released, he is liable to be detained in pursuance of his sentence.'

(4) In section 23 of the Criminal Justice Act 1961 (c. 39) (prison rules), in subsection (3) for 'The days' there is substituted 'Subject to subsection (3A), the days' and after subsection (3) there is inserted –

'(3A) In relation to a prisoner to whom an intermittent custody order under section 183 of the Criminal Justice Act 2003 relates, the only days to which subsection (3) applies are Christmas Day, Good Friday and any day which under the Banking and Financial Dealings Act 1971 is a bank holiday in England and Wales.'

(5) In section 1 of the Prisoners (Return to Custody) Act 1995 (c. 16) (remaining at large after temporary release) after subsection (1) there is inserted –

'(1A) A person who has been temporarily released in pursuance of an intermittent custody order made under section 183 of the Criminal Justice Act 2003 is guilty of an offence if, without reasonable excuse, he remains unlawfully at large at any time after becoming so at large by virtue of the expiry of the period for which he was temporarily released.'

(6) In this section 'the 1952 Act' means the Prison Act 1952 (c. 52).

Further provision about custody plus orders and intermittent custody orders

187 Revocation or amendment of order

Schedule 10 (which contains provisions relating to the revocation or amendment of custody plus orders and the amendment of intermittent custody orders) shall have effect.

188 Transfer of custody plus orders and intermittent custody orders to Scotland or Northern Ireland

Schedule 11 (transfer of custody plus orders and intermittent custody orders to Scotland or Northern Ireland) shall have effect.

Suspended sentences

189 Suspended sentences of imprisonment

(1) A court which passes a sentence of imprisonment for a term of at least 28 weeks but not more than 51 weeks in accordance with section 181 may –

(a) order the offender to comply during a period specified for the purposes of this paragraph in the order (in this Chapter referred to as 'the supervision period') with one or more requirements falling within section 190(1) and specified in the order, and

(b) order that the sentence of imprisonment is not to take effect unless either –

   (i) during the supervision period the offender fails to comply with a requirement imposed under paragraph (a), or

   (ii) during a period specified in the order for the purposes of this sub-paragraph (in this Chapter referred to as 'the operational period') the offender commits in the United Kingdom another offence (whether or not punishable with imprisonment),

and (in either case) a court having power to do so subsequently orders under paragraph 8 of Schedule 12 that the original sentence is to take effect.

(2) Where two or more sentences imposed on the same occasion are to be served consecutively, the power conferred by subsection (1) is not exercisable in relation to any of them unless the aggregate of the terms of the sentences does not exceed 65 weeks.

(3) The supervision period and the operational period must each be a period of not less than six months and not more than two years beginning with the date of the order.

(4) The supervision period must not end later than the operational period.

(5) A court which passes a suspended sentence on any person for an offence may not impose a community sentence in his case in respect of that offence or any other offence of which he is convicted by or before the court or for which he is dealt with by the court.

(6) Subject to any provision to the contrary contained in the Criminal Justice Act 1967 (c. 80), the Sentencing Act or any other enactment passed or instrument made under any enactment after 31st December 1967, a suspended sentence which has not taken effect under paragraph 8 of Schedule 12 is to be treated as a sentence of imprisonment for the purposes of all enactments and instruments made under enactments.

(7) In this Part –

(a) 'suspended sentence order' means an order under subsection (1),
(b) 'suspended sentence' means a sentence to which a suspended sentence order relates, and
(c) 'community requirement', in relation to a suspended sentence order, means a requirement imposed under subsection (1)(a).

190 Imposition of requirements by suspended sentence order

(1) The requirements falling within this subsection are –

(a) an unpaid work requirement (as defined by section 199),
(b) an activity requirement (as defined by section 201),
(c) a programme requirement (as defined by section 202),
(d) a prohibited activity requirement (as defined by section 203),
(e) a curfew requirement (as defined by section 204),
(f) an exclusion requirement (as defined by section 205),
(g) a residence requirement (as defined by section 206),
(h) a mental health treatment requirement (as defined by section 207),
(i) a drug rehabilitation requirement (as defined by section 209),
(j) an alcohol treatment requirement (as defined by section 212),
(k) a supervision requirement (as defined by section 213), and
(l) in a case where the offender is aged under 25, an attendance centre requirement (as defined by section 214).

(2) Section 189(1)(a) has effect subject to section 218 and to the following provisions of Chapter 4 relating to particular requirements –

(a) section 199(3) (unpaid work requirement),
(b) section 201(3) and (4) (activity requirement),
(c) section 202(4) and (5) (programme requirement),
(d) section 203(2) (prohibited activity requirement),
(e) section 207(3) (mental health treatment requirement),
(f) section 209(2) (drug rehabilitation requirement), and
(g) section 212(2) and (3) (alcohol treatment requirement).

(3) Where the court makes a suspended sentence order imposing a curfew requirement or an exclusion requirement, it must also impose an electronic monitoring requirement (as defined by section 215) unless –

(a) the court is prevented from doing so by section 215(2) or 218(4), or
(b) in the particular circumstances of the case, it considers it inappropriate to do so.

(4) Where the court makes a suspended sentence order imposing an unpaid work requirement, an activity requirement, a programme requirement, a prohibited activity requirement, a residence requirement, a mental health treatment requirement, a drug rehabilitation requirement, an alcohol treatment requirement, a supervision requirement or an attendance centre requirement, the court may also impose an

electronic monitoring requirement unless the court is prevented from doing so by section 215(2) or 218(4).

(5) Before making a suspended sentence order imposing two or more different requirements falling within subsection (1), the court must consider whether, in the circumstances of the case, the requirements are compatible with each other.

191 Power to provide for review of suspended sentence order

(1) A suspended sentence order may –

    (a) provide for the order to be reviewed periodically at specified intervals,

    (b) provide for each review to be made, subject to section 192(4), at a hearing held for the purpose by the court responsible for the order (a 'review hearing'),

    (c) require the offender to attend each review hearing, and

    (d) provide for the responsible officer to make to the court responsible for the order, before each review, a report on the offender's progress in complying with the community requirements of the order.

(2) Subsection (1) does not apply in the case of an order imposing a drug rehabilitation requirement (provision for such a requirement to be subject to review being made by section 210).

(3) In this section references to the court responsible for a suspended sentence order are references –

    (a) where a court is specified in the order in accordance with subsection (4), to that court;

    (b) in any other case, to the court by which the order is made.

(4) Where the area specified in a suspended sentence order made by a magistrates' court is not the area for which the court acts, the court may, if it thinks fit, include in the order provision specifying for the purpose of subsection (3) a magistrates' court which acts for the area specified in the order.

(5) Where a suspended sentence order has been made on an appeal brought from the Crown Court or from the criminal division of the Court of Appeal, it is to be taken for the purposes of subsection (3)(b) to have been made by the Crown Court.

192 Periodic reviews of suspended sentence order

(1) At a review hearing (within the meaning of subsection (1) of section 191) the court may, after considering the responsible officer's report referred to in that subsection, amend the community requirements of the suspended sentence order, or any provision of the order which relates to those requirements.

(2) The court –

    (a) may not amend the community requirements of the order so as to impose a requirement of a different kind unless the offender expresses his willingness to comply with that requirement,

    (b) may not amend a mental health treatment requirement, a drug rehabilitation requirement or an alcohol treatment requirement unless the offender expresses his willingness to comply with the requirement as amended,

    (c) may amend the supervision period only if the period as amended complies with section 189(3) and (4),

    (d) may not amend the operational period of the suspended sentence, and

    (e)   except with the consent of the offender, may not amend the order while an appeal against the order is pending.

(3) For the purposes of subsection (2)(a) –

    (a)   a community requirement falling within any paragraph of section 190(1) is of the same kind as any other community requirement falling within that paragraph, and

    (b)   an electronic monitoring requirement is a community requirement of the same kind as any requirement falling within section 190(1) to which it relates.

(4) If before a review hearing is held at any review the court, after considering the responsible officer's report, is of the opinion that the offender's progress in complying with the community requirements of the order is satisfactory, it may order that no review hearing is to be held at that review; and if before a review hearing is held at any review, or at a review hearing, the court, after considering that report, is of that opinion, it may amend the suspended sentence order so as to provide for each subsequent review to be held without a hearing.

(5) If at a review held without a hearing the court, after considering the responsible officer's report, is of the opinion that the offender's progress under the order is no longer satisfactory, the court may require the offender to attend a hearing of the court at a specified time and place.

(6) If at a review hearing the court is of the opinion that the offender has without reasonable excuse failed to comply with any of the community requirements of the order, the court may adjourn the hearing for the purpose of dealing with the case under paragraph 8 of Schedule 12.

(7) At a review hearing the court may amend the suspended sentence order so as to vary the intervals specified under section 191(1).

(8) In this section any reference to the court, in relation to a review without a hearing, is to be read –

    (a)   in the case of the Crown Court, as a reference to a judge of the court, and

    (b)   in the case of a magistrates' court, as a reference to a justice of the peace acting for the commission area for which the court acts.

193 Breach, revocation or amendment of suspended sentence order, and effect of further conviction

Schedule 12 (which relates to the breach, revocation or amendment of the community requirements of suspended sentence orders, and to the effect of any further conviction) shall have effect.

194 Transfer of suspended sentence orders to Scotland or Northern Ireland

Schedule 13 (transfer of suspended sentence orders to Scotland or Northern Ireland) shall have effect.

Interpretation of Chapter

195 Interpretation of Chapter 3

In this Chapter –

'custodial period', in relation to a term of imprisonment imposed in accordance with section 181, has the meaning given by subsection (3)(a) of that section;

'licence period' –

(a)   in relation to a term of imprisonment imposed in accordance with section 181, has the meaning given by subsection (3)(b) of that section, and

(b)   in relation to a term of imprisonment to which an intermittent custody order relates, has the meaning given by section 183(3);

'the number of custodial days', in relation to a term of imprisonment to which an intermittent custody order relates, has the meaning given by section 183(3);

'operational period' and 'supervision period', in relation to a suspended sentence, are to be read in accordance with section 189(1);

'sentence of imprisonment' does not include a committal for contempt of court or any kindred offence.

CHAPTER 4

FURTHER PROVISIONS ABOUT ORDERS UNDER CHAPTERS 2 AND 3

Introductory

196 Meaning of 'relevant order'

(1) In this Chapter 'relevant order' means –

(a)   a community order,
(b)   a custody plus order,
(c)   a suspended sentence order, or
(d)   an intermittent custody order.

(2) In this Chapter any reference to a requirement being imposed by, or included in, a relevant order is, in relation to a custody plus order or an intermittent custody order, a reference to compliance with the requirement being required by the order to be a condition of a licence.

197 Meaning of 'the responsible officer'

(1) For the purposes of this Part, 'the responsible officer', in relation to an offender to whom a relevant order relates, means –

(a)   in a case where the order –

(i)   imposes a curfew requirement or an exclusion requirement but no other requirement mentioned in section 177(1) or, as the case requires, section 182(1) or 190(1), and

(ii)   imposes an electronic monitoring requirement,

the person who under section 215(3) is responsible for the electronic monitoring required by the order;

(b)   in a case where the offender is aged 18 or over and the only requirement imposed by the order is an attendance centre requirement, the officer in charge of the attendance centre in question;

    (c) in any other case, the qualifying officer who, as respects the offender, is for the time being responsible for discharging the functions conferred by this Part on the responsible officer.

(2) The following are qualifying officers for the purposes of subsection (1)(c) –

    (a) in a case where the offender is aged under 18 at the time when the relevant order is made, an officer of a local probation board appointed for or assigned to the petty sessions area for the time being specified in the order or a member of a youth offending team established by a local authority for the time being specified in the order;

    (b) in any other case, an officer of a local probation board appointed for or assigned to the petty sessions area for the time being specified in the order.

(3) The Secretary of State may by order –

    (a) amend subsections (1) and (2), and

    (b) make any other amendments of this Part that appear to him to be necessary or expedient in consequence of any amendment made by virtue of paragraph (a).

(4) An order under subsection (3) may, in particular, provide for the court to determine which of two or more descriptions of 'responsible officer' is to apply in relation to any relevant order.

198 Duties of responsible officer

(1) Where a relevant order has effect, it is the duty of the responsible officer –

    (a) to make any arrangements that are necessary in connection with the requirements imposed by the order,

    (b) to promote the offender's compliance with those requirements, and

    (c) where appropriate, to take steps to enforce those requirements.

(2) In this section 'responsible officer' does not include a person falling within section 197(1)(a).

Requirements available in case of all offenders

199 Unpaid work requirement

(1) In this Part 'unpaid work requirement', in relation to a relevant order, means a requirement that the offender must perform unpaid work in accordance with section 200.

(2) The number of hours which a person may be required to work under an unpaid work requirement must be specified in the relevant order and must be in the aggregate –

    (a) not less than 40, and

    (b) not more than 300.

(3) A court may not impose an unpaid work requirement in respect of an offender unless after hearing (if the courts thinks necessary) an appropriate officer, the court is satisfied that the offender is a suitable person to perform work under such a requirement.

(4) In subsection (3) 'an appropriate officer' means –

    (a) in the case of an offender aged 18 or over, an officer of a local probation board, and

(b) in the case of an offender aged under 18, an officer of a local probation board, a social worker of a local authority social services department or a member of a youth offending team.

(5) Where the court makes relevant orders in respect of two or more offences of which the offender has been convicted on the same occasion and includes unpaid work requirements in each of them, the court may direct that the hours of work specified in any of those requirements is to be concurrent with or additional to those specified in any other of those orders, but so that the total number of hours which are not concurrent does not exceed the maximum specified in subsection (2)(b).

200 Obligations of person subject to unpaid work requirement

(1) An offender in respect of whom an unpaid work requirement of a relevant order is in force must perform for the number of hours specified in the order such work at such times as he may be instructed by the responsible officer.

(2) Subject to paragraph 20 of Schedule 8 and paragraph 18 of Schedule 12 (power to extend order), the work required to be performed under an unpaid work requirement of a community order or a suspended sentence order must be performed during a period of twelve months.

(3) Unless revoked, a community order imposing an unpaid work requirement remains in force until the offender has worked under it for the number of hours specified in it.

(4) Where an unpaid work requirement is imposed by a suspended sentence order, the supervision period as defined by section 189(1)(a) continues until the offender has worked under the order for the number of hours specified in the order, but does not continue beyond the end of the operational period as defined by section 189(1)(b)(ii).

201 Activity requirement

(1) In this Part 'activity requirement', in relation to a relevant order, means a requirement that the offender must do either or both of the following –

(a) present himself to a person or persons specified in the relevant order at a place or places so specified on such number of days as may be so specified;
(b) participate in activities specified in the order on such number of days as may be so specified.

(2) The specified activities may consist of or include activities whose purpose is that of reparation, such as activities involving contact between offenders and persons affected by their offences.

(3) A court may not include an activity requirement in a relevant order unless –

(a) it has consulted –
  (i) in the case of an offender aged 18 or over, an officer of a local probation board,
  (ii) in the case of an offender aged under 18, either an officer of a local probation board or a member of a youth offending team, and
(b) it is satisfied that it is feasible to secure compliance with the requirement.

(4) A court may not include an activity requirement in a relevant order if compliance with that requirement would involve the co-operation of a person other than the offender and the offender's responsible officer, unless that other person consents to its inclusion.

(5) The aggregate of the number of days specified under subsection (1)(a) and (b) must not exceed 60.

(6) A requirement such as is mentioned in subsection (1)(a) operates to require the offender –

(a) in accordance with instructions given by his responsible officer, to present himself at a place or places on the number of days specified in the order, and
(b) while at any place, to comply with instructions given by, or under the authority of, the person in charge of that place.

(7) A place specified under subsection (1)(a) must be –

(a) a community rehabilitation centre, or
(b) a place that has been approved by the local probation board for the area in which the premises are situated as providing facilities suitable for persons subject to activity requirements.

(8) Where the place specified under subsection (1)(a) is a community rehabilitation centre, the reference in subsection (6)(a) to the offender presenting himself at the specified place includes a reference to him presenting himself elsewhere than at the centre for the purpose of participating in activities in accordance with instructions given by, or under the authority of, the person in charge of the centre.

(9) A requirement to participate in activities operates to require the offender –

(a) in accordance with instructions given by his responsible officer, to participate in activities on the number of days specified in the order, and
(b) while participating, to comply with instructions given by, or under the authority of, the person in charge of the activities.

(10) In this section 'community rehabilitation centre' means premises –

(a) at which non-residential facilities are provided for use in connection with the rehabilitation of offenders, and
(b) which are for the time being approved by the Secretary of State as providing facilities suitable for persons subject to relevant orders.

202 Programme requirement

(1) In this Part 'programme requirement', in relation to a relevant order, means a requirement that the offender must participate in an accredited programme specified in the order at a place so specified on such number of days as may be so specified.

(2) In this Part 'accredited programme' means a programme that is for the time being accredited by the accreditation body.

(3) In this section –

(a) 'programme' means a systematic set of activities, and
(b) 'the accreditation body' means such body as the Secretary of State may designate for the purposes of this section by order.

(4) A court may not include a programme requirement in a relevant order unless –

(a) the accredited programme which the court proposes to specify in the order has been recommended to the court as being suitable for the offender –
    (i) in the case of an offender aged 18 or over, by an officer of a local probation board, or

(ii)   in the case of an offender aged under 18, either by an officer of a local probation board or by a member of a youth offending team, and

(b)   the court is satisfied that the programme is (or, where the relevant order is a custody plus order or an intermittent custody order, will be) available at the place proposed to be specified.

(5) A court may not include a programme requirement in a relevant order if compliance with that requirement would involve the co-operation of a person other than the offender and the offender's responsible officer, unless that other person consents to its inclusion.

(6) A requirement to attend an accredited programme operates to require the offender –

(a)   in accordance with instructions given by the responsible officer, to participate in the accredited programme at the place specified in the order on the number of days specified in the order, and

(b)   while at that place, to comply with instructions given by, or under the authority of, the person in charge of the programme.

(7) A place specified in an order must be a place that has been approved by the local probation board for the area in which the premises are situated as providing facilities suitable for persons subject to programme requirements.

203 Prohibited activity requirement

(1) In this Part 'prohibited activity requirement', in relation to a relevant order, means a requirement that the offender must refrain from participating in activities specified in the order –

(a)   on a day or days so specified, or

(b)   during a period so specified.

(2) A court may not include a prohibited activity requirement in a relevant order unless it has consulted –

(a)   in the case of an offender aged 18 or over, an officer of a local probation board;

(b)   in the case of an offender aged under 18, either an officer of a local probation board or a member of a youth offending team.

(3) The requirements that may by virtue of this section be included in a relevant order include a requirement that the offender does not possess, use or carry a firearm within the meaning of the Firearms Act 1968 (c. 27).

204 Curfew requirement

(1) In this Part 'curfew requirement', in relation to a relevant order, means a requirement that the offender must remain, for periods specified in the relevant order, at a place so specified.

(2) A relevant order imposing a curfew requirement may specify different places or different periods for different days, but may not specify periods which amount to less than two hours or more than twelve hours in any day.

(3) A community order or suspended sentence order which imposes a curfew requirement may not specify periods which fall outside the period of six months beginning with the day on which it is made.

(4) A custody plus order which imposes a curfew requirement may not specify a period which falls outside the period of six months beginning with the first day of the licence period as defined by section 181(3)(b).

(5) An intermittent custody order which imposes a curfew requirement must not specify a period if to do so would cause the aggregate number of days on which the offender is subject to the requirement for any part of the day to exceed 182.

(6) Before making a relevant order imposing a curfew requirement, the court must obtain and consider information about the place proposed to be specified in the order (including information as to the attitude of persons likely to be affected by the enforced presence there of the offender).

205 Exclusion requirement

(1) In this Part 'exclusion requirement', in relation to a relevant order, means a provision prohibiting the offender from entering a place specified in the order for a period so specified.

(2) Where the relevant order is a community order, the period specified must not be more than two years.

(3) An exclusion requirement –

(a) may provide for the prohibition to operate only during the periods specified in the order, and
(b) may specify different places for different periods or days.

(4) In this section 'place' includes an area.

206 Residence requirement

(1) In this Part, 'residence requirement', in relation to a community order or a suspended sentence order, means a requirement that, during a period specified in the relevant order, the offender must reside at a place specified in the order.

(2) If the order so provides, a residence requirement does not prohibit the offender from residing, with the prior approval of the responsible officer, at a place other than that specified in the order.

(3) Before making a community order or suspended sentence order containing a residence requirement, the court must consider the home surroundings of the offender.

(4) A court may not specify a hostel or other institution as the place where an offender must reside, except on the recommendation of an officer of a local probation board.

207 Mental health treatment requirement

(1) In this Part, 'mental health treatment requirement', in relation to a community order or suspended sentence order, means a requirement that the offender must submit, during a period or periods specified in the order, to treatment by or under the direction of a registered medical practitioner or a chartered psychologist (or both, for different periods) with a view to the improvement of the offender's mental condition.

(2) The treatment required must be such one of the following kinds of treatment as may be specified in the relevant order –

(a) treatment as a resident patient in an independent hospital or care home within the meaning of the Care Standards Act 2000 (c. 14) or a hospital within the meaning of the Mental Health Act 1983 (c. 20), but not in hospital premises where high security psychiatric services within the meaning of that Act are provided;

(b) treatment as a non-resident patient at such institution or place as may be specified in the order;

(c) treatment by or under the direction of such registered medical practitioner or chartered psychologist (or both) as may be so specified;

but the nature of the treatment is not to be specified in the order except as mentioned in paragraph (a), (b) or (c).

(3) A court may not by virtue of this section include a mental health treatment requirement in a relevant order unless –

(a) the court is satisfied, on the evidence of a registered medical practitioner approved for the purposes of section 12 of the Mental Health Act 1983, that the mental condition of the offender –
 (i) is such as requires and may be susceptible to treatment, but
 (ii) is not such as to warrant the making of a hospital order or guardianship order within the meaning of that Act;

(b) the court is also satisfied that arrangements have been or can be made for the treatment intended to be specified in the order (including arrangements for the reception of the offender where he is to be required to submit to treatment as a resident patient); and

(c) the offender has expressed his willingness to comply with such a requirement.

(4) While the offender is under treatment as a resident patient in pursuance of a mental health requirement of a relevant order, his responsible officer shall carry out the supervision of the offender to such extent only as may be necessary for the purpose of the revocation or amendment of the order.

(5) Subsections (2) and (3) of section 54 of the Mental Health Act 1983 (c. 20) have effect with respect to proof for the purposes of subsection (3)(a) of an offender's mental condition as they have effect with respect to proof of an offender's mental condition for the purposes of section 37(2)(a) of that Act.

(6) In this section and section 208, 'chartered psychologist' means a person for the time being listed in the British Psychological Society's Register of Chartered Psychologists.

208 Mental health treatment at place other than that specified in order

(1) Where the medical practitioner or chartered psychologist by whom or under whose direction an offender is being treated for his mental condition in pursuance of a mental health treatment requirement is of the opinion that part of the treatment can be better or more conveniently given in or at an institution or place which –

(a) is not specified in the relevant order, and

(b) is one in or at which the treatment of the offender will be given by or under the direction of a registered medical practitioner or chartered psychologist,

he may, with the consent of the offender, make arrangements for him to be treated accordingly.

(2) Such arrangements as are mentioned in subsection (1) may provide for the offender to receive part of his treatment as a resident patient in an institution or place

notwithstanding that the institution or place is not one which could have been specified for that purpose in the relevant order.

(3) Where any such arrangements as are mentioned in subsection (1) are made for the treatment of an offender –

(a) the medical practitioner or chartered psychologist by whom the arrangements are made shall give notice in writing to the offender's responsible officer, specifying the institution or place in or at which the treatment is to be carried out; and

(b) the treatment provided for by the arrangements shall be deemed to be treatment to which he is required to submit in pursuance of the relevant order.

209 Drug rehabilitation requirement

(1) In this Part 'drug rehabilitation requirement', in relation to a community order or suspended sentence order, means a requirement that during a period specified in the order ('the treatment and testing period') the offender –

(a) must submit to treatment by or under the direction of a specified person having the necessary qualifications or experience with a view to the reduction or elimination of the offender's dependency on or propensity to misuse drugs, and

(b) for the purpose of ascertaining whether he has any drug in his body during that period, must provide samples of such description as may be so determined, at such times or in such circumstances as may (subject to the provisions of the order) be determined by the responsible officer or by the person specified as the person by or under whose direction the treatment is to be provided.

(2) A court may not impose a drug rehabilitation requirement unless –

(a) it is satisfied –
   (i) that the offender is dependent on, or has a propensity to misuse, drugs, and
   (ii) that his dependency or propensity is such as requires and may be susceptible to treatment,

(b) it is also satisfied that arrangements have been or can be made for the treatment intended to be specified in the order (including arrangements for the reception of the offender where he is to be required to submit to treatment as a resident),

(c) the requirement has been recommended to the court as being suitable for the offender –
   (i) in the case of an offender aged 18 or over, by an officer of a local probation board, or
   (ii) in the case of an offender aged under 18, either by an officer of a local probation board or by a member of a youth offending team, and

(d) the offender expresses his willingness to comply with the requirement.

(3) The treatment and testing period must be at least six months.

(4) The required treatment for any particular period must be –

(a) treatment as a resident in such institution or place as may be specified in the order, or

(b) treatment as a non-resident in or at such institution or place, and at such intervals, as may be so specified;

but the nature of the treatment is not to be specified in the order except as mentioned in paragraph (a) or (b) above.

(5) The function of making a determination as to the provision of samples under provision included in the community order or suspended sentence order by virtue of subsection (1)(b) is to be exercised in accordance with guidance given from time to time by the Secretary of State.

(6) A community order or suspended sentence order imposing a drug rehabilitation requirement must provide that the results of tests carried out on any samples provided by the offender in pursuance of the requirement to a person other than the responsible officer are to be communicated to the responsible officer.

(7) In this section 'drug' means a controlled drug as defined by section 2 of the Misuse of Drugs Act 1971 (c. 38).

210 Drug rehabilitation requirement: provision for review by court

(1) A community order or suspended sentence order imposing a drug rehabilitation requirement may (and must if the treatment and testing period is more than 12 months) –

(a) provide for the requirement to be reviewed periodically at intervals of not less than one month,

(b) provide for each review of the requirement to be made, subject to section 211(6), at a hearing held for the purpose by the court responsible for the order (a 'review hearing'),

(c) require the offender to attend each review hearing,

(d) provide for the responsible officer to make to the court responsible for the order, before each review, a report in writing on the offender's progress under the requirement, and

(e) provide for each such report to include the test results communicated to the responsible officer under section 209(6) or otherwise and the views of the treatment provider as to the treatment and testing of the offender.

(2) In this section references to the court responsible for a community order or suspended sentence order imposing a drug rehabilitation requirement are references –

(a) where a court is specified in the order in accordance with subsection (3), to that court;

(b) in any other case, to the court by which the order is made.

(3) Where the area specified in a community order or suspended sentence order which is made by a magistrates' court and imposes a drug rehabilitation requirement is not the area for which the court acts, the court may, if it thinks fit, include in the order provision specifying for the purposes of subsection (2) a magistrates' court which acts for the area specified in the order.

(4) Where a community order or suspended sentence order imposing a drug rehabilitation requirement has been made on an appeal brought from the Crown Court or from the criminal division of the Court of Appeal, for the purposes of subsection (2)(b) it shall be taken to have been made by the Crown Court.

211 Periodic review of drug rehabilitation requirement

(1) At a review hearing (within the meaning given by subsection (1) of section 210) the court may, after considering the responsible officer's report referred to in that subsection, amend the community order or suspended sentence order, so far as it relates to the drug rehabilitation requirement.

(2) The court –

(a) may not amend the drug rehabilitation requirement unless the offender expresses his willingness to comply with the requirement as amended,

(b) may not amend any provision of the order so as to reduce the period for which the drug rehabilitation requirement has effect below the minimum specified in section 209(3), and

(c) except with the consent of the offender, may not amend any requirement or provision of the order while an appeal against the order is pending.

(3) If the offender fails to express his willingness to comply with the drug rehabilitation requirement as proposed to be amended by the court, the court may –

(a) revoke the community order, or the suspended sentence order and the suspended sentence to which it relates, and

(b) deal with him, for the offence in respect of which the order was made, in any way in which he could have been dealt with for that offence by the court which made the order if the order had not been made.

(4) In dealing with the offender under subsection (3)(b), the court –

(a) shall take into account the extent to which the offender has complied with the requirements of the order, and

(b) may impose a custodial sentence (where the order was made in respect of an offence punishable with such a sentence) notwithstanding anything in section 152(2).

(5) Where the order is a community order made by a magistrates' court in the case of an offender under 18 years of age in respect of an offence triable only on indictment in the case of an adult, any powers exercisable under subsection (3)(b) in respect of the offender after he attains the age of 18 are powers to do either or both of the following –

(a) to impose a fine not exceeding £5,000 for the offence in respect of which the order was made;

(b) to deal with the offender for that offence in any way in which the court could deal with him if it had just convicted him of an offence punishable with imprisonment for a term not exceeding twelve months.

(6) If at a review hearing (as defined by section 210(1)(b)) the court, after considering the responsible officer's report, is of the opinion that the offender's progress under the requirement is satisfactory, the court may so amend the order as to provide for each subsequent review to be made by the court without a hearing.

(7) If at a review without a hearing the court, after considering the responsible officer's report, is of the opinion that the offender's progress under the requirement is no longer satisfactory, the court may require the offender to attend a hearing of the court at a specified time and place.

(8) At that hearing the court, after considering that report, may –

(a) exercise the powers conferred by this section as if the hearing were a review hearing, and

(b) so amend the order as to provide for each subsequent review to be made at a review hearing.

(9) In this section any reference to the court, in relation to a review without a hearing, is to be read –

(a)   in the case of the Crown Court, as a reference to a judge of the court;
(b)   in the case of a magistrates' court, as a reference to a justice of the peace acting for the commission area for which the court acts.

212 Alcohol treatment requirement

(1) In this Part 'alcohol treatment requirement', in relation to a community order or suspended sentence order, means a requirement that the offender must submit during a period specified in the order to treatment by or under the direction of a specified person having the necessary qualifications or experience with a view to the reduction or elimination of the offender's dependency on alcohol.

(2) A court may not impose an alcohol treatment requirement in respect of an offender unless it is satisfied –

(a)   that he is dependent on alcohol,
(b)   that his dependency is such as requires and may be susceptible to treatment, and
(c)   that arrangements have been or can be made for the treatment intended to be specified in the order (including arrangements for the reception of the offender where he is to be required to submit to treatment as a resident).

(3) A court may not impose an alcohol treatment requirement unless the offender expresses his willingness to comply with its requirements.

(4) The period for which the alcohol treatment requirement has effect must be not less than six months.

(5) The treatment required by an alcohol treatment requirement for any particular period must be –

(a)   treatment as a resident in such institution or place as may be specified in the order,
(b)   treatment as a non-resident in or at such institution or place, and at such intervals, as may be so specified, or
(c)   treatment by or under the direction of such person having the necessary qualification or experience as may be so specified;

but the nature of the treatment shall not be specified in the order except as mentioned in paragraph (a), (b) or (c) above.

213 Supervision requirement

(1) In this Part 'supervision requirement', in relation to a relevant order, means a requirement that, during the relevant period, the offender must attend appointments with the responsible officer or another person determined by the responsible officer, at such time and place as may be determined by the officer.

(2) The purpose for which a supervision requirement may be imposed is that of promoting the offender's rehabilitation.

(3) In subsection (1) 'the relevant period' means –

(a)   in relation to a community order, the period for which the community order remains in force,
(b)   in relation to a custody plus order, the licence period as defined by section 181(3)(b),
(c)   in relation to an intermittent custody order, the licence periods as defined by section 183(3), and

(d) in relation to a suspended sentence order, the supervision period as defined by section 189(1)(a).

Requirements available only in case of offenders aged under 25

214 Attendance centre requirement

(1) In this Part 'attendance centre requirement', in relation to a relevant order, means a requirement that the offender must attend at an attendance centre specified in the relevant order for such number of hours as may be so specified.

(2) The aggregate number of hours for which the offender may be required to attend at an attendance centre must not be less than 12 or more than 36.

(3) The court may not impose an attendance centre requirement unless the court is satisfied that the attendance centre to be specified in it is reasonably accessible to the offender concerned, having regard to the means of access available to him and any other circumstances.

(4) The first time at which the offender is required to attend at the attendance centre is a time notified to the offender by the responsible officer.

(5) The subsequent hours are to be fixed by the officer in charge of the centre, having regard to the offender's circumstances.

(6) An offender may not be required under this section to attend at an attendance centre on more than one occasion on any day, or for more than three hours on any occasion.

Electronic monitoring

215 Electronic monitoring requirement

(1) In this Part 'electronic monitoring requirement', in relation to a relevant order, means a requirement for securing the electronic monitoring of the offender's compliance with other requirements imposed by the order during a period specified in the order, or determined by the responsible officer in accordance with the relevant order.

(2) Where –

(a) it is proposed to include in a relevant order a requirement for securing electronic monitoring in accordance with this section, but
(b) there is a person (other than the offender) without whose co-operation it will not be practicable to secure the monitoring,

the requirement may not be included in the order without that person's consent.

(3) A relevant order which includes an electronic monitoring requirement must include provision for making a person responsible for the monitoring; and a person who is made so responsible must be of a description specified in an order made by the Secretary of State.

(4) Where an electronic monitoring requirement is required to take effect during a period determined by the responsible officer in accordance with the relevant order, the responsible officer must, before the beginning of that period, notify –

(a) the offender,
(b) the person responsible for the monitoring, and

(c) any person falling within subsection (2)(b),

of the time when the period is to begin.

Provisions applying to relevant orders generally

216 Petty sessions area to be specified in relevant order

(1) A community order or suspended sentence order must specify the petty sessions area in which the offender resides or will reside.

(2) A custody plus order or an intermittent custody order must specify the petty sessions area in which the offender will reside –

    (a) in the case of a custody plus order, during the licence period as defined by section 181(3)(b), or

    (b) in the case of an intermittent custody order, during the licence periods as defined by section 183(3).

217 Requirement to avoid conflict with religious beliefs, etc.

(1) The court must ensure, as far as practicable, that any requirement imposed by a relevant order is such as to avoid –

    (a) any conflict with the offender's religious beliefs or with the requirements of any other relevant order to which he may be subject; and

    (b) any interference with the times, if any, at which he normally works or attends school or any other educational establishment.

(2) The responsible officer in relation to an offender to whom a relevant order relates must ensure, as far as practicable, that any instruction given or requirement imposed by him in pursuance of the order is such as to avoid the conflict or interference mentioned in subsection (1).

(3) The Secretary of State may by order provide that subsection (1) or (2) is to have effect with such additional restrictions as may be specified in the order.

218 Availability of arrangements in local area

(1) A court may not include an unpaid work requirement in a relevant order unless the court is satisfied that provision for the offender to work under such a requirement can be made under the arrangements for persons to perform work under such a requirement which exist in the petty sessions area in which he resides or will reside.

(2) A court may not include an activity requirement in a relevant order unless the court is satisfied that provision for the offender to participate in the activities proposed to be specified in the order can be made under the arrangements for persons to participate in such activities which exist in the petty sessions area in which he resides or will reside.

(3) A court may not include an attendance centre requirement in a relevant order in respect of an offender unless the court has been notified by the Secretary of State that an attendance centre is available for persons of his description.

(4) A court may not include an electronic monitoring requirement in a relevant order in respect of an offender unless the court –

(a) has been notified by the Secretary of State that electronic monitoring arrangements are available in the relevant areas mentioned in subsections (5) to (7), and

(b) is satisfied that the necessary provision can be made under those arrangements.

(5) In the case of a relevant order containing a curfew requirement or an exclusion requirement, the relevant area for the purposes of subsection (4) is the area in which the place proposed to be specified in the order is situated.

(6) In the case of a relevant order containing an attendance centre requirement, the relevant area for the purposes of subsection (4) is the area in which the attendance centre proposed to be specified in the order is situated.

(7) In the case of any other relevant order, the relevant area for the purposes of subsection (4) is the petty sessions area proposed to be specified in the order.

(8) In subsection (5) 'place', in relation to an exclusion requirement, has the same meaning as in section 205.

219 Provision of copies of relevant orders

(1) The court by which any relevant order is made must forthwith provide copies of the order –

(a) to the offender,

(b) if the offender is aged 18 or over, to an officer of a local probation board assigned to the court,

(c) if the offender is aged 16 or 17, to an officer of a local probation board assigned to the court or to a member of a youth offending team assigned to the court, and

(d) where the order specifies a petty sessions area for which the court making the order does not act, to the local probation board acting for that area.

(2) Where a relevant order imposes any requirement specified in the first column of Schedule 14, the court by which the order is made must also forthwith provide the person specified in relation to that requirement in the second column of that Schedule with a copy of so much of the order as relates to that requirement.

(3) Where a relevant order specifies a petty sessions area for which the court making the order does not act, the court making the order must provide to the magistrates's court acting for that area –

(a) a copy of the order, and

(b) such documents and information relating to the case as it considers likely to be of assistance to a court acting for that area in the exercise of its functions in relation to the order.

220 Duty of offender to keep in touch with responsible officer

(1) An offender in respect of whom a community order or a suspended sentence order is in force –

(a) must keep in touch with the responsible officer in accordance with such instructions as he may from time to time be given by that officer, and

(b) must notify him of any change of address.

(2) The obligation imposed by subsection (1) is enforceable as if it were a requirement imposed by the order.

Powers of Secretary of State

221 Provision of attendance centres

(1) The Secretary of State may continue to provide attendance centres.

(2) In this Part 'attendance centre' means a place at which offenders aged under 25 may be required to attend and be given under supervision appropriate occupation or instruction in pursuance of –

  (a) attendance centre requirements of relevant orders, or
  (b) attendance centre orders under section 60 of the Sentencing Act.

(3) For the purpose of providing attendance centres, the Secretary of State may make arrangements with any local authority or police authority for the use of premises of that authority.

222 Rules

(1) The Secretary of State may make rules for regulating –

  (a) the supervision of persons who are subject to relevant orders,
  (b) without prejudice to the generality of paragraph (a), the functions of responsible officers in relation to offenders subject to relevant orders,
  (c) the arrangements to be made by local probation boards for persons subject to unpaid work requirements to perform work and the performance of such work,
  (d) the provision and carrying on of attendance centres and community rehabilitation centres,
  (e) the attendance of persons subject to activity requirements or attendance centre requirements at the places at which they are required to attend, including hours of attendance, reckoning days of attendance and the keeping of attendance records,
  (f) electronic monitoring in pursuance of an electronic monitoring requirement, and
  (g) without prejudice to the generality of paragraph (f), the functions of persons made responsible for securing electronic monitoring in pursuance of such a requirement.

(2) Rules under subsection (1)(c) may, in particular, make provision –

  (a) limiting the number of hours of work to be done by a person on any one day,
  (b) as to the reckoning of hours worked and the keeping of work records, and
  (c) for the payment of travelling and other expenses in connection with the performance of work.

223 Power to amend limits

(1) The Secretary of State may by order amend –

  (a) subsection (2) of section 199 (unpaid work requirement), or
  (b) subsection (2) of section 204 (curfew requirement),
by substituting, for the maximum number of hours for the time being specified in that subsection, such other number of hours as may be specified in the order.

(2) The Secretary of State may by order amend any of the provisions mentioned in subsection (3) by substituting, for any period for the time being specified in the provision, such other period as may be specified in the order.

(3) Those provisions are –

(a) section 204(3) (curfew requirement);
(b) section 205(2) (exclusion requirement);
(c) section 209(3) (drug rehabilitation requirement);
(d) section 212(4) (alcohol treatment requirement).

CHAPTER 5

DANGEROUS OFFENDERS

224 Meaning of 'specified offence' etc.

(1) An offence is a 'specified offence' for the purposes of this Chapter if it is a specified violent offence or a specified sexual offence.

(2) An offence is a 'serious offence' for the purposes of this Chapter if and only if –

(a) it is a specified offence, and
(b) it is, apart from section 225, punishable in the case of a person aged 18 or over by –
  (i)   imprisonment for life, or
  (ii)   imprisonment for a determinate period of ten years or more.

(3) In this Chapter –

'relevant offence' has the meaning given by section 229(4);
'serious harm' means death or serious personal injury, whether physical or psychological;
'specified violent offence' means an offence specified in Part 1 of Schedule 15;
'specified sexual offence' means an offence specified in Part 2 of that Schedule.

225 Life sentence or imprisonment for public protection for serious offences

(1) This section applies where –

(a) a person aged 18 or over is convicted of a serious offence committed after the commencement of this section, and
(b) the court is of the opinion that there is a significant risk to members of the public of serious harm occasioned by the commission by him of further specified offences.

(2) If –

(a) the offence is one in respect of which the offender would apart from this section be liable to imprisonment for life, and
(b) the court considers that the seriousness of the offence, or of the offence and one or more offences associated with it, is such as to justify the imposition of a sentence of imprisonment for life,

the court must impose a sentence of imprisonment for life.

(3) In a case not falling within subsection (2), the court must impose a sentence of imprisonment for public protection.

(4) A sentence of imprisonment for public protection is a sentence of imprisonment for an indeterminate period, subject to the provisions of Chapter 2 of Part 2 of the Crime (Sentences) Act 1997 (c. 43) as to the release of prisoners and duration of licences.

(5) An offence the sentence for which is imposed under this section is not to be regarded as an offence the sentence for which is fixed by law.

226 Detention for life or detention for public protection for serious offences committed by those under 18

(1) This section applies where –

(a) a person aged under 18 is convicted of a serious offence committed after the commencement of this section, and

(b) the court is of the opinion that there is a significant risk to members of the public of serious harm occasioned by the commission by him of further specified offences.

(2) If –

(a) the offence is one in respect of which the offender would apart from this section be liable to a sentence of detention for life under section 91 of the Sentencing Act, and

(b) the court considers that the seriousness of the offence, or of the offence and one or more offences associated with it, is such as to justify the imposition of a sentence of detention for life,

the court must impose a sentence of detention for life under that section.

(3) If, in a case not falling within subsection (2), the court considers that an extended sentence under section 228 would not be adequate for the purpose of protecting the public from serious harm occasioned by the commission by the offender of further specified offences, the court must impose a sentence of detention for public protection.

(4) A sentence of detention for public protection is a sentence of detention for an indeterminate period, subject to the provisions of Chapter 2 of Part 2 of the Crime (Sentences) Act 1997 (c. 43) as to the release of prisoners and duration of licences.

(5) An offence the sentence for which is imposed under this section is not to be regarded as an offence the sentence for which is fixed by law.

227 Extended sentence for certain violent or sexual offences: persons 18 or over

(1) This section applies where –

(a) a person aged 18 or over is convicted of a specified offence, other than a serious offence, committed after the commencement of this section, and

(b) the court considers that there is a significant risk to members of the public of serious harm occasioned by the commission by the offender of further specified offences.

(2) The court must impose on the offender an extended sentence of imprisonment, that is to say, a sentence of imprisonment the term of which is equal to the aggregate of –

(a) the appropriate custodial term, and

(b) a further period ('the extension period') for which the offender is to be subject to a licence and which is of such length as the court considers necessary for the purpose of protecting members of the public from serious harm occasioned by the commission by him of further specified offences.

(3) In subsection (2) 'the appropriate custodial term' means a term of imprisonment (not exceeding the maximum term permitted for the offence) which –

(a) is the term that would (apart from this section) be imposed in compliance with section 153(2), or

(b) where the term that would be so imposed is a term of less than 12 months, is a term of 12 months.

(4) The extension period must not exceed –

(a) five years in the case of a specified violent offence, and
(b) eight years in the case of a specified sexual offence.

(5) The term of an extended sentence of imprisonment passed under this section in respect of an offence must not exceed the maximum term permitted for the offence.

228 Extended sentence for certain violent or sexual offences: persons under 18

(1) This section applies where –

(a) a person aged under 18 is convicted of a specified offence committed after the commencement of this section, and
(b) the court considers –
    (i) that there is a significant risk to members of the public of serious harm occasioned by the commission by the offender of further specified offences, and
    (ii) where the specified offence is a serious offence, that the case is not one in which the court is required by section 226(2) to impose a sentence of detention for life under section 91 of the Sentencing Act or by section 226(3) to impose a sentence of detention for public protection.

(2) The court must impose on the offender an extended sentence of detention, that is to say, a sentence of detention the term of which is equal to the aggregate of –

(a) the appropriate custodial term, and
(b) a further period ('the extension period') for which the offender is to be subject to a licence and which is of such length as the court considers necessary for the purpose of protecting members of the public from serious harm occasioned by the commission by him of further specified offences.

(3) In subsection (2) 'the appropriate custodial term' means such term as the court considers appropriate, which –

(a) must be at least 12 months, and
(b) must not exceed the maximum term of imprisonment permitted for the offence.

(4) The extension period must not exceed –

(a) five years in the case of a specified violent offence, and
(b) eight years in the case of a specified sexual offence.

(5) The term of an extended sentence of detention passed under this section in respect of an offence must not exceed the maximum term of imprisonment permitted for the offence.

(6) Any reference in this section to the maximum term of imprisonment permitted for an offence is a reference to the maximum term of imprisonment that is, apart from section 225, permitted for the offence in the case of a person aged 18 or over.

229 The assessment of dangerousness

(1) This section applies where –

    (a) a person has been convicted of a specified offence, and

    (b) it falls to a court to assess under any of sections 225 to 228 whether there is a significant risk to members of the public of serious harm occasioned by the commission by him of further such offences.

(2) If at the time when that offence was committed the offender had not been convicted in any part of the United Kingdom of any relevant offence or was aged under 18, the court in making the assessment referred to in subsection (1)(b) –

    (a) must take into account all such information as is available to it about the nature and circumstances of the offence,

    (b) may take into account any information which is before it about any pattern of behaviour of which the offence forms part, and

    (c) may take into account any information about the offender which is before it.

(3) If at the time when that offence was committed the offender was aged 18 or over and had been convicted in any part of the United Kingdom of one or more relevant offences, the court must assume that there is such a risk as is mentioned in subsection (1)(b) unless, after taking into account –

    (a) all such information as is available to it about the nature and circumstances of each of the offences,

    (b) where appropriate, any information which is before it about any pattern of behaviour of which any of the offences forms part, and

    (c) any information about the offender which is before it,

the court considers that it would be unreasonable to conclude that there is such a risk.

(4) In this Chapter 'relevant offence' means –

    (a) a specified offence,

    (b) an offence specified in Schedule 16 (offences under the law of Scotland), or

    (c) an offence specified in Schedule 17 (offences under the law of Northern Ireland).

230 Imprisonment or detention for public protection: release on licence

Schedule 18 (release of prisoners serving sentences of imprisonment or detention for public protection) shall have effect.

231 Appeals where previous convictions set aside

(1) This section applies where –

    (a) a sentence has been imposed on any person under section 225 or 227, and

    (b) any previous conviction of his without which the court would not have been required to make the assumption mentioned in section 229(3) has been subsequently set aside on appeal.

(2) Notwithstanding anything in section 18 of the Criminal Appeal Act 1968 (c. 19), notice of appeal against the sentence may be given at any time within 28 days from the date on which the previous conviction was set aside.

232 Certificates of convictions for purposes of section 229

Where –

(a) on any date after the commencement of this section a person is convicted in England and Wales of a relevant offence, and
(b) the court by or before which he is so convicted states in open court that he has been convicted of such an offence on that date, and
(c) that court subsequently certifies that fact,

that certificate shall be evidence, for the purposes of section 229, that he was convicted of such an offence on that date.

233 Offences under service law

Where –

(a) a person has at any time been convicted of an offence under section 70 of the Army Act 1955 (3 & 4 Eliz. 2 c. 18), section 70 of the Air Force Act 1955 (3 & 4 Eliz. 2 c. 19) or section 42 of the Naval Discipline Act 1957 (c. 53), and
(b) the corresponding civil offence (within the meaning of that Act) was a relevant offence,

section 229 shall have effect as if he had at that time been convicted in England and Wales of the corresponding civil offence.

234 Determination of day when offence committed

Where an offence is found to have been committed over a period of two or more days, or at some time during a period of two or more days, it shall be taken for the purposes of section 229 to have been committed on the last of those days.

235 Detention under sections 226 and 228

A person sentenced to be detained under section 226 or 228 is liable to be detained in such place, and under such conditions, as may be determined by the Secretary of State or by such other person as may be authorised by him for the purpose.

236 Conversion of sentences of detention into sentences of imprisonment

For section 99 of the Sentencing Act (conversion of sentence of detention and custody into sentence of imprisonment) there is substituted –

'*Conversion of sentence of detention to sentence of imprisonment*

99 Conversion of sentence of detention to sentence of imprisonment

(1) Subject to the following provisions of this section, where an offender has been sentenced by a relevant sentence of detention to a term of detention and either –

(a) he has attained the age of 21, or
(b) he has attained the age of 18 and has been reported to the Secretary of State by the board of visitors of the institution in which he is detained as exercising a bad influence on the other inmates of the institution or as behaving in a disruptive manner to the detriment of those inmates,

the Secretary of State may direct that he shall be treated as if he had been sentenced to imprisonment for the same term.

(2) Where the Secretary of State gives a direction under subsection (1) above in relation to an offender, the portion of the term of detention imposed under the relevant sentence of detention which he has already served shall be deemed to have been a portion of a term of imprisonment.

(3) Where the Secretary of State gives a direction under subsection (1) above in relation to an offender serving a sentence of detention for public protection under section 226 of the Criminal Justice Act 2003 the offender shall be treated as if he had been sentenced under section 225 of that Act; and where the Secretary of State gives such a direction in relation to an offender serving an extended sentence of detention under section 228 of that Act the offender shall be treated as if he had been sentenced under section 227 of that Act.

(4) Rules under section 47 of the Prison Act 1952 may provide that any award for an offence against discipline made in respect of an offender serving a relevant sentence of detention shall continue to have effect after a direction under subsection (1) has been given in relation to him.

(5) In this section 'relevant sentence of detention' means –

    (a) a sentence of detention under section 90 or 91 above,

    (b) a sentence of detention for public protection under section 226 of the Criminal Justice Act 2003, or

    (c) an extended sentence of detention under section 228 of that Act.'

CHAPTER 6

RELEASE ON LICENCE

Preliminary

237 Meaning of 'fixed-term prisoner'

(1) In this Chapter 'fixed-term prisoner' means –

    (a) a person serving a sentence of imprisonment for a determinate term, or

    (b) a person serving a determinate sentence of detention under section 91 of the Sentencing Act or under section 228 of this Act.

(2) In this Chapter, unless the context otherwise requires, 'prisoner' includes a person serving a sentence falling within subsection (1)(b); and 'prison' includes any place where a person serving such a sentence is liable to be detained.

Power of court to recommend licence conditions

238 Power of court to recommend licence conditions for certain prisoners

(1) A court which sentences an offender to a term of imprisonment of twelve months or more in respect of any offence may, when passing sentence, recommend to the Secretary of State particular conditions which in its view should be included in any licence granted to the offender under this Chapter on his release from prison.

(2) In exercising his powers under section 250(4)(b) in respect of an offender, the Secretary of State must have regard to any recommendation under subsection (1).

(3) A recommendation under subsection (1) is not to be treated for any purpose as part of the sentence passed on the offender.

(4) This section does not apply in relation to a sentence of detention under section 91 of the Sentencing Act or section 228 of this Act.

239 The Parole Board

(1) The Parole Board is to continue to be, by that name, a body corporate and as such is –

(a) to be constituted in accordance with this Chapter, and
(b) to have the functions conferred on it by this Chapter in respect of fixed-term prisoners and by Chapter 2 of Part 2 of the Crime (Sentences) Act 1997 (c. 43) (in this Chapter referred to as 'the 1997 Act') in respect of life prisoners within the meaning of that Chapter.

(2) It is the duty of the Board to advise the Secretary of State with respect to any matter referred to it by him which is to do with the early release or recall of prisoners.

(3) The Board must, in dealing with cases as respects which it makes recommendations under this Chapter or under Chapter 2 of Part 2 of the 1997 Act, consider –

(a) any documents given to it by the Secretary of State, and
(b) any other oral or written information obtained by it;

and if in any particular case the Board thinks it necessary to interview the person to whom the case relates before reaching a decision, the Board may authorise one of its members to interview him and must consider the report of the interview made by that member.

(4) The Board must deal with cases as respects which it gives directions under this Chapter or under Chapter 2 of Part 2 of the 1997 Act on consideration of all such evidence as may be adduced before it.

(5) Without prejudice to subsections (3) and (4), the Secretary of State may make rules with respect to the proceedings of the Board, including proceedings authorising cases to be dealt with by a prescribed number of its members or requiring cases to be dealt with at prescribed times.

(6) The Secretary of State may also give to the Board directions as to the matters to be taken into account by it in discharging any functions under this Chapter or under Chapter 2 of Part 2 of the 1997 Act; and in giving any such directions the Secretary of State must have regard to –

(a) the need to protect the public from serious harm from offenders, and
(b) the desirability of preventing the commission by them of further offences and of securing their rehabilitation.

(7) Schedule 19 shall have effect with respect to the Board.

Effect of remand in custody

240 Crediting of periods of remand in custody: terms of imprisonment and detention

(1) This section applies where –

(a) a court sentences an offender to imprisonment for a term in respect of an offence committed after the commencement of this section, and
(b) the offender has been remanded in custody (within the meaning given by section 242) in connection with the offence or a related offence, that is to say, any other offence the charge for which was founded on the same facts or evidence.

(2) It is immaterial for that purpose whether the offender –

    (a)   has also been remanded in custody in connection with other offences; or

    (b)   has also been detained in connection with other matters.

(3) Subject to subsection (4), the court must direct that the number of days for which the offender was remanded in custody in connection with the offence or a related offence is to count as time served by him as part of the sentence.

(4) Subsection (3) does not apply if and to the extent that –

    (a)   rules made by the Secretary of State so provide in the case of –

        (i)   a remand in custody which is wholly or partly concurrent with a sentence of imprisonment, or

        (ii)   sentences of imprisonment for consecutive terms or for terms which are wholly or partly concurrent, or

    (b)   it is in the opinion of the court just in all the circumstances not to give a direction under that subsection.

(5) Where the court gives a direction under subsection (3), it shall state in open court –

    (a)   the number of days for which the offender was remanded in custody, and

    (b)   the number of days in relation to which the direction is given.

(6) Where the court does not give a direction under subsection (3), or gives such a direction in relation to a number of days less than that for which the offender was remanded in custody, it shall state in open court –

    (a)   that its decision is in accordance with rules made under paragraph (a) of subsection (4), or

    (b)   that it is of the opinion mentioned in paragraph (b) of that subsection and what the circumstances are.

(7) For the purposes of this section a suspended sentence –

    (a)   is to be treated as a sentence of imprisonment when it takes effect under paragraph 8(2)(a) or (b) of Schedule 12, and

    (b)   is to be treated as being imposed by the order under which it takes effect.

(8) For the purposes of the reference in subsection (3) to the term of imprisonment to which a person has been sentenced (that is to say, the reference to his 'sentence'), consecutive terms and terms which are wholly or partly concurrent are to be treated as a single term if –

    (a)   the sentences were passed on the same occasion, or

    (b)   where they were passed on different occasions, the person has not been released under this Chapter at any time during the period beginning with the first and ending with the last of those occasions.

(9) Where an offence is found to have been committed over a period of two or more days, or at some time during a period of two or more days, it shall be taken for the purposes of subsection (1) to have been committed on the last of those days.

(10) This section applies to a determinate sentence of detention under section 91 of the Sentencing Act or section 228 of this Act as it applies to an equivalent sentence of imprisonment.

241 Effect of direction under section 240 on release on licence

(1) In determining for the purposes of this Chapter or Chapter 3 (prison sentences of less than twelve months) whether a person to whom a direction under section 240 relates –

    (a) has served, or would (but for his release) have served, a particular proportion of his sentence, or

    (b) has served a particular period,

the number of days specified in the direction are to be treated as having been served by him as part of that sentence or period.

(2) In determining for the purposes of section 183 (intermittent custody) whether any part of a sentence to which an intermittent custody order relates is a licence period, the number of custodial days, as defined by subsection (3) of that section, is to be taken to be reduced by the number of days specified in a direction under section 240.

242 Interpretation of sections 240 and 241

(1) For the purposes of sections 240 and 241, the definition of 'sentence of imprisonment' in section 305 applies as if for the words from the beginning of the definition to the end of paragraph (a) there were substituted –

    ' "sentence of imprisonment" does not include a committal –

        (a) in default of payment of any sum of money, other than one adjudged to be paid on a conviction,';

and references in those sections to sentencing an offender to imprisonment, and to an offender's sentence, are to be read accordingly.

(2) References in sections 240 and 241 to an offender's being remanded in custody are references to his being –

    (a) remanded in or committed to custody by order of a court,

    (b) remanded or committed to local authority accommodation under section 23 of the Children and Young Persons Act 1969 (c. 54) and kept in secure accommodation or detained in a secure training centre pursuant to arrangements under subsection (7A) of that section, or

    (c) remanded, admitted or removed to hospital under section 35, 36, 38 or 48 of the Mental Health Act 1983 (c. 20).

(3) In subsection (2), 'secure accommodation' has the same meaning as in section 23 of the Children and Young Persons Act 1969.

243 Persons extradited to the United Kingdom

(1) A fixed-term prisoner is an extradited prisoner for the purposes of this section if –

    (a) he was tried for the offence in respect of which his sentence was imposed –

        (i)   after having been extradited to the United Kingdom, and

        (ii) without having first been restored or had an opportunity of leaving the United Kingdom, and

    (b) he was for any period kept in custody while awaiting his extradition to the United Kingdom as mentioned in paragraph (a).

(2) In the case of an extradited prisoner, section 240 has effect as if the days for which he was kept in custody while awaiting extradition were days for which he was remanded in

custody in connection with the offence, or any other offence the charge for which was founded on the same facts or evidence.

(3) In this section –

'extradited to the United Kingdom' means returned to the United Kingdom –

    (a)   in pursuance of extradition arrangements,

    (b)   under any law of a designated Commonwealth country corresponding to the Extradition Act 1989 (c. 33),

    (c)   under that Act as extended to a British overseas territory or under any corresponding law of a British overseas territory,

    (d)   in pursuance of a warrant of arrest endorsed in the Republic of Ireland under the law of that country corresponding to the Backing of Warrants (Republic of Ireland) Act 1965 (c. 45), or

    (e)   in pursuance of arrangements with a foreign state in respect of which an Order in Council under section 2 of the Extradition Act 1870 (c. 52) is in force;

'extradition arrangements' has the meaning given by section 3 of the Extradition Act 1989;

'designated Commonwealth country' has the meaning given by section 5(1) of that Act.

Release on licence

244 Duty to release prisoners

(1) As soon as a fixed-term prisoner, other than a prisoner to whom section 247 applies, has served the requisite custodial period, it is the duty of the Secretary of State to release him on licence under this section.

(2) Subsection (1) is subject to section 245.

(3) In this section 'the requisite custodial period' means –

    (a)   in relation to a person serving a sentence of imprisonment for a term of twelve months or more or any determinate sentence of detention under section 91 of the Sentencing Act, one-half of his sentence,

    (b)   in relation to a person serving a sentence of imprisonment for a term of less than twelve months (other than one to which an intermittent custody order relates), the custodial period within the meaning of section 181,

    (c)   in relation to a person serving a sentence of imprisonment to which an intermittent custody order relates, any part of the term which is not a licence period as defined by section 183(3), and

    (d)   in relation to a person serving two or more concurrent or consecutive sentences, the period determined under sections 263(2) and 264(2).

245 Restrictions on operation of section 244(1) in relation to intermittent custody prisoners

(1) Where an intermittent custody prisoner returns to custody after being unlawfully at large within the meaning of section 49 of the Prison Act 1952 (c. 52) at any time during the currency of his sentence, section 244(1) does not apply until –

    (a)   the relevant time (as defined in subsection (2)), or

    (b)   if earlier, the date on which he has served in prison the number of custodial days required by the intermittent custody order.

(2) In subsection (1)(a) 'the relevant time' means –

    (a) in a case where, within the period of 72 hours beginning with the return to custody of the intermittent custody prisoner, the Secretary of State or the responsible officer has applied to the court for the amendment of the intermittent custody order under paragraph 6(1)(b) of Schedule 10, the date on which the application is withdrawn or determined, and

    (b) in any other case, the end of that 72–hour period.

(3) Section 244(1) does not apply in relation to an intermittent custody prisoner at any time after he has been recalled under section 254, unless after his recall the Board has directed his further release on licence.

246 Power to release prisoners on licence before required to do so

(1) Subject to subsections (2) to (4), the Secretary of State may –

    (a) release on licence under this section a fixed-term prisoner, other than an intermittent custody prisoner, at any time during the period of 135 days ending with the day on which the prisoner will have served the requisite custodial period, and

    (b) release on licence under this section an intermittent custody prisoner when 135 or less of the required custodial days remain to be served.

(2) Subsection (1)(a) does not apply in relation to a prisoner unless –

    (a) the length of the requisite custodial period is at least 6 weeks,

    (b) he has served –

        (i)   at least 4 weeks of his sentence, and

        (ii)   at least one-half of the requisite custodial period.

(3) Subsection (1)(b) does not apply in relation to a prisoner unless –

    (a) the number of required custodial days is at least 42, and

    (b) the prisoner has served –

        (i)   at least 28 of those days, and

        (ii)   at least one-half of the total number of those days.

(4) Subsection (1) does not apply where –

    (a) the sentence is imposed under section 227 or 228,

    (b) the sentence is for an offence under section 1 of the Prisoners (Return to Custody) Act 1995 (c. 16),

    (c) the prisoner is subject to a hospital order, hospital direction or transfer direction under section 37, 45A or 47 of the Mental Health Act 1983 (c. 20),

    (d) the sentence was imposed by virtue of paragraph 9(1)(b) or (c) or 10(1)(b) or (c) of Schedule 8 in a case where the prisoner has failed to comply with a curfew requirement of a community order,

    (e) the prisoner is subject to the notification requirements of Part 2 of the Sexual Offences Act 2003 (c. 42),

    (f) the prisoner is liable to removal from the United Kingdom,

    (g) the prisoner has been released on licence under this section during the currency of the sentence, and has been recalled to prison under section 255(1)(a),

    (h) the prisoner has been released on licence under section 248 during the currency of the sentence, and has been recalled to prison under section 254, or

(i)   in the case of a prisoner to whom a direction under section 240 relates, the interval between the date on which the sentence was passed and the date on which the prisoner will have served the requisite custodial period is less than 14 days or, where the sentence is one of intermittent custody, the number of the required custodial days remaining to be served is less than 14.

(5) The Secretary of State may by order –

(a)   amend the number of days for the time being specified in subsection (1) (a) or (b), (3) or (4)(i),

(b)   amend the number of weeks for the time being specified in subsection (2)(a) or (b)(i), and

(c)   amend the fraction for the time being specified in subsection (2)(b)(ii) or (3)(b)(ii).

(6) In this section –

'the required custodial days', in relation to an intermittent custody prisoner, means –
(a)   the number of custodial days specified under section 183, or
(b)   in the case of two or more sentences of intermittent custody, the aggregate of the numbers so specified;

'the requisite custodial period' in relation to a person serving any sentence other than a sentence of intermittent custody, has the meaning given by paragraph (a), (b) or (d) of section 244(3);

'sentence of intermittent custody' means a sentence to which an intermittent custody order relates.

247 Release on licence of prisoner serving extended sentence under section 227 or 228

(1) This section applies to a prisoner who is serving an extended sentence imposed under section 227 or 228.

(2) As soon as –

(a)   a prisoner to whom this section applies has served one-half of the appropriate custodial term, and

(b)   the Parole Board has directed his release under this section,

it is the duty of the Secretary of State to release him on licence.

(3) The Parole Board may not give a direction under subsection (2) unless the Board is satisfied that it is no longer necessary for the protection of the public that the prisoner should be confined.

(4) As soon as a prisoner to whom this section applies has served the appropriate custodial term, it is the duty of the Secretary of State to release him on licence unless the prisoner has previously been recalled under section 254.

(5) Where a prisoner to whom this section applies is released on a licence, the Secretary of State may not by virtue of section 250(4)(b) include, or subsequently insert, a condition in the licence, or vary or cancel a condition in the licence, except after consultation with the Board.

(6) For the purposes of subsection (5), the Secretary of State is to be treated as having consulted the Board about a proposal to include, insert, vary or cancel a condition in any

case if he has consulted the Board about the implementation of proposals of that description generally or in that class of case.

(7) In this section 'the appropriate custodial term' means the period determined by the court as the appropriate custodial term under section 227 or 228.

248 Power to release prisoners on compassionate grounds

(1) The Secretary of State may at any time release a fixed-term prisoner on licence if he is satisfied that exceptional circumstances exist which justify the prisoner's release on compassionate grounds.

(2) Before releasing under this section a prisoner to whom section 247 applies, the Secretary of State must consult the Board, unless the circumstances are such as to render such consultation impracticable.

249 Duration of licence

(1) Subject to subsections (2) and (3), where a fixed-term prisoner is released on licence, the licence shall, subject to any revocation under section 254 or 255, remain in force for the remainder of his sentence.

(2) Where an intermittent custody prisoner is released on licence under section 244, the licence shall, subject to any revocation under section 254, remain in force –

(a) until the time when he is required to return to prison at the beginning of the next custodial period of the sentence, or
(b) where it is granted at the end of the last custodial period, for the remainder of his sentence.

(3) Subsection (1) has effect subject to sections 263(2) (concurrent terms) and 264(3) and (4) (consecutive terms).

(4) In subsection (2) 'custodial period', in relation to a sentence to which an intermittent custody order relates, means any period which is not a licence period as defined by 183(3).

250 Licence conditions

(1) In this section –

(a) 'the standard conditions' means such conditions as may be prescribed for the purposes of this section as standard conditions, and
(b) 'prescribed' means prescribed by the Secretary of State by order.

(2) Subject to subsection (6) and section 251, any licence under this Chapter in respect of a prisoner serving one or more sentences of imprisonment of less than twelve months and no sentence of twelve months or more –

(a) must include –
  (i) the conditions required by the relevant court order, and
  (ii) so far as not inconsistent with them, the standard conditions, and
(b) may also include –
  (i) any condition which is authorised by section 62 of the Criminal Justice and Court Services Act 2000 (c. 43) (electronic monitoring) or section 64 of that Act (drug testing requirements) and which is compatible with the conditions required by the relevant court order, and

    (ii)   such other conditions of a kind prescribed for the purposes of this paragraph as the Secretary of State may for the time being consider to be necessary for the protection of the public and specify in the licence.

(3) For the purposes of subsection (2)(a)(i), any reference in the relevant court order to the licence period specified in the order is, in relation to a prohibited activity requirement, exclusion requirement, residence requirement or supervision requirement, to be taken to include a reference to any other period during which the prisoner is released on licence under section 246 or 248.

(4) Any licence under this Chapter in respect of a prisoner serving a sentence of imprisonment for a term of twelve months or more (including such a sentence imposed under section 227) or any sentence of detention under section 91 of the Sentencing Act or section 228 of this Act –

    (a)   must include the standard conditions, and
    (b)   may include –
        (i)   any condition authorised by section 62 or 64 of the Criminal Justice and Court Services Act 2000, and
        (ii)   such other conditions of a kind prescribed by the Secretary of State for the purposes of this paragraph as the Secretary of State may for the time being specify in the licence.

(5) A licence under section 246 must also include a curfew condition complying with section 253.

(6) Where –

    (a)   a licence under section 246 is granted to a prisoner serving one or more sentences of imprisonment of less than 12 months and no sentence of 12 months or more, and
    (b)   the relevant court order requires the licence to be granted subject to a condition requiring his compliance with a curfew requirement (as defined by section 204),

that condition is not to be included in the licence at any time while a curfew condition required by section 253 is in force.

(7) The preceding provisions of this section have effect subject to section 263(3) (concurrent terms) and section 264(3) and (4) (consecutive terms).

(8) In exercising his powers to prescribe standard conditions or the other conditions referred to in subsection (4)(b)(ii), the Secretary of State must have regard to the following purposes of the supervision of offenders while on licence under this Chapter –

    (a)   the protection of the public,
    (b)   the prevention of re-offending, and
    (c)   securing the successful re-integration of the prisoner into the community.

251 Licence conditions on re-release of prisoner serving sentence of less than 12 months

(1) In relation to any licence under this Chapter which is granted to a prisoner serving one or more sentences of imprisonment of less than twelve months and no sentence of twelve months or more on his release in pursuance of a decision of the Board under section 254 or 256, subsections (2) and (3) apply instead of section 250(2).

(2) The licence –

  (a) must include the standard conditions, and
  (b) may include –
      (i)   any condition authorised by section 62 or 64 of the Criminal Justice and Court Services Act 2000 (c. 43), and
      (ii)   such other conditions of a kind prescribed by the Secretary of State for the purposes of section 250(4)(b)(ii) as the Secretary of State may for the time being specify in the licence.

(3) In exercising his powers under subsection (2)(b)(ii), the Secretary of State must have regard to the terms of the relevant court order.

(4) In this section 'the standard conditions' has the same meaning as in section 250.

252 Duty to comply with licence conditions

A person subject to a licence under this Chapter must comply with such conditions as may for the time being be specified in the licence.

253 Curfew condition to be included in licence under section 246

(1) For the purposes of this Chapter, a curfew condition is a condition which –

  (a) requires the released person to remain, for periods for the time being specified in the condition, at a place for the time being so specified (which may be premises approved by the Secretary of State under section 9 of the Criminal Justice and Court Services Act 2000 (c. 43)), and
  (b) includes requirements for securing the electronic monitoring of his whereabouts during the periods for the time being so specified.

(2) The curfew condition may specify different places or different periods for different days, but may not specify periods which amount to less than 9 hours in any one day (excluding for this purpose the first and last days of the period for which the condition is in force).

(3) The curfew condition is to remain in force until the date when the released person would (but for his release) fall to be released on licence under section 244.

(4) Subsection (3) does not apply in relation to a released person to whom an intermittent custody order relates; and in relation to such a person the curfew condition is to remain in force until the number of days during which it has been in force is equal to the number of the required custodial days, as defined in section 246(6), that remained to be served at the time when he was released under section 246.

(5) The curfew condition must include provision for making a person responsible for monitoring the released person's whereabouts during the periods for the time being specified in the condition; and a person who is made so responsible shall be of a description specified in an order made by the Secretary of State.

(6) Nothing in this section is to be taken to require the Secretary of State to ensure that arrangements are made for the electronic monitoring of released persons' whereabouts in any particular part of England and Wales.

Recall after release

254 Recall of prisoners while on licence

(1) The Secretary of State may, in the case of any prisoner who has been released on licence under this Chapter, revoke his licence and recall him to prison.

(2) A person recalled to prison under subsection (1) –

    (a) may make representations in writing with respect to his recall, and

    (b) on his return to prison, must be informed of the reasons for his recall and of his right to make representations.

(3) The Secretary of State must refer to the Board the case of a person recalled under subsection (1).

(4) Where on a reference under subsection (3) relating to any person the Board recommends his immediate release on licence under this Chapter, the Secretary of State must give effect to the recommendation.

(5) In the case of an intermittent custody prisoner who has not yet served in prison the number of custodial days specified in the intermittent custody order, any recommendation by the Board as to immediate release on licence is to be a recommendation as to his release on licence until the end of one of the licence periods specified by virtue of section 183(1)(b) in the intermittent custody order.

(6) On the revocation of the licence of any person under this section, he shall be liable to be detained in pursuance of his sentence and, if at large, is to be treated as being unlawfully at large.

(7) Nothing in subsections (2) to (6) applies in relation to a person recalled under section 255.

255 Recall of prisoners released early under section 246

(1) If it appears to the Secretary of State, as regards a person released on licence under section 246 –

    (a) that he has failed to comply with any condition included in his licence, or

    (b) that his whereabouts can no longer be electronically monitored at the place for the time being specified in the curfew condition included in his licence,

the Secretary of State may, if the curfew condition is still in force, revoke the licence and recall the person to prison under this section.

(2) A person whose licence under section 246 is revoked under this section –

    (a) may make representations in writing with respect to the revocation, and

    (b) on his return to prison, must be informed of the reasons for the revocation and of his right to make representations.

(3) The Secretary of State, after considering any representations under subsection (2)(b) or any other matters, may cancel a revocation under this section.

(4) Where the revocation of a person's licence is cancelled under subsection (3), the person is to be treated for the purposes of section 246 as if he had not been recalled to prison under this section.

(5) On the revocation of a person's licence under section 246, he is liable to be detained in pursuance of his sentence and, if at large, is to be treated as being unlawfully at large.

256 Further release after recall

(1) Where on a reference under section 254(3) in relation to any person, the Board does not recommend his immediate release on licence under this Chapter, the Board must either –

(a) fix a date for the person's release on licence, or
(b) fix a date as the date for the next review of the person's case by the Board.

(2) Any date fixed under subsection (1)(a) or (b) must not be later than the first anniversary of the date on which the decision is taken.

(3) The Board need not fix a date under subsection (1)(a) or (b) if the prisoner will fall to be released unconditionally at any time within the next 12 months.

(4) Where the Board has fixed a date under subsection (1)(a), it is the duty of the Secretary of State to release him on licence on that date.

(5) On a review required by subsection (1)(b) in relation to any person, the Board may –

(a) recommend his immediate release on licence, or
(b) fix a date under subsection (1)(a) or (b).

Additional days

257 Additional days for disciplinary offences

(1) Prison rules, that is to say, rules made under section 47 of the Prison Act 1952 (c. 52), may include provision for the award of additional days –

(a) to fixed-term prisoners, or
(b) conditionally on their subsequently becoming such prisoners, to persons on remand,

who (in either case) are guilty of disciplinary offences.

(2) Where additional days are awarded to a fixed-term prisoner, or to a person on remand who subsequently becomes such a prisoner, and are not remitted in accordance with prison rules –

(a) any period which he must serve before becoming entitled to or eligible for release under this Chapter,
(b) any period which he must serve before he can be removed from prison under section 260, and
(c) any period for which a licence granted to him under this Chapter remains in force,

is extended by the aggregate of those additional days.

Fine defaulters and contemnors

258 Early release of fine defaulters and contemnors

(1) This section applies in relation to a person committed to prison –

(a) in default of payment of a sum adjudged to be paid by a conviction, or
(b) for contempt of court or any kindred offence.

(2) As soon as a person to whom this section applies has served one-half of the term for which he was committed, it is the duty of the Secretary of State to release him unconditionally.

(3) Where a person to whom this section applies is also serving one or more sentences of imprisonment, nothing in this section requires the Secretary of State to release him until he is also required to release him in respect of that sentence or each of those sentences.

(4) The Secretary of State may at any time release unconditionally a person to whom this section applies if he is satisfied that exceptional circumstances exist which justify the person's release on compassionate grounds.

Persons liable to removal from the United Kingdom

259 Persons liable to removal from the United Kingdom

For the purposes of this Chapter a person is liable to removal from the United Kingdom if –

- (a) he is liable to deportation under section 3(5) of the Immigration Act 1971 (c. 77) and has been notified of a decision to make a deportation order against him,
- (b) he is liable to deportation under section 3(6) of that Act,
- (c) he has been notified of a decision to refuse him leave to enter the United Kingdom,
- (d) he is an illegal entrant within the meaning of section 33(1) of that Act, or
- (e) he is liable to removal under section 10 of the Immigration and Asylum Act 1999 (c. 33).

260 Early removal of prisoners liable to removal from United Kingdom

(1) Subject to subsections (2) and (3), where a fixed-term prisoner is liable to removal from the United Kingdom, the Secretary of State may remove him from prison under this section at any time during the period of 135 days ending with the day on which the prisoner will have served the requisite custodial period.

(2) Subsection (1) does not apply in relation to a prisoner unless –

- (a) the length of the requisite custodial period is at least 6 weeks, and
- (b) he has served –
  - (i) at least 4 weeks of his sentence, and
  - (ii) at least one-half of the requisite custodial period.

(3) Subsection (1) does not apply where –

- (a) the sentence is imposed under section 227 or 228,
- (b) the sentence is for an offence under section 1 of the Prisoners (Return to Custody) Act 1995 (c. 16),
- (c) the prisoner is subject to a hospital order, hospital direction or transfer direction under section 37, 45A or 47 of the Mental Health Act 1983 (c. 20),
- (d) the prisoner is subject to the notification requirements of Part 2 of the Sexual Offences Act 2003 (c. 42), or
- (e) in the case of a prisoner to whom a direction under section 240 relates, the interval between the date on which the sentence was passed and the date on which the prisoner will have served the requisite custodial period is less than 14 days.

(4) A prisoner removed from prison under this section –

(a) is so removed only for the purpose of enabling the Secretary of State to remove him from the United Kingdom under powers conferred by –
  (i) Schedule 2 or 3 to the Immigration Act 1971, or
  (ii) section 10 of the Immigration and Asylum Act 1999 (c. 33), and
(b) so long as remaining in the United Kingdom, remains liable to be detained in pursuance of his sentence until he has served the requisite custodial period.

(5) So long as a prisoner removed from prison under this section remains in the United Kingdom but has not been returned to prison, any duty or power of the Secretary of State under section 244 or 248 is exercisable in relation to him as if he were in prison.

(6) The Secretary of State may by order –

(a) amend the number of days for the time being specified in subsection (1) or (3)(e),
(b) amend the number of weeks for the time being specified in subsection (2)(a) or (b)(i), and
(c) amend the fraction for the time being specified in subsection (2)(b)(ii).

(7) In this section 'the requisite custodial period' has the meaning given by paragraph (a), (b) or (d) of section 244(3).

261 Re-entry into United Kingdom of offender removed from prison early

(1) This section applies in relation to a person who, after being removed from prison under section 260, has been removed from the United Kingdom before he has served the requisite custodial period.

(2) If a person to whom this section applies enters the United Kingdom at any time before his sentence expiry date, he is liable to be detained in pursuance of his sentence from the time of his entry into the United Kingdom until whichever is the earlier of the following –

(a) the end of a period ('the further custodial period') beginning with that time and equal in length to the outstanding custodial period, and
(b) his sentence expiry date.

(3) A person who is liable to be detained by virtue of subsection (2) is, if at large, to be taken for the purposes of section 49 of the Prison Act 1952 (c. 52) (persons unlawfully at large) to be unlawfully at large.

(4) Subsection (2) does not prevent the further removal from the United Kingdom of a person falling within that subsection.

(5) Where, in the case of a person returned to prison by virtue of subsection (2), the further custodial period ends before the sentence expiry date, section 244 has effect in relation to him as if the reference to the requisite custodial period were a reference to the further custodial period.

(6) In this section –

'further custodial period' has the meaning given by subsection (2)(a);
'outstanding custodial period', in relation to a person to whom this section applies, means the period beginning with the date of his removal from the United Kingdom and ending with the date on which he would, but for his removal, have served the requisite custodial period;
'requisite custodial period' has the meaning given by paragraph (a), (b) or (d) of section 244(3);

'sentence expiry date', in relation to a person to whom this section applies, means the date on which, but for his removal from the United Kingdom, he would have ceased to be subject to a licence.

262 Prisoners liable to removal from United Kingdom: modifications of Criminal Justice Act 1991

Part 2 of the Criminal Justice Act 1991 (c. 53) (early release of prisoners) shall (until the coming into force of its repeal by this Act) have effect subject to the modifications set out in Schedule 20 (which relate to persons liable to removal from the United Kingdom).

Consecutive or concurrent terms

263 Concurrent terms

(1) This section applies where –

(a) a person ('the offender') has been sentenced by any court to two or more terms of imprisonment which are wholly or partly concurrent, and

(b) the sentences were passed on the same occasion or, where they were passed on different occasions, the person has not been released under this Chapter at any time during the period beginning with the first and ending with the last of those occasions.

(2) Where this section applies –

(a) nothing in this Chapter requires the Secretary of State to release the offender in respect of any of the terms unless and until he is required to release him in respect of each of the others,

(b) section 244 does not authorise the Secretary of State to release him on licence under that section in respect of any of the terms unless and until that section authorises the Secretary of State to do so in respect of each of the others,

(c) on and after his release under this Chapter the offender is to be on licence for so long, and subject to such conditions, as is required by this Chapter in respect of any of the sentences.

(3) Where the sentences include one or more sentences of twelve months or more and one or more sentences of less than twelve months, the terms of the licence may be determined by the Secretary of State in accordance with section 250(4)(b), without regard to the requirements of any custody plus order or intermittent custody order.

(4) In this section 'term of imprisonment' includes a determinate sentence of detention under section 91 of the Sentencing Act or under section 228 of this Act.

264 Consecutive terms

(1) This section applies where –

(a) a person ('the offender') has been sentenced to two or more terms of imprisonment which are to be served consecutively on each other, and

(b) the sentences were passed on the same occasion or, where they were passed on different occasions, the person has not been released under this Chapter at any time during the period beginning with the first and ending with the last of those occasions.

(2) Nothing in this Chapter requires the Secretary of State to release the offender on licence until he has served a period equal in length to the aggregate of the length of the custodial periods in relation to each of the terms of imprisonment.

(3) Where any of the terms of imprisonment is a term of twelve months or more, the offender is, on and after his release under this Chapter, to be on licence –

(a) until he would, but for his release, have served a term equal in length to the aggregate length of the terms of imprisonment, and

(b) subject to such conditions as are required by this Chapter in respect of each of those terms of imprisonment.

(4) Where each of the terms of imprisonment is a term of less than twelve months, the offender is, on and after his release under this Chapter, to be on licence until the relevant time, and subject to such conditions as are required by this Chapter in respect of any of the terms of imprisonment, and none of the terms is to be regarded for any purpose as continuing after the relevant time.

(5) In subsection (4) 'the relevant time' means the time when the offender would, but for his release, have served a term equal in length to the aggregate of –

(a) all the custodial periods in relation to the terms of imprisonment, and

(b) the longest of the licence periods in relation to those terms.

(6) In this section –

(a) 'custodial period' –
   (i) in relation to an extended sentence imposed under section 227 or 228, means the appropriate custodial term determined under that section,
   (ii) in relation to a term of twelve months or more, means one-half of the term, and
   (iii) in relation to a term of less than twelve months complying with section 181, means the custodial period as defined by subsection (3)(a) of that section;

(b) 'licence period', in relation to a term of less than twelve months complying with section 181, has the meaning given by subsection (3)(b) of that section.

(7) This section applies to a determinate sentence of detention under section 91 of the Sentencing Act or under section 228 of this Act as it applies to a term of imprisonment of 12 months or more.

Restriction on consecutive sentences for released prisoners

265 Restriction on consecutive sentences for released prisoners

(1) A court sentencing a person to a term of imprisonment may not order or direct that the term is to commence on the expiry of any other sentence of imprisonment from which he has been released early under this Chapter.

(2) In this section 'sentence of imprisonment' includes a sentence of detention under section 91 of the Sentencing Act or section 228 of this Act, and 'term of imprisonment' is to be read accordingly.

Drug testing requirements

266 Release on licence etc: drug testing requirements

(1) Section 64 of the Criminal Justice and Court Services Act 2000 (c. 43) (release on licence etc: drug testing requirements) is amended as follows.

(2) In subsection (1) for paragraph (a) there is substituted –

'(a) the Secretary of State releases from prison a person aged 14 or over on whom a sentence of imprisonment has been imposed,
(aa) a responsible officer is of the opinion –
    (i) that the offender has a propensity to misuse specified Class A drugs, and
    (ii) that the misuse by the offender of any specified Class A drug caused or contributed to any offence of which he has been convicted, or is likely to cause or contribute to the commission of further offences, and'.

(3) After subsection (4) there is inserted –

'(4A) A person under the age of 17 years may not be required by virtue of this section to provide a sample otherwise than in the presence of an appropriate adult.'

(4) In subsection (5), after paragraph (e) there is inserted 'and
(f) a sentence of detention under section 226 or 228 of the Criminal Justice Act 2003,'.

(5) After subsection (5) there is inserted –

'(6) In this section –

'"appropriate adult", in relation to a person aged under 17, means –
    (a) his parent or guardian or, if he is in the care of a local authority or voluntary organisation, a person representing that authority or organisation,
    (b) a social worker of a local authority social services department, or
    (c) if no person falling within paragraph (a) or (b) is available, any responsible person aged 18 or over who is not a police officer or a person employed by the police;
"responsible officer" means –
    (a) in relation to an offender aged under 18, an officer of a local probation board or a member of a youth offending team;
    (b) in relation to an offender aged 18 or over, an officer of a local probation board.'

Supplemental

267 Alteration by order of relevant proportion of sentence

The Secretary of State may by order provide that any reference in section 244(3)(a), section 247(2) or section 264(6)(a)(ii) to a particular proportion of a prisoner's sentence is to be read as a reference to such other proportion of a prisoner's sentence as may be specified in the order.

268 Interpretation of Chapter 6

In this Chapter –

'the 1997 Act' means the Crime (Sentences) Act 1997 (c. 43);
'the Board' means the Parole Board;
'fixed-term prisoner' has the meaning given by section 237(1);
'intermittent custody prisoner' means a prisoner serving a sentence of imprisonment to which an intermittent custody order relates;
'prison' and 'prisoner' are to be read in accordance with section 237(2);
'release', in relation to a prisoner serving a sentence of imprisonment to which an intermittent custody order relates, includes temporary release;
'relevant court order', in relation to a person serving a sentence of imprisonment to which a custody plus order or intermittent custody order relates, means that order.

CHAPTER 7

EFFECT OF LIFE SENTENCE

269 Determination of minimum term in relation to mandatory life sentence

(1) This section applies where after the commencement of this section a court passes a life sentence in circumstances where the sentence is fixed by law.

(2) The court must, unless it makes an order under subsection (4), order that the provisions of section 28(5) to (8) of the Crime (Sentences) Act 1997 (referred to in this Chapter as 'the early release provisions') are to apply to the offender as soon as he has served the part of his sentence which is specified in the order.

(3) The part of his sentence is to be such as the court considers appropriate taking into account –

   (a) the seriousness of the offence, or of the combination of the offence and any one or more offences associated with it, and
   (b) the effect of any direction which it would have given under section 240 (crediting periods of remand in custody) if it had sentenced him to a term of imprisonment.

(4) If the offender was 21 or over when he committed the offence and the court is of the opinion that, because of the seriousness of the offence, or of the combination of the offence and one or more offences associated with it, no order should be made under subsection (2), the court must order that the early release provisions are not to apply to the offender.

(5) In considering under subsection (3) or (4) the seriousness of an offence (or of the combination of an offence and one or more offences associated with it), the court must have regard to –

   (a) the general principles set out in Schedule 21, and
   (b) any guidelines relating to offences in general which are relevant to the case and are not incompatible with the provisions of Schedule 21.

(6) The Secretary of State may by order amend Schedule 21.

(7) Before making an order under subsection (6), the Secretary of State shall consult the Sentencing Guidelines Council.

270 Duty to give reasons

(1) Any court making an order under subsection (2) or (4) of section 269 must state in open court, in ordinary language, its reasons for deciding on the order made.

(2) In stating its reasons the court must, in particular –

   (a)   state which of the starting points in Schedule 21 it has chosen and its reasons for doing so, and
   (b)   state its reasons for any departure from that starting point.

271 Appeals

(1) In section 9 of the Criminal Appeal Act 1968 (c. 19) (appeal against sentence following conviction on indictment), after subsection (1) there is inserted –

   '(1A) In subsection (1) of this section, the reference to a sentence fixed by law does not include a reference to an order made under subsection (2) or (4) of section 269 of the Criminal Justice Act 2003 in relation to a life sentence (as defined in section 277 of that Act) that is fixed by law.'.

(2) In section 8 of the Courts-Martial (Appeals) Act 1968 (c. 20) (right of appeal from court-martial to Courts-Martial Appeal Court) after subsection (1) there is inserted –

   '(1ZA) In subsection (1) above, the reference to a sentence fixed by law does not include a reference to an order made under subsection (2) or (4) of section 269 of the Criminal Justice Act 2003 in relation to a life sentence (as defined in section 277 of that Act) that is fixed by law.'.

272 Review of minimum term on a reference by Attorney General

(1) In section 36 of the Criminal Justice Act 1988 (c. 33) (reviews of sentencing) after subsection (3) there is inserted –

   '(3A) Where a reference under this section relates to an order under subsection (2) of section 269 of the Criminal Justice Act 2003 (determination of minimum term in relation to mandatory life sentence), the Court of Appeal shall not, in deciding what order under that section is appropriate for the case, make any allowance for the fact that the person to whom it relates is being sentenced for a second time.'.

(2) Each of the following sections (which relate to the review by the Courts-Martial Appeal Court of sentences passed by courts-martial) –

   (a)   section 113C of the Army Act 1955 (3 & 4 Eliz. 2 c. 18),
   (b)   section 113C of the Air Force Act 1955 (3 & 4 Eliz. 2 c. 19), and
   (c)   section 71AC of the Naval Discipline Act 1957 (c. 53),

is amended as follows.

(3) After subsection (3) there is inserted –

   '(3A) Where a reference under this section relates to an order under subsection (2) of section 269 of the Criminal Justice Act 2003 (determination of minimum term in relation to mandatory life sentence), the Courts-Martial Appeal Court shall not, in deciding what order under that section is appropriate for the case, make any allowance for the fact that the person to whom it relates is being sentenced for a second time.'.

273 Life prisoners transferred to England and Wales

(1) The Secretary of State must refer the case of any transferred life prisoner to the High Court for the making of one or more relevant orders.

(2) In subsection (1) 'transferred life prisoner' means a person –

(a) on whom a court in a country or territory outside the British Islands has imposed one or more sentences of imprisonment or detention for an indeterminate period, and

(b) who has been transferred to England and Wales after the commencement of this section in pursuance of –

(i) an order made by the Secretary of State under section 2 of the Colonial Prisoners Removal Act 1884 (c. 31), or

(ii) a warrant issued by the Secretary of State under the Repatriation of Prisoners Act 1984 (c. 47),

there to serve his sentence or sentences or the remainder of his sentence or sentences.

(3) In subsection (1) 'a relevant order' means –

(a) in the case of an offence which appears to the court to be an offence for which, if it had been committed in England and Wales, the sentence would have been fixed by law, an order under subsection (2) or (4) of section 269, and

(b) in any other case, an order under subsection (2) or (4) of section 82A of the Sentencing Act.

(4) In section 34(1) of the Crime (Sentences) Act 1997 (c. 43) (meaning of 'life prisoner' in Chapter 2 of Part 2 of that Act) at the end there is inserted 'and includes a transferred life prisoner as defined by section 273 of the Criminal Justice Act 2003'.

274 Further provisions about references relating to transferred life prisoners

(1) A reference to the High Court under section 273 is to be determined by a single judge of that court without an oral hearing.

(2) In relation to a reference under that section, any reference to 'the court' in subsections (2) to (5) of section 269, in Schedule 21 or in section 82A(2) to (4) of the Sentencing Act is to be read as a reference to the High Court.

(3) A person in respect of whom a reference has been made under section 273 may with the leave of the Court of Appeal appeal to the Court of Appeal against the decision of the High Court on the reference.

(4) Section 1(1) of the Administration of Justice Act 1960 (c. 65) (appeal to House of Lords from decision of High Court in a criminal cause or matter) and section 18(1)(a) of the Supreme Court Act 1981 (c. 54) (exclusion of appeal from High Court to Court of Appeal in a criminal cause or matter) do not apply in relation to a decision to which subsection (3) applies.

(5) The jurisdiction conferred on the Court of Appeal by subsection (3) is to be exercised by the criminal division of that court.

(6) Section 33(3) of the Criminal Appeal Act 1968 (c. 19) (limitation on appeal from criminal division of Court of Appeal) does not prevent an appeal to the House of Lords under this section.

(7) In relation to appeals to the Court of Appeal or the House of Lords under this section, the Secretary of State may make an order containing provision corresponding to any provision in the Criminal Appeal Act 1968 (subject to any specified modifications).

275 Duty to release certain life prisoners

(1) Section 28 of the Crime (Sentences) Act 1997 (c. 43) (duty to release certain life prisoners) is amended as follows.

(2) For subsection (1A) there is substituted –

> '(1A) This section applies to a life prisoner in respect of whom a minimum term order has been made; and any reference in this section to the relevant part of such a prisoner's sentence is a reference to the part of the sentence specified in the order.'

(3) In subsection (1B)(a) –

   (a) for the words from the beginning to 'applies' there is substituted 'this section does not apply to him', and

   (b) for the words from 'such an order' to 'appropriate stage' there is substituted 'a minimum term order has been made in respect of each of those sentences'.

(4) After subsection (8) there is inserted –

> '(8A) In this section 'minimum term order' means an order under –
>
>   (a) subsection (2) of section 82A of the Powers of Criminal Courts (Sentencing) Act 2000 (determination of minimum term in respect of life sentence that is not fixed by law), or
>
>   (b) subsection (2) of section 269 of the Criminal Justice Act 2003 (determination of minimum term in respect of mandatory life sentence).'.

276 Mandatory life sentences: transitional cases

Schedule 22 (which relates to the effect in transitional cases of mandatory life sentences) shall have effect.

277 Interpretation of Chapter 7

In this Chapter –

> 'court' includes a court-martial;
> 'guidelines' has the same meaning as in section 172(1);
> 'life sentence' means –
>
>   (a) a sentence of imprisonment for life,
>
>   (b) a sentence of detention during Her Majesty's pleasure, or
>
>   (c) a sentence of custody for life passed before the commencement of section 61(1) of the Criminal Justice and Court Services Act 2000 (c. 43) (which abolishes that sentence).

CHAPTER 8

OTHER PROVISIONS ABOUT SENTENCING

Deferment of sentence

278 Deferment of sentence

Schedule 23 (deferment of sentence) shall have effect.

Power to include drug treatment and testing requirement in certain orders in respect of young offenders

279 Drug treatment and testing requirement in action plan order or supervision order

Schedule 24 (which enables a requirement as to drug treatment and testing to be included in an action plan order or a supervision order) shall have effect.

Alteration of penalties for offences

280 Alteration of penalties for specified summary offences

(1) The summary offences listed in Schedule 25 are no longer punishable with imprisonment.

(2) Schedule 26 (which contains amendments increasing the maximum term of imprisonment for certain summary offences from 4 months or less to 51 weeks) shall have effect.

(3) This section does not affect the penalty for any offence committed before the commencement of this section.

281 Alteration of penalties for other summary offences

(1) Subsection (2) applies to any summary offence which –

   (a) is an offence under a relevant enactment,
   (b) is punishable with a maximum term of imprisonment of five months or less, and
   (c) is not listed in Schedule 25 or Schedule 26.

(2) The Secretary of State may by order amend any relevant enactment so as to –

   (a) provide that any summary offence to which this subsection applies is no longer punishable with imprisonment, or
   (b) increase to 51 weeks the maximum term of imprisonment to which a person is liable on conviction of the offence.

(3) An order under subsection (2) may make such supplementary, incidental or consequential provision as the Secretary of State considers necessary or expedient, including provision amending any relevant enactment.

(4) Subsection (5) applies to any summary offence which –

   (a) is an offence under a relevant enactment, and
   (b) is punishable with a maximum term of imprisonment of six months.

(5) The maximum term of imprisonment to which a person is liable on conviction of an offence to which this subsection applies is, by virtue of this subsection, 51 weeks (and the relevant enactment in question is to be read as if it had been amended accordingly).

(6) Neither of the following –

   (a) an order under subsection (2), or
   (b) subsection (5),
affects the penalty for any offence committed before the commencement of that order or subsection (as the case may be).

(7) In this section and section 282 'relevant enactment' means any enactment contained in –

(a) an Act passed before or in the same Session as this Act, or
(b) any subordinate legislation made before the passing of this Act.

(8) In subsection (7) 'subordinate legislation' has the same meaning as in the Interpretation Act 1978 (c. 30).

282 Increase in maximum term that may be imposed on summary conviction of offence triable either way

(1) In section 32 of the Magistrates' Courts Act 1980 (c. 43) (penalties on summary conviction for offences triable either way) in subsection (1) (offences listed in Schedule 1 to that Act) for 'not exceeding 6 months' there is substituted 'not exceeding 12 months'.

(2) Subsection (3) applies to any offence triable either way which –

(a) is an offence under a relevant enactment,
(b) is punishable with imprisonment on summary conviction, and
(c) is not listed in Schedule 1 to the Magistrates' Courts Act 1980.

(3) The maximum term of imprisonment to which a person is liable on summary conviction of an offence to which this subsection applies is by virtue of this subsection 12 months (and the relevant enactment in question is to be read as if it had been amended accordingly).

(4) Nothing in this section affects the penalty for any offence committed before the commencement of this section.

283 Enabling powers: power to alter maximum penalties

(1) The Secretary of State may by order, in accordance with subsection (2) or (3), amend any relevant enactment which confers a power (however framed or worded) by subordinate legislation to make a person –

(a) as regards a summary offence, liable on conviction to a term of imprisonment;
(b) as regards an offence triable either way, liable on summary conviction to a term of imprisonment.

(2) An order made by virtue of paragraph (a) of subsection (1) may amend the relevant enactment in question so as to –

(a) restrict the power so that a person may no longer be made liable on conviction of a summary offence to a term of imprisonment, or
(b) increase to 51 weeks the maximum term of imprisonment to which a person may be made liable on conviction of a summary offence under the power.

(3) An order made by virtue of paragraph (b) of that subsection may amend the relevant enactment in question so as to increase the maximum term of imprisonment to which a person may be made liable on summary conviction of an offence under the power to 12 months.

(4) Schedule 27 (which amends the maximum penalties which may be imposed by virtue of certain enabling powers) shall have effect.

(5) The power conferred by subsection (1) shall not apply to the enactments amended under Schedule 27.

(6) An order under subsection (1) may make such supplementary, incidental or consequential provision as the Secretary of State considers necessary or expedient, including provision amending any relevant enactment.

(7) None of the following –

(a) an order under subsection (1), or
(b) Schedule 27,

affects the penalty for any offence committed before the commencement of that order or Schedule (as the case may be).

(8) In subsection (1) 'subordinate legislation' has the same meaning as in the Interpretation Act 1978 (c. 30).

(9) In this section 'relevant enactment' means any enactment contained in an Act passed before or in the same Session as this Act.

284 Increase in penalties for drug-related offences

(1) Schedule 28 (increase in penalties for certain drug-related offences) shall have effect.

(2) That Schedule does not affect the penalty for any offence committed before the commencement of that Schedule.

285 Increase in penalties for certain driving-related offences

(1) In section 12A of the Theft Act 1968 (c. 60) (aggravated vehicle-taking), in subsection (4), for 'five years' there is substituted 'fourteen years'.

(2) Part 1 of Schedule 2 to the Road Traffic Offenders Act 1988 (c. 53) (prosecution and punishment of offences) is amended in accordance with subsections (3) and (4).

(3) In the entry relating to section 1 of the Road Traffic Act 1988 (c. 52) (causing death by dangerous driving), in column 4, for '10 years' there is substituted '14 years'.

(4) In the entry relating to section 3A of that Act (causing death by careless driving when under influence of drink or drugs), in column 4, for '10 years' there is substituted '14 years'.

(5) Part I of Schedule 1 to the Road Traffic Offenders (Northern Ireland) Order 1996 (S.I. 1996/1320 (N.I. 10)) (prosecution and punishment of offences) is amended in accordance with subsections (6) and (7).

(6) In the entry relating to Article 9 of the Road Traffic (Northern Ireland) Order 1995 (S.I. 1995/2994 (N.I. 18)) (causing death or grievous bodily injury by dangerous driving), in column 4, for '10 years' there is substituted '14 years'.

(7) In the entry relating to Article 14 of that Order (causing death or grievous bodily injury by careless driving when under the influence of drink or drugs), in column 4, for '10 years' there is substituted '14 years'.

(8) This section does not affect the penalty for any offence committed before the commencement of this section.

286 Increase in penalties for offences under section 174 of Road Traffic Act 1988

(1) In Part 1 of Schedule 2 to the Road Traffic Offenders Act 1988 (c. 53) (prosecution and punishment of offences), in the entry relating to section 174 of the Road Traffic Act

1988 (c. 52) (false statements and withholding material information), for columns (3) and (4) there is substituted –

'(a) Summarily	(a) 6 months or the statutory maximum or both
(b) On indictment	(b) 2 years or a fine or both'.

(2) Section 282(3) (increase in maximum term that may be imposed on summary conviction of offence triable either way) has effect in relation to the entry amended by subsection (1) as it has effect in relation to any other enactment contained in an Act passed before this Act.

(3) This section does not apply in relation to any offence committed before the commencement of this section.

Firearms offences

287 Minimum sentence for certain firearms offences

After section 51 of the Firearms Act 1968 (c. 27) there is inserted the following section –

'51A Minimum sentence for certain offences under s. 5

(1) This section applies where –

    (a) an individual is convicted of –
        (i)   an offence under section 5(1)(a), (ab), (aba), (ac), (ad), (ae), (af) or (c) of this Act, or
        (ii)   an offence under section 5(1A)(a) of this Act, and
    (b) the offence was committed after the commencement of this section and at a time when he was aged 16 or over.

(2) The court shall impose an appropriate custodial sentence (or order for detention) for a term of at least the required minimum term (with or without a fine) unless the court is of the opinion that there are exceptional circumstances relating to the offence or to the offender which justify its not doing so.

(3) Where an offence is found to have been committed over a period of two or more days, or at some time during a period of two or more days, it shall be taken for the purposes of this section to have been committed on the last of those days.

(4) In this section 'appropriate custodial sentence (or order for detention)' means –

    (a) in relation to England and Wales –
        (i)   in the case of an offender who is aged 18 or over when convicted, a sentence of imprisonment, and
        (ii)   in the case of an offender who is aged under 18 at that time, a sentence of detention under section 91 of the Powers of Criminal Courts (Sentencing) Act 2000;
    (b) in relation to Scotland –
        (i)   in the case of an offender who is aged 21 or over when convicted, a sentence of imprisonment,

  (ii) in the case of an offender who is aged under 21 at that time (not being an offender mentioned in sub-paragraph (iii)), a sentence of detention under section 207 of the Criminal Procedure (Scotland) Act 1995, and

  (iii) in the case of an offender who is aged under 18 at that time and is subject to a supervision requirement, an order for detention under section 44, or sentence of detention under section 208, of that Act.

(5) In this section 'the required minimum term' means –

  (a) in relation to England and Wales –
  (i) in the case of an offender who was aged 18 or over when he committed the offence, five years, and
  (ii) in the case of an offender who was under 18 at that time, three years, and
  (b) in relation to Scotland –
  (i) in the case of an offender who was aged 21 or over when he committed the offence, five years, and
  (ii) in the case of an offender who was aged under 21 at that time, three years.'

288 Certain firearms offences to be triable only on indictment

In Part 1 of Schedule 6 to the Firearms Act 1968 (c. 27) (prosecution and punishment of offences) for the entries relating to offences under section 5(1) (possessing or distributing prohibited weapons or ammunition) and section 5(1A) (possessing or distributing other prohibited weapons) there is substituted –

'Section 5(1)(a), (ab), (aba), (ac), (ad), (ae), (af) or (c)	Possessing or distributing prohibited weapons or ammunition.	On indictment	10 years or a fine, or both.
Section 5(1)(b)	Possessing or distributing prohibited weapon designed for discharge of noxious liquid etc.	(a) Summary (b) On indictment	6 months or a fine of the statutory maximum, or both. 10 years or a fine or both.
Section 5(1A)(a)	Possessing or distributing firearm disguised as other object.	On indictment	10 years or a fine, or both.
Section 5(1A)(b), (c), (d), (e), (f) or (g)	Possessing or distributing other prohibited weapons.	(a) Summary (b) On indictment	6 months or a fine of the statutory maximum, or both. 10 years or a fine, or both.'

289 Power to sentence young offender to detention in respect of certain firearms offences: England and Wales

(1) Section 91 of the Sentencing Act (offenders under 18 convicted of certain serious offences: power to detain for specified period) is amended as follows.

(2) After subsection (1) there is inserted –

'(1A) Subsection (3) below also applies where –

    (a) a person aged under 18 is convicted on indictment of an offence –
        (i)   under subsection (1)(a), (ab), (aba), (ac), (ad), (ae), (af) or (c) of section 5 of the Firearms Act 1968 (prohibited weapons), or
        (ii)   under subsection (1A)(a) of that section,
    (b) the offence was committed after the commencement of section 51A of that Act and at a time when he was aged 16 or over, and
    (c) the court is of the opinion mentioned in section 51A(2) of that Act (exceptional circumstances which justify its not imposing required custodial sentence).'

(3) After subsection (4) there is inserted –

'(5) Where subsection (2) of section 51A of the Firearms Act 1968 requires the imposition of a sentence of detention under this section for a term of at least the required minimum term (within the meaning of that section), the court shall sentence the offender to be detained for such period, of at least that term but not exceeding the maximum term of imprisonment with which the offence is punishable in the case of a person aged 18 or over, as may be specified in the sentence.'.

290 Power to sentence young offender to detention in respect of certain firearms offences: Scotland

(1) The Criminal Procedure (Scotland) Act 1995 (c. 46) is amended as follows.

(2) In section 49(3) (children's hearing for purpose of obtaining advice as to treatment of child), at the end there is added 'except that where the circumstances are such as are mentioned in paragraphs (a) and (b) of section 51A(1) of the Firearms Act 1968 it shall itself dispose of the case.'

(3) In section 208 (detention of children convicted on indictment), the existing provisions become subsection (1); and after that subsection there is added –

'(2) Subsection (1) does not apply where the circumstances are such as are mentioned in paragraphs (a) and (b) of section 51A(1) of the Firearms Act 1968.'.

291 Power by order to exclude application of minimum sentence to those under 18

(1) The Secretary of State may by order –

    (a) amend section 51A(1)(b) of the Firearms Act 1968 (c. 27) by substituting for the word '16' the word '18',
    (b) repeal section 91(1A)(c) and (5) of the Sentencing Act,
    (c) amend subsection (3) of section 49 of the Criminal Procedure (Scotland) Act 1995 by repealing the exception to that subsection,
    (d) repeal section 208(2) of that Act, and
    (e) make such other provision as he considers necessary or expedient in consequence of, or in connection with, the provision made by virtue of paragraphs (a) to (d).

(2) The provision that may be made by virtue of subsection (1)(e) includes, in particular, provision amending or repealing any provision of an Act (whenever passed), including any provision of this Act.

292 Sentencing for firearms offences in Northern Ireland

Schedule 29 (which contains amendments of the Firearms (Northern Ireland) Order 1981 (S.I. 1981/155 (N.I. 2)) relating to sentencing) shall have effect.

293 Increase in penalty for offences relating to importation or exportation of certain firearms

(1) The Customs and Excise Management Act 1979 (c. 2) is amended as follows.

(2) In section 50 (penalty for improper importation of goods), for subsection (5A) there is substituted –

'(5A) In the case of –

   (a) an offence under subsection (2) or (3) above committed in Great Britain in connection with a prohibition or restriction on the importation of any weapon or ammunition that is of a kind mentioned in section 5(1)(a), (ab), (aba), (ac), (ad), (ae), (af) or (c) or (1A)(a) of the Firearms Act 1968,

   (b) any such offence committed in Northern Ireland in connection with a prohibition or restriction on the importation of any weapon or ammunition that is of a kind mentioned in Article 6(1)(a), (ab), (ac), (ad), (ae) or (c) or (1A)(a) of the Firearms (Northern Ireland) Order 1981, or

   (c) any such offence committed in connection with the prohibition contained in section 20 of the Forgery and Counterfeiting Act 1981,

subsection (4)(b) above shall have effect as if for the words "7 years" there were substituted the words "10 years".'

(3) In section 68 (offences in relation to exportation of prohibited or restricted goods) for subsection (4A) there is substituted –

'(4A) In the case of –

   (a) an offence under subsection (2) or (3) above committed in Great Britain in connection with a prohibition or restriction on the exportation of any weapon or ammunition that is of a kind mentioned in section 5(1)(a), (ab), (aba), (ac), (ad), (ae), (af) or (c) or (1A)(a) of the Firearms Act 1968,

   (b) any such offence committed in Northern Ireland in connection with a prohibition or restriction on the exportation of any weapon or ammunition that is of a kind mentioned in Article 6(1)(a), (ab), (ac), (ad), (ae) or (c) or (1A)(a) of the Firearms (Northern Ireland) Order 1981, or

   (c) any such offence committed in connection with the prohibition contained in section 21 of the Forgery and Counterfeiting Act 1981,

subsection (3)(b) above shall have effect as if for the words "7 years" there were substituted the words "10 years".'

(4) In section 170 (penalty for fraudulent evasion of duty, etc), for subsection (4A) there is substituted –

'(4A) In the case of –

   (a) an offence under subsection (2) or (3) above committed in Great Britain in connection with a prohibition or restriction on the importation or exportation of any weapon or ammunition that is of a kind mentioned in section 5(1)(a), (ab), (aba), (ac), (ad), (ae), (af) or (c) or (1A)(a) of the Firearms Act 1968,

(b) any such offence committed in Northern Ireland in connection with a prohibition or restriction on the importation or exportation of any weapon or ammunition that is of a kind mentioned in Article 6(1)(a), (ab), (ac), (ad), (ae) or (c) or (1A)(a) of the Firearms (Northern Ireland) Order 1981, or

(c) any such offence committed in connection with the prohibitions contained in sections 20 and 21 of the Forgery and Counterfeiting Act 1981,

subsection (3)(b) above shall have effect as if for the words "7 years" there were substituted the words "10 years".'

(5) This section does not affect the penalty for any offence committed before the commencement of this section.

Offenders transferred to mental hospital

294 Duration of directions under Mental Health Act 1983 in relation to offenders

(1) Section 50 of the Mental Health Act 1983 (c. 20) (further provisions as to prisoners under sentence) is amended as follows.

(2) In subsection (1), for 'the expiration of that person's sentence' there is substituted 'his release date'.

(3) For subsections (2) and (3) there is substituted –

'(2) A restriction direction in the case of a person serving a sentence of imprisonment shall cease to have effect, if it has not previously done so, on his release date.

(3) In this section, references to a person's release date are to the day (if any) on which he would be entitled to be released (whether unconditionally or on licence) from any prison or other institution in which he might have been detained if the transfer direction had not been given; and in determining that day there shall be disregarded –

(a) any powers that would be exercisable by the Parole Board if he were detained in such a prison or other institution, and

(b) any practice of the Secretary of State in relation to the early release under discretionary powers of persons detained in such a prison or other institution.'.

295 Access to Parole Board for certain patients serving prison sentences

In section 74 of the Mental Health Act 1983 (restricted patients subject to restriction directions) after subsection (5) there is inserted –

'(5A) Where the tribunal have made a recommendation under subsection (1)(b) above in the case of a patient who is subject to a restriction direction or a limitation direction –

(a) the fact that the restriction direction or limitation direction remains in force does not prevent the making of any application or reference to the Parole Board by or in respect of him or the exercise by him of any power to require the Secretary of State to refer his case to the Parole Board, and

(b) if the Parole Board make a direction or recommendation by virtue of which the patient would become entitled to be released (whether unconditionally or on licence) from any prison or other institution in which he might have been detained if he had not been removed to hospital, the restriction direction or limitation direction shall cease to have effect at the time when he would become entitled to be so released.'

296 Duration of directions under Mental Health (Northern Ireland) Order 1986 in relation to offenders

(1) Article 56 of the Mental Health (Northern Ireland) Order 1986 (S.I. 1986/ 595 (N.I. 4)) (further provisions as to prisoners under sentence) is amended as follows.

(2) In paragraph (1), for 'the expiration of that person's sentence' there is substituted 'his release date'.

(3) For paragraphs (2) and (3) there is substituted –

'(2) A restriction direction in the case of a person serving a sentence of imprisonment shall cease to have effect, if it has not previously done so, on his release date.

(3) In this Article, references to a person's release date are to the day (if any) on which he would be entitled to be released (whether unconditionally or on licence) from any prison or juvenile justice centre in which he might have been detained if the transfer direction had not been given; and in determining that day any powers that would be exercisable by the Sentence Review Commissioners or the Life Sentence Review Commissioners if he were detained in such a prison or juvenile justice centre shall be disregarded.'

297 Access to Sentence Review Commissioners and Life Sentence Review Commissioners for certain Northern Ireland patients

In Article 79 of the Mental Health (Northern Ireland) Order 1986 (restricted patients subject to restriction directions) after paragraph (5) there is inserted –

'(5A) Where the tribunal have made a recommendation under paragraph (1)(b) in the case of a patient who is subject to a restriction direction –

(a) the fact that the restriction direction remains in force does not prevent –
  (i) the making of any application or reference to the Life Sentence Review Commissioners by or in respect of him or the exercise by him of any power to require the Secretary of State to refer his case to those Commissioners, or
  (ii) the making of any application by him to the Sentence Review Commissioners, and
(b) if –
  (i) the Life Sentence Review Commissioners give a direction by virtue of which the patient would become entitled to be released (whether unconditionally or on licence) from any prison or juvenile justice centre in which he might have been detained if the transfer direction had not been given, or
  (ii) the Sentence Review Commissioners grant a declaration by virtue of which he would become so entitled,

the restriction direction shall cease to have effect at the time at which he would become so entitled.'.

Term of detention and training order

298 Term of detention and training order

(1) Section 101 of the Sentencing Act (which relates to detention and training orders) is amended as follows.

(2) In subsection (1), for 'subsection (2)' there is substituted 'subsections (2) and (2A)'.

(3) After subsection (2) there is inserted –

'(2A) Where –

    (a) the offence is a summary offence,

    (b) the maximum term of imprisonment that a court could (in the case of an offender aged 18 or over) impose for the offence is 51 weeks,

the term of a detention and training order may not exceed 6 months.'

Disqualification from working with children

299 Disqualification from working with children

Schedule 30 (which contains amendments of Part 2 of the Criminal Justice and Court Services Act 2000 (c. 43) relating to disqualification orders under that Part) shall have effect.

Fine defaulters

300 Power to impose unpaid work requirement or curfew requirement on fine defaulter

(1) Subsection (2) applies in any case where, in respect of a person aged 16 or over, a magistrates' court –

    (a) has power under Part 3 of the Magistrates' Courts Act 1980 (c. 43) to issue a warrant of commitment for default in paying a sum adjudged to be paid by a conviction (other than a sum ordered to be paid under section 6 of the Proceeds of Crime Act 2002 (c. 29)), or

    (b) would, but for section 89 of the Sentencing Act (restrictions on custodial sentences for persons under 18), have power to issue such a warrant for such default.

(2) The magistrates' court may, instead of issuing a warrant of commitment or, as the case may be, proceeding under section 81 of the Magistrates' Courts Act 1980 (enforcement of fines imposed on young offender), order the person in default to comply with –

    (a) an unpaid work requirement (as defined by section 199), or

    (b) a curfew requirement (as defined by section 204).

(3) In this Part 'default order' means an order under subsection (2).

(4) Subsections (3) and (4) of section 177 (which relate to electronic monitoring) have effect in relation to a default order as they have effect in relation to a community order.

(5) Where a magistrates' court has power to make a default order, it may, if it thinks it expedient to do so, postpone the making of the order until such time and on such conditions (if any) as it thinks just.

(6) Schedule 8 (breach, revocation or amendment of community order), Schedule 9 (transfer of community orders to Scotland or Northern Ireland) and Chapter 4 (further provisions about orders under Chapters 2 and 3) have effect in relation to default orders as they have effect in relation to community orders, but subject to the modifications contained in Schedule 31.

(7) Where a default order has been made for default in paying any sum –

(a) on payment of the whole sum to any person authorised to receive it, the order shall cease to have effect, and

(b) on payment of a part of the sum to any such person, the total number of hours or days to which the order relates is to be taken to be reduced by a proportion corresponding to that which the part paid bears to the whole sum.

(8) In calculating any reduction required by subsection (7)(b), any fraction of a day or hour is to be disregarded.

301 Fine defaulters: driving disqualification

(1) Subsection (2) applies in any case where a magistrates' court –

(a) has power under Part 3 of the Magistrates' Courts Act 1980 (c. 43) to issue a warrant of commitment for default in paying a sum adjudged to be paid by a conviction (other than a sum ordered to be paid under section 6 of the Proceeds of Crime Act 2002 (c. 29)), or

(b) would, but for section 89 of the Sentencing Act (restrictions on custodial sentences for persons under 18), have power to issue such a warrant for such default.

(2) The magistrates' court may, instead of issuing a warrant of commitment or, as the case may be, proceeding under section 81 of the Magistrates' Courts Act 1980 (enforcement of fines imposed on young offenders), order the person in default to be disqualified, for such period not exceeding twelve months as it thinks fit, for holding or obtaining a driving licence.

(3) Where an order has been made under subsection (2) for default in paying any sum –

(a) on payment of the whole sum to any person authorised to receive it, the order shall cease to have effect, and

(b) on payment of part of the sum to any such person, the total number of weeks or months to which the order relates is to be taken to be reduced by a proportion corresponding to that which the part paid bears to the whole sum.

(4) In calculating any reduction required by subsection (3)(b) any fraction of a week or month is to be disregarded.

(5) The Secretary of State may by order amend subsection (2) by substituting, for the period there specified, such other period as may be specified in the order.

(6) A court which makes an order under this section disqualifying a person for holding or obtaining a driving licence shall require him to produce –

(a) any such licence held by him together with its counterpart; or

(b) in the case where he holds a Community licence (within the meaning of Part 3 of the Road Traffic Act 1988 (c. 52)), his Community licence and its counterpart (if any).

(7) In this section –

'driving licence' means a licence to drive a motor vehicle granted under Part 3 of the Road Traffic Act 1988;
'counterpart' –
   (a) in relation to a driving licence, has the meaning given in relation to such a licence by section 108(1) of that Act; and
   (b) in relation to a Community licence, has the meaning given by section 99B of that Act.

CHAPTER 9

SUPPLEMENTARY

302 Execution of process between England and Wales and Scotland

Section 4 of the Summary Jurisdiction (Process) Act 1881 (c. 24) (execution of process of English and Welsh courts in Scotland) applies to any process issued by a magistrates' court under –

paragraph 7(2) or (4), 13(6) or 25(1) of Schedule 8,
paragraph 12 of Schedule 9,
paragraph 8(1) of Schedule 10, or
paragraph 6(2) or (4), 12(1) or 20(1) of Schedule 12,
as it applies to process issued under the Magistrates' Courts Act 1980 by a magistrates' court.

303 Sentencing: repeals

The following enactments (which are superseded by the provisions of this Part) shall cease to have effect –

   (a) Part 2 of the Criminal Justice Act 1991 (c. 53) (early release of prisoners),
   (b) in the Crime (Sentences) Act 1997 (c. 43) –
       (i)   section 29 (power of Secretary of State to release life prisoners to whom section 28 of that Act does not apply),
       (ii)   section 33 (transferred prisoners), and
       (iii) sections 35 and 40 (fine defaulters),
   (c) sections 80 and 81 of the Crime and Disorder Act 1998 (c. 37) (sentencing guidelines), and
   (d) in the Sentencing Act –
       (i)   Chapter 3 of Part 4 (community orders available only where offender 16 or over),
       (ii)   section 85 (sexual or violent offences: extension of custodial term for licence purposes),
       (iii) sections 87 and 88 (remand in custody),
       (iv)   section 109 (life sentence for second serious offence), and
       (v)   Chapter 5 of Part 5 (suspended sentences).

304 Amendments relating to sentencing

Schedule 32 (which contains amendments related to the provisions of this Part) shall have effect.

305 Interpretation of Part 12

(1) In this Part, except where the contrary intention appears –

'accredited programme' has the meaning given by section 202(2);

'activity requirement', in relation to a community order, custody plus order, intermittent custody order or suspended sentence order, has the meaning given by section 201;

'alcohol treatment requirement', in relation to a community order or suspended sentence order, has the meaning given by section 212;

'the appropriate officer of the court' means, in relation to a magistrates' court, the clerk of the court;

'associated', in relation to offences, is to be read in accordance with section 161(1) of the Sentencing Act;

'attendance centre' has the meaning given by section 221(2);

'attendance centre requirement', in relation to a community order, custody plus order, intermittent custody order or suspended sentence order, has the meaning given by section 214;

'community order' has the meaning given by section 177(1);

'community requirement', in relation to a suspended sentence order, has the meaning given by section 189(7);

'community sentence' has the meaning given by section 147(1);

'court' (without more), except in Chapter 7, does not include a service court;

'curfew requirement', in relation to a community order, custody plus order, intermittent custody order or suspended sentence order, has the meaning given by section 204;

'custodial sentence' has the meaning given by section 76 of the Sentencing Act;

'custody plus order' has the meaning given by section 181(4);

'default order' has the meaning given by section 300(3);

'drug rehabilitation requirement', in relation to a community order or suspended sentence order, has the meaning given by section 209;

'electronic monitoring requirement', in relation to a community order, custody plus order, intermittent custody order or suspended sentence order, has the meaning given by section 215;

'exclusion requirement', in relation to a community order, custody plus order, intermittent custody order or suspended sentence order, has the meaning given by section 205;

'guardian' has the same meaning as in the Children and Young Persons Act 1933 (c. 12);

'intermittent custody order' has the meaning given by section 183(2);

'licence' means a licence under Chapter 6;

'local probation board' means a local probation board established under section 4 of the Criminal Justice and Court Services Act 2000 (c. 43);

'mental health treatment requirement', in relation to a community order or suspended sentence order, has the meaning given by section 207;

'pre-sentence report' has the meaning given by section 158(1);

'programme requirement', in relation to a community order, custody plus order, intermittent custody order or suspended sentence order, has the meaning given by section 202;

'prohibited activity requirement', in relation to a community order, custody plus order, intermittent custody order or suspended sentence order, has the meaning given by section 203;

'residence requirement', in relation to a community order or suspended sentence order, has the meaning given by section 206;

'responsible officer', in relation to an offender to whom a community order, a custody plus order, an intermittent custody order or a suspended sentence order relates, has the meaning given by section 197;

'sentence of imprisonment' does not include a committal –

(a) in default of payment of any sum of money,

(b) for want of sufficient distress to satisfy any sum of money, or

(c) for failure to do or abstain from doing anything required to be done or left undone,

and references to sentencing an offender to imprisonment are to be read accordingly;

'the Sentencing Act' means the Powers of Criminal Courts (Sentencing) Act 2000 (c. 6);

'service court' means –

(a) a court-martial constituted under the Army Act 1955 (3 & 4 Eliz. 2 c. 18), the Air Force Act 1955 (3 & 4 Eliz. 2 c. 19) or the Naval Discipline Act 1957 (c. 53);

(b) a summary appeal court constituted under section 83ZA of the Army Act 1955, section 83ZA of the Air Force Act 1955 or section 52FF of the Naval Discipline Act 1957;

(c) the Courts-Martial Appeal Court; or

(d) a Standing Civilian Court;

'service disciplinary proceedings' means –

(a) any proceedings under the Army Act 1955, the Air Force Act 1955 or the Naval Discipline Act 1957 (whether before a court-martial or any other court or person authorised under any of those Acts to award a punishment in respect of any offence), and

(b) any proceedings before a Standing Civilian Court;

'supervision requirement', in relation to a community order, custody plus order, intermittent custody order or suspended sentence order, has the meaning given by section 213;

'suspended sentence' and 'suspended sentence order' have the meaning given by section 189(7);

'unpaid work requirement', in relation to a community order, custody plus order, intermittent custody order or suspended sentence order, has the meaning given by section 199;

'youth offending team' means a team established under section 39 of the Crime and Disorder Act 1998 (c. 37).

(2) For the purposes of any provision of this Part which requires the determination of the age of a person by the court or the Secretary of State, his age is to be taken to be that which it appears to the court or (as the case may be) the Secretary of State to be after considering any available evidence.

(3) Any reference in this Part to an offence punishable with imprisonment is to be read without regard to any prohibition or restriction imposed by or under any Act on the imprisonment of young offenders.

(4) For the purposes of this Part –

(a) a sentence falls to be imposed under subsection (2) of section 51A of the Firearms Act 1968 (c. 27) if it is required by that subsection and the court is not of the opinion there mentioned,

(b) a sentence falls to be imposed under section 110(2) or 111(2) of the Sentencing Act if it is required by that provision and the court is not of the opinion there mentioned,

(c) a sentence falls to be imposed under section 225 or 227 if, because the court is of the opinion mentioned in subsection (1)(b) of that section, the court is obliged to pass a sentence complying with that section,

(d) a sentence falls to be imposed under section 226 if, because the court is of the opinion mentioned in subsection (1)(b) of that section and considers that the case falls within subsection (2) or (3) of that section, the court is obliged to pass a sentence complying with that section, and

(e) a sentence falls to be imposed under section 228 if, because the court is of the opinion mentioned in subsection (1)(b)(i) and (ii) of that section, the court is obliged to pass a sentence complying with that section.

PART 13

MISCELLANEOUS

Detention of suspected terrorists

306 Limit on period of detention without charge of suspected terrorists

(1) Schedule 8 to the Terrorism Act 2000 (c. 11) (detention) is amended as follows.

(2) At the beginning of paragraph 29(3) (duration of warrants of further detention) there is inserted 'Subject to paragraph 36(3A),'.

(3) In sub-paragraph (3) of paragraph 36 (extension of warrants) –

(a) at the beginning there is inserted 'Subject to sub-paragraph (3A),', and

(b) for the words from 'beginning' onwards there is substituted 'beginning with the relevant time'.

(4) After that sub-paragraph there is inserted –

'(3A) Where the period specified in a warrant of further detention –

(a) ends at the end of the period of seven days beginning with the relevant time, or

(b) by virtue of a previous extension (or further extension) under this sub-paragraph, ends after the end of that period,

the specified period may, on an application under this paragraph, be extended or further extended to a period ending not later than the end of the period of fourteen days beginning with the relevant time.

(3B) In this paragraph "the relevant time", in relation to a person, means –

(a) the time of his arrest under section 41, or

(b) if he was being detained under Schedule 7 when he was arrested under section 41, the time when his examination under that Schedule began.'

Enforcement of legislation on endangered species

307 Enforcement of regulations implementing Community legislation on endangered species

(1) In this section –

'the 1972 Act' means the European Communities Act 1972 (c. 68);
'relevant Community instrument' means –

- (a) Council Regulation 338/97/EC on the protection of species of wild fauna and flora by regulating the trade therein, and
- (b) Commission Regulation 1808/01/EC on the implementation of the Council Regulation mentioned in paragraph (a).

(2) Regulations made under section 2(2) of the 1972 Act for the purpose of implementing any relevant Community instrument may, notwithstanding paragraph 1(1)(d) of Schedule 2 to the 1972 Act, create offences punishable on conviction on indictment with imprisonment for a term not exceeding five years.

(3) In relation to Scotland and Northern Ireland, regulations made under section 2(2) of the 1972 Act for the purpose of implementing any relevant Community instrument may, notwithstanding paragraph 1(1)(d) of Schedule 2 to the 1972 Act, create offences punishable on summary conviction with imprisonment for a term not exceeding six months.

(4) In Scotland, a constable may arrest without a warrant a person –

- (a) who has committed or attempted to commit an offence under regulations made under section 2(2) of the 1972 Act for the purpose of implementing any relevant Community instrument, or
- (b) whom he has reasonable grounds for suspecting to have committed or to have attempted to commit such an offence.

(5) Until the coming into force of paragraph 3 of Schedule 27 (which amends paragraph 1 of Schedule 2 to the 1972 Act), subsection (3) has effect –

- (a) with the omission of the words 'in relation to Scotland and Northern Ireland', and
- (b) as if, in relation to England and Wales, the definition of 'relevant Community instrument' also included Council Directive 92/43/EEC on the conservation of natural habitats and wild fauna and flora as amended by the Act of Accession to the European Union of Austria, Finland and Sweden and by Council Directive 97/62/EC.

(6) Any reference in this section to a Community instrument is to be read –

- (a) as a reference to that instrument as amended from time to time, and
- (b) where any provision of that instrument has been repealed, as including a reference to any instrument that re-enacts the repealed provision (with or without amendment).

Miscellaneous provisions about criminal proceedings

308 Non-appearance of defendant: plea of guilty

In section 12 of the Magistrates' Courts Act 1980 (c. 43) (non-appearance of accused: plea of guilty) subsection (1)(a)(i) (which excludes offences punishable with imprisonment for term exceeding 3 months) is omitted.

309 Preparatory hearings for serious offences not involving fraud

In section 29 of the Criminal Procedure and Investigations Act 1996 (c. 25) (power to order preparatory hearings) in subsection (1) (preparatory hearing may be held in complex or lengthy trial) after 'complexity' there is inserted 'a case of such seriousness'.

310 Preparatory hearings to deal with severance and joinder of charges

(1) In section 7(1) of the Criminal Justice Act 1987 (c. 38) (which sets out the purposes of preparatory hearings in fraud cases) after paragraph (d) there is inserted 'or

    (e)   considering questions as to the severance or joinder of charges'.

(2) In section 9(3) of that Act (determinations as to the admissibility of evidence etc) after paragraph (c) there is inserted 'and

    (d)   any question as to the severance or joinder of charges'.

(3) In section 9(11) of that Act (appeals against orders or rulings under section 9(3)(b) or (c)) for 'or (c)' there is substituted '(c) or (d)'.

(4) In section 29(2) of the Criminal Procedure and Investigations Act 1996 (purposes of preparatory hearings in non-fraud cases) after paragraph (d) there is inserted –

    '(e)   considering questions as to the severance or joinder of charges,'.

(5) In section 31(3) of that Act (rulings as to the admissibility of evidence etc) after paragraph (b) there is inserted –

    '(c)   any question as to the severance or joinder of charges'.

311 Reporting restrictions for preparatory hearings

(1) The Criminal Justice Act 1987 is amended as follows.

(2) In paragraphs (a) and (b) of section 11(1) (restrictions on reporting) for 'Great Britain' there is substituted 'the United Kingdom'.

(3) In section 11A (offences in connection with reporting) after subsection (3) there is inserted –

'(3A) Proceedings for an offence under this section shall not be instituted in Northern Ireland otherwise than by or with the consent of the Attorney General for Northern Ireland.'

(4) In section 17(3) (extent) after 'sections 2 and 3;' there is inserted 'sections 11 and 11A;'.

(5) The Criminal Procedure and Investigations Act 1996 (c. 25) is amended as follows.

(6) In paragraphs (a) and (b) of section 37(1) (restrictions on reporting) for 'Great Britain' there is substituted 'the United Kingdom'.

(7) In section 38 (offences in connection with reporting) after subsection (3) there is inserted –

'(3A) Proceedings for an offence under this section shall not be instituted in Northern Ireland otherwise than by or with the consent of the Attorney General for Northern Ireland.'

(8) In paragraphs (a) and (b) of section 41(1) (restrictions on reporting) for 'Great Britain' there is substituted 'the United Kingdom'.

(9) In section 79(3) (extent) after 'Parts III' there is inserted '(other than sections 37 and 38)'.

(10) In Schedule 4 (modifications for Northern Ireland) paragraph 16 is omitted.

312 Awards of costs

(1) The Prosecution of Offences Act 1985 (c. 23) is amended as follows.

(2) In section 16(4A) (defence costs on an appeal under section 9(11) of Criminal Justice Act 1987 (c. 38) may be met out of central funds) after '1987' there is inserted 'or section 35(1) of the Criminal Procedure and Investigations Act 1996'.

(3) In section 18(2) (award of costs against accused in case of dismissal of appeal under section 9(11) of the Criminal Justice Act 1987 etc) after paragraph (c) there is inserted 'or

> (d) an appeal or application for leave to appeal under section 35(1) of the Criminal Procedure and Investigations Act 1996.'

313 Extension of investigations by Criminal Cases Review Commission in England and Wales

(1) Section 23A of the Criminal Appeal Act 1968 (c. 19) (power to order investigations by Criminal Cases Review Commission) is amended as follows.

(2) In subsection (1) after 'conviction' there is inserted 'or an application for leave to appeal against conviction,'.

(3) In paragraph (a) of that subsection –

> (a) at the beginning there is inserted 'in the case of an appeal,', and
> (b) for 'case', in both places where it occurs, there is substituted 'appeal'.

(4) After paragraph (a) of that subsection there is inserted –

> '(aa) in the case of an application for leave to appeal, the matter is relevant to the determination of the application and ought, if possible, to be resolved before the application is determined;'.

(5) After that subsection there is inserted –

> '(1A) A direction under subsection (1) above may not be given by a single judge, notwithstanding that, in the case of an application for leave to appeal, the application may be determined by a single judge as provided for by section 31 of this Act.'

(6) After subsection (4) there is inserted –

> '(5) In this section 'respondent' includes a person who will be a respondent if leave to appeal is granted.'

314 Extension of investigations by Criminal Cases Review Commission in Northern Ireland

(1) Section 25A of the Criminal Appeal (Northern Ireland) Act 1980 (c. 47) (power to order investigations by Criminal Cases Review Commission) is amended as follows.

(2) In subsection (1) after 'conviction' there is inserted 'or an application for leave to appeal against conviction,'.

(3) In paragraph (a) of that subsection –

   (a) at the beginning there is inserted 'in the case of an appeal,', and
   (b) for 'case', in both places where it occurs, there is substituted 'appeal'.

(4) After paragraph (a) of that subsection there is inserted –

   '(aa) in the case of an application for leave to appeal, the matter is relevant to the determination of the application and ought, if possible, to be resolved before the application is determined;'.

(5) After that subsection there is inserted –

   '(1A) A direction under subsection (1) above may not be given by a single judge, notwithstanding that, in the case of an application for leave to appeal, the application may be determined by a single judge as provided for by section 45 below.'

(6) After subsection (4) there is inserted –

   '(5) In this section 'respondent' includes a person who will be a respondent if leave to appeal is granted.'

315 Appeals following reference by Criminal Cases Review Commission

(1) Section 14 of the Criminal Appeal Act 1995 (c. 35) (further provision about references by Criminal Cases Review Commission) is amended as follows.

(2) After subsection (4) there is inserted –

   '(4A) Subject to subsection (4B), where a reference under section 9 or 10 is treated as an appeal against any conviction, verdict, finding or sentence, the appeal may not be on any ground which is not related to any reason given by the Commission for making the reference.

   (4B) The Court of Appeal may give leave for an appeal mentioned in subsection (4A) to be on a ground relating to the conviction, verdict, finding or sentence which is not related to any reason given by the Commission for making the reference'.

(3) In subsection (5) for 'any of sections 9 to' there is substituted 'section 11 or'.

316 Power to substitute conviction of alternative offence on appeal in England and Wales

(1) The Criminal Appeal Act 1968 (c. 19) is amended as follows.

(2) In section 3 (power to substitute conviction of alternative offence) in subsection (1) after 'an offence' there is inserted 'to which he did not plead guilty'.

(3) After section 3 there is inserted –

'3A Power to substitute conviction of alternative offence after guilty plea

(1) This section applies on an appeal against conviction where –

    (a)   an appellant has been convicted of an offence to which he pleaded guilty,

    (b)   if he had not so pleaded, he could on the indictment have pleaded, or been found, guilty of some other offence, and

    (c)   it appears to the Court of Appeal that the plea of guilty indicates an admission by the appellant of facts which prove him guilty of the other offence.

(2) The Court of Appeal may, instead of allowing or dismissing the appeal, substitute for the appellant's plea of guilty a plea of guilty of the other offence and pass such sentence in substitution for the sentence passed at the trial as may be authorised by law for the other offence, not being a sentence of greater severity.'

317 Power to substitute conviction of alternative offence on appeal in Northern Ireland

(1) The Criminal Appeal (Northern Ireland) Act 1980 (c. 47) is amended as follows.

(2) In section 3 (power to substitute conviction of alternative offence) in subsection (1) after 'an offence' there is inserted 'to which he did not plead guilty'.

(3) After section 3 there is inserted –

'3A Power to substitute conviction of alternative offence after guilty plea

(1) This section applies where –

    (a)   an appellant has been convicted of an offence to which he pleaded guilty,

    (b)   if he had not so pleaded, he could on the indictment have pleaded, or been found, guilty of some other offence, and

    (c)   it appears to the Court of Appeal that the plea of guilty indicates an admission by the appellant of facts which prove him guilty of that other offence.

(2) The Court may, instead of allowing or dismissing the appeal, substitute for the appellant's plea of guilty a plea of guilty of that other offence and pass such sentence in substitution for the sentence passed at the trial as may be warranted in law by the plea so substituted.'

318 Substitution of conviction on different charge on appeal from court-martial

(1) The Courts-Martial (Appeals) Act 1968 (c. 20) is amended as follows.

(2) In section 14 (substitution of conviction on different charge) in subsection (1) after 'an offence' there is inserted 'to which he did not plead guilty'.

(3) After section 14 there is inserted –

'14A Substitution of conviction on different charge after guilty plea

(1) This section applies where –

    (a)   an appellant has been convicted of an offence to which he pleaded guilty,

    (b)   if he had not so pleaded, he could lawfully have pleaded, or been found, guilty of some other offence, and

    (c)   it appears to the Appeal Court on an appeal against conviction that the plea of guilty indicates an admission by the appellant of facts which prove him guilty of that other offence.

(2) The Appeal Court may, instead of allowing or dismissing the appeal, substitute for the appellant's plea of guilty a plea of guilty of the other offence, and may pass on the appellant, in substitution for the sentence passed on him by the court-martial, such sentence as they think proper, being a sentence warranted by the relevant Service Act for that other offence, but not a sentence of greater severity.'

319 Appeals against sentences in England and Wales

(1) The Criminal Appeal Act 1968 (c. 19) is amended as follows.

(2) In section 10 (appeal against sentence in certain cases) for subsection (3) there is substituted –

'(3) An offender dealt with for an offence before the Crown Court in a proceeding to which subsection (2) of this section applies may appeal to the Court of Appeal against any sentence passed on him for the offence by the Crown Court.'

(3) In section 11 (supplementary provisions as to appeal against sentence) after subsection (6) there is inserted –

'(7) For the purposes of this section, any two or more sentences are to be treated as passed in the same proceeding if –

(a) they are passed on the same day; or
(b) they are passed on different days but the court in passing any one of them states that it is treating that one together with the other or others as substantially one sentence.'

Outraging public decency

320 Offence of outraging public decency triable either way

(1) After paragraph 1 of Schedule 1 to the Magistrates' Courts Act 1980 (c. 43) (offences triable either way by virtue of section 17) there is inserted –

'1A An offence at common law of outraging public decency.'

(2) This section does not apply in relation to any offence committed before the commencement of this section.

Jury service

321 Jury service

Schedule 33 (jury service) shall have effect.

Individual support orders

322 Individual support orders

After section 1A of the Crime and Disorder Act 1998 (c. 37) there is inserted –

'1AA Individual support orders

(1) Where a court makes an anti-social behaviour order in respect of a defendant who is a child or young person when that order is made, it must consider whether the individual support conditions are fulfilled.

(2) If it is satisfied that those conditions are fulfilled, the court must make an order under this section ("an individual support order") which –

(a) requires the defendant to comply, for a period not exceeding six months, with such requirements as are specified in the order; and

(b) requires the defendant to comply with any directions given by the responsible officer with a view to the implementation of the requirements under paragraph (a) above.

(3) The individual support conditions are –

(a) that an individual support order would be desirable in the interests of preventing any repetition of the kind of behaviour which led to the making of the anti-social behaviour order;

(b) that the defendant is not already subject to an individual support order; and

(c) that the court has been notified by the Secretary of State that arrangements for implementing individual support orders are available in the area in which it appears to it that the defendant resides or will reside and the notice has not been withdrawn.

(4) If the court is not satisfied that the individual support conditions are fulfilled, it shall state in open court that it is not so satisfied and why it is not.

(5) The requirements that may be specified under subsection (2)(a) above are those that the court considers desirable in the interests of preventing any repetition of the kind of behaviour which led to the making of the anti-social behaviour order.

(6) Requirements included in an individual support order, or directions given under such an order by a responsible officer, may require the defendant to do all or any of the following things –

(a) to participate in activities specified in the requirements or directions at a time or times so specified;

(b) to present himself to a person or persons so specified at a place or places and at a time or times so specified;

(c) to comply with any arrangements for his education so specified.

(7) But requirements included in, or directions given under, such an order may not require the defendant to attend (whether at the same place or at different places) on more than two days in any week; and "week" here means a period of seven days beginning with a Sunday.

(8) Requirements included in, and directions given under, an individual support order shall, as far as practicable, be such as to avoid –

(a) any conflict with the defendant's religious beliefs; and

(b) any interference with the times, if any, at which he normally works or attends school or any other educational establishment.

(9) Before making an individual support order, the court shall obtain from a social worker of a local authority social services department or a member of a youth offending team any information which it considers necessary in order –

(a) to determine whether the individual support conditions are fulfilled, or

(b) to determine what requirements should be imposed by an individual support order if made,

and shall consider that information.

(10) In this section and section 1AB below "responsible officer", in relation to an individual support order, means one of the following who is specified in the order, namely –

    (a) a social worker of a local authority social services department;

    (b) a person nominated by a person appointed as chief education officer under section 532 of the Education Act 1996 (c. 56);

    (c) a member of a youth offending team.

1AB Individual support orders: explanation, breach, amendment etc

(1) Before making an individual support order, the court shall explain to the defendant in ordinary language –

    (a) the effect of the order and of the requirements proposed to be included in it;

    (b) the consequences which may follow (under subsection (3) below) if he fails to comply with any of those requirements; and

    (c) that the court has power (under subsection (6) below) to review the order on the application either of the defendant or of the responsible officer.

(2) The power of the Secretary of State under section 174(4) of the Criminal Justice Act 2003 includes power by order to –

    (a) prescribe cases in which subsection (1) above does not apply; and

    (b) prescribe cases in which the explanation referred to in that subsection may be made in the absence of the defendant, or may be provided in written form.

(3) If the person in respect of whom an individual support order is made fails without reasonable excuse to comply with any requirement included in the order, he is guilty of an offence and liable on summary conviction to a fine not exceeding –

    (a) if he is aged 14 or over at the date of his conviction, £1,000;

    (b) if he is aged under 14 then, £250.

(4) No referral order under section 16(2) or (3) of the Powers of Criminal Courts (Sentencing) Act 2000 (referral of young offenders to youth offender panels) may be made in respect of an offence under subsection (3) above.

(5) If the anti-social behaviour order as a result of which an individual support order was made ceases to have effect, the individual support order (if it has not previously ceased to have effect) ceases to have effect when the anti-social behaviour order does.

(6) On an application made by complaint by –

    (a) the person subject to an individual support order, or

    (b) the responsible officer,

        the court which made the individual support order may vary or discharge it by a further order.

(7) If the anti-social behaviour order as a result of which an individual support order was made is varied, the court varying the anti-social behaviour order may by a further order vary or discharge the individual support order.'

323 Individual support orders: consequential amendments

(1) The Crime and Disorder Act 1998 (c. 37) is amended as mentioned in subsections (2) to (5).

(2) In section 4 of that Act (appeals against orders) –

    (a) in subsection (1) after 'an anti-social behaviour order' there is inserted ', an individual support order', and

    (b) in subsection (3) after '1(8)' there is inserted ', 1AB(6)'.

(3) In section 18(1) of that Act (interpretation of Chapter 1) –

    (a) after the definition of 'curfew notice' there is inserted –

    '"individual support order" has the meaning given by section 1AA(2) above;', and

    (b) in the definition of 'responsible officer', before paragraph (a) there is inserted –

    '(za) in relation to an individual support order, has the meaning given by section 1AA(10) above;'.

(4) In section 18(4) of that Act (cases where social worker or member of a youth offending team to give supervision or directions) –

    (a) after 'directions under' there is inserted 'an individual support order or', and

    (b) for 'the child or, as the case may be, the parent' there is substituted 'the child, defendant or parent, as the case may be,'.

(5) In section 38 of that Act (local provision of youth justice services), in subsection (4)(f) after 'in relation to' there is inserted 'individual support orders,'.

(6) In section 143(2) (provisions in which sums may be altered) of the Magistrates' Courts Act 1980 (c. 43), after paragraph (d) there is inserted –

    '(da) section 1AB(3) of the Crime and Disorder Act 1998 (failure to comply with individual support order);'.

Parenting orders and referral orders

324 Parenting orders and referral orders

Schedule 34 (parenting orders and referral orders) shall have effect.

Assessing etc. risks posed by sexual or violent offenders

325 Arrangements for assessing etc risks posed by certain offenders

(1) In this section –

    'relevant sexual or violent offender' has the meaning given by section 327;
    'responsible authority', in relation to any area, means the chief officer of police, the local probation board for that area and the Minister of the Crown exercising functions in relation to prisons, acting jointly.

(2) The responsible authority for each area must establish arrangements for the purpose of assessing and managing the risks posed in that area by –

    (a) relevant sexual and violent offenders, and

    (b) other persons who, by reason of offences committed by them (wherever committed), are considered by the responsible authority to be persons who may cause serious harm to the public.

(3) In establishing those arrangements, the responsible authority must act in co-operation with the persons specified in subsection (6); and it is the duty of those persons to co-operate in the establishment by the responsible authority of those arrangements, to the extent that such co-operation is compatible with the exercise by those persons of their functions under any other enactment.

(4) Co-operation under subsection (3) may include the exchange of information.

(5) The responsible authority for each area ('the relevant area') and the persons specified in subsection (6) must together draw up a memorandum setting out the ways in which they are to co-operate.

(6) The persons referred to in subsections (3) and (5) are –

(a) every youth offending team established for an area any part of which falls within the relevant area,

(b) the Ministers of the Crown exercising functions in relation to social security, child support, war pensions, employment and training,

(c) every local education authority any part of whose area falls within the relevant area,

(d) every local housing authority or social services authority any part of whose area falls within the relevant area,

(e) every registered social landlord which provides or manages residential accommodation in the relevant area in which persons falling within subsection (2)(a) or (b) reside or may reside,

(f) every Health Authority or Strategic Health Authority any part of whose area falls within the relevant area,

(g) every Primary Care Trust or Local Health Board any part of whose area falls within the relevant area,

(h) every NHS trust any part of whose area falls within the relevant area, and

(i) every person who is designated by the Secretary of State by order for the purposes of this paragraph as a provider of electronic monitoring services.

(7) The Secretary of State may by order amend subsection (6) by adding or removing any person or description of person.

(8) The Secretary of State may issue guidance to responsible authorities on the discharge of the functions conferred by this section and section 326.

(9) In this section –

'local education authority' has the same meaning as in the Education Act 1996 (c. 56);

'local housing authority' has the same meaning as in the Housing Act 1985 (c. 68);

'Minister of the Crown' has the same meaning as in the Ministers of the Crown Act 1975 (c. 26);

'NHS trust' has the same meaning as in the National Health Service Act 1977 (c. 49);

'prison' has the same meaning as in the Prison Act 1952 (c. 52);

'registered social landlord' has the same meaning as in Part 1 of the Housing Act 1996 (c. 52);

'social services authority' means a local authority for the purposes of the Local Authority Social Services Act 1970 (c. 42).

326 Review of arrangements

(1) The responsible authority for each area must keep the arrangements established by it under section 325 under review with a view to monitoring their effectiveness and making any changes to them that appear necessary or expedient.

(2) The responsible authority for any area must exercise their functions under subsection (1) in consultation with persons appointed by the Secretary of State as lay advisers in relation to that authority.

(3) The Secretary of State must appoint two lay advisers under subsection (2) in relation to each responsible authority.

(4) The responsible authority must pay to or in respect of the persons so appointed such allowances as the Secretary of State may determine.

(5) As soon as practicable after the end of each period of 12 months beginning with 1st April, the responsible authority for each area must –

  (a) prepare a report on the discharge by it during that period of the functions conferred by section 325 and this section, and
  (b) publish the report in that area.

(6) The report must include –

  (a) details of the arrangements established by the responsible authority, and
  (b) information of such descriptions as the Secretary of State has notified to the responsible authority that he wishes to be included in the report.

327 Section 325: interpretation

(1) For the purposes of section 325, a person is a relevant sexual or violent offender if he falls within one or more of subsections (2) to (5).

(2) A person falls within this subsection if he is subject to the notification requirements of Part 2 of the Sexual Offences Act 2003 (c. 42).

(3) A person falls within this subsection if –

  (a) he is convicted by a court in England or Wales of murder or an offence specified in Schedule 15, and
  (b) one of the following sentences is imposed on him in respect of the conviction –
    (i)   a sentence of imprisonment for a term of 12 months or more,
    (ii)   a sentence of detention in a young offender institution for a term of 12 months or more,
    (iii) a sentence of detention during Her Majesty's pleasure,
    (iv)   a sentence of detention for public protection under section 226,
    (v)   a sentence of detention for a period of 12 months or more under section 91 of the Sentencing Act (offenders under 18 convicted of certain serious offences),
    (vi)   a sentence of detention under section 228,
    (vii) a detention and training order for a term of 12 months or more, or
    (viii) a hospital or guardianship order within the meaning of the Mental Health Act 1983 (c. 20).

(4) A person falls within this subsection if –

(a) he is found not guilty by a court in England and Wales of murder or an offence specified in Schedule 15 by reason of insanity or to be under a disability and to have done the act charged against him in respect of such an offence, and

(b) one of the following orders is made in respect of the act charged against him as the offence –
 (i) an order that he be admitted to hospital, or
 (ii) a guardianship order within the meaning of the Mental Health Act 1983.

(5) A person falls within this subsection if –

(a) the first condition set out in section 28(2) or 29(2) of the Criminal Justice and Court Services Act 2000 (c. 43) or the second condition set out in section 28(3) or 29(3) of that Act is satisfied in his case, or

(b) an order under section 29A of that Act has been made in respect of him.

(6) In this section 'court' does not include a service court, as defined by section 305(1).

Criminal record certificates

328 Criminal record certificates: amendments of Part 5 of Police Act 1997

Schedule 35 (which contains amendments of Part 5 of the Police Act 1997 (c. 50)) shall have effect.

Civil proceedings brought by offenders

329 Civil proceedings for trespass to the person brought by offender

(1) This section applies where –

(a) a person ('the claimant') claims that another person ('the defendant') did an act amounting to trespass to the claimant's person, and

(b) the claimant has been convicted in the United Kingdom of an imprisonable offence committed on the same occasion as that on which the act is alleged to have been done.

(2) Civil proceedings relating to the claim may be brought only with the permission of the court.

(3) The court may give permission for the proceedings to be brought only if there is evidence that either –

(a) the condition in subsection (5) is not met, or

(b) in all the circumstances, the defendant's act was grossly disproportionate.

(4) If the court gives permission and the proceedings are brought, it is a defence for the defendant to prove both –

(a) that the condition in subsection (5) is met, and

(b) that, in all the circumstances, his act was not grossly disproportionate.

(5) The condition referred to in subsection (3)(a) and (4)(a) is that the defendant did the act only because –

(a) he believed that the claimant –
 (i) was about to commit an offence,
 (ii) was in the course of committing an offence, or
 (iii) had committed an offence immediately beforehand; and

(b) he believed that the act was necessary to –

(i)   defend himself or another person,
(ii)   protect or recover property,
(iii)   prevent the commission or continuation of an offence, or
(iv)   apprehend, or secure the conviction, of the claimant after he had committed an offence;

or was necessary to assist in achieving any of those things.

(6) Subsection (4) is without prejudice to any other defence.

(7) Where –

(a)   in service disciplinary proceedings, as defined by section 305(1), a person has been found guilty of an offence under section 70 of the Army Act 1955 (3 & 4 Eliz. 2 c. 18), section 70 of the Air Force Act 1955 (3 & 4 Eliz. 2 c. 19) or section 42 of the Naval Discipline Act 1957 (c. 53), and
(b)   the corresponding civil offence (within the meaning of that Act) was an imprisonable offence,

he is to be treated for the purposes of this section as having been convicted in the United Kingdom of the corresponding civil offence.

(8) In this section –

(a)   the reference to trespass to the person is a reference to –
        (i)   assault,
        (ii)   battery, or
        (iii)   false imprisonment;
(b)   references to a defendant's belief are to his honest belief, whether or not the belief was also reasonable;
(c)   'court' means the High Court or a county court; and
(d)   'imprisonable offence' means an offence which, in the case of a person aged 18 or over, is punishable by imprisonment.

PART 14

GENERAL

330 Orders and rules

(1) This section applies to –

(a)   any power conferred by this Act on the Secretary of State to make an order or rules;
(b)   the power conferred by section 168 on the Lord Chancellor to make an order.

(2) The power is exercisable by statutory instrument.

(3) The power –

(a)   may be exercised so as to make different provision for different purposes or different areas, and
(b)   may be exercised either for all the purposes to which the power extends, or for those purposes subject to specified exceptions, or only for specified purposes.

(4) The power includes power to make –

(a)   any supplementary, incidental or consequential provision, and
(b)   any transitory, transitional or saving provision,

which the Minister making the instrument considers necessary or expedient.

(5) A statutory instrument containing –

(a)   an order under any of the following provisions –

section 25(5),
section 103,
section 161(7),
section 178,
section 197(3),
section 223,
section 246(5),
section 260,
section 267,
section 269(6),
section 281(2),
section 283(1),
section 291,
section 301(5),
section 325(7), and
paragraph 5 of Schedule 31,

(b)   an order under section 336(3) bringing section 43 into force,
(c)   an order making any provision by virtue of section 333(2)(b) which adds to, replaces or omits any part of the text of an Act, or
(d)   rules under section 240(4)(a),

may only be made if a draft of the statutory instrument has been laid before, and approved by a resolution of, each House of Parliament.

(6) Any other statutory instrument made in the exercise of a power to which this section applies is subject to annulment in pursuance of a resolution of either House of Parliament.

(7) Subsection (6) does not apply to a statutory instrument containing only an order made under one or more of the following provisions –

section 202(3)(b),
section 215(3),
section 253(5),
section 325(6)(i), and
section 336.

331 Further minor and consequential amendments

Schedule 36 (further minor and consequential amendments) shall have effect.

332 Repeals

Schedule 37 (repeals) shall have effect.

333 Supplementary and consequential provision, etc.

(1) The Secretary of State may by order make –

(a)   any supplementary, incidental or consequential provision, and
(b)   any transitory, transitional or saving provision,

which he considers necessary or expedient for the purposes of, in consequence of, or for giving full effect to any provision of this Act.

(2) An order under subsection (1) may, in particular –

(a) provide for any provision of this Act which comes into force before another such provision has come into force to have effect, until that other provision has come into force, with such modifications as are specified in the order, and

(b) amend or repeal –

    (i) any Act passed before, or in the same Session as, this Act, and

    (ii) subordinate legislation made before the passing of this Act.

(3) Nothing in this section limits the power by virtue of section 330(4)(b) to include transitional or saving provision in an order under section 336.

(4) The amendments that may be made under subsection (2)(b) are in addition to those made by or under any other provision of this Act.

(5) In this section 'subordinate legislation' has the same meaning as in the Interpretation Act 1978 (c. 30).

(6) Schedule 38 (which contains transitory and transitional provisions and savings) shall have effect.

334 Provision for Northern Ireland

(1) An Order in Council under section 85 of the Northern Ireland Act 1998 (c. 47) (provision dealing with certain reserved matters) which contains a statement that it is made only for purposes corresponding to those of any provisions of this Act specified in subsection (2) –

(a) shall not be subject to subsections (3) to (9) of that section (affirmative resolution of both Houses of Parliament), but

(b) shall be subject to annulment in pursuance of a resolution of either House of Parliament.

(2) The provisions are –

(a) in Part 1, sections 1, 3(3), 4, 7 to 10 and 12 and paragraphs 1, 2, 5 to 10 and 20 of Schedule 1, and

(b) Parts 8, 9 and 11.

(3) In relation to any time when section 1 of the Northern Ireland Act 2000 (c. 1) is in force (suspension of devolved government in Northern Ireland) –

(a) the reference in subsection (1) above to section 85 of the Northern Ireland Act 1998 shall be read as a reference to paragraph 1 of the Schedule to the Northern Ireland Act 2000 (legislation by Order in Council during suspension), and

(b) the reference in subsection (1)(a) above to subsections (3) to (9) of that section shall be read as a reference to paragraph 2 of that Schedule.

(4) The reference in section 41(2) of the Justice (Northern Ireland) Act 2002 (c. 26) (transfer of certain functions to Director of Public Prosecutions for Northern Ireland) to any function of the Attorney General for Northern Ireland of consenting to the institution of criminal proceedings includes any such function which is conferred by an amendment made by this Act.

(5) Any reference to any provision of the Criminal Appeal (Northern Ireland) Act 1980 (c. 47) in the Access to Justice (Northern Ireland) Order 2003 (S.I. 2003/435 (N.I. 10)) is to be read as a reference to that provision as amended by this Act.

335 Expenses

There shall be paid out of money provided by Parliament –

(a) any expenditure incurred by a Minister of the Crown by virtue of this Act, and
(b) any increase attributable to this Act in the sums payable out of money so provided under any other enactment.

336 Commencement

(1) The following provisions of this Act come into force on the passing of this Act –

section 168(1) and (2),
section 183(8),
section 307(1) to (3), (5) and (6),
section 330,
section 333(1) to (5),
sections 334 and 335,
this section and sections 337, 338 and 339, and
the repeal in Part 9 of Schedule 37 of section 81(2) and (3) of the Countryside and Rights of Way Act 2000 (c. 37) (and section 332 so far as relating to that repeal), and
paragraphs 1 and 6 of Schedule 38 (and section 333(6) so far as relating to those paragraphs).

(2) The following provisions of this Act come into force at the end of the period of four weeks beginning with the day on which this Act is passed –

Chapter 7 of Part 12 (and Schedules 21 and 22);
section 303(b)(i) and (ii);
paragraphs 42, 43(3), 66, 83(1) to (3), 84 and 109(2), (3)(b), (4) and (5) of Schedule 32 (and section 304 so far as relating to those provisions);
Part 8 of Schedule 37 (and section 332 so far as relating to that Part of that Schedule).

(3) The remaining provisions of this Act come into force in accordance with provision made by the Secretary of State by order.

(4) Different provision may be made for different purposes and different areas.

337 Extent

(1) Subject to the following provisions of this section and to section 338, this Act extends to England and Wales only.

(2) The following provisions extend also to Scotland and Northern Ireland –

sections 71 and 72;
sections 82 and 83;
section 180 and Schedule 9;
section 188 and Schedule 11;
section 194 and Schedule 13;
section 293;
section 306
section 307;
section 311;

this Part, except sections 331, 332 and 334(5);
paragraphs 19, 70 and 71 of Schedule 3;
paragraph 12(3) of Schedule 12;
paragraphs 3, 6, 7 and 8 of Schedule 27;
paragraphs 6 to 8 of Schedule 31.

(3) The following provisions extend also to Scotland –

section 50(14);
section 286;
sections 287, 288, and 291;
section 302;
paragraph 2 of Schedule 23;
paragraphs 1, 2 and 5 of Schedule 27;
paragraph 7 of Schedule 38.

(4) Section 290 extends to Scotland only.

(5) The following provisions extend also to Northern Ireland –

Part 5;
Part 7;
sections 75 to 81;
sections 84 to 93;
sections 95 to 97;
section 315;
Schedule 5.

(6) The following provisions extend to Northern Ireland only –

section 292 and Schedule 29;
sections 296 and 297;
section 314;
section 317;
section 334(5).

(7) The amendment or repeal of any enactment by any provision of –

(a) Part 1,
(b) section 285,
(c) Part 2 of Schedule 3 (except as mentioned in subsection (8)),
(d) Schedule 27,
(e) Schedule 28,
(f) Part 1 of Schedule 32,
(g) Parts 1 to 4 and 6 of Schedule 36, and
(h) Parts 1 to 4, 6 to 8, 10 and 12 of Schedule 37 (except as mentioned in subsection (9)),

extends to the part or parts of the United Kingdom to which the enactment extends.

(8) Paragraphs 29, 30, 31, 39, 41, 50, 53 and 63 of Schedule 3 do not extend to Northern Ireland.

(9) The repeals in Part 4 of Schedule 37 relating to –

(a) the Bankers' Books Evidence Act 1879 (c. 11),
(b) the Explosive Substances Act 1883 (c. 3),
(c) the Backing of Warrants (Republic of Ireland) Act 1965 (c. 45),
(d) the Customs and Excise Management Act 1979 (c. 2), and

(e) the Contempt of Court Act 1981 (c. 49),

do not extend to Northern Ireland.

(10) The provisions mentioned in subsection (11), so far as relating to proceedings before a particular service court, have the same extent as the Act under which the court is constituted.

(11) Those provisions are –

section 113 and Schedule 6;
section 135 and Schedule 7.

(12) Nothing in subsection (1) affects –

(a) the extent of Chapter 7 of Part 12 so far as relating to sentences passed by a court-martial, or

(b) the extent of section 299 and Schedule 30 so far as relating to the making of orders by, or orders made by, courts-martial or the Courts-Martial Appeal Court.

(13) Any provision of this Act which –

(a) relates to any enactment contained in –
    (i)   the Army Act 1955 (3 & 4 Eliz. 2 c. 18),
    (ii)   the Air Force Act 1955 (3 & 4 Eliz. 2 c. 19),
    (iii) the Naval Discipline Act 1957 (c. 53),
    (iv)   the Courts-Martial (Appeals) Act 1968 (c. 20),
    (v)   the Armed Forces Act 1976 (c. 52),
    (vi)   section 113 of the Police and Criminal Evidence Act 1984 (c. 60),
    (vii) the Reserve Forces Act 1996 (c. 14), or
    (viii) the Armed Forces Act 2001 (c. 19), and

(b) is not itself contained in Schedule 25 or Part 9 of Schedule 37,

has the same extent as the enactment to which it relates.

338 Channel Islands and Isle of Man

(1) Subject to subsections (2) and (3), Her Majesty may by Order in Council extend any provision of this Act, with such modifications as appear to Her Majesty in Council to be appropriate, to any of the Channel Islands or the Isle of Man.

(2) Subsection (1) does not authorise the extension to any place of a provision of this Act so far as the provision amends an enactment that does not itself extend there and is not itself capable of being extended there in the exercise of a power conferred on Her Majesty in Council.

(3) Subsection (1) does not apply in relation to any provision that extends to the Channel Islands or the Isle of Man by virtue of any of subsections (10) to (13) of section 337.

(4) Subsection (4) of section 330 applies to the power to make an Order in Council under subsection (1) as it applies to any power of the Secretary of State to make an order under this Act, but as if references in that subsection to the Minister making the instrument were references to Her Majesty in Council.

339 Short title

This Act may be cited as the Criminal Justice Act 2003.

SCHEDULES

SCHEDULE 1 Section 12

AMENDMENTS RELATED TO PART 1

The 1984 Act

1 The 1984 Act is amended as follows.

2 In section 18 (entry and search after arrest), for subsection (5) there is substituted –

'(5) A constable may conduct a search under subsection (1) –

(a) before the person is taken to a police station or released on bail under section 30A, and
(b) without obtaining an authorisation under subsection (4),

if the condition in subsection (5A) is satisfied.

(5A) The condition is that the presence of the person at a place (other than a police station) is necessary for the effective investigation of the offence.'

3 In section 21 (access and copying), at the end there is inserted –

'(9) The references to a constable in subsections (1), (2), (3)(a) and (5) include a person authorised under section 16(2) to accompany a constable executing a warrant.'

4 In section 22 (retention), at the end there is inserted –

'(7) The reference in subsection (1) to anything seized by a constable includes anything seized by a person authorised under section 16(2) to accompany a constable executing a warrant.'

5 In section 34 (limitation on police detention), for subsection (7) there is substituted –

'(7) For the purposes of this Part a person who –

(a) attends a police station to answer to bail granted under section 30A,
(b) returns to a police station to answer to bail granted under this Part, or
(c) is arrested under section 30D or 46A,

is to be treated as arrested for an offence and that offence is the offence in connection with which he was granted bail.'

6 In section 35(1) (designated police stations), for 'section 30(3) and (5) above' there is substituted 'sections 30(3) and (5), 30A(5) and 30D(2)'.

7 In section 36 (custody officers at police stations), after subsection (7) there is inserted –

'(7A) Subject to subsection (7B), subsection (7) applies where a person attends a police station which is not a designated station to answer to bail granted under section 30A as it applies where a person is taken to such a station.

(7B) Where subsection (7) applies because of subsection (7A), the reference in subsection (7)(b) to the officer who took him to the station is to be read as a reference to the officer who granted him bail.'

8 In section 41(2) (calculation of periods of time), after paragraph (c) there is inserted –

'(ca) in the case of a person who attends a police station to answer to bail granted under section 30A, the time when he arrives at the police station;'.

9 In section 45A(2)(a) (functions which may be performed by video-conferencing), after 'taken to' there is inserted ', or answering to bail at,'.

10 In section 47 (bail after arrest) –

(a)   in subsection (6), after 'granted bail' there is inserted 'under this Part', and
(b)   in subsection (7), after 'released on bail' there is inserted 'under this Part'.

Criminal Justice Act 1987 (c. 38)

11 In section 2 of the Criminal Justice Act 1987 (director's investigation powers), after subsection (6) there is inserted –

'(6A) Where an appropriate person accompanies a constable, he may exercise the powers conferred by subsection (5) but only in the company, and under the supervision, of the constable.'

12 In subsection (7) of that section (meaning of appropriate person), for 'subsection (6) above' there is substituted 'this section'.

13 In subsection (8D) of that section (references to evidence obtained by Director), after 'by a constable' there is inserted 'or by an appropriate person'.

Criminal Justice and Police Act 2001 (c. 16)

14 In section 56 of the Criminal Justice and Police Act 2001 (property seized by constables etc.), after subsection (4) there is inserted –

'(4A) Subsection (1)(a) includes property seized on any premises –

(a)   by a person authorised under section 16(2) of the 1984 Act to accompany a constable executing a warrant, or
(b)   by a person accompanying a constable under section 2(6) of the Criminal Justice Act 1987 in the execution of a warrant under section 2(4) of that Act.'

Armed Forces Act 2001 (c. 19)

15 In section 2(9) of the Armed Forces Act 2001 (offences for purpose of definition of prohibited article), at the end of paragraph (d) there is inserted '; and

(e) offences under section 1 of the Criminal Damage Act 1971 (destroying or damaging property).'

Police Reform Act 2002 (c. 30)

16 Schedule 4 to the Police Reform Act 2002 (powers exercisable by police civilians) is amended as follows.

17 In paragraph 17 (access to excluded and special procedure material) after paragraph (b) there is inserted –

'(bb) section 15 of that Act (safeguards) shall have effect in relation to the issue of any warrant under paragraph 12 of that Schedule to that person as it has effect in relation to the issue of a warrant under that paragraph to a constable;

(bc)　section 16 of that Act (execution of warrants) shall have effect in relation to any warrant to enter and search premises that is issued under paragraph 12 of that Schedule (whether to that person or to any other person) in respect of premises in the relevant police area as if references in that section to a constable included references to that person;'.

18　In paragraph 20 (access and copying in case of things seized by constables) after 'by a constable' there is inserted 'or by a person authorised to accompany him under section 16(2) of that Act'.

19　After paragraph 24 (extended powers of seizure) there is inserted –

'Persons accompanying investigating officers

24A(1) This paragraph applies where a person ("an authorised person") is authorised by virtue of section 16(2) of the 1984 Act to accompany an investigating officer designated for the purposes of paragraph 16 (or 17) in the execution of a warrant.

(2) The reference in paragraph 16(h) (or 17(e)) to the seizure of anything by a designated person in exercise of a particular power includes a reference to the seizure of anything by the authorised person in exercise of that power by virtue of section 16(2A) of the 1984 Act.

(3) In relation to any such seizure, paragraph 16(h) (or 17(e)) is to be read as if it provided for the references to a constable and to an officer in section 21(1) and (2) of the 1984 Act to include references to the authorised person.

(4) The reference in paragraph 16(i) (or 17(f)) to anything seized by a designated person in exercise of a particular power includes a reference to anything seized by the authorised person in exercise of that power by virtue of section 16(2A) of the 1984 Act.

(5) In relation to anything so seized, paragraph 16(i)(ii) (or 17(f)(ii)) is to be read as if it provided for –

(a)　the references to the supervision of a constable in subsections (3) and (4) of section 21 of the 1984 Act to include references to the supervision of a person designated for the purposes of paragraph 16 (or paragraph 17), and

(b)　the reference to a constable in subsection (5) of that section to include a reference to such a person or an authorised person accompanying him.

(6) Where an authorised person accompanies an investigating officer who is also designated for the purposes of paragraph 24, the references in sub-paragraphs (a) and (b) of that paragraph to the designated person include references to the authorised person.'

20　In paragraph 34 (powers of escort officer to take arrested person to prison), in sub-paragraph (1)(a), for 'subsection (1) of section 30' there is substituted 'subsection (1A) of section 30'.

SCHEDULE 2　　　　　　　　　　　　　　　　　　Section 28

CHARGING OR RELEASE OF PERSONS IN POLICE DETENTION

1　The Police and Criminal Evidence Act 1984 (c. 60) is amended as follows.

2(1) Section 37 (duties of custody officers before charge) is amended as follows.

(2) In subsection (7) for paragraphs (a) and (b) there is substituted –

'(a) shall be released without charge and on bail for the purpose of enabling the Director of Public Prosecutions to make a decision under section 37B below,

(b) shall be released without charge and on bail but not for that purpose,

(c) shall be released without charge and without bail, or

(d) shall be charged.'

(3) After that subsection there is inserted –

'(7A) The decision as to how a person is to be dealt with under subsection (7) above shall be that of the custody officer.

(7B) Where a person is released under subsection (7)(a) above, it shall be the duty of the custody officer to inform him that he is being released to enable the Director of Public Prosecutions to make a decision under section 37B below.'

(4) In subsection (8)(a) after '(7)(b)' there is inserted 'or (c)'.

3 After that section there is inserted –

'37A Guidance

(1) The Director of Public Prosecutions may issue guidance –

(a) for the purpose of enabling custody officers to decide how persons should be dealt with under section 37(7) above or 37C(2) below, and

(b) as to the information to be sent to the Director of Public Prosecutions under section 37B(1) below.

(2) The Director of Public Prosecutions may from time to time revise guidance issued under this section.

(3) Custody officers are to have regard to guidance under this section in deciding how persons should be dealt with under section 37(7) above or 37C(2) below.

(4) A report under section 9 of the Prosecution of Offences Act 1985 (report by DPP to Attorney General) must set out the provisions of any guidance issued, and any revisions to guidance made, in the year to which the report relates.

(5) The Director of Public Prosecutions must publish in such manner as he thinks fit –

(a) any guidance issued under this section, and

(b) any revisions made to such guidance.

(6) Guidance under this section may make different provision for different cases, circumstances or areas.

37B Consultation with the Director of Public Prosecutions

(1) Where a person is released on bail under section 37(7)(a) above, an officer involved in the investigation of the offence shall, as soon as is practicable, send to the Director of Public Prosecutions such information as may be specified in guidance under section 37A above.

(2) The Director of Public Prosecutions shall decide whether there is sufficient evidence to charge the person with an offence.

(3) If he decides that there is sufficient evidence to charge the person with an offence, he shall decide –

(a) whether or not the person should be charged and, if so, the offence with which he should be charged, and

(b) whether or not the person should be given a caution and, if so, the offence in respect of which he should be given a caution.

(4) The Director of Public Prosecutions shall give written notice of his decision to an officer involved in the investigation of the offence.

(5) If his decision is –

(a) that there is not sufficient evidence to charge the person with an offence, or

(b) that there is sufficient evidence to charge the person with an offence but that the person should not be charged with an offence or given a caution in respect of an offence,

a custody officer shall give the person notice in writing that he is not to be prosecuted.

(6) If the decision of the Director of Public Prosecutions is that the person should be charged with an offence, or given a caution in respect of an offence, the person shall be charged or cautioned accordingly.

(7) But if his decision is that the person should be given a caution in respect of the offence and it proves not to be possible to give the person such a caution, he shall instead be charged with the offence.

(8) For the purposes of this section, a person is to be charged with an offence either –

(a) when he is in police detention after returning to a police station to answer bail or is otherwise in police detention at a police station, or

(b) in accordance with section 29 of the Criminal Justice Act 2003.

(9) In this section "caution" includes –

(a) a conditional caution within the meaning of Part 3 of the Criminal Justice Act 2003, and

(b) a warning or reprimand under section 65 of the Crime and Disorder Act 1998.

37C Breach of bail following release under section 37(7)(a)

(1) This section applies where –

(a) a person released on bail under section 37(7)(a) above or subsection (2)(b) below is arrested under section 46A below in respect of that bail, and

(b) at the time of his detention following that arrest at the police station mentioned in section 46A(2) below, notice under section 37B(4) above has not been given.

(2) The person arrested –

(a) shall be charged, or

(b) shall be released without charge, either on bail or without bail.

(3) The decision as to how a person is to be dealt with under subsection (2) above shall be that of a custody officer.

(4) A person released on bail under subsection (2)(b) above shall be released on bail subject to the same conditions (if any) which applied immediately before his arrest.

37D Release under section 37(7)(a): further provision

(1) Where a person is released on bail under section 37(7)(a) or section 37C(2)(b) above, a custody officer may subsequently appoint a different time, or an additional time, at which the person is to attend at the police station to answer bail.

(2) The custody officer shall give the person notice in writing of the exercise of the power under subsection (1).

(3) The exercise of the power under subsection (1) shall not affect the conditions (if any) to which bail is subject.

(4) Where a person released on bail under section 37(7)(a) or 37C(2)(b) above returns to a police station to answer bail or is otherwise in police detention at a police station, he may be kept in police detention to enable him to be dealt with in accordance with section 37B or 37C above or to enable the power under subsection (1) above to be exercised.

(5) If the person is not in a fit state to enable him to be so dealt with or to enable that power to be exercised, he may be kept in police detention until he is.

(6) Where a person is kept in police detention by virtue of subsection (4) or (5) above, section 37(1) to (3) and (7) above (and section 40(8) below so far as it relates to section 37(1) to (3)) shall not apply to the offence in connection with which he was released on bail under section 37(7)(a) or 37C(2)(b) above.'

4 In section 40 (review of police detention) in subsection (9) after '37(9)' there is inserted 'or 37D(5)'.

5 In section 46A (power of arrest for failure to answer police bail) after subsection (1) insert –

'(1A) A person who has been released on bail under section 37(7)(a) or 37C(2)(b) above may be arrested without warrant by a constable if the constable has reasonable grounds for suspecting that the person has broken any of the conditions of bail.'

6(1) Section 47 (bail after arrest) is amended as follows.

(2) In subsection (1) (release on bail under Part 4 shall be release on bail granted in accordance with certain provisions of the Bail Act 1976) for 'Subject to subsection (2) below' there is substituted 'Subject to the following provisions of this section'.

(3) In subsection (1A) (bail conditions may be imposed when a person is released under section 38(1)) after 'section', in the first place where it occurs, there is inserted '37(7)(a) above or section'.

(4) After that subsection there is inserted –

'(1B) No application may be made under section 5B of the Bail Act 1976 if a person is released on bail under section 37(7)(a) or 37C(2)(b) above.

(1C) Subsections (1D) to (1F) below apply where a person released on bail under section 37(7)(a) or 37C(2)(b) above is on bail subject to conditions.

(1D) The person shall not be entitled to make an application under section 43B of the Magistrates' Courts Act 1980.

(1E) A magistrates' court may, on an application by or on behalf of the person, vary the conditions of bail; and in this subsection 'vary' has the same meaning as in the Bail Act 1976.

(1F) Where a magistrates' court varies the conditions of bail under subsection (1E) above, that bail shall not lapse but shall continue subject to the conditions as so varied.'

SCHEDULE 3   Section 41

ALLOCATION OF CASES TRIABLE EITHER WAY, AND SENDING CASES TO THE CROWN COURT ETC

PART 1

PRINCIPAL AMENDMENTS

Magistrates' Courts Act 1980 (c. 43)

1 The Magistrates' Courts Act 1980 is amended as follows.

2(1) Section 17A (initial indication as to plea) is amended as follows.

(2) For paragraph (b) of subsection (4) there is substituted –

'(b) he may (unless section 17D(2) below were to apply) be committed to the Crown Court under section 3 or (if applicable) 3A of the Powers of Criminal Courts (Sentencing) Act 2000 if the court is of such opinion as is mentioned in subsection (2) of the applicable section.'

(3) After subsection (9) there is inserted –

'(10) If in respect of the offence the court receives a notice under section 51B or 51C of the Crime and Disorder Act 1998 (which relate to serious or complex fraud cases and to certain cases involving children respectively), the preceding provisions of this section and the provisions of section 17B below shall not apply, and the court shall proceed in relation to the offence in accordance with section 51 or, as the case may be, section 51A of that Act.'

3 After section 17C there is inserted –

'17D Maximum penalty under section 17A(6) or 17B(2)(c) for certain offences

(1) If –

(a) the offence is a scheduled offence (as defined in section 22(1) below);
(b) the court proceeds in relation to the offence in accordance with section 17A(6) or 17B(2)(c) above; and
(c) the court convicts the accused of the offence,

the court shall consider whether, having regard to any representations made by him or by the prosecutor, the value involved (as defined in section 22(10) below) appears to the court to exceed the relevant sum (as specified for the purposes of section 22 below).

(2) If it appears to the court clear that the value involved does not exceed the relevant sum, or it appears to the court for any reason not clear whether the value involved does or does not exceed the relevant sum –

(a) subject to subsection (4) below, the court shall not have power to impose on the accused in respect of the offence a sentence in excess of the limits mentioned in section 33(1)(a) below; and
(b) sections 3 and 4 of the Powers of Criminal Courts (Sentencing) Act 2000 shall not apply as regards that offence.

(3) Subsections (9) to (12) of section 22 below shall apply for the purposes of this section as they apply for the purposes of that section (reading the reference to subsection (1) in section 22(9) as a reference to subsection (1) of this section).

(4) Subsection (2)(a) above does not apply to an offence under section 12A of the Theft Act 1968 (aggravated vehicle-taking).

17E Functions under sections 17A to 17D capable of exercise by single justice

(1) The functions of a magistrates' court under sections 17A to 17D above may be discharged by a single justice.

(2) Subsection (1) above shall not be taken as authorising –

(a) the summary trial of an information (otherwise than in accordance with section 17A(6) or 17B(2)(c) above); or
(b) the imposition of a sentence,

by a magistrates' court composed of fewer than two justices.'

4 In section 18 (initial procedure on information against adult for offence triable either way), for subsection (5) there is substituted –

'(5) The functions of a magistrates' court under sections 19 to 23 below may be discharged by a single justice, but this subsection shall not be taken as authorising –

(a) the summary trial of an information (otherwise than in accordance with section 20(7) below); or
(b) the imposition of a sentence,

by a magistrates' court composed of fewer than two justices.'

5 For section 19 (court to begin by considering which mode of trial appears more suitable) there is substituted –

'19 Decision as to allocation

(1) The court shall decide whether the offence appears to it more suitable for summary trial or for trial on indictment.

(2) Before making a decision under this section, the court –

(a) shall give the prosecution an opportunity to inform the court of the accused's previous convictions (if any); and
(b) shall give the prosecution and the accused an opportunity to make representations as to whether summary trial or trial on indictment would be more suitable.

(3) In making a decision under this section, the court shall consider –

(a) whether the sentence which a magistrates' court would have power to impose for the offence would be adequate; and
(b) any representations made by the prosecution or the accused under subsection (2)(b) above,

and shall have regard to any allocation guidelines (or revised allocation guidelines) issued as definitive guidelines under section 170 of the Criminal Justice Act 2003.

(4) Where –

(a) the accused is charged with two or more offences; and

(b) it appears to the court that the charges for the offences could be joined in the same indictment or that the offences arise out of the same or connected circumstances,

subsection (3)(a) above shall have effect as if references to the sentence which a magistrates' court would have power to impose for the offence were a reference to the maximum aggregate sentence which a magistrates' court would have power to impose for all of the offences taken together.

(5) In this section any reference to a previous conviction is a reference to –

(a) a previous conviction by a court in the United Kingdom; or
(b) a previous finding of guilt in –
    (i) any proceedings under the Army Act 1955, the Air Force Act 1955 or the Naval Discipline Act 1957 (whether before a court-martial or any other court or person authorised under any of those Acts to award a punishment in respect of any offence); or
    (ii) any proceedings before a Standing Civilian Court.

(6) If, in respect of the offence, the court receives a notice under section 51B or 51C of the Crime and Disorder Act 1998 (which relate to serious or complex fraud cases and to certain cases involving children respectively), the preceding provisions of this section and sections 20, 20A and 21 below shall not apply, and the court shall proceed in relation to the offence in accordance with section 51(1) of that Act.'

6 For section 20 (procedure where summary trial appears more suitable) there is substituted –

'20 Procedure where summary trial appears more suitable

(1) If the court decides under section 19 above that the offence appears to it more suitable for summary trial, the following provisions of this section shall apply (unless they are excluded by section 23 below).

(2) The court shall explain to the accused in ordinary language –

(a) that it appears to the court more suitable for him to be tried summarily for the offence;
(b) that he can either consent to be so tried or, if he wishes, be tried on indictment; and
(c) in the case of a specified offence (within the meaning of section 224 of the Criminal Justice Act 2003), that if he is tried summarily and is convicted by the court, he may be committed for sentence to the Crown Court under section 3A of the Powers of Criminal Courts (Sentencing) Act 2000 if the committing court is of such opinion as is mentioned in subsection (2) of that section.

(3) The accused may then request an indication ('an indication of sentence') of whether a custodial sentence or non-custodial sentence would be more likely to be imposed if he were to be tried summarily for the offence and to plead guilty.

(4) If the accused requests an indication of sentence, the court may, but need not, give such an indication.

(5) If the accused requests and the court gives an indication of sentence, the court shall ask the accused whether he wishes, on the basis of the indication, to reconsider the indication of plea which was given, or is taken to have been given, under section 17A or 17B above.

(6) If the accused indicates that he wishes to reconsider the indication under section 17A or 17B above, the court shall ask the accused whether (if the offence were to proceed to trial) he would plead guilty or not guilty.

(7) If the accused indicates that he would plead guilty the court shall proceed as if –

(a) the proceedings constituted from that time the summary trial of the information; and
(b) section 9(1) above were complied with and he pleaded guilty under it.

(8) Subsection (9) below applies where –

(a) the court does not give an indication of sentence (whether because the accused does not request one or because the court does not agree to give one);
(b) the accused either –
  (i) does not indicate, in accordance with subsection (5) above, that he wishes; or
  (ii) indicates, in accordance with subsection (5) above, that he does not wish,
  to reconsider the indication of plea under section 17A or 17B above; or
(c) the accused does not indicate, in accordance with subsection (6) above, that he would plead guilty.

(9) The court shall ask the accused whether he consents to be tried summarily or wishes to be tried on indictment and –

(a) if he consents to be tried summarily, shall proceed to the summary trial of the information; and
(b) if he does not so consent, shall proceed in relation to the offence in accordance with section 51(1) of the Crime and Disorder Act 1998.

20A Procedure where summary trial appears more suitable: supplementary

(1) Where the case is dealt with in accordance with section 20(7) above, no court (whether a magistrates' court or not) may impose a custodial sentence for the offence unless such a sentence was indicated in the indication of sentence referred to in section 20 above.

(2) Subsection (1) above is subject to sections 3A(4), 4(8) and 5(3) of the Powers of Criminal Courts (Sentencing) Act 2000.

(3) Except as provided in subsection (1) above –

(a) an indication of sentence shall not be binding on any court (whether a magistrates' court or not); and
(b) no sentence may be challenged or be the subject of appeal in any court on the ground that it is not consistent with an indication of sentence.

(4) Subject to section 20(7) above, the following shall not for any purpose be taken to constitute the taking of a plea –

(a) asking the accused under section 20 above whether (if the offence were to proceed to trial) he would plead guilty or not guilty; or
(b) an indication by the accused under that section of how he would plead.

(5) Where the court gives an indication of sentence under section 20 above, it shall cause each such indication to be entered in the register.

(6) In this section and in section 20 above, references to a custodial sentence are to a custodial sentence within the meaning of section 76 of the Powers of Criminal Courts (Sentencing) Act 2000, and references to a non-custodial sentence shall be construed accordingly.'

7 For section 21 (procedure where trial on indictment appears more suitable) there is substituted –

'21 Procedure where trial on indictment appears more suitable

If the court decides under section 19 above that the offence appears to it more suitable for trial on indictment, the court shall tell the accused that the court has decided that it is more suitable for him to be tried on indictment, and shall proceed in relation to the offence in accordance with section 51(1) of the Crime and Disorder Act 1998.'

8(1) Section 23 (power of court, with consent of legally represented accused, to proceed in his absence) is amended as follows.

(2) In subsection (4) –

   (a) for the words preceding paragraph (a) there is substituted 'If the court decides under section 19 above that the offence appears to it more suitable for trial on indictment then— ', and
   (b) in paragraph (b), for the words from 'to inquire' to the end there is substituted 'in relation to the offence in accordance with section 51(1) of the Crime and Disorder Act 1998.'.

(3) For subsection (5) there is substituted –

   '(5) If the court decides under section 19 above that the offence appears to it more suitable for trial on indictment, section 21 above shall not apply and the court shall proceed in relation to the offence in accordance with section 51(1) of the Crime and Disorder Act 1998.'

9(1) Section 24 (summary trial of information against child or young persons for indictable offence), as amended by section 42 of this Act, is amended as follows.

(2) For subsection (1) there is substituted –

   '(1) Where a person under the age of 18 years appears or is brought before a magistrates' court on an information charging him with an indictable offence he shall, subject to sections 51 and 51A of the Crime and Disorder Act 1998 and to sections 24A and 24B below, be tried summarily.'

(3) Subsections (1A) and (2) are omitted.

10 After section 24 there is inserted –

'24A Child or young person to indicate intention as to plea in certain cases

   (1) This section applies where –

   (a) a person under the age of 18 years appears or is brought before a magistrates' court on an information charging him with an offence other than one falling within section 51A(12) of the Crime and Disorder Act 1998 ("the 1998 Act"); and
   (b) but for the application of the following provisions of this section, the court would be required at that stage, by virtue of section 51(7) or (8) or 51A(3)(b), (4) or (5) of the 1998 Act to determine, in relation to the offence, whether to send the person to the Crown Court for trial (or to determine any

matter, the effect of which would be to determine whether he is sent to the Crown Court for trial).

(2) Where this section applies, the court shall, before proceeding to make any such determination as is referred to in subsection (1)(b) above (the 'relevant determination'), follow the procedure set out in this section.

(3) Everything that the court is required to do under the following provisions of this section must be done with the accused person in court.

(4) The court shall cause the charge to be written down, if this has not already been done, and to be read to the accused.

(5) The court shall then explain to the accused in ordinary language that he may indicate whether (if the offence were to proceed to trial) he would plead guilty or not guilty, and that if he indicates that he would plead guilty –

(a) the court must proceed as mentioned in subsection (7) below; and
(b) (in cases where the offence is one mentioned in section 91(1) of the Powers of Criminal Courts (Sentencing) Act 2000) he may be sent to the Crown Court for sentencing under section 3B or (if applicable) 3C of that Act if the court is of such opinion as is mentioned in subsection (2) of the applicable section.

(6) The court shall then ask the accused whether (if the offence were to proceed to trial) he would plead guilty or not guilty.

(7) If the accused indicates that he would plead guilty, the court shall proceed as if –

(a) the proceedings constituted from the beginning the summary trial of the information; and
(b) section 9(1) above was complied with and he pleaded guilty under it,

and, accordingly, the court shall not (and shall not be required to) proceed to make the relevant determination or to proceed further under section 51 or (as the case may be) section 51A of the 1998 Act in relation to the offence.

(8) If the accused indicates that he would plead not guilty, the court shall proceed to make the relevant determination and this section shall cease to apply.

(9) If the accused in fact fails to indicate how he would plead, for the purposes of this section he shall be taken to indicate that he would plead not guilty.

(10) Subject to subsection (7) above, the following shall not for any purpose be taken to constitute the taking of a plea –

(a) asking the accused under this section whether (if the offence were to proceed to trial) he would plead guilty or not guilty;
(b) an indication by the accused under this section of how he would plead.

24B Intention as to plea by child or young person: absence of accused

(1) This section shall have effect where –

(a) a person under the age of 18 years appears or is brought before a magistrates' court on an information charging him with an offence other than one falling within section 51A(12) of the Crime and Disorder Act 1998;
(b) but for the application of the following provisions of this section, the court would be required at that stage to make one of the determinations referred to in paragraph (b) of section 24A(1) above ('the relevant determination');
(c) the accused is represented by a legal representative;

(d) the court considers that by reason of the accused's disorderly conduct before the court it is not practicable for proceedings under section 24A above to be conducted in his presence; and

(e) the court considers that it should proceed in the absence of the accused.

(2) In such a case –

(a) the court shall cause the charge to be written down, if this has not already been done, and to be read to the representative;

(b) the court shall ask the representative whether (if the offence were to proceed to trial) the accused would plead guilty or not guilty;

(c) if the representative indicates that the accused would plead guilty the court shall proceed as if the proceedings constituted from the beginning the summary trial of the information, and as if section 9(1) above was complied with and the accused pleaded guilty under it;

(d) if the representative indicates that the accused would plead not guilty the court shall proceed to make the relevant determination and this section shall cease to apply.

(3) If the representative in fact fails to indicate how the accused would plead, for the purposes of this section he shall be taken to indicate that the accused would plead not guilty.

(4) Subject to subsection (2)(c) above, the following shall not for any purpose be taken to constitute the taking of a plea –

(a) asking the representative under this section whether (if the offence were to proceed to trial) the accused would plead guilty or not guilty;

(b) an indication by the representative under this section of how the accused would plead.

24C Intention as to plea by child or young person: adjournment

(1) A magistrates' court proceeding under section 24A or 24B above may adjourn the proceedings at any time, and on doing so on any occasion when the accused is present may remand the accused.

(2) Where the court remands the accused, the time fixed for the resumption of proceedings shall be that at which he is required to appear or be brought before the court in pursuance of the remand or would be required to be brought before the court but for section 128(3A) below.

24D Functions under sections 24A to 24C capable of exercise by single justice

(1) The functions of a magistrates' court under sections 24A to 24C above may be discharged by a single justice.

(2) Subsection (1) above shall not be taken as authorising –

(a) the summary trial of an information (other than a summary trial by virtue of section 24A(7) or 24B(2)(c) above); or

(b) the imposition of a sentence,

by a magistrates' court composed of fewer than two justices.'

11(1) Section 25 (power to change from summary trial to committal proceedings and vice versa), as amended by section 42 of this Act, is amended as follows.

(2) In subsection (1), for '(2) to (4)' there is substituted '(2) to (2D)'.

(3) For subsection (2) there is substituted –

'(2) Where the court is required under section 20(9) above to proceed to the summary trial of the information, the prosecution may apply to the court for the offence to be tried on indictment instead.

(2A) An application under subsection (2) above –

    (a)   must be made before the summary trial begins; and

    (b)   must be dealt with by the court before any other application or issue in relation to the summary trial is dealt with.

(2B) The court may grant an application under subsection (2) above but only if it is satisfied that the sentence which a magistrates' court would have power to impose for the offence would be inadequate.

(2C) Where –

    (a)   the accused is charged on the same occasion with two or more offences; and

    (b)   it appears to the court that they constitute or form part of a series of two or more offences of the same or a similar character,

subsection (2B) above shall have effect as if references to the sentence which a magistrates' court would have power to impose for the offence were a reference to the maximum aggregate sentence which a magistrates' court would have power to impose for all of the offences taken together.

(2D) Where the court grants an application under subsection (2) above, it shall proceed in relation to the offence in accordance with section 51(1) of the Crime and Disorder Act 1998.'

(4) Subsections (3) to (8) are omitted.

12 For subsections (1) and (2) of section 26 (power to issue summons to accused in certain circumstances) there is substituted –

'(1) Where, in the circumstances mentioned in section 23(1)(a) above, the court is not satisfied that there is good reason for proceeding in the absence of the accused, the justice or any of the justices of which the court is composed may issue a summons directed to the accused requiring his presence before the court.

(2) In a case within subsection (1) above, if the accused is not present at the time and place appointed for the proceedings under section 19 or section 22(1) above, the court may issue a warrant for his arrest.'

13 In section 33 (maximum penalties on summary conviction in pursuance of section 22), in subsection (1), paragraph (b) and the word 'and' immediately preceding it are omitted.

14 Section 42 (restriction on justices sitting after dealing with bail) shall cease to have effect.

Crime and Disorder Act 1998 (c. 37)

15 The Crime and Disorder Act 1998 is amended as follows.

16 In section 50 (early administrative hearings), in subsection (1) (court may consist of single justice unless accused falls to be dealt with under section 51), the words 'unless the accused falls to be dealt with under section 51 below' are omitted.

17 After section 50 there is inserted –

'50A Order of consideration for either-way offences

(1) Where an adult appears or is brought before a magistrates' court charged with an either-way offence (the 'relevant offence'), the court shall proceed in the manner described in this section.

(2) If notice is given in respect of the relevant offence under section 51B or 51C below, the court shall deal with the offence as provided in section 51 below.

(3) Otherwise –

    (a) if the adult (or another adult with whom the adult is charged jointly with the relevant offence) is or has been sent to the Crown Court for trial for an offence under section 51(2)(a) or 51(2)(c) below –

        (i)   the court shall first consider the relevant offence under subsection (3), (4), (5) or, as the case may be, (6) of section 51 below and, where applicable, deal with it under that subsection;

        (ii)   if the adult is not sent to the Crown Court for trial for the relevant offence by virtue of sub-paragraph (i) above, the court shall then proceed to deal with the relevant offence in accordance with sections 17A to 23 of the 1980 Act;

    (b) in all other cases –

        (i)   the court shall first consider the relevant offence under sections 17A to 20 (excluding subsections (8) and (9) of section 20) of the 1980 Act;

        (ii)   if, by virtue of sub-paragraph (i) above, the court would be required to proceed in relation to the offence as mentioned in section 17A(6), 17B(2)(c) or 20(7) of that Act (indication of guilty plea), it shall proceed as so required (and, accordingly, shall not consider the offence under section 51 or 51A below);

        (iii) if sub-paragraph (ii) above does not apply –

            (a) the court shall consider the relevant offence under sections 51 and 51A below and, where applicable, deal with it under the relevant section;

            (b) if the adult is not sent to the Crown Court for trial for the relevant offence by virtue of paragraph (a) of this sub-paragraph, the court shall then proceed to deal with the relevant offence as contemplated by section 20(9) or, as the case may be, section 21 of the 1980 Act.

(4) Subsection (3) above is subject to any requirement to proceed as mentioned in subsections (2) or (6)(a) of section 22 of the 1980 Act (certain offences where value involved is small).

(5) Nothing in this section shall prevent the court from committing the adult to the Crown Court for sentence pursuant to any enactment, if he is convicted of the relevant offence.'

18 For section 51 (no committal proceedings for indictable-only offences) there is substituted –

'51 Sending cases to the Crown Court: adults

(1) Where an adult appears or is brought before a magistrates' court ('the court') charged with an offence and any of the conditions mentioned in subsection (2) below is satisfied, the court shall send him forthwith to the Crown Court for trial for the offence.

(2) Those conditions are –

(a) that the offence is an offence triable only on indictment other than one in respect of which notice has been given under section 51B or 51C below;

(b) that the offence is an either-way offence and the court is required under section 20(9)(b), 21, 23(4)(b) or (5) or 25(2D) of the Magistrates' Courts Act 1980 to proceed in relation to the offence in accordance with subsection (1) above;

(c) that notice is given to the court under section 51B or 51C below in respect of the offence.

(3) Where the court sends an adult for trial under subsection (1) above, it shall at the same time send him to the Crown Court for trial for any either-way or summary offence with which he is charged and which –

(a) (if it is an either-way offence) appears to the court to be related to the offence mentioned in subsection (1) above; or

(b) (if it is a summary offence) appears to the court to be related to the offence mentioned in subsection (1) above or to the either-way offence, and which fulfils the requisite condition (as defined in subsection (11) below).

(4) Where an adult who has been sent for trial under subsection (1) above subsequently appears or is brought before a magistrates' court charged with an either-way or summary offence which –

(a) appears to the court to be related to the offence mentioned in subsection (1) above; and

(b) (in the case of a summary offence) fulfils the requisite condition,

the court may send him forthwith to the Crown Court for trial for the either-way or summary offence.

(5) Where –

(a) the court sends an adult ("A") for trial under subsection (1) or (3) above;

(b) another adult appears or is brought before the court on the same or a subsequent occasion charged jointly with A with an either-way offence; and

(c) that offence appears to the court to be related to an offence for which A was sent for trial under subsection (1) or (3) above,

the court shall where it is the same occasion, and may where it is a subsequent occasion, send the other adult forthwith to the Crown Court for trial for the either-way offence.

(6) Where the court sends an adult for trial under subsection (5) above, it shall at the same time send him to the Crown Court for trial for any either-way or summary offence with which he is charged and which –

(a) (if it is an either-way offence) appears to the court to be related to the offence for which he is sent for trial; and

(b) (if it is a summary offence) appears to the court to be related to the offence for which he is sent for trial or to the either-way offence, and which fulfils the requisite condition.

(7) Where –

(a) the court sends an adult ('A') for trial under subsection (1), (3) or (5) above; and

(b) a child or young person appears or is brought before the court on the same or a subsequent occasion charged jointly with A with an indictable offence for which A is sent for trial under subsection (1), (3) or (5) above, or an indictable offence which appears to the court to be related to that offence,

the court shall, if it considers it necessary in the interests of justice to do so, send the child or young person forthwith to the Crown Court for trial for the indictable offence.

(8) Where the court sends a child or young person for trial under subsection (7) above, it may at the same time send him to the Crown Court for trial for any indictable or summary offence with which he is charged and which –

(a) (if it is an indictable offence) appears to the court to be related to the offence for which he is sent for trial; and
(b) (if it is a summary offence) appears to the court to be related to the offence for which he is sent for trial or to the indictable offence, and which fulfils the requisite condition.

(9) Subsections (7) and (8) above are subject to sections 24A and 24B of the Magistrates' Courts Act 1980 (which provide for certain cases involving children and young persons to be tried summarily).

(10) The trial of the information charging any summary offence for which a person is sent for trial under this section shall be treated as if the court had adjourned it under section 10 of the 1980 Act and had not fixed the time and place for its resumption.

(11) A summary offence fulfils the requisite condition if it is punishable with imprisonment or involves obligatory or discretionary disqualification from driving.

(12) In the case of an adult charged with an offence –

(a) if the offence satisfies paragraph (c) of subsection (2) above, the offence shall be dealt with under subsection (1) above and not under any other provision of this section or section 51A below;
(b) subject to paragraph (a) above, if the offence is one in respect of which the court is required to, or would decide to, send the adult to the Crown Court under –
  (i) subsection (5) above; or
  (ii) subsection (6) of section 51A below,

the offence shall be dealt with under that subsection and not under any other provision of this section or section 51A below.

(13) The functions of a magistrates' court under this section, and its related functions under section 51D below, may be discharged by a single justice.

51A Sending cases to the Crown Court: children and young persons

(1) This section is subject to sections 24A and 24B of the Magistrates' Courts Act 1980 (which provide for certain offences involving children or young persons to be tried summarily).

(2) Where a child or young person appears or is brought before a magistrates' court ("the court") charged with an offence and any of the conditions mentioned in subsection (3) below is satisfied, the court shall send him forthwith to the Crown Court for trial for the offence.

(3) Those conditions are –

(a) that the offence falls within subsection (12) below;
(b) that the offence is such as is mentioned in subsection (1) of section 91 of the Powers of Criminal Courts (Sentencing) Act 2000 (other than one mentioned in paragraph (d) below in relation to which it appears to the court as mentioned there) and the court considers that if he is found guilty of the offence it ought to be possible to sentence him in pursuance of subsection (3) of that section;
(c) that notice is given to the court under section 51B or 51C below in respect of the offence;
(d) that the offence is a specified offence (within the meaning of section 224 of the Criminal Justice Act 2003) and it appears to the court that if he is found guilty of the offence the criteria for the imposition of a sentence under section 226(3) or 228(2) of that Act would be met.

(4) Where the court sends a child or young person for trial under subsection (2) above, it may at the same time send him to the Crown Court for trial for any indictable or summary offence with which he is charged and which –

(a) (if it is an indictable offence) appears to the court to be related to the offence mentioned in subsection (2) above; or
(b) (if it is a summary offence) appears to the court to be related to the offence mentioned in subsection (2) above or to the indictable offence, and which fulfils the requisite condition (as defined in subsection (9) below).

(5) Where a child or young person who has been sent for trial under subsection (2) above subsequently appears or is brought before a magistrates' court charged with an indictable or summary offence which –

(a) appears to the court to be related to the offence mentioned in subsection (2) above; and
(b) (in the case of a summary offence) fulfils the requisite condition,

the court may send him forthwith to the Crown Court for trial for the indictable or summary offence.

(6) Where –

(a) the court sends a child or young person ('C') for trial under subsection (2) or (4) above; and
(b) an adult appears or is brought before the court on the same or a subsequent occasion charged jointly with C with an either-way offence for which C is sent for trial under subsection (2) or (4) above, or an either-way offence which appears to the court to be related to that offence,

the court shall where it is the same occasion, and may where it is a subsequent occasion, send the adult forthwith to the Crown Court for trial for the either-way offence.

(7) Where the court sends an adult for trial under subsection (6) above, it shall at the same time send him to the Crown Court for trial for any either-way or summary offence with which he is charged and which –

(a) (if it is an either-way offence) appears to the court to be related to the offence for which he was sent for trial; and
(b) (if it is a summary offence) appears to the court to be related to the offence for which he was sent for trial or to the either-way offence, and which fulfils the requisite condition.

(8) The trial of the information charging any summary offence for which a person is sent for trial under this section shall be treated as if the court had adjourned it under section 10 of the 1980 Act and had not fixed the time and place for its resumption.

(9) A summary offence fulfils the requisite condition if it is punishable with imprisonment or involves obligatory or discretionary disqualification from driving.

(10) In the case of a child or young person charged with an offence –

    (a) if the offence satisfies any of the conditions in subsection (3) above, the offence shall be dealt with under subsection (2) above and not under any other provision of this section or section 51 above;

    (b) subject to paragraph (a) above, if the offence is one in respect of which the requirements of subsection (7) of section 51 above for sending the child or young person to the Crown Court are satisfied, the offence shall be dealt with under that subsection and not under any other provision of this section or section 51 above.

(11) The functions of a magistrates' court under this section, and its related functions under section 51D below, may be discharged by a single justice.

(12) An offence falls within this subsection if –

    (a) it is an offence of homicide; or

    (b) each of the requirements of section 51A(1) of the Firearms Act 1968 would be satisfied with respect to –

        (i)   the offence; and

        (ii) the person charged with it,

if he were convicted of the offence.

51B Notices in serious or complex fraud cases

(1) A notice may be given by a designated authority under this section in respect of an indictable offence if the authority is of the opinion that the evidence of the offence charged –

    (a) is sufficient for the person charged to be put on trial for the offence; and

    (b) reveals a case of fraud of such seriousness or complexity that it is appropriate that the management of the case should without delay be taken over by the Crown Court.

(2) That opinion must be certified by the designated authority in the notice.

(3) The notice must also specify the proposed place of trial, and in selecting that place the designated authority must have regard to the same matters as are specified in paragraphs (a) to (c) of section 51D(4) below.

(4) A notice under this section must be given to the magistrates' court at which the person charged appears or before which he is brought.

(5) Such a notice must be given to the magistrates' court before any summary trial begins.

(6) The effect of such a notice is that the functions of the magistrates' court cease in relation to the case, except –

    (a) for the purposes of section 51D below;

    (b) as provided by paragraph 2 of Schedule 3 to the Access to Justice Act 1999; and

    (c) as provided by section 52 below.

(7) The functions of a designated authority under this section may be exercised by an officer of the authority acting on behalf of the authority.

(8) A decision to give a notice under this section shall not be subject to appeal or liable to be questioned in any court (whether a magistrates' court or not).

(9) In this section "designated authority" means –

    (a) the Director of Public Prosecutions;
    (b) the Director of the Serious Fraud Office;
    (c) the Commissioners of the Inland Revenue;
    (d) the Commissioners of Customs and Excise; or
    (e) the Secretary of State.

51C Notices in certain cases involving children

(1) A notice may be given by the Director of Public Prosecutions under this section in respect of an offence falling within subsection (3) below if he is of the opinion –

    (a) that the evidence of the offence would be sufficient for the person charged to be put on trial for the offence;
    (b) that a child would be called as a witness at the trial; and
    (c) that, for the purpose of avoiding any prejudice to the welfare of the child, the case should be taken over and proceeded with without delay by the Crown Court.

(2) That opinion must be certified by the Director of Public Prosecutions in the notice.

(3) This subsection applies to an offence –

    (a) which involves an assault on, or injury or a threat of injury to, a person;
    (b) under section 1 of the Children and Young Persons Act 1933 (cruelty to persons under 16);
    (c) under the Sexual Offences Act 1956, the Protection of Children Act 1978 or the Sexual Offences Act 2003;
    (d) of kidnapping or false imprisonment, or an offence under section 1 or 2 of the Child Abduction Act 1984;
    (e) which consists of attempting or conspiring to commit, or of aiding, abetting, counselling, procuring or inciting the commission of, an offence falling within paragraph (a), (b), (c) or (d) above.

(4) Subsections (4), (5) and (6) of section 51B above apply for the purposes of this section as they apply for the purposes of that.

(5) The functions of the Director of Public Prosecutions under this section may be exercised by an officer acting on behalf of the Director.

(6) A decision to give a notice under this section shall not be subject to appeal or liable to be questioned in any court (whether a magistrates' court or not).

(7) In this section "child" means –

    (a) a person who is under the age of 17; or
    (b) any person of whom a video recording (as defined in section 63(1) of the Youth Justice and Criminal Evidence Act 1999) was made when he was under the age of 17 with a view to its admission as his evidence in chief in the trial referred to in subsection (1) above.

51D Notice of offence and place of trial

(1) The court shall specify in a notice –

- (a) the offence or offences for which a person is sent for trial under section 51 or 51A above; and
- (b) the place at which he is to be tried (which, if a notice has been given under section 51B above, must be the place specified in that notice).

(2) A copy of the notice shall be served on the accused and given to the Crown Court sitting at that place.

(3) In a case where a person is sent for trial under section 51 or 51A above for more than one offence, the court shall specify in that notice, for each offence –

- (a) the subsection under which the person is so sent; and
- (b) if applicable, the offence to which that offence appears to the court to be related.

(4) Where the court selects the place of trial for the purposes of subsection (1) above, it shall have regard to –

- (a) the convenience of the defence, the prosecution and the witnesses;
- (b) the desirability of expediting the trial; and
- (c) any direction given by or on behalf of the Lord Chief Justice with the concurrence of the Lord Chancellor under section 75(1) of the Supreme Court Act 1981.

51E Interpretation of sections 50A to 51D

For the purposes of sections 50A to 51D above –

- (a) "adult" means a person aged 18 or over, and references to an adult include a corporation;
- (b) "either-way offence" means an offence triable either way;
- (c) an either-way offence is related to an indictable offence if the charge for the either-way offence could be joined in the same indictment as the charge for the indictable offence;
- (d) a summary offence is related to an indictable offence if it arises out of circumstances which are the same as or connected with those giving rise to the indictable offence.'

19(1) After section 52 there is inserted –

'52A Restrictions on reporting

(1) Except as provided by this section, it shall not be lawful –

- (a) to publish in the United Kingdom a written report of any allocation or sending proceedings in England and Wales; or
- (b) to include in a relevant programme for reception in the United Kingdom a report of any such proceedings,

if (in either case) the report contains any matter other than that permitted by this section.

(2) Subject to subsections (3) and (4) below, a magistrates' court may, with reference to any allocation or sending proceedings, order that subsection (1) above shall not apply to reports of those proceedings.

(3) Where there is only one accused and he objects to the making of an order under subsection (2) above, the court shall make the order if, and only if, it is satisfied,

after hearing the representations of the accused, that it is in the interests of justice to do so.

(4) Where in the case of two or more accused one of them objects to the making of an order under subsection (2) above, the court shall make the order if, and only if, it is satisfied, after hearing the representations of the accused, that it is in the interests of justice to do so.

(5) An order under subsection (2) above shall not apply to reports of proceedings under subsection (3) or (4) above, but any decision of the court to make or not to make such an order may be contained in reports published or included in a relevant programme before the time authorised by subsection (6) below.

(6) It shall not be unlawful under this section to publish or include in a relevant programme a report of allocation or sending proceedings containing any matter other than that permitted by subsection (7) below –

    (a) where, in relation to the accused (or all of them, if there are more than one), the magistrates' court is required to proceed as mentioned in section 20(7) of the 1980 Act, after the court is so required;

    (b) where, in relation to the accused (or any of them, if there are more than one), the court proceeds other than as mentioned there, after conclusion of his trial or, as the case may be, the trial of the last to be tried.

(7) The following matters may be contained in a report of allocation or sending proceedings published or included in a relevant programme without an order under subsection (2) above before the time authorised by subsection (6) above –

    (a) the identity of the court and the name of the justice or justices;

    (b) the name, age, home address and occupation of the accused;

    (c) in the case of an accused charged with an offence in respect of which notice has been given to the court under section 51B above, any relevant business information;

    (d) the offence or offences, or a summary of them, with which the accused is or are charged;

    (e) the names of counsel and solicitors engaged in the proceedings;

    (f) where the proceedings are adjourned, the date and place to which they are adjourned;

    (g) the arrangements as to bail;

    (h) whether a right to representation funded by the Legal Services Commission as part of the Criminal Defence Service was granted to the accused or any of the accused.

(8) The addresses that may be published or included in a relevant programme under subsection (7) above are addresses –

    (a) at any relevant time; and

    (b) at the time of their publication or inclusion in a relevant programme.

(9) The following is relevant business information for the purposes of subsection (7) above –

    (a) any address used by the accused for carrying on a business on his own account;

    (b) the name of any business which he was carrying on on his own account at any relevant time;

    (c) the name of any firm in which he was a partner at any relevant time or by which he was engaged at any such time;

(d)   the address of any such firm;
(e)   the name of any company of which he was a director at any relevant time or by which he was otherwise engaged at any such time;
(f)   the address of the registered or principal office of any such company;
(g)   any working address of the accused in his capacity as a person engaged by any such company;

and here "engaged" means engaged under a contract of service or a contract for services.

(10) Subsection (1) above shall be in addition to, and not in derogation from, the provisions of any other enactment with respect to the publication of reports of court proceedings.

(11) In this section –

"allocation or sending proceedings" means, in relation to an information charging an indictable offence –
(a)   any proceedings in the magistrates' court at which matters are considered under any of the following provisions –
(i)   sections 19 to 23 of the 1980 Act;
(ii)   section 51, 51A or 52 above;
(b)   any proceedings in the magistrates' court before the court proceeds to consider any matter mentioned in paragraph (a) above; and
(c)   any proceedings in the magistrates' court at which an application under section 25(2) of the 1980 Act is considered;

"publish", in relation to a report, means publish the report, either by itself or as part of a newspaper or periodical, for distribution to the public;
"relevant programme" means a programme included in a programme service (within the meaning of the Broadcasting Act 1990);
"relevant time" means a time when events giving rise to the charges to which the proceedings relate occurred.

52B   Offences in connection with reporting

(1) If a report is published or included in a relevant programme in contravention of section 52A above, each of the following persons is guilty of an offence –

(a)   in the case of a publication of a written report as part of a newspaper or periodical, any proprietor, editor or publisher of the newspaper or periodical;
(b)   in the case of a publication of a written report otherwise than as part of a newspaper or periodical, the person who publishes it;
(c)   in the case of the inclusion of a report in a relevant programme, any body corporate which is engaged in providing the service in which the programme is included and any person having functions in relation to the programme corresponding to those of the editor of a newspaper.

(2) A person guilty of an offence under this section is liable on summary conviction to a fine not exceeding level 5 on the standard scale.

(3) Proceedings for an offence under this section shall not, in England and Wales, be instituted otherwise than by or with the consent of the Attorney General.

(4) Proceedings for an offence under this section shall not, in Northern Ireland, be instituted otherwise than by or with the consent of the Attorney General for Northern Ireland.

(5) Subsection (11) of section 52A above applies for the purposes of this section as it applies for the purposes of that section.'.

(2) In section 121 (short title, commencement and extent) –

- (a) in subsection (6), after paragraph (b) there is inserted –
'(bb) sections 52A and 52B;', and
- (b) in subsection (8), after '(5) above,' there is inserted 'sections 52A and 52B above,'.

20(1) Schedule 3 (procedure where persons are sent for trial under section 51 of the Crime and Disorder Act 1998) is amended as follows.

(2) In paragraph 1(1) –

- (a) after '51' there is inserted 'or 51A', and
- (b) in paragraph (b), for 'subsection (7) of that section' there is substituted 'section 51D(1) of this Act'.

(3) In paragraph 2 –

- (a) in sub-paragraph (1) –
  - (i) after '51' there is inserted 'or 51A', and
  - (ii) for 'subsection (7) of that section' there is substituted 'section 51D(1) of this Act', and
- (b) sub-paragraphs (4) and (5) are omitted.

(4) In paragraph 4, in sub-paragraph (1)(a), after '51' there is inserted 'or 51A'.

(5) In paragraph 5, in sub-paragraph (2), after '51' there is inserted 'or 51A'.

(6) Paragraph 6 is amended as follows –

- (a) in sub-paragraph (1), after '51' there is inserted 'or 51A',
- (b) in sub-paragraph (2), for the words from the second 'offence' to the end there is substituted 'indictable offence for which he was sent for trial or, as the case may be, any of the indictable offences for which he was so sent', and
- (c) in sub-paragraph (9), for 'indictable-only' there is substituted 'indictable'.

(7) In paragraph 7 –

- (a) in sub-paragraph (1)(a), after '51' there is inserted 'or 51A',
- (b) in sub-paragraph (1)(b), for 'offence that is triable only on indictment' there is substituted 'main offence',
- (c) in sub-paragraph (3), after 'each' there is inserted 'remaining',
- (d) in sub-paragraph (7), for 'consider' there is substituted 'decide', and
- (e) after sub-paragraph (8) there is inserted –

  '(9) In this paragraph, a "main offence" is –

  - (a) an offence for which the person has been sent to the Crown Court for trial under section 51(1) of this Act; or
  - (b) an offence –
    - (i) for which the person has been sent to the Crown Court for trial under subsection (5) of section 51 or subsection (6) of section 51A of this Act ("the applicable subsection"); and
    - (ii) in respect of which the conditions for sending him to the Crown Court for trial under the applicable subsection (as set out in paragraphs (a) to (c) of section 51(5) or paragraphs (a) and (b) of section 51A(6)) continue to be satisfied.'

(8) In paragraph 8 –

    (a) in sub-paragraph (1)(a), after '51' there is inserted 'or 51A',

    (b) in sub-paragraph (1)(b), for 'offence that is triable only on indictment' there is substituted 'main offence (within the meaning of paragraph 7 above)',

        (c) in sub-paragraph (2)(a), after 'each' there is inserted 'remaining', and

        (d) in sub-paragraph (2)(d), for 'consider' there is substituted 'decide'.

(9) In paragraph 9 –

    (a) in sub-paragraph (1), for 'consider' there is substituted 'decide', and

    (b) for sub-paragraphs (2) and (3), there is substituted-

'(2) Before deciding the question, the court –

    (a) shall give the prosecution an opportunity to inform the court of the accused's previous convictions (if any); and

    (b) shall give the prosecution and the accused an opportunity to make representations as to whether summary trial or trial on indictment would be more suitable.

(3) In deciding the question, the court shall consider –

    (a) whether the sentence which a magistrates' court would have power to impose for the offence would be adequate; and

    (b) any representations made by the prosecution or the accused under sub-paragraph (2)(b) above,

and shall have regard to any allocation guidelines (or revised allocation guidelines) issued as definitive guidelines under section 170 of the Criminal Justice Act 2003.

(4) Where –

    (a) the accused is charged on the same occasion with two or more offences; and

    (b) it appears to the court that they constitute or form part of a series of two or more offences of the same or a similar character;

sub-paragraph (3)(a) above shall have effect as if references to the sentence which a magistrates' court would have power to impose for the offence were a reference to the maximum aggregate sentence which a magistrates' court would have power to impose for all of the offences taken together.

(5) In this paragraph any reference to a previous conviction is a reference to –

    (a) a previous conviction by a court in the United Kingdom, or

    (b) a previous finding of guilt in –

        (i)   any proceedings under the Army Act 1955, the Air Force Act 1955 or the Naval Discipline Act 1957 (whether before a court-martial or any other court or person authorised under any of those Acts to award a punishment in respect of any offence), or

        (ii) any proceedings before a Standing Civilian Court.'

(10) In paragraph 10 –

    (a) for sub-paragraph (2), there is substituted –

'(2) The court shall explain to the accused in ordinary language –

    (a) that it appears to the court more suitable for him to be tried summarily for the offence;

(b) that he can either consent to be so tried or, if he wishes, be tried on indictment; and

(c) in the case of a specified offence (within the meaning of section 224 of the Criminal Justice Act 2003), that if he is tried summarily and is convicted by the court, he may be committed for sentence to the Crown Court under section 3A of the Powers of Criminal Courts (Sentencing) Act 2000 if the committing court is of such opinion as is mentioned in subsection (2) of that section.', and

(b) in sub-paragraph (3), for 'by a jury' there is substituted 'on indictment'.

(11) In paragraph 11, in sub-paragraph (a), for 'by a jury' there is substituted 'on indictment'.

(12) Paragraph 12 shall cease to have effect.

(13) In paragraph 13 –

(a) in sub-paragraph (1)(a), after '51' there is inserted 'or 51A',
(b) in sub-paragraph (1)(b), for 'offence that is triable only on indictment' there is substituted 'main offence',
(c) in sub-paragraph (2), the words from 'unless' to the end are omitted, and
(d) for sub-paragraph (3) there is substituted –

'(3) In this paragraph, a "main offence" is –

(a) an offence for which the child or young person has been sent to the Crown Court for trial under section 51A(2) of this Act; or
(b) an offence –
  (i) for which the child or young person has been sent to the Crown Court for trial under subsection (7) of section 51 of this Act; and
  (ii) in respect of which the conditions for sending him to the Crown Court for trial under that subsection (as set out in paragraphs (a) and (b) of that subsection) continue to be satisfied.'

(14) In paragraph 15, in each of sub-paragraphs (3) and (4), for 'considered' there is substituted 'decided'.

Powers of Criminal Courts (Sentencing) Act 2000 (c. 6)

21 The Powers of Criminal Courts (Sentencing) Act 2000 is amended as follows.

22 For section 3 (committal for sentence on summary trial of offence triable either way) there is substituted –

'3 Committal for sentence on indication of guilty plea to serious offence triable either way

(1) Subject to subsection (4) below, this section applies where –

(a) a person aged 18 or over appears or is brought before a magistrates' court ("the court") on an information charging him with an offence triable either way ("the offence");
(b) he or his representative indicates under section 17A or (as the case may be) 17B of the Magistrates' Courts Act 1980 (initial procedure: accused to indicate intention as to plea), but not section 20(7) of that Act, that he would plead guilty if the offence were to proceed to trial; and

(c) proceeding as if section 9(1) of that Act were complied with and he pleaded guilty under it, the court convicts him of the offence.

(2) If the court is of the opinion that –

(a) the offence; or
(b) the combination of the offence and one or more offences associated with it,

was so serious that the Crown Court should, in the court's opinion, have the power to deal with the offender in any way it could deal with him if he had been convicted on indictment, the court may commit him in custody or on bail to the Crown Court for sentence in accordance with section 5(1) below.

(3) Where the court commits a person under subsection (2) above, section 6 below (which enables a magistrates' court, where it commits a person under this section in respect of an offence, also to commit him to the Crown Court to be dealt with in respect of certain other offences) shall apply accordingly.

(4) This section does not apply in relation to an offence as regards which this section is excluded by section 17D of the Magistrates' Courts Act 1980 (certain offences where value involved is small).

(5) The preceding provisions of this section shall apply in relation to a corporation as if –

(a) the corporation were an individual aged 18 or over; and
(b) in subsection (2) above, the words "in custody or on bail" were omitted.'

23 After section 3 there is inserted –

'3A Committal for sentence of dangerous adult offenders

(1) This section applies where on the summary trial of a specified offence triable either way a person aged 18 or over is convicted of the offence.

(2) If, in relation to the offence, it appears to the court that the criteria for the imposition of a sentence under section 225(3) or 227(2) of the Criminal Justice Act 2003 would be met, the court must commit the offender in custody or on bail to the Crown Court for sentence in accordance with section 5(1) below.

(3) Where the court commits a person under subsection (2) above, section 6 below (which enables a magistrates' court, where it commits a person under this section in respect of an offence, also to commit him to the Crown Court to be dealt with in respect of certain other offences) shall apply accordingly.

(4) In reaching any decision under or taking any step contemplated by this section –

(a) the court shall not be bound by any indication of sentence given in respect of the offence under section 20 of the Magistrates' Courts Act 1980 (procedure where summary trial appears more suitable); and
(b) nothing the court does under this section may be challenged or be the subject of any appeal in any court on the ground that it is not consistent with an indication of sentence.

(5) Nothing in this section shall prevent the court from committing a specified offence to the Crown Court for sentence under section 3 above if the provisions of that section are satisfied.

(6) In this section, references to a specified offence are to a specified offence within the meaning of section 224 of the Criminal Justice Act 2003.

3B Committal for sentence on indication of guilty plea by child or young person

(1) This section applies where –

   (a) a person aged under 18 appears or is brought before a magistrates' court ("the court") on an information charging him with an offence mentioned in subsection (1) of section 91 below ("the offence");

   (b) he or his representative indicates under section 24A or (as the case may be) 24B of the Magistrates' Courts Act 1980 (child or young person to indicate intention as to plea in certain cases) that he would plead guilty if the offence were to proceed to trial; and

   (c) proceeding as if section 9(1) of that Act were complied with and he pleaded guilty under it, the court convicts him of the offence.

(2) If the court is of the opinion that –

   (a) the offence; or

   (b) the combination of the offence and one or more offences associated with it,

was such that the Crown Court should, in the court's opinion, have power to deal with the offender as if the provisions of section 91(3) below applied, the court may commit him in custody or on bail to the Crown Court for sentence in accordance with section 5A(1) below.

(3) Where the court commits a person under subsection (2) above, section 6 below (which enables a magistrates' court, where it commits a person under this section in respect of an offence, also to commit him to the Crown Court to be dealt with in respect of certain other offences) shall apply accordingly.

3C Committal for sentence of dangerous young offenders

(1) This section applies where on the summary trial of a specified offence a person aged under 18 is convicted of the offence.

(2) If, in relation to the offence, it appears to the court that the criteria for the imposition of a sentence under section 226(3) or 228(2) of the Criminal Justice Act 2003 would be met, the court must commit the offender in custody or on bail to the Crown Court for sentence in accordance with section 5A(1) below.

(3) Where the court commits a person under subsection (2) above, section 6 below (which enables a magistrates' court, where it commits a person under this section in respect of an offence, also to commit him to the Crown Court to be dealt with in respect of certain other offences) shall apply accordingly.

(4) Nothing in this section shall prevent the court from committing a specified offence to the Crown Court for sentence under section 3B above if the provisions of that section are satisfied.

(5) In this section, references to a specified offence are to a specified offence within the meaning of section 224 of the Criminal Justice Act 2003.'

24(1) Section 4 (committal for sentence on indication of guilty plea to offence triable either way) is amended as follows.

(2) For subsection (1)(b), there is substituted –

   '(b) he or (where applicable) his representative indicates under section 17A, 17B or 20(7) of the Magistrates' Courts Act 1980 that he would plead guilty if the offence were to proceed to trial; and'.

(3) In subsection (1)(c), for 'the Magistrates' Courts Act 1980' there is substituted 'that Act'.

(4) After subsection (1) there is inserted –

'(1A) But this section does not apply to an offence as regards which this section is excluded by section 17D of that Act (certain offences where value involved is small).'

(5) For subsection (3), there is substituted –

'(3) If the power conferred by subsection (2) above is not exercisable but the court is still to determine to, or to determine whether to, send the offender to the Crown Court for trial under section 51 or 51A of the Crime and Disorder Act 1998 for one or more related offences –

(a) it shall adjourn the proceedings relating to the offence until after it has made those determinations; and

(b) if it sends the offender to the Crown Court for trial for one or more related offences, it may then exercise that power.'

(6) In subsection (4)(b), after 'section 3(2)' there is inserted 'or, as the case may be, section 3A(2)'.

(7) After subsection (7) there is inserted –

'(8) In reaching any decision under or taking any step contemplated by this section –

(a) the court shall not be bound by any indication of sentence given in respect of the offence under section 20 of the Magistrates' Courts Act 1980 (procedure where summary trial appears more suitable); and

(b) nothing the court does under this section may be challenged or be the subject of any appeal in any court on the ground that it is not consistent with an indication of sentence.'

25 After section 4 there is inserted –

'4A Committal for sentence on indication of guilty plea by child or young person with related offences

(1) This section applies where –

(a) a person aged under 18 appears or brought before a magistrates' court ("the court") on an information charging him with an offence mentioned in subsection (1) of section 91 below ("the offence");

(b) he or his representative indicates under section 24A or (as the case may be) 24B of the Magistrates' Courts Act 1980 (child or young person to indicate intention as to plea in certain cases) that he would plead guilty if the offence were to proceed to trial; and

(c) proceeding as if section 9(1) of that Act were complied with and he pleaded guilty under it, the court convicts him of the offence.

(2) If the court has sent the offender to the Crown Court for trial for one or more related offences, that is to say one or more offences which, in its opinion, are related to the offence, it may commit him in custody or on bail to the Crown Court to be dealt with in respect of the offence in accordance with section 5A(1) below.

(3) If the power conferred by subsection (2) above is not exercisable but the court is still to determine to, or to determine whether to, send the offender to the Crown

Court for trial under section 51 or 51A of the Crime and Disorder Act 1998 for one or more related offences –

(a) it shall adjourn the proceedings relating to the offence until after it has made those determinations; and

(b) if it sends the offender to the Crown Court for trial for one or more related offences, it may then exercise that power.

(4) Where the court –

(a) under subsection (2) above commits the offender to the Crown Court to be dealt with in respect of the offence; and

(b) does not state that, in its opinion, it also has power so to commit him under section 3B(2) or, as the case may be, section 3C(2) above,

section 5A(1) below shall not apply unless he is convicted before the Crown Court of one or more of the related offences.

(5) Where section 5A(1) below does not apply, the Crown Court may deal with the offender in respect of the offence in any way in which the magistrates' court could deal with him if it had just convicted him of the offence.

(6) Where the court commits a person under subsection (2) above, section 6 below (which enables a magistrates' court, where it commits a person under this section in respect of an offence, also to commit him to the Crown Court to be dealt with in respect of certain other offences) shall apply accordingly.

(7) Section 4(7) above applies for the purposes of this section as it applies for the purposes of that section.'

26 For section 5 (power of Crown Court on committal for sentence under sections 3 and 4) there is substituted –

'5 Power of Crown Court on committal for sentence under sections 3, 3A and 4

(1) Where an offender is committed by a magistrates' court for sentence under section 3, 3A or 4 above, the Crown Court shall inquire into the circumstances of the case and may deal with the offender in any way in which it could deal with him if he had just been convicted of the offence on indictment before the court.

(2) In relation to committals under section 4 above, subsection (1) above has effect subject to section 4(4) and (5) above.

(3) Section 20A(1) of the Magistrates' Courts Act 1980 (which relates to the effect of an indication of sentence under section 20 of that Act) shall not apply in respect of any specified offence (within the meaning of section 224 of the Criminal Justice Act 2003) –

(a) in respect of which the offender is committed under section 3A(2) above; or

(b) in respect of which –

(i) the offender is committed under section 4(2) above; and

(ii) the court states under section 4(4) above that, in its opinion, it also has power to commit the offender under section 3A(2) above.'

27 After section 5 there is inserted –

'5A Power of Crown Court on committal for sentence under sections 3B, 3C and 4A

(1) Where an offender is committed by a magistrates' court for sentence under section 3B, 3C or 4A above, the Crown Court shall inquire into the circumstances of

the case and may deal with the offender in any way in which it could deal with him if he had just been convicted of the offence on indictment before the court.

(2) In relation to committals under section 4A above, subsection (1) above has effect subject to section 4A(4) and (5) above.'

28 In section 6 (committal for sentence in certain cases where offender committed in respect of another offence), in subsection (4)(b), for '3 and 4' there is substituted '3 to 4A'.

PART 2

MINOR AND CONSEQUENTIAL AMENDMENTS

Territorial Waters Jurisdiction Act 1878 (c. 73)

29 In section 4 of the Territorial Waters Jurisdiction Act 1878 (provisions as to procedure), in the paragraph beginning 'Proceedings before a justice of the peace', for the words from the beginning to 'his trial' there is substituted –

'Any stage of proceedings –

(a) before the summary trial of the offence; or
(b) before the offender has been sent for trial for the offence,'.

Bankers' Books Evidence Act 1879 (c. 11)

30(1) The Bankers' Books Evidence Act 1879 is amended as follows.

(2) In section 4 (proof that book is a banker's book), the paragraph beginning 'Where the proceedings' is omitted.

(3) In section 5 (verification of copy), the paragraph beginning 'Where the proceedings' is omitted.

Explosive Substances Act 1883 (c. 3)

31 In section 6 of the Explosive Substances Act 1883 (inquiry by Attorney-General, and apprehension of absconding witnesses), subsection (3) is omitted.

Criminal Justice Act 1925 (c. 86)

32 In section 49 of the Criminal Justice Act 1925 (interpretation, etc), subsection (2) is omitted.

Children and Young Persons Act 1933 (c. 12)

33 In section 42 of the Children and Young Persons Act 1933 (extension of power to take deposition of child or young person), in subsection (2)(a), for 'committed' in both places there is substituted 'sent'.

Administration of Justice (Miscellaneous Provisions) Act 1933 (c. 36)

34(1) Section 2 of the Administration of Justice (Miscellaneous Provisions) Act 1933 (procedure for indictment of offenders) is amended as follows.

(2) In subsection (2) –

(a) in paragraph (a), for 'committed' there is substituted 'sent',

(b) paragraphs (aa) to (ac) are omitted,

(c) for paragraph (i) there is substituted –

'(i)   where the person charged has been sent for trial, the bill of indictment against him may include, either in substitution for or in addition to any count charging an offence specified in the notice under section 57D(1) of the Crime and Disorder Act 1998, any counts founded on material which, in pursuance of regulations made under paragraph 1 of Schedule 3 to that Act, was served on the person charged, being counts which may lawfully be joined in the same indictment;',

(d) paragraphs (iA) and (iB) are omitted,

(e) in paragraph (ii), for 'the committal' there is substituted 'such notice', and

(f) the words from 'and in paragraph (iA)' to the end are omitted.

(3) In subsection (3)(b), for 'committed' there is substituted 'sent'.

Criminal Justice Act 1948 (c. 58)

35(1) The Criminal Justice Act 1948 is amended as follows.

(2) In section 27 (remand and committal of persons aged 17 to 20), in subsection (1), for 'commits him for trial or' there is substituted 'sends him to the Crown Court for trial or commits him there for'.

(3) In section 41 (evidence by certificate), subsection (5A) is omitted.

(4) In section 80 (interpretation), the definition of 'Court of summary jurisdiction' is omitted.

Prison Act 1952 (c. 52)

36   Until their repeal by (respectively) section 59 of, and paragraph 10(a)(ii) of Schedule 7 to, the Criminal Justice and Court Services Act 2000, paragraph (a) of subsection (1), and paragraphs (b) and (c) of subsection (2), of section 43 of the Prison Act 1952 (remand centres, detention centres and youth custody centres) are to have effect as if references to being committed for trial were references to being sent for trial.

Army Act 1955 (3 & 4 Eliz. 2 c. 18)

37   In section 187 of the Army Act 1955 (proceedings before a civil court where persons suspected of illegal absence), at the end of subsection (4) there is inserted –

'The references in this subsection to provisions of the Magistrates' Courts Act 1980 and to corresponding enactments are to be taken to refer to those provisions and enactments as if no amendment to them had been made by the Criminal Justice Act 2003.'

Air Force Act 1955 (3 & 4 Eliz. 2 c. 19)

38   In section 187 of the Air Force Act 1955 (proceedings before a civil court where persons suspected of illegal absence), at the end of subsection (4) there is inserted –

'The references in this subsection to provisions of the Magistrates' Courts Act 1980 and to corresponding enactments are to be taken to refer to those provisions and enactments as if no amendment to them had been made by the Criminal Justice Act 2003.'

Geneva Conventions Act 1957 (c. 52)

39 In section 5 of the Geneva Conventions Act 1957 (reduction of sentence and custody of protected persons) –

    (a)   in subsection (1), for 'committal' there is substituted 'having been sent',

    (b)   in subsection (2), for 'committal', where it first appears, there is substituted 'having been sent'.

Naval Discipline Act 1957 (c. 53)

40 In section 109 of the Naval Discipline Act 1957 (proceedings before summary courts), at the end of subsection (4) there is inserted –

'The references in this subsection to provisions are to be taken to refer to those provisions as if no amendment to them had been made by the Criminal Justice Act 2003.'

Backing of Warrants (Republic of Ireland) Act 1965 (c. 45)

41 In paragraph 4 of the Schedule to the Backing of Warrants (Republic of Ireland) Act 1965 (supplementary procedures as to proceedings under section 2) –

    (a)   the words 'and section 2 of the Poor Prisoners Defence Act 1930 (legal aid before examining justices)' are omitted, and

    (b)   for 'it had determined not to commit for trial' there is substituted 'the offence were to be dealt with summarily and the court had dismissed the information'.

Criminal Procedure (Attendance of Witnesses) Act 1965 (c. 69)

42 In section 2 of the Criminal Procedure (Attendance of Witnesses) Act 1965 (issue of witness summons on application to Crown Court) –

    (a)   for subsection (4) there is substituted –

'(4) Where a person has been sent for trial for any offence to which the proceedings concerned relate, an application must be made as soon as is reasonably practicable after service on that person, in pursuance of regulations made under paragraph 1 of Schedule 3 to the Crime and Disorder Act 1998, of the documents relevant to that offence.', and

    (b)   subsection (5) is omitted.

Criminal Justice Act 1967 (c. 80)

43(1) The Criminal Justice Act 1967 is amended as follows.

(2) In section 9 (proof by written statement), in subsection (1), the words ', other than committal proceedings,' are omitted.

(3) In section 36 (interpretation), in subsection (1), the definition of 'committal proceedings' is omitted.

Criminal Appeal Act 1968 (c. 19)

44(1) The Criminal Appeal Act 1968 is amended as follows.

(2) In section 1 (right of appeal), in subsection (3), for 'committed him' there is substituted 'sent him to the Crown Court'.

(3) In section 9 (appeal against sentence following conviction on indictment), in subsection (2), the words from 'section 41' to 'either way offence' are omitted.

Firearms Act 1968 (c. 27)

45 In Schedule 6 to the Firearms Act 1968 (prosecution and punishment of offences), in Part 2, paragraph 3 is omitted.

Theft Act 1968 (c. 60)

46 In section 27 of the Theft Act 1968 (evidence and procedure on charge of theft or handling stolen goods), subsection (4A) is omitted.

Criminal Justice Act 1972 (c. 71)

47 In section 46 of the Criminal Justice Act 1972 (admissibility of written statements outside England and Wales), subsections (1A) to (1C) are omitted.

Bail Act 1976 (c. 63)

48(1) The Bail Act 1976 is amended as follows.

(2) In section 3 (general provisions) –

  (a) in subsection (8) –
    (i) for 'committed' there is substituted 'sent', and
    (ii) after 'for trial or' there is inserted 'committed him on bail to the Crown Court', and
  (b) subsections (8A) and (8B), and the subsection (10) inserted by paragraph 12(b) of Schedule 9 to the Criminal Justice and Public Order Act 1994 (c. 33), are omitted.

(3) In section 5 (supplementary provisions about decisions on bail) –
  (a) in subsection (6)(a), for 'committing' there is substituted 'sending', and
  (b) in subsection (6A)(a) –
    (i) after 'under' there is inserted 'section 52(5) of the Crime and Disorder Act 1998,',
    (ii) sub-paragraph (i) is omitted,
    (iii) after sub-paragraph (ii) there is inserted –

    '(iia) section 17C (intention as to plea: adjournment);', and

  (iv) at the end of sub-paragraph (iii) there is inserted 'or

    (iv) section 24C (intention as to plea by child or young person: adjournment),'.

(4) In section 6 (offence of absconding by person released on bail), in subsection (6)(b), for 'commits' there is substituted 'sends'.

(5) In section 9 (offence of agreeing to indemnify sureties in criminal proceedings), in subsection (3)(b), for 'commits' there is substituted 'sends'.

Interpretation Act 1978 (c. 30)

49 In Schedule 1 to the Interpretation Act 1978 (words and expressions defined) –

  (a) in the definition of 'Committed for trial', paragraph (a) is omitted,

(b) after the entry for 'Secretary of State' there is inserted –

'Sent for trial' means, in relation to England and Wales, sent by a magistrates' court to the Crown Court for trial pursuant to section 51 or 51A of the Crime and Disorder Act 1998.'

Customs and Excise Management Act 1979 (c. 2)

50 In section 147 of the Customs and Excise Management Act 1979 (proceedings for offences), subsection (2) is omitted.

Magistrates' Courts Act 1980 (c. 43)

51(1) The Magistrates' Courts Act 1980 is amended as follows.

(2) In section 2, as substituted by the Courts Act 2003 (trial of summary offences), in subsection (2), for 'as examining justices over' there is substituted 'under sections 51 and 51A of the Crime and Disorder Act 1998 in respect of'.

(3) Sections 4 to 8 (which relate to committal proceedings) shall cease to have effect and the cross-heading preceding section 4 is omitted.

(4) In section 8B, as inserted by the Courts Act 2003 (effect of rulings at pre-trial hearing), in subsection (6), the words 'commits or' are omitted.

(5) In section 29 (power of magistrates' court to remit a person under 17 for trial to a juvenile court in certain circumstances), in subsection (2)(b)(i), for the words from 'proceeds' to the end there is substituted 'sends him to the Crown Court for trial under section 51 or 51A of the Crime and Disorder Act 1998; and'.

(6) The following sections shall cease to have effect –

(a) section 97A (summons or warrant as to committal proceedings),
(b) section 103 (evidence of persons under 14 in committal proceedings for assault, sexual offences etc), and
(c) section 106 (false written statements tendered in evidence).

(7) In section 128 (remand in custody or on bail) –

(a) in subsection (1)(b), the words 'inquiring into or' are omitted,
(b) in subsection (1A)(a) –
    (i) '5,' is omitted, and
    (ii) for 'or 18(4)' there is substituted ', 18(4) or 24C',
(c) in subsection (3A) –
    (i) '5,' is omitted, and
    (ii) for 'or 18(4)' there is substituted ', 18(4) or 24C',
(d) in subsection (3C)(a) –
    (i) '5,' is omitted, and
    (ii) for 'or 18(4)' there is substituted ', 18(4) or 24C', and
(e) in subsection (3E)(a) –
    (i) '5,' is omitted, and
    (ii) for 'or 18(4)' there is substituted ', 18(4) or 24C'.

(8) In section 129 (further remand), in subsection (4) –

(a) for 'commits a person' there is substituted 'sends a person to the Crown Court', and
(b) for 'committed' there is substituted 'sent'.

(9) In section 130 (transfer of remand hearings), in subsection (1) –

   (a) '5,' is omitted, and
   (b) for 'or 18(4)' there is substituted ', 18(4) or 24C'.

(10) In section 145 (rules: supplementary provisions), in subsection (1), paragraph (f) is omitted.

(11) In section 150 (interpretation of other terms), in subsection (1), the definition of 'committal proceedings' is omitted.

(12) In section 155 (short title, extent and commencement), in subsection (2)(a), the words '8 (except subsection (9))' are omitted.

(13) In Schedule 3 (corporations) –

   (a) in paragraph 2, sub-paragraph (a) is omitted,
   (b) in paragraph 6, for 'inquiry into, and trial of,' there is substituted 'trial of'.

(14) In Schedule 5 (transfer of remand hearings) –

   (a) paragraph 2 is omitted, and
   (b) in paragraph 5, for '5, 10 or 18(4)' there is substituted '10, 17C, 18(4) or 24C'.

Criminal Attempts Act 1981 (c. 47)

52 In section 2 of the Criminal Attempts Act 1981 (application of procedures and other provisions to offences under section 1), in subsection (2)(g), the words 'or committed for trial' are omitted.

Contempt of Court Act 1981 (c. 49)

53 In section 4 of the Contempt of Court Act 1981 (contemporary reports of proceedings), in subsection (3), for paragraph (b) there is substituted –

   '(b) in the case of a report of allocation or sending proceedings of which publication is permitted by virtue only of subsection (6) of section 52A of the Crime and Disorder Act 1998 ('the 1998 Act'), if published as soon as practicable after publication is so permitted;
   (c) in the case of a report of an application of which publication is permitted by virtue only of sub-paragraph (5) or (7) of paragraph 3 of Schedule 3 to the 1998 Act, if published as soon as practicable after publication is so permitted.'

Supreme Court Act 1981 (c. 54)

54(1) The Supreme Court Act 1981 is amended as follows.

(2) In section 76 (committal for trial: alteration of place of trial) –

   (a) in subsection (1), for the words from 'varying' (where it first appears) to 'to Crown Court)' there is substituted 'substituting some other place for the place specified in a notice under section 51D(1) of the Crime and Disorder Act 1998 (a 'section 51D notice'),
   (b) in subsection (3), for the words 'fixed by the magistrates' court, as specified in a notice under a relevant transfer provision' there is substituted 'specified in a section 51D notice',
   (c) subsection (5) is omitted, and
   (d) in the heading, for '**Committal**' there is substituted '**Sending**'.

(3) In section 77 (committal for trial: date of trial) –

(a) in subsection (1), for 'committal for trial or the giving of a notice of transfer under a relevant transfer provision' there is substituted 'being sent for trial',

(b) in subsection (2), for 'committed by a magistrates' court or in respect of whom a notice of transfer under a relevant transfer provision has been given' there is substituted 'sent for trial',

(c) in subsection (3), for 'of committal for trial or of a notice of transfer' there is substituted 'when the defendant is sent for trial',

(d) subsection (4) is omitted, and

(e) in the heading, for '**Committal**' there is substituted '**Sending**'.

(4) In section 80 (process to compel appearance), in subsection (2), for 'committed' there is substituted 'sent'.

(5) In section 81 –

(a) in subsection (1) –
  (i) in paragraph (a) –
    (a) the words 'who has been committed in custody for appearance before the Crown Court or in relation to whose case a notice of transfer has been given under a relevant transfer provision or' are omitted, and
    (b) after '51' there is inserted 'or 51A',
  (ii) in paragraph (g), sub-paragraph (i) is omitted, and
(b) subsection (7) is omitted.

Mental Health Act 1983 (c. 20)

55(1) The Mental Health Act 1983 is amended as follows.

(2) In section 43 (power of magistrates' court to commit for restriction order), for subsection (4) there is substituted –

'(4) The powers of a magistrates' court under section 3 or 3B of the Powers of Criminal Courts (Sentencing) Act 2000 (which enable such a court to commit an offender to the Crown Court where the court is of the opinion, or it appears to the court, as mentioned in the section in question) shall also be exercisable by a magistrates' court where it is of that opinion (or it so appears to it) unless a hospital order is made in the offender's case with a restriction order.'

(3) In section 52 (further provisions as to persons remanded by magistrates' courts) –

(a) in subsection (2), for 'committed' there is substituted 'sent',
(b) in subsection (5), for 'committed' there is substituted 'sent',
(c) in subsection (6), for 'committed' there is substituted 'sent', and
(d) in subsection (7), for the words from 'inquire' to '1980' there is substituted 'send him to the Crown Court for trial under section 51 or 51A of the Crime and Disorder Act 1998', and in paragraph (b) of that subsection, the words 'where the court proceeds under subsection (1) of that section' are omitted.

Police and Criminal Evidence Act 1984 (c. 60)

56(1) The Police and Criminal Evidence Act 1984 is amended as follows.

(2) In section 62 (intimate samples), in subsection (10) –

(a) sub-paragraph (i) of paragraph (a) is omitted, and

(b) in paragraph (aa), for sub-paragraphs (i) and (ii) there is substituted 'paragraph 2 of Schedule 3 to the Crime and Disorder Act 1998 (applications for dismissal); and'.

(3) In section 71 (microfilm copies), the paragraph beginning 'Where the proceedings' is omitted.

(4) In section 76 (confessions), subsection (9) is omitted.

(5) In section 78 (exclusion of unfair evidence), subsection (3) is omitted.

Prosecution of Offences Act 1985 (c. 23)

57(1) The Prosecution of Offences Act 1985 is amended as follows.

(2) In section 7A (powers of non-legal staff), for subsection (6) there is substituted –

'(6) This section applies to an offence if it is triable only on indictment or is an offence for which the accused has been sent for trial.'

(3) In section 16 (defence costs) –

    (a) in subsection (1), paragraph (b) is omitted, and
    (b) in subsection (2) –
        (i) in paragraph (a), for 'committed' there is substituted 'sent', and
        (ii) paragraph (aa) is omitted, and
    (c) subsection (12) is omitted.

(4) In section 21 (interpretation), in subsection (6)(b), for 'committed' there is substituted 'sent'.

(5) In section 22 (power of Secretary of State to set time limits in relation to preliminary stages of criminal proceedings), in subsection (11) –

    (a) in paragraph (a) of the definition of 'appropriate court', for 'committed for trial, sent for trial under section 51 of the Crime and Disorder Act 1998' there is substituted 'sent for trial',
    (b) for the definition of 'custody of the Crown Court' there is substituted –

'custody of the Crown Court' includes custody to which a person is committed in pursuance of –

    (a) section 43A of the Magistrates' Courts Act 1980 (magistrates' court dealing with a person brought before it following his arrest in pursuance of a warrant issued by the Crown Court); or
    (b) section 52 of the Crime and Disorder Act 1998 (provisions supplementing section 51);'.

(6) In section 23 (discontinuance of proceedings in magistrates' court), in subsection (2), for paragraphs (a) to (c) there is substituted –

    '(a) any stage of the proceedings after the court has begun to hear evidence for the prosecution at a summary trial of the offence; or
    (b) any stage of the proceedings after the accused has been sent for trial for the offence.'

(7) In section 23A (discontinuance of proceedings after accused has been sent for trial) –

    (a) in paragraph (b) of subsection (1), the words from 'under' to '1998' are omitted, and

   (b) in subsection (2), for '51(7)' there is substituted '51D(1)'.

Criminal Justice Act 1987 (c. 38)

58(1) The Criminal Justice Act 1987 is amended as follows.

(2) Sections 4 to 6 (which relate to the transfer of cases to the Crown Court) shall cease to have effect.

(3) In section 11 (restrictions on reporting) –
   (a) in subsection (2), paragraph (a) is omitted,

   (b) subsection (3) is omitted,
   (c) in subsection (7), '(3),' is omitted,
   (d) in subsection (8), '(3),' is omitted,
   (e) subsections (9) and (10) are omitted,
   (f) in subsection (11), paragraphs (a) and (d) are omitted.

Coroners Act 1988 (c. 13)

59(1) The Coroners Act 1988 is amended as follows.

(2) In section 16 (adjournment of inquest in event of criminal proceedings) –

   (a) in subsection (1)(b), for 'charged before examining justices with' there is substituted 'sent for trial for', and
   (b) for subsection (8) there is substituted –

   '(8) In this section, the 'relevant criminal proceedings' means the proceedings –

     (a) before a magistrates' court to determine whether the person charged is to be sent to the Crown Court for trial; or
     (b) before any court to which that person is sent for trial.'

(3) In section 17 (provisions supplementary to section 16) –

   (a) in subsection (2), for 'committed' there is substituted 'sent', and
   (b) in subsection (3)(b), for 'committed' there is substituted 'sent'.

Criminal Justice Act 1988 (c. 33)

60(1) The Criminal Justice Act 1988 is amended as follows.

(2) In section 23 (first-hand hearsay), subsection (5) is omitted.

(3) In section 24 (business etc documents), subsection (5) is omitted.

(4) In section 26 (statements in certain documents), the paragraph beginning 'This section shall not apply' is omitted.

(5) In section 27 (proof of statements contained in documents), the paragraph beginning 'This section shall not apply' is omitted.

(6) In section 30 (expert reports), subsection (4A) is omitted.

(7) In section 40 (power to join in indictment count for common assault etc), in subsection (1) –

   (a) the words 'were disclosed to a magistrates' court inquiring into the offence as examining justices or' are omitted,
   (b) after '51' there is inserted 'or 51A'.

(8) Section 41 (power of Crown Court to deal with summary offence where person committed for either way offence) shall cease to have effect.

Road Traffic Offenders Act 1988 (c. 53)

61(1) The Road Traffic Offenders Act 1988 is amended as follows.

(2) In section 11 (evidence by certificate as to driver, user or owner), subsection (3A) is omitted.

(3) In section 13 (admissibility of records as evidence), subsection (7) is omitted.

(4) In section 16 (documentary evidence as to specimens), subsection (6A) is omitted.

(5) In section 20 (speeding offences etc), subsection (8A) is omitted.

Criminal Justice Act 1991 (c. 53)

62(1) The Criminal Justice Act 1991 is amended as follows.

(2) Section 53 (notices of transfer in certain cases involving children) shall cease to have effect.

(3) Schedule 6 (notices of transfer: procedures in lieu of committal) shall cease to have effect.

Sexual Offences (Amendment) Act 1992 (c. 34)

63 In section 6 of the Sexual Offences (Amendment) Act 1992 (interpretation), in subsection (3)(c), for 'commits him' there is substituted 'sends him to the Crown Court'.

Criminal Justice and Public Order Act 1994 (c. 33)

64(1) The Criminal Justice and Public Order Act 1994 is amended as follows.

(2) In section 34 (effect of accused's failure to mention facts when questioned or charged), in subsection (2) –

    (a) paragraph (a) is omitted, and
    (b) in paragraph (b), for sub-paragraphs (i) and (ii), there is substituted 'paragraph 2 of Schedule 3 to the Crime and Disorder Act 1998'.

(3) In section 36 (effect of accused's failure or refusal to account for objects, substances or marks), in subsection (2) –

    (a) paragraph (a) is omitted, and
    (b) in paragraph (b), for sub-paragraphs (i) and (ii), there is substituted 'paragraph 2 of Schedule 3 to the Crime and Disorder Act 1998'.

(4) In section 37 (effect of accused's failure or refusal to account for presence at a particular place), in subsection (2) –

    (a) paragraph (a) is omitted, and
    (b) in paragraph (b), for sub-paragraphs (i) and (ii), there is substituted 'paragraph 2 of Schedule 3 to the Crime and Disorder Act 1998'.

Reserve Forces Act 1996 (c. 14)

65 In Schedule 2 to the Reserve Forces Act 1996 (deserters and absentees without leave), in paragraph 3, after sub-paragraph (2) there is inserted –

'(2A) The reference in sub-paragraph (2) to provisions of the Magistrates' Courts Act 1980 is to be taken to refer to those provisions as if no amendment to them had been made by the Criminal Justice Act 2003.'

Criminal Procedure and Investigations Act 1996 (c. 25)

66(1) The Criminal Procedure and Investigations Act 1996 is amended as follows.

(2) In section 1 (application of this Part), in subsection (2) –

    (a) paragraphs (a) to (c) are omitted, and
    (b) in paragraph (cc), the words from 'under' to the end are omitted.

(3) In section 5 (compulsory disclosure by accused) –

    (a) in subsection (1), for '(2) to' there is substituted '(3A) and',
    (b) subsections (2) and (3) are omitted, and
    (c) in subsection (3A), in paragraph (b), for 'subsection (7) of section 51' there is substituted 'subsection (1) of section 51D'.

(4) In section 13 (time limits: transitional), in subsection (1), paragraphs (a) to (c) of the modified section 3(8) are omitted.

(5) In section 21 (common law rules as to disclosure), in subsection (3), for paragraphs (b) and (c) there is substituted –

    '(b) the accused is sent for trial (where this Part applies by virtue of section 1(2)(cc)),'.

(6) In section 28 (introduction to Part 3), in subsection (1) –

    (a) for paragraph (a) there is substituted –

       '(a) on or after the appointed day the accused is sent for trial for the offence concerned,', and

    (b) paragraph (b) is omitted.

(7) In section 39 (meaning of pre-trial hearing), in subsection (1), for paragraph (a) there is substituted –

    '(a) after the accused has been sent for trial for the offence, and'.

(8) Section 68 (use of written statements and depositions at trial) and Schedule 2 (statements and depositions) shall cease to have effect.

Sexual Offences (Protected Material) Act 1997 (c. 39)

67 In section 9 of the Sexual Offences (Protected Material) Act 1997 (modification and amendment of certain enactments), subsection (1) is omitted.

Crime and Disorder Act 1998 (c. 37)

68 The Crime and Disorder Act 1998 is amended as follows.

69 In section 52 (provisions supplementing section 51) –

    (a) in subsection (1), after '51' there is inserted 'or 51A',
    (b) in subsection (3), after '51' there is inserted 'or 51A',

(c) in subsection (5), after '51' there is inserted 'or 51A',

(d) in subsection (6), after '51' there is inserted 'or 51A', and

(e) in the heading, after '**51**' there is inserted '**and 51A**'.

70 In section 121 (short title, commencement and extent), in subsection (8), before 'paragraphs 7(1)' there is inserted 'paragraph 3 of Schedule 3 to this Act, section 52(6) above so far as relating to that paragraph,'.

71 In paragraph 3 of Schedule 3 (reporting restrictions) –

(a) in each of paragraphs (a) and (b) of sub-paragraph (1), for 'Great Britain' there is substituted 'the United Kingdom',

(b) in sub-paragraph (8), after paragraph (b) there is inserted –

'(bb) where the application made by the accused under paragraph 2(1) above relates to a charge for an offence in respect of which notice has been given to the court under section 51B of this Act, any relevant business information;',

(c) after sub-paragraph (9) there is inserted –

'(9A) The following is relevant business information for the purposes of sub-paragraph (8) above –

(a) any address used by the accused for carrying on a business on his own account;

(b) the name of any business which he was carrying on on his own account at any relevant time;

(c) the name of any firm in which he was a partner at any relevant time or by which he was engaged at any such time;

(d) the address of any such firm;

(e) the name of any company of which he was a director at any relevant time or by which he was otherwise engaged at any such time;

(f) the address of the registered or principal office of any such company;

(g) any working address of the accused in his capacity as a person engaged by any such company;

and here 'engaged' means engaged under a contract of service or a contract for services.', and

(d) after sub-paragraph (11) there is inserted –

'(11A) Proceedings for an offence under this paragraph shall not, in Northern Ireland, be instituted otherwise than by or with the consent of the Attorney General for Northern Ireland.'

72 In paragraph 4 of Schedule 3 (power of justice to take depositions etc), in sub-paragraph (12), for the definition of 'the relevant date' there is substituted –

'"the relevant date" means the expiry of the period referred to in paragraph 1(1) above.'

Youth Justice and Criminal Evidence Act 1999 (c. 23)

73(1) The Youth Justice and Criminal Evidence Act 1999 is amended as follows.

(2) In section 27 (video recorded evidence in chief), subsection (10) is omitted.

(3) In section 42 (interpretation and application of section 41), in subsection (3) –

(a) paragraphs (a) and (b) are omitted, and

(b) in paragraph (c), after '51' there is inserted 'or 51A'.

Powers of Criminal Courts (Sentencing) Act 2000 (c. 6)

74(1) The Powers of Criminal Courts (Sentencing) Act 2000 is amended as follows.

(2) In section 8 (power and duty to remit young offenders to youth courts for sentence), in subsection (2), for paragraph (a) there is substituted –

'(a) if the offender was sent to the Crown Court for trial under section 51 or 51A of the Crime and Disorder Act 1998, to a youth court acting for the place where he was sent to the Crown Court for trial;'.

(3) In section 89 (restriction on imposing imprisonment), in subsection (2) –

(a) in paragraph (b), the words 'trial or' are omitted, and
(b) in paragraph (c), after '51' there is inserted 'or 51A'.

(4) In section 140 (enforcement of fines etc), in subsection (1)(b) –

(a) the words 'was committed to the Crown Court to be tried or dealt with or by which he' are omitted, and
(b) after '51' there is inserted 'or 51A'.

(5) In section 148 (restitution orders), in subsection (6), for paragraph (b) there is substituted –

'(b) such documents as were served on the offender in pursuance of regulations made under paragraph 1 of Schedule 3 to the Crime and Disorder Act 1998.'

(6) In Schedule 11, paragraph 9 is omitted.

Proceeds of Crime Act 2002 (c. 29)

75(1) The Proceeds of Crime Act 2002 is amended as follows.

(2) In section 6 (making of confiscation order), in subsection (2)(b), for 'section 3, 4 or 6' there is substituted 'section 3, 3A, 3B, 3C, 4, 4A or 6'.

(3) In section 27 (defendant absconds after being convicted or committed), in subsection (2)(b), for 'section 3, 4 or 6' there is substituted 'section 3, 3A, 3B, 3C, 4, 4A or 6'.

(4) In section 70 (committal by magistrates' court), in subsection (5), after 'way)' there is inserted 'or under section 3B(2) of that Act (committal of child or young person)'.

SCHEDULE 4   Section 62

QUALIFYING OFFENCES FOR PURPOSES OF SECTION 62

PART 1

LIST OF OFFENCES

Offences Against the Person

Murder

1 Murder.

Attempted murder

2 An offence under section 1 of the Criminal Attempts Act 1981 (c. 47) of attempting to commit murder.

Soliciting murder

3 An offence under section 4 of the Offences against the Person Act 1861 (c. 100).

Manslaughter

4 Manslaughter.

Wounding or causing grievous bodily harm with intent

5 An offence under section 18 of the Offences against the Person Act 1861 (c. 100).

Kidnapping

6 Kidnapping.

Sexual Offences

Rape

7 An offence under section 1 of the Sexual Offences Act 1956 (c. 69) or section 1 of the Sexual Offences Act 2003 (c. 42).

Attempted rape

8 An offence under section 1 of the Criminal Attempts Act 1981 (c. 47) of attempting to commit an offence under section 1 of the Sexual Offences Act 1956 or section 1 of the Sexual Offences Act 2003.

Intercourse with a girl under thirteen

9 An offence under section 5 of the Sexual Offences Act 1956.

Incest by a man with a girl under thirteen

10 An offence under section 10 of the Sexual Offences Act 1956 alleged to have been committed with a girl under thirteen.

Assault by penetration

11 An offence under section 2 of the Sexual Offences Act 2003.

Causing a person to engage in sexual activity without consent

12 An offence under section 4 of the Sexual Offences Act 2003 where it is alleged that the activity caused involved penetration within subsection (4)(a) to (d) of that section.

Rape of a child under thirteen

13 An offence under section 5 of the Sexual Offences Act 2003.

Attempted rape of a child under thirteen

14 An offence under section 1 of the Criminal Attempts Act 1981 of attempting to commit an offence under section 5 of the Sexual Offences Act 2003.

Assault of a child under thirteen by penetration

15 An offence under section 6 of the Sexual Offences Act 2003.

Causing a child under thirteen to engage in sexual activity

16 An offence under section 8 of the Sexual Offences Act 2003 (c. 42) where it is alleged that an activity involving penetration within subsection (2)(a) to (d) of that section was caused.

Sexual activity with a person with a mental disorder impeding choice

17 An offence under section 30 of the Sexual Offences Act 2003 where it is alleged that the touching involved penetration within subsection (3)(a) to (d) of that section.

Causing or inciting a person with a mental disorder impeding choice to engage in sexual activity

18 An offence under section 31 of the Sexual Offences Act 2003 where it is alleged that an activity involving penetration within subsection (3)(a) to (d) of that section was caused.

Drugs Offences

Unlawful importation of Class A drug

19 An offence under section 50(2) of the Customs and Excise Management Act 1979 (c. 2) alleged to have been committed in respect of a Class A drug (as defined by section 2 of the Misuse of Drugs Act 1971 (c. 38)).

Unlawful exportation of Class A drug

20 An offence under section 68(2) of the Customs and Excise Management Act 1979 alleged to have been committed in respect of a Class A drug (as defined by section 2 of the Misuse of Drugs Act 1971).

Fraudulent evasion in respect of Class A drug

21 An offence under section 170(1) or (2) of the Customs and Excise Management Act 1979 alleged to have been committed in respect of a Class A drug (as defined by section 2 of the Misuse of Drugs Act 1971).

Producing or being concerned in production of Class A drug

22 An offence under section 4(2) of the Misuse of Drugs Act 1971 alleged to have been committed in relation to a Class A drug (as defined by section 2 of that Act).

Supplying or offering to supply Class A drug

23 An offence under section 4(3) of the Misuse of Drugs Act 1971 alleged to have been committed in relation to a Class A drug (as defined by section 2 of that Act).

Theft Offences

Robbery

24 An offence under section 8(1) of the Theft Act 1968 (c. 60) where it is alleged that, at some time during the commission of the offence, the defendant had in his possession a firearm or imitation firearm (as defined by section 57 of the Firearms Act 1968 (c. 27)).

Criminal Damage Offences

Arson endangering life

25 An offence under section 1(2) of the Criminal Damage Act 1971 (c. 48) alleged to have been committed by destroying or damaging property by fire.

Causing explosion likely to endanger life or property

26 An offence under section 2 of the Explosive Substances Act 1883 (c. 3).

Intent or conspiracy to cause explosion likely to endanger life or property

27 An offence under section 3(1)(a) of the Explosive Substances Act 1883.

War Crimes and Terrorism

Genocide, crimes against humanity and war crimes

28 An offence under section 51 or 52 of the International Criminal Court Act 2001 (c. 17).

Grave breaches of the Geneva Conventions

29 An offence under section 1 of the Geneva Conventions Act 1957 (c. 52).

Directing terrorist organisation

30 An offence under section 56 of the Terrorism Act 2000 (c. 11).

Hostage-taking

31 An offence under section 1 of the Taking of Hostages Act 1982 (c. 28).

Hijacking and Other Offences Relating to Aviation, Maritime and Rail Security

Hijacking of aircraft

32 An offence under section 1 of the Aviation Security Act 1982 (c. 36).

Destroying, damaging or endangering the safety of an aircraft

33 An offence under section 2 of the Aviation Security Act 1982.

Hijacking of ships

34 An offence under section 9 of the Aviation and Maritime Security Act 1990 (c. 31).

Seizing or exercising control of fixed platforms

35 An offence under section 10 of the Aviation and Maritime Security Act 1990.

Destroying ships or fixed platforms or endangering their safety

36 An offence under section 11 of the Aviation and Maritime Security Act 1990.

Hijacking of Channel Tunnel trains

37 An offence under article 4 of the Channel Tunnel (Security) Order 1994 (S.I.1994/ 570).

Seizing or exercising control of the Channel Tunnel system

38 An offence under article 5 of the Channel Tunnel (Security) Order 1994 (S.I.1994/ 570).

Conspiracy

Conspiracy

39 An offence under section 1 of the Criminal Law Act 1977 (c. 45) of conspiracy to commit an offence listed in this Part of this Schedule.

PART 2

SUPPLEMENTARY

40 A reference in Part 1 of this Schedule to an offence includes a reference to an offence of aiding, abetting, counselling or procuring the commission of the offence.

41 A reference in Part 1 of this Schedule to an enactment includes a reference to the enactment as enacted and as amended from time to time.

SCHEDULE 5   Section 75

QUALIFYING OFFENCES FOR PURPOSES OF PART 10

PART 1

LIST OF OFFENCES FOR ENGLAND AND WALES

Offences Against the Person

Murder

1 Murder.

Attempted murder

2 An offence under section 1 of the Criminal Attempts Act 1981 (c. 47) of attempting to commit murder.

Soliciting murder

3 An offence under section 4 of the Offences against the Person Act 1861 (c. 100).

Manslaughter

4 Manslaughter.

Kidnapping

5 Kidnapping.

Sexual Offences

Rape

6 An offence under section 1 of the Sexual Offences Act 1956 (c. 69) or section 1 of the Sexual Offences Act 2003 (c. 42).

Attempted rape

7 An offence under section 1 of the Criminal Attempts Act 1981 of attempting to commit an offence under section 1 of the Sexual Offences Act 1956 or section 1 of the Sexual Offences Act 2003.

Intercourse with a girl under thirteen

8 An offence under section 5 of the Sexual Offences Act 1956.

Incest by a man with a girl under thirteen

9 An offence under section 10 of the Sexual Offences Act 1956 alleged to have been committed with a girl under thirteen.

Assault by penetration

10 An offence under section 2 of the Sexual Offences Act 2003 (c. 42).

Causing a person to engage in sexual activity without consent

11 An offence under section 4 of the Sexual Offences Act 2003 where it is alleged that the activity caused involved penetration within subsection (4)(a) to (d) of that section.

Rape of a child under thirteen

12 An offence under section 5 of the Sexual Offences Act 2003.

Attempted rape of a child under thirteen

13 An offence under section 1 of the Criminal Attempts Act 1981 (c. 47) of attempting to commit an offence under section 5 of the Sexual Offences Act 2003.

Assault of a child under thirteen by penetration

14 An offence under section 6 of the Sexual Offences Act 2003.

Causing a child under thirteen to engage in sexual activity

15 An offence under section 8 of the Sexual Offences Act 2003 where it is alleged that an activity involving penetration within subsection (2)(a) to (d) of that section was caused.

Sexual activity with a person with a mental disorder impeding choice

16 An offence under section 30 of the Sexual Offences Act 2003 where it is alleged that the touching involved penetration within subsection (3)(a) to (d) of that section.

Causing a person with a mental disorder impeding choice to engage in sexual activity

17 An offence under section 31 of the Sexual Offences Act 2003 where it is alleged that an activity involving penetration within subsection (3)(a) to (d) of that section was caused.

Drugs Offences

Unlawful importation of Class A drug

18 An offence under section 50(2) of the Customs and Excise Management Act 1979 (c. 2) alleged to have been committed in respect of a Class A drug (as defined by section 2 of the Misuse of Drugs Act 1971 (c. 38)).

Unlawful exportation of Class A drug

19 An offence under section 68(2) of the Customs and Excise Management Act 1979 alleged to have been committed in respect of a Class A drug (as defined by section 2 of the Misuse of Drugs Act 1971).

Fraudulent evasion in respect of Class A drug

20 An offence under section 170(1) or (2) of the Customs and Excise Management Act 1979 (c. 2) alleged to have been committed in respect of a Class A drug (as defined by section 2 of the Misuse of Drugs Act 1971 (c. 38)).

Producing or being concerned in production of Class A drug

21 An offence under section 4(2) of the Misuse of Drugs Act 1971 alleged to have been committed in relation to a Class A drug (as defined by section 2 of that Act).

Criminal Damage Offences

Arson endangering life

22 An offence under section 1(2) of the Criminal Damage Act 1971 (c. 48) alleged to have been committed by destroying or damaging property by fire.

Causing explosion likely to endanger life or property

23 An offence under section 2 of the Explosive Substances Act 1883 (c. 3).

Intent or conspiracy to cause explosion likely to endanger life or property

24 An offence under section 3(1)(a) of the Explosive Substances Act 1883.

War Crimes and Terrorism

Genocide, crimes against humanity and war crimes

25 An offence under section 51 or 52 of the International Criminal Court Act 2001 (c. 17).

Grave breaches of the Geneva Conventions

26 An offence under section 1 of the Geneva Conventions Act 1957 (c. 52).

Directing terrorist organisation

27 An offence under section 56 of the Terrorism Act 2000 (c. 11).

Hostage-taking

28 An offence under section 1 of the Taking of Hostages Act 1982 (c. 28).

Conspiracy

Conspiracy

29 An offence under section 1 of the Criminal Law Act 1977 (c. 45) of conspiracy to commit an offence listed in this Part of this Schedule.

PART 2

LIST OF OFFENCES FOR NORTHERN IRELAND

Offences Against the Person

Murder

30 Murder.

Attempted murder

31 An offence under Article 3 of the Criminal Attempts and Conspiracy (Northern Ireland) Order 1983 of attempting to commit murder.

Soliciting murder

32 An offence under section 4 of the Offences against the Person Act 1861 (c. 100).

Manslaughter

33 Manslaughter.

Kidnapping

34 Kidnapping.

Sexual Offences

Rape

35 Rape.

Attempted rape

36 An offence under section 2 of the Attempted Rape, etc., Act (Northern Ireland) 1960.

Intercourse with a girl under fourteen

37 An offence under section 4 of the Criminal Law Amendment Act 1885 (c. 69) of unlawfully and carnally knowing a girl under fourteen.

Incest by a man with a girl under fourteen

38 An offence under section 1(1) of the Punishment of Incest Act 1908 (c.45) alleged to have been committed with a girl under fourteen.

Drugs Offences

Unlawful importation of Class A drug

39 An offence under section 50(2) of the Customs and Excise Management Act 1979 (c. 2) alleged to have been committed in respect of a Class A drug (as defined by section 2 of the Misuse of Drugs Act 1971 (c. 38)).

Unlawful exportation of Class A drug

40 An offence under section 68(2) of the Customs and Excise Management Act 1979 alleged to have been committed in respect of a Class A drug (as defined by section 2 of the Misuse of Drugs Act 1971).

Fraudulent evasion in respect of Class A drug

41 An offence under section 170(1) or (2) of the Customs and Excise Management Act 1979 alleged to have been committed in respect of a Class A drug (as defined by section 2 of the Misuse of Drugs Act 1971).

Producing or being concerned in production of Class A drug

42 An offence under section 4(2) of the Misuse of Drugs Act 1971 alleged to have been committed in respect of a Class A drug (as defined by section 2 of that Act).

Criminal Damage Offences

Arson endangering life

43 An offence under Article 3(2) of the Criminal Damage (Northern Ireland) Order 1977 alleged to have been committed by destroying or damaging property by fire.

Causing explosion likely to endanger life or property

44 An offence under section 2 of the Explosive Substances Act 1883 (c. 3).

Intent or conspiracy to cause explosion likely to endanger life or property

45 An offence under section 3(1)(a) of the Explosive Substances Act 1883.

War Crimes and Terrorism

Genocide, crimes against humanity and war crimes

46 An offence under section 51 or 52 of the International Criminal Court Act 2001 (c. 17).

Grave breaches of the Geneva Conventions

47 An offence under section 1 of the Geneva Conventions Act 1957 (c. 52).

Directing terrorist organisation

48 An offence under section 56 of the Terrorism Act 2000 (c. 11).

Hostage-taking

49 An offence under section 1 of the Taking of Hostages Act 1982 (c. 28).

Conspiracy

Conspiracy

50 An offence under Article 9 of the Criminal Attempts and Conspiracy (Northern Ireland) Order 1983 of conspiracy to commit an offence listed in this Part of this Schedule.

PART 3

SUPPLEMENTARY

51 A reference in this Schedule to an offence includes a reference to an offence of aiding, abetting, counselling or procuring the commission of the offence.

52 A reference in this Schedule to an enactment includes a reference to the enactment as enacted and as amended from time to time.

SCHEDULE 6 Section 113

EVIDENCE OF BAD CHARACTER: ARMED FORCES

1 Sections 98 to 106, 109, 110 and 112, in so far as they are not applied in relation to proceedings before service courts by provision contained in or made under any other Act, have effect in relation to such proceedings (whether in the United Kingdom or elsewhere) as they have effect in relation to criminal proceedings.

2 Section 103, as it applies in relation to proceedings before service courts, has effect with the substitution in subsection (4)(a) of 'charge sheet' for 'written charge or indictment'.

3(1) Section 107 has effect in relation to proceedings before courts-martial (whether in the United Kingdom or elsewhere) with the following modifications.

(2) In subsection (1) –

    (a) for 'judge and jury' substitute 'court-martial';
    (b) for 'the court is satisfied' substitute 'the judge advocate is satisfied';
    (c) for the words after paragraph (b) substitute 'the judge advocate must either direct the court to acquit the defendant of the offence or, if he considers that there ought to be a retrial, dissolve the court.'

(3) In subsection (2) –

    (a) for 'jury' substitute 'court';
    (b) for 'the court is satisfied' substitute 'the judge advocate is satisfied'.

(4) In subsection (3) –

    (a) for paragraph (a) substitute –

        '(a) a court is required to determine under section 115B(2) of the Army Act 1955, section 115B(2) of the Air Force Act 1955 or section 62B(2) of the Naval Discipline Act 1957 whether a person charged with an offence did the act or made the omission charged,';

(b) for 'the court is satisfied' substitute 'the judge advocate is satisfied';

(c) for the words after paragraph (c) substitute 'the judge advocate must either direct the court to acquit the defendant of the offence or, if he considers that there ought to be a rehearing, dissolve the court.'

(5) For subsection (4) substitute –

'(4) This section does not prejudice any other power a judge advocate may have to direct a court to acquit a person of an offence or to dissolve a court.'

4 Section 110, as it applies in relation to proceedings before service courts, has effect with the substitution of the following for subsection (1) –

'(1) Where the court makes a relevant ruling –

(a) it must state in open court (but, in the case of a ruling by a judge advocate in proceedings before a court-martial, in the absence of the other members of the court) its reasons for the ruling;

(b) if it is a Standing Civilian Court, it must cause the ruling and the reasons for it to be entered in the note of the court's proceedings.'

5 Section 111 has effect as if, in subsection (7), the definition of 'rules of court' included rules regulating the practice and procedure of service courts.

6(1) In this Schedule, and in section 107 as applied by this Schedule, 'court-martial' means a court-martial constituted under the Army Act 1955 (3 & 4 Eliz. 2 c. 18), the Air Force Act 1955 (3 & 4 Eliz. 2 c. 19) or the Naval Discipline Act 1957 (c. 53).

(2) In this Schedule 'service court' means –

(a) a court-martial;

(b) a summary appeal court constituted under section 83ZA of the Army Act 1955, section 83ZA of the Air Force Act 1955 or section 52FF of the Naval Discipline Act 1957;

(c) the Courts-Martial Appeal Court;

(d) a Standing Civilian Court.

SCHEDULE 7   Section 135

HEARSAY EVIDENCE: ARMED FORCES

Application to proceedings before service courts

1 Sections 114 to 121, 123, 124, 126, 127 to 129 and 133 and 134, in so far as they are not applied in relation to proceedings before service courts by provision contained in or made under any other Act, have effect in relation to such proceedings (whether in the United Kingdom or elsewhere) as they have effect in relation to criminal proceedings.

2(1) In their application to such proceedings those sections have effect with the following modifications.

(2) In section 116(2)(c) for 'United Kingdom' substitute 'country where the court is sitting'.

(3) In section 117 insert after subsection (7) –

'(8) In subsection (4) "criminal proceedings" includes summary proceedings under section 76B of the Army Act 1955, section 76B of the Air Force Act 1955 or section 52D of the Naval Discipline Act 1957; and the definition of 'criminal proceedings' in section 134(1) has effect accordingly.'

(4) In section 123(4) for paragraph (a) substitute –

'(a) in the case of proceedings before a court-martial, proceedings held for the determination of the issue must take place before the judge advocate in the absence of the other members of the court;'.

(5) In section 127, for subsection (7) substitute –

'(7) The appropriate rules are those regulating the practice and procedure of service courts.'

(6) In section 132(10), at the end of the definition of 'rules of court' insert –

'(d) rules regulating the practice and procedure of service courts.'

(7) In section 134 insert after subsection (1) –

'(1A) In this Part "criminal investigation" includes any investigation which may lead –

(a) to proceedings before a court-martial or Standing Civilian Court, or
(b) to summary proceedings under section 76B of the Army Act 1955, section 76B of the Air Force Act 1955 or section 52D of the Naval Discipline Act 1957.'

3(1) Section 122 has effect in relation to proceedings before courts-martial (whether in the United Kingdom or elsewhere) with the following modifications.

(2) In subsection (1) for 'judge and jury' substitute 'court-martial'.

(3) In subsection (2) –

(a) for 'jury when they retire to consider their' substitute 'court when it retires to consider its'.
(b) for 'the court' in paragraph (a) substitute 'the judge advocate';
(c) for 'the jury' in paragraph (b) substitute 'the court'.

4(1) Section 125 has effect in relation to proceedings before courts-martial (whether in the United Kingdom or elsewhere) with the following modifications.

(2) In subsection (1) –

(a) for 'judge and jury' substitute 'court-martial';
(b) for 'the court is satisfied' substitute 'the judge advocate is satisfied';
(c) for the words after paragraph (b) substitute 'the judge advocate must either direct the court to acquit the defendant of the offence or, if he considers that there ought to be a retrial, dissolve the court.'

(3) In subsection (2) –

(a) for 'jury' substitute 'court';
(b) for 'the court is satisfied' substitute 'the judge advocate is satisfied'.

(4) In subsection (3) –

(a) for paragraph (a) substitute –

'(a) a court is required to determine under section 115B(2) of the Army Act 1955, section 115B(2) of the Air Force Act 1955 or section 62B(2) of the Naval Discipline Act 1957 whether a person charged with an offence did the act or made the omission charged,';

(b) for 'the court is satisfied' substitute 'the judge advocate is satisfied';
(c) for the words after paragraph (b) substitute 'the judge advocate must either direct the court to acquit the defendant of the offence or, if he considers that there ought to be a rehearing, dissolve the court.'

(5) For subsection (4) substitute –

'(4) This section does not prejudice any other power a judge advocate may have to direct a court to acquit a person of an offence or to dissolve a court.'

Amendments

5 For paragraph 1 of Schedule 1 to the Courts-Martial (Appeals) Act 1968 (c. 20) (use at retrial under Naval Discipline Act 1957 of record of evidence given at original trial) substitute –

'1 Evidence given at the retrial of any person under section 19 of this Act shall be given orally if it was given orally at the original trial, unless –

(a) all the parties to the retrial agree otherwise;
(b) section 116 of the Criminal Justice Act 2003 applies (admissibility of hearsay evidence where a witness is unavailable); or
(c) the witness is unavailable to give evidence, otherwise than as mentioned in subsection (2) of that section, and section 114(1)(d) of that Act applies (admission of hearsay evidence under residual discretion).'

6 For paragraph 3 of that Schedule (use at retrial under Army Act 1955 of record of evidence given at original trial) substitute –

'3 Evidence given at the retrial of any person under section 19 of this Act shall be given orally if it was given orally at the original trial, unless –

(a) all the parties to the retrial agree otherwise;
(b) section 116 of the Criminal Justice Act 2003 applies (admissibility of hearsay evidence where a witness is unavailable); or
(c) the witness is unavailable to give evidence, otherwise than as mentioned in subsection (2) of that section, and section 114(1)(d) of that Act applies (admission of hearsay evidence under residual discretion).'

7 For paragraph 5 of that Schedule (use at retrial under Air Force Act 1955 of record of evidence given at original trial) substitute –

'5 Evidence given at the retrial of any person under section 19 of this Act shall be given orally if it was given orally at the original trial, unless –

(a) all the parties to the retrial agree otherwise;
(b) section 116 of the Criminal Justice Act 2003 applies (admissibility of hearsay evidence where a witness is unavailable); or
(c) the witness is unavailable to give evidence, otherwise than as mentioned in subsection (2) of that section, and section 114(1)(d) of that Act applies (admission of hearsay evidence under residual discretion).'

Interpretation

8 In this Schedule, and in any provision of this Part as applied by this Schedule –

'court-martial' means a court-martial constituted under the Army Act 1955 (3 & 4

Eliz. 2 c. 18), the Air Force Act 1955 (3 & 4 Eliz. 2 c. 19) or the Naval Discipline Act 1957 (c. 53);

'service court' means –

(a) a court-martial;

(b) a summary appeal court constituted under section 83ZA of the Army Act 1955, section 83ZA of the Air Force Act 1955 or section 52FF of the Naval Discipline Act 1957;

(c) the Courts-Martial Appeal Court;

(d) a Standing Civilian Court.

SCHEDULE 8   Section 179

BREACH, REVOCATION OR AMENDMENT OF COMMUNITY ORDER

PART 1

PRELIMINARY

Interpretation

1 In this Schedule –

'the offender', in relation to a community order, means the person in respect of whom the order is made;

'the petty sessions area concerned', in relation to a community order, means the petty sessions area for the time being specified in the order;

'the responsible officer' has the meaning given by section 197.

2 In this Schedule –

(a) references to a drug rehabilitation requirement of a community order being subject to review are references to that requirement being subject to review in accordance with section 210(1)(b);

(b) references to the court responsible for a community order imposing a drug rehabilitation requirement which is subject to review are to be construed in accordance with section 210(2).

3 For the purposes of this Schedule –

(a) a requirement falling within any paragraph of section 177(1) is of the same kind as any other requirement falling within that paragraph, and

(b) an electronic monitoring requirement is a requirement of the same kind as any requirement falling within section 177(1) to which it relates.

Orders made on appeal

4 Where a community order has been made on appeal, it is to be taken for the purposes of this Schedule to have been made by the Crown Court.

PART 2

BREACH OF REQUIREMENT OF ORDER

Duty to give warning

5(1) If the responsible officer is of the opinion that the offender has failed without reasonable excuse to comply with any of the requirements of a community order, the officer must give him a warning under this paragraph unless –

(a)   the offender has within the previous twelve months been given a warning under this paragraph in relation to a failure to comply with any of the requirements of the order, or

(b)   the officer causes an information to be laid before a justice of the peace in respect of the failure.

(2) A warning under this paragraph must –

(a)   describe the circumstances of the failure,

(b)   state that the failure is unacceptable, and

(c)   inform the offender that, if within the next twelve months he again fails to comply with any requirement of the order, he will be liable to be brought before a court.

(3) The responsible officer must, as soon as practicable after the warning has been given, record that fact.

(4) In relation to any community order which was made by the Crown Court and does not include a direction that any failure to comply with the requirements of the order is to be dealt with by a magistrates' court, the reference in sub-paragraph (1)(b) to a justice of the peace is to be read as a reference to the Crown Court.

Breach of order after warning

6(1) If –

(a)   the responsible officer has given a warning under paragraph 5 to the offender in respect of a community order, and

(b)   at any time within the twelve months beginning with the date on which the warning was given, the responsible officer is of the opinion that the offender has since that date failed without reasonable excuse to comply with any of the requirements of the order,

the officer must cause an information to be laid before a justice of the peace in respect of the failure in question.

(2) In relation to any community order which was made by the Crown Court and does not include a direction that any failure to comply with the requirements of the order is to be dealt with by a magistrates' court, the reference in sub-paragraph (1) to a justice of the peace is to be read as a reference to the Crown Court.

Issue of summons or warrant by justice of the peace

7(1) This paragraph applies to –

(a)   a community order made by a magistrates' court, or

(b)   any community order which was made by the Crown Court and includes a direction that any failure to comply with the requirements of the order is to be dealt with by a magistrates' court.

(2) If at any time while a community order to which this paragraph applies is in force it appears on information to a justice of the peace acting for the petty sessions area concerned that the offender has failed to comply with any of the requirements of the order, the justice may –

(a)   issue a summons requiring the offender to appear at the place and time specified in it, or

(b) if the information is in writing and on oath, issue a warrant for his arrest.

(3) Any summons or warrant issued under this paragraph must direct the offender to appear or be brought –

(a) in the case of a community order imposing a drug rehabilitation requirement which is subject to review, before the magistrates' court responsible for the order, or

(b) in any other case, before a magistrates' court acting for the petty sessions area concerned.

(4) Where a summons issued under sub-paragraph (2)(a) requires the offender to appear before a magistrates' court and the offender does not appear in answer to the summons, the magistrates' court may issue a warrant for the arrest of the offender.

Issue of summons or warrant by Crown Court

8(1) This paragraph applies to a community order made by the Crown Court which does not include a direction that any failure to comply with the requirements of the order is to be dealt with by a magistrates' court.

(2) If at any time while a community order to which this paragraph applies is in force it appears on information to the Crown Court that the offender has failed to comply with any of the requirements of the order, the Crown Court may –

(a) issue a summons requiring the offender to appear at the place and time specified in it, or

(b) if the information is in writing and on oath, issue a warrant for his arrest.

(3) Any summons or warrant issued under this paragraph must direct the offender to appear or be brought before the Crown Court.

(4) Where a summons issued under sub-paragraph (2)(a) requires the offender to appear before the Crown Court and the offender does not appear in answer to the summons, the Crown Court may issue a warrant for the arrest of the offender.

Powers of magistrates' court

9(1) If it is proved to the satisfaction of a magistrates' court before which an offender appears or is brought under paragraph 7 that he has failed without reasonable excuse to comply with any of the requirements of the community order, the court must deal with him in respect of the failure in any one of the following ways –

(a) by amending the terms of the community order so as to impose more onerous requirements which the court could include if it were then making the order;

(b) where the community order was made by a magistrates' court, by dealing with him, for the offence in respect of which the order was made, in any way in which the court could deal with him if he had just been convicted by it of the offence;

(c) where –

(i) the community order was made by a magistrates' court,

(ii) the offence in respect of which the order was made was not an offence punishable by imprisonment,

(iii) the offender is aged 18 or over, and

(iv) the offender has wilfully and persistently failed to comply with the requirements of the order, by dealing with him, in respect of that offence, by imposing a sentence of imprisonment for a term not exceeding 51 weeks.

(2) In dealing with an offender under sub-paragraph (1), a magistrates' court must take into account the extent to which the offender has complied with the requirements of the community order.

(3) In dealing with an offender under sub-paragraph (1)(a), the court may extend the duration of particular requirements (subject to any limit imposed by Chapter 4 of Part 12 of this Act) but may not extend the period specified under section 177(5).

(4) In dealing with an offender under sub-paragraph (1)(b), the court may, in the case of an offender who has wilfully and persistently failed to comply with the requirements of the community order, impose a custodial sentence (where the order was made in respect of an offence punishable with such a sentence) notwithstanding anything in section 152(2).

(5) Where a magistrates' court deals with an offender under sub-paragraph (1)(b) or (c), it must revoke the community order if it is still in force.

(6) Where a community order was made by the Crown Court and a magistrates' court would (apart from this sub-paragraph) be required to deal with the offender under sub-paragraph (1)(a), (b) or (c), it may instead commit him to custody or release him on bail until he can be brought or appear before the Crown Court.

(7) A magistrates' court which deals with an offender's case under sub-paragraph (6) must send to the Crown Court –

   (a)   a certificate signed by a justice of the peace certifying that the offender has failed
         to comply with the requirements of the community order in the respect specified
         in the certificate, and
   (b)   such other particulars of the case as may be desirable;
and a certificate purporting to be so signed is admissible as evidence of the failure before the Crown Court.

(8) A person sentenced under sub-paragraph (1)(b) or (c) for an offence may appeal to the Crown Court against the sentence.

Powers of Crown Court

10(1) Where under paragraph 8 or by virtue of paragraph 9(6) an offender appears or is brought before the Crown Court and it is proved to the satisfaction of that court that he has failed without reasonable excuse to comply with any of the requirements of the community order, the Crown Court must deal with him in respect of the failure in any one of the following ways –

   (a)   by amending the terms of the community order so as to impose more onerous
         requirements which the Crown Court could impose if it were then making the
         order;
   (b)   by dealing with him, for the offence in respect of which the order was made, in
         any way in which he could have been dealt with for that offence by the court
         which made the order if the order had not been made;
   (c)   where –
         (i)   the offence in respect of which the order was made was not an offence
                punishable by imprisonment,
         (ii)   the offender is aged 18 or over,

    (iii)   the offender has wilfully and persistently failed to comply with the requirements of the order,

by dealing with him, in respect of that offence, by imposing a sentence of imprisonment for a term not exceeding 51 weeks.

(2) In dealing with an offender under sub-paragraph (1), the Crown Court must take into account the extent to which the offender has complied with the requirements of the community order.

(3) In dealing with an offender under sub-paragraph (1)(a), the court may extend the duration of particular requirements (subject to any limit imposed by Chapter 4 of Part 12 of this Act) but may not extend the period specified under section 177(5).

(4) In dealing with an offender under sub-paragraph (1)(b), the Crown Court may, in the case of an offender who has wilfully and persistently failed to comply with the requirements of the community order, impose a custodial sentence (where the order was made in respect of an offence punishable with such a sentence) notwithstanding anything in section 152(2).

(5) Where the Crown Court deals with an offender under sub-paragraph (1)(b) or (c), it must revoke the community order if it is still in force.

(6) In proceedings before the Crown Court under this paragraph any question whether the offender has failed to comply with the requirements of the community order is to be determined by the court and not by the verdict of a jury.

Restriction of powers in paragraphs 9 and 10 where treatment required

11(1) An offender who is required by any of the following requirements of a community order –

    (a)   a mental health treatment requirement,
    (b)   a drug rehabilitation requirement, or
    (c)   an alcohol treatment requirement,

to submit to treatment for his mental condition, or his dependency on or propensity to misuse drugs or alcohol, is not to be treated for the purposes of paragraph 9 or 10 as having failed to comply with that requirement on the ground only that he had refused to undergo any surgical, electrical or other treatment if, in the opinion of the court, his refusal was reasonable having regard to all the circumstances.

(2) A court may not under paragraph 9(1)(a) or 10(1)(a) amend a mental health treatment requirement, a drug rehabilitation requirement or an alcohol treatment requirement unless the offender expresses his willingness to comply with the requirement as amended.

Supplementary

12 Where a community order was made by a magistrates' court in the case of an offender under 18 years of age in respect of an offence triable only on indictment in the case of an adult, any powers exercisable under paragraph 9(1)(b) in respect of the offender after he attains the age of 18 are powers to do either or both of the following –

    (a)   to impose a fine not exceeding £5,000 for the offence in respect of which the order was made;

(b) to deal with the offender for that offence in any way in which a magistrates' court could deal with him if it had just convicted him of an offence punishable with imprisonment for a term not exceeding 51 weeks.

PART 3

REVOCATION OF ORDER

Revocation of order with or without re-sentencing: powers of magistrates' court

13(1) This paragraph applies where a community order, other than an order made by the Crown Court and falling within paragraph 14(1)(a), is in force and on the application of the offender or the responsible officer it appears to the appropriate magistrates' court that, having regard to circumstances which have arisen since the order was made, it would be in the interests of justice –

(a) for the order to be revoked, or
(b) for the offender to be dealt with in some other way for the offence in respect of which the order was made.

(2) The appropriate magistrates' court may –

(a) revoke the order, or
(b) both –
    (i)   revoke the order, and
    (ii) deal with the offender, for the offence in respect of which the order was made, in any way in which it could deal with him if he had just been convicted by the court of the offence.

(3) The circumstances in which a community order may be revoked under sub-paragraph (2) include the offender's making good progress or his responding satisfactorily to supervision or treatment (as the case requires).

(4) In dealing with an offender under sub-paragraph (2)(b), a magistrates' court must take into account the extent to which the offender has complied with the requirements of the community order.

(5) A person sentenced under sub-paragraph (2)(b) for an offence may appeal to the Crown Court against the sentence.

(6) Where a magistrates' court proposes to exercise its powers under this paragraph otherwise than on the application of the offender, it must summon him to appear before the court and, if he does not appear in answer to the summons, may issue a warrant for his arrest.

(7) In this paragraph 'the appropriate magistrates' court' means –

(a) in the case of an order imposing a drug rehabilitation requirement which is subject to review, the magistrates' court responsible for the order, and
(b) in the case of any other community order, a magistrates' court acting for the petty sessions area concerned.

Revocation of order with or without re-sentencing: powers of Crown Court

14(1) This paragraph applies where –

(a) there is in force a community order made by the Crown Court which does not include a direction that any failure to comply with the requirements of the order is to be dealt with by a magistrates' court, and

(b) the offender or the responsible officer applies to the Crown Court for the order to be revoked or for the offender to be dealt with in some other way for the offence in respect of which the order was made.

(2) If it appears to the Crown Court to be in the interests of justice to do so, having regard to circumstances which have arisen since the order was made, the Crown Court may –

(a) revoke the order, or
(b) both –
    (i) revoke the order, and
    (ii) deal with the offender, for the offence in respect of which the order was made, in any way in which he could have been dealt with for that offence by the court which made the order if the order had not been made.

(3) The circumstances in which a community order may be revoked under sub-paragraph (2) include the offender's making good progress or his responding satisfactorily to supervision or treatment (as the case requires).

(4) In dealing with an offender under sub-paragraph (2)(b), the Crown Court must take into account the extent to which the offender has complied with the requirements of the order.

(5) Where the Crown Court proposes to exercise its powers under this paragraph otherwise than on the application of the offender, it must summon him to appear before the court and, if he does not appear in answer to the summons, may issue a warrant for his arrest.

Supplementary

15 Paragraph 12 applies for the purposes of paragraphs 13 and 14 as it applies for the purposes of paragraph 9 above, but as if for the words 'paragraph 9(1)(b)' there were substituted 'paragraph 13(2)(b)(ii) or 14(2)(b)(ii)'.

PART 4

AMENDMENT OF ORDER

Amendment by reason of change of residence

16(1) This paragraph applies where, at any time while a community order is in force in respect of an offender, the appropriate court is satisfied that the offender proposes to change, or has changed, his residence from the petty sessions area concerned to another petty sessions area.

(2) Subject to sub-paragraphs (3) and (4), the appropriate court may, and on the application of the responsible officer must, amend the community order by substituting the other petty sessions area for the area specified in the order.

(3) The court may not under this paragraph amend a community order which contains requirements which, in the opinion of the court, cannot be complied with unless the offender continues to reside in the petty sessions area concerned unless, in accordance with paragraph 17, it either –

(a) cancels those requirements, or
(b) substitutes for those requirements other requirements which can be complied with if the offender ceases to reside in that area.

(4) The court may not amend under this paragraph a community order imposing a programme requirement unless it appears to the court that the accredited programme specified in the requirement is available in the other petty sessions area.

(5) In this paragraph 'the appropriate court' means –

    (a)   in relation to any community order imposing a drug rehabilitation requirement which is subject to review, the court responsible for the order,

    (b)   in relation to any community order which was made by the Crown Court and does not include any direction that any failure to comply with the requirements of the order is to be dealt with by a magistrates' court, the Crown Court, and

    (c)   in relation to any other community order, a magistrates' court acting for the petty sessions area concerned.

Amendment of requirements of community order

17(1) The appropriate court may, on the application of the offender or the responsible officer, by order amend a community order –

    (a)   by cancelling any of the requirements of the order, or

    (b)   by replacing any of those requirements with a requirement of the same kind, which the court could include if it were then making the order.

(2) The court may not under this paragraph amend a mental health treatment requirement, a drug rehabilitation requirement or an alcohol treatment requirement unless the offender expresses his willingness to comply with the requirement as amended.

(3) If the offender fails to express his willingness to comply with a mental health treatment requirement, drug rehabilitation requirement or alcohol treatment requirement as proposed to be amended by the court under this paragraph, the court may –

    (a)   revoke the community order, and

    (b)   deal with him, for the offence in respect of which the order was made, in any way in which he could have been dealt with for that offence by the court which made the order if the order had not been made.

(4) In dealing with the offender under sub-paragraph (3)(b), the court –

    (a)   must take into account the extent to which the offender has complied with the requirements of the order, and

    (b)   may impose a custodial sentence (where the order was made in respect of an offence punishable with such a sentence) notwithstanding anything in section 152(2).

(5) Paragraph 12 applies for the purposes of this paragraph as it applies for the purposes of paragraph 9, but as if for the words 'paragraph 9(1)(b)' there were substituted 'paragraph 17(3)(b)'.

(6) In this paragraph 'the appropriate court' has the same meaning as in paragraph 16.

Amendment of treatment requirements of community order on report of practitioner

18(1) Where the medical practitioner or other person by whom or under whose direction an offender is, in pursuance of any requirement to which this sub-paragraph applies, being treated for his mental condition or his dependency on or propensity to misuse drugs or alcohol –

   (a) is of the opinion mentioned in sub-paragraph (3), or

   (b) is for any reason unwilling to continue to treat or direct the treatment of the offender,

he must make a report in writing to that effect to the responsible officer and that officer must apply under paragraph 17 to the appropriate court for the variation or cancellation of the requirement.

(2) The requirements to which sub-paragraph (1) applies are –

   (a) a mental health treatment requirement,

   (b) a drug rehabilitation requirement, and

   (c) an alcohol treatment requirement.

(3) The opinion referred to in sub-paragraph (1) is –

   (a) that the treatment of the offender should be continued beyond the period specified in that behalf in the order,

   (b) that the offender needs different treatment,

   (c) that the offender is not susceptible to treatment, or

   (d) that the offender does not require further treatment.

(4) In this paragraph 'the appropriate court' has the same meaning as in paragraph 16.

Amendment in relation to review of drug rehabilitation requirement

19 Where the responsible officer is of the opinion that a community order imposing a drug rehabilitation requirement which is subject to review should be so amended as to provide for each subsequent periodic review (required by section 211) to be made without a hearing instead of at a review hearing, or vice versa, he must apply under paragraph 17 to the court responsible for the order for the variation of the order.

Extension of unpaid work requirement

20(1) Where –

   (a) a community order imposing an unpaid work requirement is in force in respect of any offender, and

   (b) on the application of the offender or the responsible officer, it appears to the appropriate court that it would be in the interests of justice to do so having regard to circumstances which have arisen since the order was made,

the court may, in relation to the order, extend the period of twelve months specified in section 200(2).

(2) In this paragraph 'the appropriate court' has the same meaning as in paragraph 16.

PART 5

POWERS OF COURT IN RELATION TO ORDER FOLLOWING SUBSEQUENT CONVICTION

Powers of magistrates' court following subsequent conviction

21(1) This paragraph applies where –

   (a) an offender in respect of whom a community order made by a magistrates' court is in force is convicted of an offence by a magistrates' court, and

(b) it appears to the court that it would be in the interests of justice to exercise its powers under this paragraph, having regard to circumstances which have arisen since the community order was made.

(2) The magistrates' court may –

(a) revoke the order, or
(b) both –
    (i) revoke the order, and
    (ii) deal with the offender, for the offence in respect of which the order was made, in any way in which he could have been dealt with for that offence by the court which made the order if the order had not been made.

(3) In dealing with an offender under sub-paragraph (2)(b), a magistrates' court must take into account the extent to which the offender has complied with the requirements of the community order.

(4) A person sentenced under sub-paragraph (2)(b) for an offence may appeal to the Crown Court against the sentence.

22(1) Where an offender in respect of whom a community order made by the Crown Court is in force is convicted of an offence by a magistrates' court, the magistrates' court may commit the offender in custody or release him on bail until he can be brought before the Crown Court.

(2) Where the magistrates' court deals with an offender's case under sub-paragraph (1), it must send to the Crown Court such particulars of the case as may be desirable.

Powers of Crown Court following subsequent conviction

23(1) This paragraph applies where –

(a) an offender in respect of whom a community order is in force –
    (i) is convicted of an offence by the Crown Court, or
    (ii) is brought or appears before the Crown Court by virtue of paragraph 22 or having been committed by the magistrates' court to the Crown Court for sentence, and
(b) it appears to the Crown Court that it would be in the interests of justice to exercise its powers under this paragraph, having regard to circumstances which have arisen since the community order was made.

(2) The Crown Court may –

(a) revoke the order, or
(b) both –
    (i) revoke the order, and
    (ii) deal with the offender, for the offence in respect of which the order was made, in any way in which he could have been dealt with for that offence by the court which made the order if the order had not been made.

(3) In dealing with an offender under sub-paragraph (2)(b), the Crown Court must take into account the extent to which the offender has complied with the requirements of the community order.

PART 6

SUPPLEMENTARY

24(1) No order may be made under paragraph 16, and no application may be made under paragraph 13, 17 or 20, while an appeal against the community order is pending.

(2) Sub-paragraph (1) does not apply to an application under paragraph 17 which –

(a) relates to a mental health treatment requirement, a drug rehabilitation requirement or an alcohol treatment requirement, and

(b) is made by the responsible officer with the consent of the offender.

25(1) Subject to sub-paragraph (2), where a court proposes to exercise its powers under Part 4 or 5 of this Schedule, otherwise than on the application of the offender, the court –

(a) must summon him to appear before the court, and

(b) if he does not appear in answer to the summons, may issue a warrant for his arrest.

(2) This paragraph does not apply to an order cancelling a requirement of a community order or reducing the period of any requirement, or substituting a new petty sessions area or a new place for the one specified in the order.

26 Paragraphs 9(1)(a), 10(1)(a) and 17(1)(b) have effect subject to the provisions mentioned in subsection (2) of section 177, and to subsections (3) and (6) of that section.

27(1) On the making under this Schedule of an order revoking or amending a community order, the proper officer of the court must –

(a) provide copies of the revoking or amending order to the offender and the responsible officer,

(b) in the case of an amending order which substitutes a new petty sessions area, provide a copy of the amending order to –

(i)   the local probation board acting for that area, and

(ii)   the magistrates' court acting for that area, and

(c) in the case of an amending order which imposes or amends a requirement specified in the first column of Schedule 14, provide a copy of so much of the amending order as relates to that requirement to the person specified in relation to that requirement in the second column of that Schedule.

(2) Where under sub-paragraph (1)(b) the proper officer of the court provides a copy of an amending order to a magistrates' court acting for a different area, the officer must also provide to that court such documents and information relating to the case as it considers likely to be of assistance to a court acting for that area in the exercise of its functions in relation to the order.

(3) In this paragraph 'proper officer' means –

(a) in relation to a magistrates' court, the justices' chief executive for the court; and

(b) in relation to the Crown Court, the appropriate officer.

SCHEDULE 9   Section 180

TRANSFER OF COMMUNITY ORDERS TO SCOTLAND OR NORTHERN IRELAND

PART 1

SCOTLAND

1(1) Where the court considering the making of a community order is satisfied that the offender resides in Scotland, or will reside there when the order comes into force, the court may not make a community order in respect of the offender unless it appears to the court –

    (a) in the case of an order imposing a requirement mentioned in sub-paragraph (2), that arrangements exist for persons to comply with such a requirement in the locality in Scotland in which the offender resides, or will be residing when the order comes into force, and that provision can be made for him to comply with the requirement under those arrangements, and

    (b) in any case, that suitable arrangements for his supervision can be made by the council constituted under section 2 of the Local Government etc. (Scotland) Act 1994 (c. 39) in whose area he resides, or will be residing when the order comes into force.

(2) The requirements referred to in sub-paragraph (1)(a) are –

    (a) an unpaid work requirement,
    (b) an activity requirement,
    (c) a programme requirement,
    (d) a mental health treatment requirement,
    (e) a drug rehabilitation requirement,
    (f) an alcohol treatment requirement, and
    (g) an electronic monitoring requirement.

(3) Where –

    (a) the appropriate court for the purposes of paragraph 16 of Schedule 8 (amendment by reason of change of residence) is satisfied that an offender in respect of whom a community order is in force proposes to reside or is residing in Scotland, and

    (b) it appears to the court that the conditions in sub-paragraph (1)(a) and (b) are satisfied,

the power of the court to amend the order under Part 4 of Schedule 8 includes power to amend it by requiring it to be complied with in Scotland and the offender to be supervised in accordance with the arrangements referred to in sub-paragraph (1)(b).

(4) For the purposes of sub-paragraph (3), any reference in sub-paragraph (1)(a) and (b) to the time when the order comes into force is to be treated as a reference to the time when the amendment comes into force.

(5) The court may not by virtue of sub-paragraph (1) or (3) require an attendance centre requirement to be complied with in Scotland.

(6) A community order made or amended in accordance with this paragraph must –

    (a) specify the locality in Scotland in which the offender resides or will be residing when the order or amendment comes into force;

    (b) specify as the corresponding order for the purposes of this Schedule an order that may be made by a court in Scotland;

(c) specify as the appropriate court for the purposes of subsection (4) of section 228 of the Criminal Procedure (Scotland) Act 1995 (c. 46) a court of summary jurisdiction (which, in the case of an offender convicted on indictment, must be the sheriff court) having jurisdiction in the locality specified under paragraph (a);

and section 216 (petty sessions area to be specified) does not apply in relation to an order so made or amended.

2(1) Where a court is considering the making or amendment of a community order by virtue of paragraph 1, Chapter 4 of Part 12 of this Act has effect subject to the following modifications.

(2) Any reference to the responsible officer has effect as a reference to the officer of a council constituted under section 2 of the Local Government etc. (Scotland) Act 1994 (c. 39) responsible for the offender's supervision or, as the case may be, discharging in relation to him the functions in respect of community service orders assigned by sections 239 to 245 of the Criminal Procedure (Scotland) Act 1995.

(3) The following provisions are omitted –

(a) subsection (7) of section 201 (activity requirement),
(b) subsection (7) of section 202 (programme requirement),
(c) subsection (4) of section 206 (residence requirement), and
(d) subsection (4) of section 218 (availability of arrangements in local area).

(4) In section 207 (mental health treatment requirement), for subsection (2)(a) there is substituted –

'(a) treatment as a resident patient in a hospital within the meaning of the Mental Health (Care and Treatment) (Scotland) Act 2003, not being a State hospital within the meaning of that Act;'.

(5) In section 215 (electronic monitoring requirement), in subsection (3), the words from 'and' onwards are omitted.

PART 2

NORTHERN IRELAND

3(1) Where the court considering the making of a community order is satisfied that the offender resides in Northern Ireland, or will reside there when the order comes into force, the court may not make a community order in respect of the offender unless it appears to the court –

(a) in the case of an order imposing a requirement mentioned in sub-paragraph (2), that arrangements exist for persons to comply with such a requirement in the petty sessions district in Northern Ireland in which the offender resides, or will be residing when the order comes into force, and that provision can be made for him to comply with the requirement under those arrangements, and
(b) in any case, that suitable arrangements for his supervision can be made by the Probation Board for Northern Ireland.

(2) The requirements referred to in sub-paragraph (1) are –

(a) an unpaid work requirement,
(b) an activity requirement,
(c) a programme requirement,
(d) a mental health treatment requirement,
(e) a drug rehabilitation requirement,

    (f)   an alcohol treatment requirement,

    (g)   an attendance centre requirement, and

    (h)   an electronic monitoring requirement.

(3) Where –

    (a)   the appropriate court for the purposes of paragraph 16 of Schedule 8 (amendment by reason of change of residence) is satisfied that the offender to whom a community order relates proposes to reside or is residing in Northern Ireland, and

    (b)   it appears to the court that the conditions in sub-paragraphs (1)(a) and (b) are satisfied,

the power of the court to amend the order under Part 4 of Schedule 8 includes power to amend it by requiring it to be complied with in Northern Ireland and the offender to be supervised in accordance with the arrangements referred to in sub-paragraph (1)(b).

(4) For the purposes of sub-paragraph (3), any reference in sub-paragraph (1)(a) and (b) to the time when the order comes into force is to be treated as a reference to the time when the amendment comes into force.

(5) A community order made or amended in accordance with this paragraph must specify the petty sessions district in Northern Ireland in which the offender resides or will be residing when the order or amendment comes into force; and section 216 (petty sessions area to be specified) does not apply in relation to an order so made or amended.

(6) A community order made or amended in accordance with this paragraph must also specify as the corresponding order for the purposes of this Schedule an order that may be made by a court in Northern Ireland.

4(1) Where a court is considering the making or amendment of a community order by virtue of paragraph 3, Chapter 4 of Part 12 of this Act has effect subject to the following modifications.

(2) Any reference to the responsible officer has effect as a reference to the probation officer responsible for the offender's supervision or, as the case may be, discharging in relation to the offender the functions conferred by Part 2 of the Criminal Justice (Northern Ireland) Order 1996 (S.I. 1996/3160 (N.I. 24)).

(3) The following provisions are omitted –

    (a)   subsection (7) of section 201 (activity requirement),

    (b)   subsection (7) of section 202 (programme requirement),

    (c)   subsection (4) of section 206 (residence requirement), and

    (d)   subsection (4) of section 218 (availability of arrangements in local area).

(4) In section 207 (mental health treatment requirement), for subsection (2)(a) there is substituted –

    '(a)   treatment (whether as an in-patient or an out-patient) at such hospital as may be specified in the order, being a hospital within the meaning of the Health and Personal Social Services (Northern Ireland) Order 1972, approved by the Department of Health, Social Services and Public Safety for the purposes of paragraph 4(3) of Schedule 1 to the Criminal Justice (Northern Ireland) Order 1996 (S.I. 1996/3160 (N.I. 24));'.

(5) In section 214 (attendance centre requirement), any reference to an attendance centre has effect as a reference to a day centre, as defined by paragraph 3(6) of Schedule 1 to the Criminal Justice (Northern Ireland) Order 1996 (S.I. 1996/3160 (N.I. 24)).

(6) In section 215 (electronic monitoring requirement), in subsection (3), the words from 'and' onwards are omitted.

PART 3

GENERAL PROVISIONS

5 In this Part of this Schedule –

'corresponding order' means the order specified under paragraph 1(6)(b) or 3(6);

'home court' means –

    (a) if the offender resides in Scotland, or will be residing there at the relevant time, the sheriff court having jurisdiction in the locality in which he resides or proposes to reside, and

    (b) if he resides in Northern Ireland, or will be residing there at the relevant time, the court of summary jurisdiction acting for the petty sessions district in which he resides or proposes to reside;

'the local authority officer concerned', in relation to an offender, means the officer of a council constituted under section 2 of the Local Government etc. (Scotland) Act 1994 (c. 39) responsible for his supervision or, as the case may be, discharging in relation to him the functions in respect of community service orders assigned by sections 239 to 245 of the Criminal Procedure (Scotland) Act 1995 (c. 46);

'the probation officer concerned', in relation to an offender, means the probation officer responsible for his supervision or, as the case may be, discharging in relation to him the functions conferred by Part 2 of the Criminal Justice (Northern Ireland) Order 1996;

'the relevant time' means the time when the order or the amendment to it comes into force.

6 Where a community order is made or amended in accordance with paragraph 1 or 3, the court which makes or amends the order must provide the home court with a copy of the order as made or amended, together with such other documents and information relating to the case as it considers likely to be of assistance to that court; and paragraphs (b) to (d) of subsection (1) of section 219 (provision of copies of relevant orders) do not apply.

7 In section 220 (duty of offender to keep in touch with responsible officer) the reference to the responsible officer is to be read in accordance with paragraph 2(2) or 4(2).

8 Where a community order is made or amended in accordance with paragraph 1 or 3, then, subject to the following provisions of this Part of this Schedule –

    (a) the order is to be treated as if it were a corresponding order made in the part of the United Kingdom in which the offender resides, or will be residing at the relevant time, and

    (b) the legislation relating to such orders which has effect in that part of the United Kingdom applies accordingly.

9 Before making or amending a community order in those circumstances the court must explain to the offender in ordinary language –

    (a) the requirements of the legislation relating to corresponding orders which has effect in the part of the United Kingdom in which he resides or will be residing at the relevant time,

(b) the powers of the home court under that legislation, as modified by this Part of this Schedule, and

(c) its own powers under this Part of this Schedule.

10 The home court may exercise in relation to the community order any power which it could exercise in relation to the corresponding order made by a court in the part of the United Kingdom in which the home court exercises jurisdiction, by virtue of the legislation relating to such orders which has effect in that part, except the following –

(a) any power to discharge or revoke the order (other than a power to revoke the order where the offender has been convicted of a further offence and the court has imposed a custodial sentence),

(b) any power to deal with the offender for the offence in respect of which the order was made,

(c) in the case of a community order imposing an unpaid work requirement, any power to vary the order by substituting for the number of hours of work specified in it any greater number than the court which made the order could have specified, and

(d) in the case of a community order imposing a curfew requirement, any power to vary the order by substituting for the period specified in it any longer period than the court which made the order could have specified.

11 If at any time while legislation relating to corresponding orders which has effect in Scotland or Northern Ireland applies by virtue of paragraph 7 to a community order made in England and Wales –

(a) it appears to the home court –
  (i)   if that court is in Scotland, on information from the local authority officer concerned, or
  (ii) if that court is in Northern Ireland, upon a complaint being made to a justice of the peace acting for the petty sessions district for the time being specified in the order,

that the offender has failed to comply with any of the requirements of the order, or

(b) it appears to the home court –
  (i)   if that court is in Scotland, on the application of the offender or of the local authority officer concerned, or
  (ii) if it is in Northern Ireland, on the application of the offender or of the probation officer concerned,

  that it would be in the interests of justice for a power conferred by paragraph 13 or 14 of Schedule 8 to be exercised,

the home court may require the offender to appear before the court which made the order or the court which last amended the order in England and Wales.

12 Where an offender is required by virtue of paragraph 11 to appear before a court in England and Wales that court –

(a) may issue a warrant for his arrest, and

(b) may exercise any power which it could exercise in respect of the community order if the offender resided in England and Wales,

and any enactment relating to the exercise of such powers has effect accordingly, and with any reference to the responsible officer being read as a reference to the local authority officer or probation officer concerned.

13 Paragraph 12(b) does not enable the court to amend the community order unless –

(a) where the offender resides in Scotland, it appears to the court that the conditions in paragraph 1(1)(a) and (b) are satisfied in relation to any requirement to be imposed, or

(b) where the offender resides in Northern Ireland, it appears to the court that the conditions in paragraph 3(1)(a) and (b) are satisfied in relation to any requirement to be imposed.

14 The preceding paragraphs of this Schedule have effect in relation to the amendment of a community order by virtue of paragraph 12(b) as they have effect in relation to the amendment of such an order by virtue of paragraph 1(3) or 3(3).

15 Where an offender is required by virtue of paragraph (a) of paragraph 11 to appear before a court in England and Wales –

(a) the home court must send to that court a certificate certifying that the offender has failed to comply with such of the requirements of the order as may be specified in the certificate, together with such other particulars of the case as may be desirable, and

(b) a certificate purporting to be signed by the clerk of the home court is admissible as evidence of the failure before the court which made the order.

SCHEDULE 10 Section 187

REVOCATION OR AMENDMENT OF CUSTODY PLUS ORDERS AND AMENDMENT OF INTERMITTENT CUSTODY ORDERS

Interpretation

1(1) In this Schedule –

'the appropriate court' means –
(a) where the custody plus order or intermittent custody order was made by the Crown Court, the Crown Court, and
(b) in any other case, a magistrates' court acting for the petty sessions area concerned;
'the offender', in relation to a custody plus order or intermittent custody order, means the person in respect of whom the order is made;
'the petty sessions area concerned', in relation to a custody plus order or intermittent custody order, means the petty sessions area for the time being specified in the order;
'the responsible officer' has the meaning given by section 197.

(2) In this Schedule any reference to a requirement being imposed by, or included in, a custody plus order or intermittent custody order is to be read as a reference to compliance with the requirement being required by the order to be a condition of a licence.

Orders made on appeal

2 Where a custody plus order or intermittent custody order has been made on appeal, it is to be taken for the purposes of this Schedule to have been made by the Crown Court.

Revocation of custody plus order or removal from intermittent custody order of requirements as to licence conditions

3(1) Where at any time while a custody plus order or intermittent custody order is in force, it appears to the appropriate court on the application of the offender or the responsible officer that, having regard to circumstances which have arisen since the order was made, it would be in the interests of justice to do so, the court may –

(a) in the case of a custody plus order, revoke the order, and
(b) in the case of an intermittent custody order, amend the order so that it contains only provision specifying periods for the purposes of section 183(1)(b)(i).

(2) The revocation under this paragraph of a custody plus order does not affect the sentence of imprisonment to which the order relates, except in relation to the conditions of the licence.

Amendment by reason of change of residence

4(1) This paragraph applies where, at any time during the term of imprisonment to which a custody plus order or intermittent custody order relates, the appropriate court is satisfied that the offender proposes to change, or has changed, his residence during the licence period from the petty sessions area concerned to another petty sessions area.

(2) Subject to sub-paragraphs (3) and (4), the appropriate court may, and on the application of the Secretary of State or the responsible officer must, amend the custody plus order or intermittent custody order by substituting the other petty sessions area for the area specified in the order.

(3) The court may not amend under this paragraph a custody plus order or intermittent custody order which contains requirements which, in the opinion of the court, cannot be complied with unless the offender resides in the petty sessions area concerned unless, in accordance with paragraph 5, it either –

(a) cancels those requirements, or
(b) substitutes for those requirements other requirements which can be complied with if the offender does not reside in that area.

(4) The court may not amend under this paragraph any custody plus order or intermittent custody order imposing a programme requirement unless it appears to the court that the accredited programme specified in the requirement is available in the other petty sessions area.

Amendment of requirements of custody plus order or intermittent custody order

5(1) At any time during the term of imprisonment to which a custody plus order or intermittent custody order relates, the appropriate court may, on the application of the offender, the Secretary of State or the responsible officer, by order amend any requirement of the custody plus order or intermittent custody order –

(a) by cancelling the requirement, or
(b) by replacing it with a requirement of the same kind imposing different obligations, which the court could include if it were then making the order.

(2) For the purposes of sub-paragraph (1) –

(a) a requirement falling within any paragraph of section 182(1) is of the same kind as any other requirement falling within that paragraph, and
(b) an electronic monitoring requirement is a requirement of the same kind as any requirement falling within section 182(1) to which it relates.

(3) Sub-paragraph (1)(b) has effect subject to the provisions mentioned in subsection (2) of section 182, and to subsections (3) and (5) of that section.

Alteration of pattern of temporary release

6(1) At any time during the term of imprisonment to which an intermittent custody order relates, the appropriate court may, on the application of the offender, the Secretary of State or the responsible officer, amend the order –

    (a) so as to specify different periods for the purposes of section 183(1)(b)(i), or

    (b) so as to provide that he is to remain in prison until the number of days served by him in prison is equal to the number of custodial days.

(2) The appropriate court may not by virtue of sub-paragraph (1) amend an intermittent custody order unless it has received from the Secretary of State notification that suitable prison accommodation is available for the offender during the periods which, under the order as amended, will be custodial periods.

(3) In this paragraph 'custodial period' has the same meaning as in section 184(3).

Supplementary

7 No application may be made under paragraph 3(1), 5(1) or 6(1) while an appeal against the sentence of which the custody plus or intermittent custody order forms part is pending.

8(1) Subject to sub-paragraph (2), where a court proposes to exercise its powers under paragraph 5 or 6, otherwise than on the application of the offender, the court –

    (a) must summon him to appear before the court, and

    (b) if he does not appear in answer to the summons, may issue a warrant for his arrest.

(2) This paragraph does not apply to an order cancelling any requirement of a custody plus or intermittent custody order.

9(1) On the making under this Schedule of an order revoking or amending a custody plus order or amending an intermittent custody order, the proper officer of the court must –

    (a) provide copies of the revoking or amending order to the offender and the responsible officer,

    (b) in the case of an amending order which substitutes a new petty sessions area, provide a copy of the amending order to –

        (i)   the local probation board acting for that area, and

        (ii) the magistrates' court acting for that area,

    (c) in the case of an order which cancels or amends a requirement specified in the first column of Schedule 14, provide a copy of so much of the amending order as relates to that requirement to the person specified in relation to that requirement in the second column of that Schedule.

(2) Where under sub-paragraph (1)(b) the proper officer of the court provides a copy of an amending order to a magistrates' court acting for a different area, the officer must also provide to that court such documents and information relating to the case as it considers likely to be of assistance to a court acting for that area in the exercise of its functions in relation to the order.

SCHEDULE 11   Section 188

TRANSFER OF CUSTODY PLUS ORDERS AND INTERMITTENT CUSTODY ORDERS TO SCOTLAND OR NORTHERN IRELAND

PART 1

INTRODUCTORY

1 In this Schedule –

    (a) 'the 1997 Act' means the Crime (Sentences) Act 1997 (c. 43), and

    (b) any reference to a requirement being imposed by, or included in a custody plus order or intermittent custody order is a reference to compliance with the requirement being required by the order to be a condition of a licence.

PART 2

SCOTLAND

2(1) Where the court making a custody plus order is satisfied that the offender resides in Scotland, or will reside there during the licence period, the court may, subject to sub-paragraph (2), impose requirements that are to be complied with in Scotland and require the offender's compliance with the order to be supervised in accordance with arrangements made by the local authority in Scotland in whose area he resides or will reside.

(2) The court may not make an order by virtue of this paragraph unless it appears to the court –

    (a) in the case of an order imposing a requirement mentioned in sub-paragraph (3), that arrangements exist for persons to comply with such a requirement in the locality in Scotland in which the offender resides, or will be residing during the licence period, and that provision can be made for him to comply with the requirement under those arrangements, and

    (b) in any case, that suitable arrangements for supervising his compliance with the order can be made by the local authority in whose area he resides, or will be residing during the licence period.

(3) The requirements referred to in sub-paragraph (2)(a) are –

    (a) an unpaid work requirement,

    (b) an activity requirement,

    (c) a programme requirement, and

    (d) an electronic monitoring requirement.

(4) If an order has been made in accordance with this paragraph in relation to an offender but –

    (a) the Secretary of State decides not to make an order under paragraph 1 or 4 of Schedule 1 to the 1997 Act in relation to him, and

    (b) the offender has not applied under paragraph 22 of this Schedule for the amendment of the custody plus order or intermittent custody order,

the Secretary of State must apply to the court under paragraph 22 of this Schedule for the amendment of the order.

3 Where –

(a) the appropriate court for the purposes of paragraph 4 of Schedule 10 (amendment by reason of change of residence) is satisfied that the offender in respect of whom a custody plus order or intermittent custody order is in force is residing in Scotland, or proposes to reside there during the licence period,

(b) the Secretary of State has made, or has indicated his willingness to make, an order under paragraph 1 or 4 of Schedule 1 to the 1997 Act in relation to the offender, and

(c) it appears to the court that the conditions in paragraph 2(2)(a) and (b) are satisfied,

the power of the court to amend the order under Schedule 10 includes power to amend it by requiring the requirements included in the order to be complied with in Scotland and the offender's compliance with them to be supervised in accordance with the arrangements referred to in paragraph 2(2)(b).

4 A court may not by virtue of paragraph 2 or 3 require an attendance centre requirement to be complied with in Scotland.

5 A custody plus order made in accordance with paragraph 2 or a custody plus order or intermittent order amended in accordance with paragraph 3 must –

(a) specify the local authority area in which the offender resides or will reside during the licence period, and

(b) require the local authority for that area to appoint or assign an officer who will be responsible for discharging in relation to him the functions conferred on responsible officers by Part 12 of this Act;
and section 216 (petty sessions area to be specified) does not apply in relation to an order so made or amended.

6(1) Where a court makes a custody plus order in accordance with paragraph 2 or amends a custody plus order or intermittent custody order in accordance with paragraph 3, the court must provide the relevant documents to –

(a) the local authority for the area specified in the order, and

(b) the sheriff court having jurisdiction in the locality in which the offender resides or proposes to reside;

and paragraphs (b) to (d) of subsection (1) of section 219 (which relate to the provision of copies) do not apply in relation to an order so made or amended.

(2) In this paragraph, 'the relevant documents' means –

(a) a copy of the order as made or amended, and

(b) such other documents and information relating to the case as the court making or amending the order considers likely to be of assistance.

7(1) In relation to the making of a custody plus order by virtue of paragraph 2, in relation to the amendment of a custody plus order or intermittent custody order by virtue of paragraph 3, and (except for the purposes of paragraph 22) in relation to an order so made or amended, Chapter 4 of Part 12 of this Act has effect subject to the following modifications.

(2) Any reference to the responsible officer has effect as a reference to the officer appointed or assigned under paragraph 5(b).

(3) The following provisions are omitted –

(a) subsection (7) of section 201 (activity requirement);

(b) subsection (7) of section 202 (programme requirement);

(c) subsection (4) of section 218 (availability of arrangements in local area).

(4) In section 215 (electronic monitoring requirement), in subsection (3), the words from 'and' onwards are omitted.

8 In this Part of this Schedule 'local authority' means a council constituted under section 2 of the Local Government etc. (Scotland) Act 1994 (c. 39); and any reference to the area of such an authority is a reference to the local government area within the meaning of that Act.

PART 3

NORTHERN IRELAND

9(1) Where the court making a custody plus order is satisfied that the offender resides in Northern Ireland, or will reside there during the licence period, the court may, subject to sub-paragraph (2), impose requirements that are to be complied with in Northern Ireland and require the offender's compliance with the order to be supervised in accordance with arrangements made by the Probation Board for Northern Ireland.

(2) The court may not make an order by virtue of this paragraph unless it appears to the court –

(a) in the case of an order imposing a requirement mentioned in sub-paragraph (3), that arrangements exist for persons to comply with such a requirement in the petty sessions district in Northern Ireland in which the offender resides, or will be residing during the licence period, and that provision can be made for him to comply with the requirement under those arrangements, and

(b) in any case, that suitable arrangements for supervising his compliance with the order can be made by the Probation Board for Northern Ireland.

(3) The requirements referred to in sub-paragraph (1)(a) are –

(a) an unpaid work requirement,

(b) an activity requirement,

(c) a programme requirement,

(d) an attendance centre requirement, and

(e) an electronic monitoring requirement.

(4) If an order has been made in accordance with this paragraph in relation to an offender but –

(a) the Secretary of State decides not to make an order under paragraph 1 or 4 of Schedule 1 to the 1997 Act in relation to him, and

(b) the offender has not applied under paragraph 22 of this Schedule for the amendment of the custody plus order or intermittent custody order,

the Secretary of State must apply to the court under paragraph 22 for the amendment of the order.

10 Where –

(a) the appropriate court for the purposes of paragraph 4 of Schedule 10 (amendment by reason of change of residence) is satisfied that the offender in respect of whom a custody plus order or intermittent custody order is in force is residing in Northern Ireland, or proposes to reside there during the licence period,

(b) the Secretary of State has made, or has indicated his willingness to make, an order under paragraph 1 or 4 of Schedule 1 to the 1997 Act in relation to the offender, and

(c) it appears to the court that the conditions in paragraph 9(2)(a) and (b) are satisfied,

the power of the court to amend the order under Schedule 10 includes power to amend it by requiring the requirements included in the order to be complied with in Northern Ireland and the offender's compliance with them to be supervised in accordance with the arrangements referred to in paragraph 9(2)(b).

11 A custody plus order made in accordance with paragraph 9 or a custody plus order or intermittent custody order amended in accordance with paragraph 10 must –

(a) specify the petty sessions district in Northern Ireland in which the offender resides or will reside during the licence period, and

(b) require the Probation Board for Northern Ireland to appoint or assign a probation officer who will be responsible for discharging in relation to him the functions conferred on responsible officers by Part 11 of this Act;

and section 216 (petty sessions area to be specified) does not apply in relation to an order so made or amended.

12(1) Where a court makes a custody plus order in accordance with paragraph 9 or amends a custody plus order or intermittent custody order in accordance with paragraph 10, the court must provide the relevant documents to –

(a) the Probation Board for Northern Ireland, and

(b) the court of summary jurisdiction acting for the petty sessions district in which the offender resides or proposes to reside;

and paragraphs (b) to (d) of subsection (1) of section 219 (which relate to the provision of copies) do not apply in relation to an order so made or amended.

(2) In this paragraph, 'the relevant documents' means –

(a) a copy of the order as made or amended, and

(b) such other documents and information relating to the case as the court making or amending the order considers likely to be of assistance.

13(1) In relation to the making of a custody plus order by virtue of paragraph 9, in relation to the amendment of a custody plus order or intermittent custody order by virtue of paragraph 10, and (except for the purposes of paragraph 22) in relation to an order so made or amended, Chapter 4 of Part 12 of this Act has effect subject to the following modifications.

(2) Any reference to the responsible officer has effect as a reference to the probation officer appointed or assigned under paragraph 11(b).

(3) The following provisions are omitted –

(a) subsection (7) of section 201 (activity requirement);

(b) subsection (7) of section 202 (programme requirement);

(c) subsection (4) of section 218 (availability of arrangements in local area).

(4) In section 214 (attendance centre requirement), any reference to an attendance centre has effect as a reference to a day centre, as defined by paragraph 3(6) of Schedule 1 to the Criminal Justice (Northern Ireland) Order 1996 (S.I. 1996/3160 (N.I. 24).

(5) In section 215 (electronic monitoring requirement), in subsection (3), the words from 'and' onwards are omitted.

PART 4

GENERAL PROVISIONS

14 This Part of this Schedule applies at any time while a custody plus order made in accordance with paragraph 2 or 9 or amended in accordance with paragraph 3 or 10, or an intermittent custody order amended in accordance with paragraph 3 or 10, is in force in respect of an offender.

15 In this Part of this Schedule –

'home court' means –

    (a) if the offender resides in Scotland, or will be residing there during the licence period, the sheriff court having jurisdiction in the locality in which the offender resides or proposes to reside, and

    (b) if he resides in Northern Ireland, or will be residing there during the licence period, the court of summary jurisdiction acting for the petty sessions district in which he resides or proposes to reside;

'local authority' and 'local authority area' are to be read in accordance with paragraph 8;

'original court' means the court in England and Wales which made or last amended the custody plus order or intermittent custody order;

'the relevant officer' means –

    (a) where the order specifies a local authority area in Scotland, the local authority officer appointed or assigned under paragraph 5(b), and

    (b) where the order specifies a local authority district in Northern Ireland, the probation officer appointed or assigned under paragraph 11(b).

16(1) Where this Part of this Schedule applies, Schedule 10 has effect subject to the following modifications.

(2) Any reference to the responsible officer has effect as a reference to the relevant officer.

(3) Any reference to the appropriate court has effect as a reference to the original court.

(4) Where the order specifies a local authority area in Scotland –

    (a) any reference to the petty sessions area concerned has effect as a reference to that local authority area, and

    (b) any other reference to a petty sessions area has effect as a reference to a local authority area.

(5) Where the order specifies a petty sessions district in Northern Ireland –

    (a) any reference to the petty sessions area concerned has effect as a reference to that petty sessions district, and

    (b) any other reference to a petty sessions area has effect as a reference to a petty sessions district.

(6) Paragraph 9 is omitted.

17(1) The home court may exercise any power under paragraph 4 or 5 of Schedule 10 (amendment of custody plus order or intermittent custody order) as if it were the original court.

(2) Subject to sub-paragraph (3), where the home court proposes to exercise the power conferred by paragraph 5 of Schedule 10, otherwise than on the application of the offender, the court –

(a) if it is in Scotland –
    (i) must issue a citation requiring the offender to appear before it, and
    (ii) if he does not appear in answer to the citation, may issue a warrant for the offender's arrest;
(b) if it is in Northern Ireland –
    (i) must issue a summons requiring the offender to appear before it, and
    (ii) if he does not appear in answer to the summons, may issue a warrant for the offender's arrest;

and paragraph 8 of Schedule 10 does not apply to the home court.

(3) Sub-paragraph (2) does not apply to any order cancelling any requirement of a custody plus order or intermittent custody order.

(4) Where the home court is considering amending a custody plus or intermittent custody order, any reference in Chapter 4 of Part 12 of this Act to a local probation board has effect as a reference to a local authority in Scotland or, as the case may be, the Probation Board for Northern Ireland.

18 Where by virtue of paragraph 17 any application is made to the home court under paragraph 4 or 5 of Schedule 10, the home court may (instead of dealing with the application) require the offender to appear before the original court.

19 No court may amend or further amend a custody plus order or an intermittent custody order unless it appears to the court that the conditions in paragraph 2(2)(a) and (b) or, as the case may be, the conditions in paragraph 9(2)(a) and (b) are satisfied in relation to any requirement to be imposed; but this paragraph does not apply to any amendment made by virtue of paragraph 22(1).

20 The preceding paragraphs of this Schedule have effect in relation to any amendment of a custody plus or intermittent custody order by any court as they have effect in relation to the amendment of such an order by virtue of paragraph 3 or 10.

21 On the making of an order amending a custody plus order or intermittent custody order –

(a) the court must provide copies of the amending order to the offender and the relevant officer, and
(b) in the case of an amending order which substitutes a new local authority area or petty sessions district, paragraphs 5 and 6, or as the case may be paragraphs 11 and 12, have effect in relation to the order as they have effect in relation to an order made or amended in accordance with paragraph 2 or 3, or as the case may be, 9 or 10.

22(1) Where –

(a) a custody plus order has been made in accordance with paragraph 2 or 9 or a custody plus or intermittent custody order has been amended in accordance with paragraph 3 or 10, but (in any of those cases) the Secretary of State has not made an order under paragraph 1 or 4 of Schedule 1 to the 1997 Act in relation to the offender, or
(b) the Secretary of State has made, or indicated his willingness to make, an order under paragraph 7(1) of Schedule 1 to the 1997 Act transferring the offender or his supervision back to England and Wales,

the court may, on the application of the offender or the Secretary of State, amend the custody plus order or intermittent custody order by requiring it to be complied with in England and Wales.

(2) In sub-paragraph (1) 'the court', in a case falling within paragraph (a) of that sub-paragraph, means the original court.

(3) In a case where paragraph 2(4) or 9(4) requires the Secretary of State to apply under this paragraph, the court must make an amending order under this paragraph.

(4) Where under this paragraph the court amends a custody plus order or intermittent custody order which contains requirements which, in the opinion of the court, cannot be complied with in the petty sessions area in which the offender is residing or proposes to reside, the court must, in accordance with paragraph 5 of Schedule 10, either –

(a) cancel those requirements, or
(b) substitute for those requirements other requirements which can be complied with if the offender resides in that area.

(5) Where the court amends under this paragraph any custody plus order or intermittent custody order imposing a programme requirement, the court must ensure that the requirement as amended specifies a programme which is available in the petty sessions area in England and Wales in which the offender is residing or proposes to reside.

(6) The custody plus order or intermittent custody order as amended under this paragraph must specify the petty sessions area in which the offender resides or proposes to reside in the licence period.

(7) On the making under this paragraph of an order amending a custody plus order or intermittent custody order, the court must –

(a) provide copies of the amending order to the offender, the relevant officer and the local probation board acting for the new petty sessions area, and
(b) provide the magistrates' court acting for that area with a copy of the amending order and such other documents and information relating to the case as the home court considers likely to be of assistance to the court acting for that area in the exercise of its functions in relation to the order.

(8) Where an order has been amended under this paragraph, the preceding paragraphs of this Schedule shall cease to apply to the order as amended.

PART 5

SUPPLEMENTARY

23 Subsections (1) and (3) of section 245C of the Criminal Procedure (Scotland) Act 1995 (c. 46) (provision of remote monitoring) have effect as if they included a reference to the electronic monitoring of the requirements of a custody plus order made in accordance with paragraph 2 or a custody plus order or intermittent custody order made in accordance with paragraph 3.

24(1) Section 4 of the Summary Jurisdiction (Process) Act 1881 (c. 24) (which provides, among other things, for service in England and Wales of Scottish citations or warrants) applies to any citation or warrant issued under paragraph 17(2)(a) as it applies to a citation or warrant granted under section 134 of the Criminal Procedure (Scotland) Act 1995.

(2) A summons issued by a court in Northern Ireland under paragraph 17(2)(b) may, in such circumstances as may be prescribed by rules of court, be served in England and Wales or Scotland.

SCHEDULE 12 Section 193

BREACH OR AMENDMENT OF SUSPENDED SENTENCE ORDER, AND EFFECT OF FURTHER CONVICTION

PART 1

PRELIMINARY

Interpretation

1 In this Schedule –

'the offender', in relation to a suspended sentence order, means the person in respect of whom the order is made;

'the petty sessions area concerned', in relation to a suspended sentence order, means the petty sessions area for the time being specified in the order;

'the responsible officer' has the meaning given by section 197.

2 In this Schedule –

(a) any reference to a suspended sentence order being subject to review is a reference to such an order being subject to review in accordance with section 191(1)(b) or to a drug rehabilitation requirement of such an order being subject to review in accordance with section 210(1)(b);

(b) any reference to the court responsible for a suspended sentence order which is subject to review is to be construed in accordance with section 191(3) or, as the case may be, 210(2).

Orders made on appeal

3 Where a suspended sentence order is made on appeal it is to be taken for the purposes of this Schedule to have been made by the Crown Court.

PART 2

BREACH OF COMMUNITY REQUIREMENT OR CONVICTION OF FURTHER OFFENCE

Duty to give warning in relation to community requirement

4(1) If the responsible officer is of the opinion that the offender has failed without reasonable excuse to comply with any of the community requirements of a suspended sentence order, the officer must give him a warning under this paragraph unless –

(a) the offender has within the previous twelve months been given a warning under this paragraph in relation to a failure to comply with any of the community requirements of the order, or

(b) the officer causes an information to be laid before a justice of the peace in respect of the failure.

(2) A warning under this paragraph must –

(a) describe the circumstances of the failure,

(b) state that the failure is unacceptable, and

(c) inform the offender that if within the next twelve months he again fails to comply with any requirement of the order, he will be liable to be brought before a court.

(3) The responsible officer must, as soon as practicable after the warning has been given, record that fact.

(4) In relation to any suspended sentence order which is made by the Crown Court and does not include a direction that any failure to comply with the community requirements of the order is to be dealt with by a magistrates' court, the reference in sub-paragraph (1)(b) to a justice of the peace is to be read as a reference to the Crown Court.

Breach of order after warning

5(1) If –

- (a) the responsible officer has given a warning under paragraph 4 to the offender in respect of a suspended sentence order, and
- (b) at any time within the twelve months beginning with the date on which the warning was given, the responsible officer is of the opinion that the offender has since that date failed without reasonable excuse to comply with any of the community requirements of the order,

the officer must cause an information to be laid before a justice of the peace in respect of the failure in question.

(2) In relation to any suspended sentence order which is made by the Crown Court and does not include a direction that any failure to comply with the community requirements of the order is to be dealt with by a magistrates' court, the reference in sub-paragraph (1) to a justice of the peace is to be read as a reference to the Crown Court.

Issue of summons or warrant by justice of the peace

6(1) This paragraph applies to –

- (a) a suspended sentence order made by a magistrates' court, or
- (b) any suspended sentence order which was made by the Crown Court and includes a direction that any failure to comply with the community requirements of the order is to be dealt with by a magistrates' court.

(2) If at any time while a suspended sentence order to which this paragraph applies is in force it appears on information to a justice of the peace acting for the petty sessions area concerned that the offender has failed to comply with any of the community requirements of the order, the justice may –

- (a) issue a summons requiring the offender to appear at the place and time specified in it, or
- (b) if the information is in writing and on oath, issue a warrant for his arrest.

(3) Any summons or warrant issued under this paragraph must direct the offender to appear or be brought –

- (a) in the case of a suspended sentence order which is subject to review, before the court responsible for the order,
- (b) in any other case, before a magistrates' court acting for the petty sessions area concerned.

(4) Where a summons issued under sub-paragraph (2)(a) requires the offender to appear before a magistrates' court and the offender does not appear in answer to the summons, the magistrates' court may issue a warrant for the arrest of the offender.

Issue of summons or warrant by Crown Court

7(1) This paragraph applies to a suspended sentence order made by the Crown Court which does not include a direction that any failure to comply with the community requirements of the order is to be dealt with by a magistrates' court.

(2) If at any time while a suspended sentence order to which this paragraph applies is in force it appears on information to the Crown Court that the offender has failed to comply with any of the community requirements of the order, the Crown Court may –

(a) issue a summons requiring the offender to appear at the place and time specified in it, or

(b) if the information is in writing and on oath, issue a warrant for his arrest.

(3) Any summons or warrant issued under this paragraph must direct the offender to appear or be brought before the Crown Court.

(4) Where a summons issued under sub-paragraph (1)(a) requires the offender to appear before the Crown Court and the offender does not appear in answer to the summons, the Crown Court may issue a warrant for the arrest of the offender.

Powers of court on breach of community requirement or conviction of further offence

8(1) This paragraph applies where –

(a) it is proved to the satisfaction of a court before which an offender appears or is brought under paragraph 6 or 7 or by virtue of section 192(6) that he has failed without reasonable excuse to comply with any of the community requirements of the suspended sentence order, or

(b) an offender is convicted of an offence committed during the operational period of a suspended sentence (other than one which has already taken effect) and either –

(i) he is so convicted by or before a court having power under paragraph 11 to deal with him in respect of the suspended sentence, or

(ii) he subsequently appears or is brought before such a court.

(2) The court must consider his case and deal with him in one of the following ways –

(a) the court may order that the suspended sentence is to take effect with its original term and custodial period unaltered,

(b) the court may order that the sentence is to take effect with either or both of the following modifications –

(i) the substitution for the original term of a lesser term complying with section 181(2), and

(ii) the substitution for the original custodial period of a lesser custodial period complying with section 181(5) and (6),

(c) the court may amend the order by doing any one or more of the following –

(i) imposing more onerous community requirements which the court could include if it were then making the order,

(ii) subject to subsections (3) and (4) of section 189, extending the supervision period, or

(iii) subject to subsection (3) of that section, extending the operational period.

(3) The court must make an order under sub-paragraph (2)(a) or (b) unless it is of the opinion that it would be unjust to do so in view of all the circumstances, including the matters mentioned in sub-paragraph (4); and where it is of that opinion the court must state its reasons.

(4) The matters referred to in sub-paragraph (3) are –

(a) the extent to which the offender has complied with the community requirements of the suspended sentence order, and

(b) in a case falling within sub-paragraph (1)(b), the facts of the subsequent offence.

(5) Where a court deals with an offender under sub-paragraph (2) in respect of a suspended sentence, the appropriate officer of the court must notify the appropriate officer of the court which passed the sentence of the method adopted.

(6) Where a suspended sentence order was made by the Crown Court and a magistrates' court would (apart from this sub-paragraph) be required to deal with the offender under sub-paragraph (2)(a), (b) or (c) it may instead commit him to custody or release him on bail until he can be brought or appear before the Crown Court.

(7) A magistrates' court which deals with an offender's case under sub-paragraph (6) must send to the Crown Court –

  (a) a certificate signed by a justice of the peace certifying that the offender has failed to comply with the community requirements of the suspended sentence order in the respect specified in the certificate, and
  (b) such other particulars of the case as may be desirable;

and a certificate purporting to be so signed is admissible as evidence of the failure before the Crown Court.

(8) In proceedings before the Crown Court under this paragraph any question whether the offender has failed to comply with the community requirements of the suspended sentence order and any question whether the offender has been convicted of an offence committed during the operational period of the suspended sentence is to be determined by the court and not by the verdict of a jury.

Further provisions as to order that suspended sentence is to take effect

9(1) When making an order under paragraph 8(2)(a) or (b) that a sentence is to take effect (with or without any variation of the original term and custodial period), the court –

  (a) must also make a custody plus order, and
  (b) may order that the sentence is to take effect immediately or that the term of that sentence is to commence on the expiry of another term of imprisonment passed on the offender by that or another court.

(2) The power to make an order under sub-paragraph (1)(b) has effect subject to section 265 (restriction on consecutive sentences for released prisoners).

(3) For the purpose of any enactment conferring rights of appeal in criminal cases, any order made by the court under paragraph 8(2)(a) or (b) is to be treated as a sentence passed on the offender by that court for the offence for which the suspended sentence was passed.

Restriction of powers in paragraph 8 where treatment required

10(1) An offender who is required by any of the following community requirements of a suspended sentence order –

  (a) a mental health treatment requirement,
  (b) a drug rehabilitation requirement, or
  (c) an alcohol treatment requirement,

to submit to treatment for his mental condition, or his dependency on or propensity to misuse drugs or alcohol, is not to be treated for the purposes of paragraph 8(1)(a) as having failed to comply with that requirement on the ground only that he had refused to undergo any surgical, electrical or other treatment if, in the opinion of the court, his refusal was reasonable having regard to all the circumstances.

(2) A court may not under paragraph 8(2)(c)(i) amend a mental health treatment requirement, a drug rehabilitation requirement or an alcohol treatment requirement unless the offender expresses his willingness to comply with the requirement as amended.

Court by which suspended sentence may be dealt with under paragraph 8(1)(b)

11(1) An offender may be dealt with under paragraph 8(1)(b) in respect of a suspended sentence by the Crown Court or, where the sentence was passed by a magistrates' court, by any magistrates' court before which he appears or is brought.

(2) Where an offender is convicted by a magistrates' court of any offence and the court is satisfied that the offence was committed during the operational period of a suspended sentence passed by the Crown Court –

    (a)   the court may, if it thinks fit, commit him in custody or on bail to the Crown Court, and

    (b)   if it does not, must give written notice of the conviction to the appropriate officer of the Crown Court.

Procedure where court convicting of further offence does not deal with suspended sentence

12(1) If it appears to the Crown Court, where that court has jurisdiction in accordance with sub-paragraph (2), or to a justice of the peace having jurisdiction in accordance with that sub-paragraph –

    (a)   that an offender has been convicted in the United Kingdom of an offence committed during the operational period of a suspended sentence, and

    (b)   that he has not been dealt with in respect of the suspended sentence,

that court or justice may, subject to the following provisions of this paragraph, issue a summons requiring the offender to appear at the place and time specified in it, or a warrant for his arrest.

(2) Jurisdiction for the purposes of sub-paragraph (1) may be exercised –

    (a)   if the suspended sentence was passed by the Crown Court, by that court;

    (b)   if it was passed by a magistrates' court, by a justice acting for the petty sessions area for which that court acted.

(3) Where –

    (a)   an offender is convicted in Scotland or Northern Ireland of an offence, and

    (b)   the court is informed that the offence was committed during the operational period of a suspended sentence passed in England or Wales,

the court must give written notice of the conviction to the appropriate officer of the court by which the suspended sentence was passed.

(4) Unless he is acting in consequence of a notice under sub-paragraph (3), a justice of the peace may not issue a summons under this paragraph except on information and may not issue a warrant under this paragraph except on information in writing and on oath.

(5) A summons or warrant issued under this paragraph must direct the offender to appear or be brought before the court by which the suspended sentence was passed.

PART 3

AMENDMENT OF SUSPENDED SENTENCE ORDER

Cancellation of community requirements of suspended sentence order

13(1) Where at any time while a suspended sentence order is in force, it appears to the appropriate court on the application of the offender or the responsible officer that, having regard to the circumstances which have arisen since the order was made, it would be in the interests of justice to do so, the court may cancel the community requirements of the suspended sentence order.

(2) The circumstances in which the appropriate court may exercise its power under sub-paragraph (1) include the offender's making good progress or his responding satisfactorily to supervision.

(3) In this paragraph 'the appropriate court' means –

  (a) in the case of a suspended sentence order which is subject to review, the court responsible for the order,
  (b) in the case of a suspended sentence order which was made by the Crown Court and does not include any direction that any failure to comply with the community requirements of the order is to be dealt with by a magistrates' court, the Crown Court, and
  (c) in any other case, a magistrates' court acting for the petty sessions area concerned.

Amendment by reason of change of residence

14(1) This paragraph applies where, at any time while a suspended sentence order is in force, the appropriate court is satisfied that the offender proposes to change, or has changed, his residence from the petty sessions area concerned to another petty sessions area.

(2) Subject to sub-paragraphs (3) and (4), the appropriate court may, and on the application of the responsible officer must, amend the suspended sentence order by substituting the other petty sessions area for the area specified in the order.

(3) The court may not amend under this paragraph a suspended sentence order which contains requirements which, in the opinion of the court, cannot be complied with unless the offender resides in the petty sessions area concerned unless, in accordance with paragraph 15 it either –

  (a) cancels those requirements, or
  (b) substitutes for those requirements other requirements which can be complied with if the offender does not reside in that area.

(4) The court may not amend under this paragraph any suspended sentence order imposing a programme requirement unless it appears to the court that the accredited programme specified in the requirement is available in the other petty sessions area.

(5) In this paragraph 'the appropriate court' has the same meaning as in paragraph 13.

Amendment of community requirements of suspended sentence order

15(1) At any time during the supervision period, the appropriate court may, on the application of the offender or the responsible officer, by order amend any community requirement of a suspended sentence order –

(a) by cancelling the requirement, or

(b) by replacing it with a requirement of the same kind, which the court could include if it were then making the order.

(2) For the purposes of sub-paragraph (1) –

(a) a requirement falling within any paragraph of section 190(1) is of the same kind as any other requirement falling within that paragraph, and

(b) an electronic monitoring requirement is a requirement of the same kind as any requirement falling within section 190(1) to which it relates.

(3) The court may not under this paragraph amend a mental health treatment requirement, a drug rehabilitation requirement or an alcohol treatment requirement unless the offender expresses his willingness to comply with the requirement as amended.

(4) If the offender fails to express his willingness to comply with a mental health treatment requirement, drug rehabilitation requirement or alcohol treatment requirement as proposed to be amended by the court under this paragraph, the court may –

(a) revoke the suspended sentence order and the suspended sentence to which it relates, and

(b) deal with him, for the offence in respect of which the suspended sentence was imposed, in any way in which it could deal with him if he had just been convicted by or before the court of the offence.

(5) In dealing with the offender under sub-paragraph (4)(b), the court must take into account the extent to which the offender has complied with the requirements of the order.

(6) In this paragraph 'the appropriate court' has the same meaning as in paragraph 13.

Amendment of treatment requirements on report of practitioner

16(1) Where the medical practitioner or other person by whom or under whose direction an offender is, in pursuance of any requirement to which this sub-paragraph applies, being treated for his mental condition or his dependency on or propensity to misuse drugs or alcohol –

(a) is of the opinion mentioned in sub-paragraph (3), or

(b) is for any reason unwilling to continue to treat or direct the treatment of the offender,

he must make a report in writing to that effect to the responsible officer and that officer must apply under paragraph 15 to the appropriate court for the variation or cancellation of the requirement.

(2) The requirements to which sub-paragraph (1) applies are –

(a) a mental health treatment requirement,

(b) a drug rehabilitation requirement, and

(c) an alcohol treatment requirement.

(3) The opinion referred to in sub-paragraph (1) is –

(a) that the treatment of the offender should be continued beyond the period specified in that behalf in the order,

(b) that the offender needs different treatment,

    (c)   that the offender is not susceptible to treatment, or

    (d)   that the offender does not require further treatment.

(4) In this paragraph 'the appropriate court' has the same meaning as in paragraph 13.

Amendment in relation to review of drug rehabilitation requirement

17 Where the responsible officer is of the opinion that a suspended sentence order imposing a drug rehabilitation requirement which is subject to review should be so amended as to provide for each periodic review (required by section 211) to be made without a hearing instead of at a review hearing, or vice versa, he must apply under paragraph 15 to the court responsible for the order for the variation of the order.

Extension of unpaid work requirement

18(1) Where –

    (a)   a suspended sentence order imposing an unpaid work requirement is in force in respect of the offender, and

    (b)   on the application of the offender or the responsible officer, it appears to the appropriate court that it would be in the interests of justice to do so having regard to circumstances which have arisen since the order was made,

the court may, in relation to the order, extend the period of twelve months specified in section 200(2).

(2) In this paragraph 'the appropriate court' has the same meaning as in paragraph 13.

Supplementary

19(1) No application may be made under paragraph 13, 15 or 18, and no order may be made under paragraph 14, while an appeal against the suspended sentence is pending.

(2) Sub-paragraph (1) does not apply to an application under paragraph 15 which –

    (a)   relates to a mental health treatment requirement, a drug rehabilitation requirement or an alcohol treatment requirement, and

    (b)   is made by the responsible officer with the consent of the offender.

20(1) Subject to sub-paragraph (2), where a court proposes to exercise its powers under paragraph 15, otherwise than on the application of the offender, the court –

    (a)   must summon him to appear before the court, and

    (b)   if he does not appear in answer to the summons, may issue a warrant for his arrest.

(2) This paragraph does not apply to an order cancelling any community requirement of a suspended sentence order.

21 Paragraphs 8(2)(c) and 15(1)(b) have effect subject to the provisions mentioned in subsection (2) of section 190, and to subsections (3) and (5) of that section.

22(1) On the making under this Schedule of an order amending a suspended sentence order, the proper officer of the court must –

    (a)   provide copies of the amending order to the offender and the responsible officer,

    (b)   in the case of an amending order which substitutes a new petty sessions area, provide a copy of the amending order to –

        (i)   the local probation board acting for that area, and

        (ii)   the magistrates' court acting for that area, and

(c) in the case of an amending order which imposes or amends a requirement specified in the first column of Schedule 14, provide a copy of so much of the amending order as relates to that requirement to the person specified in relation to that requirement in the second column of that Schedule.

(2) Where under sub-paragraph (1)(b) the proper officer of the court provides a copy of an amending order to a magistrates' court acting for a different area, the officer must also provide to that court such documents and information relating to the case as it considers likely to be of assistance to a court acting for that area in the exercise of its functions in relation to the order.

(3) In this paragraph 'proper officer' means –

(a) in relation to a magistrates' court, the justices' chief executive for the court; and
(b) in relation to the Crown Court, the appropriate officer.

SCHEDULE 13   Section 194

TRANSFER OF SUSPENDED SENTENCE ORDERS TO SCOTLAND OR
NORTHERN IRELAND

PART 1

SCOTLAND

1(1) Where the court considering the making of a suspended sentence order is satisfied that the offender resides in Scotland, or will reside there when the order comes into force, the court may not make a suspended sentence order in respect of the offender unless it appears to the court –

(a) in the case of an order imposing a requirement mentioned in sub-paragraph (2), that arrangements exist for persons to comply with such a requirement in the locality in Scotland in which the offender resides, or will be residing when the order comes into force, and that provision can be made for him to comply with the requirement under those arrangements, and
(b) in any case, that suitable arrangements for his supervision can be made by the local authority in whose area he resides, or will be residing when the order comes into force.

(2) The requirements referred to in sub-paragraph (1)(a) are –

(a) an unpaid work requirement,
(b) an activity requirement,
(c) a programme requirement,
(d) a mental health treatment requirement,
(e) a drug rehabilitation requirement,
(f) an alcohol treatment requirement, and
(g) an electronic monitoring requirement.

(3) Where –

(a) the appropriate court for the purposes of paragraph 14 of Schedule 12 (amendment by reason of change of residence) is satisfied that an offender in respect of whom a suspended sentence order is in force proposes to reside or is residing in Scotland, and
(b) it appears to the court that the conditions in sub-paragraph (1)(a) and (b) are satisfied,

the power of the court to amend the order under Part 3 of Schedule 12 includes power to amend it by requiring it to be complied with in Scotland and the offender to be supervised in accordance with the arrangements referred to in sub-paragraph (1)(b).

(4) For the purposes of sub-paragraph (3), any reference in sub-paragraph (1)(a) and (b) to the time when the order comes into force is to be treated as a reference to the time when the amendment comes into force.

(5) The court may not by virtue of sub-paragraph (1) or (3) require an attendance centre requirement to be complied with in Scotland.

(6) The court may not provide for an order made in accordance with this paragraph to be subject to review under section 191 or 210; and where an order which is subject to review under either of those sections is amended in accordance with this paragraph, the order shall cease to be so subject.

2 A suspended sentence order made or amended in accordance with paragraph 1 must –

    (a) specify the local authority area in which the offender resides or will be residing when the order or amendment comes into force, and

    (b) require the local authority for that area to appoint or assign an officer who will be responsible for discharging in relation to him the functions conferred on responsible officers by Part 12 of this Act;

and section 216 (petty sessions area to be specified) does not apply in relation to an order so made or amended.

3(1) Where a court makes or amends a suspended sentence order in accordance with paragraph 1, the court must provide the relevant documents to –

    (a) the local authority for the area specified in the order, and

    (b) the sheriff court having jurisdiction in the locality in which the offender resides or proposes to reside;

and paragraphs (b) to (d) of subsection (1) of section 219 (provision of copies of relevant orders) do not apply in relation to an order so made or amended.

(2) In this paragraph, 'the relevant documents' means –

    (a) a copy of the order as made or amended, and

    (b) such other documents and information relating to the case as the court making or amending the order considers likely to be of assistance.

4(1) In relation to the making or amendment of a suspended sentence order in accordance with paragraph 1, and (except for the purposes of paragraph 20) in relation to an order so made or amended, Chapter 4 of Part 12 of this Act has effect subject to the following modifications.

(2) Any reference to the responsible officer has effect as a reference to the officer appointed or assigned under paragraph 2(b).

(3) The following provisions are omitted –

    (a) subsection (7) of section 201 (activity requirement),

    (b) subsection (7) of section 202 (programme requirement),

    (c) subsection (4) of section 206 (residence requirement),

    (d) subsection (4) of section 218 (availability of arrangements in local area).

(4) In section 207 (mental health treatment requirement), for subsection (2)(a) there is substituted –

'(a) treatment as a resident patient in a hospital within the meaning of the Mental Health (Care and Treatment) (Scotland) Act 2003, not being a state hospital within the meaning of that Act;'.

(5) In section 215 (electronic monitoring requirement), in subsection (3), the words from 'and' onwards are omitted.

5 In this Part of this Schedule 'local authority' means a council constituted under section 2 of the Local Government etc. (Scotland) Act 1994 (c. 39); and any reference to the area of such an authority is a reference to the local government area within the meaning of that Act.

PART 2

NORTHERN IRELAND

6(1) Where the court considering the making of a suspended sentence order is satisfied that the offender resides in Northern Ireland, or will reside there when the order comes into force, the court may not make a suspended sentence order in respect of the offender unless it appears to the court –

(a) in the case of an order imposing a requirement mentioned in sub-paragraph (2), that arrangements exist for persons to comply with such a requirement in the petty sessions district in Northern Ireland in which the offender resides, or will be residing when the order comes into force, and that provision can be made for him to comply with the requirement under those arrangements, and

(b) in any case, that suitable arrangements for his supervision can be made by the Probation Board for Northern Ireland.

(2) The requirements referred to in sub-paragraph (1)(a) are –

(a) an unpaid work requirement,
(b) an activity requirement,
(c) a programme requirement,
(d) a mental health treatment requirement,
(e) a drug rehabilitation requirement,
(f) an alcohol treatment requirement,
(g) an attendance centre requirement, and
(h) an electronic monitoring requirement.

(3) Where –

(a) the appropriate court for the purposes of paragraph 14 of Schedule 12 (amendment by reason of change of residence) is satisfied that an offender in respect of whom a suspended sentence order is in force proposes to reside or is residing in Northern Ireland, and

(b) it appears to the court that the conditions in sub-paragraphs (1)(a) and (b) are satisfied,

the power of the court to amend the order under Part 3 of Schedule 12 includes power to amend it by requiring it to be complied with in Northern Ireland and the offender to be supervised in accordance with the arrangements referred to in sub-paragraph (1)(b).

(4) For the purposes of sub-paragraph (3), any reference in sub-paragraph (1)(a) and (b) to the time when the order comes into force is to be treated as a reference to the time when the amendment comes into force.

(5) The court may not provide for an order made in accordance with this paragraph to be subject to review under section 191 or 210; and where an order which is subject to review

under either of those sections is amended in accordance with this paragraph, the order shall cease to be so subject.

7 A suspended sentence order made or amended in accordance with paragraph 6 must –

(a) specify the petty sessions district in Northern Ireland in which the offender resides or will be residing when the order or amendment comes into force, and

(b) require the Probation Board for Northern Ireland to appoint or assign a probation officer who will be responsible for discharging in relation to him the functions conferred on responsible officers by Part 12 of this Act;

and section 216 (petty sessions area to be specified) does not apply in relation to an order so made or amended.

8(1) Where a court makes or amends a suspended sentence order in accordance with paragraph 6, the court must provide the relevant documents to –

(a) the Probation Board for Northern Ireland, and

(b) the court of summary jurisdiction acting for the petty sessions district in which the offender resides or proposes to reside;

and paragraphs (b) to (d) of subsection (1) of section 219 (provision of copies of relevant orders) do not apply in relation to an order so made or amended.

(2) In this paragraph, 'the relevant documents' means –

(a) a copy of the order as made or amended, and

(b) such other documents and information relating to the case as the court making or amending the order considers likely to be of assistance.

9(1) In relation to the making or amendment of a suspended sentence order in accordance with paragraph 6, and (except for the purposes of paragraph 20) in relation to an order so made or amended, Chapter 4 of Part 12 of this Act has effect subject to the following modifications.

(2) Any reference to the responsible officer has effect as a reference to the probation officer appointed or assigned under paragraph 7(b).

(3) The following provisions are omitted –

(a) subsection (7) of section 201 (activity requirement),

(b) subsection (7) of section 202 (programme requirement),

(c) subsection (4) of section 206 (residence requirement),

(d) subsection (4) of section 218 (availability of arrangements in local area).

(4) In section 207 (mental health treatment requirement), for subsection (2)(a) there is substituted –

'(a) treatment (whether as an in-patient or an out-patient) at such hospital as may be specified in the order, being a hospital within the meaning of the Health and Personal Social Services (Northern Ireland) Order 1972, approved by the Department of Health, Social Services and Public Safety for the purposes of paragraph 4(3) of Schedule 1 to the Criminal Justice (Northern Ireland) Order 1996 (S.I. 1996/ 3160 (N.I. 24));'.

(5) In section 214 (attendance centre requirement), any reference to an attendance centre has effect as a reference to a day centre, as defined by paragraph 3(6) of Schedule 1 to the Criminal Justice (Northern Ireland) Order 1996 (S.I. 1996/3160 (N.I. 24).

(6) In section 215 (electronic monitoring requirement), in subsection (3), the words from 'and' onwards are omitted.

PART 3

GENERAL PROVISIONS: BREACH OR AMENDMENT

10 This Part of this Schedule applies at any time while a suspended sentence order made or amended in accordance with paragraph 1 or 6 is in force in respect of an offender.

11 In this Part of this Schedule –

'home court' means –
- (a) if the offender resides in Scotland, or will be residing there at the relevant time, the sheriff court having jurisdiction in the locality in which the offender resides or proposes to reside, and
- (b) if he resides in Northern Ireland, or will be residing there at the relevant time, the court of summary jurisdiction acting for the petty sessions district in which he resides or proposes to reside;

'local authority' and 'local authority area' are to be read in accordance with paragraph 5;

'original court' means the court in England and Wales which made or last amended the order;

'the relevant officer' means –
- (a) where the order specifies a local authority area in Scotland, the local authority officer appointed or assigned under paragraph 2(b), and
- (b) where the court specifies a petty sessions district in Northern Ireland, the probation officer appointed or assigned under paragraph 7(b);

'the relevant time' means the time when the order or the amendment to it comes into force.

12(1) Where this Part of this Schedule applies, Schedule 12 has effect subject to the following modifications.

(2) Any reference to the responsible officer has effect as a reference to the relevant officer.

(3) Any reference to a magistrates' court acting for the petty sessions area concerned has effect as a reference to a magistrates' court acting for the same petty sessions area as the original court; and any reference to a justice of the peace acting for the petty sessions area concerned has effect as a reference to a justice of the peace acting for the same petty sessions area as that court.

(4) Any reference to the appropriate court has effect as a reference to the original court.

(5) In paragraphs 4 and 5, any reference to causing an information to be laid before a justice of the peace has effect –

- (a) if the home court is in Scotland, as a reference to providing information to the home court with a view to it issuing a citation, and
- (b) if the home court is in Northern Ireland, as a reference to making a complaint to a justice of the peace in Northern Ireland.

(6) In paragraph 14 –

- (a) if the home court is in Scotland –
    - (i) any reference to the petty sessions area concerned has effect as a reference to the local authority area specified in the order, and
    - (ii) any other reference to a petty sessions area has effect as a reference to a local authority area, and
- (b) if the home court is in Northern Ireland –

(i) any reference to the petty sessions area concerned has effect as a reference to the petty sessions district specified in the order, and

(ii) any other reference to a petty sessions area has effect as a reference to a petty sessions district.

(7) Paragraph 22 is omitted.

(8) No court in England and Wales may –

(a) exercise any power in relation to any failure by the offender to comply with any community requirement of the order unless the offender has been required in accordance with paragraph 14(1)(b) or (2)(a) of this Schedule to appear before that court;

(b) exercise any power under Part 3 of Schedule 12 unless the offender has been required in accordance with paragraph 15(2) or 16 of this Schedule to appear before that court.

13(1) Sub-paragraph (2) applies where it appears to the home court –

(a) if that court is in Scotland, on information from the relevant officer, or

(b) if that court is in Northern Ireland, upon a complaint being made by the relevant officer,

that the offender has failed without reasonable excuse to comply with any of the community requirements of the suspended sentence order.

(2) The home court may –

(a) if it is in Scotland –
   (i) issue a citation requiring the offender to appear before it at the time specified in the citation, or
   (ii) issue a warrant for the offender's arrest;

(b) if it is in Northern Ireland –
   (i) issue a summons requiring the offender to appear before it at the time specified in the summons, or
   (ii) issue a warrant for the offender's arrest.

14(1) The court before which an offender appears or is brought by virtue of paragraph 13 must –

(a) determine whether the offender has failed without reasonable excuse to comply with any of the community requirements of the suspended sentence order, or

(b) require the offender to appear before the original court.

(2) If the home court determines that the offender has failed without reasonable excuse to comply with any of the community requirements of the order –

(a) the home court must require the offender to appear before the original court, and

(b) when the offender appears before the original court, paragraph 8 of Schedule 12 applies as if it had already been proved to the satisfaction of the original court that the offender failed without reasonable excuse to comply with such of the community requirements of the order as may have been determined.

(3) An offender who is required by any of the following community requirements of a suspended sentence order –

(a) a mental health treatment requirement,

(b) a drug rehabilitation requirement, or

(c) an alcohol treatment requirement,

to submit to treatment for his mental condition, or his dependency on or propensity to misuse drugs or alcohol, is not to be treated for the purposes of sub-paragraph (2) as having failed to comply with that requirement on the ground only that he had refused to undergo any surgical, electrical or other treatment if, in the opinion of the court, his refusal was reasonable having regard to all the circumstances.

(4) The evidence of one witness shall, for the purposes of sub-paragraph (2), be sufficient.

(5) Where the home court is in Scotland and the order contains an electronic monitoring requirement, section 245H of the Criminal Procedure (Scotland) Act 1995 (c. 46) (documentary evidence) applies to proceedings under this paragraph as it applies to proceedings under section 245F of that Act (breach of restriction of liberty order).

(6) Where an offender is required by virtue of sub-paragraph (2) to appear before the original court –

    (a) the home court must send to the original court a certificate certifying that the offender has failed without reasonable excuse to comply with the requirements of the order in the respect specified, and

    (b) such a certificate signed by the clerk of the home court is admissible before the original court as conclusive evidence of the matters specified in it.

15(1) The home court may exercise any power under Part 3 of Schedule 12 (amendment of suspended sentence order) as if it were the original court, except that the home court may not exercise the power conferred by paragraph 15(4) of that Schedule.

(2) Where paragraph 15(4) of Schedule 12 applies the home court must require the offender to appear before the original court.

(3) Subject to sub-paragraph (4), where the home court proposes to exercise the power conferred by paragraph 15(1) of Schedule 12, otherwise than on the application of the offender, the court –

    (a) if it is in Scotland –
        (i)   must issue a citation requiring the offender to appear before it, and
        (ii) if he does not appear in answer to the citation, may issue a warrant for the offender's arrest;

    (b) if it is in Northern Ireland –
        (i)   must issue a summons requiring the offender to appear before it, and
        (ii) if he does not appear in answer to the summons, may issue a warrant for the offender's arrest;

and paragraph 20 of Schedule 12 does not apply to the home court.

(4) Sub-paragraph (3) does not apply to an order cancelling any community requirement of a suspended sentence order.

(5) Where the home court is considering amending a suspended sentence order, any reference in Chapter 4 of Part 12 of this Act to a local probation board has effect as a reference to a local authority in Scotland or, as the case may be, the Probation Board for Northern Ireland.

16 Where by virtue of paragraph 15 any application is made to the home court under Part 3 of Schedule 12, the home court may (instead of dealing with the application) require the offender to appear before the original court.

17 No court may amend or further amend a suspended sentence order unless it appears to the court that the conditions in paragraph 1(1)(a) and (b) or, as the case may be,

paragraph 6(1)(a) and (b) are satisfied in relation to any requirement to be imposed; but this paragraph does not apply to any amendment by virtue of paragraph 20(2).

18 The preceding paragraphs of this Schedule have effect in relation to any amendment of a suspended order by any court as they have effect in relation to the amendment of such an order by virtue of paragraph 1(3) or 6(3).

19 On the making of an order amending a suspended sentence order –

(a) the court must provide copies of the amending order to the offender and the relevant officer, and

(b) in the case of an amending order which substitutes a new local authority area or petty sessions district, paragraphs 2 and 3 or, as the case may be, 7 and 8 have effect in relation to the order as they have effect in relation to an order made or amended in accordance with paragraph 1 or 6.

20(1) This paragraph applies where the home court is satisfied that the offender is residing or proposes to reside in England and Wales.

(2) Subject to sub-paragraphs (3) and (4), the home court may, and on the application of the relevant officer must, amend the suspended sentence order by requiring it to be complied with in England and Wales.

(3) The court may not amend under this paragraph a suspended sentence order which contains requirements which, in the opinion of the court, cannot be complied with in the petty sessions area in which the offender is residing or proposes to reside unless, in accordance with paragraph 15 of Schedule 12 it either –

(a) cancels those requirements, or

(b) substitutes for those requirements other requirements which can be complied with if the offender resides in that area.

(4) The court may not amend under this paragraph any suspended sentence order imposing a programme requirement unless it appears to the court that the accredited programme specified in the requirement is available in the petty sessions area in England and Wales in which the offender is residing or proposes to reside.

(5) The suspended sentence order as amended must specify the petty sessions area in which the offender resides or proposes to reside.

(6) On the making under this paragraph of an order amending a suspended sentence order, the home court must –

(a) provide copies of the amending order to the offender, the relevant officer and the local probation board acting for the new petty sessions area, and

(b) provide the magistrates' court acting for that area with a copy of the amending order and such other documents and information relating to the case as the home court considers likely to be of assistance to a court acting for that area in the exercise of its functions in relation to the order.

(7) Where an order has been amended under this paragraph, the preceding paragraphs of this Schedule shall cease to apply to the order as amended.

PART 4

SUPPLEMENTARY

21 Subsections (1) and (3) of section 245C of the Criminal Procedure (Scotland) Act 1995 (c. 46) (provision of remote monitoring) have effect as if they included a reference

to the electronic monitoring of the community requirements of a suspended sentence order made or amended in accordance with paragraph 1 of this Schedule.

22(1) Section 4 of the Summary Jurisdiction (Process) Act 1881 (c. 24) (which provides, among other things, for service in England and Wales of Scottish citations or warrants) applies to any citation or warrant issued under paragraph 13(2)(a) or 15(3)(a) as it applies to a citation or warrant granted under section 134 of the Criminal Procedure (Scotland) Act 1995.

(2) A summons issued by a court in Northern Ireland under paragraph 13(2)(b) or 15(3)(b) may, in such circumstances as may be prescribed by rules of court, be served in England and Wales or Scotland.

SCHEDULE 14   Section 219

PERSONS TO WHOM COPIES OF REQUIREMENTS TO BE PROVIDED IN PARTICULAR CASES

Requirement	*Person to whom copy of requirement is to be given*
An activity requirement.	The person specified under section 201(1)(a).
An exclusion requirement imposed for the purpose (or partly for the purpose) of protecting a person from being approached by the offender.	The person intended to be protected.
A residence requirement relating to residence in an institution.	The person in charge of the institution.
A mental health treatment requirement.	The person specified under section 207(2)(c) or the person in charge of the institution or place specified under section 207(2)(a) or (b).
A drug rehabilitation requirement.	The person in charge of the institution or place specified under section 209(4)(a) or (b).
An alcohol treatment requirement.	The person specified under section 212(5)(c) or the person in charge of the institution or place specified under section 212(5)(a) or (b).
An attendance centre requirement.	The officer in charge of the attendance centre specified in the requirement.
An electronic monitoring requirement.	Any person who by virtue of section 215(3) will be responsible for the electronic monitoring. Any person by virtue of whose consent the requirement is included in the order.

SCHEDULE 15   Section 224

SPECIFIED OFFENCES FOR PURPOSES OF CHAPTER 5 OF PART 12

PART 1

SPECIFIED VIOLENT OFFENCES

1 Manslaughter.

2 Kidnapping.

3 False imprisonment.

4 An offence under section 4 of the Offences against the Person Act 1861 (c. 100) (soliciting murder).

5 An offence under section 16 of that Act (threats to kill).

6 An offence under section 18 of that Act (wounding with intent to cause grievous bodily harm).

7 An offence under section 20 of that Act (malicious wounding).

8 An offence under section 21 of that Act (attempting to choke, suffocate or strangle in order to commit or assist in committing an indictable offence).

9 An offence under section 22 of that Act (using chloroform etc. to commit or assist in the committing of any indictable offence).

10 An offence under section 23 of that Act (maliciously administering poison etc. so as to endanger life or inflict grievous bodily harm).

11 An offence under section 27 of that Act (abandoning children).

12 An offence under section 28 of that Act (causing bodily injury by explosives).

13 An offence under section 29 of that Act (using explosives etc. with intent to do grievous bodily harm).

14 An offence under section 30 of that Act (placing explosives with intent to do bodily injury).

15 An offence under section 31 of that Act (setting spring guns etc. with intent to do grievous bodily harm).

16 An offence under section 32 of that Act (endangering the safety of railway passengers).

17 An offence under section 35 of that Act (injuring persons by furious driving).

18 An offence under section 37 of that Act (assaulting officer preserving wreck).

19 An offence under section 38 of that Act (assault with intent to resist arrest).

20 An offence under section 47 of that Act (assault occasioning actual bodily harm).

21 An offence under section 2 of the Explosive Substances Act 1883 (c. 3) (causing explosion likely to endanger life or property).

22 An offence under section 3 of that Act (attempt to cause explosion, or making or keeping explosive with intent to endanger life or property).

23 An offence under section 1 of the Infant Life (Preservation) Act 1929 (c. 34) (child destruction).

24 An offence under section 1 of the Children and Young Persons Act 1933 (c. 12) (cruelty to children).

25 An offence under section 1 of the Infanticide Act 1938 (c. 36) (infanticide).

26 An offence under section 16 of the Firearms Act 1968 (c. 27) (possession of firearm with intent to endanger life).

27 An offence under section 16A of that Act (possession of firearm with intent to cause fear of violence).

28 An offence under section 17(1) of that Act (use of firearm to resist arrest).

29 An offence under section 17(2) of that Act (possession of firearm at time of committing or being arrested for offence specified in Schedule 1 to that Act).

30 An offence under section 18 of that Act (carrying a firearm with criminal intent).

31 An offence under section 8 of the Theft Act 1968 (c. 60) (robbery or assault with intent to rob).

32 An offence under section 9 of that Act of burglary with intent to –

   (a) inflict grievous bodily harm on a person, or
   (b) do unlawful damage to a building or anything in it.

33 An offence under section 10 of that Act (aggravated burglary).

34 An offence under section 12A of that Act (aggravated vehicle-taking) involving an accident which caused the death of any person.

35 An offence of arson under section 1 of the Criminal Damage Act 1971 (c. 48).

36 An offence under section 1(2) of that Act (destroying or damaging property) other than an offence of arson.

37 An offence under section 1 of the Taking of Hostages Act 1982 (c. 28) (hostage-taking).

38 An offence under section 1 of the Aviation Security Act 1982 (c. 36) (hijacking).

39 An offence under section 2 of that Act (destroying, damaging or endangering safety of aircraft).

40 An offence under section 3 of that Act (other acts endangering or likely to endanger safety of aircraft).

41 An offence under section 4 of that Act (offences in relation to certain dangerous articles).

42 An offence under section 127 of the Mental Health Act 1983 (c. 20) (ill-treatment of patients).

43 An offence under section 1 of the Prohibition of Female Circumcision Act 1985 (c. 38) (prohibition of female circumcision).

44 An offence under section 1 of the Public Order Act 1986 (c. 64) (riot).

45 An offence under section 2 of that Act (violent disorder).

46 An offence under section 3 of that Act (affray).

47 An offence under section 134 of the Criminal Justice Act 1988 (c. 33) (torture).

48 An offence under section 1 of the Road Traffic Act 1988 (c. 52) (causing death by dangerous driving).

49 An offence under section 3A of that Act (causing death by careless driving when under influence of drink or drugs).

50 An offence under section 1 of the Aviation and Maritime Security Act 1990 (c. 31) (endangering safety at aerodromes).

51 An offence under section 9 of that Act (hijacking of ships).

52 An offence under section 10 of that Act (seizing or exercising control of fixed platforms).

53 An offence under section 11 of that Act (destroying fixed platforms or endangering their safety).

54 An offence under section 12 of that Act (other acts endangering or likely to endanger safe navigation).

55 An offence under section 13 of that Act (offences involving threats).

56 An offence under Part II of the Channel Tunnel (Security) Order 1994 (S.I. 1994/570) (offences relating to Channel Tunnel trains and the tunnel system).

57 An offence under section 4 of the Protection from Harassment Act 1997 (c. 40) (putting people in fear of violence).

58 An offence under section 29 of the Crime and Disorder Act 1998 (c. 37) (racially or religiously aggravated assaults).

59 An offence falling within section 31(1)(a) or (b) of that Act (racially or religiously aggravated offences under section 4 or 4A of the Public Order Act 1986 (c. 64)).

60 An offence under section 51 or 52 of the International Criminal Court Act 2001 (c. 17) (genocide, crimes against humanity, war crimes and related offences), other than one involving murder.

61 An offence under section 1 of the Female Genital Mutilation Act 2003 (c. 31) (female genital mutilation).

62 An offence under section 2 of that Act (assisting a girl to mutilate her own genitalia).

63 An offence under section 3 of that Act (assisting a non-UK person to mutilate overseas a girl's genitalia).

64 An offence of –

   (a) aiding, abetting, counselling, procuring or inciting the commission of an offence specified in this Part of this Schedule,
   (b) conspiring to commit an offence so specified, or
   (c) attempting to commit an offence so specified.

65 An attempt to commit murder or a conspiracy to commit murder.

PART 2

SPECIFIED SEXUAL OFFENCES

66 An offence under section 1 of the Sexual Offences Act 1956 (c. 69) (rape).

67 An offence under section 2 of that Act (procurement of woman by threats).

68 An offence under section 3 of that Act (procurement of woman by false pretences).

69 An offence under section 4 of that Act (administering drugs to obtain or facilitate intercourse).

70 An offence under section 5 of that Act (intercourse with girl under thirteen).

71 An offence under section 6 of that Act (intercourse with girl under 16).

72 An offence under section 7 of that Act (intercourse with a defective).

73 An offence under section 9 of that Act (procurement of a defective).

74 An offence under section 10 of that Act (incest by a man).

75 An offence under section 11 of that Act (incest by a woman).

76 An offence under section 14 of that Act (indecent assault on a woman).

77 An offence under section 15 of that Act (indecent assault on a man).

78 An offence under section 16 of that Act (assault with intent to commit buggery).

79 An offence under section 17 of that Act (abduction of woman by force or for the sake of her property).

80 An offence under section 19 of that Act (abduction of unmarried girl under eighteen from parent or guardian).

81 An offence under section 20 of that Act (abduction of unmarried girl under sixteen from parent or guardian).

82 An offence under section 21 of that Act (abduction of defective from parent or guardian).

83 An offence under section 22 of that Act (causing prostitution of women).

84 An offence under section 23 of that Act (procuration of girl under twenty-one).

85 An offence under section 24 of that Act (detention of woman in brothel).

86 An offence under section 25 of that Act (permitting girl under thirteen to use premises for intercourse).

87 An offence under section 26 of that Act (permitting girl under sixteen to use premises for intercourse).

88 An offence under section 27 of that Act (permitting defective to use premises for intercourse).

89 An offence under section 28 of that Act (causing or encouraging the prostitution of, intercourse with or indecent assault on girl under sixteen).

90 An offence under section 29 of that Act (causing or encouraging prostitution of defective).

91 An offence under section 32 of that Act (soliciting by men).

92 An offence under section 33 of that Act (keeping a brothel).

93 An offence under section 128 of the Mental Health Act 1959 (c. 72) (sexual intercourse with patients).

94 An offence under section 1 of the Indecency with Children Act 1960 (c. 33) (indecent conduct towards young child).

95 An offence under section 4 of the Sexual Offences Act 1967 (c. 60) (procuring others to commit homosexual acts).

96 An offence under section 5 of that Act (living on earnings of male prostitution).

97 An offence under section 9 of the Theft Act 1968 (c. 60) of burglary with intent to commit rape.

98 An offence under section 54 of the Criminal Law Act 1977 (c. 45) (inciting girl under sixteen to have incestuous sexual intercourse).

99 An offence under section 1 of the Protection of Children Act 1978 (c. 37) (indecent photographs of children).

100 An offence under section 170 of the Customs and Excise Management Act 1979 (c. 2) (penalty for fraudulent evasion of duty etc.) in relation to goods prohibited to be imported under section 42 of the Customs Consolidation Act 1876 (c. 36) (indecent or obscene articles).

101 An offence under section 160 of the Criminal Justice Act 1988 (c. 33) (possession of indecent photograph of a child).

102 An offence under section 1 of the Sexual Offences Act 2003 (c. 42) (rape).

103 An offence under section 2 of that Act (assault by penetration).

104 An offence under section 3 of that Act (sexual assault).

105 An offence under section 4 of that Act (causing a person to engage in sexual activity without consent).

106 An offence under section 5 of that Act (rape of a child under 13).

107 An offence under section 6 of that Act (assault of a child under 13 by penetration).

108 An offence under section 7 of that Act (sexual assault of a child under 13).

109 An offence under section 8 of that Act (causing or inciting a child under 13 to engage in sexual activity).

110 An offence under section 9 of that Act (sexual activity with a child).

111 An offence under section 10 of that Act (causing or inciting a child to engage in sexual activity).

112 An offence under section 11 of that Act (engaging in sexual activity in the presence of a child).

113 An offence under section 12 of that Act (causing a child to watch a sexual act).

114 An offence under section 13 of that Act (child sex offences committed by children or young persons).

115 An offence under section 14 of that Act (arranging or facilitating commission of a child sex offence).

116 An offence under section 15 of that Act (meeting a child following sexual grooming etc.).

117 An offence under section 16 of that Act (abuse of position of trust: sexual activity with a child).

118 An offence under section 17 of that Act (abuse of position of trust: causing or inciting a child to engage in sexual activity).

119 An offence under section 18 of that Act (abuse of position of trust: sexual activity in the presence of a child).

120 An offence under section 19 of that Act (abuse of position of trust: causing a child to watch a sexual act).

121 An offence under section 25 of that Act (sexual activity with a child family member).

122 An offence under section 26 of that Act (inciting a child family member to engage in sexual activity).

123 An offence under section 30 of that Act (sexual activity with a person with a mental disorder impeding choice).

124 An offence under section 31 of that Act (causing or inciting a person with a mental disorder impeding choice to engage in sexual activity).

125 An offence under section 32 of that Act (engaging in sexual activity in the presence of a person with a mental disorder impeding choice).

126 An offence under section 33 of that Act (causing a person with a mental disorder impeding choice to watch a sexual act).

127 An offence under section 34 of that Act (inducement, threat or deception to procure sexual activity with a person with a mental disorder).

128 An offence under section 35 of that Act (causing a person with a mental disorder to engage in or agree to engage in sexual activity by inducement, threat or deception).

129 An offence under section 36 of that Act (engaging in sexual activity in the presence, procured by inducement, threat or deception, of a person with a mental disorder).

130 An offence under section 37 of that Act (causing a person with a mental disorder to watch a sexual act by inducement, threat or deception).

131 An offence under section 38 of that Act (care workers: sexual activity with a person with a mental disorder).

132 An offence under section 39 of that Act (care workers: causing or inciting sexual activity).

133 An offence under section 40 of that Act (care workers: sexual activity in the presence of a person with a mental disorder).

134 An offence under section 41 of that Act (care workers: causing a person with a mental disorder to watch a sexual act).

135 An offence under section 47 of that Act (paying for sexual services of a child).

136 An offence under section 48 of that Act (causing or inciting child prostitution or pornography).

137 An offence under section 49 of that Act (controlling a child prostitute or a child involved in pornography).

138 An offence under section 50 of that Act (arranging or facilitating child prostitution or pornography).

139 An offence under section 52 of that Act (causing or inciting prostitution for gain).

140 An offence under section 53 of that Act (controlling prostitution for gain).

141 An offence under section 57 of that Act (trafficking into the UK for sexual exploitation).

142 An offence under section 58 of that Act (trafficking within the UK for sexual exploitation).

143 An offence under section 59 of that Act (trafficking out of the UK for sexual exploitation).

144 An offence under section 61 of that Act (administering a substance with intent).

145 An offence under section 62 of that Act (committing an offence with intent to commit a sexual offence).

146 An offence under section 63 of that Act (trespass with intent to commit a sexual offence).

147 An offence under section 64 of that Act (sex with an adult relative: penetration).

148 An offence under section 65 of that Act (sex with an adult relative: consenting to penetration).

149 An offence under section 66 of that Act (exposure).

150 An offence under section 67 of that Act (voyeurism).

151 An offence under section 69 of that Act (intercourse with an animal).

152 An offence under section 70 of that Act (sexual penetration of a corpse).

153 An offence of –

(a) aiding, abetting, counselling, procuring or inciting the commission of an offence specified in this Part of this Schedule,
(b) conspiring to commit an offence so specified, or
(c) attempting to commit an offence so specified.

SCHEDULE 16   Section 229

SCOTTISH OFFENCES SPECIFIED FOR THE PURPOSES OF
SECTION 229(4)

1 Rape.

2 Clandestine injury to women.

3 Abduction of woman or girl with intent to rape or ravish.

4 Assault with intent to rape or ravish.

5 Indecent assault.

6 Lewd, indecent or libidinous behaviour or practices.

7 Shameless indecency.

8 Sodomy.

9 An offence under section 170 of the Customs and Excise Management Act 1979 (c. 2) in relation to goods prohibited to be imported under section 42 of the Customs Consolidation Act 1876 (c. 36), but only where the prohibited goods include indecent photographs of persons.

10 An offence under section 52 of the Civic Government (Scotland) Act 1982 (c. 45) (taking and distribution of indecent images of children).

11 An offence under section 52A of that Act (possession of indecent images of children).

12 An offence under section 1 of the Criminal Law (Consolidation) (Scotland) Act 1995 (c. 39) (incest).

13 An offence under section 2 of that Act (intercourse with a stepchild).

14 An offence under section 3 of that Act (intercourse with child under 16 by person in position of trust).

15 An offence under section 5 of that Act (unlawful intercourse with girl under 16).

16 An offence under section 6 of that Act (indecent behaviour towards girl between 12 and 16).

17 An offence under section 8 of that Act (detention of woman in brothel or other premises).

18 An offence under section 10 of that Act (person having parental responsibilities causing or encouraging sexual activity in relation to a girl under 16).

19 An offence under subsection (5) of section 13 of that Act (homosexual offences).

20 An offence under section 3 of the Sexual Offences (Amendment) Act 2000 (c. 44) (abuse of position of trust).

21 An offence of –

  (a) attempting, conspiring or inciting another to commit any offence specified in the preceding paragraphs, or
  (b) aiding, abetting, counselling or procuring the commission of any offence specified in paragraphs 9 to 20.

22 Any offence (other than an offence specified in any of the preceding paragraphs) inferring personal violence.

SCHEDULE 17   Section 229

NORTHERN IRELAND OFFENCES SPECIFIED FOR THE PURPOSES OF
SECTION 229(4)

PART 1

VIOLENT OFFENCES

1 Manslaughter.

2 Kidnapping.

3 Riot.

4 Affray.

5 False imprisonment.

6 An offence under section 4 of the Offences against the Person Act 1861 (c. 100) (soliciting murder).

7 An offence under section 16 of that Act (threats to kill).

8 An offence under section 18 of that Act (wounding with intent to cause grievous bodily harm).

9 An offence under section 20 of that Act (malicious wounding).

10 An offence under section 21 of that Act (attempting to choke, suffocate or strangle in order to commit or assist in committing an indictable offence).

11 An offence under section 22 of that Act (using chloroform etc. to commit or assist in the committing of any indictable offence).

12 An offence under section 23 of that Act (maliciously administering poison etc. so as to endanger life or inflict grievous bodily harm).

13 An offence under section 27 of that Act (abandoning children).

14 An offence under section 28 of that Act (causing bodily injury by explosives).

15 An offence under section 29 of that Act (using explosives etc. with intent to do grievous bodily harm).

16 An offence under section 30 of that Act (placing explosives with intent to do bodily injury).

17 An offence under section 31 of that Act (setting spring guns etc. with intent to do grievous bodily harm).

18 An offence under section 32 of that Act (endangering the safety of railway passengers).

19 An offence under section 35 of that Act (injuring persons by furious driving).

20 An offence under section 37 of that Act (assaulting officer preserving wreck).

21 An offence under section 47 of that Act of assault occasioning actual bodily harm.

22 An offence under section 2 of the Explosive Substances Act 1883 (c. 3) (causing explosion likely to endanger life or property).

23 An offence under section 3 of that Act (attempt to cause explosion, or making or keeping explosive with intent to endanger life or property).

24 An offence under section 25 of the Criminal Justice (Northern Ireland) Act 1945 (c. 15) (child destruction).

25 An offence under section 1 of the Infanticide Act (Northern Ireland) 1939 (c. 5) (infanticide).

26 An offence under section 7(1)(b) of the Criminal Justice (Miscellaneous Provisions) Act (Northern Ireland) 1968 (c. 28) (assault with intent to resist arrest).

27 An offence under section 20 of the Children and Young Persons Act (Northern Ireland) 1968 (c. 34) (cruelty to children).

28 An offence under section 8 of the Theft Act (Northern Ireland) 1969 (c. 16) (robbery or assault with intent to rob).

29 An offence under section 9 of that Act of burglary with intent to –

  (a) inflict grievous bodily harm on a person, or
  (b) do unlawful damage to a building or anything in it.

30 An offence under section 10 of that Act (aggravated burglary).

31 An offence of arson under Article 3 of the Criminal Damage Northern Ireland) Order 1977 (S.I. 1977/426 (N.I. 4)).

32 An offence under Article 3(2) of that Order (destroying or damaging property) other than an offence of arson.

33 An offence under Article 17 of the Firearms (Northern Ireland) Order 1981 (S.I. 1981/155 (N.I. 2)) (possession of firearm with intent to endanger life).

34 An offence under Article 17A of that Order (possession of firearm with intent to cause fear of violence).

35 An offence under Article 18(1) of that Order (use of firearm to resist arrest).

36 An offence under Article 18(2) of that Order (possession of firearm at time of committing or being arrested for an offence specified in Schedule 1 to that Order).

37 An offence under Article 19 of that Order (carrying a firearm with criminal intent).

38 An offence under section 1 of the Taking of Hostages Act 1982 (c. 28) (hostage-taking).

39 An offence under section 1 of the Aviation Security Act 1982 (c. 36) (hijacking).

40 An offence under section 2 of that Act (destroying, damaging or endangering safety of aircraft).

41 An offence under section 3 of that Act (other acts endangering or likely to endanger safety of aircraft).

42 An offence under section 4 of that Act (offences in relation to certain dangerous articles).

43 An offence under section 1 of the Prohibition of Female Circumcision Act 1985 (c. 38) (prohibition of female circumcision).

44 An offence under Article 121 of the Mental Health (Northern Ireland) Order 1986 (S.I. 1986/595 (N.I.4) (ill-treatment of patients).

45 An offence under section 134 of the Criminal Justice Act 1988 (c. 33) (torture).

46 An offence under section 1 of the Aviation and Maritime Security Act 1990 (c. 31) (endangering safety at aerodromes).

47 An offence under section 9 of that Act (hijacking of ships).

48 An offence under section 10 of that Act (seizing or exercising control of fixed platforms).

49 An offence under section 11 of that Act (destroying fixed platforms or endangering their safety).

50 An offence under section 12 of that Act (other acts endangering or likely to endanger safe navigation).

51 An offence under section 13 of that Act (offences involving threats).

52 An offence under Part II of the Channel Tunnel (Security) Order 1994 (S.I. 1994/570) (offences relating to Channel Tunnel trains and the tunnel system).

53 An offence under Article 9 of the Road Traffic (Northern Ireland) Order 1995 (S.I. 1995/2994 (N.I. 18)) (causing death or grievous bodily injury by dangerous driving).

54 An offence under Article 14 of that Order (causing death or grievous bodily injury by careless driving when under the influence of drink or drugs).

55 An offence under Article 6 of the Protection from Harassment (Northern Ireland) Order 1997 (S.I. 1997/1180 (N.I. 9)) (putting people in fear of violence).

56 An offence under section 66 of the Police (Northern Ireland) Act 1998 (c. 32) (assaulting or obstructing a constable etc.).

57 An offence under section 51 or 52 of the International Criminal Court Act 2001 (c. 17) (genocide, crimes against humanity, war crimes and related offences), other than one involving murder.

58 An offence under section 1 of the Female Genital Mutilation Act 2003 (c. 31) (female genital mutilation).

59 An offence under section 2 of that Act (assisting a girl to mutilate her own genitalia).

60 An offence under section 3 of that Act (assisting a non-UK person to mutilate overseas a girl's genitalia).

61 An offence of –

   (a) aiding, abetting, counselling, procuring or inciting the commission of an offence specified in this Part of this Schedule,
   (b) conspiring to commit an offence so specified, or
   (c) attempting to commit an offence so specified.

62 An attempt to commit murder or a conspiracy to commit murder.

PART 2

SEXUAL OFFENCES

63 Rape.

64 Indecent assault upon a female.

65 An offence under section 52 of the Offences against the Person Act 1861 (c. 100) (indecent assault upon a female).

66 An offence under section 53 of that Act (abduction of woman etc.).

67 An offence under section 54 of that Act (abduction of woman by force).

68 An offence under section 55 of that Act (abduction of unmarried girl under 16 from parent or guardian).

69 An offence under section 2 of the Criminal Law Amendment Act 1885 (c. 69) (procuration).

70 An offence under section 3 of that Act (procurement of woman or girl by threats etc. or administering drugs).

71 An offence under section 4 of that Act (intercourse or attempted intercourse with girl under 14).

72 An offence under section 5 of that Act (intercourse or attempted intercourse with girl under 17).

73 An offence under section 6 of that Act (permitting girl under 17 to use premises for intercourse).

74 An offence under section 7 of that Act (abduction of girl under 18 from parent or guardian).

75 An offence under section 8 of that Act (unlawful detention of woman or girl in brothel etc.).

76 An offence under section 1 of the Vagrancy Act 1898 (c. 39) (living on earnings of prostitution or soliciting or importuning in a public place).

77 An offence under section 1 of the Punishment of Incest Act 1908 (c. 45) (incest by a man).

78 An offence under section 2 of that Act (incest by a woman).

79 An offence under section 21 of the Children and Young Persons Act (Northern Ireland) 1968 (c. 34) (causing or encouraging seduction or prostitution of girl under 17).

80 An offence under section 22 of that Act (indecent conduct towards child).

81 An offence under section 9 of the Theft Act (Northern Ireland) 1969 (c. 16) of burglary with intent to commit rape.

82 An offence under Article 3 of the Protection of Children (Northern Ireland) Order 1978 (S.I. 1978/1047 (N.I. 17)) (indecent photographs of children).

83 An offence under section 170 of the Customs and Excise Management Act 1979 (c. 2) (penalty for fraudulent evasion of duty etc.) in relation to goods prohibited to be imported under section 42 of the Customs Consolidation Act 1876 (c. 36) (indecent or obscene articles).

84 An offence under Article 9 of the Criminal Justice (Northern Ireland) Order 1980 (S.I. 1980/704 (N.I. 6)) (inciting girl under 16 to have incestuous sexual intercourse).

85 An offence under Article 7 of the Homosexual Offences (Northern Ireland) Order 1982 (S.I. 1982/1536 (N.I. 19)) (procuring others to commit homosexual acts).

86 An offence under Article 8 of that Order (living on earnings of male prostitution).

87 An offence under Article 122 of the Mental Health (Northern Ireland) Order 1986 (S.I. 1986/595 (N.I. 4)) (protection of women suffering from severe mental handicap).

88 An offence under Article 123 of that Order (protection of patients).

89 An offence under Article 15 of the Criminal Justice (Evidence, etc.) (Northern Ireland) Order 1988 (S.I. 1988/1847 (N.I. 17) (possession of indecent photograph of a child).

90 An offence under section 15 of the Sexual Offences Act 2003 (c. 42) (meeting a child following sexual grooming etc.).

91 An offence under section 16 of that Act (abuse of position of trust: sexual activity with a child).

92 An offence under section 17 of that Act (abuse of position of trust: causing or inciting a child to engage in sexual activity).

93 An offence under section 18 of that Act (abuse of position of trust: sexual activity in the presence of a child).

94 An offence under section 19 of that Act (abuse of position of trust: causing a child to watch a sexual act).

95 An offence under section 47 of that Act (paying for sexual services of a child).

96 An offence under section 48 of that Act (causing or inciting child prostitution or pornography).

97 An offence under section 49 of that Act (controlling a child prostitute or a child involved in pornography).

98 An offence under section 50 of that Act (arranging or facilitating child prostitution or pornography).

99 An offence under section 52 of that Act (causing or inciting prostitution for gain).

100 An offence under section 53 of that Act (controlling prostitution for gain).

101 An offence under section 57 of that Act (trafficking into the UK for sexual exploitation).

102 An offence under section 58 of that Act (trafficking within the UK for sexual exploitation).

103 An offence under section 59 of that Act (trafficking out of the UK for sexual exploitation).

104 An offence under section 66 of that Act (exposure).

105 An offence under section 67 of that Act (voyeurism).

106 An offence under section 69 of that Act (intercourse with an animal).

107 An offence under section 70 of that Act (sexual penetration of a corpse).

108 An offence under Article 20 of the Criminal Justice (Northern Ireland) Order 2003 (S.I. 2003/1247 (N.I. 13)) (assault with intent to commit buggery).

109 An offence under Article 21 of that Order (indecent assault on a male).

110 An offence of –

   (a) aiding, abetting, counselling, procuring or inciting the commission of an offence specified in this Part of this Schedule,
   (b) conspiring to commit an offence so specified, or
   (c) attempting to commit an offence so specified.

SCHEDULE 18   Section 230

RELEASE OF PRISONERS SERVING SENTENCES OF IMPRISONMENT OR
DETENTION FOR PUBLIC PROTECTION

Release on licence

1(1) Section 31 of the Crime (Sentences) Act 1997 (c. 43) (duration and conditions of licences for life prisoners), is amended as follows.

(2) In subsection (1) (licence to remain in force until death), after 'life prisoner' there is inserted ', other than a prisoner to whom section 31A below applies,'.

(3) After that subsection there is inserted –

   '(1A) Where a prisoner to whom section 31A below applies is released on licence, the licence shall remain in force until his death unless –

      (a) it is previously revoked under section 32(1) or (2) below; or
      (b) it ceases to have effect in accordance with an order made by the Secretary of State under section 31A below.'

2 After that section there is inserted –

'31A Imprisonment or detention for public protection: termination of licences

(1) This section applies to a prisoner who –

(a) is serving one or more preventive sentences, and
(b) is not serving any other life sentence.

(2) Where –

(a) the prisoner has been released on licence under this Chapter; and
(b) the qualifying period has expired,

the Secretary of State shall, if directed to do so by the Parole Board, order that the licence is to cease to have effect.

(3) Where –

(a) the prisoner has been released on licence under this Chapter;
(b) the qualifying period has expired; and
(c) if he has made a previous application under this subsection, a period of at least twelve months has expired since the disposal of that application,

the prisoner may make an application to the Parole Board under this subsection.

(4) Where an application is made under subsection (3) above, the Parole Board –

(a) shall, if it is satisfied that it is no longer necessary for the protection of the public that the licence should remain in force, direct the Secretary of State to make an order that the licence is to cease to have effect;
(b) shall otherwise dismiss the application.

(5) In this section –

"preventive sentence" means a sentence of imprisonment for public protection under section 225 of the Criminal Justice Act 2003 or a sentence of detention for public protection under section 226 of that Act;
"the qualifying period", in relation to a prisoner who has been released on licence, means the period of ten years beginning with the date of his release.'

3 In section 34(2) of that Act (meaning of 'life sentence'), after paragraph (c) there is inserted –

'(d) a sentence of imprisonment for public protection under section 225 of the Criminal Justice Act 2003, and
(e) a sentence of detention for public protection under section 226 of that Act.'

Determination of tariffs

4 In section 82A of the Sentencing Act (determination of tariffs), after subsection (4) there is inserted –

'(4A) No order under subsection (4) above may be made where the life sentence is –

(a) a sentence of imprisonment for public protection under section 225 of the Criminal Justice Act 2003, or
(b) a sentence of detention for public protection under section 226 of that Act.'

SCHEDULE 19   Section 239(7)

THE PAROLE BOARD: SUPPLEMENTARY PROVISIONS

Status and Capacity

1(1) The Board is not to be regarded as the servant or agent of the Crown or as enjoying any status, immunity or privilege of the Crown; and the Board's property is not to be regarded as property of, or held on behalf of, the Crown.

(2) It is within the capacity of the Board as a statutory corporation to do such things and enter into such transactions as are incidental to or conducive to the discharge of –

(a) its functions under Chapter 6 of Part 12 in respect of fixed-term prisoners, and
(b) its functions under Chapter 2 of Part 2 of the Crime (Sentences) Act 1997 (c. 43) in relation to life prisoners within the meaning of that Chapter.

Membership

2(1) The Board is to consist of a chairman and not less than four other members appointed by the Secretary of State.

(2) The Board must include among its members –

(a) a person who holds or has held judicial office;
(b) a registered medical practitioner who is a psychiatrist;
(c) a person appearing to the Secretary of State to have knowledge and experience of the supervision or after-care of discharged prisoners; and
(d) a person appearing to the Secretary of State to have made a study of the causes of delinquency or the treatment of offenders.

(3) A member of the Board –

(a) holds and vacates office in accordance with the terms of his appointment;
(b) may resign his office by notice in writing addressed to the Secretary of State;

and a person who ceases to hold office as a member of the Board is eligible for re-appointment.

Payments to members

3(1) The Board may pay to each member such remuneration and allowances as the Secretary of State may determine.

(2) The Board may pay or make provision for paying to or in respect of any member such sums by way of pension, allowances or gratuities as the Secretary of State may determine.

(3) If a person ceases to be a member otherwise than on the expiry of his term of office and it appears to the Secretary of State that there are special circumstances that make it right that he should receive compensation, the Secretary of State may direct the Board to make to that person a payment of such amount as the Secretary of State may determine.

(4) A determination or direction of the Secretary of State under this paragraph requires the approval of the Treasury.

Proceedings

4(1) Subject to the provisions of section 239(5), the arrangements relating to meetings of the Board are to be such as the Board may determine.

(2) The arrangements may provide for the discharge, under the general direction of the Board, of any of the Board's functions by a committee or by one or more of the members or employees of the Board.

(3) The validity of the proceedings of the Board are not to be affected by any vacancy among the members or by any defect in the appointment of a member.

Staff

5(1) The Board may appoint such number of employees as it may determine.

(2) The remuneration and other conditions of service of the persons appointed under this paragraph are to be determined by the Board.

(3) Any determination under sub-paragraph (1) or (2) requires the approval of the Secretary of State given with the consent of the Treasury.

(4) The Employers' Liability (Compulsory Insurance) Act 1969 (c. 57) shall not require insurance to be effected by the Board.

6(1) Employment with the Board shall continue to be included among the kinds of employment to which a scheme under section 1 of the Superannuation Act 1972 (c. 11) can apply, and accordingly in Schedule 1 to that Act (in which those kinds of employment are listed) at the end of the list of Other Bodies there shall continue to be inserted –

'Parole Board.'.

(2) The Board shall pay to the Treasury, at such times as the Treasury may direct, such sums as the Treasury may determine in respect of the increase attributable to this paragraph in the sums payable under the Superannuation Act 1972 out of money provided by Parliament.

Financial provisions

7(1) The Secretary of State shall pay to the Board –

(a) any expenses incurred or to be incurred by the Board by virtue of paragraph 3 or 5; and
(b) with the consent of the Treasury, such sums as he thinks fit for enabling the Board to meet other expenses.

(2) Any sums required by the Secretary of State for making payments under sub-paragraph (1) are to be paid out of money provided by Parliament.

Authentication of Board's seal

8 The application of the seal of the Board is to be authenticated by the signature of the Chairman or some other person authorised for the purpose.

Presumption of authenticity of documents issued by Board

9 Any document purporting to be an instrument issued by the Board and to be duly executed under the seal of the Board or to be signed on behalf of the Board shall be received in evidence and shall be deemed to be such an instrument unless the contrary is shown.

Accounts and audit

10(1) It is the duty of the Board –

    (a) to keep proper accounts and proper records in relation to the accounts;

    (b) to prepare in respect of each financial year a statement of accounts in such form as the Secretary of State may direct with the approval of the Treasury; and

    (c) to send copies of each such statement to the Secretary of State and the Comptroller and Auditor General not later than 31st August next following the end of the financial year to which the statement relates.

(2) The Comptroller and Auditor General shall examine, certify and report on each statement of accounts sent to him by the Board and shall lay a copy of every such statement and of his report before each House of Parliament.

(3) In this paragraph and paragraph 11 'financial year' means a period of 12 months ending with 31st March.

Reports

11 The Board must as soon as practicable after the end of each financial year make to the Secretary of State a report on the performance of its functions during the year; and the Secretary of State must lay a copy of the report before each House of Parliament.

SCHEDULE 20   Section 262

PRISONERS LIABLE TO REMOVAL FROM UNITED KINGDOM:
MODIFICATIONS OF CRIMINAL JUSTICE ACT 1991

1 In this Schedule 'the 1991 Act' means the Criminal Justice Act 1991 (c. 53).

2 In section 42 of the 1991 Act (additional days for disciplinary offences), in subsection (2) before the word 'and' at the end of paragraph (a) there is inserted –

    '(aa) any period which he must serve before he can be removed under section 46A below;'.

3(1) In section 46 of the 1991 Act (persons liable to removal from the United Kingdom) in subsection (3) after paragraph (d) there is inserted 'or

    (e) he is liable to removal under section 10 of the Immigration and Asylum Act 1999'.

(2) Sub-paragraph (1) does not apply to any prisoner whose sentence relates to an offence committed before the commencement of this Schedule.

4 After section 46 of the 1991 Act there is inserted –

'46A Early removal of persons liable to removal from United Kingdom

(1) Subject to subsection (2) below, where a short-term or long-term prisoner is liable to removal from the United Kingdom, the Secretary of State may under this section remove him from prison at any time after he has served the requisite period.

(2) Subsection (1) above does not apply where –

    (a) the sentence is an extended sentence within the meaning of section 85 of the Powers of Criminal Courts (Sentencing) Act 2000,

    (b) the sentence is for an offence under section 1 of the Prisoners (Return to Custody) Act 1995,

(c) the prisoner is subject to a hospital order, hospital direction or transfer direction under section 37, 45A or 47 of the Mental Health Act 1983,

(d) the prisoner is subject to the notification requirements of Part 2 of the Sexual Offences Act 2003, or

(e) the interval between –

    (i) the date on which the prisoner will have served the requisite period for the term of the sentence, and

    (ii) the date on which he will have served one-half of the sentence,

is less than 14 days.

(3) A prisoner removed from prison under this section –

(a) is so removed only for the purpose of enabling the Secretary of State to remove him from the United Kingdom under powers conferred by –

    (i) Schedule 2 or 3 to the Immigration Act 1971, or

    (ii) section 10 of the Immigration and Asylum Act 1999, and

(b) so long as remaining in the United Kingdom, remains liable to be detained in pursuance of his sentence until he falls to be released under section 33 or 35 above.

(4) So long as a prisoner removed from prison under this section remains in the United Kingdom but has not been returned to prison, any duty or power of the Secretary of State under section 33, 35 or 36 is exercisable in relation to him as if he were in prison.

(5) In this section "the requisite period" means –

(a) for a term of three months or more but less than four months, a period of 30 days;

(b) for a term of four months or more but less than 18 months, a period equal to one-quarter of the term;

(c) for a term of 18 months or more, a period that is 135 days less than one-half of the term.

(6) The Secretary of State may by order made by statutory instrument –

(a) amend the definition of 'the requisite period' in subsection (5) above,

(b) make such transitional provision as appears to him necessary or expedient in connection with the amendment.

(7) No order shall be made under subsection (6) above unless a draft of the order has been laid before and approved by a resolution of each House of Parliament.

(8) In relation to any time before the commencement of sections 80 and 81 of the Sexual Offences Act 2003, the reference in subsection (2)(d) above to Part 2 of that Act is to be read as a reference to Part 1 of the Sex Offenders Act 1997.

46B Re-entry into United Kingdom of offender removed early from prison

(1) This section applies in relation to a person who, after being removed from prison under section 46A above, has been removed from the United Kingdom before he has served one-half of his sentence.

(2) If a person to whom this section applies enters the United Kingdom at any time before his sentence expiry date, he is liable to be detained in pursuance of his sentence from the time of his entry into the United Kingdom until whichever is the earlier of the following –

(a) the end of a period ("the further custodial period") beginning with that time and equal in length to the outstanding custodial period, and

(b) his sentence expiry date.

(3) A person who is liable to be detained by virtue of subsection (2) above is, if at large, to be taken for the purposes of section 49 of the Prison Act 1952 (persons unlawfully at large) to be unlawfully at large.

(4) Subsection (2) above does not prevent the further removal from the United Kingdom of a person falling within that subsection.

(5) Where, in the case of a person returned to prison by virtue of subsection (2) above, the further custodial period ends before the sentence expiry date, subsections (1) and (2) of section 33 above apply in relation to him as if any reference to one-half or two-thirds of the prisoner's sentence were a reference to the further custodial period.

(6) If a person returned to prison by virtue of subsection (2) above falls by virtue of subsection (5) above to be released on licence under section 33(1) or (2) above after the date on which (but for his removal from the United Kingdom) he would have served three-quarters of his sentence, section 37(1) above has effect in relation to him as if for the reference to three-quarters of his sentence there were substituted a reference to the whole of his sentence.

(7) If a person who is released on licence under section 33(1) or (2) above at the end of the further custodial period is recalled to prison under section 39(1) or (2) above, section 33A(3) above shall not apply, but it shall be the duty of the Secretary of State –

(a) if the person is recalled before the date on which (but for his removal from the United Kingdom) he would have served three-quarters of his sentence, to release him on licence on that date, and

(b) if he is recalled after that date, to release him on the sentence expiry date.

(8) A licence granted by virtue of subsection (7)(a) above shall remain in force until the sentence expiry date.

(9) In this section –

"further custodial period" has the meaning given by subsection (2)(a) above;
"outstanding custodial period", in relation to a person to whom this section applies, means the period beginning with the date on which he was removed from the United Kingdom and ending with the date on which (but for his removal) he would have served one-half of his sentence;
"sentence expiry date", in relation to a person to whom this section applies, means the date on which (but for his removal from the United Kingdom) he would have served the whole of this sentence.'

SCHEDULE 21

Section 269(5)

DETERMINATION OF MINIMUM TERM IN RELATION TO MANDATORY
LIFE SENTENCE

Interpretation

1 In this Schedule –

'child' means a person under 18 years;
'mandatory life sentence' means a life sentence passed in circumstances where the sentence is fixed by law;
'minimum term', in relation to a mandatory life sentence, means the part of the sentence to be specified in an order under section 269(2);

'whole life order' means an order under subsection (4) of section 269.

2 Section 28 of the Crime and Disorder Act 1998 (c. 37) (meaning of 'racially or religiously aggravated') applies for the purposes of this Schedule as it applies for the purposes of sections 29 to 32 of that Act.

3 For the purposes of this Schedule an offence is aggravated by sexual orientation if it is committed in circumstances falling within subsection (2)(a)(i) or (b)(i) of section 146.

Starting points

4(1) If –

    (a) the court considers that the seriousness of the offence (or the combination of the offence and one or more offences associated with it) is exceptionally high, and

    (b) the offender was aged 21 or over when he committed the offence,

the appropriate starting point is a whole life order.

(2) Cases that would normally fall within sub-paragraph (1)(a) include –

    (a) the murder of two or more persons, where each murder involves any of the following –

        (i)   a substantial degree of premeditation or planning,

        (ii) the abduction of the victim, or

        (iii) sexual or sadistic conduct,

    (b) the murder of a child if involving the abduction of the child or sexual or sadistic motivation,

    (c) a murder done for the purpose of advancing a political, religious or ideological cause, or

    (d) a murder by an offender previously convicted of murder.

5(1) If –

    (a) the case does not fall within paragraph 4(1) but the court considers that the seriousness of the offence (or the combination of the offence and one or more offences associated with it) is particularly high, and

    (b) the offender was aged 18 or over when he committed the offence,

the appropriate starting point, in determining the minimum term, is 30 years.

(2) Cases that (if not falling within paragraph 4(1)) would normally fall within sub-paragraph (1)(a) include –

    (a) the murder of a police officer or prison officer in the course of his duty,

    (b) a murder involving the use of a firearm or explosive,

    (c) a murder done for gain (such as a murder done in the course or furtherance of robbery or burglary, done for payment or done in the expectation of gain as a result of the death),

    (d) a murder intended to obstruct or interfere with the course of justice,

    (e) a murder involving sexual or sadistic conduct,

    (f) the murder of two or more persons,

    (g) a murder that is racially or religiously aggravated or aggravated by sexual orientation, or

    (h) a murder falling within paragraph 4(2) committed by an offender who was aged under 21 when he committed the offence.

6 If the offender was aged 18 or over when he committed the offence and the case does not fall within paragraph 4(1) or 5(1), the appropriate starting point, in determining the minimum term, is 15 years.

7 If the offender was aged under 18 when he committed the offence, the appropriate starting point, in determining the minimum term, is 12 years.

Aggravating and mitigating factors

8 Having chosen a starting point, the court should take into account any aggravating or mitigating factors, to the extent that it has not allowed for them in its choice of starting point.

9 Detailed consideration of aggravating or mitigating factors may result in a minimum term of any length (whatever the starting point), or in the making of a whole life order.

10 Aggravating factors (additional to those mentioned in paragraph 4(2) and 5(2)) that may be relevant to the offence of murder include –

(a) a significant degree of planning or premeditation,
(b) the fact that the victim was particularly vulnerable because of age or disability,
(c) mental or physical suffering inflicted on the victim before death,
(d) the abuse of a position of trust,
(e) the use of duress or threats against another person to facilitate the commission of the offence,
(f) the fact that the victim was providing a public service or performing a public duty, and
(g) concealment, destruction or dismemberment of the body.

11 Mitigating factors that may be relevant to the offence of murder include –

(a) an intention to cause serious bodily harm rather than to kill,
(b) lack of premeditation,
(c) the fact that the offender suffered from any mental disorder or mental disability which (although not falling within section 2(1) of the Homicide Act 1957 (c. 11)), lowered his degree of culpability,
(d) the fact that the offender was provoked (for example, by prolonged stress) in a way not amounting to a defence of provocation,
(e) the fact that the offender acted to any extent in self-defence,
(f) a belief by the offender that the murder was an act of mercy, and
(g) the age of the offender.

12 Nothing in this Schedule restricts the application of –

(a) section 143(2) (previous convictions),
(b) section 143(3) (bail), or
(c) section 144 (guilty plea).

SCHEDULE 22 Section 276

MANDATORY LIFE SENTENCES: TRANSITIONAL CASES

Interpretation

1 In this Schedule –

'the commencement date' means the day on which section 269 comes into force;
'the early release provisions' means the provisions of section 28(5) to (8) of the Crime (Sentences) Act 1997 (c. 43);
'existing prisoner' means a person serving one or more mandatory life sentences passed before the commencement date (whether or not he is also serving any other sentence);

'life sentence' means a sentence of imprisonment for life or custody for life passed in England and Wales or by a court-martial outside England and Wales;

'mandatory life sentence' means a life sentence passed in circumstances where the sentence was fixed by law.

Existing prisoners notified by Secretary of State

2 Paragraph 3 applies in relation to any existing prisoner who, in respect of any mandatory life sentence, has before the commencement date been notified in writing by the Secretary of State (otherwise than in a notice that is expressed to be provisional) either –

(a) of a minimum period which in the view of the Secretary of State should be served before the prisoner's release on licence, or

(b) that the Secretary of State does not intend that the prisoner should ever be released on licence.

3(1) On the application of the existing prisoner, the High Court must, in relation to the mandatory life sentence, either –

(a) order that the early release provisions are to apply to him as soon as he has served the part of the sentence which is specified in the order, which in a case falling within paragraph 2(a) must not be greater than the notified minimum term, or

(b) in a case falling within paragraph 2(b), order that the early release provisions are not to apply to the offender.

(2) In a case falling within paragraph 2(a), no application may be made under this paragraph after the end of the notified minimum term.

(3) Where no application under this paragraph is made in a case falling within paragraph 2(a), the early release provisions apply to the prisoner in respect of the sentence as soon as he has served the notified minimum term (or, if he has served that term before the commencement date but has not been released, from the commencement date).

(4) In this paragraph 'the notified minimum term' means the minimum period notified as mentioned in paragraph 2(a), or where the prisoner has been so notified on more than one occasion, the period most recently so notified.

4(1) In dealing with an application under paragraph 3, the High Court must have regard to –

(a) the seriousness of the offence, or of the combination of the offence and one or more offences associated with it,

(b) where the court is satisfied that, if the prisoner had been sentenced to a term of imprisonment, the length of his sentence would have been treated by section 67 of the Criminal Justice Act 1967 (c. 80) as being reduced by a particular period, the effect which that section would have had if he had been sentenced to a term of imprisonment, and

(c) the length of the notified minimum term or, where a notification falling within paragraph 2(b) has been given to the prisoner, to the fact that such a notification has been given.

(2) In considering under sub-paragraph (1) the seriousness of the offence, or of the combination of the offence and one or more offences associated with it, the High Court must have regard to –

(a) the general principles set out in Schedule 21, and

(b) any recommendation made to the Secretary of State by the trial judge or the Lord Chief Justice as to the minimum term to be served by the offender before release on licence.

(3) In this paragraph 'the notified minimum term' has the same meaning as in paragraph 3.

Existing prisoners not notified by Secretary of State

5 Paragraph 6 applies in relation to any existing prisoner who, in respect of any mandatory life sentence, has not before the commencement date been notified as mentioned in paragraph 2(a) or (b) by the Secretary of State.

6 The Secretary of State must refer the prisoner's case to the High Court for the making by the High Court of an order under subsection (2) or (4) of section 269 in relation to the mandatory life sentence.

7 In considering under subsection (3) or (4) of section 269 the seriousness of an offence (or the combination of an offence and one or more offences associated with it) in a case referred to the High Court under paragraph 6, the High Court must have regard not only to the matters mentioned in subsection (5) of that section but also to any recommendation made to the Secretary of State by the trial judge or the Lord Chief Justice as to the minimum term to be served by the offender before release on licence.

8 In dealing with a reference under paragraph 6, the High Court –

(a) may not make an order under subsection (2) of section 269 specifying a part of the sentence which in the opinion of the court is greater than that which, under the practice followed by the Secretary of State before December 2002, the Secretary of State would have been likely to notify as mentioned in paragraph 2(a), and

(b) may not make an order under subsection (4) of section 269 unless the court is of the opinion that, under the practice followed by the Secretary of State before December 2002, the Secretary of State would have been likely to give the prisoner a notification falling within paragraph 2(b).

Sentences passed on or after commencement date in respect of offences committed before that date

9 Paragraph 10 applies where –

(a) on or after the commencement date a court passes a life sentence in circumstances where the sentence is fixed by law, and

(b) the offence to which the sentence relates was committed before the commencement date.

10 The court –

(a) may not make an order under subsection (2) of section 269 specifying a part of the sentence which in the opinion of the court is greater than that which, under the practice followed by the Secretary of State before December 2002, the Secretary of State would have been likely to notify as mentioned in paragraph 2(a), and

(b) may not make an order under subsection (4) of section 269 unless the court is of the opinion that, under the practice followed by the Secretary of State before December 2002, the Secretary of State would have been likely to give the prisoner a notification falling within paragraph 2(b).

Proceedings in High Court

11(1) An application under paragraph 3 or a reference under paragraph 6 is to be determined by a single judge of the High Court without an oral hearing.

(2) In relation to such an application or reference, any reference to 'the court' in section 269(2) to (5) and Schedule 21 is to be read as a reference to the High Court.

Giving of reasons

12(1) Where the High Court makes an order under paragraph 3(1)(a) or (b), it must state in open court, in ordinary language, its reasons for deciding on the order made.

(2) Where the order is an order under paragraph 3(1)(a) specifying a part of the sentence shorter than the notified minimum term the High Court must, in particular, state its reasons for departing from the notified minimum term.

13 Where the High Court makes an order under subsection (2) or (4) of section 269 on a reference under paragraph 6, subsection (2) of section 270 does not apply.

Right of appeal

14(1) A person who has made an application under paragraph 3 or in respect of whom a reference has been made under paragraph 6 may with the leave of the Court of Appeal appeal to the Court of Appeal against the decision of the High Court on the application or reference.

(2) Section 1(1) of the Administration of Justice Act 1960 (c. 65) (appeal to House of Lords from decision of High Court in a criminal cause or matter) and section 18(1)(a) of the Supreme Court Act 1981 (c. 54) (exclusion of appeal from High Court to Court of Appeal in a criminal cause or matter) do not apply in relation to a decision to which sub-paragraph (1) applies.

(3) The jurisdiction conferred on the Court of Appeal by this paragraph is to be exercised by the criminal division of that court.

(4) Section 33(3) of the Criminal Appeal Act 1968 (c. 19) (limitation on appeal from criminal division of Court of Appeal) does not prevent an appeal to the House of Lords under this paragraph.

(5) In relation to appeals to the Court of Appeal or the House of Lords under this paragraph, the Secretary of State may make an order containing provision corresponding to any provision in the Criminal Appeal Act 1968 (subject to any specified modifications).

Review of minimum term on reference by Attorney General

15 Section 36 of the Criminal Justice Act 1988 (c. 33) applies in relation to an order made by the High Court under paragraph 3(1)(a) as it applies in relation to an order made by the Crown Court under section 269(2).

Modification of early release provisions

16(1) In relation to an existing prisoner, section 28 of the Crime (Sentences) Act 1997 (c. 43) has effect subject to the following modifications.

(2) Any reference to a life prisoner in respect of whom a minimum term order has been made includes a reference to –

(a) an existing prisoner in respect of whom an order under paragraph 3(1)(a) has been made, and

(b) an existing prisoner serving a sentence in respect of which paragraph 3(3) applies.

(3) Any reference to the relevant part of the sentence is to be read –

(a) in relation to a sentence in respect of which an order under paragraph 3(1)(a) has been made, as a reference to the part specified in the order, and

(b) in relation to a sentence in respect of which paragraph 3(3) applies, as a reference to the notified minimum term as defined by paragraph 3(4).

(4) In subsection (1B) (life prisoner serving two or more sentences), paragraph (a) is to be read as if it referred to each of the sentences being one –

(a) in respect of which a minimum term order or an order under paragraph 3(1)(a) has been made, or

(b) in respect of which paragraph 3(3) applies.

17 In section 34(1) of the Crime (Sentences) Act 1997 (c. 43) (interpretation of Chapter 2 of that Act), in the definition of 'life prisoner', the reference to a transferred prisoner as defined by section 273 of this Act includes a reference to an existing prisoner who immediately before the commencement date is a transferred life prisoner for the purposes of section 33 of that Act.

Transferred life prisoners

18 In relation to an existing prisoner who immediately before the commencement date is a transferred life prisoner for the purposes of section 33 of the Crime (Sentences) Act 1997, this Schedule is to be read as if –

(a) any certificate under subsection (2) of that section were a notification falling within paragraph 2(a) of this Schedule, and

(b) references to any recommendation of the trial judge or the Lord Chief Justice were omitted.

SCHEDULE 23   Section 278

DEFERMENT OF SENTENCE

1 For sections 1 and 2 of the Sentencing Act (deferment of sentence) there is substituted –

'*Deferment of sentence*

1 Deferment of sentence

(1) The Crown Court or a magistrates' court may defer passing sentence on an offender for the purpose of enabling the court, or any other court to which it falls to deal with him, to have regard in dealing with him to –

(a) his conduct after conviction (including, where appropriate, the making by him of reparation for his offence); or

(b) any change in his circumstances;

but this is subject to subsections (3) and (4) below.

(2) Without prejudice to the generality of subsection (1) above, the matters to which the court to which it falls to deal with the offender may have regard by virtue

of paragraph (a) of that subsection include the extent to which the offender has complied with any requirements imposed under subsection (3)(b) below.

(3) The power conferred by subsection (1) above shall be exercisable only if –

(a) the offender consents;

(b) the offender undertakes to comply with any requirements as to his conduct during the period of the deferment that the court considers it appropriate to impose; and

(c) the court is satisfied, having regard to the nature of the offence and the character and circumstances of the offender, that it would be in the interests of justice to exercise the power.

(4) Any deferment under this section shall be until such date as may be specified by the court, not being more than six months after the date on which the deferment is announced by the court; and, subject to section 1D(3) below, where the passing of sentence has been deferred under this section it shall not be further so deferred.

(5) Where a court has under this section deferred passing sentence on an offender, it shall forthwith give a copy of the order deferring the passing of sentence and setting out any requirements imposed under subsection (3)(b) above –

(a) to the offender,

(b) where an officer of a local probation board has been appointed to act as a supervisor in relation to him, to that board, and

(c) where a person has been appointed under section 1A(2)(b) below to act as a supervisor in relation to him, to that person.

(6) Notwithstanding any enactment, a court which under this section defers passing sentence on an offender shall not on the same occasion remand him.

(7) Where –

(a) a court which under this section has deferred passing sentence on an offender proposes to deal with him on the date originally specified by the court, or

(b) the offender does not appear on the day so specified,

the court may issue a summons requiring him to appear before the court at a time and place specified in the summons, or may issue a warrant to arrest him and bring him before the court at a time and place specified in the warrant.

(8) Nothing in this section or sections 1A to 1D below shall affect –

(a) the power of the Crown Court to bind over an offender to come up for judgment when called upon; or

(b) the power of any court to defer passing sentence for any purpose for which it may lawfully do so apart from this section.

1A Further provision about undertakings

(1) Without prejudice to the generality of paragraph (b) of section 1(3) above, the requirements that may be imposed by virtue of that paragraph include requirements as to the residence of the offender during the whole or any part of the period of deferment.

(2) Where an offender has undertaken to comply with any requirements imposed under section 1(3)(b) above the court may appoint –

(a) an officer of a local probation board, or

(b) any other person whom the court thinks appropriate,

to act as a supervisor in relation to him.

(3) A person shall not be appointed under subsection (2)(b) above without his consent.

(4) It shall be the duty of a supervisor appointed under subsection (2) above –

    (a)   to monitor the offender's compliance with the requirements; and

    (b)   to provide the court to which it falls to deal with the offender in respect of the offence in question with such information as the court may require relating to the offender's compliance with the requirements.

1B Breach of undertakings

(1) A court which under section 1 above has deferred passing sentence on an offender may deal with him before the end of the period of deferment if –

    (a)   he appears or is brought before the court under subsection (3) below; and

    (b)   the court is satisfied that he has failed to comply with one or more requirements imposed under section 1(3)(b) above in connection with the deferment.

(2) Subsection (3) below applies where –

    (a)   a court has under section 1 above deferred passing sentence on an offender;

    (b)   the offender undertook to comply with one or more requirements imposed under section 1(3)(b) above in connection with the deferment; and

    (c)   a person appointed under section 1A(2) above to act as a supervisor in relation to the offender has reported to the court that the offender has failed to comply with one or more of those requirements.

(3) Where this subsection applies, the court may issue –

    (a)   a summons requiring the offender to appear before the court at a time and place specified in the summons; or

    (b)   a warrant to arrest him and bring him before the court at a time and place specified in the warrant.

1C Conviction of offence during period of deferment

(1) A court which under section 1 above has deferred passing sentence on an offender may deal with him before the end of the period of deferment if during that period he is convicted in Great Britain of any offence.

(2) Subsection (3) below applies where a court has under section 1 above deferred passing sentence on an offender in respect of one or more offences and during the period of deferment the offender is convicted in England and Wales of any offence ("the later offence").

(3) Where this subsection applies, then (without prejudice to subsection (1) above and whether or not the offender is sentenced for the later offence during the period of deferment), the court which passes sentence on him for the later offence may also, if this has not already been done, deal with him for the offence or offences for which passing of sentence has been deferred, except that –

    (a)   the power conferred by this subsection shall not be exercised by a magistrates' court if the court which deferred passing sentence was the Crown Court; and

    (b)   the Crown Court, in exercising that power in a case in which the court which deferred passing sentence was a magistrates' court, shall not pass any sentence which could not have been passed by a magistrates' court in exercising that power.

(4) Where a court which under section 1 above has deferred passing sentence on an offender proposes to deal with him by virtue of subsection (1) above before the end of the period of deferment, the court may issue –

(a) a summons requiring him to appear before the court at a time and place specified in the summons; or

(b) a warrant to arrest him and bring him before the court at a time and place specified in the warrant.

1D Deferment of sentence: supplementary

(1) In deferring the passing of sentence under section 1 above a magistrates' court shall be regarded as exercising the power of adjourning the trial conferred by section 10(1) of the Magistrates' Courts Act 1980, and accordingly sections 11(1) and 13(1) to (3A) and (5) of that Act (non-appearance of the accused) apply (without prejudice to section 1(7) above) if the offender does not appear on the date specified under section 1(4) above.

(2) Where the passing of sentence on an offender has been deferred by a court ("the original court") under section 1 above, the power of that court under that section to deal with the offender at the end of the period of deferment and any power of that court under section 1B(1) or 1C(1) above, or of any court under section 1C(3) above, to deal with the offender –

(a) is power to deal with him, in respect of the offence for which passing of sentence has been deferred, in any way in which the original court could have dealt with him if it had not deferred passing sentence; and

(b) without prejudice to the generality of paragraph (a) above, in the case of a magistrates' court, includes the power conferred by section 3 below to commit him to the Crown Court for sentence.

(3) Where –

(a) the passing of sentence on an offender in respect of one or more offences has been deferred under section 1 above, and

(b) a magistrates' court deals with him in respect of the offence or any of the offences by committing him to the Crown Court under section 3 below,

the power of the Crown Court to deal with him includes the same power to defer passing sentence on him as if he had just been convicted of the offence or offences on indictment before the court.

(4) Subsection (5) below applies where –

(a) the passing of sentence on an offender in respect of one or more offences has been deferred under section 1 above;

(b) it falls to a magistrates' court to determine a relevant matter; and

(c) a justice of the peace is satisfied –

(i) that a person appointed under section 1A(2)(b) above to act as a supervisor in relation to the offender is likely to be able to give evidence that may assist the court in determining that matter; and

(ii) that that person will not voluntarily attend as a witness.

(5) The justice may issue a summons directed to that person requiring him to attend before the court at the time and place appointed in the summons to give evidence.

(6) For the purposes of subsection (4) above a court determines a relevant matter if it –

(a) deals with the offender in respect of the offence, or any of the offences, for which the passing of sentence has been deferred; or

(b) determines, for the purposes of section 1B(1)(b) above, whether the offender has failed to comply with any requirements imposed under section 1(3)(b) above.'

2 In section 159 of the Sentencing Act (execution of process between England and Wales and Scotland), for 'section 2(4),' there is substituted 'section 1(7), 1B(3), 1C(4),'.

SCHEDULE 24   Section 279

DRUG TREATMENT AND TESTING REQUIREMENT IN ACTION PLAN
ORDER OR SUPERVISION ORDER

1(1) Section 70 of the Sentencing Act (requirements which may be included in action plan orders and directions) is amended as follows.

(2) After subsection (4) there is inserted –

'(4A) Subsection (4B) below applies where a court proposing to make an action plan order is satisfied –

(a) that the offender is dependent on, or has a propensity to misuse, drugs, and
(b) that his dependency or propensity is such as requires and may be susceptible to treatment.

(4B) Where this subsection applies, requirements included in an action plan order may require the offender for a period specified in the order ('the treatment period') to submit to treatment by or under the direction of a specified person having the necessary qualifications and experience ('the treatment provider') with a view to the reduction or elimination of the offender's dependency on or propensity to misuse drugs.

(4C) The required treatment shall be –

(a) treatment as a resident in such institution or place as may be specified in the order, or
(b) treatment as a non-resident at such institution or place, and at such intervals, as may be so specified;

but the nature of the treatment shall not be specified in the order except as mentioned in paragraph (a) or (b) above.

(4D) A requirement shall not be included in an action plan order by virtue of subsection (4B) above –

(a) in any case, unless –
    (i) the court is satisfied that arrangements have been or can be made for the treatment intended to be specified in the order (including arrangements for the reception of the offender where he is to be required to submit to treatment as a resident), and
    (ii) the requirement has been recommended to the court as suitable for the offender by an officer of a local probation board or by a member of a youth offending team; and
(b) in the case of an order made or to be made in respect of a person aged 14 or over, unless he consents to its inclusion.

(4E) Subject to subsection (4F), an action plan order which includes a requirement by virtue of subsection (4B) above may, if the offender is aged 14 or over, also include a requirement ('a testing requirement') that, for the purpose of ascertaining whether he has any drug in his body during the treatment period, the offender shall during that period, at such times or in such circumstances as may (subject to the provisions of the order) be determined by the responsible officer or the treatment provider, provide samples of such description as may be so determined.

(4F) A testing requirement shall not be included in an action plan order by virtue of subsection (4E) above unless –

    (a) the offender is aged 14 or over and consents to its inclusion, and

    (b) the court has been notified by the Secretary of State that arrangements for implementing such requirements are in force in the area proposed to be specified in the order

(4G) A testing requirement shall specify for each month the minimum number of occasions on which samples are to be provided.

(4H) An action plan order including a testing requirement shall provide for the results of tests carried out on any samples provided by the offender in pursuance of the requirement to a person other than the responsible officer to be communicated to the responsible officer.'

2(1) Schedule 6 to the Sentencing Act (requirements which may be included in supervision orders) is amended as follows.

(2) In paragraph 1, after '6' there is inserted ',6A'.

(3) After paragraph 6 there is inserted –

'Requirements as to drug treatment and testing

6A(1) This paragraph applies where a court proposing to make a supervision order is satisfied –

    (a) that the offender is dependent on, or has a propensity to misuse, drugs, and

    (b) that his dependency or propensity is such as requires and may be susceptible to treatment.

(2) Where this paragraph applies, the court may include in the supervision order a requirement that the offender shall, for a period specified in the order ("the treatment period"), submit to treatment by or under the direction of a specified person having the necessary qualifications and experience ("the treatment provider") with a view to the reduction or elimination of the offender's dependency on or propensity to misuse drugs.

(3) The required treatment shall be –

    (a) treatment as a resident in such institution or place as may be specified in the order, or

    (b) treatment as a non-resident at such institution or place, and at such intervals, as may be so specified;

but the nature of the treatment shall not be specified in the order except as mentioned in paragraph (a) or (b) above.

(4) A requirement shall not be included in a supervision order by virtue of sub-paragraph (2) above –

    (a) in any case, unless –

        (i) the court is satisfied that arrangements have been or can be made for the treatment intended to be specified in the order (including arrangements for the reception of the offender where he is to be required to submit to treatment as a resident), and

(ii)   the requirement has been recommended to the court as suitable for the offender by an officer of a local probation board or by a member of a youth offending team; and

(b)   in the case of an order made or to be made in respect of a person aged 14 or over, unless he consents to its inclusion.

(5) Subject to sub-paragraph (6), a supervision order which includes a treatment requirement may also include a requirement ("a testing requirement") that, for the purpose of ascertaining whether he has any drug in his body during the treatment period, the offender shall during that period, at such times or in such circumstances as may (subject to the provisions of the order) be determined by the supervisor or the treatment provider, provide samples of such description as may be so determined.

(6) A testing requirement shall not be included in a supervision order by virtue of sub-paragraph (5) above unless –

(a)   the offender is aged 14 or over and consents to its inclusion, and

(b)   the court has been notified by the Secretary of State that arrangements for implementing such requirements are in force in the area proposed to be specified in the order.

(7) A testing requirement shall specify for each month the minimum number of occasions on which samples are to be provided.

(8) A supervision order including a testing requirement shall provide for the results of tests carried out on any samples provided by the offender in pursuance of the requirement to a person other than the supervisor to be communicated to the supervisor.'

3 In Schedule 7 to the Sentencing Act (breach, revocation and amendment of supervision orders), in paragraph 2(1), before 'or 7' there is inserted ',6A'.

SCHEDULE 25   Section 280(1)

SUMMARY OFFENCES NO LONGER PUNISHABLE WITH IMPRISONMENT

Vagrancy Act 1824 (c. 83)

1 The offence under section 3 of the Vagrancy Act 1824 (idle and disorderly persons) of causing or procuring or encouraging any child or children to wander abroad, or place himself or herself in any public place, street, highway, court, or passage, to beg or gather alms.

2 The following offences under section 4 of that Act (rogues and vagabonds) –

(a)   the offence of going about as a gatherer or collector of alms, or endeavouring to procure charitable contributions of any nature or kind, under any false or fraudulent pretence,

(b)   the offence of being found in or upon any dwelling house, warehouse, coach-house, stable, or outhouse, or in any inclosed yard, garden, or area, for any unlawful purpose, and

(c)   the offence of being apprehended as an idle and disorderly person, and violently resisting any constable, or other peace officer so apprehending him or her, and being subsequently convicted of the offence for which he or she shall have been so apprehended.

Railway Regulation Act 1842 (c. 55)

3 An offence under section 17 of the Railway Regulation Act 1842 (punishment of railway employees guilty of misconduct).

London Hackney Carriages Act 1843 (c. 86)

4 An offence under section 28 of the London Hackney Carriages Act 1843 (punishment for furious driving etc.).

Town Police Clauses Act 1847 (c. 89)

5 An offence under section 26 of the Town Police Clauses Act 1847 (unlawful release of impounded stray cattle).

6 An offence under section 28 of that Act (offences relating to obstructions and nuisances).

7 An offence under section 29 of that Act (drunken persons, etc. guilty of violent or indecent behaviour).

8 An offence under section 36 of that Act (keeping places for bear-baiting, cock-fighting etc.).

Ecclesiastical Courts Jurisdiction Act 1860 (c. 32)

9 An offence under section 2 of the Ecclesiastical Courts Jurisdiction Act 1860 (making a disturbance in churches, chapels, churchyards, etc.).

Town Gardens Protection Act 1863 (c. 13)

10 An offence under section 5 of the Town Gardens Protection Act 1863 (injuring gardens).

Public Stores Act 1875 (c. 25)

11 An offence under section 8 of the Public Stores Act 1875 (sweeping, etc., near dockyards, artillery ranges, etc.).

North Sea Fisheries Act 1893 (c. 17)

12 An offence under section 2 of the North Sea Fisheries Act 1893 (penalty for supplying, exchanging, or otherwise selling spirits).

13 An offence under section 3 of that Act (penalty for purchasing spirits by exchange or otherwise).

Seamen's and Soldiers' False Characters Act 1906 (c. 5)

14 An offence under section 1 of the Seamen's and Soldiers' False Characters Act 1906 (forgery of service or discharge certificate and personation).

Aliens Restriction (Amendment) Act 1919 (c. 92)

15 An offence under section 3(2) of the Aliens Restriction (Amendment) Act 1919 (promoting industrial unrest).

Children and Young Persons Act 1933 (c. 12)

16 An offence under section 4 of the Children and Young Persons Act 1933 (causing or allowing persons under sixteen to be used for begging).

Protection of Animals Act 1934 (c. 21)

17 An offence under section 2 of the Protection of Animals Act 1934 (offences relating to the prohibition of certain public contests, performances, and exhibitions with animals).

Public Health Act 1936 (c. 49)

18 An offence under section 287 of the Public Health Act 1936 (power to enter premises).

Essential Commodities Reserves Act 1938 (c. 51)

19 An offence under section 4(2) of the Essential Commodities Reserves Act 1938 (enforcement).

London Building Acts (Amendment) Act 1939 (c. xcvii)

20 An offence under section 142 of the London Building Acts (Amendment) Act 1939 (power of Council and others to enter buildings etc).

Cancer Act 1939 (c. 13)

21 An offence under section 4 of the Cancer Act 1939 (prohibition of certain advertisements).

Civil Defence Act 1939 (c. 31)

22 An offence under section 77 of the Civil Defence Act 1939 (penalty for false statements).

Hill Farming Act 1946 (c. 73)

23 An offence under section 19(2) or (3) of the Hill Farming Act 1946 (offences in relation to the control of rams).

Polish Resettlement Act 1947 (c. 19)

24 An offence under paragraph 7 of the Schedule to the Polish Resettlement Act 1947 (false representation or making a false statement).

Agriculture Act 1947 (c. 48)

25 An offence under section 14(7) of the Agriculture Act 1947, as remaining in force for the purposes of section 95 of that Act, (directions to secure good estate management and good husbandry).

26 An offence under section 95 of that Act (failure to comply with a direction to secure production).

Civil Defence Act 1948 (c. 5)

27 An offence under section 4 of the Civil Defence Act 1948 (powers as to land).

Agricultural Wages Act 1948 (c. 47)

28 An offence under section 12 of the Agricultural Wages Act 1948 (hindering investigation of complaints etc.).

Wireless Telegraphy Act 1949 (c. 54)

29 An offence under section 11(7) of the Wireless Telegraphy Act 1949 (enforcement of regulations as to use of apparatus), other than one within section 14(1A)(c) of that Act.

Prevention of Damage by Pests Act 1949 (c. 55)

30 An offence under section 22(5) of the Prevention of Damage by Pests Act 1949 (wrongful disclosure of information).

Coast Protection Act 1949 (c. 74)

31 An offence under section 25(9) of the Coast Protection Act 1949 (powers of entry and inspection).

Pet Animals Act 1951 (c. 35)

32 An offence under the Pet Animals Act 1951 (offences relating to licensing of pet shops and the sale of pets), other than one under section 4 of that Act.

Cockfighting Act 1952 (c. 59)

33 An offence under section 1 of the Cockfighting Act 1952 (possession of appliances for use in fighting of domestic fowl).

Agricultural Land (Removal of Surface Soil) Act 1953 (c. 10)

34 An offence under the Agricultural Land (Removal of Surface Soil) Act 1953 (removal of surface soil without planning permission).

Accommodation Agencies Act 1953 (c. 23)

35 An offence under section 1 of the Accommodation Agencies Act 1953 (illegal commissions and advertisements).

Army Act 1955 (3 & 4 Eliz. 2 c. 18)

36 An offence under section 19 of the Army Act 1955 (false answers in attestation paper).

37 An offence under section 161 of that Act (refusal to receive persons billeted, etc.).

38 An offence under section 171 of that Act (offences relating to the enforcement of provisions as to requisitioning).

39 An offence under section 191 of that Act (pretending to be a deserter).

40 An offence under section 193 of that Act (obstructing members of regular forces in execution of duty).

41 An offence under section 196 of that Act (illegal dealings in documents relating to pay, pensions, mobilisation etc.).

42 An offence under section 197 of that Act (unauthorised use of and dealing in decorations etc.).

Air Force Act 1955 (3 & 4 Eliz. 2 c. 19)

43 An offence under section 19 of the Air Force Act 1955 (false answers in attestation paper).

44 An offence under section 161 of that Act (refusal to receive persons billeted, etc.).

45 An offence under section 171 of that Act (offences relating to the enforcement of provisions as to requisitioning).

46 An offence under section 191 of that Act (pretending to be a deserter).

47 An offence under section 193 of that Act (obstructing members of regular air force in execution of duty).

48 An offence under section 196 of that Act (illegal dealings in documents relating to pay, pensions, mobilisation etc.).

49 An offence under section 197 of that Act (unauthorised use of and dealing in decorations etc.).

Naval Discipline Act 1957 (c. 53)

50 An offence under section 96 of the Naval Discipline Act 1957 (false pretence of desertion or absence without leave).

51 An offence under section 99 of that Act (illegal dealings in official documents).

Agricultural Marketing Act 1958 (c. 47)

52 An offence under section 45 of the Agricultural Marketing Act 1958 (failure to comply with demand for information or knowingly making any false statement in reply thereto).

Rivers (Prevention of Pollution) Act 1961 (c. 50)

53 An offence under section 12(1) of the Rivers (Prevention of Pollution) Act 1961 (restriction of disclosure of information).

Betting, Gaming and Lotteries Act 1963 (c. 2)

54 An offence under section 8 of the Betting, Gaming and Lotteries Act 1963 (betting in streets and public places).

Children and Young Persons Act 1963 (c. 37)

55 An offence under section 40 of the Children and Young Persons Act 1963 (offences relating to persons under 16 taking part in public performances etc.).

Animal Boarding Establishments Act 1963 (c. 43)

56 An offence under the Animal Boarding Establishments Act 1963 (offences in connection with the licensing and inspection of boarding establishments for animals), other than an offence under section 2 of that Act.

Agriculture and Horticulture Act 1964 (c. 28)

57 An offence under Part 3 of the Agriculture and Horticulture Act 1964 (offences relating to the grading and transport of fresh horticultural produce), other than an offence under section 15(1) of that Act.

Emergency Laws (Re-enactments and Repeals) Act 1964 (c. 60)

58 An offence under paragraph 1(3) or 2(4) of Schedule 1 to the Emergency Laws (Re-enactments and Repeals) Act 1964 (offences relating to the production of documents).

Riding Establishments Act 1964 (c. 70)

59 An offence under the Riding Establishments Act 1964 (offences relating to the keeping of riding establishments), other than an offence under section 2(4) of that Act.

Industrial and Provident Societies Act 1965 (c. 12)

60 An offence under section 16 of the Industrial and Provident Societies Act 1965 (cancellation of registration of society).

61 An offence under section 48 of that Act (production of documents and provision of information for certain purposes).

Cereals Marketing Act 1965 (c. 14)

62 An offence under section 17(1) of the Cereals Marketing Act 1965 (failure to comply with a requirement of a scheme).

Gas Act 1965 (c. 36)

63 An offence under paragraph 9 of Schedule 6 to the Gas Act 1965 (wrongful disclosure of information).

Armed Forces Act 1966 (c. 45)

64 An offence under section 8 of the Armed Forces Act 1966 (false statements on entry into Royal Navy).

Agriculture Act 1967 (c. 22)

65 An offence under section 6(9) of the Agriculture Act 1967 (compulsory use of systems of classification of carcases).

66 An offence under section 14(2) of that Act (levy schemes: requirements in relation to registration, returns and records).

67 An offence under section 69 of that Act (false statements to obtain grants etc).

Sea Fisheries (Shellfish) Act 1967 (c. 83)

68 An offence under section 14(2) of the Sea Fisheries (Shellfish) Act 1967 (offences relating to the deposit and importation of shellfish).

Theatres Act 1968 (c. 54)

69 An offence under section 13(1) or (2) of the Theatres Act 1968 (offences relating to licensing of premises for public performances of plays).

Theft Act 1968 (c. 60)

70 An offence under paragraph 2(1) of Schedule 1 to the Theft Act 1968 (taking or destroying fish).

Agriculture Act 1970 (c. 40)

71 An offence under section 106(8) of the Agriculture Act 1970 (eradication of brucellosis: obstructing or impeding an officer in the exercise of powers to obtain information).

Breeding of Dogs Act 1973 (c. 60)

72 An offence under the Breeding of Dogs Act 1973 (offences connected with the licensing of breeding establishments for dogs), other than under section 2 of that Act.

Slaughterhouses Act 1974 (c. 3)

73 An offence under section 4(5) of the Slaughterhouses Act 1974 (knacker's yard licences and applications for such licences).

National Health Service Act 1977 (c. 49)

74 An offence under paragraph 8(3) or 9(4) of Schedule 11 to the National Health Service Act 1977 (offences relating to the production of documents etc.).

Magistrates' Courts Act 1980 (c. 43)

75 An offence under section 84(3) of the Magistrates' Courts Act 1980 (making of false statement as to means).

Animal Health Act 1981 (c. 22)

76 An offence under paragraph 6 of Schedule 1 to the Animal Health Act 1981 (offences relating to the manufacture of veterinary therapeutic substances).

Fisheries Act 1981 (c. 29)

77 An offence under section 5(4) of the Fisheries Act 1981 (alteration of records or furnishing false information).

Civil Aviation Act 1982 (c. 16)

78 An offence under section 82 of the Civil Aviation Act 1982 (using an aircraft for advertising, etc.).

Mental Health Act 1983 (c. 20)

79 An offence under section 103 of the Mental Health Act 1983 (wrongful disclosure of a report made by a Visitor).

80 An offence under section 129 of that Act (obstruction).

Building Act 1984 (c. 55)

81 An offence under section 96(3) of the Building Act 1984 (wrongful disclosure of information).

Surrogacy Arrangements Act 1985 (c. 49)

82 An offence under section 2 of the Surrogacy Arrangements Act 1985 (negotiating surrogacy arrangements on a commercial basis, etc.).

Animals (Scientific Procedures) Act 1986 (c. 14)

83 An offence under section 22(3), 23 or 25(3) of the Animals (Scientific Procedures) Act 1986 (false statements and offences in relation to powers of entry).

Motor Cycle Noise Act 1987 (c. 34)

84 An offence under paragraph 1 of Schedule 1 to the Motor Cycle Noise Act 1987 (supply of exhaust systems etc. not complying with prescribed requirements).

Human Organ Transplants Act 1989 (c. 31)

85 An offence under section 2 of the Human Organ Transplants Act 1989 (restrictions on organ transplants).

Town and Country Planning Act 1990 (c. 8)

86 An offence under paragraph 14(4) of Schedule 15 to the Town and Country Planning Act 1990 (wrongful disclosure of information).

Environmental Protection Act 1990 (c. 43)

87 An offence under section 118(1)(g), (h) or (i) of the Environmental Protection Act 1990 (offences relating to inspection of genetically modified organisms).

Criminal Justice Act 1991 (c. 53)

88 An offence under section 20A of the Criminal Justice Act 1991 (false statements as to financial circumstances).

Deer Act 1991 (c. 54)

89 An offence under section 10(3) of the Deer Act 1991 (offences relating to sale and purchase etc. of venison).

Water Industry Act 1991 (c. 56)

90 An offence under section 206(2) of the Water Industry Act 1991 (wrongful disclosure of information).

91 An offence that falls within paragraph 5(5) of Schedule 6 to that Act (wrongful disclosure of information).

Social Security Administration Act 1992 (c. 5)

92 An offence under section 105 of the Social Security Administration Act 1992 (failure of person to maintain himself or another).

93 An offence under section 182 of that Act (illegal possession of documents).

Local Government Finance Act 1992 (c. 14)

94 An offence under section 27(5) of the Local Government Finance Act 1992 (false statements in relation to properties).

Trade Union and Labour Relations (Consolidation) Act 1992 (c. 52)

95 An offence under section 240 of the Trade Union and Labour Relations (Consolidation) Act 1992 (breach of contract involving injury to persons or property).

Merchant Shipping Act 1995 (c. 21)

96 An offence under section 57 of the Merchant Shipping Act 1995 (offences relating to merchant navy uniforms).

Reserve Forces Act 1996 (c. 14)

97 An offence under section 75(5) of the Reserve Forces Act 1996 (making false statements).

98 An offence under section 82(1) of that Act (offences in connection with regulations under sections 78 and 79 of that Act).

99 An offence under section 87(1) of that Act (offences in connection with claims for payment).

100 An offence under section 99 of that Act (false pretence of illegal absence).

101 An offence under paragraph 5(1) of Schedule 1 to that Act (false answers in attestation papers).

Housing Act 1996 (c. 52)

102 An offence under paragraph 23 or 24 of Schedule 1 to the Housing Act 1996 (contravening order not to part with money etc. held on behalf of a social landlord).

Broadcasting Act 1996 (c. 55)

103 An offence under section 144 of the Broadcasting Act 1996 (providing false information in connection with licences).

Breeding and Sale of Dogs (Welfare) Act 1999 (c. 11)

104 An offence under section 8 or 9(6) of the Breeding and Sale of Dogs (Welfare) Act 1999 (offences relating to the sale of dogs and connected matters).

Transport Act 2000 (c. 38)

105 An offence under section 82(2) of the Transport Act 2000 (wrongful disclosure of information).

SCHEDULE 26 Section 280(2)

INCREASE IN MAXIMUM TERM FOR CERTAIN SUMMARY OFFENCES

Railway Regulation Act 1840 (c. 97)

1 In section 16 of the Railway Regulation Act 1840 (obstructing officers or trespassing upon railway), for 'one month', there is substituted '51 weeks'.

Licensing Act 1872 (c. 94)

2 In section 12 of the Licensing Act 1872 (penalty for being found drunk), for 'one month' there is substituted '51 weeks'.

Regulation of Railways Act 1889 (c. 57)

3 In section 5 of the Regulation of Railways Act 1889 (avoiding payment of fares, etc.), in subsection (3), for 'three months' there is substituted '51 weeks'.

Witnesses (Public Inquiries) Protection Act 1892 (c. 64)

4 In section 2 of the Witnesses (Public Inquiries) Protection Act 1892 (persons obstructing or intimidating witnesses), for 'three months' there is substituted '51 weeks'.

Licensing Act 1902 (c. 28)

5 In section 2 of the Licensing Act 1902 (penalty for being drunk while in charge of a child), in subsection (1), for 'one month' there is substituted '51 weeks'.

Emergency Powers Act 1920 (c. 55)

6 In section 2 of the Emergency Powers Act 1920 (emergency regulations), in subsection (3), for 'three months' there is substituted '51 weeks'.

Judicial Proceedings (Regulation of Reports) Act 1926 (c. 61)

7 In section 1 of the Judicial Proceedings (Regulation of Reports) Act 1926 (restriction on publication of reports of judicial proceedings), in subsection (2), for 'four months' there is substituted '51 weeks'.

Public Order Act 1936 (1 Edw. 8 & 1 Geo. 6 c. 6)

8 In section 7 of the Public Order Act 1936 (enforcement), in subsection (2), for 'three months' there is substituted '51 weeks'.

Cinematograph Films (Animals) Act 1937 (c. 59)

9 In section 1 of the Cinematograph Films (Animals) Act 1937 (prohibition of films involving cruelty to animals), in subsection (3), for 'three months' there is substituted '51 weeks'.

House to House Collections Act 1939 (c. 44)

10 In section 8 of the House to House Collections Act 1939, in subsection (2), for 'three months' there is substituted '51 weeks'.

Fire Services Act 1947 (c. 41)

11 In section 31 of the Fire Services Act 1947 (false alarms of fire), in subsection (1), for 'three months' there is substituted '51 weeks'.

National Assistance Act 1948 (c. 29)

12(1) The National Assistance Act 1948 is amended as follows.

(2) In section 51 (failure to maintain), in subsection (3)(a) and (b), for 'three months' there is substituted '51 weeks'.

(3) In section 52 (false statements), in subsection (1), for 'three months' there is substituted '51 weeks'.

Docking and Nicking of Horses Act 1949 (c. 70)

13(1) The Docking and Nicking of Horses Act 1949 is amended as follows.

(2) In section 1 (prohibition of docking and nicking except in certain cases), in subsection (3), for 'three months' there is substituted '51 weeks'.

(3) In section 2 (restriction on landing docked horses) –

    (a) in subsection (3), and
    (b) in subsection (4),
for '3 months' there is substituted '51 weeks'.

Protection of Animals (Amendment) Act 1954 (c. 40)

14 In section 2 of the Protection of Animals (Amendment) Act 1954 (breach of disqualification order), for 'three months' there is substituted '51 weeks'.

Children and Young Persons (Harmful Publications) Act 1955 (c. 28)

15 In section 2 of the Children and Young Persons (Harmful Publications) Act 1955 (penalty for publishing certain works etc.), in subsection (1), for 'four months' there is substituted '51 weeks'.

Agriculture Act 1957 (c. 57)

16 In section 7 of the Agriculture Act 1957 (penalties) –

    (a) in subsection (1), for 'three months' there is substituted '51 weeks', and
    (b) in subsection (2), for 'one month' there is substituted '51 weeks'.

Animals (Cruel Poisons) Act 1962 (c. 26)

17 In section 1 of the Animals (Cruel Poisons) Act 1962 (offences and penalties under regulations), in paragraph (b), for 'three months' there is substituted '51 weeks'.

Plant Varieties and Seeds Act 1964 (c. 14)

18 In section 27 of the Plant Varieties and Seeds Act 1964 (tampering with samples), in subsection (1), for 'three months' there is substituted '51 weeks'.

Agriculture Act 1967 (c. 22)

19(1) The Agriculture Act 1967 is amended as follows.

(2) In section 6 (penalties), in subsection (4), for 'three months' there is substituted '51 weeks'.

(3) In section 21 (inquiry by Meat and Livestock Commission), in subsection (11), for 'three months' there is substituted '51 weeks'.

Firearms Act 1968 (c. 27)

20(1) Part 1 of Schedule 6 to the Firearms Act 1968 (prosecution and punishment of offences) is amended as follows.

(2) In the entry relating to section 3(6) of that Act (business and other transactions with firearms and ammunition), in the fourth column, for '3 months' there is substituted '51 weeks'.

(3) In the entry relating to section 6(3) of that Act (power to prohibit movement of arms and ammunition), in the fourth column, for '3 months' there is substituted '51 weeks'.

(4) In the entry relating to section 20(2) of that Act (trespassing with firearm), in the fourth column, for '3 months' there is substituted '51 weeks'.

(5) In the entry relating to section 22(1A) of that Act (acquisition and possession of firearms by minors), in the fourth column, for '3 months' there is substituted '51 weeks'.

(6) In the entry relating to section 25 of that Act (supplying firearm to person drunk or insane), in the fourth column, for '3 months' there is substituted '51 weeks'.

(7) In the entry relating to section 32C(6) of that Act (variation endorsement etc. of European documents), in the fourth column, for '3 months' there is substituted '51 weeks'.

(8) In the entry relating to section 42A of that Act (information as to transactions under visitors' permits), in the fourth column, for '3 months' there is substituted '51 weeks'.

(9) In the entry relating to section 47(2) of that Act (powers of constables to stop and search), in the fourth column, for '3 months' there is substituted '51 weeks'.

(10) In the entry relating to section 49(3) of that Act (police powers in relation to arms traffic), in the fourth column, for '3 months' there is substituted '51 weeks'.

Agriculture (Miscellaneous Provisions) Act 1968 (c. 34)

21 In section 7 of the Agriculture (Miscellaneous Provisions) Act 1968 (punishment of offences under Part 1), in subsection (1), for 'three months' there is substituted '51 weeks'.

Agriculture Act 1970 (c. 40)

22(1) The Agriculture Act 1970 is amended as follows.

(2) In section 68 (duty to give statutory statement), in subsection (4), for 'three months' there is substituted '51 weeks'.

(3) In section 69 (marking of material prepared for sale), in subsection (4), for 'three months' there is substituted '51 weeks'.

(4) In section 70 (use of names or expressions with prescribed meanings), in subsection (2), for 'three months' there is substituted '51 weeks'.

(5) In section 71 (particulars to be given of attributes if claimed to be present), in subsection (2), for 'three months' there is substituted '51 weeks'.

(6) In section 73 (deleterious ingredients in feeding stuff), in subsection (4), for 'three months' there is substituted '51 weeks'.

(7) In section 73A (unwholesome feeding stuff), in subsection (4), for 'three months' there is substituted '51 weeks'.

(8) In section 74A (regulations controlling the contents of feeding stuff), in subsection (3), for 'three months' there is substituted '51 weeks'.

(9) In section 79 (supplementary provision relating to samples and analysis), in subsection (10), for 'three months' there is substituted '51 weeks'.

(10) In section 83 (exercise of powers by inspectors), in subsection (3), for 'three months' there is substituted '51 weeks'.

(11) In section 106 (eradication of brucellosis), in subsection (7), for 'three months' there is substituted '51 weeks'.

Slaughterhouses Act 1974 (c. 3)

23(1) The Slaughterhouses Act 1974 is amended as follows.

(2) In section 20 (wrongful disclosure of information), in subsection (4), for 'three months' there is substituted '51 weeks'.

(3) In section 21 (obstruction), in subsection (1), for 'one month' there is substituted '51 weeks'.

(4) In section 23 (prosecution and punishment of offences), in subsection (2)(a), for 'three months' there is substituted '51 weeks'.

Criminal Law Act 1977 (c. 45)

24 In section 8 of the Criminal Law Act 1977 (trespassing with a weapon of offence), in subsection (3), for 'three months' there is substituted '51 weeks'.

Refuse Disposal (Amenity) Act 1978 (c. 3)

25 In section 2 of the Refuse Disposal (Amenity) Act 1978 (penalty for unauthorised dumping), in subsection (1), for 'three months' there is substituted '51 weeks'.

Customs and Excise Management Act 1979 (c. 2)

26(1) The Customs and Excise Management Act 1979 is amended as follows.

(2) In section 21 (control of movement of aircraft), in subsection (6), for '3 months' there is substituted '51 weeks'.

(3) In section 33 (power to inspect aircraft etc.), in subsection (4), for '3 months' there is substituted '51 weeks'.

(4) In section 34 (power to prevent flight of aircraft) –

(a) in subsection (2), and

(b) in subsection (3),

for '3 months' there is substituted '51 weeks'.

Licensed Premises (Exclusion of Certain Persons) Act 1980 (c. 32)

27 In section 2 of the Licensed Premises (Exclusion of Certain Persons) Act 1980 (penalty for non-compliance with an exclusion order), in subsection (1), for 'one month' there is substituted '51 weeks'.

Criminal Attempts Act 1981 (c. 47)

28 In section 9 of the Criminal Attempts Act 1981 (interference with vehicles), in subsection (3), for 'three months' there is substituted '51 weeks'.

British Nationality Act 1981 (c. 61)

29 In section 46 of the British Nationality Act 1981 (offences and proceedings), in subsection (1) for 'three months' there is substituted '51 weeks'.

Civil Aviation Act 1982 (c. 16)

30(1) The Civil Aviation Act 1982 is amended as follows.

(2) In section 44 (offences relating to the power to obtain rights over land), in subsection (10), for 'three months' there is substituted '51 weeks'.

(3) In section 75 (investigation of accidents), in subsection (5), for 'three months' there is substituted '51 weeks'.

Anatomy Act 1984 (c. 14)

31 In section 11 of the Anatomy Act 1984 (offences), in subsection (6), for '3 months' there is substituted '51 weeks'.

Public Health (Control of Disease) Act 1984 (c. 22)

32(1) The Public Health (Control of Disease) Act 1984 is amended as follows.

(2) In section 29 (letting of house after recent case of notifiable disease), in subsection (1), for 'one month' there is substituted '51 weeks'.

(3) In section 30 (duty on ceasing to occupy house after recent case of notifiable disease), in subsection (1), for 'one month' there is substituted '51 weeks'.

(4) In section 62 (powers of entry), in subsection (3), for '3 months' there is substituted '51 weeks'.

County Courts Act 1984 (c. 28)

33(1) The County Courts Act 1984 is amended as follows.

(2) In section 14 (penalty for assaulting officers), in subsection (1)(a), for '3 months' there is substituted '51 weeks'.

(3) In section 92 (penalty for rescuing goods seized), in subsection (1)(a), for 'one month' there is substituted '51 weeks.'

Animal Health and Welfare Act 1984 (c. 40)

34 In section 10 of the Animal Health and Welfare Act 1984 (artificial breeding of livestock), in subsection (6), for 'three months' there is substituted '51 weeks'.

Police and Criminal Evidence Act 1984 (c. 60)

35 In section 63C of the Police and Criminal Evidence Act 1984 (testing for presence of drugs), in subsection (1), for 'three months' there is substituted '51 weeks'.

Sporting Events (Control of Alcohol etc.) Act 1985 (c. 57)

36 In section 8 of the Sporting Events (Control of Alcohol etc.) Act 1985 (penalties for offences), in paragraph (b), for 'three months' there is substituted '51 weeks'.

Public Order Act 1986 (c. 64)

37(1) The Public Order Act 1986 is amended as follows.

(2) In section 12 (imposing conditions on public processions) –

    (a)   in subsection (8), and
    (b)   in subsection (10),

for '3 months' there is substituted '51 weeks'.

(3) In section 13 (prohibiting public processions) –

    (a)   in subsection (11), and
    (b)   in subsection (13),

for '3 months' there is substituted '51 weeks'.

(4) In section 14 (imposing conditions on public assemblies) –

    (a)   in subsection (8), and
    (b)   in subsection (10),

for '3 months' there is substituted '51 weeks'.

(5) In section 14B (offences in connection with trespassory assemblies and arrest therefor) –

    (a)   in subsection (5), and
    (b)   in subsection (7),

for '3 months' there is substituted '51 weeks'.

Road Traffic Offenders Act 1988 (c. 53)

38(1) Part 1 of Schedule 2 to the Road Traffic Offenders Act 1988 (prosecution and punishment of offenders) is amended as follows.

(2) In the entry relating to section 4(2) of the Road Traffic Act 1988 (driving, or being in charge, when under the influence of drink or drugs), in column 4, for '3 months' there is substituted '51 weeks'.

(3) In the entry relating to section 5(1)(b) of that Act (driving or being in charge of a motor vehicle with alcohol concentration above prescribed limit), in column 4, for '3 months' there is substituted '51 weeks'.

(4) In the entry relating to section 7 of that Act (provision of specimens for analysis), in column 4, for '3 months' there is substituted '51 weeks'.

(5) In the entry relating to section 7A of that Act (failing to allow specimen to be subjected to analysis), in column 4, for '3 months' there is substituted '51 weeks'.

Official Secrets Act 1989 (c. 6)

39 In section 10 of the Official Secrets Act 1989 (penalties), in subsection (2), for 'three months' there is substituted '51 weeks'.

Human Organ Transplants Act 1989 (c. 31)

40 In section 1 of the Human Organ Transplants Act 1989 (prohibition of commercial dealings in human organs), in subsection (5), for 'three months' there is substituted '51 weeks'.

Football Spectators Act 1989 (c. 37)

41 In section 2 of the Football Spectators Act 1989 (unauthorised attendance at designated football matches), in subsection (3), for 'one month' there is substituted '51 weeks'.

Food Safety Act 1990 (c. 16)

42 In section 35 of the Food Safety Act 1990 (punishment of offences), in subsection (1), for 'three months' there is substituted '51 weeks'.

Deer Act 1991 (c. 54)

43 In section 9 of the Deer Act 1991 (penalties for offences relating to deer), in subsection (1), for 'three months' there is substituted '51 weeks'.

Social Security Administration Act 1992 (c. 5)

44 In section 112 of the Social Security Administration Act 1992 (false representations for obtaining benefit etc.), in subsection (2), for '3 months' there is substituted '51 weeks'.

Criminal Justice and Public Order Act 1994 (c. 33)

45(1) The Criminal Justice and Public Order Act 1994 is amended as follows.

(2) In section 60 (failing to stop), in subsection (8), for 'one month' there is substituted '51 weeks'.

(3) In section 60AA (powers to require removal of disguises), in subsection (7), for 'one month' there is substituted '51 weeks'.

(4) In section 61 (power to remove trespasser on land), in subsection (4), for 'three months' there is substituted '51 weeks'.

(5) In section 62B (failure to comply with direction under section 62A: offences), in subsection (3), for '3 months' there is substituted '51 weeks'.

(6) In section 63 (powers to remove persons attending or preparing for a rave), in subsections (6) and (7B), for 'three months' there is substituted '51 weeks'.

(7) In section 68 (offence of aggravated trespass), in subsection (3), for 'three months' there is substituted '51 weeks'.

(8) In section 69 (powers to remove persons committing or participating in aggravated trespass), in subsection (3), for 'three months' there is substituted '51 weeks'.

London Local Authorities Act 1995 (c. x)

46 In section 24 of the London Local Authorities Act 1995 (enforcement), in subsection (1), for 'three months' there is substituted '51 weeks'.

Police Act 1996 (c. 16)

47 In section 89 of the Police Act 1996 (assaults on constables etc.), in subsection (2), for 'one month' there is substituted '51 weeks'.

Treasure Act 1996 (c. 24)

48 In section 8 of the Treasure Act 1996 (duty of finder of treasure to notify coroner), in subsection (3)(a), for 'three months' there is substituted '51 weeks'.

Education Act 1996 (c. 56)

49(1) The Education Act 1996 is amended as follows.

(2) In section 444 (failure to secure regular attendance at school), in subsection (8A)(b), for 'three months' there is substituted '51 weeks'.

(3) In section 559 (prohibition or restriction on employment of children), in subsection (4)(b), for 'one month' there is substituted '51 weeks'.

Government of Wales Act 1998 (c. 38)

50 In section 75 of the Government of Wales Act 1998 (witnesses and documents: supplementary), in subsection (3)(b), for 'three months' there is substituted '51 weeks'.

Access to Justice Act 1999 (c. 22)

51 In section 21 of the Access to Justice Act 1999 (misrepresentation etc), in subsection (2)(b), for 'three months' there is substituted '51 weeks'.

Greater London Authority Act 1999 (c. 29)

52 In section 64 of the Greater London Authority Act 1999 (failure to attend proceedings etc), in subsection (2)(b), for 'three months' there is substituted '51 weeks'.

Immigration and Asylum Act 1999 (c. 33)

53(1) The Immigration and Asylum Act 1999 is amended as follows.

(2) In section 105 (false representation), in subsection (2), for 'three months' there is substituted '51 weeks'.

(3) In section 108 (failure of sponsor to maintain), in subsection (2), for '3 months' there is substituted '51 weeks'.

Financial Services and Markets Act 2000 (c. 8)

54(1) The Financial Services and Markets Act 2000 is amended as follows.

(2) In section 177 (offences), in subsection (6), for 'three months' there is substituted '51 weeks'.

(3) In section 352 (offences), in subsection (5), for 'three months' there is substituted '51 weeks'.

Terrorism Act 2000 (c. 11)

55(1) The Terrorism Act 2000 is amended as follows.

(2) In section 36 (police powers), in subsection (4)(a), for 'three months' there is substituted '51 weeks'.

(3) In section 51 (offences in relation to parking), in subsection (6)(a), for 'three months' there is substituted '51 weeks'.

(4) In Schedule 5 (terrorist investigations: information) –

    (a) in paragraph 3(8)(a), and
    (b) in paragraph 15(5)(a),

for 'three months' there is substituted '51 weeks'.

(5) In Schedule 7 (ports and border controls), in paragraph 18(2)(a), for 'three months' there is substituted '51 weeks'.

Criminal Justice and Police Act 2001 (c. 16)

56(1) The Criminal Justice and Police Act 2001 is amended as follows.

(2) In section 25 (enforcement of closure orders) –

    (a) in subsection (3)(a), for 'one month' there is substituted '51 weeks', and
    (b) in subsections (4) and (5), for 'three months' there is substituted '51 weeks'.

(3) In section 42 (prevention of intimidation), in subsection (7), for 'three months' there is substituted '51 weeks'.

Police Reform Act 2002 (c. 30)

57 In section 46 of the Police Reform Act 2002 (offences against designated and accredited persons etc.), in subsection (2), for 'one month' there is substituted '51 weeks'.

Nationality, Immigration and Asylum Act 2002 (c. 41)

58 In section 137 of the Nationality, Immigration and Asylum Act 2002 (offences relating to the disclosure of information), in subsection (2)(a), for 'three months' there is substituted '51 weeks'.

Anti-social Behaviour Act 2003 (c. 38)

59 In section 40 of the Anti-social Behaviour Act 2003 (closure of noisy premises), in subsection (5)(a), for 'three months' there is substituted '51 weeks'.

SCHEDULE 27   Section 283

ENABLING POWERS: ALTERATION OF MAXIMUM PENALTIES ETC.

Plant Health Act 1967 (c. 8)

1(1) Section 3 of the Plant Health Act 1967 (control of spread of pests in Great Britain) is amended as follows.

(2) In subsection (4A), for 'three months' there is substituted 'the prescribed term'.

(3) After that subsection there is inserted –

'(4B) In subsection (4A) above, "the prescribed term" means –

(a) in relation to England and Wales, 51 weeks;
(b) in relation to Scotland, three months.'

Agriculture Act 1967 (c. 22)

2(1) Section 9 of the Agriculture Act 1967 (powers to meet future developments in livestock and livestock products industries) is amended as follows.

(2) In subsection (10), for 'three months' there is substituted 'the prescribed term'.

(3) After that subsection there is inserted –

'(10A) In subsection (10), "the prescribed term" means –

(a) in relation to England and Wales, 51 weeks;
(b) in relation to Scotland, three months.'

European Communities Act 1972 (c. 68)

3(1) Paragraph 1 of Schedule 2 to the European Communities Act 1972 (provisions as to powers conferred by section 2(2)) is amended as follows.

(2) In sub-paragraph (1)(d), for 'three months' there is substituted 'the prescribed term'.

(3) After sub-paragraph (2) there is inserted –

'(3) In sub-paragraph (1)(d), "the prescribed term" means –

(a) in relation to England and Wales, where the offence is a summary offence, 51 weeks;
(b) in relation to England and Wales, where the offence is triable either way, twelve months;
(c) in relation to Scotland and Northern Ireland, three months.'

Slaughterhouses Act 1974 (c. 3)

4 In section 38(5) of the Slaughterhouses Act 1974 (maximum penalties to be prescribed by regulations), the words 'or imprisonment for a term of three months or both' are omitted.

Anatomy Act 1984 (c. 14)

5(1) Section 11 of the Anatomy Act 1984 (offences) is amended as follows.

(2) In subsection (7), for '3 months' there is substituted 'the prescribed term'.

(3) After that subsection there is inserted –

'(7A) In subsection (7), "the prescribed term" means –

(a) in relation to England and Wales, 51 weeks;
(b) in relation to Scotland, 3 months.'

Environmental Protection Act 1990 (c. 43)

6(1) Section 141 of the Environmental Protection Act 1990 (power to prohibit or restrict the importation or exportation of waste) is amended as follows.

(2) In paragraph (g) of subsection (5), for 'six months' there is substituted 'the prescribed term'.

(3) After that subsection there is inserted –

'(5A) In subsection (5)(g), "the prescribed term" means –

  (a) in relation to England and Wales, where the offence is a summary offence, 51 weeks;
  (b) in relation to England and Wales, where the offence is triable either way, twelve months;
  (c) in relation to Scotland and Northern Ireland, six months.'

Scotland Act 1998 (c. 46)

7(1) Section 113 of the Scotland Act 1998 (subordinate legislation: scope of powers) is amended as follows.

(2) In paragraph (a) of subsection (10), for 'three months' there is substituted 'the prescribed term'.

(3) After that subsection there is inserted –

'(10A) In subsection (10)(a), "the prescribed term" means –

  (a) in relation to England and Wales, where the offence is a summary offence, 51 weeks;
  (b) in relation to England and Wales, where the offence is triable either way, twelve months;
  (c) in relation to Scotland and Northern Ireland, three months.'

Regulatory Reform Act 2001 (c. 6)

8(1) Section 3 of the Regulatory Reform Act 2001 (limitations on order-making power) is amended as follows.

(2) In paragraph (b) of subsection (3), for 'six months' there is substituted 'the prescribed term'.

(3) After that subsection there is inserted –

'(3A) In subsection (3)(b), "the prescribed term" means –

  (a) in relation to England and Wales, where the offence is a summary offence, 51 weeks;
  (b) in relation to England and Wales, where the offence is triable either way, twelve months;
  (c) in relation to Scotland and Northern Ireland, six months.'

SCHEDULE 28   Section 284

INCREASE IN PENALTIES FOR DRUG-RELATED OFFENCES

Misuse of Drugs Act 1971 (c. 38)

1(1) Schedule 4 to the Misuse of Drugs Act 1971 (prosecution and punishment of offences) is amended as follows.

(2) In column 6 of that Schedule (punishments for offences under that Act committed in relation to Class C drugs), in each of the following entries, for '5 years' there is substituted '14 years'.

(3) Those entries are the entries relating to the punishment, on conviction on indictment, of offences under the following provisions of that Act –

(a)   section 4(2) (production, or being concerned in the production, of a controlled drug),
(b)   section 4(3) (supplying or offering to supply a controlled drug or being concerned in the doing of either activity by another),
(c)   section 5(3) (having possession of a controlled drug with intent to supply it to another),
(d)   section 8 (being the occupier, or concerned in the management, of premises and permitting or suffering certain activities to take place there),
(e)   section 12(6) (contravention of direction prohibiting practitioner etc from possessing, supplying etc controlled drugs), and
(f)   section 13(3) (contravention of direction prohibiting practitioner etc from prescribing, supplying etc controlled drugs).

Customs and Excise Management Act 1979 (c. 2)

2 In Schedule 1 to the Customs and Excise Management Act 1979 (controlled drugs: variation of punishments for certain offences under that Act), in paragraph 2(c) (punishment on conviction on indictment of offences under that Act committed in relation to Class C drugs), for '5 years' there is substituted '14 years'.

Criminal Justice (International Co-operation) Act 1990 (c. 5)

3 In section 19 of the Criminal Justice (International Co-operation) Act 1990 (ships used for illicit traffic), in subsection (4)(c)(ii) (punishment on conviction on indictment of offences under that section committed in relation to Class C drugs), for 'five years' there is substituted 'fourteen years'.

SCHEDULE 29   Section 292

SENTENCING FOR FIREARMS OFFENCES IN NORTHERN IRELAND

1 The Firearms (Northern Ireland) Order 1981 (S.I. 1981/155 (N.I. 2)) is amended as follows.

2 In Article 2(2) (interpretation) after the definition of 'firearms dealer' there is inserted –

'"handgun" means any firearm which either has a barrel less than 30 centimetres in length or is less than 60 centimetres in length overall, other than an air weapon, a muzzle-loading gun or a firearm designed as signalling apparatus;'.

3 In Article 3(1) (requirement of firearm certificate) for sub-paragraph (a) there is substituted –

'(aa) has in his possession, or purchases or acquires, a handgun without holding a firearm certificate in force at the time, or otherwise than as authorised by such a certificate;

(ab) has in his possession, or purchases or acquires, any firearm, other than a handgun, without holding a firearm certificate in force at the time, or otherwise than as authorised by such a certificate; or'.

4 After Article 52 of that Order there is inserted –

'52A Minimum sentence for certain offences

(1) This Article applies where –

   (a) an individual is convicted of –
      (i)   an offence under Article 3(1)(aa),
      (ii)   an offence under Article 6(1)(a), (ab), (ac), (ad), (ae) or (c), or
      (iii) an offence under Article 6(1A)(a), and
   (b) the offence was committed after the commencement of this Article and at a time when he was aged 16 or over.

(2) The court shall –

   (a) in the case of an offence under Article 3(1)(aa) committed by a person who was aged 21 or over when he committed the offence, impose a sentence of imprisonment for a term of five years (with or without a fine), and

   (b) in any other case, impose an appropriate custodial sentence for a term of at least the required minimum term (with or without a fine)

unless (in any of those cases) the court is of the opinion that there are exceptional circumstances relating to the offence or to the offender which justify its not doing so.

(3) Where an offence is found to have been committed over a period of two or more days, or at some time during a period of two or more days, it shall be taken for the purposes of this Article to have been committed on the last of those days.

(4) In this Article –

"appropriate custodial sentence" means –
   (a) in the case of an offender who is aged 21 or over when convicted, a sentence of imprisonment, and
   (b) in the case of an offender who is aged under 21 at that time, a sentence of detention under section 5(1) of the Treatment of Offenders Act (Northern Ireland) 1968;
"the required minimum term" means –
   (a) in the case of an offender who was aged 21 or over when he committed the offence, five years, and
   (b) in the case of an offender who was aged under 21 at that time, three years.'

5 After Article 52A there is inserted –

'52B Power by order to exclude application of minimum sentence to those under 18

(1) The Secretary of State may by order –

   (a) amend Article 52A(1)(b) by substituting for the word "16" the word "18", and

(b) make such other provision as he considers necessary or expedient in consequence of, or in connection with, the provision made by virtue of sub-paragraph (a).

(2) The provision that may be made by virtue of paragraph (1)(b) includes, in particular, provision amending or repealing any statutory provision within the meaning of section 1(f) of the Interpretation Act (Northern Ireland) 1954 (whenever passed or made).

(3) An order under paragraph (1) shall be subject to annulment in pursuance of a resolution of either House of Parliament in like manner as a statutory instrument and section 5 of the Statutory Instruments Act 1946 shall apply accordingly.'

6(1) Schedule 2 (table of punishments) is amended as follows.

(2) For the entry relating to offences under Article 3(1) (purchase, acquisition or possession of firearm or ammunition without firearm certificate) there is substituted –

'Article 3(1)(aa)	Purchase, acquisition or possession of handgun without firearm certificate	Indictment	10 years or a fine, or both
Article 3(1)(ab)	Purchase, acquisition or possession without firearm certificate of firearm other than handgun	(a) Summary	1 year or a fine of the statutory maximum, or both
		(b) Indictment	5 years or a fine, or both
Article 3(1)(b)	Purchase, acquisition or possession of ammunition without firearm certificate	(a) Summary	1 year or a fine of the statutory maximum, or both
		(b) Indictment	5 years or a fine, or both'

(3) For the entries relating to offences under Article 6(1) (manufacture, dealing in or possession of prohibited weapons) and Article 6(1A) (possession of or dealing in other prohibited weapons) there is substituted –

'Article 6(1)(a), (ab), (ac), (ad), (ae) and (c)	Manufacture, dealing in or possession of prohibited weapons.	Indictment	10 years or a fine, or both

Article 6(1)(b)	Manfacture, dealing in or possession of prohibited weapon designed for discharge of noxious liquid etc.	(a) Summary	1 year or a fine of the statutory maximum, or both
		(b) Indictment	10 years or a fine, or both
Article 6 (1A)(a)	Possession of or dealing in firearm disguised as other object	Indictment	10 years or a fine, or both
Article 6(1A)(b), (c), (d), (e), (f) or (g)	Possession of or dealing in other prohibited weapons	(a) Summary	6 months or a fine of the statutory maximum, or both
		(b) Indictment	10 years or a fine, or both'

SCHEDULE 30   Section 299

DISQUALIFICATION FROM WORKING WITH CHILDREN

1 The Criminal Justice and Court Services Act 2000 (c. 43) is amended as follows.

2 After section 29 there is inserted –

'29A Disqualification at discretion of court: adults and juveniles

(1) This section applies where –

   (a) an individual is convicted of an offence against a child (whether or not committed when he was aged 18 or over),
   (b) the individual is sentenced by a senior court, and
   (c) no qualifying sentence is imposed in respect of the conviction.

(2) If the court is satisfied, having regard to all the circumstances, that it is likely that the individual will commit a further offence against a child, it may order the individual to be disqualified from working with children.

(3) If the court makes an order under this section, it must state its reasons for doing so and cause those reasons to be included in the record of the proceedings.

29B Subsequent application for order under section 28 or 29

(1) Where –

   (a) section 28 applies but the court has neither made an order under that section nor complied with subsection (6) of that section, or
   (b) section 29 applies but the court has not made an order under that section, and it appears to the prosecutor that the court has not considered the making of an order under that section,

the prosecutor may at any time apply to that court for an order under section 28 or 29.

(2) Subject to subsection (3), on an application under subsection (1) –

    (a) in a case falling within subsection (1)(a), the court –
        (i)   must make an order under section 28 unless it is satisfied as mentioned in subsection (5) of that section, and
        (ii) if it does not make an order under that section, must comply with subsection (6) of that section,
    (b) in a case falling within subsection (1)(b), the court –
        (i)   must make an order under section 29 if it is satisfied as mentioned in subsection (4) of that section, and
        (ii) if it does so, must comply with subsection (5) of that section.

(3) Subsection (2) does not enable or require an order under section 28 or 29 to be made where the court is satisfied that it had considered the making of an order under that section at the time when it imposed the qualifying sentence or made the relevant order.'

3(1) Section 30 (supplemental provisions) is amended as follows.

(2) In the heading for 'and 29' there is substituted 'to 29B'.

(3) In subsection (1) –

    (a) for 'and 29' there is substituted 'to 29B', and
    (b) in the definition of 'qualifying sentence', after paragraph (d) there is inserted –

    '(dd) a sentence of detention under section 198 or 200 of the Criminal Justice Act 2003,'.

(4) In subsection (5) –

    (a) in paragraph (a), for 'or 29' there is substituted ', 29 or 29A',
    (b) after paragraph (b) there is inserted –

    '(c) in relation to an individual to whom section 29A applies and on whom a sentence has been passed, references to his sentence are to that sentence.'

4 In section 31 (appeals), in subsection (1), after paragraph (b) there is inserted –

    '(c) where an order is made under section 29A, as if the order were a sentence passed on him for the offence of which he has been convicted.'

5(1) Section 33 (conditions for application under section 32) is amended as follows.

(2) In subsection (6), after paragraph (d) there is inserted –

    '(e) in relation to an individual not falling within any of paragraphs (a) to (d), the day on which the disqualification order is made.'.

(3) For subsection (8) there is substituted –

    '(8) In subsection (7) "detention" means detention (or detention and training) –

    (a) under any sentence or order falling within paragraphs (b) to (f) of the definition of "qualifying sentence" in section 30(1), or
    (b) under any sentence or order which would fall within those paragraphs if it were for a term or period of 12 months or more.'.

SCHEDULE 31 Section 300

DEFAULT ORDERS: MODIFICATION OF PROVISIONS RELATING TO
COMMUNITY ORDERS

General

1 Any reference to the offender is, in relation to a default order, to be read as a
reference to the person in default.

Unpaid work requirement

2(1) In its application to a default order, section 199 (unpaid work requirement) is
modified as follows.

(2) In subsection (2), for paragraphs (a) and (b) there is substituted –

'(a) not less than 20 hours, and
 (b) in the case of an amount in default which is specified in the first column of
      the following Table, not more than the number of hours set out opposite
      that amount in the second column.

TABLE

Amount	Number of Hours
An amount not exceeding £200	40 hours
An amount exceeding £20 but not exceeding £500	60 hours
An amount exceeding £500	100 hours'

(3) Subsection (5) is omitted.

Curfew requirement

3(1) In its application to a default order, section 204 (curfew requirement) is modified as
follows.

(2) After subsection (2) there is inserted –

'(2A) In the case of an amount in default which is specified in the first column of the
following Table, the number of days on which the person in default is subject to the
curfew requirement must not exceed the number of days set out opposite that
amount in the second column.

TABLE

Amount	Number of days
An amount not exceeding £200	20 days
An amount exceeding £200 but not exceeding £500	30 days
An amount exceeding £500 but not exceeding £1,000	60 days
An amount exceeding £1,000 but not exceeding £2,500	90 days
An amount exceeding £2,500	180 days'

Enforcement, revocation and amendment of default order

4(1) In its application to a default order, Schedule 8 (breach, revocation or amendment of community orders) is modified as follows.

(2) Any reference to the offence in respect of which the community order was made is to be taken to be a reference to the default in respect of which the default order was made.

(3) Any power of the court to revoke the community order and deal with the offender for the offence is to be taken to be a power to revoke the default order and deal with him in any way in which the court which made the default order could deal with him for his default in paying the sum in question.

(4) In paragraph 4 the reference to the Crown Court is to be taken as a reference to a magistrates' court.

(5) The following provisions are omitted –

   (a) paragraph 9(1)(c), (5) and (8),
   (b) paragraph 12,
   (c) paragraph 13(5),
   (d) paragraph 15,
   (e) paragraph 17(5),
   (f) paragraph 21(4), and
   (g) paragraph 23(2)(b).

Power to alter amount of money or number of hours or days

5 The Secretary of State may by order amend paragraph 2 or 3 by substituting for any reference to an amount of money or a number of hours or days there specified a reference to such other amount or number as may be specified in the order.

Transfer of default orders to Scotland or Northern Ireland

6 In its application to a default order, Schedule 9 (transfer of community orders to Scotland or Northern Ireland) is modified as follows.

7 After paragraph 8 there is inserted –

'8A Nothing in paragraph 8 affects the application of section 300(7) to a default order made or amended in accordance with paragraph 1 or 3.'

8 In paragraph 10, after paragraph (b) there is inserted –

'(bb) any power to impose a fine on the offender.'

SCHEDULE 32   Section 304

AMENDMENTS RELATING TO SENTENCING

PART 1

GENERAL

Piracy Act 1837 (c. 88)

1 Section 3 of the Piracy Act 1837 (punishment for offence under certain repealed Acts relating to piracy) shall cease to have effect.

Children and Young Persons Act 1933 (c. 12)

2(1) Section 49 of the Children and Young Persons Act 1933 (restrictions on reports of proceedings in which young persons are concerned) is amended as follows.

(2) In subsection (4A)(d), for 'section 62(3) of the Powers of Criminal Courts (Sentencing) Act 2000' there is substituted 'section 222(1)(d) or (e) of the Criminal Justice Act 2003'.

(3) In subsection (11) –

(a) in the definition of 'sexual offence', for 'has the same meaning as in the Powers of Criminal Courts (Sentencing) Act 2000' there is substituted 'means an offence listed in Part 2 of Schedule 15 to the Criminal Justice Act 2003', and
(b) in the definition of 'violent offence', for 'has the same meaning as in the Powers of Criminal Courts (Sentencing) Act 2000' there is substituted 'means an offence listed in Part 1 of Schedule 15 to the Criminal Justice Act 2003'.

Prison Act 1952 (c. 52)

3 In section 53 of the Prison Act 1952 (interpretation), for 'section 62 of the Powers of Criminal Courts (Sentencing) Act 2000' there is substituted 'section 221 of the Criminal Justice Act 2003'.

Criminal Justice Act 1967 (c. 80)

4 The Criminal Justice Act 1967 is amended as follows.

5 In section 32 (amendments of Costs in Criminal Cases Act 1952), in subsection (3)(a), for 'make an order under paragraph 5 of Schedule 2 to the Powers of Criminal Courts (Sentencing) Act 2000 (probation orders requiring treatment for mental condition) or' there is substituted 'include in a community order (within the meaning of Part 12 of the Criminal Justice Act 2003) a mental health requirement under section 207 of that Act or make an order under'.

6 In section 104 (general provisions as to interpretation) –

(a) in subsection (1), the definition of 'suspended sentence' is omitted, and
(b) subsection (2) is omitted.

Criminal Appeal Act 1968 (c. 19)

7 The Criminal Appeal Act 1968 is amended as follows.

8(1) Section 10 (appeal against sentence in cases dealt with by Crown Court otherwise than on conviction on indictment) is amended as follows.

(2) In subsection (2) –

(a) in paragraph (b), for 'or a community order within the meaning of the Powers of Criminal Courts (Sentencing) Act 2000' there is substituted 'a youth community order within the meaning of the Powers of Criminal Courts (Sentencing) Act 2000 or a community order within the meaning of Part 12 of the Criminal Justice Act 2003', and

(b) paragraph (c) and the word 'or' immediately preceding it are omitted.

9 In section 11 (supplementary provisions as to appeal against sentence), subsection (4) is omitted.

10 In Schedule 2 (procedural and other provisions applicable on order for retrial), in paragraph 2(4), for the words from the beginning to 'apply' there is substituted 'Section 240 of the Criminal Justice Act 2003 (crediting of periods of remand in custody: terms of imprisonment and detention) shall apply'.

Firearms Act 1968 (c. 27)

11 The Firearms Act 1968 is amended as follows.

12(1) Section 21 (possession of firearms by persons previously convicted of crime) is amended as follows.

(2) In subsection (2A), after paragraph (c) there is inserted –

'(d) in the case of a person who has been subject to a sentence of imprisonment to which an intermittent custody order under section 183(1)(b) of the Criminal Justice Act 2003 relates, the date of his final release.'

(3) After subsection (2A) there is inserted –

'(2B) A person who is serving a sentence of imprisonment to which an intermittent custody order under section 183 of the Criminal Justice Act 2003 relates shall not during any licence period specified for the purposes of subsection (1)(b)(i) of that section have a firearm or ammunition in his possession.'.

(4) In subsection (3)(b), for 'probation order' there is substituted 'community order'.

(5) After subsection (3) there is inserted –

'(3ZA) In subsection (3)(b) above, "community order" means –

(a) a community order within the meaning of Part 12 of the Criminal Justice Act 2003 made in England and Wales, or

(b) a probation order made in Scotland.'

(6) In subsection (6), after '(2)' there is inserted ', (2B)'.

13(1) Section 52 (forfeiture and disposal of firearms; cancellation of certificate by convicting court) is amended as follows.

(2) In subsection (1)(c), for 'probation order' there is substituted 'community order'.

(3) After subsection (1) there is inserted –

'(1A) In subsection (1)(c) "community order" means –

(a) a community order within the meaning of Part 12 of the Criminal Justice Act 2003 made in England and Wales, or
(b) a probation order made in Scotland.'

Social Work (Scotland) Act 1968 (c. 49)

14 In section 94 of the Social Work (Scotland) Act 1968 (interpretation), in the definition of 'probation order' in subsection (1), for 'community rehabilitation order' there is substituted 'community order within the meaning of Part 12 of the Criminal Justice Act 2003'.

Children and Young Persons Act 1969 (c. 54)

15 In section 23 of the Children and Young Persons Act 1969 (remands and committals to local authority accommodation), for the definition of 'sexual offence' and "violent offence" in subsection (12) there is substituted –

' "sexual offence" means an offence specified in Part 2 of Schedule 15 to the Criminal Justice Act 2003;
"violent offence" means murder or an offence specified in Part 1 of Schedule 15 to the Criminal Justice Act 2003;'.

Immigration Act 1971 (c. 77)

16 In section 7 of the Immigration Act 1971 (exemption from deportation for certain existing residents), in subsection (4), for 'section 67 of the Criminal Justice Act 1967' there is substituted 'section 240 of the Criminal Justice Act 2003'.

Thames Barrier and Flood Prevention Act 1972 (c. xiv)

17 In section 56 of the Thames Barrier and Flood Prevention Act 1972 (orders for carrying out certain defence works), in subsection (3)(a)(ii), for 'six months' there is substituted '12 months'.

Rehabilitation of Offenders Act 1974 (c. 53)

18(1) Section 5 of the Rehabilitation of Offenders Act 1974 (rehabilitation periods for particular offences) is amended as follows.

(2) In subsection (1) –

(a) at the end of paragraph (e), there is inserted 'and', and
(b) after that paragraph, there is inserted the following paragraph –

'(f) a sentence of imprisonment for public protection under section 225 of the Criminal Justice Act 2003, a sentence of detention for public protection under section 226 of that Act or an extended sentence under section 227 or 228 of that Act'

(3) In subsection (4A), after the words 'probation order' there is inserted 'or a community order under section 177 of the Criminal Justice Act 2003'.

Armed Forces Act 1976 (c. 52)

19(1) Section 8 of the Armed Forces Act 1976 (powers of Standing Civilian Courts in relation to civilians) is amended as follows.

(2) In subsection (1)(a), for 'six months' there is substituted 'twelve months'.

(3) In subsection (2), for '12 months' there is substituted '65 weeks'.

Bail Act 1976 (c. 63)

20 The Bail Act 1976 is amended as follows.

21(1) Section 2 (other definitions) is amended as follows.

(2) In subsection (1)(d) –

    (a) the words 'placing the offender on probation or' are omitted, and
    (b) for 'him' there is substituted 'the offender'.

(3) In subsection (2), in the definition of 'probation hostel', for the words from 'by' onwards there is substituted 'by a community order under section 177 of the Criminal Justice Act 2003'.

22 In section 4 (general right to bail of accused persons and others), in subsection (3), for the words from 'to be dealt with' onwards there is substituted 'or the Crown Court to be dealt with under –

    (a) Part 2 of Schedule 3 to the Powers of Criminal Courts (Sentencing) Act 2000 (breach of certain youth community orders), or
    (b) Part 2 of Schedule 8 to the Criminal Justice Act 2003 (breach of requirement of community order).'

23 In Part 3 of Schedule 1 (interpretation), in the definition of 'default' in paragraph 4, for the words from 'Part II' onwards there is substituted 'Part 2 of Schedule 8 to the Criminal Justice Act 2003 (breach of requirement of order)'.

Criminal Law Act 1977 (c. 45)

24 In section 3 of the Criminal Law Act 1977 (penalties for conspiracy), in subsection (1), for 'section 127 of the Powers of Criminal Courts (Sentencing) Act 2000' there is substituted 'section 163 of the Criminal Justice Act 2003'.

Magistrates' Courts Act 1980 (c. 43)

25 The Magistrates' Courts Act 1980 is amended as follows.

26 In section 11 (non appearance of accused), in subsection (3), for 'section 119 of the Powers of Criminal Courts (Sentencing) Act 2000' there is substituted 'paragraph 8(2)(a) or (b) of Schedule 12 to the Criminal Justice Act 2003'.

27 In section 33 (maximum penalties on summary conviction in pursuance of section 22), in subsection (1)(a), for '3 months' there is substituted '51 weeks'.

28 In section 85 (power to remit fine), in subsection (2A), for 'section 35(2)(a) or (b) of the Crime (Sentences) Act 1997' there is substituted 'section 300(2) of the Criminal Justice Act 2003'.

29 In section 131 (remand of accused already in custody), after subsection (2) there is inserted –

    '(2A) Where the accused person is serving a sentence of imprisonment to which an intermittent custody order under section 183 of the Criminal Justice Act 2003 relates, the reference in subsection (2) to the expected date of his release is to be read as a reference to the expected date of his next release on licence.'.

30 In section 133 (consecutive terms of imprisonment), in subsection (1), for 'Subject to section 84 of the Powers of Criminal Courts (Sentencing) Act 2000,' there is substituted 'Subject to section 265 of the Criminal Justice Act 2003,'.

Law Reform (Miscellaneous Provisions) (Scotland) Act 1980 (c. 55)

31 In Schedule 1 to the Law Reform (Miscellaneous Provisions) (Scotland) Act 1980 (ineligibility for and disqualification and excusal from jury service), in Part 2, in paragraph (bb), for sub-paragraph (v) there is substituted –

> '(v) a community order within the meaning of section 177 of the Criminal Justice Act 2003;
> (va) a youth community order as defined by section 33 of the Powers of Criminal Courts (Sentencing) Act 2000;'.

Public Passenger Vehicles Act 1981 (c. 14)

32(1) In Schedule 3 to the Public Passenger Vehicles Act 1981 (supplementary provisions as to qualifications for PSV operators licence), paragraph 1 is amended as follows.

(2) In sub-paragraph (4)(a), for 'a community service order for more than sixty hours' there is substituted 'a community order requiring the offender to perform unpaid work for more than sixty hours'.

(3) In sub-paragraph (6), for the words from "a community' onwards there is substituted "a community order' means an order under section 177 of the Criminal Justice Act 2003, a community punishment order made before the commencement of that section or a community service order under the Community Service by Offenders (Scotland) Act 1978'.

Criminal Attempts Act 1981 (c. 47)

33 In section 4 of the Criminal Attempts Act 1981 (trials and penalties), in subsection (5)(b), for sub-paragraph (ii) there is substituted –

> '(ii) in section 154(1) and (2) (general limit on magistrates' court's powers to impose imprisonment) of the Criminal Justice Act 2003.'.

Criminal Justice Act 1982 (c. 48)

34 The Criminal Justice Act 1982 is amended as follows.

35 In section 32 (early release of prisoners), in subsection (1)(a), after 'life' there is inserted ', imprisonment for public protection under section 225 of the Criminal Justice Act 2003 or an extended sentence under section 227 of that Act'.

36(1) Part 3 of Schedule 13 (reciprocal arrangements (Northern Ireland): persons residing in England and Wales or Scotland) is amended as follows.

(2) In paragraph 7 –

(a) in sub-paragraph (2)(b), for 'such orders' there is substituted 'an unpaid work requirement of a community order (within the meaning of Part 12 of the Criminal Justice Act 2003)', and

(b) in sub-paragraph (3)(b), for the words from 'community service orders' onwards there is substituted 'community orders within the meaning of Part 12 of the Criminal Justice Act 2003 conferred on responsible officers by that Part of that Act.'.

(3) For paragraph 9(3) there is substituted –

'(3) Subject to the following provisions of this paragraph –

(a) a community service order made or amended in the circumstances specified in paragraph 7 above shall be treated as if it were a community order made in England and Wales under section 177 of the Criminal Justice Act 2003 and the provisions of Part 12 of that Act (so far as relating to such orders) shall apply accordingly; and

(b) a community service order made or amended in the circumstances specified in paragraph 8 above shall be treated as if it were a community service order made in Scotland and the legislation relating to community service orders in Scotland shall apply accordingly.'

(4) In paragraph 9(4)(a), after 'community service orders' there is inserted 'or, as the case may be, community orders (within the meaning of Part 12 of the Criminal Justice Act 2003)'.

(5) In paragraph 9(5), after 'a community service order' there is inserted 'or, as the case may be, a community order (within the meaning of Part 12 of the Criminal Justice Act 2003)'.

(6) In paragraph 9(6) –

(a) after 'community service orders', where first occurring, there is inserted 'or, as the case may be, community orders (within the meaning of Part 12 of the Criminal Justice Act 2003)', and

(b) in paragraph (b)(i), for 'the Powers of Criminal Courts (Sentencing) Act 2000' there is substituted 'Part 12 of the Criminal Justice Act 2003'.

Mental Health Act 1983 (c. 20)

37 The Mental Health Act 1983 is amended as follows.

38 In section 37 (powers of courts to order hospital admission or guardianship) –

(a) in subsection (1), the words 'or falls to be imposed under section 109(2) of the Powers of Criminal Courts (Sentencing) Act 2000' are omitted,

(b) for subsections (1A) and (1B) there is substituted -

'(1A) In the case of an offence the sentence for which would otherwise fall to be imposed –

(a) under section 51A(2) of the Firearms Act 1968,

(b) under section 110(2) or 111(2) of the Powers of Criminal Courts (Sentencing) Act 2000, or

(c) under any of sections 225 to 228 of the Criminal Justice Act 2003,

nothing in those provisions shall prevent a court from making an order under subsection (1) above for the admission of the offender to a hospital.

(1B) References in subsection (1A) above to a sentence falling to be imposed under any of the provisions mentioned in that subsection are to be read in accordance with section 305(4) of the Criminal Justice Act 2003.'

(c) in subsection (8), for 'probation order' there is substituted 'community order (within the meaning of Part 12 of the Criminal Justice Act 2003)'.

39 In section 45A (powers of higher courts to direct hospital admission), in subsection (1)(b), the words from 'except' to '1997' are omitted.

Repatriation of Prisoners Act 1984 (c. 47)

40 The Repatriation of Prisoners Act 1984 is amended as follows.

41 In section 2 (transfer out of the United Kingdom), in subsection (4)(b), for sub-paragraph (i) there is substituted –

'(i)   released on licence under section 28(5) of the Crime (Sentences) Act 1997 or under section 244 or 246 of the Criminal Justice Act 2003; or'.

42 In section 3 (transfer into the United Kingdom), subsection (9) is omitted.

43(1) The Schedule (operation of certain enactments in relation to the prisoner) is amended as follows in relation to prisoners repatriated to England and Wales.

(2) In paragraph 2, for sub-paragraphs (1A) and (2) there is substituted –

'(2) If the warrant specifies a period to be taken into account for the purposes of this paragraph, the amount of time the prisoner has served shall, so far only as the question whether he has served a particular part of a life sentence is concerned, be deemed to be increased by that period.

(3) Where the prisoner's sentence is for a term of less than twelve months, Chapter 6 of Part 12 of the Criminal Justice Act 2003 shall apply as if the sentence were for a term of twelve months or more.

(4) In this paragraph –

"the enactments relating to release on licence" means section 28(5) and (7) of the Crime (Sentences) Act 1997 and Chapter 6 of Part 12 of the Criminal Justice Act 2003;
"sentence", means the provision included in the warrant which is equivalent to sentence.'.

(3) Paragraph 3 is omitted.

Police and Criminal Evidence Act 1984 (c. 60)

44 In section 38 of the Police and Criminal Evidence Act 1984 (duties of custody officer after charge), for the definitions of 'sexual offence' and 'violent offence' in subsection (6A) there is substituted –

'"sexual offence" means an offence specified in Part 2 of Schedule 15 to the Criminal Justice Act 2003;
"violent offence" means murder or an offence specified in Part 1 of that Schedule;'.

Criminal Justice Act 1988 (c. 33)

45 The Criminal Justice Act 1988 is amended as follows.

46 In section 36 (reviews of sentencing), in subsection (2), for the words from 'erred in law' onwards there is substituted –

'(a)   erred in law as to his powers of sentencing; or

    (b)   failed to impose a sentence required by –
        (i)   section 51A(2) of the Firearms Act 1968;
        (ii)   section 110(2) or 111(2) of the Powers of Criminal Courts (Sentencing) Act 2000; or
        (iii)   any of sections 225 to 228 of the Criminal Justice Act 2003.'

47 In section 50 (suspended and partly suspended sentences on certain civilians in courts-martial and Standing Civilian Courts), in subsection (3)(b)(i), for 'Powers of Criminal Courts (Sentencing) Act 2000' there is substituted 'Criminal Justice Act 2003'.

Firearms (Amendment) Act 1988 (c. 45)

48 The Firearms (Amendment) Act 1988 is amended as follows.

49 In section 1 (prohibited weapons and ammunition), in subsection (4A) after paragraph (b) there is inserted –

    '(bb) may amend subsection (1A)(a) of section 91 of the Powers of Criminal Courts (Sentencing) Act 2000 (offenders under 18 convicted of certain serious offences: power to detain for specified period) so as to include a reference to any provision added by the order to section 5(1) of the principal Act,
    (bc) may amend section 50(5A)(a), 68(4A)(a) or 170(4A)(a) of the Customs and Excise Management Act 1979 (offences relating to improper importation or exportation) so as to include a reference to anything added by the order to section 5(1) of the principal Act,'.

50 In section 27(4) (which relates to Northern Ireland), after 'Except for' there is inserted 'section 1, so far as enabling provision to be made amending the Customs and Excise Management Act 1979, and'.

Road Traffic Act 1988 (c. 52)

51 In section 164 of the Road Traffic Act 1988 (power of constables to require production of driving licence and in certain cases statement of date of birth), in subsection (5), for 'section 40 of the Crime (Sentences) Act 1997' there is substituted 'section 301 of the Criminal Justice Act 2003'.

Road Traffic Offenders Act 1988 (c. 53)

52 The Road Traffic Offenders Act 1988 is amended as follows.

53 In section 27 (production of licence), in subsection (3), for 'section 40 of the Crime (Sentences) Act 1997' there is substituted 'section 301 of the Criminal Justice Act 2003'.

54 In section 46 (combination of disqualification and endorsement with probation orders and orders for discharge), in subsection (1), paragraph (a) and the word 'or' following it shall cease to have effect.

Football Spectators Act 1989 (c. 37)

55 The Football Spectators Act 1989 is amended as follows.

56 In section 7 (disqualification for membership of scheme), subsection (9) is omitted.

57 In section 14E (banning orders: general), after subsection (6) there is inserted –

    '(7) A person serving a sentence of imprisonment to which an intermittent custody order under section 183 of the Criminal Justice Act 2003 relates is to be treated for the purposes of this section as having been detained in legal custody until his final release; and accordingly any reference in this section to release is, in relation to a person serving such a sentence, a reference to his final release.'

58 In section 18 (information), after subsection (4) there is inserted –

'(5) In relation to a person serving a sentence of imprisonment to which an intermittent custody order under section 183 of the Criminal Justice Act 2003 relates, any reference in this section to his detention or to his release shall be construed in accordance with section 14E(7).'

Children Act 1989 (c. 41)

59 The Children Act 1989 is amended as follows.

60(1) Section 68 (persons disqualified from being foster parents) is amended as follows.

(2) In subsection (2)(d), the words 'a probation order has been made in respect of him or he has been' are omitted.

(3) After subsection (2) there is inserted –

'(2A) A conviction in respect of which a probation order was made before 1st October 1992 (which would not otherwise be treated as a conviction) is to be treated as a conviction for the purposes of subsection (2)(d).'

61(1) In Schedule 9A (child minding and day care for young children), paragraph 4 is amended as follows.

(2) In sub-paragraph (2)(g), the words 'placed on probation or' are omitted.

(3) At the end there is inserted –

'(7) A conviction in respect of which a probation order was made before 1st October 1992 (which would not otherwise be treated as a conviction) is to be treated as a conviction for the purposes of this paragraph.'.

Criminal Justice Act 1991 (c. 53)

62 The Criminal Justice Act 1991 is amended as follows.

63 Section 65 (supervision of young offenders after release) is omitted.

64(1) Schedule 3 (reciprocal enforcement of certain orders) is amended as follows.

(2) In paragraph 10(3)(d), for the words from 'paragraph 3 of Schedule 2' onwards there is substituted 'section 201 of the Criminal Justice Act 2003'.

(3) In paragraph 11(2) –

    (a) in paragraph (a) –
        (i)   for 'probation order' there is substituted 'community order', and
        (ii)   after 'England and Wales' there is inserted 'under section 177 of the Criminal Justice Act 2003', and
    (b) for paragraph (b) there is substituted –

    '(b) the provisions of Part 12 of that Act (so far as relating to such orders) shall apply accordingly.'.

(4) In paragraph 11(3), for paragraphs (a) and (b) there is substituted –

'(a) the requirements of Part 12 of the Criminal Justice Act 2003 relating to community orders (within the meaning of that Part);

(b) the powers of the home court under Schedule 8 to that Act, as modified by this paragraph; and'.

(5) In paragraph 11(4), for the words from 'probation order made by a court' onwards there is substituted 'community order made by a court in England and Wales under section 177 of the Criminal Justice Act 2003, except a power conferred by paragraph 9(1)(b) or (c) or 13(2) of Schedule 8 to that Act'.

(6) In paragraph 11(5), for 'the Powers of Criminal Courts (Sentencing) Act 2000' there is substituted 'Part 12 of the Criminal Justice Act 2003'.

Aggravated Vehicle-Taking Act 1992 (c. 11)

65 In section 1 of the Aggravated Vehicle-Taking Act 1992 (new offence of aggravated vehicle taking), in subsection (2)(a), for 'section 127 of the Powers of Criminal Courts (Sentencing) Act 2000' there is substituted 'section 163 of the Criminal Justice Act 2003'.

Prisoners and Criminal Proceedings (Scotland) Act 1993 (c. 9)

66 In section 10 of the Prisoners and Criminal Proceedings (Scotland) Act 1993 (life prisoners transferred to Scotland) –

(a) in subsection (1) –

(i) in paragraph (a), sub-paragraph (i), and the succeeding 'or', are omitted, and

(ii) after paragraph (a)(ii) there is inserted 'or

(iii) subsections (5) to (8) of section 28 (early release of life prisoners to whom that section applies) of the Crime (Sentences) Act 1997 (c. 43) (in this section, the "1997 Act") apply by virtue of an order made under section 28(2)(b) of that Act (while that provision was in force) or an order made under section 269(2) of, or paragraph 3(1)(a) of Schedule 22 to, the Criminal Justice Act 2003;', and

(iii) for '28(2)(b) or 82A(2) or paragraph' there is substituted '82A(2), 28(2)(b) or 269(2) or paragraph 3(1)(a) or';

(b) after subsection (1) there is inserted –

'(1AA) This Part of this Act, except section 2(9), applies also to a transferred life prisoner –

(a) who is transferred from England and Wales on or after the date on which section 269 of the Criminal Justice Act 2003 comes into force,

(b) in relation to whom paragraph 3 of Schedule 22 to that Act applies by virtue of paragraph 2(a) of that Schedule, but

(c) in respect of whom, under the paragraph so applying, no order has been made,

as if the prisoner were a life prisoner within the meaning of section 2 of this Act and the punishment part of his sentence within the meaning of that section were the notified minimum term defined by paragraph 3(4) of that Schedule.'; and

(c) in subsection (5)(b) –

(i) for 'the Crime (Sentences) Act 1997' there is substituted 'the 1997 Act', and (ii)　after the words 'Powers of Criminal Courts (Sentencing) Act 2000 (c. 6)' there is inserted 'section 269(2) of, or paragraph 3(1)(a) of Schedule 22 to, the Criminal Justice Act 2003,'.

Criminal Justice and Public Order Act 1994 (c. 33)

67 In section 25 of the Criminal Justice and Public Order Act 1994 (no bail for defendants charged with or convicted of homicide or rape after previous conviction of such offences), in paragraph (c) of the definition of 'conviction' in subsection (5) –

(a)　the words 'placing the offender on probation or' are omitted, and
(b)　for 'him' there is substituted 'the offender'.

Goods Vehicles (Licensing of Operators) Act 1995 (c. 23)

68(1) In Schedule 3 to the Goods Vehicles (Licensing of Operators) Act 1995 (qualifications for standard licence), paragraph 3 is amended as follows.

(2) In sub-paragraph (2)(a), for 'exceeding three months' there is substituted 'of 12 months or more or, before the commencement of section 181 of the Criminal Justice Act 2003, a term exceeding 3 months'.

(3) In sub-paragraph (2)(c), for 'community service order' there is substituted 'community order'.

(4) For sub-paragraph (3)(b), there is substituted –

'(b)　"community order" means a community order under section 177 of the Criminal Justice Act 2003, a community punishment order made under section 46 of the Powers of Criminal Courts (Sentencing) Act 2000 or a community service order under the Community Service by Offenders (Scotland) Act 1978.'.

Criminal Procedure (Scotland) Act 1995 (c. 46)

69 The Criminal Procedure (Scotland) Act 1995 is amended as follows.

70(1) Section 234 (probation orders: persons residing in England and Wales) is amended as follows.

(2) In subsection (1), the words after paragraph (b) are omitted.

(3) For subsection (2) there is substituted –

'(2) Subsection (1) above applies to any probation order made under section 228 unless the order includes requirements which are more onerous than those which a court in England and Wales could impose on an offender under section 177 of the Criminal Justice Act 2003.'

(4) In subsection (3), the words from 'or to vary' to 'one hundred' are omitted.

(5) In subsection (4) –

(a)　in paragraph (a) –
(i)　for 'paragraph 5(3) of Schedule 2 to the 2000 Act' there is substituted 'section 207(2) of the Criminal Justice Act 2003',
(ii)　for 'or, as the case may be, community rehabilitation orders' there is substituted 'or, as the case may be, community orders under Part 12 of that Act', and

      (iii)   for 'paragraph 5 of the said Schedule 2' there is substituted 'section 207 of the Criminal Justice Act 2003', and

  (b) in paragraph (b), for 'sub-paragraphs (5) to (7) of the said paragraph 5' there is substituted 'sections 207(4) and 208(1) and (2) of the Criminal Justice Act 2003'.

(6) After subsection (4) there is inserted –

'(4A) A probation order made or amended under this section must specify as the corresponding requirements for the purposes of this section requirements which could be included in a community order made under section 177 of the Criminal Justice Act 2003.'

(7) In subsection (5), for 'Schedule 3' onwards there is substituted 'Schedule 8 to the Criminal Justice Act 2003 shall apply as if it were a community order made by a magistrates' court under section 177 of that Act and imposing the requirements specified under subsection (4A) above'.

(8) For subsection (6) there is substituted –

'(6) In its application to a probation order made or amended under this section, Schedule 8 to the Criminal Justice Act 2003 has effect subject to the following modifications –

  (a) any reference to the responsible officer has effect as a reference to the person appointed or assigned under subsection (1)(a) above,

  (b) in paragraph 9 –
      (i)   paragraphs (b) and (c) of sub-paragraph (1) are omitted,
      (ii) in sub-paragraph (6), the first reference to the Crown Court has effect as a reference to a court in Scotland, and
      (iii) any other reference in sub-paragraphs (6) or (7) to the Crown Court has effect as a reference to the court in Scotland, and

  (c) Parts 3 and 5 are omitted.'

(9) In subsection (10) –

  (a) for the words from 'paragraph 6' to 'community rehabilitation orders' there is substituted 'paragraph 8 of Schedule 9 (which relates to community orders', and

  (b) for 'an order made under section 41' there is substituted 'a community order made under Part 12'.

71 In section 242 (community service orders: persons residing in England and Wales) –

  (a) in subsection (1) –
      (i)   in paragraph (a)(ii), for 'a community punishment order' there is substituted 'an unpaid work requirement imposed by a community order (within the meaning of Part 12 of the Criminal Justice Act 2003)', and
      (ii) in paragraph (a)(iii), for 'community punishment orders made under section 46 of the Powers of Criminal Courts (Sentencing) Act 2000' there is substituted 'unpaid work requirements imposed by community orders made under section 177 of the Criminal Justice Act 2003',

  (b) in subsection (2)(b), for 'community punishment orders made under section 46 of the Powers of Criminal Courts (Sentencing) Act 2000' there is substituted 'unpaid work requirements imposed by community orders made under section 177 of the Criminal Justice Act 2003', and

  (c) in subsection (3)(b), for 'in respect of community punishment orders conferred on responsible officers by the Powers of Criminal Courts (Sentencing) Act 2000' there is substituted 'conferred on responsible officers by Part 12 of the Criminal

Justice Act 2003 in respect of unpaid work requirements imposed by community orders (within the meaning of that Part)'.

72 In section 244 (community service orders: provisions relating to persons living in England and Wales or Northern Ireland) –

(a) in subsection (3)(a) –
  (i) for 'community punishment order' there is substituted 'community order (within the meaning of Part 12 of the Criminal Justice Act 2003)', and
  (ii) for 'community punishment orders' there is substituted 'such community orders',
(b) in subsection (4)(a), for 'community punishment orders' there is substituted 'community orders (within the meaning of Part 12 of the Criminal Justice Act 2003)',
(c) in subsection (5), for 'community punishment order' there is substituted 'a community order (within the meaning of Part 12 of the Criminal Justice Act 2003)', and
(d) in subsection (6) –
  (i) for 'community punishment orders', where first occurring, there is substituted 'community orders (within the meaning of Part 12 of the Criminal Justice Act 2003)', and
  (ii) in paragraph (b)(ii), for 'the Powers of Criminal Courts (Sentencing) Act 2000' there is substituted 'Part 12 of the Criminal Justice Act 2003'.

Education Act 1996 (c. 56)

73 In section 562 of the Education Act 1996 (Act not to apply to persons detained under order of a court), for 'probation order' there is substituted 'community order under section 177 the Criminal Justice Act 2003'.

Criminal Justice (Northern Ireland) Order 1996 (S.I. 1996/3160 (N.I.24))

74 The Criminal Justice (Northern Ireland) Order 1996 is amended as follows.

75 In Article 2 (interpretation) after paragraph (8) there is inserted –

'(9) For the purposes of this Order, a sentence falls to be imposed under paragraph (2) of Article 52A of the Firearms (Northern Ireland) Order 1981 if it is required by that paragraph and the court is not of the opinion there mentioned.'

76 In Article 4 (absolute and conditional discharge), in paragraph (1), for '(not being an offence for which the sentence is fixed by law)' there is substituted '(not being an offence for which the sentence is fixed by law or falls to be imposed under Article 52A(2) of the Firearms (Northern Ireland) Order 1981)'.

77 In Article 10 (probation orders), in paragraph (1) for '(not being an offence for which the sentence is fixed by law)' there is substituted '(not being an offence for which the sentence is fixed by law or falls to be imposed under Article 52A(2) of the Firearms (Northern Ireland) Order 1981)'.

78(1) Article 13 (community service orders) is amended as follows.

(2) In paragraph (1) for '(not being an offence for which the sentence is fixed by law)' there is substituted '(not being an offence for which the sentence is fixed by law or falls to be imposed under Article 52A(2) of the Firearms (Northern Ireland) Order 1981)'.

(3) In paragraph (4)(b) as it has effect pursuant to paragraph 7(1) of Schedule 13 to the Criminal Justice Act 1982 (reciprocal arrangements), for 'such orders' there is

substituted 'an unpaid work requirement of a community order (within the meaning of Part 12 of the Criminal Justice Act 2003)'.

79 In Article 15 (orders combining probation and community service), in paragraph (1) for '(not being an offence for which the sentence is fixed by law)' there is substituted '(not being an offence for which the sentence is fixed by law or falls to be imposed under Article 52A(2) of the Firearms (Northern Ireland) Order 1981)'.

80 In Article 19 (restrictions on imposing custodial sentences), at the end of paragraph (1) there is inserted 'or falling to be imposed under Article 52A(2) of the Firearms (Northern Ireland) Order 1981'.

81(1) In Article 20 (length of custodial sentences), at the end of paragraph (1) there is inserted 'or falling to be imposed under Article 52A(2) of the Firearms (Northern Ireland) Order 1981'.

(2) In Article 24 (custody probation orders), in paragraph (1) for 'other than one fixed by law' there is substituted ', other than an offence for which the sentence is fixed by law or falls to be imposed under Article 52A(2) of the Firearms (Northern Ireland) Order 1981,'.

Crime (Sentences) Act 1997 (c. 43)

82 The Crime (Sentences) Act 1997 is amended as follows.

83(1) Section 31 (duration and conditions of licences) is amended as follows.

(2) In subsection (3), for the words from 'except' onwards there is substituted 'except in accordance with recommendations of the Parole Board'.

(3) Subsection (4) is omitted.

(4) In subsection (6), for 'section 46(3) of the 1991 Act' there is substituted 'section 259 of the Criminal Justice Act 2003'.

84 In section 32 (recall of life prisoners while on licence) for subsection (5) there is substituted –

'(5) Where on a reference under subsection (4) above the Parole Board directs the immediate release on licence under this section of the life prisoner, the Secretary of State shall give effect to the direction.'

85(1) Schedule 1 (transfers of prisoners within the British Islands) is amended as follows.

(2) In paragraph 6, after sub-paragraph (3) there is inserted –

'(4) In this Part of this Schedule –

"the 2003 Act" means the Criminal Justice Act 2003;
"custody plus order" has the meaning given by section 181(4) of that Act;
"intermittent custody order" has the meaning given by section 183(2) of that Act.'

(3) In paragraph 8 (restricted transfers from England and Wales to Scotland) –

  (a) for sub-paragraph (2)(a) there is substituted –

     '(a) sections 241, 244, 247 to 252 and 254 to 264 of the 2003 Act (fixed-term prisoners) or, as the case may require, sections 102 to 104 of the Powers of Criminal Courts (Sentencing) Act 2000 (detention and training orders) or sections 28 to 34 of this Act (life sentences) shall apply to him in place of the corresponding provisions of the law of Scotland;

(aa) sections 62 and 64 of the Criminal Justice and Court Services Act 2000 (which relate to licence conditions) shall apply to him in place of the corresponding provisions of the law of Scotland;

(ab) where a custody plus order or intermittent custody order has effect in relation to him, the provisions of Chapters 3 and 4 of Part 12 of the 2003 Act relating to such orders shall also apply to him (subject to Schedule 11 to that Act); and',

(b) for sub-paragraph (4)(a) there is substituted –

'(a) sections 241, 249 to 252 and 254 to 264 of the 2003 Act (fixed-term prisoners) or, as the case may require, sections 103 and 104 of the Powers of Criminal Courts (Sentencing) Act 2000 (detention and training orders) or sections 31 to 34 of this Act (life sentences) shall apply to him in place of the corresponding provisions of the law of Scotland;

(aa) sections 62 and 64 of the Criminal Justice and Court Services Act 2000 (which relate to licence conditions) shall apply to him in place of the corresponding provisions of the law of Scotland;

(ab) where a custody plus order or intermittent custody order has effect in relation to him, the provisions of Chapters 3 and 4 of Part 12 of the 2003 Act relating to such orders shall also apply to him (subject to Schedule 11 to that Act); and', and

(c) for sub-paragraphs (5) to (7) there is substituted –

'(5) Section 31(2A) of this Act (conditions as to supervision after release), as applied by sub-paragraph (2) or (4) above, shall have effect as if for paragraphs (a) to (c) there were substituted the words "a relevant officer of such local authority as may be specified in the licence".

(6) Any provision of sections 102 to 104 of the Powers of Criminal Courts (Sentencing) Act 2000 which is applied by sub-paragraph (2) or (4) above shall have effect (as so applied) as if –

(a) any reference to secure accommodation were a reference to secure accommodation within the meaning of Part 2 of the Children (Scotland) Act 1995 or a young offenders institution provided under section 19(1)(b) of the Prisons (Scotland) Act 1989,

(b) except in section 103(2), any reference to the Secretary of State were a reference to the Scottish Ministers,

(c) any reference to an officer of a local probation board were a reference to a relevant officer as defined by section 27(1) of the Prisoners and Criminal Proceedings (Scotland) Act 1993,

(d) any reference to a youth court were a reference to a sheriff court,

(e) in section 103, any reference to a petty sessions area were a reference to a local government area within the meaning of the Local Government etc. (Scotland) Act 1994,

(f) in section 103(3), for paragraphs (b) and (c) there were substituted a reference to an officer of a local authority constituted under that Act for the local government area in which the offender resides for the time being,

(g) section 103(5) were omitted,

(h) in section 104, for subsection (1) there were substituted –

"(1) Where a detention and training order is in force in respect of an offender and it appears on information to a sheriff court having jurisdiction in the locality in which the offender resides that the offender has failed to comply with requirements under section 103(6)(b), the court may –

    (a) issue a citation requiring the offender to appear before it at the time specified in the citation, or

    (b) issue a warrant for the offender's arrest.",

    (i) section 104(2) were omitted, and

    (j) in section 104(6), the reference to the Crown Court were a reference to the High Court of Justiciary.'

(4) In paragraph 9 (restricted transfers from England and Wales to Northern Ireland) –

    (a) for sub-paragraph (2)(a) there is substituted –

    '(a) sections 241, 244, 247 to 252 and 254 to 264 of the 2003 Act (fixed-term prisoners) or, as the case may require, sections 102 to 104 of the Powers of Criminal Courts (Sentencing) Act 2000 (detention and training orders) or sections 28 to 34 of this Act (life sentences) shall apply to him in place of the corresponding provisions of the law of Northern Ireland;

    (aa) sections 62 and 64 of the Criminal Justice and Court Services Act 2000 (which relate to licence conditions) shall apply to him in place of the corresponding provisions of the law of Northern Ireland;

    (ab) where a custody plus order or intermittent custody order has effect in relation to him, the provisions of Chapters 3 and 4 of Part 12 of the 2003 Act relating to such orders shall apply to him (subject to Schedule 11 to that Act); and',

    (b) for sub-paragraph (4)(a) there is substituted –

    '(a) sections 241, 249 to 252 and 254 to 264 of the 2003 Act (fixed-term prisoners) or, as the case may require, sections 103 and 104 of the Powers of Criminal Courts (Sentencing) Act 2000 (detention and training orders) or sections 31 to 34 of this Act (life sentences) shall apply to him in place of the corresponding provisions of the law of Northern Ireland;

    (aa) sections 62 and 64 of the Criminal Justice and Court Services Act 2000 (which relate to licence conditions) shall apply to him in place of the corresponding provisions of the law of Northern Ireland;

    (ab) where a custody plus order or intermittent custody order has effect in relation to him, the provisions of Chapters 3 and 4 of Part 12 of the 2003 Act relating to such orders shall apply to him (subject to Schedule 11 to that Act); and',

    (c) for sub-paragraphs (5) to (7) there is substituted –

'(5) Section 31(2A) of this Act (conditions as to supervision after release), as applied by sub-paragraph (2) or (4) above, shall have effect as if for paragraphs (a) to (c) there were substituted the words "a probation appointed for or assigned to the petty sessions district within which the prisoner for the time being resides".'

(5) In paragraph 15 (unrestricted transfers: general provisions), sub-paragraph (5) is omitted.

86 In Schedule 2 (repatriation of prisoners to the British Islands) paragraphs 2 and 3 are omitted.

Crime and Disorder Act 1998 (c. 37)

87 The Crime and Disorder Act 1998 is amended as follows.

88 In section 18 (interpretation etc. of Chapter 1) –

   (a) after the definition of 'responsible officer' in subsection (1) there is inserted –

   '"serious harm" shall be construed in accordance with section 224 of the Criminal Justice Act 2003;'; and

   (b) subsection (2) is omitted.

89(1) Section 38 (local provision of youth justice services) is amended as follows.

(2) In subsection (4)(g), for 'probation order, a community service order or a combination order' there is substituted 'community order under section 177 of the Criminal Justice Act 2003'.

(3) In subsection (4)(i), after '1997 Act')' there is inserted 'or by virtue of conditions imposed under section 250 of the Criminal Justice Act 2003'.

Powers of Criminal Courts (Sentencing) Act 2000 (c. 6)

90 The Powers of Criminal Courts (Sentencing) Act 2000 is amended as follows.

91(1) Section 6 (committal for sentence in certain cases where offender committed in respect of another offence) is amended as follows.

(2) In subsection (3)(b), for 'section 120(1) below' there is substituted 'paragraph 11(1) of Schedule 12 to the Criminal Justice Act 2003'.

(3) For subsection (4)(e), there is substituted –

   '(e) paragraph 11(2) of Schedule 12 to the Criminal Justice Act 2003 (committal to Crown Court where offender convicted during operational period of suspended sentence).'.

92 In section 7 (power of Crown Court on committal for sentence under section 6), in subsection (2), for 'section 119 below' there is substituted 'paragraphs 8 and 9 of Schedule 12 to the Criminal Justice Act 2003'.

93 In section 12 (absolute and conditional discharge) –

   (a) in subsection (1) for '109(2), 110(2) or 111(2) below' there is substituted 'section 110(2) or 111(2) below, section 51A(2) of the Firearms Act 1968 or section 225, 226, 227 or 228 of the Criminal Justice Act 2003)', and

   (b) subsection (4) (duty to explain effect of order for conditional discharge) is omitted.

94 In the heading to Part 4, and the heading to Chapter 1 of that Part, for 'COMMUNITY ORDERS' there is substituted 'YOUTH COMMUNITY ORDERS'.

95 For section 33 there is substituted –

   '33 Meaning of "youth community order" and "community sentence"

   (1) In this Act "youth community order" means any of the following orders –

      (a) a curfew order;
      (b) an exclusion order;
      (c) an attendance centre order;
      (d) a supervision order;

(e) an action plan order.

(2) In this Act "community sentence" means a sentence which consists of or includes –

(a) a community order under section 177 of the Criminal Justice Act 2003, or
(b) one or more youth community orders.'

96(1) Section 36B (electronic monitoring of requirements in community orders) is amended as follows.

(2) In the heading for '**community orders**' there is substituted '**youth community orders**', and

(3) In subsection (1) –

(a) for 'to (4)' there is substituted 'and (3)', and
(b) for 'community order' there is substituted 'youth community order'.

(4) In subsection (2) and (6)(a), for 'community order' there is substituted 'youth community order'.

97(1) Section 37 (curfew orders) is amended as follows.

(2) In subsection (1) –

(a) after the word 'person' there is inserted 'aged under 16', and
(b) for 'sections 34 to 36 above' there is substituted 'sections 148, 150 and 156 of the Criminal Justice Act 2003'.

(3) In subsection (5), for 'community order' there is substituted 'youth community order'.

(4) Subsection (10) is omitted.

98 In section 39 (breach, revocation and amendment of curfew orders), for 'community orders' there is substituted 'youth community orders'.

99 In section 40 (curfew orders: supplementary), in subsection (3), for 'paragraphs 2A(4) and (5) and 19(3)' there is substituted 'paragraph 16(2)'.

100(1) Section 40A (exclusion orders) is amended as follows.

(2) In subsection (1) –

(a) after 'person' there is inserted 'aged under 16',
(b) for 'sections 34 to 36 above' there is substituted 'sections 148, 150 and 156 of the Criminal Justice Act 2003', and
(c) for 'two years' there is substituted 'three months'.

(3) In subsection (5), for 'community order' there is substituted 'youth community order'.

(4) Subsection (10) is omitted.

101 In section 40B (breach, revocation and amendment of exclusion orders), for 'community orders' there is substituted 'youth community orders'.

102(1) Section 60 (attendance centre orders) is amended as follows.

(2) In subsection (1) –

(a) in paragraph (a), for 'sections 34 to 36 above' there is substituted 'sections 148, 150 and 156 of the Criminal Justice Act 2003' and for '21' there is substituted '16', and
(b) in paragraph (b), for '21' there is substituted '16', and

(c)   paragraph (c) and the word 'or' immediately preceding it are omitted.

(3) In subsection (4), for paragraphs (a) and (b) there is substituted 'shall not exceed 24'.

(4) In subsection (7), for 'community order' there is substituted 'youth community order'.

103 In section 63 (supervision orders), in subsection (1), for 'sections 34 to 36 above' there is substituted 'sections 148, 150 and 156 of the Criminal Justice Act 2003'.

104(1) Section 69 (action plan orders) is amended as follows.

(2) In subsection (1), for 'sections 34 to 36 above' there is substituted 'sections 148, 150 and 156 of the Criminal Justice Act 2003', and

(3) In subsection (5)(b), for 'a community rehabilitation order, a community punishment order, a community punishment and rehabilitation order,' there is substituted 'a community order under section 177 of the Criminal Justice Act 2003'.

(4) Subsection (11) is omitted.

105 In section 70 (requirements which may be included in action plan orders and directions), in subsection (5)(a), after the word 'other' there is inserted 'youth community order or any'.

106(1) Section 73 (reparation orders) is amended as follows.

(2) In subsection (4)(b), for 'a community punishment order, a community punishment and rehabilitation order,' there is substituted 'a community order under section 177 of the Criminal Justice Act 2003'.

(3) Subsection (7) is omitted.

107 In section 74 (requirements and provisions of reparation order, and obligations of person subject to it), in subsection (3)(a), after 'community order' there is inserted 'or any youth community order'.

108 In section 76 (meaning of custodial sentence), in subsection (1) after paragraph (b) there is inserted –

'(bb)   a sentence of detention for public protection under section 226 of the Criminal Justice Act 2003;
(bc)   a sentence of detention under section 228 of that Act;'.

109(1) Section 82A (determination of tariffs) is amended as follows.

(2) In subsection (1), for the words from 'where' onwards there is substituted 'where the sentence is not fixed by law'.

(3) In subsection (3) –

(a)   in paragraph (b), for 'section 87' there is substituted 'section 240 of the Criminal Justice Act 2003', and
(b)   in paragraph (c), for 'sections 33(2) and 35(1) of the Criminal Justice Act 1991' there is substituted 'section 244(1) of the Criminal Justice Act 2003'.

(4) In subsection (4) –

(a)   after 'If' there is inserted 'the offender was aged 21 or over when he committed the offence and', and
(b)   the words 'subject to subsection (5) below' are omitted.

(5) Subsections (5) and (6) are omitted.

110(1) Section 91 (offenders under 18 convicted of certain serious offences) is amended as follows.

(2) In subsection (3), for 'none of the other methods in which the case may legally be dealt with' there is substituted 'neither a community sentence nor a detention and training order'.

(3) In subsection (4), for 'section 79 and 80 above' there is substituted 'section 152 and 153 of the Criminal Justice Act 2003'.

111(1) Section 100 (detention and training orders) is amended as follows.

(2) In subsection (1) –

  (a) for the words from the beginning to 'subsection (2)' there is substituted 'Subject to sections 90 and 91 above, sections 226 and 228 of the Criminal Justice Act 2003, and subsection (2)', and

  (b) for paragraph (b) there is substituted –

    '(b) the court is of the opinion that subsection (2) of section 152 of the Criminal Justice Act 2003 applies or the case falls within subsection (3) of that section,'.

(3) Subsection (4) is omitted.

112 In section 106 (interaction of detention and training orders with sentences of detention in a young offender institution), subsections (2) and (3) are omitted.

113 After section 106 there is inserted –

'106A Interaction with sentences of detention

(1) In this section –

"the 2003 Act" means the Criminal Justice Act 2003;
"sentence of detention" means –
  (a) a sentence of detention under section 91 above, or
  (b) a sentence of detention under section 228 of the 2003 Act (extended sentence for certain violent or sexual offences: persons under 18).

(2) Where a court passes a sentence of detention in the case of an offender who is subject to a detention and training order, the sentence shall take effect as follows –

  (a) if the offender has at any time been released by virtue of subsection (2), (3), (4) or (5) of section 102 above, at the beginning of the day on which the sentence is passed, and

  (b) if not, either as mentioned in paragraph (a) above or, if the court so orders, at the time when the offender would otherwise be released by virtue of subsection (2), (3), (4) or (5) of section 102.

(3) Where a court makes a detention and training order in the case of an offender who is subject to a sentence of detention, the order shall take effect as follows –

  (a) if the offender has at any time been released under Chapter 6 of Part 12 of the 2003 Act (release on licence of fixed-term prisoners), at the beginning of the day on which the order is made, and

  (b) if not, either as mentioned in paragraph (a) above or, if the court so orders, at the time when the offender would otherwise be released under that Chapter.

(4) Where an order under section 102(5) above is made in the case of a person in respect of whom a sentence of detention is to take effect as mentioned in subsection

(2)(b) above, the order is to be expressed as an order that the period of detention attributable to the detention and training order is to end at the time determined under section 102(5)(a) or (b) above.

(5) In determining for the purposes of subsection (3)(b) the time when an offender would otherwise be released under Chapter 6 of Part 12 of the 2003 Act, section 246 of that Act (power of Secretary of State to release prisoners on licence before he is required to do so) is to be disregarded.

(6) Where by virtue of subsection (3)(b) above a detention and training order made in the case of a person who is subject to a sentence of detention under section 228 of the 2003 Act is to take effect at the time when he would otherwise be released under Chapter 6 of Part 12 of that Act, any direction by the Parole Board under subsection (2)(b) of section 247 of that Act in respect of him is to be expressed as a direction that the Board would, but for the detention and training order, have directed his release under that section.

(7) Subject to subsection (9) below, where at any time an offender is subject concurrently –

    (a)   to a detention and training order, and
    (b)   to a sentence of detention,

he shall be treated for the purposes of the provisions specified in subsection (8) below as if he were subject only to the sentence of detention.

(8) Those provisions are –

    (a)   sections 102 to 105 above,
    (b)   section 92 above and section 235 of the 2003 Act (place of detention, etc.), and
    (c)   Chapter 6 of Part 12 of the 2003 Act.

(9) Nothing in subsection (7) above shall require the offender to be released in respect of either the order or the sentence unless and until he is required to be released in respect of each of them.'

114 In section 110 (required custodial sentence for third class A drug trafficking offence), subsection (3) is omitted.

115 In section 111 (minimum of three years for third domestic burglary) subsection (3) is omitted.

116 Sections 116 and 117 (return to prison etc. where offence committed during original sentence) shall cease to have effect.

117 In section 130 (compensation orders against convicted persons), in subsection (2), for '109(2), 110(2) or 111(2) above,' there is substituted '110(2) or 111(2) above, section 51A(2) of the Firearms Act 1968 or section 225, 226, 227 or 228 of the Criminal Justice Act 2003,'.

118 In section 136 (power to order statement as to financial circumstances of parent or guardian) in subsection (2), for 'section 126 above' there is substituted 'section 162 of the Criminal Justice Act 2003'.

119(1) Section 138 (fixing of fine or compensation to be paid by parent or guardian) is amended as follows.

(2) In subsection (1)(a), for 'section 128 above' there is substituted 'section 164 of the Criminal Justice Act 2003'.

(3) In subsection (2), for 'sections 128(1) (duty to inquire into financial circumstances) and' there is substituted 'section 164(1) of the Criminal Justice Act 2003 and section'.

(4) In subsection (4) –
- (a) for 'section 129 above' there is substituted 'section 165 of the Criminal Justice Act 2003',
- (b) for 'section 129(1)' there is substituted 'section 165(1)', and
- (c) for 'section 129(2)' there is substituted 'section 165(2)'.

120 In section 146 (driving disqualification for any offence), in subsection (2), for '109(2), 110(2) or 111(2) above' there is substituted '110(2) or 111(2) above, section 51A(2) of the Firearms Act 1968 or section 225, 226, 227 or 228 of the Criminal Justice Act 2003'.

121 In section 154 (commencement of Crown Court sentence), in subsection (2), for 'section 84 above' there is substituted 'section 265 of the Criminal Justice Act 2003'.

122 In section 159 (execution of process between England and Wales and Scotland), for '10(7) or 24(1)' there is substituted '10(6) or 18(1)'.

123(1) Section 163 (interpretation) is amended as follows.

(2) In the definition of 'attendance centre' for 'section 62(2) above' there is substituted 'section 221(2) of the Criminal Justice Act 2003'.

(3) In the definition of 'attendance centre order' for the words from 'by virtue of' to 'Schedule 3' there is substituted 'by virtue of paragraph 4(2)(b) or 5(2)(b) of Schedule 3'.

(4) In the definition of 'community order', for 'section 33(1) above' there is substituted 'section 177(1) of the Criminal Justice Act 2003'.

(5) For the definition of 'curfew order' there is substituted –

' "curfew order" means an order under section 37(1) above (and, except where the contrary intention is shown by paragraph 7 of Schedule 3 or paragraph 3 of Schedule 7 or 8, includes orders made under section 37(1) by virtue of paragraph 4(2)(a) or 5(2)(a) of Schedule 3 or paragraph 2(2)(a) of Schedule 7 or 8).'.

(6) In the definition of 'operational period', for 'section 118(3) above' there is substituted 'section 189(1)(b)(ii) of the Criminal Justice Act 2003'.

(7) In the definition of 'suspended sentence', for 'section 118(3) above' there is substituted 'section 189(7) of the Criminal Justice Act 2003'.

(8) At the end there is inserted –

' "youth community order" has the meaning given by section 33(1) above.'.

124 In section 164 (further interpretative provision) for subsection (3) there is substituted –

'(3) References in this Act to a sentence falling to be imposed –

- (a) under section 110(2) or 111(2) above,
- (b) under section 51A(2) of the Firearms Act 1968, or
- (c) under any of sections 225 to 228 of the Criminal Justice Act 2003,

are to be read in accordance with section 305(4) of the Criminal Justice Act 2003.'

125 For Schedule 3 (breach revocation and amendment of certain community orders) there is substituted –

'SCHEDULE 3

BREACH, REVOCATION AND AMENDMENT OF CURFEW ORDERS AND EXCLUSION ORDERS

PART 1

PRELIMINARY

Definitions

1 In this Schedule –

"the petty sessions area concerned" means –
   (a) in relation to a curfew order, the petty sessions area in which the place for the time being specified in the order is situated; and
   (b) in relation to an exclusion order, the petty sessions area for the time being specified in the order;
"relevant order" means a curfew order or an exclusion order.

Orders made on appeal

2 Where a relevant order has been made on appeal, for the purposes of this Schedule it shall be deemed –

   (a) if it was made on an appeal brought from a magistrates' court, to have been made by a magistrates' court;
   (b) if it was made on an appeal brought from the Crown Court or from the criminal division of the Court of Appeal, to have been made by the Crown Court.

PART 2

BREACH OF REQUIREMENT OF ORDER

Issue of summons or warrant

3(1) If at any time while a relevant order is in force in respect of an offender it appears on information to a justice of the peace acting for the petty sessions area concerned that the offender has failed to comply with any of the requirements of the order, the justice may –

   (a) issue a summons requiring the offender to appear at the place and time specified in it; or
   (b) if the information is in writing and on oath, issue a warrant for his arrest.

(2) Any summons or warrant issued under this paragraph shall direct the offender to appear or be brought –

   (a) in the case of any relevant order which was made by the Crown Court and included a direction that any failure to comply with any of the requirements of the order be dealt with by the Crown Court, before the Crown Court; and
   (b) in the case of a relevant order which is not an order to which paragraph (a) above applies, before a magistrates' court acting for the petty sessions area concerned.

(3) Where a summons issued under sub-paragraph (1)(a) above requires an offender to appear before the Crown Court and the offender does not appear in

answer to the summons, the Crown Court may issue a further summons requiring the offender to appear at the place and time specified in it.

(4) Where a summons issued under sub-paragraph (1)(a) above or a further summons issued under sub-paragraph (3) above requires an offender to appear before the Crown Court and the offender does not appear in answer to the summons, the Crown Court may issue a warrant for the arrest of the offender.

Powers of magistrates' court

4(1) This paragraph applies if it is proved to the satisfaction of a magistrates' court before which an offender appears or is brought under paragraph 3 above that he has failed without reasonable excuse to comply with any of the requirements of the relevant order.

(2) The magistrates' court may deal with the offender in respect of the failure in one of the following ways (and must deal with him in one of those ways if the relevant order is in force) –

  (a) by making a curfew order in respect of him (subject to paragraph 7 below);
  (b) by making an attendance centre order in respect of him (subject to paragraph 8 below); or
  (c) where the relevant order was made by a magistrates' court, by dealing with him, for the offence in respect of which the order was made, in any way in which he could have been dealt with for that offence by the court which made the order if the order had not been made.

(3) In dealing with an offender under sub-paragraph (2)(c) above, a magistrates' court –

  (a) shall take into account the extent to which the offender has complied with the requirements of the relevant order; and
  (b) in the case of an offender who has wilfully and persistently failed to comply with those requirements, may impose a custodial sentence (where the relevant order was made in respect of an offence punishable with such a sentence) notwithstanding anything in section 152(2) of the Criminal Justice Act 2003.

(4) Where a magistrates' court deals with an offender under sub-paragraph (2)(c) above, it shall revoke the relevant order if it is still in force.

(5) Where a relevant order was made by the Crown Court and a magistrates' court has power to deal with the offender under sub-paragraph (2)(a) or (b) above, it may instead commit him to custody or release him on bail until he can be brought or appear before the Crown Court.

(6) A magistrates' court which deals with an offender's case under sub-paragraph (5) above shall send to the Crown Court –

  (a) a certificate signed by a justice of the peace certifying that the offender has failed to comply with the requirements of the relevant order in the respect specified in the certificate; and
  (b) such other particulars of the case as may be desirable;

and a certificate purporting to be so signed shall be admissible as evidence of the failure before the Crown Court.

(7) A person sentenced under sub-paragraph (2)(c) above for an offence may appeal to the Crown Court against the sentence.

Powers of Crown Court

5(1) This paragraph applies where under paragraph 3 or by virtue of paragraph 4(5) above an offender is brought or appears before the Crown Court and it is proved to the satisfaction of that court that he has failed without reasonable excuse to comply with any of the requirements of the relevant order.

(2) The Crown Court may deal with the offender in respect of the failure in one of the following ways (and must deal with him in one of those ways if the relevant order is in force) –

    (a) by making a curfew order in respect of him (subject to paragraph 7 below);
    (b) by making an attendance centre order in respect of him (subject to paragraph 8 below); or
    (c) by dealing with him, for the offence in respect of which the order was made, in any way in which he could have been dealt with for that offence by the court which made the order if the order had not been made.

(3) In dealing with an offender under sub-paragraph (2)(c) above, the Crown Court –

    (a) shall take into account the extent to which the offender has complied with the requirements of the relevant order; and
    (b) in the case of an offender who has wilfully and persistently failed to comply with those requirements, may impose a custodial sentence (where the relevant order was made in respect of an offence punishable with such a sentence) notwithstanding anything in section 152(2) of the Criminal Justice Act 2003.

(4) Where the Crown Court deals with an offender under sub-paragraph (2)(c) above, it shall revoke the relevant order if it is still in force.

(5) In proceedings before the Crown Court under this paragraph any question whether the offender has failed to comply with the requirements of the relevant order shall be determined by the court and not by the verdict of a jury.

Exclusions from paragraphs 4 and 5

6 Without prejudice to paragraphs 10 and 11 below, an offender who is convicted of a further offence while a relevant order is in force in respect of him shall not on that account be liable to be dealt with under paragraph 4 or 5 in respect of a failure to comply with any requirement of the order.

Curfew orders imposed for breach of relevant order

7(1) Section 37 of this Act (curfew orders) shall apply for the purposes of paragraphs 4(2)(a) and 5(2)(a) above as if for the words from the beginning to "make" there were substituted "Where a court has power to deal with an offender under Part 2 of Schedule 3 to this Act for failure to comply with any of the requirements of a relevant order, the court may make in respect of the offender".

(2) The following provisions of this Act, namely –

(a) section 37(3) to (12), and

(b) so far as applicable, sections 36B and 40 and this Schedule so far as relating to curfew orders;

have effect in relation to a curfew order made by virtue of paragraphs 4(2)(a) and 5(2)(a) as they have effect in relation to any other curfew order, subject to sub-paragraph (3) below.

(3) This Schedule shall have effect in relation to such a curfew order as if –

(a) the power conferred on the court by each of paragraphs 4(2)(c), 5(2)(c) and 10(3)(b) to deal with the offender for the offence in respect of which the order was made were a power to deal with the offender, for his failure to comply with the relevant order, in any way in which the appropriate court could deal with him for that failure if it had just been proved to the satisfaction of the court;

(b) the reference in paragraph 10(1)(b) to the offence in respect of which the order was made were a reference to the failure to comply in respect of which the curfew order was made; and

(c) the power conferred on the Crown Court by paragraph 11(2)(b) to deal with the offender for the offence in respect of which the order was made were a power to deal with the offender, for his failure to comply with the relevant order, in any way in which the appropriate court (if the relevant order was made by the magistrates' court) or the Crown Court (if that order was made by the Crown Court) could deal with him for that failure if it had just been proved to its satisfaction.

(4) For the purposes of the provisions mentioned in paragraphs (a) and (c) of sub-paragraph (3) above, as applied by that sub-paragraph, if the relevant order is no longer in force the appropriate court's powers shall be determined on the assumption that it is still in force.

(5) Sections 148 and 156 of the Criminal Justice Act 2003 (restrictions and procedural requirements for community sentences) do not apply in relation to a curfew order made by virtue of paragraph 4(2)(a) or 5(2)(a) above.

Attendance centre orders imposed for breach of relevant order

8(1) Section 60(1) of this Act (attendance centre orders) shall apply for the purposes of paragraphs 4(2)(b) and 5(2)(b) above as if for the words from the beginning to 'the court may,' there were substituted 'Where a court has power to deal with an offender under Part 2 of Schedule 3 to this Act for failure to comply with any of the requirements of a relevant order, the court may,'.

(2) The following provisions of this Act, namely –

(a) subsections (3) to (11) of section 60, and

(b) so far as applicable, section 36B and Schedule 5,

have effect in relation to an attendance centre order made by virtue of paragraph 4(2)(b) or 5(2)(b) above as they have effect in relation to any other attendance centre order, but as if there were omitted from each of paragraphs 2(1)(b), 3(1) and 4(3) of Schedule 5 the words ", for the offence in respect of which the order was made," and "for that offence".

(3) Sections 148 and 156 of the Criminal Justice Act 2003 (restrictions and procedural requirements for community sentences) do not apply in relation to an attendance centre order made by virtue of paragraph 4(2)(b) or 5(2)(b) above.

Supplementary

9 Any exercise by a court of its powers under paragraph 4(2)(a) or (b) or 5(2)(a) or (b) above shall be without prejudice to the continuance of the relevant order.

PART 3

REVOCATION OF ORDER

Revocation of order with or without re-sentencing: powers of magistrates' court

10(1) This paragraph applies where a relevant order made by a magistrates' court is in force in respect of any offender and on the application of the offender or the responsible officer it appears to the appropriate magistrates' court that, having regard to circumstances which have arisen since the order was made, it would be in the interests of justice –

    (a) for the order to be revoked; or

    (b) for the offender to be dealt with in some other way for the offence in respect of which the order was made.

(2) In this paragraph "the appropriate magistrates' court" means a magistrates' court acting for the petty sessions area concerned.

(3) The appropriate magistrates' court may –

    (a) revoke the order; or

    (b) both –

        (i)   revoke the order; and

        (ii)   deal with the offender for the offence in respect of which the order was made, in any way in which he could have been dealt with for that offence by the court which made the order if the order had not been made.

(4) In dealing with an offender under sub-paragraph (3)(b) above, a magistrates' court shall take into account the extent to which the offender has complied with the requirements of the relevant order.

(5) A person sentenced under sub-paragraph (3)(b) above for an offence may appeal to the Crown Court against the sentence.

(6) Where a magistrates' court proposes to exercise its powers under this paragraph otherwise than on the application of the offender, it shall summon him to appear before the court and, if he does not appear in answer to the summons, may issue a warrant for his arrest.

(7) No application may be made by the offender under sub-paragraph (1) above while an appeal against the relevant order is pending.

Revocation of order with or without re-sentencing: powers of Crown Court on conviction etc

11(1) This paragraph applies where –

    (a) a relevant order made by the Crown Court is in force in respect of an offender and the offender or the responsible officer applies to the Crown Court for the order to be revoked or for the offender to be dealt with in some other way for the offence in respect of which the order was made; or

(b) an offender in respect of whom a relevant order is in force is convicted of an offence before the Crown Court or, having been committed by a magistrates' court to the Crown Court for sentence, is brought or appears before the Crown Court.

(2) If it appears to the Crown Court to be in the interests of justice to do so, having regard to circumstances which have arisen since the order was made, the Crown Court may –

(a) revoke the order; or
(b) both –
   (i)   revoke the order; and
   (ii) deal with the offender for the offence in respect of which the order was made, in any way in which he could have been dealt with for that offence by the court which made the order if the order had not been made.

(3) In dealing with an offender under sub-paragraph (2)(b) above, the Crown Court shall take into account the extent to which the offender has complied with the requirements of the relevant order.

Revocation following custodial sentence by magistrates' court unconnected with order

12(1) This paragraph applies where –

(a) an offender in respect of whom a relevant order is in force is convicted of an offence by a magistrates' court unconnected with the order;
(b) the court imposes a custodial sentence on the offender; and
(c) it appears to the court, on the application of the offender or the responsible officer, that it would be in the interests of justice to exercise its powers under this paragraph having regard to circumstances which have arisen since the order was made.

(2) In sub-paragraph (1) above "a magistrates' court unconnected with the order" means a magistrates' court not acting for the petty sessions area concerned.

(3) The court may –

(a) if the order was made by a magistrates' court, revoke it;
(b) if the order was made by the Crown Court, commit the offender in custody or release him on bail until he can be brought or appear before the Crown Court.

(4) Where the court deals with an offender's case under sub-paragraph (3)(b) above, it shall send to the Crown Court such particulars of the case as may be desirable.

13 Where by virtue of paragraph 12(3)(b) above an offender is brought or appears before the Crown Court and it appears to the Crown Court to be in the interests of justice to do so, having regard to circumstances which have arisen since the relevant order was made, the Crown Court may revoke the order.

Supplementary

14(1) On the making under this Part of this Schedule of an order revoking a relevant order, the proper officer of the court shall forthwith give copies of the revoking order to the responsible officer.

(2) In sub-paragraph (1) above "proper officer" means –

    (a) in relation to a magistrates' court, the justices' chief executive for the court; and
    (b) in relation to the Crown Court, the appropriate officer.

(3) A responsible officer to whom in accordance with sub-paragraph (1) above copies of a revoking order are given shall give a copy to the offender and to the person in charge of any institution in which the offender was required by the order to reside.

PART 4

AMENDMENT OF ORDER

Amendment by reason of change of residence

15(1) This paragraph applies where, at any time while a relevant order is in force in respect of an offender, a magistrates' court acting for the petty sessions area concerned is satisfied that the offender proposes to change, or has changed, his residence from that petty sessions area to another petty sessions area.

(2) Subject to sub-paragraph (3) below, the court may, and on the application of the responsible officer shall, amend the relevant order by substituting the other petty sessions area for the area specified in the order or, in the case of a curfew order, a place in that other area for the place so specified.

(3) The court shall not amend under this paragraph a curfew order which contains requirements which, in the opinion of the court, cannot be complied with unless the offender continues to reside in the petty sessions area concerned unless, in accordance with paragraph 16 below, it either –

    (a) cancels those requirements; or
    (b) substitutes for those requirements other requirements which can be complied with if the offender ceases to reside in that area.

Amendment of requirements of order

16(1) Without prejudice to the provisions of paragraph 15 above but subject to the following provisions of this paragraph, a magistrates' court acting for the petty sessions area concerned may, on the application of an eligible person, by order amend a relevant order –

    (a) by cancelling any of the requirements of the order; or
    (b) by inserting in the order (either in addition to or in substitution for any of its requirements) any requirement which the court could include if it were then making the order.

(2) A magistrates' court shall not under sub-paragraph (1) above amend a curfew order by extending the curfew periods beyond the end of six months from the date of the original order.

(3) A magistrates' court shall not under sub-paragraph (1) above amend an exclusion order by extending the period for which the offender is prohibited from entering the place in question beyond the end of three months from the date of the original order.

(4) For the purposes of this paragraph the eligible persons are –

(a) the offender;

(b) the responsible officer; and

(c) in relation to an exclusion order, any affected person.

But an application under sub-paragraph (1) by a person such as is mentioned in paragraph (c) above must be for the cancellation of a requirement which was included in the order by virtue of his consent or for the purpose (or partly for the purpose) of protecting him from being approached by the offender, or for the insertion of a requirement which will, if inserted, be such a requirement.

Supplementary

17 No order may be made under paragraph 15 above, and no application may be made under paragraph 16 above, while an appeal against the relevant order is pending.

18(1) Subject to sub-paragraph (2) below, where a court proposes to exercise its powers under this Part of this Schedule, otherwise than on the application of the offender, the court –

(a) shall summon him to appear before the court; and

(b) if he does not appear in answer to the summons, may issue a warrant for his arrest.

(2) This paragraph shall not apply to an order cancelling a requirement of a relevant order or reducing the period of any requirement, or to an order under paragraph 15 above substituting a new petty sessions area or a new place for the one specified in a relevant order.

19(1) On the making under this Part of this Schedule of an order amending a relevant order, the justices' chief executive for the court shall forthwith –

(a) if the order amends the relevant order otherwise than by substituting, by virtue of paragraph 15 above, a new petty session area or a new place for the one specified in the relevant order, give copies of the amending order to the responsible officer;

(b) if the order amends the relevant order in the manner excepted by paragraph (a) above, send to the chief executive to the justices for the new petty sessions area or, as the case may be, for the petty sessions area in which the new place is situated –

(i)   copies of the amending order; and

(ii)   such documents and information relating to the case as he considers likely to be of assistance to a court acting for that area in the exercise of its functions in relation to the order;

and in a case falling within paragraph (b) above the chief executive of the justices for that area shall give copies of the amending order to the responsible officer.

(2) A responsible officer to whom in accordance with sub-paragraph (1) above copies of an order are given shall give a copy to the offender and to the person in charge of any institution in which the offender is or was required by the order to reside.'

126 In Schedule 5 (breach, revocation and amendment of attendance centre orders) –

(a) in paragraph 1(1)(b), for 'section 62(3) of this Act' there is substituted 'section 222(1)(d) or (e) of the Criminal Justice Act 2003',

(b) in paragraph 2(5)(b), for 'section 79(2) of this Act' there is substituted 'section 152(2) of the Criminal Justice Act 2003', and

(c) in paragraph 3(3)(b), for 'section 79(2) of this Act' there is substituted 'section 152(2) of the Criminal Justice Act 2003'.

127 In Schedule 6 (requirements which may be included in supervision orders) –

(a) in paragraph 2(7)(a), after the word 'other' there is inserted 'youth community order or any', and

(b) in paragraph 3(6)(a), for 'community order' there is substituted 'youth community order'.

128 In Schedule 7 (breach, revocation and amendment of supervision orders) –

(a) in paragraph 3 –
   (i) in sub-paragraph (2), for 'sub-paragraphs (4) and (5)' there is substituted 'sub-paragraph (5)',
   (ii) in sub-paragraph (3), for 'Sections 35 and 36 of this Act' there is substituted 'Sections 148 and 156 of the Criminal Justice Act 2003',
   (iii) sub-paragraph (4) is omitted, and
   (iv) in sub-paragraph (5)(a), for the words from the beginning to 'and' there is substituted 'the power conferred on the court by each of paragraphs 4(2)(c) and', and

(b) in paragraph 4(3), for 'Sections 35 and 36 of this Act' there is substituted 'Sections 148 and 156 of the Criminal Justice Act 2003'.

129 In Schedule 8 (breach, revocation and amendment of action plan orders and reparation orders) –

(a) in paragraph 3 –
   (i) in sub-paragraph (2), for 'sub-paragraphs (4) and (5)' there is substituted 'sub-paragraph (5)',
   (ii) in sub-paragraph (3), for 'Sections 35 and 36 of this Act' there is substituted 'Sections 148 and 156 of the Criminal Justice Act 2003',
   (iii) sub-paragraph (4) is omitted, and
   (iv) in sub-paragraph (5)(a), for the words from the beginning to 'and' there is substituted 'The power conferred on the court by each of paragraphs 4(2)(c) and', and

(b) in paragraph 4(3), for 'Sections 35 and 36 of this Act' there is substituted 'Sections 148 and 156 of the Criminal Justice Act 2003'.

Child Support, Pensions and Social Security Act 2000 (c. 19)

130 The Child Support, Pensions and Social Security Act 2000 is amended as follows.

131(1) Section 62 (loss of benefit for breach of community order) is amended as follows.

(2) In subsection (8), for the definition of 'relevant community order' there is substituted –

'"relevant community order" means –
   (a) a community order made under section 177 of the Criminal Justice Act 2003; or
   (b) any order falling in England or Wales to be treated as such an order.'

(3) In subsection (11)(c)(ii), for 'to (e)' there is substituted 'and (b)'.

132 In section 64 (information provision), in subsection (6)(a), after 'community orders' there is inserted '(as defined by section 177 of the Criminal Justice Act 2003)'.

Criminal Justice and Court Services Act 2000 (c. 43)

133 The Criminal Justice and Court Services Act 2000 is amended as follows.

134 In section 1 (purposes of Chapter 1 of Part 1 of the Act), in subsection (2) –

  (a) in paragraph (a), after 'community orders' there is inserted '(as defined by section 177 of the Criminal Justice Act 2003)', and
  (b) after paragraph (c) there is inserted –

    '(d) giving effect to suspended sentence orders (as defined by section 189 of the Criminal Justice Act 2003).'

135 In section 42 (interpretation of Part 2), in subsection (2)(a), for 'section 119 of the Powers of Criminal Court (Sentencing) Act 2000' there is substituted 'paragraph 8(2)(a) or (b) of Schedule 11 of the Criminal Justice Act 2003'.

136(1) Section 62 (release on licence etc: conditions as to monitoring) is amended as follows.

(2) For subsection (3) there is substituted –

    '(3) In relation to a prisoner released under section 246 of the Criminal Justice Act 2003 (power to release prisoners on licence before required to do so), the monitoring referred to in subsection (2)(a) does not include the monitoring of his compliance with conditions imposed under section 253 of that Act (curfew condition).'

(3) In subsection (5) after paragraph (e) there is inserted ', and

    (f) a sentence of detention under section 226 or 228 of the Criminal Justice Act 2003'.

137 In section 69 (duties of local probation boards in connection with victims of certain offences), in subsection (8), for paragraph (a) there is substituted –

    '(a) murder or an offence specified in Schedule 15 to the Criminal Justice Act 2003,'.

138 In section 70 (general interpretation), in subsection (5), for the words 'any community order' there is substituted 'a curfew order, an exclusion order, a community rehabilitation order, a community punishment order, a community punishment and rehabilitation order, a drug treatment and testing order, a drug abstinence order, an attendance centre order, a supervision order or an action plan order'.

International Criminal Court Act 2001 (c. 17)

139(1) Schedule 7 to the International Criminal Court Act 2001 (domestic provisions not applicable to ICC prisoners), is amended as follows.

(2) In paragraph 2(1), for paragraph (d) there is substituted –

    '(d) section 240 of the Criminal Justice Act 2003 (crediting of periods of remand in custody).'

(3) In paragraph 3(1), for 'Part 2 of the Criminal Justice Act 1991' there is substituted 'sections 244 to 264 of the Criminal Justice Act 2003'.

Armed Forces Act 2001 (c. 19)

140 In section 30 of the Armed Forces Act 2001 (conditional release from custody), in subsection (6)(a) for 'six months' there is substituted 'the term specified in subsection (1)(a) of section 8 of the Armed Forces Act 1976 (powers of courts in relation to civilians)'.

Proceeds of Crime Act 2002 (c. 29)

141 In section 38 of the Proceeds of Crime Act 2002 (provisions about imprisonment or detention), in subsection (4)(a), for 'section 118(1) of the Sentencing Act' there is substituted 'section 189(1) of the Criminal Justice Act 2003'.

Sexual Offences Act 2003 (c. 42)

142 The Sexual Offences Act 2003 is amended as follows.

143 In section 131 (application of Part 2 to young offenders), after paragraph (j) there is inserted –

'(k) a sentence of detention for public protection under section 226 of the Criminal Justice Act 2003,
(l) an extended sentence under section 228 of that Act,'.

144 In section 133 (general interpretation), at the end of paragraph (a) of the definition of 'community order' there is inserted '(as that Act had effect before the passing of the Criminal Justice Act 2003)'.

PART 2

OFFENCES: ABOLITION OF IMPRISONMENT AND CONVERSION TO SUMMARY OFFENCE

Vagrancy Act 1824 (c. 83)

145 In section 3 of the Vagrancy Act 1824 (idle and disorderly persons), for the words from 'subject to' to the end there is substituted 'it shall be lawful for any justice of the peace to impose on such person (being thereof convicted before him by his own view, or by the confession of such person, or by the evidence on oath of one or more credible witnesses) a fine not exceeding level 3 on the standard scale'.

146(1) Section 4 of that Act (rogues and vagabonds) is amended as follows.

(2) In that section, for the words from 'shall be' to the end there is substituted 'commits an offence under this section'.

(3) At the end of that section (which becomes subsection (1)) there is inserted –

'(2) It shall be lawful for any justice of the peace to impose on any person who commits an offence under this section (being thereof convicted before him by the confession of such person, or by the evidence on oath of one or more credible witnesses) –

(a) in the case of a person convicted of the offence of wandering abroad and lodging in any barn or outhouse, or in any deserted or unoccupied building, or in the open air, or under a tent, or in any cart or waggon, and not giving a good account of himself, a fine not exceeding level 1 on the standard scale, and

    (b) in the case of a person convicted of any other offence under this section, a fine not exceeding level 3 on the standard scale.'

London Hackney Carriages Act 1843 (c. 86)

147 In section 28 of the London Hackney Carriages Act 1843, after 'for every such offence', there is inserted 'of which he is convicted before the justice'.

Town Police Clauses Act 1847 (c. 89)

148 In section 26 of the Town Police Clauses Act 1847, for the words from 'committed by them' to the end, there is substituted 'liable to a fine not exceeding level 3 on the standard scale'.

149 In section 28 of that Act, after 'for each offence', there is inserted 'of which he is convicted before the justice'.

150 In section 29 of that Act, after 'for every such offence', there is inserted 'of which he is convicted before the justice'.

151 In section 36 of that Act, after 'liable', there is inserted 'on conviction before the justices'.

Seamen's and Soldiers' False Characters Act 1906 (c. 5)

152 In section 1 of the Seamen's and Soldiers' False Characters Act 1906, for 'imprisonment for a term not exceeding three months' there is substituted 'a fine not exceeding level 2 on the standard scale'.

Aliens Restriction (Amendment) Act 1919 (c. 92)

153 In section 3(2) of the Aliens Restriction (Amendment) Act 1919, for 'imprisonment for a term not exceeding three months' there is substituted 'a fine not exceeding level 3 on the standard scale'.

Polish Resettlement Act 1947 (c. 19)

154 In the Schedule to the Polish Resettlement Act 1947, in paragraph 7, for 'imprisonment for a term not exceeding three months' there is substituted 'a fine not exceeding level 1 on the standard scale'.

Army Act 1955 (3 & 4 Eliz. 2 c. 18)

155 In section 61 of the Army Act 1955, for the words from 'the like' to 'section nineteen of this Act' there is substituted 'dismissal from Her Majesty's service with or without disgrace, to detention for a term not exceeding three months,'.

Air Force Act 1955 (3 & 4 Eliz. 2 c. 19)

156 In section 61 of the Air Force Act 1955, for the words from 'the like' to 'section nineteen of this Act' there is substituted 'dismissal from Her Majesty's service with or without disgrace, to detention for a term not exceeding three months,'.

Naval Discipline Act 1957 (c. 53)

157 In section 34A of the Naval Discipline Act 1957, for the words 'imprisonment for a term not exceeding three months' there is substituted 'dismissal from Her Majesty's service with or without disgrace, detention for a term not exceeding three months,'.

Slaughterhouses Act 1974 (c. 3)

158 In section 4 of the Slaughterhouses Act 1974, after subsection (5) there is inserted –

'(5A) A person guilty of an offence under subsection (5) above shall be liable to a fine not exceeding level 3 on the standard scale.'

Water Industry Act 1991 (c. 56)

159 In Schedule 6 to the Water Industry Act 1991, in paragraph 5(4), for paragraphs (a) and (b) there is substituted ', on summary conviction, to a fine not exceeding level 5 on the standard scale'.

Water Resources Act 1991 (c.57)

160 In section 205(6) of the Water Resources Act 1991, for paragraphs (a) and (b) there is substituted 'on summary conviction to a fine not exceeding level 5 on the standard scale'.

Transport Act 2000 (c. 38)

161 In section 82(4) of the Transport Act 2000, after 'subsection (1)' there is inserted 'or (2)'.

Reserve Forces Act 1996 (c. 14)

162 In paragraph 5(3) of Schedule 1 to the Reserve Forces Act 1996, for the words 'imprisonment for a term not exceeding three months' there is substituted 'dismissal from Her Majesty's service with or without disgrace, to detention for a term not exceeding 3 months,'.

SCHEDULE 33 Section 321

JURY SERVICE

1 The Juries Act 1974 (c. 23) is amended as follows.

2 For section 1 (qualification for jury service) there is substituted –

'1 Qualification for jury service

(1) Subject to the provisions of this Act, every person shall be qualified to serve as a juror in the Crown Court, the High Court and county courts and be liable accordingly to attend for jury service when summoned under this Act if –

> (a) he is for the time being registered as a parliamentary or local government elector and is not less than eighteen nor more than seventy years of age;
>
> (b) he has been ordinarily resident in the United Kingdom, the Channel Islands or the Isle of Man for any period of at least five years since attaining the age of thirteen;
>
> (c) he is not a mentally disordered person; and

    (d) he is not disqualified for jury service.

(2) In subsection (1) above 'mentally disordered person' means any person listed in Part 1 of Schedule 1 to this Act.

(3) The persons who are disqualified for jury service are those listed in Part 2 of that Schedule.'

3 Section 9(1) (certain persons entitled to be excused from jury service) shall cease to have effect.

4 In section 9(2) (discretionary excusal) after 'may' there is inserted ', subject to section 9A(1A) of this Act,'.

5 After section 9(2) (discretionary excusal) there is inserted –

'(2A) Without prejudice to subsection (2) above, the appropriate officer shall excuse a full-time serving member of Her Majesty's naval, military or air forces from attending in pursuance of a summons if –

    (a) that member's commanding officer certifies to the appropriate officer that it would be prejudicial to the efficiency of the service if that member were to be required to be absent from duty, and
    (b) subsection (2A) or (2B) of section 9A of this Act applies.

(2B) Subsection (2A) above does not affect the application of subsection (2) above to a full-time serving member of Her Majesty's naval, military or air forces in a case where he is not entitled to be excused under subsection (2A).'

6 In section 9(3) (discretionary excusal) after 'above' there is inserted 'or any failure by the appropriate officer to excuse him as required by subsection (2A) above'.

7 In section 9A(1) (discretionary deferral) after 'may' there is inserted ', subject to subsection (2) below,'.

8 After section 9A(1) (discretionary deferral) there is inserted –

'(1A) Without prejudice to subsection (1) above and subject to subsection (2) below, the appropriate officer –

    (a) shall defer the attendance of a full-time serving member of Her Majesty's naval, military or air forces in pursuance of a summons if subsection (1B) below applies, and
    (b) for this purpose, shall vary the dates upon which that member is summoned to attend and the summons shall have effect accordingly.

(1B) This subsection applies if that member's commanding officer certifies to the appropriate officer that it would be prejudicial to the efficiency of the service if that member were to be required to be absent from duty.

(1C) Nothing in subsection (1A) or (1B) above shall affect the application of subsection (1) above to a full-time serving member of Her Majesty's naval, military or air forces in a case where subsection (1B) does not apply.'

9 For section 9A(2) (discretionary deferral) there is substituted –

'(2) The attendance of a person in pursuance of a summons shall not be deferred under subsection (1) or (1A) above if subsection (2A) or (2B) below applies.'

10 After section 9A(2) (discretionary deferral) there is inserted –

'(2A) This subsection applies where a deferral of the attendance of the person in pursuance of the summons has previously been made or refused under subsection (1) above or has previously been made under subsection (1A) above.

(2B) This subsection applies where –

(a) the person is a full-time serving member of Her Majesty's naval, military or air forces, and
(b) in addition to certifying to the appropriate officer that it would be prejudicial to the efficiency of the service if that member were to be required to be absent from duty, that member's commanding officer certifies that this position is likely to remain for any period specified for the purpose of this subsection in guidance issued under section 9AA of this Act.'

11 In section 9A(3) (discretionary deferral) after 'above' there is inserted 'or any failure by the appropriate officer to defer his attendance as required by subsection (1A) above'.

12 After section 9A (discretionary deferral) there is inserted –

'9AA Requirement to issue guidance

(1) The Lord Chancellor shall issue guidance as to the manner in which the functions of the appropriate officer under sections 9 and 9A of this Act are to be exercised.

(2) The Lord Chancellor shall –

(a) lay before each House of Parliament the guidance, and any revised guidance, issued under this section, and
(b) arrange for the guidance, or revised guidance, to be published in a manner which he considers appropriate.'

13 In section 19 (payment for jury service), after subsection (1) there is inserted –

'(1A) The reference in subsection (1) above to payments by way of allowance for subsistence includes a reference to vouchers and other benefits which may be used to pay for subsistence, whether or not their use is subject to any limitations.'

14 In section 20 (offences), for subsection (5)(d) there is substituted –

'(d) knowing that he is disqualified under Part 2 of Schedule 1 to this Act, serves on a jury;'

15 For Schedule 1 (ineligibility and disqualification for and excusal from jury service) there is substituted –

'SCHEDULE 1

MENTALLY DISORDERED PERSONS AND PERSONS DISQUALIFIED
FOR JURY SERVICE

PART 1

MENTALLY DISORDERED PERSONS

1 A person who suffers or has suffered from mental illness, psychopathic disorder, mental handicap or severe mental handicap and on account of that condition either –

(a) is resident in a hospital or similar institution; or
(b) regularly attends for treatment by a medical practitioner.

2 A person for the time being under guardianship under section 7 of the Mental Health Act 1983.

3 A person who, under Part 7 of that Act, has been determined by a judge to be incapable, by reason of mental disorder, of managing and administering his property and affairs.

4(1) In this Part of this Schedule –

    (a) "mental handicap" means a state of arrested or incomplete development of mind (not amounting to severe mental handicap) which includes significant impairment of intelligence and social functioning;

    (b) "severe mental handicap" means a state of arrested or incomplete development of mind which includes severe impairment of intelligence and social functioning;

    (c) other expressions are to be construed in accordance with the Mental Health Act 1983.

(2) For the purposes of this Part a person is to be treated as being under guardianship under section 7 of the Mental Health Act 1983 at any time while he is subject to guardianship pursuant to an order under section 116A(2)(b) of the Army Act 1955, section 116A(2)(b) of the Air Force Act 1955 or section 63A(2)(b) of the Naval Discipline Act 1957.

PART 2

PERSONS DISQUALIFIED

5 A person who is on bail in criminal proceedings (within the meaning of the Bail Act 1976).

6 A person who has at any time been sentenced in the United Kingdom, the Channel Islands or the Isle of Man –

    (a) to imprisonment for life, detention for life or custody for life,

    (b) to detention during her Majesty's pleasure or during the pleasure of the Secretary of State,

    (c) to imprisonment for public protection or detention for public protection,

    (d) to an extended sentence under section 227 or 228 of the Criminal Justice Act 2003 or section 210A of the Criminal Procedure (Scotland) Act 1995, or

    (e) to a term of imprisonment of five years or more or a term of detention of five years or more.

7 A person who at any time in the last ten years has –

    (a) in the United Kingdom, the Channel Islands or the Isle of Man –

        (i) served any part of a sentence of imprisonment or a sentence of detention, or

        (ii) had passed on him a suspended sentence of imprisonment or had made in respect of him a suspended order for detention,

    (b) in England and Wales, had made in respect of him a community order under section 177 of the Criminal Justice Act 2003, a community rehabilitation order, a community punishment order, a community punishment and rehabilitation order, a drug treatment and testing order or a drug abstinence order, or

    (c) had made in respect of him any corresponding order under the law of Scotland, Northern Ireland, the Isle of Man or any of the Channel Islands.

8 For the purposes of this Part of this Schedule –

    (a) a sentence passed by a court-martial is to be treated as having been passed in the United Kingdom, and

    (b) a person is sentenced to a term of detention if, but only if –

        (i) a court passes on him, or makes in respect of him on conviction, any sentence or order which requires him to be detained in custody for any period, and

        (ii) the sentence or order is available only in respect of offenders below a certain age,

and any reference to serving a sentence of detention is to be construed accordingly.'

SCHEDULE 34   Section 324

PARENTING ORDERS AND REFERRAL ORDERS

Crime and Disorder Act 1998 (c. 37)

1 In section 8 of the Crime and Disorder Act 1998 (parenting orders), in subsection (2) the words from 'and to section 19(5)' to '2000' shall cease to have effect.

2(1) Section 9 of that Act (parenting orders: supplemental) is amended as follows.

(2) For subsection (1A) there is substituted –

    '(1A) The requirements of subsection (1) do not apply where the court makes a referral order in respect of the offence.'

(3) After subsection (2) there is inserted –

    '(2A) In a case where a court proposes to make both a referral order in respect of a child or young person convicted of an offence and a parenting order, before making the parenting order the court shall obtain and consider a report by an appropriate officer –

        (a) indicating the requirements proposed by that officer to be included in the parenting order;

        (b) indicating the reasons why he considers those requirements would be desirable in the interests of preventing the commission of any further offence by the child or young person; and

        (c) if the child or young person is aged under 16, containing the information required by subsection (2) above.

    (2B) In subsection (2A) above "an appropriate officer" means –

        (a) an officer of a local probation board;

        (b) a social worker of a local authority social services department; or

        (c) a member of a youth offending team.'

(4) After subsection (7) there is inserted –

    '(7A) In this section 'referral order' means an order under section 16(2) or (3) of the Powers of Criminal Courts (Sentencing) Act 2000 (referral of offender to youth offender panel).'

Powers of Criminal Courts (Sentencing) Act 2000 (c. 6)

3 In section 19(5) of the Powers of Criminal Courts (Sentencing) Act 2000 (orders that cannot be made with referral orders) –

(a) at the end of paragraph (a) there is inserted 'or', and

(b) paragraph (c) (parenting orders) and the word 'or' immediately preceding it shall cease to have effect.

4 In section 22 of that Act (referral orders: attendance at panel meetings), after subsection (2) there is inserted –

'(2A) If –

(a) a parent or guardian of the offender fails to comply with an order under section 20 above (requirement to attend the meetings of the panel), and

(b) the offender is aged under 18 at the time of the failure,

the panel may refer that parent or guardian to a youth court acting for the petty sessions area in which it appears to the panel that the offender resides or will reside.'

5(1) Section 28 of that Act (which introduces Schedule 1) is amended as follows.

(2) In the sidenote, for 'Offender referred back to court or' there is substituted 'Offender or parent referred back to court: offender'.

(3) After paragraph (a) there is inserted –

'(aa) in Part 1A makes provision for what is to happen when a youth offender panel refers a parent or guardian to the court under section 22(2A) above, and'.

6 In Schedule 1 to that Act (youth offender panels: further court proceedings), after Part 1 there is inserted –

'PART 1A

REFERRAL OF PARENT OR GUARDIAN FOR BREACH OF SECTION 20 ORDER

Introductory

9A(1) This Part of this Schedule applies where, under section 22(2A) of this Act, a youth offender panel refers an offender's parent or guardian to a youth court.

(2) In this Part of this Schedule –

(a) "the offender" means the offender whose parent or guardian is referred under section 22(2A);

(b) "the parent" means the parent or guardian so referred; and

(c) "the youth court" means a youth court as mentioned in section 22(2A).

Mode of referral to court

9B The panel shall make the referral by sending a report to the youth court explaining why the parent is being referred to it.

Bringing the parent before the court

9C(1) Where the youth court receives such a report it shall cause the parent to appear before it.

(2) For the purpose of securing the attendance of the parent before the court, a justice acting for the petty sessions area for which the court acts may –

(a) issue a summons requiring the parent to appear at the place and time specified in it; or

(b) if the report is substantiated on oath, issue a warrant for the parent's arrest.

(3) Any summons or warrant issued under sub-paragraph (2) above shall direct the parent to appear or be brought before the youth court.

Power of court to make parenting order: application of supplemental provisions

9D(1) Where the parent appears or is brought before the youth court under paragraph 9C above, the court may make a parenting order in respect of the parent if –

(a) it is proved to the satisfaction of the court that the parent has failed without reasonable excuse to comply with the order under section 20 of this Act; and

(b) the court is satisfied that the parenting order would be desirable in the interests of preventing the commission of any further offence by the offender.

(2) A parenting order is an order which requires the parent –

(a) to comply, for a period not exceeding twelve months, with such requirements as are specified in the order, and

(b) subject to sub-paragraph (4) below, to attend, for a concurrent period not exceeding three months, such counselling or guidance programme as may be specified in directions given by the responsible officer.

(3) The requirements that may be specified under sub-paragraph (2)(a) above are those which the court considers desirable in the interests of preventing the commission of any further offence by the offender.

(4) A parenting order under this paragraph may, but need not, include a requirement mentioned in subsection (2)(b) above in any case where a parenting order under this paragraph or any other enactment has been made in respect of the parent on a previous occasion.

(5) A counselling or guidance programme which a parent is required to attend by virtue of subsection (2)(b) above may be or include a residential course but only if the court is satisfied –

(a) that the attendance of the parent at a residential course is likely to be more effective than his attendance at a non-residential course in preventing the commission of any further offence by the offender, and

(b) that any interference with family life which is likely to result from the attendance of the parent at a residential course is proportionate in all the circumstances.

(6) Before making a parenting order under this paragraph where the offender is aged under 16, the court shall obtain and consider information about his family circumstances and the likely effect of the order on those circumstances.

(7) Sections 8(3) and (8), 9(3) to (7) and 18(3) and (4) of the Crime and Disorder Act 1998 apply in relation to a parenting order made under this paragraph as they apply in relation to any other parenting order.

Appeal

9E(1) An appeal shall lie to the Crown Court against the making of a parenting order under paragraph 9D above.

(2) Subsections (2) and (3) of section 10 of the Crime and Disorder Act 1998 (appeals against parenting orders) apply in relation to an appeal under this paragraph as they apply in relation to an appeal under subsection (1)(b) of that section.

Effect on section 20 order

9F(1) The making of a parenting order under paragraph 9D above is without prejudice to the continuance of the order under section 20 of this Act.

(2) Section 63(1) to (4) of the Magistrates' Courts Act 1980 (power of magistrates' court to deal with person for breach of order, etc) apply (as well as section 22(2A) of this Act and this Part of this Schedule) in relation to an order under section 20 of this Act.'

SCHEDULE 35   Section 328

CRIMINAL RECORD CERTIFICATES: AMENDMENTS OF PART 5 OF POLICE ACT 1997

1 The Police Act 1997 (c. 50) is amended as follows.

2 In section 112 (criminal conviction certificates), in subsection (1)(a), after 'prescribed' there is inserted 'manner and'.

3(1) Section 113 (criminal record certificates) is amended as follows.

(2) In subsection (1) –
  (a)   at the beginning there is inserted 'Subject to subsection (4A)',
  (b)   in paragraph (a), after 'prescribed' there is inserted 'manner and', and
  (c)   in paragraph (b), after 'pays' there is inserted 'in the prescribed manner'.

(3) After subsection (4) there is inserted –

'(4A) The Secretary of State may treat an application under this section as an application under section 115 if –

  (a)   in his opinion the certificate is required for a purpose prescribed under subsection (2) of that section,
  (b)   the registered person provides him with the statement required by subsection (2) of that section, and
  (c)   the applicant consents and pays to the Secretary of State the amount (if any) by which the fee payable in relation to an application under section 115 exceeds the fee paid in relation to the application under this section.'.

4(1) Section 115 (enhanced criminal record certificates) is amended as follows.

(2) In subsection (1) –

  (a)   at the beginning there is inserted 'Subject to subsection (9A),',
  (b)   in paragraph (a), after 'prescribed' there is inserted 'manner and', and
  (c)   in paragraph (b), after 'pays' there is inserted 'in the prescribed manner'.

(3) In subsection (2), for paragraphs (a) to (c) there is substituted 'for such purposes as may be prescribed under this subsection'.

(4) Subsections (3) to (5) and subsections (6C) to (6E) are omitted.

(5) After subsection (9) there is inserted –

'(9A) The Secretary of State may treat an application under this section as an application under section 113 if in his opinion the certificate is not required for a purpose prescribed under subsection (2).

(9B) Where by virtue of subsection (9A) the Secretary of State treats an application under this section as an application under section 113, he must refund to the applicant the amount (if any) by which the fee paid in relation to the application under this section exceeds the fee payable in relation to an application under section 113.'

5 In section 116 (enhanced criminal record certificates: judicial appointments and Crown employment), in subsection (2)(b), for the words from 'to which' onwards there is substituted 'of such description as may be prescribed'.

6(1) Section 120 (registered persons) is amended as follows.

(2) For subsection (2) there is substituted –

'(2) Subject to regulations under section 120ZA and 120AA and to section 120A the Secretary of State shall include in the register any person who –

(a) applies to him in writing to be registered,
(b) satisfies the conditions in subsections (4) to (6), and
(c) has not in the period of two years ending with the date of the application been removed from the register under section 120A or 120AA.'

(3) Subsection (3) is omitted.

7 After section 120 there is inserted –

'120ZA Regulations about registration

(1) The Secretary of State may by regulations make further provision about registration.

(2) Regulations under this section may in particular make provision for –

(a) the payment of fees,
(b) the information to be included in the register,
(c) the registration of any person to be subject to conditions,
(d) the nomination by –
    (i) a body corporate or unincorporate, or
    (ii) a person appointed to an office by virtue of any enactment,
    of the individuals authorised to act for it or, as the case may be, him in relation to the countersigning of applications under this Part, and
(e) the refusal by the Secretary of State, on such grounds as may be specified in or determined under the regulations, to accept or to continue to accept the nomination of a person as so authorised.

(3) The provision which may be made by virtue of subsection (2)(c) includes provision –

(a) for the registration or continued registration of any person to be subject to prescribed conditions or, if the regulations so provide, such conditions as the Secretary of State thinks fit, and
(b) for the Secretary of State to vary or revoke those conditions.

(4) The conditions imposed by virtue of subsection (2)(c) may in particular include conditions –

   (a)   requiring a registered person, before he countersigns an application at an individual's request, to verify the identity of that individual in the prescribed manner,

   (b)   requiring an application under section 113 or 115 to be transmitted by electronic means to the Secretary of State by the registered person who countersigns it, and

   (c)   requiring a registered person to comply with any code of practice for the time being in force under section 122.'

8 At the end of the sidenote to section 120A (refusal and cancellation of registration) there is inserted 'on grounds related to disclosure'.

9 After section 120A there is inserted –

'120AA Refusal, cancellation or suspension of registration on other grounds

(1) Regulations may make provision enabling the Secretary of State in prescribed cases to refuse to register a person who, in the opinion of the Secretary of State, is likely to countersign fewer applications under this Part in any period of twelve months than a prescribed minimum number.

(2) Subsection (3) applies where a registered person –

   (a)   is, in the opinion of the Secretary of State, no longer likely to wish to countersign applications under this Part,

   (b)   has, in any period of twelve months during which he was registered, countersigned fewer applications under this Part than the minimum number specified in respect of him by regulations under subsection (1), or

   (c)   has failed to comply with any condition of his registration.

(3) Subject to section 120AB, the Secretary of State may –

   (a)   suspend that person's registration for such period not exceeding 6 months as the Secretary of State thinks fit, or

   (b)   remove that person from the register.

120AB Procedure for cancellation or suspension under section 120AA

(1) Before cancelling or suspending a person's registration by virtue of section 120AA, the Secretary of State must send him written notice of his intention to do so.

(2) Every such notice must –

   (a)   give the Secretary of State's reasons for proposing to cancel or suspend the registration, and

   (b)   inform the person concerned of his right under subsection (3) to make representations.

(3) A person who receives such a notice may, within 21 days of service, make representations in writing to the Secretary of State as to why the registration should not be cancelled or suspended.

(4) After considering such representations, the Secretary of state must give the registered person written notice –

   (a)   that at the end of a further period of six weeks beginning with the date of service, the person's registration will be cancelled or suspended, or

    (b) that he does not propose to take any further action.

(5) If no representations are received within the period mentioned in subsection (3) the Secretary of State may cancel or suspend the person's registration at the end of the period mentioned in that subsection.

(6) Subsection (1) does not prevent the Secretary of State from imposing on the registered person a lesser sanction than that specified in the notice under that subsection.

(7) Any notice under this section that is required to be given in writing may be given by being transmitted electronically.

(8) This section does not apply where –

    (a) the Secretary of State is satisfied, in the case of a registered person other than a body, that the person has died or is incapable, by reason of physical or mental impairment, of countersigning applications under this Part, or
    (b) the registered person has requested to be removed from the register.

(9) The Secretary of State may by regulations amend subsection (4)(a) by substituting for the period there specified, such other period as may be specified in the regulations.'

10 After section 122 there is inserted –

'122A Delegation of functions of Secretary of State

(1) The Secretary of State may, to such extent and subject to such conditions as he thinks fit, delegate any relevant function of his under this Part to such person as he may determine.

(2) A function is relevant for the purposes of subsection (1) if it does not consist of a power –

    (a) to make regulations, or
    (b) to publish or revise a code of practice or to lay any such code before Parliament.

(3) A delegation under subsection (1) may be varied or revoked at any time.'

11 After section 124 (offences: disclosure) there is inserted –

'124A Further offences: disclosure of information obtained in connection with delegated function

(1) Any person who is engaged in the discharge of functions conferred by this Part on the Secretary of State commits an offence if he discloses information which has been obtained by him in connection with those functions and which relates to a particular person unless he discloses the information, in the course of his duties, –

    (a) to another person engaged in the discharge of those functions,
    (b) to the chief officer of a police force in connection with a request under this Part to provide information to the Secretary of State, or
    (c) to an applicant or registered person who is entitled under this Part to the information disclosed to him.

(2) Where information is disclosed to a person and the disclosure –

    (a) is an offence under subsection (1), or
    (b) would be an offence under subsection (1) but for subsection (3)(a), (d) or (e),

the person to whom the information is disclosed commits an offence if he discloses it to any other person.

(3) Subsection (1) does not apply to a disclosure of information which is made –

    (a)   with the written consent of the person to whom the information relates,

    (b)   to a government department,

    (c)   to a person appointed to an office by virtue of any enactment,

    (d)   in accordance with an obligation to provide information under or by virtue of any enactment, or

    (e)   for some other purpose specified in regulations made by the Secretary of State.

(4) A person who is guilty of an offence under this section shall be liable on summary conviction to imprisonment for a term not exceeding 51 weeks or to a fine not exceeding level 3 on the standard scale, or to both.

(5) In relation to an offence committed before the commencement of section 281(5) of the Criminal Justice Act 2003, the reference in subsection (4) to 51 weeks is to be read as a reference to 6 months.'

12 In section 125 (regulations) –

    (a)   subsection (3) is omitted, and

    (b)   in subsection (4), the words 'to which subsection (3) does not apply' are omitted.

[…]

SCHEDULE 37   Section 332

REPEALS

PART 1

REPEALS RELATING TO AMENDMENTS OF POLICE AND CRIMINAL EVIDENCE ACT 1984

Short title and chapter	Extent of repeal
Police and Criminal Evidence Act 1984 (c. 60)	In section 1(8), the word 'and' at the end of paragraph (c).
	In section 54(1), the words 'and record or cause to be recorded'.
	In section 63(3)(a), the words 'is in police detention or'.

	In section 67 –
	   (a) the word 'such' in subsections (9), (10)(a), (b) and (c) and in both places where it occurs in subsection (11), and
	   (b) the words 'of practice to which this section applies' in subsection (9A).

	In section 113 –
	   (a) in subsection (4), the words 'issued under that subsection',
	   (b) in subsection (8), the words 'of practice issued under this section', and
	   (c) in subsection (10), the word 'such' in both places where it occurs.

Short title and chapter	Extent of repeal
Criminal Justice and Public Order Act 1994 (c. 33)	Section 29(3).
Armed Forces Act 2001 (c. 19)	In section 2(9), the word 'and' at the end of paragraph (c).
Police Reform Act 2002 (c. 30)	In Schedule 7, paragraph 9(1) and (6).

PART 2

BAIL

Short title and chapter	Extent of repeal
Criminal Justice Act 1967 (c. 80)	In section 22, in subsection (1) the words 'subject to section 25 of the Criminal Justice and Public Order Act 1994' and in subsection (3) the words from 'except that' to the end.
Courts Act 1971 (c. 23)	In Schedule 8, in paragraph 48(b), the word '22(3)'.
Bail Act 1976 (c. 63)	In section 3(6), the words 'to secure that'.
	In section 3A(5), the words 'for the purpose of preventing that person from'.
	In section 5, in subsection (3), the words from 'with a view' to 'another court', and in subsection (6), in paragraph (a) the words 'to the High Court or' and paragraph (b).
	In section 5A(2), in the substituted version of section 5(3), the words from 'with a view' to 'vary the conditions'.
Supreme Court Act 1981 (c. 54)	In section 81(1)(g), the word 'or' at the end of sub-paragraph (ii).
Criminal Justice Act 1991 (c. 53)	In Schedule 11, in paragraph 22(2), the words 'and the words' onwards.
Criminal Justice and Public Order Act 1994 (c. 33)	Section 26.
	In Schedule 10, paragraphs 15 and 34.
Powers of Criminal Courts (Sentencing) Act 2000 (c. 6)	In Schedule 9, paragraph 87(b).

PART 3

DISCLOSURE

Short title and chapter	Extent of repeal
Criminal Justice Act 1987 (c. 38)	In section 9(5)(i) and (iii).
Criminal Justice (Serious Fraud) (Northern Ireland) Order 1988 (S.I. 1988/1846 (N.I. 16))	Article 8(5)(i) and (iii).
Criminal Procedure and Investigations Act 1996 (c. 25)	Section 5(6) to (9).
	Section 6(3).
	Section 7.
	Section 9.
	Section 20(2).
	Section 31(6)(a) and (c).

PART 4

ALLOCATION AND SENDING OF OFFENCES

Short title and chapter	Extent of repeal
Bankers' Books Evidence Act 1879 (c. 11)	In section 4, the paragraph beginning 'Where the proceedings'.
	In section 5, the paragraph beginning 'Where the proceedings'.
Explosive Substances Act 1883 (c. 3)	Section 6(3).
Criminal Justice Act 1925 (c. 86)	Section 49(2).
Administration of Justice (Miscellaneous Provisions) Act 1933 (c. 36)	In section 2(2), paragraphs (aa) to (ac), paragraphs (iA) and (iB), and the words from 'and in paragraph (iA)' to the end.
Criminal Justice Act 1948 (c. 58)	Section 41(5A).
	In section 80, the definition of 'Court of summary jurisdiction'.
Backing of Warrants (Republic of Ireland) Act 1965 (c. 45)	In the Schedule, in paragraph 4, the words 'and section 2 of the Poor Prisoners Defence Act 1930 (legal aid before examining justices)'.
Criminal Procedure (Attendance of Witnesses) Act 1965 (c. 69)	Section 2(5).
Criminal Justice Act 1967 (c. 80)	In section 9(1), the words ', other than committal proceedings'.
	In section 36(1), the definition of 'committal proceedings'.
Criminal Appeal Act 1968 (c. 19)	In section 9(2), the words from 'section 41' to 'either way offence'.
Firearms Act 1968 (c. 27)	In Schedule 6, in Part 2, paragraph 3.
Theft Act 1968 (c. 60)	Section 27(4A).
Criminal Justice Act 1972 (c. 71)	In section 46, subsections (1A) to (1C).
Bail Act 1976 (c. 63)	In section 3, subsections (8A) and (8B), and the subsection (10) inserted by paragraph 12(b) of Schedule 9 to the Criminal Justice and Public Order Act 1994 (c. 33).
	Section 5(6A)(a)(i).
Criminal Law Act 1977 (c. 45)	In Schedule 12, the entry relating to the Firearms Act 1968 (c. 27).
Interpretation Act 1978 (c. 30)	In Schedule 1, in the definition of 'Committed for trial', paragraph (a).
Customs and Excise Management Act 1979 (c. 2)	Section 147(2).

Short title and chapter	Extent of repeal
Magistrates' Courts Act 1980 (c. 43)	Sections 4 to 8, and the cross-heading preceding section 4.
	In section 8B(6)(a), the words 'commits or'.
	Section 24(1A) and (2).
	In section 25, subsections (3) to (8).
	In section 33(1), paragraph (b) and the word 'and' immediately preceding it.
	Section 42.
	Section 97A.
	Section 103.
	Section 106.
	In section 128, in subsection (1)(b), the words 'inquiring into or', and in each of subsections (1A)(a), (3A), (3C)(a) and (3E)(a), the word '5,'.
	In section 130(1), the word '5,'.
	Section 145(1)(f).
	In section 150(1), the definition of 'committal proceedings'.
	In section 155(2)(a), the words '8 (except subsection (9))'.
	In Schedule 3, paragraph 2(a).
	In Schedule 5, paragraph 2.
	In Schedule 7, paragraph 73.
Criminal Justice (Amendment) Act 1981 (c. 27)	The whole Act.
Criminal Attempts Act 1981 (c. 47)	In section 2(2)(g), the words 'or committed for trial'.
Contempt of Court Act 1981 (c. 49)	Section 4(4).
Supreme Court Act 1981 (c. 54)	Section 76(5).
	Section 77(4).
	In section 81 –
	(a) in subsection (1)(a), the words 'who has been committed in custody for appearance before the Crown Court or in relation to whose case a notice of transfer has been given under a relevant transfer provision or',
	(b) subsection (1)(g)(i),
	(c) subsection (7).
Criminal Justice Act 1982 (c. 48)	Section 61.
	In Schedule 9, paragraph 1(a).
Mental Health Act 1983 (c. 20)	In section 52(7)(b), the words 'where the court proceeds under subsection (1) of that section,'.
Police and Criminal Evidence Act 1984 (c. 60)	Section 62(10)(a)(i).
	In section 71, the paragraph beginning 'Where the proceedings'.
	Section 76(9).
	Section 78(3).
Prosecution of Offences Act 1985 (c. 23)	In section 16, subsections (1)(b), (2)(aa) and (12).
	In section 23A(1)(b), the words from 'under' to '1998'.
	In Schedule 1, paragraphs 2 and 3.

Short title and chapter	Extent of repeal
Criminal Justice Act 1987 (c. 38)	Sections 4 to 6.
	In section 11 –
	(a) subsection (2)(a),
	(b) subsection (3),
	(c) in subsection (7), the word '(3),',
	(d) in subsection (8), the word '(3),',
	(e) subsections (9) and (10),
	(f) in subsection (11), paragraphs (a) and (d).
	In Schedule 2, paragraphs 1, 9 and 14.
Criminal Justice Act 1988 (c. 33)	Section 23(5).
	Section 24(5).
	In section 26, the paragraph beginning 'This section shall not apply'.
	In section 27, the paragraph beginning 'This section shall not apply'.
	Section 30(4A).
	Section 33.
	In section 40(1), the words 'were disclosed to a magistrates' court inquiring into the offence as examining justices or'.
	Section 41.
	Section 144.
	In Schedule 15, paragraphs 10, 66 and 104.
Road Traffic Offenders Act 1988 (c. 53)	Section 11(3A).
	Section 13(7).
	Section 16(6A).
	Section 20(8A).
Courts and Legal Services Act 1990 (c. 41)	In Schedule 18, paragraph 25(5).
Broadcasting Act 1990 (c. 42)	In Schedule 20, paragraph 29(1).
Criminal Justice Act 1991 (c. 53)	Section 53.
	Section 55(1).
	Schedule 6.
	In Schedule 11, paragraph 25.
Criminal Justice and Public Order Act 1994 (c. 33)	Section 34(2)(a).
	Section 36(2)(a).
	Section 37(2)(a).
	In Schedule 9, paragraphs 12, 17(c), 18(d), 25, 27, 29 and 49.
	In Schedule 10, paragraphs 40 and 71.
Criminal Procedure and Investigations Act 1996 (c. 25)	In section 1(2), paragraphs (a) to (c) and, in paragraph (cc), the words from 'under' to the end.
	In section 5, subsections (2) and (3).
	In section 13(1), paragraphs (a) to (c) of the modified section 3(8).
	Section 28(1)(b).
	Section 44(3).
	Section 45.
	Section 49(4).
	Section 68.

Short title and chapter	Extent of repeal
	In Schedule 1, paragraphs 2 to 5, 8, 10, 12, 13, 15 to 19, 22(3), 24 to 26, 28 to 32, and 34 to 38.
	Schedule 2.
Sexual Offences (Protected Material) Act 1997 (c. 39)	Section 9(1).
Crime and Disorder Act 1998 (c. 37)	Section 47(6).
	In section 50(1), the words 'unless the accused falls to be dealt with under section 51 below'.
	In Schedule 3, in paragraph 2, sub-paragraphs (4) and (5), paragraph 12, and in paragraph 13(2), the words from 'unless' to the end.
	In Schedule 8, paragraphs 8, 37, 40, 65 and 93.
Access to Justice Act 1999 (c. 22)	Section 67(3).
	In Schedule 4, paragraphs 16, 39 and 47.
	In Schedule 13, paragraphs 96, 111 and 137.
Youth Justice and Criminal Evidence Act 1999 (c. 23)	Section 27(10).
	In section 42(3), paragraphs (a) and (b).
Powers of Criminal Courts (Sentencing) Act 2000 (c. 6)	In section 89(2)(b), the words 'trial or'.
	In section 140(1)(b), the words 'was committed to the Crown Court to be tried or dealt with or by which he'.
	In Schedule 9, paragraphs 62, 63, 64(2), 65, 91 and 201.
	In Schedule 11, paragraph 9.

PART 5

EVIDENCE OF BAD CHARACTER

Short title and chapter	Extent of repeal
Criminal Procedure Act 1865 (c. 18)	In section 6, the words 'and upon being so questioned, if'.
Criminal Evidence Act 1898 (c. 36)	Section 1(3).
Children and Young Persons Act 1963 (c. 37)	Section 16(2) and (3).
Criminal Evidence Act 1979 (c. 16)	In section 1, the words from 'each of the following' to '1898, and'.
Police and Criminal Evidence Act 1984 (c. 60)	In section 74(3), the words from 'in so far' to 'he is charged,'.
Criminal Justice and Public Order Act 1994 (c. 33)	Section 31.
Crime (Sentences) Act 1997 (c. 43)	In Schedule 4, paragraph 4.
Youth Justice and Criminal Evidence Act 1999 (c. 23)	In Schedule 4, paragraph 1(5).
Powers of Criminal Courts (Sentencing) Act 2000 (c. 6)	In Schedule 9, paragraph 23.

PART 6

HEARSAY EVIDENCE

Short title and chapter	Extent of repeal
Registered Designs Act 1949 (c. 88)	In section 17, in subsection (8) the words 'Subject to subsection (11) below,' and in subsection (10) the words ', subject to subsection (11) below,'.
Patents Act 1977 (c. 37)	In section 32, in subsection (9) the words 'Subject to subsection (12) below,' and in subsection (11) the words ', subject to subsection (12) below,'.
Criminal Justice Act 1988 (c. 33)	Part 2. Schedule 2. In Schedule 13, paragraphs 2 to 5. In Schedule 15, paragraph 32. In Schedule 4, paragraph 6(2).
Finance Act 1994 (c. 9)	Section 22(2)(b). In Schedule 7, paragraph 1(6)(b).
Value Added Tax Act 1994 (c. 23)	In Schedule 11, paragraph 6(6)(b).
Criminal Justice and Public Order Act 1994 (c. 33)	In Schedule 9, paragraph 31.
Civil Evidence Act 1995 (c. 38)	In Schedule 1, paragraph 12.
Finance Act 1996 (c. 8)	In Schedule 5, paragraph 2(6)(a).
Criminal Procedure and Investigations Act 1996 (c. 25)1	In Schedule 1, paragraphs 28 to 31.
Crime and Disorder Act 1998 (c. 37)	In Schedule 3, paragraph 5(4).
Youth Justice and Criminal Evidence Act 1999 (c. 23)	In Schedule 4, paragraph 16.
Finance Act 2000 (c. 17)	In Schedule 6, paragraph 126(2)(a).
Finance Act 2001 (c. 9)	In Schedule 7, paragraph 3(2)(a).
Crime (International Co-operation) Act 2003 (c. 32)	In section 9(4), the words 'section 25 of the Criminal Justice Act 1988 or'.

PART 7

SENTENCING: GENERAL

Short title and chapter	Extent of repeal
Piracy Act 1837 (c. 88)	Section 3.
Children and Young Persons Act 1933 (c. 12)	In section 16(3), the words 'mandatory and'.
Criminal Justice Act 1967 (c. 80)	In section 104, in subsection (1) the definition of 'suspended sentence' and subsection (2).
Criminal Appeal Act 1968 (c. 19)	In section 10 subsection (2)(c) and the word 'or' immediately preceding it. Section 11(4).
Social Work (Scotland) Act 1968 (c. 49)	In section 94(1), the definition of 'community rehabilitation order'.
Bail Act 1976 (c. 63)	In section 2(1)(d), the words 'placing the offender on probation or'.

Short title and chapter	Extent of repeal
Magistrates' Courts Act 1980 (c. 43)	In section 82(4A), paragraph (e) and the word 'or' immediately preceding it.
	Section 133(2).
	In Schedule 6A, the entry relating to section 123(3) of the Powers of Criminal Courts (Sentencing) Act 2000.
Forgery and Counterfeiting Act 1981 (c. 45)	Section 23(1)(b), (2)(b) and (3)(b).
Mental Health Act 1983 (c. 20)	In section 37(1B), the words '109(2),'.
	In section 45A(1)(b), the words from 'except' to '1997'.
Road Traffic Offenders Act 1988 (c. 53)	In section 46(1), paragraph (a) and the word 'or' following it.
Football Spectators Act 1989 (c. 37)	In section 7, subsection (9) and in subsection (10)(b) the words from '(or' to the end.
Children Act 1989 (c. 41)	In section 68(2)(d), the words 'a probation order has been made in respect of him or he has been'.
	In Schedule 9A, in paragraph 4(2)(g), the words 'placed on probation or'.
Criminal Justice Act 1991 (c. 53)	Sections 32 to 51.
	Section 65.
	Schedule 5.
	In Schedule 12 –
	(a) in paragraph 8(8), paragraph (d), and
	(b) in paragraph 9(3), paragraph (c).
Prisoners and Criminal Proceedings (Scotland) Act 1993 (c. 9)	In section 10(1)(a), sub-paragraph (i) and the succeeding 'or'.
Criminal Justice Act 1993 (c. 36)	Section 67(1).
Criminal Justice and Public Order Act 1994 (c. 33)	In section 25(3)(c), the words 'placing the offender on probation or'.
Criminal Procedure (Scotland) Act 1995 (c. 46)	In section 234 –
	(a) in subsection (1), the words after paragraph (b),
	(b) in subsection (3), the words from 'or to vary' to 'one hundred', and
	(c) subsection (11).
Crime (Sentences) Act 1997 (c. 43)	Sections 35 and 40.
	In Schedule 1, paragraph 15(5).
	In Schedule 2, paragraphs 2 and 3.
	In Schedule 4, paragraphs 6(2), 7, 10(1), 12(1), 13 and 15(10).
Crime and Disorder Act 1998 (c. 37)	In section 18, subsection (2).
	In section 38(4)(i), the words 'section 37(4A) or 65 of the 1991 Act or'.
	Sections 59 and 60.
	Sections 80 and 81.
	Sections 99 and 100.
	Sections 101(1).
	Sections 103 to 105.
	In section 121(12), the words from the beginning to 'paragraphs 56 to 60 of Schedule 8 to this Act;'.
	In Schedule 7, paragraph 50.
	In Schedule 8, paragraphs 11, 13(2), 56, 58, 59, 79 to 84, 86 to 91, 94, 97, 132 and 135(3) and (4).

Short title and chapter	Extent of repeal
Criminal Justice (Children) (Northern Ireland) Order 1998 (S.I. 1998/1504 (N.I. 9))	In Schedule 5, paragraph 28(b).
Access to Justice Act 1999 (c. 22)	Section 58(5).
Powers of Criminal Courts (Sentencing) Act 2000 (c. 6)	Section 6(4)(d).
	Section 12(4).
	Sections 34 to 36A.
	In section 36B, subsections (4) and (8) and, in subsection (9), the words from 'a community punishment order' to 'a drug abstinence order'.
	In section 37, in subsection (9) the words 'who on conviction is under 16' and subsection (10).
	In section 40A, subsection (4), in subsection (9) the words 'who on conviction is under 16' and subsection (10).
	Sections 41 to 59.
	In section 60, in subsection (1), paragraph (c) and the word 'or' immediately preceding it.
	Section 62.
	Section 69(11).
	Section 73(7).
	Sections 78 to 82.
	Section 84.
	Section 85.
	Sections 87 and 88.
	Section 91(2).
	Section 100(4).
	Section 106(2) and (3).
	Section 109.
	Section 110(3).
	Section 111(3).
	In section 112(1)(a), the words '109,'.
	In section 113, in subsection (1)(a), the words 'a serious offence or' and in subsection (3), the words ''serious offence','' and '109,'.
	In section 114(1)(b), the words 'a serious offence,'.
	In section 115, the word '109,'.
	Sections 116 and 117.
	Sections 118 to 125.
	Sections 126 to 129.
	Sections 151 to 153.
	Sections 156 to 158.
	In section 159, the words ', 121(1) or 123(1)' and 'paragraph 6(6) of Schedule 4 to this Act,'.
	In section 160 – (a) in subsection (2), in paragraph (a) the words from '42(2E)' to 'Schedule 2' and in paragraph (b) the words from '122(7)' to the end, (b) in subsection (3), in paragraph (a) the words '45, 50, 58, 58A(4), 85(7)', paragraph (b) and the word 'or' immediately preceding it, (c) subsection (4), and

Short title and chapter	Extent of repeal
	(d) in subsection (5), in paragraph (a) the words from 'or paragraph 7' to the end, and in paragraph (b) the words from '42(2E)' to the end.
	Section 161(2) to (4).
	Section 162.
	In section 163, in the definition of 'affected person', paragraphs (b) and (c), the definitions of 'the appropriate officer of the court', 'community punishment and rehabilitation order', 'community rehabilitation order', 'community rehabilitation period', 'community punishment order', the definitions of 'drug abstinence order', 'drug treatment and testing order', 'falling to be imposed under section 109(2), 110(2) or 11(2)', 'pre-sentence report', 'protecting the public from serious harm'', in the definition of 'responsible officer', paragraphs (b) to (ee) and the words from 'except that' to 'that section;', the definitions of 'review hearing', 'sexual offence', 'specified Class A drug', 'suspended sentence supervision order', 'the testing requirement', 'the treatment provider', 'the treatment requirement', 'the treatment and testing period', 'trigger offence' and 'violent offence'.
	In section 168 –
	(a) in subsection (1), the words 'to subsection (2) below and', and
	(b) subsections (2) and (3).
	Schedule 2.
	Schedule 4.
	In Schedule 7, paragraph 3(4).
	In Schedule 8, paragraph 3(4).
	In Schedule 9, paragraphs 7, 24(a), 26(2), 28, 29, 52, 54(3), 55, 61, 76, 81, 82, 89(2), 90(2), 94, 102, 137 to 145, 147(2) and (3)(a) to (d) and (e)(i), 151, 174, 176(2) to (5) and (7), 177(2) and (3), 184, 185, 186(3) and (4), 187(2), (3) and (5), 196 and 202.
Terrorism Act 2000 (c. 11)	In Schedule 15, paragraph 20.
Child Support, Pensions and Social Security Act 2000 (c. 19)	Section 62(10).
Criminal Justice and Court Services Act 2000 (c. 43)	Section 47 to 51.
	Sections 53 to 55.
	Section 63.
	Section 64(5)(e).
	In section 78(1), the definition of 'community order'.
	In Schedule 7, paragraphs 1 to 3, 104 to 107, 111(b), 123(a) and (c) to (f), 124(a) and (b), 133, 139, 140, 161, 162, 165 to 172, 177, 179, 189, 196(c)(ii) and (iii), 197(c) and (g)(ii), 198 to 200 and 206(a).
Anti-terrorism, Crime and Security Act 2001 (c. 24)	Section 39(7).
Proceeds of Crime Act 2002 (c. 29)	In Schedule 11, paragraph 32.

PART 8

LIFE SENTENCES

Short title and chapter	*Extent of repeal*
Murder (Abolition of Death Penalty) Act 1965 (c. 71)	Section 1(2).
Repatriation of Prisoners Act 1984 (c. 47)	In section 2(4)(b)(i), the words 'or 29(1)'. Section 3(9). Paragraph 3 of the Schedule.
Crime (Sentences) Act 1997 (c. 43)	Section 29. Section 31(4). Section 33. In section 34(3), the words from the beginning to 'advocate; and'.
Crime and Punishment (Scotland) Act 1977 (c. 48)	In Schedule 1, paragraph 10(3).
Crime and Disorder Act 1998 (c. 37)	In Schedule 8, paragraphs 57 and 60.
Powers of Criminal Courts (Sentencing) Act 2000 (c. 6)	In section 82A, in subsection (4) the words 'subject to subsection (5) below', and subsections (5) and (6).

PART 9

ALTERATION OF PENALTIES FOR SUMMARY OFFENCES

Short title and chapter	*Extent of repeal*
Vagrancy Act 1824 (c. 83)	Section 5. Section 10.
Railway Regulation Act 1842 (c. 55)	In section 17, the words from 'be imprisoned' (where first occurring) to 'discretion of such justice, shall'.
London Hackney Carriages Act 1843 (c. 86)	In section 28, the words from '; or it shall be lawful' to the end.
Town Police Clauses Act 1847 (c. 89)	In section 28, the words from ', or, in the discretion' to 'fourteen days'. In section 29, the words from ', or, in the discretion' to the end. In section 36, the words from ', or, in the discretion' to 'one month'.
Ecclesiastical Courts Jurisdiction Act 1860 (c. 32)	In section 2, the words from ', or may, if the justices' to the end.
Town Gardens Protection Act 1863 (c. 13)	In section 5, the words ', or to imprisonment for any period not exceeding fourteen days'.
Public Stores Act 1875 (c. 25)	In section 8, the words from ', or, in the discretion' to the end.
North Sea Fisheries Act 1893 (c. 17)	In section 2 – (a) in paragraph (a), the words from ', or, in the discretion' to the end, and (b) in paragraph (b), the words from ', or in the discretion' to the end. In section 3(a), the words from ', or, in the discretion' to the end.

Short title and chapter	*Extent of repeal*
Children and Young Persons Act 1933 (c. 12)	In section 4(1), the words from ', or alternatively' to the end.
Protection of Animals Act 1934 (c. 21)	In section 2, the words from ', or, alternatively' to the end.
Public Health Act 1936 (c. 49)	In section 287(5), the words from 'or to imprisonment' to the end.
Essential Commodities Reserves Act 1938 (c. 51)	In section 4(2), the words from 'or to imprisonment' to the end.
London Building Acts (Amendment) Act 1939 (c. xcvii)	In section 142(5), the words from 'or to imprisonment' to the end.
Cancer Act 1939 (c. 13)	In section 4(2), the words from 'or to imprisonment' to the end.
Civil Defence Act 1939 (c. 31)	In section 77, the words from 'or to imprisonment' to the end.
Hill Farming Act 1946 (c. 73)	In section 19 – (a) in subsection (2), the words from ', or to imprisonment' to the end, and (b) in subsection (3), the words from 'or to imprisonment' to the end.
Agriculture Act 1947 (c. 48)	In section 14(7) (as remaining in force for the purposes of section 95), the words – (a) 'to imprisonment for a term not exceeding three months or', and (b) 'or to both such imprisonment and such fine'. In section 95(3), the words – (a) 'to imprisonment for a term not exceeding three months or', and (b) 'or to both such imprisonment and such fine'.
Civil Defence Act 1948 (c. 5)	In section 4(4), the words from 'or to imprisonment' to the end.
Agricultural Wages Act 1948 (c. 47)	In section 12(7), the words from 'or to imprisonment' to the end.
Wireless Telegraphy Act 1949 (c. 54)	In section 14(1B), the words – (a) 'to imprisonment for a term not exceeding three months or', and (b) ', or both'.
Prevention of Damage by Pests Act 1949 (c. 55)	In section 22(5), the words from 'or to imprisonment' to the end.
Coast Protection Act 1949 (c. 74)	In section 25(9), the words from 'or to imprisonment' to the end.
Pet Animals Act 1951 (c. 35)	In section 5 – (a) in subsection (1), the words 'other than the last foregoing section' and the words from 'or to imprisonment' to the end, and (b) subsection (2).
Cockfighting Act 1952 (c. 59)	In section 1(1), the words – (a) 'to imprisonment for a term not exceeding three months, or', and (b) ', or to both such imprisonment and such fine'.

Short title and chapter	Extent of repeal

Agricultural Land (Removal of Surface Soil) Act 1953 (c. 10)	In section 2(1) –
	  (a) paragraph (a) of the proviso,
	  (b) the word '; or' immediately preceding paragraph (b) of the proviso, and
	  (c) the words 'or to both'.

Accommodation Agencies Act 1953 (c. 23)	In section 1(5), the words from 'or to imprisonment' to the end.
Army Act 1955 (3 & 4 Eliz. 2 c. 18)	In section 19(1), the words 'to imprisonment for a term not exceeding three months or'. In section 161, the words from ', or to imprisonment' to the end. In section 171(1), the words from ', or to imprisonment' to the end. In section 191, the words from 'or to imprisonment' to the end. In section 193, the words from 'or to imprisonment' to the end. In section 196(3), the words from 'or to imprisonment' to the end. In section 197(3), the words from 'or to imprisonment' to the end.
Air Force Act 1955 (3 & 4 Eliz. 2 c. 19)	In section 19(1), the words 'to imprisonment for a term not exceeding three months or'. In section 161, the words from ', or to imprisonment' to the end. In section 171(1), the words from ', or to imprisonment' to the end. In section 191, the words from 'or to imprisonment' to the end. In sections 193, the words from 'or to imprisonment' to the end. In section 196(3), the words from 'or to imprisonment' to the end. In section 197(3), the words from 'or to imprisonment' to the end.
Naval Discipline Act 1957 (c. 53)	In section 96, the words from 'or to imprisonment' to the end. In section 99(3), the words from 'or to imprisonment' to the end.

Agricultural Marketing Act 1958 (c. 47)	In section 45(6), the words –
	  (a) 'to imprisonment for a term not exceeding one month, or', and
	  (b) ', or to both such imprisonment and such fine'.

Rivers (Prevention of Pollution) Act 1961 (c. 50)	In section 12(2), the words from 'or to imprisonment' to the end.

Short title and chapter	Extent of repeal
Betting, Gaming and Lotteries Act 1963 (c. 2)	In section 8(1), the words – (a) 'or to imprisonment for a term not exceeding three months, or to both', and (b) 'in any case'.
Children and Young Persons Act 1963 (c. 37)	In section 40 – (a) in subsection (1), the words from 'or imprisonment' to the end, and (b) in subsection (2), the words from 'or imprisonment' to the end.
Animal Boarding Establishments Act 1963 (c. 43)	In section 3 – (a) in subsection (1), the words 'other than the last foregoing section' and the words from 'or to imprisonment' to the end, and (b) subsection (2).
Agriculture and Horticulture Act 1964 (c. 28)	In section 20(2), the words from 'or to imprisonment' to the end.
Emergency Laws (Re-enactments and Repeals) Act 1964 (c. 60)	In Schedule 1 – (a) in paragraph 1(3), the words 'to imprisonment for a term not exceeding three months or' and ', or to both', and (b) in paragraph 2(4), the words 'to imprisonment for a term not exceeding three months or' and ', or to both'.
Riding Establishments Act 1964 (c. 70)	In section 4(1), the words from 'or to imprisonment' to the end.
Industrial and Provident Societies Act 1965 (c. 12)	In section 16(5), the words from 'or to imprisonment' to the end. In section 48(2), the words from 'or to imprisonment' to the end.
Cereals Marketing Act 1965 (c. 14)	In section 17(1), the words from 'or to imprisonment' to the end.
Gas Act 1965 (c. 36)	In Schedule 6, in paragraph 9, the words from 'or to imprisonment' to the end.
Armed Forces Act 1966 (c. 45)	In section 8, the words 'to imprisonment for a term not exceeding three months or'.
Agriculture Act 1967 (c. 22)	In section 6(9), the words from 'or to imprisonment' to the end. In section 14(2), the words from 'or to imprisonment' to the end. In section 69, the words from 'or imprisonment' to the end.
Criminal Justice Act 1967 (c. 80)	Section 20.
Sea Fisheries (Shellfish) Act 1967 (c. 83)	In section 14(2), the words from 'or to imprisonment' to the end.
Theatres Act 1968 (c. 54)	In section 13(3), the words from 'or to imprisonment' to the end.
Theft Act 1968 (c. 60)	In Schedule 1, in paragraph 2(1), the words – (a) 'to imprisonment for a term not exceeding three months or', and (b) 'or to both'.

Short title and chapter	Extent of repeal
Agriculture Act 1970 (c. 40)	In section 106(8), the words from 'or imprisonment' to the end.
Breeding of Dogs Act 1973 (c. 60)	In section 3(1) – (a) paragraph (a), (b) the word '; or' immediately preceding paragraph (b), and (c) the words 'or to both'.
Slaughterhouses Act 1974 (c. 3)	In section 38(5), the words 'or imprisonment for a term of three months or both'.
National Health Service Act 1977 (c. 49)	In Schedule 11 – (a) in paragraph 8(3), the words 'to imprisonment for a term not exceeding three months or' and ', or to both', and (b) in paragraph 9(4), the words 'to imprisonment for a term not exceeding three months or' and ', or to both'.
Magistrates' Courts Act 1980 (c. 43)	In section 84(3), the words – (a) 'imprisonment for a term not exceeding 4 months or', and (b) 'to both'.
Animal Health Act 1981 (c. 22)	In paragraph 6 of Schedule 1, the words – (a) 'or to imprisonment for a term not exceeding 2 months,', and (b) 'in either case'.
Fisheries Act 1981 (c. 29)	In section 5(4), the words from 'or to imprisonment' to the end.
Civil Aviation Act 1982 (c. 16)	In section 82(2), the words from 'or to imprisonment' to the end.
Criminal Justice Act 1982 (c. 48)	Section 70.
Mental Health Act 1983 (c. 20)	Section 43(5). In section 103(9), the words – (a) 'to imprisonment for a term not exceeding three months or', and (b) 'or both'. In section 129(3), the words – (a) 'to imprisonment for a term not exceeding three months or', and (b) 'or to both'.
Building Act 1984 (c. 55)	In section 96(3), the words 'or to imprisonment for a term not exceeding three months'.
Surrogacy Arrangements Act 1985 (c. 49)	In section 4(1) – (a) paragraph (a), and (b) in paragraph (b), the words 'in the case of an offence under section 3'.
Animals (Scientific Procedures) Act 1986 (c. 14)	In section 22(3), the words – (a) 'to imprisonment for a term not exceeding three months or', and (b) 'or to both'.

Short title and chapter	Extent of repeal
	In section 23(2), the words –
	(a) 'to imprisonment for a term not exceeding three months or', and
	(b) 'or to both'.
	In section 25(3), the words –
	(a) 'to imprisonment for a term not exceeding three months or', and
	(b) 'or to both'.
Motor Cycle Noise Act 1987 (c. 34)	In the Schedule, in paragraph 1(1), the words 'to imprisonment for a term not exceeding three months or'.
Human Organ Transplants Act 1989 (c. 31)	In section 2(5), the words –
	(a) 'imprisonment for a term not exceeding three months or', and
	(b) 'or both'.
Town and Country Planning Act 1990 (c. 8)	In Schedule 15, in paragraph 14(4), the words from 'or to imprisonment' to the end.
Environmental Protection Act 1990 (c. 43)	In section 118(7), the words from 'or to imprisonment' to the end.
Criminal Justice Act 1991 (c. 53)	Section 26(5).
Deer Act 1991 (c. 54)	In section 10(3), the words from 'or to imprisonment' to the end.
Water Industry Act 1991 (c. 56)	In section 206(9), the words –
	(a) 'to imprisonment for a term not exceeding three months or', and
	(b) 'or to both'.
	In Schedule 6, in paragraph 5(5), the words –
	(a) 'to imprisonment for a term not exceeding three months or', and
	(b) 'or to both'.
Social Security Administration Act 1992 (c. 5)	In section 105(1), the words –
	(a) 'to imprisonment for a term not exceeding 3 months or', and
	(b) 'or to both'.
	In section 182(3), the words –
	(a) 'to imprisonment for a term not exceeding 3 months or', and
	(b) 'or to both'.
Local Government Finance Act 1992 (c. 14)	In section 27(5), the words –
	(a) 'imprisonment for a term not exceeding three months or', and
	(b) 'or both'.
Trade Union and Labour Relations (Consolidation) Act 1992 (c. 52)	In section 240(3), the words –
	(a) 'to imprisonment for a term not exceeding three months or', and
	(b) 'or both'.
Merchant Shipping Act 1995 (c. 21)	In section 57(2) –
	(a) in paragraph (a), the words 'except in a case falling within paragraph (b) below,', and
	(b) paragraph (b).

Short title and chapter	Extent of repeal
Reserve Forces Act 1996 (c. 14)	In section 75(5), the words – (a) 'imprisonment for a term not exceeding 3 months or', and (b) '(or both)'. In section 82(1), the words – (a) 'imprisonment for a term not exceeding 3 months', and (b) '(or both)'. In section 87(1), the words – (a) 'imprisonment for a term not exceeding 3 months or', and (b) '(or both)'. In section 99, the words – (a) 'imprisonment for a term not exceeding 3 months', and (b) '(or both)'. In Schedule 1, in paragraph 5(2), the words – (a) 'imprisonment for a term not exceeding 3 months or', and (b) '(or both)'.
Housing Act 1996 (c. 52)	In Schedule 1 – (a) in paragraph 23(6), the words from 'or imprisonment' to 'or both', and (b) in paragraph 24(6), the words from 'or imprisonment' to 'or both'.
Broadcasting Act 1996 (c. 55)	In section 144(4), the words – (a) 'to imprisonment for a term not exceeding three months or', and (b) 'or to both'.
Breeding and Sale of Dogs (Welfare) Act 1999 (c. 11)	In section 9 – (a) in subsection (1), paragraph (a), the word ', or' immediately preceding paragraph (b) and the words 'or to both', and (b) in subsection (7), paragraph (a), the word ', or' immediately preceding paragraph (b) and the words 'or to both'.
Powers of Criminal Courts (Sentencing) Act 2000 (c. 6)	In section 6(4), paragraph (a).
Countryside and Rights of Way Act 2000 (c. 37)	In section 81, subsections (2) and (3).
Transport Act 2000 (c. 38)	In section 82, subsection (5).

PART 10

JURY SERVICE

Short title and chapter	Extent of repeal
Juries Act 1974 (c. 23).	In section 2(5)(a), the word '9(1),'. In section 9, subsection (1) and in subsection (2) the words from 'and' to the end.

Short title and chapter	Extent of repeal
Criminal Law Act 1977 (c. 45).	In Schedule 12, the entry relating to the Juries Act 1974.
Criminal Justice Act 1982 (c. 48).	In Schedule 14, paragraph 35.
Mental Health (Amendment) Act 1982 (c. 51).	In Schedule 3, paragraph 48.
Mental Health Act 1983 (c. 20).	In Schedule 4, paragraph 37.
Juries (Disqualification) Act 1984 (c. 34).	The whole Act.
Coroners Act 1988 (c. 13).	Section 9(2).
Criminal Justice Act 1988 (c. 33).	Section 119.
	In Schedule 8, paragraph 8.
Courts and Legal Services Act 1990 (c. 41).	In Schedule 17, paragraph 7.
	In Schedule 18, paragraph 5.
Criminal Justice Act 1991 (c. 53).	In Schedule 11, paragraph 18.
Probation Service Act 1993 (c. 47).	In Schedule 3, paragraph 5.
Police and Magistrates' Courts Act 1994 (c. 29).	In Schedule 8, paragraph 28.
Criminal Justice and Public Order Act 1994 (c. 33).	Section 40.
	Section 42.
	In Schedule 10, paragraph 29.
Criminal Appeal Act 1995 (c. 35).	In Schedule 2, paragraph 8.
Police Act 1996 (c. 16).	In Schedule 7, paragraph 23.
Police Act 1997 (c. 50).	In Schedule 9, paragraph 27.
Government of Wales Act 1998 (c. 38).	In Schedule 12, paragraph 18.
Scotland Act 1998 (c. 46).	Section 85(1).
Access to Justice Act 1999 (c. 22).	In Schedule 11, paragraph 22.
Criminal Justice and Court Services Act 2000 (c. 43).	In Schedule 7, paragraph 47.
European Parliamentary Elections Act 2002 (c. 24).	In Schedule 3, paragraph 2.

PART 11

REPEALS RELATING TO AMENDMENTS OF PART 5 OF POLICE ACT 1997

Short title and chapter	Extent of repeal
Police Act 1997 (c. 50)	In section 115, subsections (3) to (5) and subsections (6C) to (6E).
	Section 120(3).
	In section 125, subsection (3) and, in subsection (4), the words 'to which subsection (3) does not apply'.
Care Standards Act 2000 (c. 14)	Section 104(3)(a).
	In Schedule 4, paragraph 25(2)(a).
Private Security Industry Act 2001 (c. 12)	Section 21.
	Section 26(3)(a).
Health and Social Care Act 2001 (c. 15)	Section 19.

Short title and chapter	Extent of repeal
Criminal Justice and Police Act 2001 (c. 16)	Section 134(3) and (4).
National Health Service Reform and Health Care Professions Act 2002 (c. 17)	Section 42(7). In Schedule 2, paragraph 64.
Education Act 2002 (c. 32)	In Schedule 12, paragraph 15(2). In Schedule 13, paragraph 8(2).
Licensing Act 2003 (c. 17)	In Schedule 6, paragraph 116.

PART 12

MISCELLANEOUS

Short title and chapter	Extent of repeal
Criminal Appeal Act 1968 (c. 19)Section 10(4).	In section 11(2), the words from '(which expression' to 'purposes of section 10)'. In section 51(1), the definition of 'the defendant'.
Bail Act 1976 (c. 63)	In section 5(1)(c), the words 'a court or officer of a court appoints'.
Magistrates' Courts Act 1980 (c. 43)	In section 1(3), the words 'and substantiated on oath'. Section 12(1)(a)(i). In section 13(3)(a), the words 'the information has been substantiated on oath and'.
Criminal Appeal (Northern Ireland) Act 1980 (c. 47)	In section 19(1A)(a), the words 'application for leave to'.
Criminal Procedure and Investigations Act 1996 (c. 25)	In Schedule 4, paragraph 16.
Crime and Disorder Act 1998 (c. 37)	In section 8(2), the words from 'and to section 19(5)' to '2000'.
Youth Justice and Criminal Evidence Act 1999 (c. 23)	In Schedule 4, paragraphs 26 and 27.
Powers of Criminal Courts (Sentencing) Act 2000 (c. 6)	In section 19(5), paragraph (c) and the word 'or' immediately preceding it. In Schedule 9, paragraphs 194 and 195.
Criminal Justice and Court Services Act 2000 (c. 43)	Sections 67 and 68.

SCHEDULE 38   Section 333(6)

TRANSITORY, TRANSITIONAL AND SAVING PROVISIONS

Sentencing of offenders aged 18 but under 21

1 If any provision of Part 12 ('the relevant provision') is to come into force before the day on which section 61 of the Criminal Justice and Court Services Act 2000 (abolition of sentences of detention in a young offender institution, custody for life, etc.) comes into force (or fully into force) the provision that may be made by order under section 333(1) includes provision modifying the relevant provision with respect to sentences passed, or other things done, at any time before section 61 of that Act comes into force (or fully into force).

Sentencing guidelines

2 The repeal by this Act of sections 80 and 81 of the Crime and Disorder Act 1998 does not affect the authority of any guidelines with respect to sentencing which have been included in any judgment of the Court of Appeal given before the commencement of that repeal ('existing guidelines'), but any existing guidelines may be superseded by sentencing guidelines published by the Sentencing Guidelines Council under section 170 of this Act as definitive guidelines.

3(1) Subject to sub-paragraph (2), the repeal by this Act of section 81 of the Crime and Disorder Act 1998 does not affect the operation of subsection (4) of that section in relation to any notification received by the Panel under subsection (2) of that section, or proposal made by the Panel under subsection (3) of that section, before the commencement of the repeal.

(2) In its application by virtue of sub-paragraph (1) after the commencement of that repeal, section 81(4) of that Act is to have effect as if any reference to 'the Court' were a reference to the Sentencing Guidelines Council.

(3) In this paragraph 'the Panel' means the Sentencing Advisory Panel.

Drug treatment and testing orders

4 A drug treatment and testing order made under section 52 of the Powers of Criminal Courts (Sentencing) Act 2000 before the repeal of that section by this Act is in force (or fully in force) need not include the provision referred to in subsection (6) of section 54 of that Act (periodic review by court) if the treatment and testing period (as defined by section 52(1) of that Act) is less than 12 months.

Drug testing as part of supervision of young offenders after release

5(1) Until the coming into force of the repeal by this Act of section 65 of the Criminal Justice Act 1991 (c. 53) (supervision of young offenders after release), that section has effect subject to the following modifications.

(2) In subsection (5B) –

(a) in paragraph (a), for '18 years' there is substituted '14 years',
(b) for paragraph (b) there is substituted –

'(b) a responsible officer is of the opinion –
  (i) that the offender has a propensity to misuse specified Class A drugs, and
  (ii) that the misuse by the offender of any specified Class A drug caused or contributed to any offence of which he has been convicted, or is likely to cause or contribute to the commission by him of further offences; and'.

(3) After subsection (5D) there is inserted –

'(5E) A person under the age of 17 years may not be required by virtue of subsection (5A) to provide a sample otherwise than in the presence of an appropriate adult.'

(4) For subsection (10) there is substituted –

'(10) In this section –

"appropriate adult", in relation to a person aged under 17, means –

    (a) his parent or guardian or, if he is in the care of a local authority or voluntary organisation, a person representing that authority or organisation,

    (b) a social worker of a local authority social services department, or

    (c) if no person falling within paragraph (a) or (b) is available, any responsible person aged 18 or over who is not a police officer or a person employed by the police;

"responsible officer" means –

    (a) in relation to an offender aged under 18, an officer of a local probation board or a member of a youth offending team;

    (b) in relation to an offender aged 18 or over, an officer of a local probation board;

"specified Class A drug" has the same meaning as in Part 3 of the Criminal Justice and Court Services Act 2000 (c. 43).'

Intermittent custody

6 If section 183 (intermittent custody) is to come into force for any purpose before the commencement of the repeal by this Act of section 78 of the Powers of Criminal Courts (Sentencing) Act 2000 (c. 6) (which imposes a general limit on the power of a magistrates' court to impose imprisonment), the provision that may be made by order under section 333(1) includes provision modifying any period or number of days specified in section 183 with respect to sentences passed by magistrates' courts before the commencement of that repeal.

Transfer to Scotland of community orders and suspended sentence orders

7(1) Until the coming into force of the repeal by the Mental Health (Care and Treatment) (Scotland) Act 2003 of the Mental Health (Scotland) Act 1984 (c. 36), in the provisions mentioned in sub-paragraph (2) the reference to the Mental Health (Care and Treatment) (Scotland) Act 2003 has effect as a reference to the Mental Health (Scotland) Act 1984.

(2) Those provisions are –

    (a) paragraph 2(4) of Schedule 9 (transfer of community orders to scotland or Northern Ireland), and

    (b) paragraph 4 of Schedule 13 (transfer of suspended sentence orders to Scotland or Northern Ireland).

Criminal Justice Act 2003: Notes as to commencement

Provisions of the Act have been brought into force in by the Act itself or by Commencement Order, as follows.

On Royal Assent (20 November 2003): see CJA 2003, s 336(1)

- s 168(1) and (2) (power to make provision relating to the Sentencing Guidelines Council);
- s 183(8) (power to make provision as to orders of intermittent custody);
- s 307(1) to (3), (5) and (6) (enforcement of legislation on endangered species);
- s 330 (orders and rules);
- s 333(1) to (5) (supplementary and consequential provision, etc);
- ss 334 to 339 (extent, expenses, commencement title, etc).

On 18 December 2003: see CJA 2003, s 336(2)

- ss 269 to 277 (effect of life sentence) and certain consequential amendments and repeals relating thereto.

On 20 January 2004: see Criminal Justice Act 2003 (Commencement No 2 and Saving Provisions) Order 2004 (SI 2004/81)

- ss 1, 2, 4, 6 to 8, 11 and 12 and Sch 1 (amendments to PACE);
- ss 294 to 297 (offenders transferred to mental hospitals);
- s 306 (limit on period of detention without charge of suspected terrorists), but subject to the transitional provision in art 2(3) of SI 2004/81;
- s 320 (offence of outraging public decency triable either way);
- s 329 (civil proceedings for trespass to the person brought by offender);
- repeals in Sch 37, Part 1 relating to PACE (but not s 63(3)(a)), the CJPOA 1994, the Armed Forces Act 2001 and the PRA 2002.

On 22 January 2004: see Criminal Justice Act 2003 (Commencement No 2 and Saving Provisions) Order 2004 (SI 2004/81)

- s 42 (mode of trial for certain firearms offences: transitory arrangements);
- ss 287 to 293 (firearms offences: sentencing) and Sch 29 (sentencing for firearms offences in Northern Ireland);
- consequential and other amendments in Sch 32, Part 1, paras 48 to 50.

On 26 January 2004: see Criminal Justice Act 2003 (Commencement No 1) Order 2003 (SI 2003/3282)

The following provisions, but only for the purposes of the passing of a sentence of imprisonment to which an intermittent custody order relates and the release on licence of a person serving such a sentence:

- s 182(1) and (3) to (5) (licence conditions);
- s 183(1) to (7) and (9) (intermittent custody);
- ss 184 to 186 (restrictions on power to make intermittent custody order; intermittent custody; licence conditions; further provisions relating to intermittent custody);
- s 187 and Sch 10 (revocation or amendment of order);
- s 195 (interpretation of Chapter 3);
- s 196(1)(d) and (2) (meaning of 'relevant order');

- ss 197 to 199 (meaning of 'the responsible officer'; duties of responsible officer; unpaid work requirement);
- s 200(1) (obligations of person subject to unpaid work requirement);
- ss 201 to 203 (activity requirement; programme requirement; prohibited activity requirement);
- s 204(1), (2), (5) and (6) (curfew requirement);
- s 205(1), (3) and (4) (exclusion requirement);
- ss 213(1), (2) and (3)(c), 214 and 215 (supervision requirement; attendance centre requirement; electronic monitoring requirement);
- s 216(2)(b), 217 and 218 (petty sessions area to be specified in relevant order; requirement to avoid conflict with religious beliefs, etc; availability of arrangements in local area);
- s 219(1)(a), (b) and (d), (2) and (3), and Sch 14 (provision of copies of relevant orders);
- ss 221, 222 and 223(1), (2), (3)(a) and (b) (powers of Secretary of State);
- ss 237 and 239 and Sch 19 (meaning of 'fixed-term prisoner'; the Parole Board);
- s 241(3) (effect of direction under s 240 on release on licence);
- s 244(1), (2) and (3)(c) and (d) (duty to release prisoners);
- s 245 (restrictions on operation of s 244(1) in relation to intermittent custody prisoners);
- s 246(1)(b), (3), (4)(b) to (i), (5) and (6) (power to release prisoners on licence before required to do so);
- s 248(1) (power to release prisoners on compassionate grounds);
- ss 249 and 250(1) to (3) and (5) to (8) (duration of licence; licence conditions);
- ss 251 to 253 (licence conditions on re-release of prisoner serving sentence of less than 12 months; duty to comply with licence condition; curfew condition to be included in licence under s 246);
- ss 254 to 256 (recall after release);
- s 257 (additional days);
- s 259 (persons liable to removal from the United Kingdom);
- ss 263 to 265 (consecutive or concurrent terms; restriction on consecutive sentences for released prisoners);
- s 268 (interpretation of Chapter 6);
- s 302 (execution of process between England and Wales and Scotland);
- s 304 and Sch 32, paras 11, 12(1) to (3) and (6), 29, 57 and 58 (amendments relating to sentencing);
- s 305(1) to (3) (interpretation of Part 12).

On 29 January 2004: see Criminal Justice Act 2003 (Commencement No 2 and Savings Provisions) Order 2004 (SI 2004/81)

- s 3 (arrestable offences);
- s 25 (code of practice);
- s 28 and Sch 2 (charging or release of persons in police detention), but not insofar as relating to s 37B(8) and (9)(a) of PACE;
- s 31 (removal of requirement to substantiate information on oath);
- ss 31, 49, 55, 73, 93, 111 and 132 (rules of court);
- s 284 and Sch 28 (increase in penalties for drug-related offences);
- s 286 (increase in penalties for offences under the Road Traffic Act 1988, s 174);
- Sch 35 (criminal record certificates: amendments of Police Act 1997, Part 5), paras 1, 2, 3(1), (2)(b) and (c), 4(1), (2)(b) and (c), 7, 10, 11 and, for the purposes of making regulations only, 4(3) and 5;
- Sch 37, Part 11 insofar as it relates to the repeal of the Police Act 1997, s 120(3).

On 27 February 2004: see Criminal Justice Act 2003 (Commencement No 2 and Savings Provisions) Order 2004 (SI 2004/81)

- ss 167, 168(3) and 169 to 173 (sentencing and allocation guidelines);
- s 285 (increase in penalties for certain driving-related offences);
- s 324 and Sch 34 (parenting orders and referral orders);
- Sch 37, Part 7 insofar as it relates to the repeal of the CDA 1998, ss 80 and 81;
- Sch 38 (transitory, transitional and saving provisions), paras 2 and 3.

Forecast dates

Home Office Circular 60/2003 indicates that s 5 (drug testing for those aged under 18) is likely to be piloted in a limited number of areas from summer 2004. It is proposed that ss 9 and 10 (which relate to fingerprints and samples) will be implemented in spring 2004. Section 28, which relates to the charging or release of persons in police custody and is largely in force from 29 January 2004, is due to be fully implemented in April 2004.

Addendum

UPDATE APRIL 2005

Since first publication of this book in March 2004 a variety of developments have occurred. A few of the most important are summarized below.

GENERAL

In the Preface to this book we highlighted the need for a pause in legislative activity in the area of criminal justice. In *R v Bradley* [2005] EWCA Crim 20 the Court of Appeal vociferously condemned legislation which was 'conspicuously unclear' (in the context of bad character) and deplored the fact that the courts were faced with real difficulties in the face of 'obfuscatory language'.

The Criminal Procedure Rules 2005 (SI 2005/384) came into effect on 4 April 2005, and provide a framework for active case management of criminal cases. In part they consolidate the various rules governing the Crown Court and magistrates' courts. But they also provide a detailed framework for the implementation of the procedural changes, which result from the implementation of provisions of the Criminal Justice Act 2003. In particular in this context the Rules set out the procedure to be followed in respect of the adducing of evidence of bad character.

COMMENCEMENT ORDERS

The following commencement orders should be noted.

Criminal Justice Act 2003 (Commencement No 4 and Saving Provisions) Order 2004 (SI 2004/1629)

Brought into force provisions relating to conditional cautions (ss 22–24, 26 and 27), and some provision relating to charging (s 28, Sch 3, para 2) on 3 July 2004.

Provisions relating to Criminal Cases Review Commission (ss 313 and 316) came into force on 1 September 2004.

Criminal Justice Act 2003 (Commencement No 5) Order 2004 (SI 2004/1867)

Brought into effect s 5 (drug testing for under 18s) on 1 August 2004 for pilots in Cleveland, Greater Manchester, Humberside, Merseyside, metropolitan police district, Nottinghamshire, and West Yorkshire.

Criminal Justice Act 2003 (Commencement No 6 and Transitional Provisions) Order 2004 (SI 2004/3033)

Brought into effect s 79 and Sch 24 (drug treatment and testing requirement in action plan order or supervision order) in Bradford, Calderdale, Keighley, Manchester and Newham, and part of Teesside, on 1 December 2004.

The character provisions (ss 98–110 and 112) and related provisions came into effect on 15 December 2004. The bad character provisions of s 101 apply in respect of trials commenced on or after that date: *R v Bradley* [2005] EWCA Crim 20.

Criminal Justice Act 2003 (Commencement No 7) Order 2004 (SI 2005/373)

Various provisions relating to sentencing and imprisonment brought into effect on 7 March 2005.

Criminal Justice Act 2003 (Commencement No 8 and Transitional and Saving Provisions) Order 2005 (SI 2005/950)

Various provisions brought into effect on 4 April 2005. These include provisions relating to prosecution appeals, retrial for serious offences, the hearsay evidence provisions, and many provisions relating to sentencing.

CONDITIONAL CAUTIONS

The commencement of the conditional caution powers was noted above. In support of that power the Criminal Justice Act 2003 (Conditional Caution: Code of Practice) Order 2004 (SI 2004/1683) made the relevant Code of Practice. This governs the detailed use, preconditions, monitoring and recording of the use of the conditional caution powers. The Code of Practice can be found at: www.cps.gov.uk/publications/others/conditionalcautioning04.htm.

BAD CHARACTER (SECTION 101)

Section 103 defines propensity for the purposes of s 101(1)(d) (which relates to matters of issue between the defendant and the prosecution). It does so, *inter alia*, by reference to offences of the same description or which fall into the same category. The Criminal Justice Act 2003 (Categories of Offences) Order 2004 (SI 2004/3346) specifies the prescribed categories of offence.

In *R v Hanson, Pickstone and Gilmore* [2005] All ER(D) 380 (Mar) the Court of Appeal gave the first guidance as to how s 101 should be used. The main features of the decision are as follows:

- Prosecution applications to adduce bad character evidence should not be made routinely simply because a defendant has previous convictions, but be based upon the particular circumstances of the case.
- Where propensity is relied on there are three questions –

(i)   whether the history of convictions establishes a propensity to commit offences of the kind charged;

(ii)   whether that propensity makes it more likely that D committed the offence charged;

(iii) whether it is unjust to rely on the convictions.

The fewer the number of convictions the weaker the evidence of propensity. The judge should take into consideration the gravity of the past and present offences, and the strength of the prosecution case.

- There is a difference between propensity to untruthfulness and propensity to dishonesty.
- In relation to s 101(1)(g) pre-existing authority remains relevant.
- Where evidence of bad character is used to show propensity the judge should warn the jury against placing undue reliance on previous convictions.

COMPLEX FRAUD CASES (NON-JURY TRIALS)

Ongoing controversy has been heightened by recent examples of unacceptably long and over-complex fraud cases. Reference should now be made to *Control and Management of Heavy Fraud and other Complex Criminal Cases – a Protocol issued by the Lord Chief Justice of England and Wales* [2005] All ER(D) 386 (Mar), which sets out protocols and guidance as to how long complex cases should be managed.

RETRIAL FOR SERIOUS OFFENCES

The retrial for serious offences provisions came into force on 4 April 2005. For their detailed implementation see Criminal Justice Act 2003 (Retrial for Serious Offences) Order 2005 (SI 2005/679).

SENTENCING

It will not generally be appropriate for the advice of the Sentencing Advisory Panel to be cited to the Court of Appeal: *R v Doidge* [2005] EWCA Crim 273.

For the licence conditions of offenders released into the community see Criminal Justice (Sentencing) (Licence Conditions) Order 2005 (SI 2005/648).

For the tariff in respect of mandatory life sentence see *The Consolidated Criminal Practice Direction (Amendment No 8) (Mandatory Life Sentences)* [2005] 1 Cr App R 8.

INDEX